KNOWLEDGE MATTERS

Knowledge
Matters

The Public Mission of the Research University

Edited by **Diana Rhoten
and Craig Calhoun**

COLUMBIA UNIVERSITY PRESS  New York

A Columbia / SSRC Book

Columbia University Press
Publishers Since 1893
New York   Chichester, West Sussex
Copyright © 2011 The Social Science Research Council

Library of Congress Cataloging-in-Publication Data
Knowledge matters : the public mission of the research university /
edited by Diana Rhoten and Craig Calhoun.
p.   cm.
"A Columbia / SRCC Book."
Includes bibliographical references and index.
ISBN 978-0-231-15114-6 (cloth : alk. paper) — ISBN 978-0-231-52183-3 (ebook)
1. Education, Higher—Research. 2. Public universities and colleges—Research.
2. Education, Higher—Aims and objectives. 4. Education, Higher—Social aspects.
5. Knowledge, Sociology of. 6. Education and globalization.
I. Rhoten, Diana. II. Calhoun, Craig J., 1952– III. Title.

LB2326.33.K63   2011
378'.013—dc22
2010022006

Columbia University Press books are printed on permanent and durable acid-free paper.
This book is printed on paper with recycled content.
Printed in the United States of America

c 10 9 8 7 6 5 4 3 2

References to Internet Web sites (URLs) were accurate at the time of writing.
Neither the editors nor Columbia University Press is responsible for URLs
that may have expired or changed since the manuscript was prepared.

Contents

Illustrations

Figures

Tables

Preface

Universities around the world are charged with public missions and often financed with public resources. The missions are many and often in tension with one another; they connect universities to different constituencies and different conceptions of the public good. The balance between public and private goals, and public funding and private property approaches to achieving goals has shifted in recent years.

At the same time, neither the universities nor their funders have clearly articulated their conceptions of the universities' public mission, particularly not how those universities should combine their mission of research with teaching and service. Rankings and assessment schemes have proliferated and greater accountability is widely sought. But this depends on a greater clarity of purpose and greater clarity about the ways in which different institutional configurations shape (or reflect) the pursuit of different goals. Debates over specific questions, like affirmative action or the imposition or increase of student fees, are seldom informed by attention to how universities should balance their private and public missions.

This book brings together contributors from Europe, Australia, Asia, Africa, Latin America, and North America. They focus on the debates in research universities—those charged with creating new knowledge—over their public mission, the implications of different decisions and policies for their organization, and different approaches to assessment and evaluation. For examples, the contributors look at individual cases, comparisons, and global patterns.

Modern research universities are central social institutions. They have grown dramatically during the last sixty years. They have become more internally complex with the rise of graduate and professional education, large-scale scientific research, the operation of subsidiary units like hospitals or TV stations, and the proliferation of "off-campus" programs, as well as engagement in local, regional, and national economic development.

Although most research universities receive substantial public funding, their public mission is not always clear. Is their "core mission" the provision of undergraduate education, and if so, what principles govern access? Is the primary goal selection on the basis of individual excellence, even if this reinforces class inequalities? Or is the goal ensuring opportunities for social mobility? Is it the job of universities to find cures for diseases, provide consultants for businesses, develop software and systems like the Internet, preserve knowledge in libraries, and distribute knowledge through extension programs? How should these different purposes be balanced? And how should the universities' success in meeting such goals be assessed?

These questions come to the fore today along with changes in funding for universities, not only curtailment in many public budgets, but also new levels of private funding. Some long-established private universities, mainly in the United States, have achieved remarkable wealth (though they also continue to receive public funds). New private and often for-profit universities are becoming prominent around the world. They come to the fore as universities compete for rankings in both domestic and increasingly global hierarchies, often with little understood and relatively arbitrary metrics. They come to the fore as governments mandate new assessment schemes, as parents question fees charged for their children, and as it becomes easier for potential students to shop for universities beyond their countries and easier for researchers and teachers to seek employment abroad. National configurations are distinct, but all these issues appear around the world.

To help answer these questions, we have brought together global perspectives on how the public mission of higher education has been conceived and debates on how it should be conceived. These perspectives are brought to bear on recent changes in university organization, funding, and assessment; in academic careers; in the marketplace for research-based knowledge; in the role of universities in promoting economic development and other public goals; and in the recent hegemony of a U.S. model and the English language.

Running throughout the chapters is a concern for the shifting relationship between public and private goods and public and private purposes for universities. Is student access an individual reward for achievement or a public good anticipating future social contributions? Is scientific research better organized as a source for private intellectual property or for open-access knowledge? Is the pursuit of knowledge for its own sake a public good or a private privilege? Should serving the economic interests of private corporations be part of the universities' mission? If so, how much should the private beneficiaries pay? These questions are addressed here not simply as binary choices about what is good or bad but through attention to the empirical implications of different approaches, the ways in which different choices are worked out in practice, and the changes—often unanticipated—that they have produced.

In the first chapter, Craig Calhoun offers a perspective on the connection between the immediate crisis—or, at least, anxieties—and longer-term structural transformations. To understand either requires situating accounts of particular universities in an understanding of the larger research university system as well as asking about its competing missions. In chapter 2, Gustavo Fischman, Sarah Igo, and Diana Rhoten delve deeper into the idea of a "crisis" specifically in public research universities. They raise questions about a previous alleged golden age and ask us to watch out for crisis-thinking informed more by nostalgia than research.

In chapter 3, Simon Marginson and Imanol Odarika explore global hegemony, higher education, and research. Using Gramsci's and Bourdieu's ideas, they analyze a field of power marked by strategic competition and the shifting structures of capital and norms across the globe. Marginson and Odarika ask whether any room will be left for transformative public roles in institutions that are so heavily shaped by structures of power and competition. In chapter 4, Mark Johnson and Andrey Kotrunov expand on this question, looking at the transformations of universities before and after the Soviet Union was dissolved. They find some new projects to be of potentially pivotal importance, although all are locked in a struggle for resources that only a few are likely to receive.

Investments in research universities are driven significantly by economic agendas. The question of how much universities actually contribute to economic development is pursued through an in-depth analysis of Latin America in chapter 5. Juan Carlos Moreno-Brid and Pablo Ruiz-Nápoles not only analyze individual cases but also situate them in relation to emerging global patterns, which include the competitive rankings regime and the effort to secure venture capital, patents, and marketable products. In chapter 6, Ka Ho Mok asks similar questions about Asia and explores the ways in which Asian policymakers integrate market fundamentalism with national development agendas.

Yusef Waghid takes up related issues in chapter 7, but in the context of African universities confronting different financial conditions and the pressures of globalization. He draws on the concept of *ubuntu* to describe distinctive orientations to collective intellectual engagement, as well as the tension between individualism and the affirmation of one's humanity in relation to others. In chapter 8, N'Drie Assié-Lumumba and Tukumbi Lumumba-Kasongo explore ways in which the university has figured as a central institution for national development projects in Africa and how its fate has been tied to theirs.

In chapter 9, Stefan Lange and Georg Krücken analyze how German universities and academics confront broader transnational structures and shifting demands in a new "knowledge ecology." They show university organization and work structures changing as German universities adapt to global competition while trying to preserve long-standing commitments such as that to professorial autonomy. John Willinsky discusses another dimension of changing knowledge ecology in chapter 10: the shifts in scholarly publication and communication. He asks both whether existing structures of libraries, presses, and journals meet the university's mission of serving the public as well as they could and how they are changing.

Questions about intellectual property rights have recently become central to debates about research universities. A shifting combination of legal, normative, and economic regimes shape the ways in which universities try to control their intellectual products and assets and often profit commercially from them. In chapter 11, Diana Rhoten and Walter Powell consider the various ways in which American public research universities have supported economic growth. They situate today's efforts to derive income from patentable technology in a longer history of applied research as academic service to the larger community. In chapter 12, Voldemar Tomusk recounts an informative debate about new intellectual property rights (IPR) policies for Cambridge University and what they can tell us about underlying issues and anxieties.

This research is, of course, committed not only to producing new knowledge and educating students but also to doing each of these things (and others) well. Quality assessment has become more and more prominent in higher education, partly because of increasingly complex regulatory systems and partly in order to manage relations among governments, markets, and the "workers" and "managers" in the universities themselves. In chapter 13, John Brennan and

Mala Singh use South African and British cases to address both what quality assessment offers and how it reflects power relations. Closely related questions concern the structure of academic work and the assessment of performance. In chapter 14, Christine Musselin takes up issues from employment patterns and gender disparities to productivity and the relationship between teaching and research. Based especially on European and American research, she assesses both what we know and what we do not but wish we did.

Finally, in chapter 15, Michael Kennedy turns his attention to a detailed local study of the tensions around globalization and diversity at the University of Michigan. These mobilize both directly academic values and values of public service, including university-state relations, and Kennedy reminds us that the ways the issues play out is always embedded in a local culture.

The authors of these varied studies do not agree with one another on everything. Moreover, even though they may discuss the same issues regarding the public mission of the research university in the face of globalization, they point to very different local conditions and contexts that influence these issues. The contributors have met to explore the insights from a comparison of the cases with which they are familiar. We are grateful to the Ford Foundation for its financial support and to the foundation's program officer, Jorge Balan, for attending and contributing to our discussions.

Collectively, the discussions point first to the importance of research universities, especially public research universities, and the range of different products, from personal mobility to national development. Research universities are important throughout the world, and some of the issues they confront are familiar everywhere. At the same time, the contributors to this book call attention to the dangers of false generalizations. While shifting economic conditions and ideologies affect universities around the world, they have different relationships with the dominant economic trends. An easy example is that universities are growing, and sometimes being created anew, in Asia in a way that they are not in Europe or America. In the latter cases, universities with strongly established ways of working are struggling to adapt to new conditions. Even as basic an issue as reconciling research expectations and teaching demands looks different in a national field that is densely populated with institutions and one in which demand is outrunning supply. Or put more simply, in some settings the research universities seem to be in crisis, and in others they seem centrally positioned in national development plans.

In all these different cases, however, there is a common struggle to articulate more clearly the ways in which knowledge matters. No one really doubts that it does, either inside universities or among their funders, regulators, and critics. But knowledge can matter in different ways. At the moment, many opinion leaders are concentrating on private interests in knowledge and the ways in which university education and research can be appropriated as a private good. But the ideal of a research university puts greater emphasis on the public: not just public support but a public mission that includes citizenship and advances in civil society as well as economic development and a public way of conducting inquiry and debate that has been crucial to modern science.

How well research universities will fare in coming years and in different contexts is up for debate. But it seems clear that clashing conceptions of their missions, both public and private, will be important.

Diana Rhoten and Craig Calhoun

KNOWLEDGE MATTERS

The Public Mission of the Research University

CRAIG CALHOUN

The university is a venerable and wonderful institution. Although it has ancient roots and played a crucial role in the Middle Ages, it has been distinctively important to the modern era. The production of knowledge and the education of a growing number of professionals are basic to both capitalist and socialist economies, to technologies that expand human capabilities, to the growth of the state and of citizen participation, and to the flourishing of civil society. The university is central to this and also to the personal development of many students and the intellectual freedom and accomplishment of many professors.

Despite its achievements, the university is an institution in upheaval. In the countries where it has been strongest, it now faces financial shortfalls, new pressures for external accountability, and competition from new ways of organizing research and scientific communication. This is partly a product of growth itself. Universities have added new functions and new fields of study and research, but they have dropped few old ones, making their operations harder to explain as well as more expensive.

Clarity of purpose also is at issue where universities are growing at breakneck pace. Should they imitate the world's most prestigious institutions? Should they narrow their missions to pursuing short-term economic payoff? Are there more appropriate forms for different settings? Is their purpose primarily to provide public goods or to support private aspirations? Easy use of the same word, *university*, to describe a wide range of different kinds of institutions masks the universities' great diversity and allows considerable confusion in both public policies and popular perceptions.

Three widely accepted conventions define what should be called universities. First, universities attempt to integrate the whole universe of knowledge, approaching and ideally connecting all or at least many subjects. That is, they are not narrowly specialized technical institutes. Second, universities combine undergraduate with advanced postgraduate education, offering master's, doctoral, and advanced professional degrees. Third, universities pursue new knowledge through research, maintain and enhance existing knowledge through scholarship, and transmit knowledge through teaching. For better or worse, however, none of these conventions is followed universally.

Even though the ideal of integration is honored by the world's most elite universities, scientific and scholarly specialization has made it hard to achieve. Popular hopes for economic advancement are focused especially on first degrees. But increasingly, only advanced degrees define a professional elite. While governments crave the economic contributions that research can bring, critics complain that much of what academics study is irrelevant. Moreover, the pursuit of new knowledge through research can conflict with both scholarly pursuits and time spent on undergraduate education.

That is not all. The full model of a research university unites freedom of intellectual inquiry (for both students and professors) with the creation of new knowledge through research, the nurturance of a scholarly community integrating disparate fields, open public communication, and the effort to make knowledge widely available as a public good. It is unclear whether those developing new universities today—in China, say, or the Arab world—will invest in this full model. It is unclear whether states and private benefactors who have sustained this model in today's most developed countries will continue to do so and whether it will be made widely available or remain the province of only a small elite.

The private gains offered by higher education are tangible. Students and their families are willing to pay ever higher fees because academic degrees and university-based networks advance careers. Private gains from research drive corporations to invest in new work in science and technology (and least in certain kinds with identifiable markets and profit potential). But the public mission of the university is often left vague.[1]

As the chapters in this book make clear, universities can and do make public contributions distinct from simply the sum of private benefits. They educate for citizenship as well as for business. They educate for public service as well as for private profit. They do research to end diseases even when they cannot make money from selling the cures. Public benefits are also the primary goals of research to strengthen social cohesion, to understand threats to peace and public security, and to help children reach their full potential.

This book focuses on the public mission of universities, what they owe in return for funding at public expense, what they may provide as public goods, how they may work in distinctively public ways, and how they may nurture public discourse. As the preceding sentence suggests, even though it is not entirely obvious how to define "publicness," it is crucial to do so.

PUBLIC MISSION

Public and private purposes are not always divided by a neat line. A better understanding of history, geography, and the world's different cultures can be useful to individuals in their jobs as well as in their roles as citizens or as international peacemakers. Knowing how science works can help venture capitalists make money and help all of us face difficult decisions about possibly catastrophic climate changes.

Just dividing higher education into a "public sector" and a "private sector" is too simple. It is true that institutions owned and governed as private property have grown rapidly. But private universities often pursue public goods, starting with the preservation and sharing of knowledge and continuing through research that addresses public needs and problems. Wealthy donors leave endowments, partly to ensure that the public goods they value are not neglected. Although for-profit universities may be more constrained in their public purposes, like the owners of any other for-profit business, those who run universities may try to combine making a profit with doing good and may resist pressures to drive all operations by short-term results alone. Conversely, state-owned universities receive private money—not least in the form of student fees but also in research contracts—and distribute private benefits like credentials that help students find jobs.

How universities are funded and governed makes a big difference. State funding of higher education grew in part precisely to make sure that they pursued key public missions: opening access; educating civil servants, teachers, and practitioners of the "helping professions"; and conducting research on problems of national need. If universities have to survive on fees paid by students, will they be tempted to concentrate their course offerings on training for the highest-paid careers? If public subsidies are minimal, will research be skewed toward corporations' short-term interests? What will become of research that provides public goods, goods for which there is typically not a market price because their consumption is shared? What will happen to the idea that the work of the university itself, teaching and research alike, should be conducted in public ways because science and scholarship depend on open communication, the chance to correct errors, and incentives to share what is learned? And what will become of the role of universities in providing knowledge and critical thinking to improve the quality of public discourse?

The growth of universities in the modern era was shaped by many purposes—from ensuring that churches would have clergy, to helping sons (and eventually daughters) of the elite and middle classes find good jobs, to producing research that would benefit states and businesses. The funding to pursue these purposes came from churches, private benefactors, student fees, and, increasingly, the state.

The primary rationale for the increase in state funding was, of course, that universities would benefit the public good. The public good could be either narrowly identified with state interests or understood more expansively. Church-supported and privately financed universities also pursued what they saw as the public good. In many cases, the public mission of these private universities was recognized and supported by tax exemptions or other subsidies from governments. So pursuing the public good was not just an obligation in return for state funding; it was part of most universities' deeper mission.

Public benefits could, of course, be construed in many ways, one of the most important being simply a fairer, more open distribution of private benefits. If a college degree helps someone launch a career, there is a public interest in the allocation of such life chances. State funding for higher education often came with the clear intent of increasing the educational opportunities of individuals. But this didn't preclude limits. In many settings, from Brazil to Turkey, publicly funded universities both expanded too slowly to accommodate demand and controlled admissions through examination systems that favored middle-class and elite students and, indeed, even students who had attended private secondary schools. In fact, publicly funded higher education sometimes became largely a subsidy for the middle and upper classes. In some cases, the recent development of private universities has served the public good of greater access to higher education (though whether it offers a better way of doing so than expanding the offerings of public universities is another question). This expansion of private universities has been largely underwritten by student fees, and one irony is how much state funding supports the higher education of students from the established middle and upper classes while students from poorer or less established backgrounds must pay for the chance to pursue their aspirations. Of course, in varying degrees, wealthy benefactors have also backed such universities and sometimes offered financial support to poorer students.

As states expanded during the modern era, especially from the eighteenth century onward, they required more and better educated civil servants. To meet this demand, universities were funded and accorded special privileges like academic freedom. Prussian support for the University of Berlin, an influential pioneer in development of the modern research university, is a good example. Indeed, the professors themselves were civil servants of a sort, and they were expected to use their knowledge in advising the state as well as in teaching and writing.[2] Hegel's *Philosophy of Right* makes clear that great Berlin professors identified with this role, but it is equally clear that Hegel's philosophy was not merely advice to the Prussian government. Universities were also founded in European colonies, as, for example, the Universities of Bombay, Calcutta, and Madras were founded in 1857 to help train an Anglo-Indian elite for government service. They reflected the growing importance of civil administration (including professional fields from medicine to architecture and accounting), complementing military power. But there was no contradiction between liberal arts and professional fields. These three pioneering Indian universities also taught English literature, reflecting but also expanding the role of the English language not just in administration but also in Indian civil and intellectual life.[3]

In the late nineteenth-century United States, the federal government helped states establish or expand public universities by making "land grants" that provided them with free building sites. These universities focused on bringing the benefits of research knowledge to more of the population, by educating large numbers of students who could not be accommodated in the existing elite universities. They developed new areas of study oriented to practical affairs, such as agricultural extension programs that brought advice and assistance from university-based scientists to farmers in sometimes remote rural areas.

Similar purposes animate programs at universities throughout the world today. In varying proportions, they combine the pursuit of economic development on a regional or national scale with the pursuit of more open access to career opportunities based on university training and credentials. Private universities have sometimes been a goad to public institutions grown complacent or too closely tied to established constituencies.[4] There is no contradiction between providing individual students with learning from which they can benefit personally and providing a broader public with knowledge it can share. Indeed, the ideal of a research university has always included a mixture of private and public benefits.

But knowledge, many have suggested, is advanced distinctively well when recognized as a "public good." Here the technical term from economics refers to goods that are "non-rivalrous."[5] Personally benefiting from them does not require excluding others from similar benefits; indeed, in some cases public goods cannot be consumed effectively without making them widely available. If you want clean air, for example, you will probably find it most efficient to keep the shared public air supply clean rather than trying to carry a private oxygen tank everywhere you go. But it is always possible that people will be persuaded that a private approach is better. In many poor countries, for example, public water supplies are inadequate, so both citizens and tourists who can afford it buy bottled water. More ironically, many residents of rich countries have been convinced that they should pay for privately marketed water rather than using public supplies that are often safer.

Knowledge is not diminished when known by more people (though certain economic benefits may be obtained by those able to keep valuable knowledge from others). There is contest over the extent to which knowledge "needs to be free" (as some open-source advocates have it) or is an essentially public good (as some economists argue). Some see enforcing intellectual property rights as a crucial source of incentives to the producers (or at least distributors) of knowledge. So publishers are jealous of copyrights, and scientists, universities, and corporations all are jealous of patents.[6]

Yet there is also tension here with a fundamental norm of science—that scientists conduct their work in public ways. That is, is there a free and open debate among researchers that can drive forward critical inquiry, correct errors, and ensure that ideas gain support from their intellectual quality—mainly on the bases of logic and evidence—as distinct from their social bases, pedigrees, or institutional and political backing? As Robert K. Merton famously argued, "Property rights in science are whittled down to a bare minimum by the rationale of the scientific ethic."[7]

The public mission of universities is closely linked to the public character of their work. Science, for example, has long been understood to depend on publication—both of results and of the bases for those results. This enables it to work as an effective institution for both error correction and the stimulation of innovation. We need to ask what is lost if patents and proprietorial interests undermine scientific openness.

At the same time, we must ask how much scholarly communication has depended on institutions, like university presses and scholarly journals, that now face serious problems. Their troubles are mostly economic, related to growing costs and shrinking markets, but they also include issues like the difficulty finding reviewers with no financial interest to bias their judgment—especially in medical research in which pharmaceutical companies have put nearly everyone on their payrolls but also increasingly in other fields in which research can affect markets—so the stakes are high. Then there is the question of how best to organize scientific and scholarly communication on the web. Here, too, a clear mission, especially whether the public interest matters, is vital to shaping the future.

Indeed, some would hold that universities themselves are models for and contributors to public debates on important public issues. It's not just that universities educate citizens, it is that in certain ways science has been one of the great models for the kind of behavior citizens need to practice for democracy or at least republican self-government to work.[8] That universities are home to student (and sometimes faculty) activism is arguably one of their positive public functions, and one to be appreciated independently of one's analysis or prioritization of any particular issue. This includes conservative activism. Perhaps ironically, the best example of the way in which free academic discourse can influence a broader public is the success of followers of Friedrich von Hayek and Milton Friedman in convincing many politicians and the public to abandon public approaches to nearly every possible public issue in favor of private-property approaches.

Open, participatory discussion is vital to the ethos of science and, indeed, of scholarship more generally (medieval universities were not democratic or scientific, but they were marvelously disputatious). From the late nineteenth century on, modern universities became dramatically more productive of new knowledge than earlier ones had been. They achieved this not only by changing their syllabi and embracing technology but also by opening up discussion and debate and reducing the control of a small number of senior faculty and administrators over this intellectual life. New intellectual agendas became easier to advance, and results that conflicted with established views became easier to publish.

As Charles Sanders Peirce wrote at the very time the modern research university was taking shape, this suggested a democratic-pragmatist way of thinking about authoritative knowledge in science: it was precisely the submission of findings to critical debate that ensured that authority would be based on the pursuit of truth rather than position or custom alone.[9] The French philosopher of science Gaston Bachelard similarly described the development of knowledge as a process of correcting errors rather than accumulating static truths.[10] All research institutions thus depend on making knowledge public in order to improve it.

IMMEDIATE CRISIS AND LARGER TRANSFORMATION

No account of higher education today can ignore the effects of the global financial crisis epitomized by the market meltdown of 2008. Budget crises are inflicting serious damage on some of the world's greatest universities, especially American universities heavily dependent on state funding. Private universities also have been hurt as their endowments have lost value, but in most cases the damage is less drastic. But it is important not to overgeneralize. Current budget cuts only aggravate the long-standing austerity in some countries, while in others, growth, not cuts, is the order of the day.

All over the world, universities are under pressure. In some countries, this is pressure to enroll more students, conduct more research, and orient both teaching and research simultaneously to national development agendas and international rankings competition. China, for example, is investing massively in higher education. One officially stated aspiration is to have one hundred "world-class universities." In fact, the new Center for World-Class Universities at Shanghai Jiao Tong University holds conferences, conducts assessments, and publishes an influential ranking of the world's top universities. Shanghai Jiao Tong itself has the goal of joining the top one hundred by 2020. New universities with similar ambitions for global leadership are also being founded in Arab states on the basis of oil wealth but with the ambition to secure prosperity beyond reliance on oil. Although these universities have been affected by the fluctuation of oil prices, their construction continues.

In China and the Persian Gulf, governments are building new universities (some with European or American partners), both to increase higher education participation rates and to compete for global leadership. In several European countries, the same goals are driving a new differentiation of higher education systems. In both France and Germany, for example, governments have provided major new resources to the top tier of the higher education system, introducing new inequality into what had been relatively egalitarian systems. The sharper differentiation responds to alarm that French and German universities have not fared well in global rankings and thus has made support for research a primary source of hierarchical distinction. The goal is to compete effectively with the U.S. universities that dominate the global rankings and with Asia's rapid development, as well as to derive economic benefits from research. At the same time, the rates of higher education participation and attainment have been increasing in Europe (and in general in the Organization for Economic Cooperation and Development [OECD] countries).[11] For the most part, the steady rise in the proportion of young adults attending universities has not increased enrollment at the research-intensive elite institutions. Rather, enrollment has increased by raising the student-faculty ratio at less prestigious institutions and absorbing those historically focused on career education into a common university structure (as, for example, Britain's renamed "polytechnics"). Functional differentiation previously gave more clarity about distinctive educational mission; this is lost in a hierarchy based largely on research prestige.

In addition, while there are new public subsidies for research excellence in several European countries, there are also are new efforts at "cost recovery." Students and their families are asked to bear increasing shares of higher education costs. In varying degrees, this is true around the world, though often without comparable public subsidies for elite research institutions. This has also long been the pattern in the United States, where private universities have been more prominent and historically state-supported universities have been relying more and more on private funds, including student fees. In the United States, government funds for the highest-level public institutions have declined. During the economic crisis, federal higher education funds have gone disproportionately to community colleges to try to increase the extent to which higher education helps the less well-off prepare for jobs. Indeed, even though the United States maintains a high rate of participation in higher education generally, it has lost its leadership in the proportion of young people actually completing college degrees.[12]

The idea of "cost recovery" is not only that governments can reduce expenditures but also that private beneficiaries should share the costs of the benefits they receive. This leaves room for governments to determine that higher education is also a public good. Increasingly, however, student fees are governed by what the market will bear. On the one hand, higher education and research have value as investments in public goods. On the other hand, they have market value and help private beneficiaries (both individual students and investors with property rights in research). When private beneficiaries pay larger shares, the return on public investment is higher. But it is the private beneficiaries who experience the highest return. So having them pay more is a logical step. The question is how to balance this with public goods like access for less wealthy students or research on issues that do not attract profit-oriented investors.

At the same time, however, reliance on student fees is not all "cost recovery" but is more and more part of a redefinition of higher education as a service industry rather than a public good. Students are not only future citizens; they are current customers. Indeed, some of the most lucrative students are specifically not citizens, and accordingly, in countries from Australia to Britain, higher education has been redefined as an export industry.[13] Differential tuition rates that make the recruitment of foreign students profitable have promoted not only international enrollments but also the creation of new courses—especially master's degrees—designed especially to produce income. In short, public universities are pushed by financial exigencies to behave more like for-profit universities.

Governments, conversely, are torn between investing in higher education to produce foreign exchange and divesting from it because families are willing to pay for it as a private career investment. What is missing from each of these approaches is a strong valuation of higher education as a public good.

Higher education faces stiff competition as well from other demands on public finances. States challenged by the recession also are struggling to fund health care, job creation, and security services, including prisons, the police, and the military.[14] The general discontent with taxation is rising. For more than thirty years, neoliberal ideologists have suggested both that private interests should take precedence over the public good and that public institutions are inherently inefficient.

The high and rising cost of university education is a source of public discontent, behind which lies uncertainty about the proportionate emphases on teaching and research. There is little evidence that private research universities are more efficient than public ones, but for-profit universities that concentrate mainly on teaching and not research are able to teach less expensively. Not least, universities also face politically motivated criticisms, religiously motivated attacks on scientific research, and calls for more accountability (often from legislators and others who are uncertain about how universities work and what they think should be counted).

But if academics in rich countries worry about the loss of support, they might compare their predicament with that of Russian scholars. The collapse of the Soviet Union also brought the collapse of a once-great educational and research system. Today Russian universities are barely mentioned in the top five hundred of the Shanghai and London rankings. As a result, Russian researchers have become a new diaspora strengthening universities throughout the West, and universities in the Confederation of Independent States have generally fared even worse.

The current financial crisis is an accelerated moment in a process of structural transformation. Although this transformation is partially economic, as the Russian example suggests, it also is political. The structural transformation is shaped not only by shifts in funding but also by new competition. Reorganization of higher education not only as a market but also as an increasingly global market is part of this. Universities also face greater competition from nonacademic research institutes, corporate laboratories, and think tanks. How universities respond to the financial crisis, the changed operating environment, and questions about whether their purposes are mainly public or private will determine what kinds of institutions they become. Focusing merely on shortfalls can obscure the longer-term reorganization of budgets—sources of funding and allocations of expenditure—and, with it, the reshaping of the university.

Private universities have not been immune from financial crisis. Even the richest found themselves caught short when the endowments on which they depend lost a third of their value. Harvard canceled free coffee for faculty meetings and slowed construction. But in fact, the financial crisis that came to a head in 2008 followed decades of massive tax-exempt transfers of wealth into endowments at the world's richest universities. Most of these are in the United States, and the gap between their resources and those of the leading state-funded universities in the United States and elsewhere grew dramatically between the 1970s and the 2008 crisis. Now, although some of these rich private universities face setbacks, none faces the potential deep cuts that some public universities do.

Many faculty members hope for a return to "normal" as the economy recovers. They expect the cuts that their departments endure today will be restored in a year or two. They worry that they may lose momentum in their plans for expansion or improvement, but they expect growth to return. Growth has defined the "normal" for many universities through most of the last six decades. Even if university budgets rise again, however, there is no guarantee that presidents and provosts will simply restore funds previously cut from departmental budgets. On the contrary, they will likely invest funds in more strategic ways. For instance, their investments may be guided by student interests or by the pursuit of new revenue streams. While the universities may strengthen the humanities, they are much more likely to concentrate on strengthening their professional schools and technology-oriented science.

The demand for higher education continues to grow. In most of the world's rich and economically developed countries, the proportion of citizens attending college or university has soared over the last hundred years, from less than 5 percent to more than 50 percent and, in some cases, more than 75 percent. By 2009 the participation rates were 71 percent in North America and western Europe, 26 percent in the East Asia/Pacific region, 23 percent in the Arab States, 11 percent in South and West Asia, and 6 percent in Africa.[15] This demand may be leveling off in Europe and America—though this is not clear—but in much of the developing and middle-income world, it is still growing rapidly. The United Nations Educational, Scientific and Cultural Organization (UNESCO) estimates that the number of postsecondary students increased by 51 million just between 2001 and 2008.[16]

To be sure, these patterns are erratic. Most of Africa was knocked off the growth track in the 1970s, and growth remained uneven during the recent boom. Many Latin American universities faced a crisis during the years of dictatorship, but recent growth has been robust. Growth was slow in China until the 1990s but has become dramatic since. On different timelines, one country after another traced the pattern from higher education as a rarity, confined mainly to a small elite and a few professions, through either gradual or abrupt expansion until it reached majority participation.

Demand is created, of course, not just by individual desire but also by institutional action. Millions of people seek university places for reasons of both careers and personal fulfillment. But effective demand depends on support from governments and on various forms of private financing from families through philanthropic foundations. And it fluctuates. In the wake of the 2008 financial crisis, universities in some wealthy countries reported a greater number of applications, partly reflecting labor market weakness. But at the same time, there have been sharp declines in other segments of higher education. The Indian Institutes of Technology, for example, had established outposts in Dubai but now face an abrupt decline in admissions.

Universities fulfill other functions as well, notably research but also information management through libraries and medical services through hospitals. Universities have assumed these functions because faculty members play multiple roles as scholars, researchers, and practitioners as well as educators. But whether these roles will remain bundled is a major question for the future of higher education. Already the opportunity and obligation to engage in research are unequally distributed among faculty members. Some universities focus more intensively on international rankings based largely on research; others make no significant investments in research; and in between are many struggling to determine a good balance as parents complain about costs but also try to send their children to the most prestigious schools.

Some U.S. universities are rich enough to be Fortune 500 corporations (like Harvard, Stanford, Yale, MIT, Duke, and Michigan).[17] Their wealth is based overwhelmingly on private endowments, even at Michigan, which was once more substantially supported by the state. For a second tier of elite universities, tuition fees are more central to budgets, which include some universities owned but not fully funded by state governments. Some universities are almost entirely dependent on state funding; other universities concentrate on the "liberal arts"; and still other universities teach them little or not at all. Some universities award doctorates, and other universities teach only undergraduates (though for many, having graduate programs defines them as "real" universities). Some universities have enormous scientific research establishments and aspirations to lead the world in scientific breakthroughs, Nobel Prizes, and citation counts; but other universities invest almost nothing in research. Indeed, some for-profit universities specialize mainly in career education.

Around the world, government funding supports most higher education, but in few other societies do private endowments play the role they do in the United States. Nonetheless, the number of private universities is growing. In Turkey, for example, several families associated with major commercial or industrial businesses created foundations to operate private universities that have become important at the elite as well as the mass levels. Bilkent, Bilgi, Koç, and Sabanci are among the most prominent. Some for-profit institutions are serving less selective student bodies with career-oriented courses. Sometimes, as in Brazil's Candido Mendes University, the two dimensions are joined as different divisions of a single enterprise. Growth is coming from both state investments, as in China, and from expansion of private universities.

This growth accelerated with the postwar dream of widespread social mobility, prosperity for all, economic development led by science and technology, and the democratic participation of an educated citizenry that would recognize its stake in the existing order and resist the extremism of left or right. New universities were built and old ones expanded. This increased the availability of opportunities, in some cases dramatically. But there was a countervailing factor. As the higher education field expanded in western Europe and the United States, its internal hierarchy became more pronounced. Just attending university ceased to mark entry into elite status; instead, this was conferred by the hierarchical position of the university attended. Admission to elite universities was both directly shaped by family background through preferential admissions and indirectly through the social and cultural capital that parents were able to spend on their offspring.[18]

The balance of openness and status reproduction varied, linked by the expansion of the higher education system and of its internal hierarchy (although the 1960s were relatively egalitarian compared with the obsession with rankings and differential resources that followed). Even where degree titles and academic departments look the same, universities are shaped by their positions in a pattern of differentiation and hierarchy.[19]

The field of higher education is fed today—as it was throughout the post–World War II baby boom—with individual and family aspirations, government plans and business interests, faculty desires for recognition, and administrative desires for order. Some hopes can be fulfilled only by open access, and some status interests can be protected only by exclusivity.

During this postwar boom, visions of an ever larger middle class and growth driven by science and technology reconciled public and private interests in higher education. In China, India, Turkey, and some other countries where higher education is growing rapidly today, we see a somewhat similar reconciliation. But higher education is now a more fraught terrain. Earlier, a broad notion of modernization guided the expansion of higher education and expectations for how it would link to economic development, improvements in government, and the expansion of activity in civil society. Something of the same idea is at work in many developing societies today, but chastened and complicated by both the experience of global power structures and a neoliberal ideology that emphasizes competition, economic ends by themselves, and private rather than public approaches.

The 1970s marked a turning point, as it followed a period in which independence encouraged high aspirations in formerly colonized countries. A peace movement challenged a neoimperialist war and dovetailed with a more general set of countercultural and political movements challenging the institutional arrangements that had reconciled capitalism, democracy, and the cold war in wealthy Western countries. At the same time, the growing middle class in Europe and America sought to extend its consumption. These issues shaped both discontent and idealism on university campuses and put the university at the center of social upheaval.

The 1973–1975 recession triggered by the production controls of the Organization of the Petroleum Exporting Countries (OPEC) and spiking oil prices was dramatic, but the crisis was broader than popular discussion typically recognized.[20] The combination of demands—for growth in less developed countries, consumption in rich countries, and more or less egalitarian social transformation—was hard to reconcile. To a large extent, the leaders of the capitalist world refused to face the crisis because it involved a widespread challenge to their authority and demands from many quarters for greater shares of wealth. They decided instead to finance continued growth with credit, driving up budget deficits and sovereign debt (and creating sovereign wealth in some other hands), and extracting profits through financial instruments and speculation rather than material production. The crisis of 2008 was in some ways a consequence of the unresolved crisis of the 1970s (which, in fact, was called "the great recession" until replaced by the still greater recession of 2008).

There is a direct connection between the larger societal crises and that in higher education. Universities were central to the projects of both the "welfare state" and the "developmental state" during the decades after World War II and became focal points for discontent when those projects failed to deliver all they had promised. Critique of the state— and of the university—came from both left and right. Indeed, it is important to remember how strong many of the left-wing attacks on universities were in the 1960s. Although these attacks usually focused on complicity with the military or capitalist exploitation, they also revealed a broadly antiauthoritarian orientation that sometimes dovetailed with right-wing libertarianism. Over the last thirty years, the right-wing "neoliberal" attack has become more prominent. This was, in fact, a radical position, different from the statist conservatism of the postwar period.

Neoliberal ideology expressed the dominance of private interests and intensified, naturalized inequality. In many different dimensions of social life, hierarchies were stretched, often with a new distance between what was accessible to the most elite and to the middle class. Income inequality quickly widened from the 1970s to the current decade, precisely the same period when university fees grew quickly as well.

A few successes rising from the bottom rungs to the top—what the French call *miraculés*—legitimated the hierarchy. For example, in the United States, public universities—including the most elite—had been the pioneers of greater inclusion of minorities in higher education. During recent decades, however, opponents of affirmative action tried to block their efforts while middle-class, mostly white families pushed for more places for their children. At the same time, wealthy private universities began to admit, and offer more scholarships to, top minority candidates. Minority enrollment in the relatively small private elite rose, becoming part of the way to maintain distinction as an elite. Growth in minority enrollments in the much larger sector of prestigious public universities, however, stalled or even retreated. Higher education overall became more unequal as participation rates went up.

Often the competitions that emerged over the last thirty years were not merely intense but nearly "winner-take-all" in their form.[21] This was true not only where the stakes were absolute matters of wealth accumulation—like the fantastic salaries and stock options granted to CEOs and investment bankers—but also where competition focused on "positional goods." Higher education figured as both a path to material success and a positional good, one that derived its value from its place in a hierarchy. Rankings were increasingly important as a gauge of quality as well as an end in themselves; a degree from a higher-ranked school had higher value.[22] Star faculty members helped secure rankings successes (and star benefits helped channel faculty effort into reproducing the system). Enormous extra benefits accrued to the top tier; for example, the richest universities found it easiest to raise additional endowments. Because this extra money freed them from dependence on student fees, they were able to recruit those students who demonstrated the most ability (however much measures of this might be contested). These in turn were most likely to be wealthy donors or prestige-generating successes in the future, and universities multiplied these odds by consecrating those they admitted with elite degrees and enrolling them not just in classes but also in elite social networks. Conversely, throughout the vast middle of the higher education system, more and more costs were passed on to students and their families (earlier and more dramatically in the United States, but in varying degree around the world). And for most, degrees were minimal conditions of remaining middle class, not tickets into an elite.

The patterns varied, of course. Private research universities remained rare in western Europe, even though private higher education expanded at the low-selectivity end of the system and in certain niche-markets like the powerful and lucrative one for business schools. Some state-funded universities, like Oxford and Cambridge, launched major "American-style" development campaigns. Others, like the LSE (London School of Economics) and Paris's Sciences Po, combined seeking private capital with developing new programs that could generate revenue from student fees (especially from international students).

In eastern Europe, reduced state funding and market-oriented transitions away from communism provided the context for new private universities. The Central European University was, however, unusual among the new private universities in attaining recognition among research universities for a range of different programs. Private universities were already more prominent in some parts of Asia (like Korea, Japan, and the Philippines), and many new private universities were founded. In most of Asia, however, the leading universities remained mainly public, even though they were integrated into national plans for economic success in a knowledge society (see chapter 6). But private money became increasingly important to some public institutions (like the Indian Institutes of Technology, which benefited from wealthy alumni abroad). In a few settings, like China, the latter part of the period saw massive new state funding for research universities.

Latin America, too, had a history of private (including church-run) universities. Their numbers expanded considerably, although public universities generally have lower costs and remain the primary source of the middle and working classes' access to higher education. Public universities are also the primary research institutions (see chapter 5). New private universities have been important to Turkey and have a smaller but strategically significant role in Russia (on Russia, see chapter 4). For the most part, these universities have focused on students from the growing middle classes and, in some cases, have considerably expanded their access. While they include schools with narrow job-training missions, some also offer broader courses and aspirations and even research centers. This was less often true in Africa, but private universities there did expand notably from the late 1990s, and in a few cases, private universities did support research centers. At the same time, as elsewhere, some public universities—like Makerere in Uganda—were able to attract new private funding to partially compensate for low state support.[23]

Two different stories were central to the growing prominence of private money in higher education. The first was an increase in the extent to which students and their families had to bear the costs of higher education. Many public universities raised the fees they charged, but seldom to levels as high as private institutions. This increase obviously was hardest for poor and working-class students seeking upward mobility. But it also affected the middle classes, whose children increasingly could stay in the middle classes only if they had a university degree. This was a global trend and involved both public universities supplementing their state funding and private universities, a growing percentage of which were for-profit.

The second story was a massive transfer of wealth, often aided by tax exemption. Private philanthropy had long played a big role in higher education, not least through the long-standing support of religiously affiliated universities. Many of Europe's public universities are, in fact, transformed versions of these. More recently, and disproportionately in the United States, private endowments funded the foundation of universities like Chicago, Stanford, Duke, and Johns Hopkins,[24] all founded as research universities. Older private universities like Harvard and Yale were remade to fit the new model and received new benefactions to maintain leadership. During the 1950s and 1960s, public universities moved into positions of increasing leadership in the United States. Although the University of California at Berkeley, the University of Michigan, the University of Wisconsin, and the University of North Carolina at Chapel Hill all were older, this was the period when they (and several other "flagship" state universities) became national leaders. From the late 1970s through 2008/2009, the balance at the elite end of the hierarchy shifted back toward the private universities. Donors gave hundreds of billions of dollars (on which they did not have to pay taxes), and university endowments also earned massive tax-free revenues (although as 2008 and 2009 proved, there was no guarantee that they could only go up).

Private funding became more important from the 1970s forward, partly because the state funding of universities slowed or was reversed. States faced new economic and fiscal pressures, including difficulty applying some traditional Keynesian macroeconomic policies. British Prime Minister Margaret Thatcher and U.S. President Ronald Reagan helped symbolize a rebellion against pubic expenditure. In much of the developing world, structural adjustment programs imposed austerity. In eastern Europe and especially the former Soviet Union, the postcommunist transition destroyed a good deal of public wealth even while it opened the doors to private accumulation and markets. In general, public support for higher education stagnated in most rich countries, although the increased reliance on private money partially compensated even the public universities. In a few cases, significant new public expenditure was linked to the agendas of market-led economic development or to international competition. An example is the new investments by the German federal state that sought to elevate a tier of universities above the more or less level playing field provided by funding from the *Lander* (state governments).[25]

In the United States, as in a number of other rich countries, the defunding of public universities started well before the 2008/2009 recession. Universities sought private funds (and federal government research funds) to compensate for this loss, some with a good deal of success. In the process, they became committed to delivering private goods, became internally differentiated by sources of funding, and lost some of their ability for autonomous and integrated planning as they began to treat units as profit centers.

The University of California, perhaps the world's greatest public university, is a case in point. During the last twenty years, state funding for the University of

California fell by 40 percent, adjusted for inflation.[26] Cuts continue. During this long decline in state support, however, the university actually expanded. It did this by increasing student-faculty ratios, by competing for large federal grants in "big science," and especially by courting private funds. For this reason, growth was most pronounced in professional schools and technology-oriented science. Undergraduate education, especially in the liberal arts, remained more dependent on state funds. Throughout the university, nonetheless, departments were urged to compete for standing on the basis of research excellence, and most were and are very highly ranked. When the state's budget crisis became severe, research excellence was not a protection in itself. Cuts were made mainly in those fields with the least access to private funds. The social sciences and humanities were hit especially hard.

The University of California was originally defined as a research university with a public mission under California's unusually explicit master plan for higher education.[27] The university proceeded with a firm commitment to serve the public in three ways: by providing education across a wide range of subjects to all students who met its stringent admissions criteria, by providing professional training that would equip the state with the experts it needed in specific fields, and by conducting research that would advance knowledge in general and also the state's economy and would address public needs. The cost was initially borne overwhelmingly by the state. Low tuition costs reflected a commitment to equality of opportunity and to the ideal of a university of elite quality open at low cost to all who were qualified (in pointed distinction to private universities available only to those able to pay). But gradually during the last thirty years and abruptly in the current crisis, the university's mission has been implicitly redefined by its shifting funding sources.

Most publicly funded systems of higher education were never thought out with the clarity of California's master plan. Most never excelled as the University of California did in meeting its range of public service missions. But to a considerable degree, all those that flourished during the postwar boom years embodied something of the same "ideal type" of a single learning community that would combine education throughout the arts and sciences, professional training, and advanced research. The integration of these missions was part of the ideal of the research university, as was a clear notion of public service that explained why each of these was worthy of state subsidy.[28]

Over the last three decades, the public research university ideal has been challenged, not just in California but also around the world.[29] State support has been less forthcoming, in some settings more because of crises in national economies, in others because of competition from other state projects, and across most settings because of the success of neoliberal ideological efforts to reduce state spending in favor of distribution of opportunities on the basis of private wealth. At the same time, the costs of research universities have grown exponentially. The costs of Big Science account for much of this. But research universities also try to create conditions for highly productive research in relatively low-cost fields. University investments are guided by competition for relative status rather than educational success, as well as by efforts to channel knowledge production into work that may yield commercial profits. Not least, the ideal is challenged by difficulties integrating the different fields and schools and missions bundled into that research university ideal. These difficulties are exacerbated by imbalanced growth and increased inequalities within the common university enterprise. A shared engagement with research-based knowledge was supposed to hold the modern university together. Now, ironically, the universities' own strategies for coping with declining state funds have increased the differentiation among their parts, creating fault lines for future tensions, reducing the commonalities among faculty members, and making the universities themselves less integrated.

THE RESEARCH UNIVERSITY SYSTEM

The term *research university* implies a distinction from nonresearch universities. To many people, this makes little sense, as they see the production of new knowledge through research as built into the very idea of a university. But in fact, this is a relatively new and unequally distributed academic mission dating mainly from the nineteenth century. That it was not how Oxford and Cambridge conceived of their core mission is part of what led to the founding of universities in London and Manchester. Scottish and German universities brought research to the forefront sooner, but in their cases, too, this was a reform of universities that predated the modern idea of an institution shaped centrally by the production of new knowledge.

Consider the definition of a university with which Cardinal Newman opens his legendary discourses on *The Idea of the University*: "It is a place of *teaching* universal *knowledge*" (italics in the original). Newman defines each term. The university is for knowledge of all sorts; it is not confined to religious training but teaches science and literature.[30] But the purpose he stresses is "the diffusion and extension of knowledge rather than the advancement. If its object were scientific and philosophical discovery, I do not see why a University should have students."[31]

The creation of a kind of institution contrary to what Newman envisaged was under way even as he wrote. From the last third of the nineteenth century on, research grew steadily more important to the dominant conception of the university, especially but not only in the German and Anglo-Saxon parts of the world. The model of public research universities flourished remarkably in the nineteenth century in Germany, Britain, Canada, the United States and in varying degrees around the world. It was the most influential model for the development of universities (albeit always with local specifics) in China, India, Uganda, Kenya, South Africa, Mexico, and Chile. This model was central to an enormous expansion of access to high-quality higher education, to amazing advances in research, and to a transformation in the relationship between universities and public constituencies ranging from schools to hospitals to social welfare institutions and agricultural extension. The integration of research and education in a single institution helped make this new sort of university more open to both talent and innovation.

But the model of public research universities is in trouble. Even where individual institutions thrive, the model has lost focus. Balance among its component missions has proved hard to maintain amid shifts in funding (an incentive system largely disconnected from teaching) and intensified competition tied to costly research.

Similar issues inform debates over the future of higher education in post-apartheid South Africa; over the reorganization and funding of the Universidad nacional autónoma de México (UNAM); over the role that universities should play and how they should be funded in Britain, France, and throughout the European Union (EU); and over the rise of private universities in Turkey and elsewhere. The stakes of the discussion include the question of whether and how public research universities and intellectual life will thrive in developing countries. Will narrow job-training and economic development agendas dominate? Will poor or marginalized people have access to the universities (and if so, will this be confined to the bottom rung)? And will the university's education and research dimensions remain integrated with each other?

That the issues are global should help us realize that the causes are not just unfortunate decisions by individual university leaders or the specific crises of certain state economies. Instead, they are situated in and perhaps exacerbated by neoliberalism (which often appears to the rest of the world as the extension of an "American model").[32] But that is not the whole story. Indeed, academics sharply critical of neoliberalism—and often of the leadership of their local universities—are also complicit in the problems: misrecognizing situations of privilege for simple reflections of merit and questioning aspects of the issue but not analyzing the whole because it would require examining situations in which they are relatively comfortable.

The relative weight given to teaching and research has been contested since the days of Cardinal Newman, but now it is a defining element in an academic hierarchy. Some universities offer doctorates and others do not. Some universities have massive scientific laboratories and others do not. Some universities have "research libraries" and others do not. Some universities limit faculty teaching loads to make time for research, and others do not. And if this is a distinction among the universities in rich countries, it is just as much a distinction among the leading universities of different countries, as brought home by the international rankings that have become popular in recent years, from the *Times Higher Education Supplement* in London and Shanghai Jiao Tong University. Both rank universities on research, but they have no meaningful way of comparing their teaching or the public service their faculties render. They also compare the prestige of research (with some bias in favor of the sciences and the English language).

Of course, universities are not the only way to organize research. Universities were marginal to the Renaissance and the early years of scientific revolution when extra-academic institutions like Britain's Royal Society brought researchers together. Isaac Newton may have done much of his most important work at Cambridge, but like many others he regarded the old university as a bastion of conservative and too often mediocre thinking. Science came on the heels of religious dissent to start a long process of renewal, often against notable resistance. Universities were more significant to the eighteenth-century Enlightenment, particularly in Scotland, but this was still largely a project of individual writers with the benefit of aristocratic patronage and profits from new print publications. Since the nineteenth century, universities have been increasingly central to intellectual production and circulation. Nonetheless, more amateur science and intellectual life could be revitalized (aided by the Internet, especially in fields that are not hugely capital intensive or whose data are routinely made public). Corporations could internalize more of the technoscience now based at universities (and are more likely to do so if subsidies are reduced). Governments could decide to support independent laboratories and split research from teaching.

Indeed, some countries have long invested more than others in specialized research institutions outside universities (like the Centre national de la recherche scientifique [CNRS] in France or the Academy of Sciences in Russia). Even though Britain's Royal Society never became a primary source of employment for many researchers, its counterparts became more or less autonomous research organizations. They have always been staffed by university graduates and thus have been part of a more or less integrated system. But they imply a greater separation of research from teaching. To a considerable extent, the Russian Academy separated postgraduate research training from undergraduate education. In France, the *grandes écoles*, with their more professional mission and expectations of direct service to the state, are also distinct from the universities, though still part of a larger academic system. Indeed, these differences in structure contribute to the differences in patterns of change today. In France, the CNRS staff are pressured to assume more teaching duties, and an institution like Sciences Po can pursue profit in trying to integrate teaching and research more like a research university. But the future is unclear.

The ideal-typical research university combines research and teaching in the same institution with the expectation that they will reinforce each other. This is an innovation associated especially with nineteenth-century German universities, notably Halle and Berlin. Scottish universities had begun to move in the same direction from the late eighteenth century, and the new universities in Britain—notably the Victorian universities in provincial cities like Manchester but also the colleges that joined to form the University of London—also combined the pursuit of new knowledge with the education of undergraduates. Oxford and Cambridge were slow to change but eventually were won over. The apotheosis of the research university model, however, came with the adaptation of the German (and, to some extent, Scottish) model to the United States.

New universities like Johns Hopkins, Cornell, and Chicago led the way in integrating the creation of new knowledge through research into a new kind of academic structure and a reformed curriculum. Faculty members were increasingly expected to hold PhD degrees, which were certifications of research competence as well as mastery of subject matter. Training new PhD students, as well as conducting and publishing research, became an important part of the work of leading universities. These research universities enjoyed influence and prestige, and so the older universities adopted many of the new structures. Undergraduate curricula were restructured with a combination of "free electives" and "majors" aligned with the research disciplines recognized in PhD programs. Departments were organized along the same lines. The last years of the nineteenth century and the first years of the twentieth produced most of the disciplines—and disciplinary departments—that remain prominent today. Even older branches of learning were reorganized in line with this approach. For example, teaching poetry and rhetoric gave way to concentrating on literature in departments that, among other things, emphasized the analysis of texts over oral performance.

The heart of the new model was the combination of research and teaching, and the university was defined as the locus of production of new knowledge. There also was an expectation of service, as the knowledge producers were expected to be advisers to the government (especially in the German version, in which professors were civil servants) and informers to the public. But the key was redefining the university through research. This meant adding a function and reshaping the organization of the faculties, the subjects taught, the curricula, and the degrees offered. The growing importance of natural and physical science was pivotal. Technical and professional courses figured prominently from early on, although until the nineteenth century, much professional education was conducted outside universities. Usually a claim to distinctive forms of research-based knowledge brought professional schools into the university. Medicine thus increasingly claimed authority from scientific research, for example, on infectious diseases, and purely practical training was complemented by experiment and theory.

The research university did not stand alone but was at the center of a larger academic system that included a variety of other components. Colleges and other institutions of higher education with less investment in research were part of this, and they were reshaped by the reorganization of knowledge that research universities pioneered and eventually by new expectations for professorial expertise. Learned societies were founded to correspond to the new academic disciplines. Thus the American Social Science Association, an organization of amateurs and professionals in fields from law to divinity as well as academics, gave way to disciplinary associations in economics, sociology, political science, history, and other fields.[33] Both university presses and other academic publishers catered to the new knowledge producers and those who would read their work. Government ministries and private foundations could also be added to the mixture in varying degrees in different countries. Despite the variations, the academic system that had the research university at its center became an impressively global model.[34]

By the early to mid-twentieth century, this academic system dominated in the production of new knowledge, the circulation of knowledge by means from publications to conferences, and the training of knowledge workers (including those organized in professions). Universities became much larger, and more of them were created (by both states and private actors). In most of the OECD countries, the majority of the population received higher education, and a rapidly growing percentage studied for postgraduate degrees. This expansion of higher education and research institutions was central to economic expansion, through both the invention of new products and processes and the training of workers. It was central to the growth and reproduction of the middle classes, and the promise of entry into the middle classes fueled the popular pursuit of higher education. Higher education helped anchor the public sphere of civil society in its debates about key social issues, and it was a source of government workers and one of the key steering mechanisms available to states to shape directions of development—whether by spending massively on research for military purposes or for medicine.

Several sectors of modern economies are largely products of academic research and remain closely tied to it. These include not only plastics and computers but also the financial technologies that have, for better or worse, increasingly driven capitalist investment and accumulation in recent decades. Despite a prestige system honoring "pure science," academic research has always been shaped by funding from rich individuals, private businesses, and government agencies trying to address specific problems, not merely to produce knowledge for its own sake.[35]

The public evidently wants research from universities. Indeed, the public generally, and those making decisions on behalf of public funders, want life-saving medical discoveries and new technologies that stimulate economic growth. They also may want research on medical ethics and the social effects of new technologies, although the latter is less sure. Literature, patent law, and the economics of the environment receive state funding as well, albeit in very unequal amounts, and are tied to very different ideas of how the public might benefit. Forced to prioritize, university leaders do make decisions, but they are seldom able to explain why a particular use of resources is in fact the best for the public. This lack of clarity is partly because most state funding comes in relatively inflexible forms, such as buildings and salaries and capitation payments for each enrolled student tied to the provision of more or less specific courses of study. Administrators are often drawn to prioritize additional income, especially funds linked not to sustaining the status quo but to new projects. The new projects, in turn, often rest on the basis provided by the more stable state funding.[36]

Many universities have, in effect, become conglomerate corporations. Like the industrial conglomerates, such as Gulf & Western and Ling-Temco-Vought (LTV), that went through a shakeout starting in the 1970s, these universities may face a shakeout today. LTV ran an airline and rented cars, made stereo equipment and golf clubs, rolled steel, and packed meat. But investors deserted it when they found that the conglomerate holding company added little to the value or profit of the firms it bought up, sometimes added costs, and often made mistakes because the central managers did not understand all the different businesses they controlled. The analogy is not far-fetched when universities offer general education (and sometimes remedial education) to eighteen-year-olds of widely different abilities, specialized education to professional students in a range of technical fields, and research training to PhD candidates even while managing giant laboratories seeking to innovate in dozens of different fields; running hospitals, radio and TV stations, housing facilities, publishing companies, and semiprofessional sports teams; providing professors a base from which to run consulting businesses; providing extension services to agricultural producers; storing books in libraries; and expanding electronic access to information. None of these is necessarily a bad thing for a university to do, nor is there is any reason not to do several. But such a proliferation of purposes challenges universities to achieve organizational structures in which the connections among these components become real advantages, not just sources of confusion or complexity. Faced with complexity, many universities adopt centralized management approaches at odds with traditions of faculty self-governance (although the tension is not always openly acknowledged). Taking on so many different tasks strains universities' capacity to provide a clear account of their purposes for themselves as well as for others.

With the proliferation of roles and functions came a proliferation of funding sources, many of which effectively operated as clients. Big Science involving massive capital investments was undertaken at the behest of governments, overwhelmingly in the United States and Europe,[37] and technoscience attracted a growing number of private investors. Professional schools were closely integrated with the professions for which they trained practitioners and often consulted or developed products. All of these grew at rates that far outstripped the humanities and social sciences (and indeed, the science fields, since they were organized for undergraduate teaching). Big Science and technoscience came to command the majority of the budgets of most of the world's leading universities. Even in the humanities and social sciences, published research became the primary criterion of evaluation, even though this was much less consistently tied to major external funding. Time spent teaching was limited in proportion to the institution's research ambitions.

To be sure, the number of students was not equally limited. On the contrary, major research universities, especially state-funded public universities, admitted many more students, with the result that class sizes expanded. Advising functions were shifted from professors to student services professionals. Throughout much of the postwar era, an implicit bargain guided university expansion. More places would be available for students seeking upward mobility (or at least to stay in the middle class). Professional schools would expand not just to provide additional training but also to help police the boundaries of professions and ensure their status and economic position. And faculty would pursue research that brought the university prestige and external funding. Producing this research determined individual professors' labor market positions, bringing them offers from other universities, salary increases, honorary chairs, and other benefits in a way that teaching and, indeed, "service" did not. This was a system that encouraged the production of new knowledge, although it may have exaggerated the importance of what was ostensibly new over the effective synthesis and mastery of what was already known. It was a system that allowed faculty members considerable autonomy, subject mainly to the scrutiny of their research fields, which acted as the primary evaluators of what was legitimate or significant work. This was, in fact, central to the notion of academic freedom as it was institutionalized in the nineteenth century: competent experts inside each field, not administrators, politicians, or economic benefactors, should pass judgment.[38]

Expansion encouraged both differentiation and new hierarchies. Universities became less integrated. Gaps among fields in salaries and resources grew more pronounced, as did the inequality among members of individual fields. A new class of casual academic laborers was created, sometimes mobilizing graduate students as teaching assistants but often extending into a longer-term status as adjunct faculty.[39] These trends were muted in most places until the 1970s but intensified thereafter. Those who produced prestige or generated new revenue streams were advantaged over others. Big Science and professional schools were relatively privileged, but support for humanities and the "human sciences" was shakier. With less external funding for research and professional services, these fields were dependent on funding for undergraduate teaching. When financial crises hit—as at the University of California in 2008/2009—they were more vulnerable. One of the lessons of the crisis was that simply being able to claim intellectual distinction within a research field was not an adequate defense against defunding if the research field commanded inadequate external resources.

Ironically, for generations the faculty members at elite institutions had been encouraged to claim distinction by research accomplishments rather than teaching. Their investments were greatest in the competition for rankings, which was vulnerable in fields without funds. Suddenly the question of how to make a virtue of relying on instructional revenues acquired new significance. It is now a challenge for the humanities and social sciences to rethink their role and claims on resources in a new era. Funding sources have shifted, and a major curricular change is under way with the disciplinary liberal arts majors in decline, along with the demand for liberal arts teaching in both issue-oriented interdisciplinary programs (like environmental studies and international studies) and professional education.

This is an issue for individual universities with their many roles and functions, and at least as much an issue for the higher education sector as a whole. This sector has come to be enormously differentiated and hierarchically organized, making it harder to develop a common articulation of a public mission. Indeed, during recent decades, public support for higher education has lagged, and universities have been regarded more and more often as providers of private goods. They offer individuals career credentials and donors, prestige connections. They offer industry-trained employees and marketable new technologies.

Knowledge is the business of the research university: creating knowledge through research, preserving and renewing knowledge through scholarship, transmitting knowledge through teaching and learning, and distributing and applying knowledge in public service. The widespread consensus is that knowledge matters and, indeed, matters more all the time to the future of contemporary societies. There is much less agreement on whether research universities have a distinctively public mission, and perhaps still less agreement on the best ways for universities to be "public."

This book is about that question of purpose. Higher education has changed dramatically over the last fifty years and still is changing today. Questions about the mission of universities must be addressed, and not just in the abstract. We thus must look, as the contributors to this book do, at how universities have been molded—and buffeted—by shifts in their national, regional, and global contexts; by shifting finances and economic agendas; by nationalist projects and internationalist projects; by dreams of social mobility and business demands for expertise; and by pressures to educate more students and to deliver research for economic purposes or prestige or both.

Universities flourished on the basis of a sometimes explicit and more often tacit expectation that they would serve public purposes. This was especially true during the postwar economic expansion when universities grew dramatically both in the world's richest countries and, at least for a time, throughout the world.

Expectations were high and certainly not all were achieved. But technological innovation, expanding trade, and growing citizen participation led to a boom to which higher education was central. They helped drive the shift from elite to mass higher education and integral connections of the university to other institutions in the "knowledge society." Academic institutions became pivotal to the development of new technologies and the training of professionals for a variety of industries. Within each university, the range of teaching programs grew wider and the economic importance of nonteaching activities, principally research, loomed larger.

Some universities have a relatively clear idea about what they do and why, and some—not always the same ones—are relatively secure in their financing. But many more have added activities and component units and costs without developing the strong institutional mechanisms for clarifying their common purpose or managing complexity effectively.

Determining how universities can and should respond to their current predicaments demands a firmer sense of mission. Simply trying to defend the status quo ante is hardly a strategy likely to strengthen universities. Such a defense will not work, and the status quo often deserves critique. The existing system is rife with unjustified inequalities, blockages to interdisciplinary collaboration and innovation, and misplaced incentives. At the same time, universities contribute enormously—if unevenly and not always efficiently—to their students and those who pursue profits based on their innovations, as well as local, national, and international publics. Whether they will continue to do so is the basic question about the public mission of research universities.

NOTES

1. In *Remaking the American University: Market-Smart and Mission-Centered* (New Brunswick, N.J.: Rutgers University Press, 2005), 4 and 6, Robert Zemsky, Gregory R. Wegner, and William F. Massy write of "the drift toward private purposes" even "to the point where many of the nation's best-known public institutions have become like private ones." See also Craig Calhoun, "The University and the Public Good," *Thesis Eleven* 84 (2005): 7–43.

2. Charles M. McClelland, *State, Society, and University in Germany, 1700–1914* (Cambridge: Cambridge University Press, 1980).

3. The first vice-chancellor of Calcutta University spoke of the role of the English language in what he understood as both a civilizing process and the formation of a foreign-oriented elite:

    We all know, that those who first undertook the task of transferring the treasures of Western learning, and Western science into the Oriental mind . . . had to choose between conveying instruction through the medium of English language, or through the medium of the Vernaculars. The first is a key which unlocks the whole treasure-house; but it is one, which only the few can acquire, and it leaves a foreign mark upon all to which it opens the door. (Sir James William Colville, quoted in Subash Battacharya, "The Domain of the Dreamers," University of Calcutta, Department of English, available at http://www.uvm.edu/~sgutman/Calcutta _University.html)

4. See chapter 4. Private universities also sometimes provided relative protection for researchers when public universities became inhospitable, notably under Latin American dictatorships.

5. The classic statement is by Paul A. Samuelson, "The Pure Theory of Public Expenditure," *The Review of Economics and Statistics* 36, no. 4 (November 1954): 387–89. See also Joseph Stiglitz, "Knowledge as a Global Public Good," in *Global Public Goods*, ed. I. Kaul, I. Grundeberg, and M. Stern (New York: Oxford University Press, 1999). For further discussion, see chapters 9, 10, and 12.

6. See chapters 9 and 10.

7. Robert K. Merton, "The Normative Structure of Science," in *The Sociology of Science*, ed. N. W. Storer (Chicago: University of Chicago Press, 1973), 267–78.

8. Michael Polanyi, "The Republic of Science: Its Political and Economic Theory," *Minerva* 1 (1962): 54–74. If Polanyi saw science as an ideal model for democracy, Yaron Ezrahi saw them as coproduced since the seventeenth century; see his *Descent of Icarus: Science and the Transformation of Contemporary Democracy* (Cambridge, Mass.: Harvard University Press, 1990).

9. "Truth is that concordance of an abstract statement with the ideal limit towards which endless investigation would tend to bring scientific belief, which concordance the abstract statement may possess by virtue of the confession of its inaccuracy and one-sidedness, and this confession is an essential ingredient of truth." See "Truth and Falsity and Error," in *Collected Papers of Charles Sanders Peirce* (Cambridge, Mass.: Harvard University Press, 1931–5), 5:565–73.

10. "Scientific thinking is essentially a rectification of knowledge." See Gaston Bachelard, *The New Scientific Spirit* (Boston: Beacon Press, 1985, orig. 1934), 173.

11. See *Education at a Glance 2009: OECD Indicators* (Paris: OECD, 2009).

12. It has fallen from second to fourteenth in OECD data. *Education at a Glance 2009*, table A.3.2.

13. See, for example, Gordon Brown's speech of January 14, 2010, "Education as a Global Growth Industry," in which the British prime minister called for Britain to "double the value of our higher education exports," available at http://www.number10.gov. uk/Page22137. As a blogger noted, the expectation of commercial growth was actu-

ally coupled not with increased investment but an austerity budget from the government, available at http://globalhighered.wordpress.com; January 15, 2010.

14. In the United States, most public universities are funded mainly by states, not the federal government. The fifty states face a fiscal squeeze without the federal government's capacity to run a deficit. Because their tax revenues are closely related to real estate values and consumer spending, they dropped quickly in the recession. The U.S. states also committed themselves to the world's highest level of spending on prisons, deciding even in an era of falling crime rates that imprisonment was as important a public purpose as higher education. State spending on prisons is about the same as state spending on universities. See Bruce Western, *Punishment and Inequality in America* (New York: Russell Sage Foundation, 2006).

15. UNESCO, "The State of Higher Education in the World Today," June 24, 2009, available at http://portal.unesco.org/es/ev.php-URL_ID=45964&URL_DO=DO _TOPIC&URL_SECTION=201.html.

16. Nicholas Burnett, assistant director-general for education, quoted in "A Global Agenda," *Inside Higher Education*, July 2, 2009.

17. Steven Brint, "Can Public Research Universities Compete?" in *Future of the American Public Research University*, ed. R. L. Geiger, C. L. Colbeck, R. L. Williams, and C. K. Anderson (Rotterdam: Sense Publishers, 2007), 91–120.

18. This is the pattern traced famously in France by Pierre Bourdieu. See Pierre Bourdieu and Jean-Claude Passeron, *The Inheritors* (Chicago: University of Chicago Press, 1979). As the more optimistic study by Yossi Shavit, Richard Arum, Adam Gamoran, and Gila Menachem, *Stratification in Higher Education: A Comparative Study* (Stanford, Calif.: Stanford University Press, 2007) demonstrates, this does not mean that expanding higher education brings no gains. They show that across fifteen countries, students from all classes tend to benefit from expansion. Hierarchical differentiation still provides the framework for elite reproduction, but educational attainment can and does mediate the impact of family background. Much depends on the selection processes that accompany expansion.

19. Of course, universities around the world have a substantial formal similarity, and they have undergone important historical shifts in concert. See the discussion in David John Frank and Jay Gabler, *Reconstructing the University: Worldwide Shifts in Academia in the 20th Century* (Stanford, Calif.: Stanford University Press, 2006). At the same time, there are significant variations in context, funding, performance and other factors, and the research university system is organized as a hierarchy rather than a sector of similarity.

20. A more substantial account would have to include attention to the turmoil in exchange rates after the United States pulled out of the Bretton Woods Accord in 1971

(which, among other things, caused the dollar to depreciate and oil producers' revenues to decline) and the Yom Kippur War of 1973, an inflection point in the ongoing entanglement of energy prices in politics (particularly, but not only, in the Middle East). Still broader factors in the background included the crises of authority and of welfare compromises represented by the range of social movements that came to the fore in the late 1960s and early 1970s, as well as the crises of Third World governments that, for example, first brought socialists to power and then led to military dictatorship in Chile and played out in different ways in different contexts.

21. See Robert H. Frank and Philip J. Cook, *The Winner-Take-All Society* (New York: Free Press, 2005).

22. On the effort to achieve quality assurance net of rankings as an end in themselves, see chapter 13.

23. See chapters 7 and 8, and also N. V. Varghese, *Private Higher Education in Africa* (Paris: UNESCO, 2004).

24. The late nineteenth and early twentieth-century transformation that produced the research university in the United States was led partly by the "land grant" public universities established to support industrialization and agricultural innovation. But it was led even more directly by several new universities established by private benefactions: Johns Hopkins, Chicago, Cornell (which also received some public support), and Stanford. There were tensions over just how tightly donors could control scientific research, and it is no accident that these private universities (and a few others, like Columbia, which sought to remake themselves as research universities) figured disproportionately in early struggles over academic freedom.

25. On the tension between change efforts and traditionally conservative and inflexible German academic administration, see chapter 11.

26. Mark Yudoff, president of the University of California system, quoted in "Before the Fall: California's Universities in Trouble," *The Economist*, August 14, 2009.

27. For the original master plan and later discussions, see http://sunsite.berkeley.edu/~ucalhist/archives_exhibits/masterplan/.

28. For a closer look at how these missions interacted and informed debate over globalization at the University of Michigan, see chapter 15.

29. According to chapter 2, more research and a longer temporal perspective will be required to gauge how deep the crisis of the public research university may be or whether it may yet be renewed for a new phase of leadership. See, too, the essays collected in Steven Brint, ed., *The Future of the City of Intellect: The Changing American University* (Stanford, Calif.: Stanford University Press, 2002); and Craig Calhoun, "Is the University in Crisis?" *Society* 43 (2006): 8–18.

30. By universality, Newman meant truth founded in the natural order, meeting the tests of reason and ever more extensive empirical investigation. He meant to ex-

clude the merely contingent, not to grapple with the issues that postmodern inquiry would raise with the idea of universality.

31. John Henry Newman, *The Idea of the University* (New Haven, Conn.: Yale University Press, 1996), 1. The book first appeared in 1873, even though Newman began his series of lectures in 1852 and an earlier print version appeared in 1859.

32. According to chapter 3, two distinct issues reinforce each other: a global ideology and American hegemony.

33. See Thomas Haskell, *The Emergence of Professional Social Science* (Baltimore: Johns Hopkins University Press, 1977)

34. See Frank and Gabler, *Reconstructing the University*, which builds on the "world polity" perspective of John Meyer, in, for example, John Meyer, Francisco O. Ramirez, and Yasemin N. Soysal, "World Expansion of Mass Education, 1870–1980," *Sociology of Education* 65: 128–49.

35. John Ziman, *Real Science* (Cambridge: Cambridge University Press, 2000).

36. Much of the pursuit of external funding actually costs universities money, but it provides administrators (as well as leading researchers) with flexible resources. Paradoxically, this makes even a money-losing operation attractive. See Roger L. Geiger, *Knowledge and Money: Research Universities and the Paradox of the Marketplace* (Stanford, Calif.: Stanford University Press, 2004). For an effort to track the relative costs of teaching intensive humanities departments and professional schools with substantial external research funding, see Christopher Newfield, *Unmaking the Public University* (Cambridge, Mass.: Harvard University Press, 2008).

37. See Derek J. de Solla Price, *Little Science, Big Science* (New York: Columbia University Press, 1963); Peter Galison and Bruce Hevly, eds., *Big Science: The Growth of Large Scale Research* (Stanford, Calif.: Stanford University Press, 1996); and much discussion since.

38. See the classic discussion in Richard Hofstadter and Walter P. Metzger, *The Development of Academic Freedom in the United States* (New York: Columbia University Press, 1955). Also see Thomas L. Haskell, "Justifying the Rights of Academic Freedom," in *The Future of Academic Freedom*, ed. Louis Menand (Chicago: University of Chicago Press, 1996); Robert Post, "The Structure of Academic Freedom," in *Academic Freedom After September 11*, ed. Beshari Doumani (New York: Zone Books, 2006); and Craig Calhoun, "Academic Freedom, Public Knowledge, and the Structural Transformation of the University," *Social Research* 76, no. 2 (2009): 1–38.

39. This particular pattern is American, but differences between more and less secure parts of the academic labor market were also pronounced elsewhere. See chapter 14.

TWO

Great Expectations, Past Promises, and Golden Ages

Rethinking the "Crisis" of Public Research Universities

GUSTAVO E. FISCHMAN, SARAH E. IGO, AND DIANA RHOTEN

The public research university (PRU) is an institution that for a great deal of its long history was perceived in almost universally positive terms.[1] Today, however, a broad set of conditions seem to be reshaping public universities, resulting in a global view of PRUs in transformation, if not turmoil and even "crisis." Despite cross-national increases in total government funding for higher education and research, diversifications in student enrollments in higher education, and upsurges in research investments and community engagements, conversations and publications the world over claim that the PRU as an archetype has lost its way and, as a result, is failing everyone from students and faculty to funders and employers. Criticisms flow from both the political left and right, from the developed and developing world, and from those concerned about privatization and the commercialization of campuses to those who complain about the unresponsiveness of academic institutions to social needs, market incentives, and technological innovations.[2] In the past, if the university was considered a "distinctive, prestigious, and even sacred institution," which by virtue of its "very name . . . is inconsistent with restrictions of any kind,"[3] it seems to have become now just another organization subject to many of the same forces of change—globalization, marketization, democratization, and digitalization—bearing down on all twenty-first-century organizations.

Numerous and often contradictory analyses of the state and the fate of PRUs under these conditions have appeared in professional journals, trade books, and public discourse.[4] Although the shape of this discussion varies greatly across geographic regions and higher education systems, certain common trends and patterns emerge when considered from a comparative approach. Most commentators seem to agree that globally, public research universities are rapidly diverging from an ideal-type model that emerged in the early twentieth century and purportedly flourished in the post–World War II period, often nostalgically referred to as the "golden age."[5] Whether this process of transformation is viewed as a steady decline into "crisis" or a necessary step toward "reform" depends in part on where the observer sits geographically, institutionally, organizationally, and even demographically. Philip Altbach, a noted analyst of contemporary changes in the university sector, captured this dualism: "Higher Education is undergoing dramatic change everywhere. It seems that the early 21st century is the 'perfect storm' of external pressures and internal responses. The current period may provide a chance of significant reform and change, although the pressures could overwhelm already stretched academic institutions."[6]

Even though the conditions creating a seemingly "perfect storm" are effecting similar changes in many private universities, they are not causing the same level of consternation. Thus in this chapter, we locate the roots of the PRU "crisis" across different eras and national cultures. To clarify the contemporary state of the PRU and its critics, we examine the history of the public university as both a model and an ideal that crystallized in the middle of the twentieth century—and then seemingly began to falter. We then explore whether the global call to arms regarding the PRU reflects a crisis of its *functionality* or its *identity* and conclude by asking whether the real or perceived crisis is in fact about public universities per se or about the state of public institutions more broadly.

THE EVOLVING MISSION OF PUBLIC RESEARCH UNIVERSITIES

One of the difficulties of analyzing the "public research university" is that this entity is not singular but plural and has had many different incarnations over time and space, including the Napoleonic model, the Cardinal Newman model, the Humboldtian model, the land grant model, and the "state-building" model.[7] Loosely speaking, although each of these models could be considered a unique national institution, they all, in fact, have been influenced by one another, borrowing and blending ideals and traditions across institutional time and space.[8] With different degrees of consistency, most modern PRUs reveal traces of the Oxford ideal of liberal undergraduate education, the medieval tradition of professional schools, the Berlin principle of research and graduate education, the Scottish concept of accessibility and social service, the applied research and practical education blueprint of the publicly funded American land grant universities, the state-building and democratizing aspirations associated with the Cordoba reform in Latin America and postcolonial African universities, and the Soviet model of using higher education to meet state manpower and industrial-technological goals.[9] Recognizing that we cannot capture all these complexities of the PRU and lose many of the cross-national variations, we sketch a rough chronological narrative at the level of transnational trends and patterns.

The "Golden Age" of the PRU

Despite the institutional multiplicity stemming from different models, traditions, and local inflections, all contemporary PRUs are organized around the production and distribution of knowledge through teaching and research activities.[10] Teaching and research as central aspects of higher education, of course, predate the modern research university and, indeed, the modern nation-state.[11] John Scott writes that "under modern, independent nation-state circumstances, three distinct missions of universities emerged . . . nationalization, democratization, and public service," which developed in turn to serve the nation-state (first in early modern European universities), the individual (first in nineteenth-century American colleges), and the public (first through the U.S. Morrill Acts of 1862 and 1890 and the 1904 "Wisconsin Idea" of state-university partnerships). Scott also states that "the missions of teaching and research were superimposed upon each of these missions."[12] This layering of functions onto the research university is thus nearly as old as the university itself.[13]

In the nineteenth century, the superimposition of several missions led to the creation of a "modern" and complex institution that contained multiple and sometimes contradictory promises. PRUs were at once central to the strengthening of nation-state identities, key players in the process of economic modernization, crucial institutions for the formation of political elites, and, in some cases, the seedbeds of practical improvements for national ends. During this period, those leading PRUs carved out an autonomous niche for creating and certifying scholarship: modernizing curricula and disciplines, committing more seriously to research, and distinguishing themselves from clerical institutions as well as competing sites of knowledge production such as museums and amateur societies. In the United States around this time, the government and universities formed an unwritten "social compact" granting universities a unique degree of autonomy, scholarly freedom, and public funding in exchange for the education of an informed citizenry and workforce.[14]

During the first half of the twentieth century, the functions, campuses, and enrollments of universities grew rapidly. This expansion coincided with the establishment of the Keynesian welfare state in Western democracies and had parallel goals: stable socioeconomic progress, democratic access to state programs and services, mass industrial development, international competitiveness, and individual (as well as group) social mobility. For Clark Kerr, former chancellor of the University of California at Berkeley, by the middle of the century, higher education had assumed a "new centrality" in modern society: "We are just now perceiving that the university's invisible product—knowledge—may be the most powerful single element in our culture, affecting the rise and fall of professions and even of social classes, of regions and even of nations." Kerr noted as well that the university's promises were obvious to the population at large. "An entire generation," he proclaimed, "is pounding at the gates and demanding admission."[15] As his words imply, this was the first period of mass higher education, a phenomenon not limited to the United States but unfolding around the globe.

The transnational recognition of the PRU as a uniquely promising social institution became even more explicit after 1945 as governments made higher education central to their political and economic projects and expanded the universities' influence and student bodies. Nations around the globe also strengthened their systems of higher education, not simply for the economic dividends they would bring, but also because PRUs were seen to play a critical role in political and cultural nationalism, in both the developed and "less developed" world. Perhaps the clearest sign of this sense of promise and the rise of national investment in public universities around the world was the pressure—from states and citizens alike—for the expansion of institutions, services, departments, enrollments, and research in the second half of the century.[16]

Research and development for national progress and the public good played a key role in the transformation of PRUs during this era, as specialized research and "Big Science" came to redefine many flagship universities' mission. Scientific research enjoyed not only government patronage but also academic autonomy in return for the priority of discovery and the disclosure of results.[17] Indeed, in many nations, universities became largely dependent on federal governments for financing during this period. Likewise, they became more closely linked to nation-building, especially to state goals of military and economic development during an age of cold war mobilization and industrial "modernization." In nations on the global periphery, universities played a leading role in creating and lending cultural legitimacy to state institutions, from health ministries to judicial systems, and in providing key personnel for the bureaucratic apparatus.

Albeit with different levels of development and speed, the growth of PRUs was accelerating around the world. A few examples illustrate this global convergence around a newly essential *national* role for PRUs in the postwar period. In the United States, these years saw the "military-industrial-academic" complex take shape. Spurred by the mobilization for World War II and the successful scientific-state partnership exemplified by the creation of the atomic bomb, government-sponsored scientific and social scientific work intensified during the cold war.[18] On the other side of the superpower divide, the Soviet Union gave priority to two functions for public universities, both linked to urgent national goals: training professionals and technicians according to the targets established in the five-year plans determined by the central government and preserving Marxism/Leninism as the dominant ideology. Universities were therefore structured primarily as teaching institutions, and research activities were conducted mostly in the "academies."[19] The importance of ideological conformity and the acceptance of the principles and targets established in the plans elaborated by the Communist Party had, in most cases, the effect of making research and teaching subordinate to political goals and weakening the development of critical scholarly activity, as well as alternative explanations to the official Marxist perspective.[20]

Similar developments marked the Eastern European countries in the Soviet orbit. Matthew S. McMullen notes that

> the Communist Party spent 40 years trying to remold Czechoslovak higher education into the image of the Soviet Union's system and the principles of international communism. The Party not only controlled all levels of higher education; it also used institutions as instruments for controlling and educating students' minds to create the "communist man." National committees, which reported to the Ministry of the Interior, administered the system. All senior appointments in the Ministry of Education and in the National Committees were to Party members. . . . Membership in the Party was an important criterion for the highest academic posts. How closely an institution conformed to the planned system was the paramount means for evaluating the effectiveness of each institution no matter its output.[21]

Across Eastern Europe, formerly autonomous institutions ceded to a centralized education ministry. By 1953, "higher education throughout the region fully approximated the Soviet variant," emphasizing training and manpower goals for the state. The Communist Party established "firm links between students' education and the needs of the planned economy. This was reflected in the rapid growth of specialized technical training, and in attempts to subordinate students' lives to planning." National centralization of curricula changed the very nature of university education, so that "at the height of Stalinism all fields of scholarship were subjected to demands for ideological conformity."[22]

In the mid-twentieth century, nationalizing projects for higher education were apparent in Asia as well. China's universities in the nineteenth and early twentieth centuries had followed multiple paths, both indigenous and Western, and pursued varied objectives, ranging from training scholars of the classics to certifying civil servants. The Communist leadership of 1949 enacted broad changes, however, closing the doors of private higher education institutions and reorganizing education after 1952, again on the Soviet model. This was a major overhaul, "designed to meet the special needs of a centrally planned economy" and sparking student resentment over the "gap between their inherited expectations and the newly enforced 'needs of national construction.'"[23] Two goals of the new government—raising "the cultural level of the people" and training workers for "national construction work"—were closely tied to these reforms.[24] In the words of the head of the Ministry of Higher Education, "Educational construction should serve economic construction," meaning heavy industry, agriculture, and national defense. It was believed that "only through . . . a totally planned system would it be possible to produce the required numbers of people trained to the specifications of each grade and level in all the various specialties required for economic development."[25] In the post–Mao Zedong era as well, "education played an instrumental role in supporting the policies of the national leadership."[26]

In Japan, the strong links between higher education and state goals date back at least to the Meiji Restoration of 1868; indeed, thirty years before that, the ruling shogunate had determined that the modern university system was an efficient means of allowing the nation to meet "the new foreign challenge."[27] But the key transformation in Japan's postwar educational system came from a different source: the U.S. Occupation forces, which imposed a program of democratization, demilitarization, and decentralization on its wartime enemy. This effort broadened access to universities as well as the mission of Japanese higher education. As a result, even after some of these reforms were reversed, the emphasis on education as a tool of state political and economic development persisted, with a "manpower approach" and "human capital approach" justifying the expansion of the system.[28]

Key universities in Latin America were similarly deemed crucial to state projects. As Imanol Ordorika and Brian Pusser have argued, institutions like the Universidad nacional autónoma de México (UNAM) and the Universidad de Buenos Aires can be considered "state-building universities," responsible in large part for "building the material conditions for the expansion and consolidation of their respective States, as well as the intellectual and social legitimacy of those states." Again, this role is relatively new. Although UNAM has a long history dating back to 1553, it was only in the mid-twentieth century that it took on these specific features. During those years, the "strength and clarity of purpose" of Latin American PRUs was "deeply connected to [their] centrality in State development projects."[29] In the 1940s and 1950s, for example, UNAM became responsible not only for designing "innumerable government bodies and offices" and "educating and credentialing the civil servants who dominate those offices" but also for shoring up "knowledge production, social mobility and political consciousness."[30]

In postcolonial Africa, hopes for the transformative power of universities—and the assumed links between national destiny and public higher education—were perhaps even stronger. The continent was home to some of the world's oldest institutions of higher learning, beginning with the Alexandria Museum and Library, established in the third century BCE. During and after World War II, new universities on the European model were established by the British and French colonial governments responding to an anticipated shift of sovereignty, to the need for an indigenous elite, and to constant demands dating from the 1920s by Pan-African and nationalist movements for more institutions of higher education.[31] Independence raised the stakes and set the foundation for tremendous growth in university building. Parallel to the emergence of state-building universities in Latin America were calls by African scholars at major conferences in Tananarive in 1962 and Accra in 1972 for a "developmental university."[32] Colonial universities were "hotbeds of the nationalist agitation for independence," and indeed, the "quintessential modern African university is a product of African nationalism."[33]

In all these cases, public universities did not grow merely by state fiat; instead, much of the growth came from demands by national populations.[34] During the 1960s, the pressures for university expansion came from the Latin American states, for example, as well as from grassroots protests by students and political activists. But the result was the same: "a large number of women, elder and poorer persons . . . started to flood the universities which were until recently all male, elite institutions of the privileged young."[35]

As the foregoing suggests, to many people, the most striking accomplishment of Latin American universities in the last half century was this rapid growth in enrollments, from half a million students to seven million in the last three decades. Accordingly, the kinds of institutions arising to meet this volume of students diversified rapidly.[36] According to Ruth Hayhoe, in China, too, the "expansion in the number of higher education institutions and in enrollments was phenomenal." Between 1957 and 1960, the number of institutions grew from 229 to 1, 289 and enrollments from 441,000 to 961,000. At the same time, following a lowering of admission standards, as well as a surge in women's participation in university life at both the student and faculty levels, there was a dramatic rise from 36.3 to 49 percent in the enrollment of students from working-class and peasant backgrounds.[37]

African universities also saw exponential growth in the second half of the twentieth century, resulting from pressures from both state elites and national populations. As one set of contemporary commentators observed in 1965,

> Education has become a major, if not the major, concern of the new independent states of Africa. At almost every point in the modernization process, education is the critical factor. . . . For millions of Africans, education is the key that will open the door to a better life and the higher living standards they were promised as the reward of the struggle for national liberation.

They went on to predict, "No government in Africa could dare, even if it were so inclined, to deny the popular demand for expansion of the educational system."[38] Before the 1960s there were forty-two universities, located mostly in North and South Africa, with student enrollments in the tens of thousands. During the first two decades of independence, university employment and degrees were in great demand as institutions were made accessible to citizens beyond those being trained for high-ranking government positions. By the end of the 1990s, there were more than four hundred African universities, enrolling 3.5 million students.[39] It is easy to cite many more examples of this demand for public higher education. In the United States, the passage of the G.I. bill in 1944 opened university doors to many working-class and middle-class veterans, making college education a key citizenship right. In Japan, the 1960s saw an "unprecedented surge in enthusiasm for expansion in education."[40]

As the previous discussion indicates, the expansion of PRUs was common to states that shared little else pertaining to history, resources, educational infrastructure, or politics. Public universities played into the ambitions of decolonizing African nations, the new Communist regimes in Eastern Europe and China, social movements in Latin America, national defense planners in the cold war Soviet Union and United States, and student movements around the world.[41] Postwar states and citizens seemed to agree that scientific, social, political, and civic rewards all would flow from much expanded higher public education systems.

Across these various national contexts, then, the promises offered by PRUs seemed to expand geometrically during this time. They newly shouldered the burden, in one account, for "the nation's defense, health, energy development, space program, and economic growth," as well as the less tangible goal of social equity.[42] They became, in our analysis, "redemptive" institutions, expected to be able to resolve or mediate all manner of social problems. In this period, public research universities were almost completely supported by national governments and were charged with distributing or making "public" certain goods that were considered socially relevant and associated with the preservation, pursuit, production, and distribution of valuable knowledge. Because such activities were undertaken on behalf of the "the common good," they were meant to be performed by publicly minded and not simply economically self-interested individuals. Public funding, institutional autonomy, and academic freedom allowed faculty to search for important, meaningful, and accurate knowledge and gave students access to new skills and upward mobility. These goals were, to a great extent, connected with ideals of national and social development, common destiny, public goods, and fairness.

THE TRANSFORMATION OF THE "GOLDEN AGE" MODEL OF THE PRU

If the postwar convergence of aspirations for national universities around the world was surprising, a shared tone of disillusionment by the late 1970s and 1980s was even more remarkable. Global developments much broader than the public university were responsible for some of this. The oil shocks of the mid-1970s and the growing acceptance of both U.S. President Ronald Reagan's and British Prime Minister Margaret Thatcher's economic policies in the 1980s had enduring negative effects on public support for state universities. Arguably the social democratic movements of the 1960s, many of which had begun on college campuses—and led to more diverse student bodies as well as a reputation for universities' cultural radicalism—did the same. High hopes and expansionary ambitions, as we have seen, marked university systems across the globe from the 1940s to the 1960s. In subsequent decades, disappointment and retrenchment, both financial and civic, were much more common themes. Indeed, from almost impossibly broad variations in origins, goals, and specific conditions emerged a relatively uniform sense of "crisis." The crisis looked quite different, of course, depending on one's vantage point. Sharp disparities in wealth and resources, deepened by the uneven hand of globalization and "structural adjustment," meant that shortages of books and equipment were a primary feature of this crisis in many African nations but not in Western Europe. Many developing nations in Asia and Africa also worried about a brain drain as students flocked to the former colonial powers for their undergraduate and postgraduate training. In other regards, however, the pressures on and the critiques of public universities were resoundingly similar, reflecting a global trend toward "marketization" or "academic capitalism" and a retreat from the ambitious civic and social visions of the middle twentieth century.

In China, for example, "disappointments and discouragements [in universities] . . . paralleled in certain ways the faltering of economic and political reforms" in other spheres of society.[43] In this context, promises regarding expanding university education for workers and peasants shifted to a more narrowly focused "modernization" program after 1978; and earlier goals of educating workers and peasants as the "main body of the nation and creator of society's wealth" gave way to policies encouraging foreign investment and technological development.[44] By the late 1980s, inflation was dramatically curbing faculty salaries, and government support barely covered the basic operating costs of higher education institutions. Historically, China's colleges and universities had been financed primarily by the government, but increasing enrollment pressures and declining resources led the government to invite the involvement of the private sector. Whereas only a handful of private higher education institutions existed in the 1980s, by 1999 the number had climbed to 1,270, outnumbering public institutions by three to four hundred. Estimates of the private sector's share of total enrollments have ranged from a fourth to a third, although only about 40,000 of these students are in programs recognized by the Ministry of Education.[45] Like everywhere else, universities were expected to become profit-making institutions in their own right rather than relying on government funding, an expectation that created new inequities between universities, departments, and employees. Chinese institutions "found themselves engulfed by broader forces of change largely outside of their control."[46]

This sense of PRUs operating in a new environment "outside their control" is echoed again and again in contemporary higher education discourse. Much of this sense stems from a bleak funding situation, combined with a critique of what PRUs "deliver," that has prompted state-supported institutions as well as students to turn to private options as solutions. Japan's PRUs, too, have been pronounced unstable and in "crisis."[47] Widespread disillusionment in Japanese national institutions of higher education has taken the form of a right-wing attack on the system's low standards and mediocrity, with some people arguing that government intervention in and financial support for education should be completely terminated.[48]

In Latin America, a tide of privatization has undercut the prominent role of the national universities, making questions about access to, and the quality of, higher education more vexing. In Brazil, although private institutions have had a strong presence since the 1940s, the number of undergraduates in private higher education institutions has increased by 84 percent since 1998, and the private sector now accounts for 70 percent of total enrollment, an industry of around US$4 billion.[49] As Lewis Tyler and colleagues write, "Not long ago, key questions in Latin American higher education could be addressed without sustained reference to a private-public distinction." Of twenty countries, they note, only two had private sectors that predated the twentieth century, and only four had private sectors reaching back to 1940. But by the mid-1970s, all but two nations had private sectors. Overall, from 1955 to 1975, the "breadth of privatization [was] impressive."[50]

Similar stories come from African nations. Since the 1980s, according to Donald Ekong, then secretary-general of the Association of African Universities, the situation of African higher education "may be described as a crisis, characterised by declining funding and the consequent deterioration of infrastructural, teaching and research facilities, while at the same time there had been growing demand for increased enrolment."[51] Citing declines in the quality of teaching and research, the impact of universities on development, and the general intellectual environment, Ekong writes: "An atmosphere of frustration or at least uncertainty about the future appears to be present throughout the higher education community in the continent."[52]

Its universities tremendously wealthy in comparison, the United States, too, has seen both state cutbacks and increasing enrollments, putting pressure on state public university systems. The University of Michigan provides a telling example. Between 2002 and 2005, state appropriations to the university fell by almost 15 percent just as enrollments at Michigan were growing, resulting in an overall decrease of public monies by more than $1,500 per student. Confronted with this situation, the university in 2005 increased in-state tuition by 12.3 percent and raised out-of-state tuition by 5.7 percent to $27,601, making it the most expensive public school in the country.[53] As a result of these twin trends, compared with the 1960s when state appropriations provided close to 70 percent of the university's total operating budget, by 2005 they covered less than 7 percent. Reflecting on this situation, President Emeritus James Duderstadt described the university as one that

> had evolved from a state-supported to a state-assisted to a state-related to a state-located university. . . . In fact, with campuses in Europe, Asia, and Latin America, we remain only a "state-molested" university, since ironically, the less support state government provides, the more it wants to micromanage its public universities through intrusive regulations.[54]

What might explain some of these developments, so geographically far-flung and yet seemingly so institutionally universal? First, the enormous increase in demand for higher education resulted in both the massification of existing institutions (mainly public universities) and the creation of numerous new institutions (mainly private ones). Second, these expansions were accompanied by a more general shift in the understanding of higher education's benefits as accruing less to the public at large than to the individuals who enrolled, and a clear decline in some of the democratizing effects of a university degree. Craig Calhoun notes that in the American university sector, as student numbers increased, public universities that once educated all the qualified students in their state became selective, and the provision of open access was pushed down to institutions of lesser status. For a time, the stratification of institutions was not fully apparent, but "a trade-off between excellence and accessibility was being exacerbated."[55] Moreover, he suggests that the tension between excellence and access is being aggravated by the growing role of research and its function of sorting institutions within the field. Research is specialized and mostly inaccessible to common discourse: "Knowledge may be in the public interest without itself being very widely disseminated to the public. Indeed, it is a striking characteristic of universities that their excellence is often measured in terms of their exclusivity."[56] The seeming retreat of universities from a common public dialogue has led, unsurprisingly, to less public support.

Indeed, university expansion was coupled with severe restrictions in financial support for public institutions, in tune with the logic of neoliberal models of higher education.[57] In the case of non-Western nations, these models were championed by empowered supranational organizations such as the International Monetary Fund and World Bank, which by the 1980s were treating higher education more like an individual benefit than a social good or an agent of social change. Such organizations emphatically defended, and, in many cases, directly conditioned governments to accept, the notion that the "rate of return" of higher education was lower than that of elementary education. The logic sustaining this discourse implied that reducing spending on universities was a matter of "equity and efficiency":

> Constraints on government finance and the need for a broader range of higher education institutions mean that the private sector should be encouraged to play a bigger role in both financing and providing higher education in LAC [Latin America and the Caribbean]. Failure to use government funds to leverage private finance will constrain access and equity of access to higher education.[58]

These arguments, coupled with the pressure applied by financial institutions and local groups that saw benefits in those policies in an atmosphere of Reagan-Thatcherite ideology, proved to be one of the most significant policy shifts for the higher education sector in developing and developed countries alike.

In Africa, for instance, "the universities were told to generate funds, and the governments were urged to encourage private universities."[59] State disinvestment based on low rates of return came at a time when the capacity of many African nations was weakening and after a period of sustained economic turmoil.[60] Yet, as debt servicing mounted and resources shrank, demands on universities actually intensified as both the population and secondary education burgeoned. All this led to growing tension between the PRUs and national governments. By the end of the 1980s, most African universities—apart from those in Namibia and Eritrea, where the national governments continued to cultivate universities and their potential for development—were in trouble.[61] As in parts of Asia and Latin America, the "development" university of the 1960s and 1970s was giving way to the "market" university of 1980s and 1990s.[62] Paul Tiyambe Zeleza and Adebayo Olukoshi argue that today

> the universities' internal and external constituencies and competitors are more plural than ever as expectations of social success and accountability expand at the same

time as the universities lose their monopoly of knowledge production and access to public resources, all of which recast their capacities to articulate a public voice and deliver public service.[63]

Despite vast differences in the university systems of Africa and North America, a nearly identical diagnosis has been made of PRUs in the United States. The *interpretation* of what has happened, too, is strangely familiar. For example, Zeleza and Olukoshi point out that changes in African higher education over the last several decades "reflect the decomposition of the old social contract between the university, the state, and society in which higher education was valued as a public and intellectual good which, moreover, dovetailed into visions of nation-building and national development."[64] Many commentators in Western nations agreed that this same social contract, outlined by Clark Kerr at the University of California at Berkeley at midcentury, also was fraying. That is, a consensus about the social and civic value of public universities can no longer be assumed, whether those universities are in Kenya, France, Argentina, or the United States.

We should emphasize a final, and powerful, undercurrent in the global PRU pattern: high expectations and unrealized hopes. This sentiment appears in commentaries spanning the globe, even among those who acknowledge how much public universities have accomplished in regard to access, research, and equity since 1945. Writing about Latin America in the late 1990s, for example, Simon Schwartzman observed,

In very broad terms, many more people have access to education now, the traditional curricula were opened to new alternatives and experimentation, and in some countries and places, full-time teaching and research were introduced for the first time in higher education. The general feeling, however, is of deterioration and loss of quality, and an idealization of the past.[65]

Daniel Levy, too, noted the simultaneous achievements of and "keen disappointment" in Latin American higher education in recent years.

The incredible development optimism generated by higher education back in the 1950s and 1960s has faded. Both heady international assistance programs and idealistic indigenous reform movements seem adventures from bygone eras. Judged by its personnel, resources, and structures, Latin American higher education falls far short of where it had been projected to be.[66]

A similar pattern was at work in other corners of the globe. As we have seen, by the 1980s, the once hopeful vision of what African universities might contribute to national development had also turned sour. In Emmanuel Ngara's words:

> Instead of being a standard bearer in finding solutions to the economic and political problems of Africa, the African university became a cause for much concern as it was beset by a plethora of problems which led to a decline in standards in terms of both the quality of life for academics and students and academic performance generally.

Ngara notes that the current conditions have led some people to question "whether African universities have had the kind of impact on social and economic development that was expected of them."[67] Looking back at the social standing of the national university in the 1960s and 1970s, Zeleza and Olukoshi observed of the higher education landscape in Africa: "It is tempting to conclude that that period represented its heyday in the hierarchy of public institutions and household priorities, as well as in the vanguard of social advancement and popular perception." If the 1960s and 1970s were the "golden age" of the African university, then to many the 1980s represented "the lowest point in its modern history."[68]

Disappointment in the seemingly failed promise of PRUs suggests not just "failure" but also what great expectations and hopes were invested in these institutions during the first half of the twentieth century. As we have seen, this general pattern holds true in Africa as well as in Latin America, Asia, Europe , and North America, thereby making the PRU "crisis" truly global in scope.

ARE PUBLIC RESEARCH UNIVERSITIES IN CRISIS?

For most of their history, PRUs were regulated by state agencies, supported by public money, and, to a large extent, at least professed to follow the stated mission of serving the public interest. That mission made PRUs responsible to society at large rather than merely to the state authorities and those individuals who took part in its educational programs. PRUs were thus seen as key social institutions that deserved special protections to warrant that teaching and research would benefit the "public mission" in autonomous ways, independent of the particular interests of either government or social groups. Increasingly, however, the PRU is losing this protected status, breaking away from its earlier "social compact" moorings to find itself tacking between the same market and managerial forces as other modern enterprises.[69]

The mutually reinforcing elements that inform most discussions of PRUs' "crisis" cross-nationally include reduced state funding and support; burgeoning populations expecting access to a university education; increased demands for accountability, efficiency, and responsiveness to a broad group of stakeholders (economic institutions, local communities, political interests, and individual students); an expanding ethos of market or quasi–market reforms; a casualization of the university workforce as permanent faculty positions are replaced by part-time staff; infringements on the autonomy of university departments and researchers; critiques of scholarly (as opposed to applied) knowledge as irrelevant to students and society at large; and competition from nontraditional knowledge institutions, including virtual universities.[70]

The combined effects of these conditions cannot be reduced to the emergence of one all-powerful, global, and consistent model of the "new public research university."[71] However, revised and, in some ways, shared perspectives on institutional arrangements for PRUs appear to be developing, with the primary underlying theme being that the PRU is just another organization for which provision, access, and benefits should be financed by the individuals who profit most directly from them.[72] In contrast to the days of Newman when the university was almost sacrosanct, seemingly untouchable by external forces, or to those days of the "golden age" when the public research university was among a nation's most cherished and distinguished institutions, the PRU today has become a site of institutional contestation and even confusion as well as a case of organizational depreciation and frustration. As George Fallis (2004) claims, PRUs are "only as strong as public understanding of what universities are for and public willingness to support their mission. . . . Today, as public support diminishes, criticisms mount, and misunderstanding persists, a loss of confidence pervades the university and the writings about it."[73]

Before accepting such analyses, we must first ask why the language of crisis with regard to public universities has become so acute. Does this language portray rhetoric or reality? What historical, political, and ideological trends inform this perception? Are we recovering from or entering into a crisis? Is this crisis internal or external to the PRU, or both? Whose crisis is this?

After ten years as president of the University of Michigan, James Duderstadt observed:

The most predictable feature of modern society is its unpredictability. We no longer believe that tomorrow will look much like today. Universities must find ways to sustain the most cherished aspects of their core values, while discovering new ways to respond vigorously to the opportunities of a rapidly changing world. This is the principal challenge to higher education as we enter a new century.[74]

Public research universities certainly are changing, but as Christine Musselin notes in chapter 14 in this volume, there is an urgent need to develop conceptual and empirical tools to "measure" the dimensions of stability and change without accepting the "bias introduced by the mirage of the 'golden age' myth" and thus without assuming that what we see for tomorrow is worse than what we remember from yesterday. But even before developing these tools, we must first agree on some common definitions and clarity in conceptions.

What Is the Meaning of "Crisis"?

Very often the term *crisis* is used in debates in education, as in individual medical situations, to describe the point at which the patient gets either better or worse.[75] This medicalized understanding reduces the character of a social "crisis" to a turning point, a distinctive moment that in its uniqueness demarcates a before and an after of momentous change. Contrary to such a narrow understanding, we follow Antonio Gramsci's notion that a crisis is a manifestation of contradictory forces within structures in which an old structure is disappearing but a newer one is not sufficiently strong to replace the old. In that sense,

> a crisis occurs, sometimes lasting for decades. This exceptional duration means that incurable structural contradictions have revealed themselves (reached maturity) and that, despite this, the political forces which are struggling to conserve and defend the existing structure itself are making every effort to cure them, within certain limits, and to overcome them.[76]

Among the many writers characterizing the changes affecting higher education in the twenty-first century as a crisis in the Gramscian sense, Boaventura de Sousa Santos proposed that the "public university" is a notion-institution operating globally under similar expectations of improving its efficiency, quality, and access. In Sousa Santos's analysis, the university is facing three fundamental crises: a crisis of hegemony because it is no longer the only institution to offer the highest levels of knowledge, a crisis of legitimacy because it no longer is consensually accepted as the only provider of the highest levels of education, and an institutional crisis because it cannot ensure its own reproduction.[77] Alberto

Amaral and Antonio Magalhães point to the same "triple crisis," adding that the collapse of the welfare state and the rise of neoliberalism have transformed the PRU from being the distinctive "social institution" that it was to being just another "social organization" by the turn of the new century.[78]

At the same time that these elements of PRU "crisis" have been emerging, however, there are counternarratives. First, we note our own critical perspective regarding a nostalgic image of the PRU's "golden age." With few exceptions, most universities were originally structured as elitist, discriminatory, and patriarchal institutions and only gradually—and incompletely—opened their doors to minorities, women, and those in the working class.[79] For us, if examined carefully, the PRU of the "golden age" in fact offers a model that few dare to defend and to which few would actually choose to return. Second, some people welcome the changing dynamics of contemporary PRUs. As Steven Brint explained,

> For every portrait of a wayward Goliath, sloughing off its commitments to the progress of all, competing narratives have been written of the necessity of evolutionary change, of the inexorable logic of altered circumstances. Indeed it is difficult to contest the central narrative: that the university has been asked to do many things for many people. . . . Many proponents of this competing narrative argue that the new university is not just inevitably more entrepreneurial than the old but also more responsive and stronger because of it.[80]

Without empirically sound studies, it is hard to accept at face value Brint's assessment about the responsiveness of the "entrepreneurial university." But it also is difficult to deny that the PRUs of the twenty-first century are, by many indicators, much more diverse than in the mid-1960s. As already noted, in the last century, the demand for higher education steadily increased, especially after the 1960s. According to Alsion Wolf, higher education everywhere has undergone meteoric expansion, and countries as far afield as China, the United States, Australia, and South Africa have developed policies to increase participation in response.[81] Since the mid-1960s, the number of university students worldwide has grown tenfold, climbing from 13 million to approximately 115 million in 2004. As Joaquim Tres, executive director of the Global University Network for Innovation, found, in seventy countries (out of 111) this growth in the number of tertiary students has been accompanied by substantial increases in higher education allocations as a percentage of total public spending on education.[82] Although this increase in public spending on higher education has not come from state sources alone, it does appear that between 1997 and

2002, the average total *government* expenditures dedicated to higher education also rose.[83]

The PRU, then, as many have come to know it, may no longer exist. But does this reflect change or crisis? Given the negative and positive options describing this transformation, we need to explore why and how the perception of "crisis" versus some alternative and perhaps more positive view of the situation has taken hold at this point in time in discussions about the fate of the PRU.

WHAT IS THE MEANING OF "PUBLICNESS"?

Probing the emergence and the timing of the perception of crisis leads us to the question of "publicness" and its meaning as applied to the public research university. The definition of *public* has always been problematic, but as a categorical and empirical concept, it is particularly in flux today. The result is a relative absence of contemporary consensus on the connotation of the term *public* and, at the same time, a comparatively strong nostalgic sense of what "publicness" once inspired. We believe that understanding the evolution of publicness and the complexity and controversy that this term incites may help explain why the transformation of the PRU has been interpreted and experienced as a "crisis." To do so, we draw on four basic notions of "public" that have been mobilized—and often misconstrued—over time in discussions of public universities.

The first meaning of public alludes directly to the concept of "public patronage" in the legal or juridical sense of government or state ownership or provision versus private or market-based support.[84] Using this frame, public universities would be identified as those supported with government monies—primarily federal and state in the form of grants or subsidies—and as distinct from private not-for-profit or for-profit institutions funded by industrial sponsors, institutional donors, and individual benefactors. In terms borrowed from political economics, this distinction represents the liberal dualism expressed in contrasting the state (public), on the one hand, with the market (private), on the other.

A second interpretation of public harks back to the idea of a "public good" in the economic sense of free and nonrival use. In this view, the idea of public as it applies to universities refers to nonrivalrous and nonexcludable goods and services.[85] Goods and services are nonrivalrous when they can be consumed by any number of people without being depleted; and they are nonexcludable when the benefits cannot be confined to individual users or buyers. Common examples of public goods are defense and law enforcement, lighthouses and street signs, environmental goods and many information goods/services (e.g., noncommercial knowledge, public television, the Internet). According to this definition of public, PRUs might be seen as institutions to which individuals may not be denied access and through which science and scholarship are produced for the unfettered consumption by all. Unlike the previous definition of public, which hinges on the source of funding, this interpretation of public is anchored in the provision of services.[86]

This economic concept of public good should not be confused with the expression "*the* public good," which is usually an application of a collective ethical notion of "for the good" in political decision making. This latter notion reflects a third articulation of public as it relates to the idea of "public interest" and the idea of contributing to the collective welfare of a polity rather than promoting the individual advantage, success, and/or profit of its members.[87] Within this frame, PRUs would be construed as sites of socially valuable research that *could* be produced by private organizations but *must be* and *should be* delivered by their public counterparts.[88] This sense of "public" has certain resonances with the idea of the "public sphere," extending the notion of broad value and usefulness inherent in university research to a public benefit. This would include the benefit of broad public discourse and dialogue about such research and thus point to societywide as well as university determinants of what is valuable and usable.[89]

The fourth and final concept of public confers the idea of "public accountability." When operating in the public sphere, an organization must necessarily name the external public as the primary entity with which it must establish trust and credibility.[90] Beyond engaging the public's trust and credibility, this conception of publicness focuses on the extent to which an organization is amenable to being held to processes of public judgment and assessment that test such trust and credibility. Through this conceptual lens, public as it applies to the PRU refers not just to the organization's role and responsibility to serve society in the interest of public writ large but also to its willingness to be responsible for society's needs, responsive to its demands, and communicative about its performance.[91]

Although these characterizations of publicness are not exhaustive, they certainly are illustrative of a shifting sense of what the "P" in PRU signifies. Indeed, if we briefly map these different possible interpretations against the history of PRUs just sketched, we will begin to see a devolving commitment to the sense of publicness on which PRUs were originally founded and that may explain the evolving sense of crisis. It could be argued that during the nineteenth century, PRUs were primarily public in the sense of public patronage. As such, the PRU was considered an institution of the nation-state for which the government had primary responsibility. At the turn of the last century, this original sense of public was intermingled with newer elements of and expectations for publicness captured in the ideas of public good and public interest. As discussed earlier, this period was marked by policy choices that turned PRUs into what could be considered a nonexclusive public good in the anticipation of their full potential to contribute to socioeconomic progress.[92] In this sense, as with other public organizations of the welfare state, the vision of the public research university as both an entity accessible by all and for the benefit of all germinated. On the one hand, as a public good, the PRU was thought to reside in the public domain for communal use, to be something from which society at large could not be denied access. On the other hand, in regard to public interest, it was believed that what the PRU produced and disseminated was for the express purpose of benefiting society and its collective progress.

Since the 1980s, these earlier values of public have been challenged by the reorientation of state policies and the introduction of market and managerial principles. With respect to marketization, many of the same countries that opted to open the doors of the PRU and expand its clientele, have, and again by policy choice, turned much of the science and scholarship produced inside these doors into an exclusive good through the dissemination of intellectual property rights.[93] With respect to managerialism, we would argue that the earlier understanding of the publicness of the PRU and other public organizations has now been subjected to and perhaps even been supplanted by ideas of public accountability. Just as exponential demands have been placed on PRUs, constantly diversifying and intensifying mechanisms of public accountability—ranging from legislative hearings, accreditation committees, and opinion polls to lobbying groups, media outlets, and grievance hearings, to name but a few—have been levied as well.

Organizational theorists have become interested in the isomorphic powers of such mechanisms of accountability. Stemming from a broader neoliberal logic of restructuration, these mechanisms, they argue, are propelling once like but still varied organizations, such as PRUs, beyond similar institutional trends toward a single organizational "design type."[94] As Stewart Ranson explains,

> Rights of possessive individualism override substantive conceptions of the common good . . . eroding any conception of the public good as collective good determined through democratic participation, contestation, and judgement in the public sphere. . . . This regime of neo-liberal accountability, designed to restore trust to

public services has, however, had the unintended consequence of further eroding public trust in the stewardship of public services because it has embodied flawed criteria of evaluation and relations of accountability.[95]

Thus, current debates about the PRU are taking place just as the very conception of publicness is being reformulated, when idealized notions of public provision, access, and benefits are being displaced by utilitarian norms of public control and liability.[96] Whether the PRU is indeed losing or is instead complicating aspects of its essential publicness raises questions about the evolution of the PRU's character and poses implications for its functioning as well as constituents' and commentators' perceptions of those functions. At the core of such concerns is the question: Is the public research *university* in ruins," as Bill Readings argues,[97] or is it individuals' "*idea* of a university" as a public entity that is in conflict?[98]

DIRECTIONS FOR NEW RESEARCH

Fundamentally, we are asking whether the sense of crisis that pervades much of the discourse today is seeded in an actual shift in the character of the PRU and, if so, to what extent that shift is either contributing to a crisis in the organization's functionality or provoking a crisis in the organization's identity. To answer these core questions, future research should start with a set of first-order prompts: How much has the PRU actually changed over time? How do we understand an organization over time as being the same entity but existing under different conditions? How can we attribute properties today to a university based on yesterday's expectations? To what extent does the current discourse of "crisis" reflect the PRUs' internal persistence and sameness (thus failure to evolve to a modern state) versus its external adaptation and difference (thus failure to persist as we know it)? Again, which version of this crisis belongs to whom? To which public?

Having sketched the critical importance of a historical appreciation for public research universities' development and highlighted the necessity of a cross-national analysis to arrive at an understanding of the PRUs' contemporary "crisis," real or perceived, we call for a series of comparative research projects that integrate theoretical approaches with empirical evidence. We also call for analyses that take a dynamic rather than static conception of the organization.[99]

Possible lines of inquiry that might help address these questions are as follows: First, using a small comparative sample, one might conduct archival analyses of documents that make overt the declarations of PRU purposes (e.g., mission statements, presidential speeches, strategic plans) to chart how the promises and expectations of PRUs have evolved longitudinally over a discrete period of time, and then compare those findings with empirical analyses of the elements of "crisis" (e.g., changes in funding, demographics, and levels of inequality/stratification) in the same sample of PRUs over the same period. Second, again with a small sample, one could combine interviews and archival research with techniques of event and content analyses to map the rhetoric of "crisis," contrasting the different PRU publics (e.g., faculty, students, public, trustees) and their discourse and perspective on the source and nature of the crisis. Third, one might conduct a comparative analysis of the new policy frameworks and regimes said to be shaping new definitions and actions of public research universities at national (e.g., Bayh Dole) as well as international (GATS, WTO, Bologna, NAFTA) levels to determine whether PRUs are being drawn toward one design type and to explore whether the dynamics of such a gravitational pull toward a model of "public accountability" and away from earlier notions of public patronage, public good and public interest may explain the current sense of crisis.

At the same time that future research examines the nature of the crisis surrounding public universities today, it should also explore the character of the nostalgia surrounding the memory of public universities in the "golden age." The 1960s and 1970s witnessed the beginnings of a global oil crisis, explosions of political and racial tensions, and years of military conflict. Given these events and the social protests and fiscal pressures they spread across public universities, why do we (re-)call this period as the "golden age"? Is the memory of the "golden age" public university as universally positive as the period's nomenclature suggests? Which of the university's many publics remember the institution this way and why? Which do not? To what extent are accounts of the public university during this period based on emotional interpretation, social reconstruction, or empirical observation? How ephemeral are these opinions or facts? Will today's "crisis" be tomorrow's remembered "golden age"?

NOTES

1. William Clark, *Academic Charisma and the Origins of the Research University* (Chicago: University of Chicago Press, 2006). We recognize that there are important international and even intranational variations among the institutions that could be grouped under the "public research university" label. It is not the goal of this chapter

to discuss all these variations but to identify and conceptualize the general dynamics affecting large universities, supported and financed (in significant ways) by the state, in which the academic personnel are considered "public employees" and appointed to teach, to do research, and to engage in service activities.

2. See, for example, Roger Geiger, *Knowledge and Money: Research Universities and the Paradox of the Marketplace* (Stanford, Calif.: Stanford University Press, 2004); Frank Newman, Lara Couturier, and Jamie Scurry, *The Future of Higher Education: Rhetoric, Reality, and the Risks of the Market* (San Francisco: Jossey-Bass, 2004); and Iris Richmond, "Las universidades argentinas en el contexto de las políticas de los 90s: El caso de la licenciatura de articulación en ciencias de la educación de la UNICEN," *Archivos analíticos de políticas educativas* 14 (2006): 1–27.

3. John Henry Newman, *The Idea of the University: Defined and Illustrated*, 3rd ed. (London: B. M. Pickering, 1873), 1, 25. Newman was reflecting about Oxford and Cambridge, which could hardly be called public research universities in his day. Nevertheless, the ideal of the "university" embodied in Newman's writings in combination with other ideals (particularly the research university proposed by Alexander von Humboldt) became basic components of the notion of what a PRU should be.

4. See, for example, Derek Bok, *Our Underachieving Colleges: A Candid Look at How Much Students Learn and Why They Should Be Learning More* (Princeton, N.J.: Princeton University Press, 2006); and Gustavo Fischman and Eric Haas, "Higher Education and Consent: The Political-Pedagogical Discourse of Editorials and Opinions in the US, 1980–2005 (paper presented at Borderlands, Borderlines in Higher Education, 31st Conference of the Association for the Study of Higher Education, Orange County, Calif., November 1–4, 2006).

5. Eric Hobsbawm, *The Age of Extremes: A History of the World, 1914–1991* (New York: Pantheon Books, 1994).

6. Philip Altbach, "Introduction: The Underlying Realities of Higher Education in the 21st Century," in *Higher Education in the New Century: Global Challenges and Innovative Ideas*, ed. Philip G. Altbach and Patti McGill Peterson (Rotterdam: Sense Publishers, 2007), xv.

7. Imanol Ordorika and Brian Pusser, "La maxima cases de estudios: The Universidad nacional autónoma de México as a State-Building University," in *Research Universities in Asia and Latin America. World Class Worldwide*, ed. Philip Altbach and Jorge Balan (Baltimore: Johns Hopkins University Press, 2007), 189–215.

8. John Scott, "The Mission of the University: Medieval to Postmodern Transformations," *Journal of Higher Education* 77 (2006): 1–39.

9. Bruce Johnstone and Olga Bain, "Universities in Transition: Privatization, Decentralization, and Institutional Autonomy as National Policy with Special Reference

to the Russian Federation," in *Higher Education in the Developing World. Changing Contexts and Institutional Responses*, ed. David W. Chapman and Ann Austin (Westport, Conn.: Greenwood Press, 2002), 47–68.

10. Again, some state university systems emphasize research (to give one example) to a much greater degree than others, depending on national traditions, aims, and resources.

11. National and colonial universities flourished between 1500 and 1800, from Russia to Peru, gradually changing from medieval scholastic institutions to humanistic centers of learning. In the late Middle Ages, teaching services and degrees were offered at both the University of Bologna and the University of Paris. Funded pure and applied research became part of universities' core mission beginning at the University of Berlin in the nineteenth century, before German unification.

12. Scott, "The Mission of the University," 4.

13. See, for example, Thomas Ehrlich, ed., *Civic Responsibility and Higher Education* (Phoenix: Oryx Press, 2000); and Bill Readings, *The University in Ruins* (Cambridge, Mass.: Harvard University Press, 1996).

14. Sheila Slaughter and Larry Leslie, *Academic Capitalism: Politics, Policies, and the Entrepreneurial University* (Baltimore: John Hopkins University Press, 1997).

15. Clark Kerr, *The Uses of the University* (Cambridge, Mass.: Harvard University Press, 1963), vii.

16. Evan Schofer and John Meyer, "The World-Wide Expansion of Higher Education in the Twentieth Century," *American Sociological Review* 70 (2005): 898–920.

17. In the United States, this institutional arrangement was ultimately known as America's "social contract for science." This logic, which continued to gain momentum after World War II, was fueled by the creation of federal units such as the Office of Naval Research (1946), the National Science Foundation (1950), the National Institutes of Health (1944–46), and the Atomic Energy Commission (1946), from which modest funding was awarded to support and sustain research conducted primarily at universities. See David Guston, *Between Politics and Science: Assuring the Integrity and Productivity of Research* (Cambridge: Cambridge University Press, 2000).

18. See Stuart Leslie, *The Cold War and American Science: The Military-Industrial-Academic Complex at MIT and Stanford* (New York: Columbia University Press, 2002); Rebecca Lowen, *Creating the Cold War University: The Transformation of Stanford* (Berkeley: University of California Press, 1997); and Ellen Schrecker, *No Ivory Tower: McCarthyism and the Universities* (New York: Oxford University Press, 1996).

19. Craig Calhoun, "The University and the Public Good," *Thesis Eleven* 84 (2006): 7–43.

20. Philip Altbach, *The Decline of the Guru: The Academic Profession in Developing and Middle-Income Countries* (Chestnut Hill, Mass.: Boston College Center for International Higher Education, 2002).

21. Matthew S. McMullen, "Higher Education Finance Reform in the Czech Republic," *Education Policy Analysis Archives* 8, no. 6 (2000), available at http://epaa.asu.edu/ojs/article/view/397 (accessed February 7, 2010).

22. John Connolly, "The Sovietization of Higher Education in the Czech Lands, East Germany, and Poland During the Stalinist Period, 1948–1954," in *Academia in Upheaval: Origins, Transfers, and Transformations of the Communist Academic Regime in Russia and East Central Europe*, ed. Michael David-Fox and György Péteri (Westport, Conn.: Bergin & Garvey, 2000), 141–79.

23. Julia Pan and Fang Yaomei, *Higher Education in the Post-Communist World: Case Studies of Eight Universities* (New York: Garland, 1999), 242; Suzanne Pepper, *Radicalism and Education Reform in 20th-Century China* (Cambridge: Cambridge University Press, 1996), 179.

24. Ruth Hayhoe, *China's Universities, 1895–1995: A Century of Cultural Conflict* (New York: Garland, 1996), 75.

25. Pepper, *Radicalism and Education Reform*, 181, 187.

26. Michael Agelasto and Bob Adamson, eds., *Higher Education in Post-Mao China* (Hong Kong: Hong Kong University Press, 1998), 2.

27. Akito Okada, "A History of the Japanese University," in *The "Big Bang" in Japanese Higher Education: The 2004 Reforms and the Dynamics of Change*, ed. J. S. Eades, Roger Goodman, and Yumiko Hada (Melbourne: Trans Pacific Press, 2005), 32–51.

28. Ibid., 39–40.

29. Ordorika and Pusser, "La maxima cases de estudios," 1, 3.

30. Ibid.

31. See, for example, Gray Cowan, James O'Connell, and David G. Scanlon, *Education and Nation-Building in Africa* (New York: Praeger, 1965); Y. G-M. Lulat, *A History of African Higher Education from Antiquity to the Present: A Critical Synthesis* (Westport, Conn.: Praeger, 2005); and J. F. Ade Ajayi, Lameck K. H. Goma, and G. Ampah Johnson, *The African Experience with Higher Education* (Athens: Association of African Universities and Ohio University Press, 1996).

32. Lulat, *A History of African Higher Education*, 473.

33. Paul Tiyambe Zeleza and Adebayo Olukoshi, eds., *African Universities in the 21st Century*, vol. 2, *Knowledge and Society* (Dakar: CODESRIA, 2004), 598–99. In the words of another observer,

> When many African countries gained control of political power in the 1960s, they regarded universities together with national airlines, as status symbols which no

nation could afford not to have. . . . Those were days of optimism when such institutions as Ibadan, Makerere, Khartoum and the University of Ghana were expected to match British universities in academic performance and prestige. (Emmanuel Ngara, *The African University and Its Mission* [Lesotho: Institute of Southern African Studies, 1995], xiii)

34. For example, in the United States, legislation such as the Civil Rights Act of 1964 and Title IX of the Higher Education Amendments of 1972 expanded the definition of women's rights to education with important consequences, like increasing access to higher education programs and scholarships.

35. Simon Schwartzman, "Policies for Higher Education in Latin America: The Context," *Higher Education* 25 (1993): 9–20.

36. Daniel Levy, "Higher Education amid the Political-Economic Changes of the 1990s: Report of the LASA Task Force on Higher Education," in *Contemporary Higher Education: International Issues for the Twenty-first Century*, ed. Lewis Tyler et al. (New York: Garland, 1997), 3–16.

37. Hayhoe, *China's Universities*, 96–97. This model of expanding enrollments did not last long, and its weaknesses became most evident and explosive in several regions, particularly during economic crisis (such as the 1979 oil crisis and the 1982 debt crisis), when international interest rates rose dramatically and regional governments could not afford their debt payments. The stress associated with the economic changes, along with the intensification of political, social, and cultural conflicts in some cases related to processes of political democratization (as in the Southern Cone) or national liberation (Nicaragua, Iran), coincided with the consolidation of social movements and NGOs as new and important political actors. Such processes, focusing mostly on the recognition of the rights of women, ethnic groups, and minorities led to the intense conflicts that often had universities as one of the main arenas of confrontation. See Boaventura de Sousa Santos, ed., *Democratizing Democracy: Beyond the Liberal Democratic Canon* (London: Verso, 2005).

38. Cowan, O'Connell, and Scanlon, *Education and Nation-Building in Africa*, v.

39. Zeleza and Olukoshi, *African Universities in the 21st Century*, vol. 2; Ajayi, Goma, and Johnson, *The African Experience with Higher Education*.

40. Okada, "A History of the Japanese University," 39–40.

41. Gustavo Fischman and Nelly P. Stromquist, "Globalización y su impacto en las universidades de los paises del tercer mundo," *Revista mexicana de educación 2001* 10 (2004): 64–71.

42. Scott, "The Mission of the University," 28.

43. Hayhoe, *China's Universities*, 120.

44. Pepper, *Radicalism and Education Reform*, 183.

45. Yingxia Cao and Daniel Levy, "The Impact of Public-Sector Privatization in China," *International Higher Education* 41 (2005): 14–15.

46. Hayhoe, *China's Universities*, 118–21.

47. Ikuo Amano and Gregory Poole, "The Japanese University in Crisis," *Higher Education* 50 (2005): 685–711.

48. Okada, "A History of the Japanese University."

49. Instituto nacional de estudos e pesquisas educacionais. "Censo da educação superior 2002," available at http://www.inep.gov.br/download/censo/2002/sinopse/Sinopse _2002_censosuperior.zip (accessed February 7, 2010).

50. Lewis Tyler et al., eds., *Contemporary Higher Education: International Issues for the Twenty-first Century* (New York: Garland, 1997).

51. Ngara, *The African University and Its Mission*, x.

52. Ibid.

53. "U-M Budget for Ann Arbor Campus to Increase Tuition, Financial Aid," available at http://www.umich.edu/news/index.html?Releases/2005/Jul05/r072105 (accessed February 7, 2010).

54. James Duderstadt, *The Crisis in Financing Public Higher Education—And a Possible Solution: A 21st Century Learn Grant Act* (Ann Arbor: University of Michigan Millennium Project, 2005), available at http://milproj.ummu.umich.edu/publications/ financing_pub_univ/ (accessed February 7, 2010).

55. Calhoun, "The University and the Public Good," 11.

56. Ibid., 16.

57. Gustavo Fischman, Stephen Ball, and Silvana Gvirtz, "Towards a Neo-Liberal Education? Tension and Change in Latin-America," in *Education, Crisis and Hope: Tension and Change in Latin-America*, ed. Stephen Ball, Gustavo Fischman and Silvan Gvirtz (New York: Routledge-Falmer), 1–19.

58. World Bank, *Educational Change in Latin America and the Caribbean* (Washington, D.C.: World Bank, 1999), 62. During the 1980s and 1990s, the IMF and World Bank exercised considerable pressure, asserting that public university education in developing countries was both "inefficient and inequitable" because most of those who benefited from public higher education came from the middle and upper classes. See World Bank, *Higher Education: Lessons from the Experience* (Washington, D.C.: World Bank, 1994). Several World Bank documents established that without equality of access to primary schooling, Third World economic development would be severely constrained. Therefore, governments that do not invest efficiently in this human capital are "delaying" their entrance into

the new global economy and "affecting" their ability to operate under the new conditions governing the world. One of the most effective arguments sustaining these policies is derived from the "ivory tower" metaphor. If higher education is only for elites, the argument goes, then what is really democratic and economically more efficient is to invest in elementary schools, which have a greater rate of return than university studies do. See Fischman and Stromquist, "Globalización y su impacto."

59. Ajayi, Goma, and Johnson, *The African Experience with Higher Education*, 113.

60. On this point, it is worth quoting Steve Klees at length:

>After twenty years of complaints from developing countries about the short-sightedness of Bank policy on higher education, the Bank completely reversed its position on the relative efficiency of investment in higher education. In a 1999 joint analysis of higher education with UNESCO, the Bank essentially says that it was wrong for the past twenty years. The report, and then-president Wolfenson himself, admitted that the Bank had miscalculated the ROR [rate of return] to higher education, thus basing its twenty-five year policy arguing for the clear superiority of investment in primary education on invalid data. . . . In particular, the report argues that, in the past, decisions based on RORs have neglected the many substantial externalities that higher education generates, including technology development; discoveries and inventions; private sector innovation; establishing a climate conducive to investment, capital flows, and growth; promoting global competitiveness and the development of new production processes; better governance and democratic functioning; etc. (Steven Klees, "A Quarter-Century of Neoliberal Thinking in Education: Misleading Analyses and Failed Policies," *Globalization, Societies, and Education* 6 (2008): 311–48.

61. Ajayi, Goma, and Johnson, *The African Experience with Higher Education*, 143.

62. Paul Tuyambe Zeleza, "Neo-Liberalism and Academic Freedom," in *African Universities in the Twenty-first Century*, vol. 1, *Liberalisation and Internationalisation*, ed. Paul Zeleza and Adebayo Olukoshi (Oxford: Oxford University Press / African Books Collective, 2004), 42–68.

63. Paul Tiyambe Zeleza and Adebayo Olukoshi, eds., *African Universities in the 21st Century*, vol. 2, *Liberalization and Internationalization* (Dakar: CODESRIA, 2004), 2.

64. Ibid., 3.

65. Schwartzman, "Policies for Higher Education in Latin America," 11.

66. Levy, "Higher Education amid the Political-Economic Changes of the 1990s," 3–4.

67. Ngara, *The African University and Its Mission*, xiv, 2.

68. Zeleza and Olukoshi, *Liberalisation and Internationalisation*, 600, 602.

69. See, for example, Martin Trow, *Problems in the Transition from Elite to Mass Higher Education* (Washington, D.C.: Carnegie Commission on Higher Education, 1973); Burton Clark, *Creating Entrepreneurial Universities: Organizational Pathways of Transformation*, Issues in Higher Education Series (Oxford: International Association of Universities and Elsevier Science, 1998); and Jurgen Enders, "Higher Education, Internationalisation, and the Nation-State: Recent Developments and Challenges to Governance Theory," *Higher Education* 47 (2004): 361–82.

70. In *The University, State, and Market: The Political Economy of Globalization in the Americas* (Stanford, Calif.: Stanford University Press, 2006), Robert Rhoads and Carlos Torres describe the crisis in terms of the "marketization" of universities. Like others, Pablo Gentili and Betina Levy understand the combined processes in terms of "privatization." See their *Espacio público y privatización del Conocimiento: Estudios sobre políticas universitarias en América Latina* (Buenos Aires: CLACSO, 2005). Other writers note that what is happening in higher education is best described as "McDonaldization" or the triumph of a model of "academic capitalism." See Dennis Hayes and Robin Wynyard, *The McDonaldization of Higher Education* (Westport, Conn.: London: Bergin & Garvey, 2002); Shelia Slaughter and Gray Rhoades, *Academic Capitalism and the New Economy: Markets, State, and Higher Education* (Baltimore: Johns Hopkins University Press, 2004).

71. Francisco Ramirez, "Growing Commonalities and Persistent Differences in Higher Education: Universities Between Globalization and National Tradition," in *The New Institutionalism in Education: Advancing Research and Policy*, ed. Heinz-Dieter Meyer and Brian Rowan (Albany: State University Press of New York, 2006): 123–41.

72. See, for example, Simon Marginson and Mark Considine, *The Enterprise University: Power, Governance and Reinvention in Australia* (Cambridge: Cambridge University Press, 2000); Helga Newotny, Michael Gibbons, and Peter Scott, *Re-thinking Science: Knowledge and the Public* (Cambridge: Polity Press, 2001); and Sheila Slaughter and Larry Leslie, *Academic Capitalism: Politics, Policies, and the Entrepreneurial University* (Baltimore: John Hopkins University Press, 1997).

73. George Fallis, "The Mission of the University" (paper submitted to *Postsecondary Review: Higher Expectations for Higher Education*), available at http://www.cou.on.ca/content/objects/The%20Mission%20V3.pdf, pp. 3, 5–6 (accessed February 7, 2010).

74. James Duderstadt, *A University for the 21st Century* (Ann Arbor: University of Michigan Press, 2000), 21.

75. David Berliner and Bruce J. Biddle, *The Manufactured Crisis: Myths, Fraud, and the Attack on America's Public Schools* (New York: Addison-Wesley, 1995).

76. Antonio Gramsci, *Selections from the Prison Notebooks* (New York: International Publishers, 1971), 178.

77. Sousa Santos, ed., *Democratizing Democracy*.

78. Alberto Amaral and Antonio Magalhães, "The Triple Crisis of the University and Its Reinvention," *Higher Education Policy* 16 (2003): 239–53.

79. Ylijoki writes of "academic nostalgia" as it relates to the notion of the "golden age" in the Finnish university: "The nostalgic yearning for the lost golden age reveals current tensions and dilemmas through which the idealized past is then socially constructed. The crucial question is therefore what purposes and functions the nostalgia has at the present time and what it tells about the current situation" (Oili-Helena Ylijoki, "Academic Nostalgia: A Narrative Approach to Academic Work," *Human Relations* 58 [2005]: 555–76).

80. Steven Brint, preface to *The Future of the City of the Intellect: The Changing American University*, ed. Steven Brint (Stanford, Calif.: Stanford University Press), xi.

81. Alsion Wolf, *Does Education Matter? Myths About Education and Economic Growth* (London: Penguin, 2002). See also Robert Cowan, ed., *The World Yearbook of Education: The Evaluation of Higher Education Systems* (London: Kogan Page, 1996); Diana Yerbury, "Ten Inter-Related Imperatives for Change and Their Implications for Australian Universities Twenty Years Hence" (paper presented at "The Global University: A 21st Century View, Second International Conference," RMIT University, Melbourne, Australia, July 14–16, 1997); and Rajani Naidoo, "Repositioning Higher Education as a Global Commodity: Opportunities and Challenges for Future Sociology of Education Work," *British Journal of Sociology of Education* 24 (2003): 249–59.

82. Global University Network for Innovation, *Higher Education in the World 2006: The Financing of Universities* (Hampshire: Palgrave Macmillan, 2006).

83. Regarding the increase of expenditures in higher education, Bikas Sanyal notes that contrary to general belief, most countries have tried to maintain or even increase the share of higher education financial support, but there is an enormous variation among countries:

Share in the national budget varied from 13.66 per cent in South Africa to 40 per cent in Romania according to a recent UNESCO survey. However, massive expansion resulted in a wide variation in resource availability per student from US$220 in Madagascar to US$13,224 in Sweden. Per student public expenditure also fell significantly all over the world owing to, among others, the massive expansion. It decreased from US$6,300 in 1980 to US$1,241 in 1995 in Africa and it decreased by 50 per cent in the United Kingdom during the last decade" (Bikas Sanyal, "Financing Higher Education: International Perspectives [paper presented at the "Second International Barcelona Conference, Higher Education in the World, 2006: The Financing of Universities," Barcelona, Spain, November 30–December 2, 2006, 6]).

84. Paul David, "Knowledge, Property and the System Dynamics of Technological Change," in *Proceedings of the World Bank Annual Conference on Development Economics 1992*, ed. Lawrence Summers and Shekhar Shah (Washington, D.C.: World Bank, 1993), 215–48.

85. Paul Samuelson, "The Pure Theory of Public Expenditure," Review of Economics and Statistics 36 (1954): 387–89.

86. Simon Marginson, "Putting the 'Public' Back into the Public University," *Thesis Eleven* 84 (2006): 44–59.

87. Jane Mansbridge, "On the Contested Nature of the Public Good," in *Private Action and the Public Good*, ed. Walter Powell and Elisabeth Clemens (New Haven, Conn.: Yale University Press, 1998), 3–19.

88. Rebecca Eisenberg and Richard Nelson, "Public vs. Proprietary Science: A Fruitful Tension?" *Daedalus* 131 (2002): 89–101.

89. Jürgen Habermas, *The Structural Transformation of the Public Sphere* (Cambridge: Polity Press, 1989).

90. Agnes Ku, "Revisiting the Notion of 'Public' in Habermas's Theory—Towards a Theory of Politics of Public Credibility," *Sociological Theory* 18 (2000): 216–40.

91. Alistair Macintyre, *Dependent Rational Animals* (London: Duckworth, 1999).

92. Inge Kaul and Ronald Mendoza, "Advancing the Concept of Public Goods," *Providing Global Public Goods* 35 (2003): 78–112.

93. Diana Rhoten and Walter Powell, "The Frontiers of Intellectual Property: Expanded Protection Versus New Models of Open Science," *Annual Review of Law and Social Science* 3 (2007): 345–73.

94. See, for example, David Frank and Jay Gabler, *Restructuring the University: Worldwide Shifts in Academia in the 20th Century* (Stanford, Calif.: Stanford University Press, 2006); John Meyer, "Globalization," *International Journal of Comparative Sociology* 48 (2007): 261–73.

95. Stewart Ranson, "Public Accountability in the Age of Neoliberalism," *Journal of Educational Change* 18 (2003): 459–80.

96. See, for example, James Perry and Hal G. Rainey, "The Public-Private Distinction in Organization Theory: A Critique and Research Strategy," *Academy of Management Review* 13 (1988): 182–201; and Jacob Hacker, *The Divided Welfare State: The Battle over Public and Private Social Benefits in the United States* (Cambridge: Cambridge University Press, 2002).

97. Readings, *The University in Ruins*.

98. John Henry Newman, *The Idea of the University*.

99. Karl Weick, "Educational Organizations as Loosely Coupled Systems," in *Organization and Governance in Higher Education: An ASHE Reader*, ed. Marvin Peterson, Ellen-Earle Chaffee, and T. H. White (Needham Heights, Mass.: Ginn Press, 1991), 103–17; John Meyer et al., "Sociology of Higher Education: An Evolving Field," in *Sociology of Higher Education: Contributions and Their Contexts*, ed. Patricia Gumport (Baltimore: Johns Hopkins University Press, 2007), 187–221.

THREE

"El central volumen de la fuerza"

Global Hegemony in
Higher Education and Research

SIMON MARGINSON AND IMANOL ORDORIKA

> es el central volumen de la fuerza,
>
> la potencia extendida de las aguas,
>
> la inmóvil soledad llena de vidas.
>
> —Pablo Neruda, *El gran océano*

A small number of nations produce more than one hundred films each year: France, Italy, Iran, China, Japan, India, the Philippines, the United Kingdom, and the United States. Although the United States is not the largest producer of films, American films are watched everywhere, and the United States exports more film and television than it imports. In most cases, the balance of trade is overwhelmingly in favor of the United States. All other nations, both rich and poor, are net importers of film and television content, and most of what they import is from the United States. For example, Mexico, an OECD (Organization for Economic Cooperation and Development) country whose per capita income in 2005 of $7,310 was just above the world average of $6,987, produced 22 films in 1999, but it imported 306 films that year, 203 of which were from the United States. Australia, a nation with a per capita income in 2005 of $32,220, produced 29 films in 1999 and imported 255 films, 174 from the United States (UNESCO Institute for Statistics 2007; World Bank 2007).

This lopsided cinematic relationship between the United States and the rest of the world is both economic and cultural. American creative industries in film, TV, music, books, and software generate more export revenue than any other industrial sector, including agriculture, aircraft, and automobiles (Drache and Froese 2005). They also fill the world with thoughts and images of Los Angeles, New York, and other U.S. cities. Just a tiny proportion of American cinema and TV time is spent on content from other nations. Although most people in the United States have no contact with the visual imaginary of people from elsewhere, the vast majority of people outside the United States are familiar with the icons and language of American popular culture.

U.S. culture has become a generic world culture, the default position in all operating systems, like the U.S. domination of film and TV, global military capacity, industrial technologies, private wealth, and infrastructure design in urban spaces. What is less well known is that the United States enjoys an equivalent domination in higher education and research. Along with U.S. economic and military power and geostrategic mobility (the capacity to intervene freely in other national sites while maintaining territorial control of the homeland), the U.S. hegemony in education and research underpins the U.S. domination of all other spheres. The planet is permeated by not just the United States' visual imaginary and iconic products but also U.S. language and knowledge and American scholars' and researchers' intellectual pursuits, assumptions, and methods. The creativity of U.S. universities, not to mention the biases and lacunae typical of mainstream U.S. academic thinking, ultimately underpin products, shape the Internet and business practices, and permeate popular culture and daily life everywhere else. Through the education of foreign students in universities in the United States, U.S. norms and ideas determine the vision of non-American elites in government, business, and intellectual life.

THE GLOBAL SPACE FOR HIGHER EDUCATION

Worldwide higher education is a relational space that includes national systems and individual institutions, global agencies such as the World Bank and the Organization for Economic Cooperation and Development (OECD) with a policy interest in education and research, and global disciplinary and professional communities. It is crisscrossed by a thickening array of networks and connected at many points with centers of power in the economy, government, and other institutions grounded in localities, cities and cross-border operations. Although the worldwide higher education environment is complex, it is open to observation and analysis. In the last two decades, global convergence and integration triggered by communications technologies (Castells 2000) and accelerated cross-border activity have made institutions and national systems more connected and more visible to one another. This does not mean that higher education and research have become a single global system that supersedes their national and local histories and identities. There *is* a global network of research universities, but they continue to function also in national systems and as local agents. Many other higher education institutions, perhaps most, are scarcely active globally. The higher education environment and its connections to other sites are simultaneously global, national, and local. The three dimensions communicate differently with one another country by country, university by university, and over time (Marginson 2006b; Marginson and Rhodes 2002; Marginson and van der Wende 2009; Valimaa 2004).

When mapping the relations of power in global higher education, a fuller picture would do justice to the variations and inequalities within nations. Here we focus mainly on the global dimension while also acknowledging the national and local distinctions, which are analytically separable. No doubt the focus on the global interpolates a globalist bias into the argument. Like economic capital, knowledge moves freely across borders, but locality-bound institutions do not have the same freedoms or reach. Indeed, national systems comprise universities, colleges, and institutes with varying fluency and resources in cross-border mobility. In the hegemonic United States, as in Indochina or sub-Saharan Africa, the most locally bound people experience the global as external and other-determining rather than internal and enabling. National powers matter also when they are configured on the scale of empire itself. Not every kind of subordination within national systems is equivalent, just as the elite research universities of some countries have more authority than those in others. One sign of the global hegemony of higher education in the United States is that U.S. community colleges and four-year institutions, while subordinated at home, are nonetheless special on the global scale, capable of attracting significant numbers of foreign students if they make the effort to recruit abroad. The Ivy League rises higher still, yet it also retains an "American" identity. Remarkably, the local and national institutions in the United States have exceptional global importance without having to look beyond the place-based mental horizons they have inherited.

Globalization

In an era of accelerated globalization (Held et al. 1999), globalization is a symbiosis of economic changes and cultural changes. On one hand, it rests on the formation of worldwide markets, operating in real time via automated processes and underpinned by the first worldwide system of financial exchange; and growth rates of foreign direct investment that far exceed capitalist growth as a whole. With the instantaneous transmission of financial information, the turnover time of economic capital tends toward zero (Harvey 1989, 2006; Mandel 1975); and the world economy moves faster and becomes more transformative of the localized parts, as Marx (1970) predicted 150 years ago in his *Grundrisse.* On the other hand, globalization rests on new worldwide systems of communications, information, culture, and knowledge. These cultural systems, which are partly subsidized by governments as public goods (e.g., universities, especially in basic research) are mobilized by nation-states and global agencies so as to support the extension of global markets that produce private goods and generate profits. In turn, these global economic forces drive further cultural integration, and the world leans toward a single cultural community (McLuhan 1964). What kind of diversity this will ultimately sustain is unclear, but the pace of change is astonishing, for example, the rollout of global English and the global evolution of research and knowledge.

Research universities are enmeshed in all aspects of globalization, especially communications, culture, and knowledge. Higher education is among the most globalized of sectors. "Although many universities still seem to perceive themselves rather as objects of processes of globalization, they are at the same time also key agents" (Enders and de Weert 2004, 27). But national systems and institutions do not participate in the global higher education environment on the basis of equality. The length of time that more than 90 percent of the population is enrolled in education varies from fifteen years in Belgium to one year in India. The United States spends more than $300 billion per year on tertiary education; some nations spend less than $10 million per year. The distribution of the competences needed to operate proactively as a self-determining global agent (Marginson 2008b)—journal access, scientific equipment, trained people, English language, communications infrastructure, modernized administration, executive steering, competitive faculty salaries, and the payment of student support—is highly uneven. Global processes tend to magnify these starting inequalities, drawing nations into common systems while at the same time excluding most of them from global power.

Any theorization of the global higher education environment must account for two aspects. The first is the *flows* across national borders via networked relationships: flows of people (students, faculty, and administrators); flows of messages and other communications; flows of information and knowledge, including published and posted research and data; flows of technologies; flows of norms, ideas, and policies; and flows of financial capital and other economic resources (Appadurai 1996; Marginson and Sawir 2005). In the *Rise of the Network Society* (2000, 71, 442–445, 500–501) and *The Internet Galaxy* (2001), Manuel Castells provides a sociology of networks and flows. "Society is constructed around flows, the expression of processes dominating our economic, political and symbolic life" (Castells 2000, 71).[1] The economics of networks sustains an inbuilt expansionary dynamic. Global flows constitute highly visible lines of communication, lines of influence and effect.

Equally important is the second aspect, the worldwide map of *difference* in the sector: both horizontal diversity, such as the variety of languages, pedagogies, approaches to scholarship, and organizational systems and cultures; and vertical diversity: relations of power and boundary making between national systems and institutions; differentiation and hierarchy, inclusion and exclusion; and the unequal distribution of resources and capabilities (Sen 2000) that channel and limit global flows in higher education. Global higher education is a relational field of power shaped by inequality and hierarchy—it is not a level playing field—and a field with relationships/networks both cooperative and competitive.

Global Higher Education as a "Field of Power"

Pierre Bourdieu[2] conceives a field of power as "a space, that is, an ensemble of positions in a relationship of mutual exclusion" (Bourdieu 1996, 232), with "a small number of distinctive features that, functioning as a system of differences," allow social differences to be expressed (Bourdieu 1984, 226).[3] Without buying into all of Bourdieu's argument concerning agency or "habitus," and his problematic claim about the interchangeability of the different Bourdieuian "capitals" (Marginson 2008a), we, like others, find that the notion of a bounded social field and its internal dynamics has wide application. In his analysis of *The Field of Cultural Production* (1993, 38–39), Bourdieu found that the cultural field is structured by a polar opposition between, at one end, the subfield of restricted production and, at the other end, the subfield of mass tending to commercial production. Each subfield has a distinct principle of hierarchization. In the mass or "popular" sites of cultural production, this principle involves economic capital and market demand and is heteronomous, although mass producers periodically renew themselves by adapting ideas from the elite sector. In the aristocratic or elite sites of cultural production, which shape the high-value products, the principle of hierarchization is cultural status, autonomous and specific to the field. Between them lie a range of intermediate institutions that combine the two opposing principles in varying degrees.

We can readily see this kind of polarity in national higher education systems as well (Naidoo 2004), and the same kind of polarity is present in the global field as in the national field. Table 3.1 provides a two-dimensional description of the global field. On the horizontal left-to-right axis, the description moves from predominantly autonomous institutions in the subfield of restricted production, to heteronomous institutions in the subfield of mass tending to commercial production. On the vertical axis, the description moves from institutions active in the global dimension (above) to institutions predominantly bound to the national and local dimensions (below). Some autonomous elite universities (category 1) exercise more worldwide influence than do others more nationally bound in activity (category 2a). Some commercial institutions (categories 3 and 6a) are significant players in global markets, and others (categories 8 and 9) are in local markets.

The numbers 1 through 9 are a ranking of the overall *global* power and prestige of institutions by category, although this must be considered approximate, as there is some overlap between categories. The overlap is considerable in the categories ranked 2a and 2b, and 4a and 4b. Note that in this vertical ranking, the overall principle of hierarchization is derived from the elite subfield and reflects cultural rather than economic status. As in the national dimension so in the global dimension: the field of universities and the most prestigious fields of knowledge are mapped according to the aristocratic sensibility. Nonprofits always tend to be ranked above for-profits, except in the case of outliers, such as the Indian IITs whose commercial position derives in part from their extreme scarcity of student places in a very large domestic market.

A field description based on the sensibilities of global business, not Harvard, would order the hierarchy differently. But such sensibilities do not determine national and global university prestige, even though the *Times Higher's* ranking now attempts to account for them.

At the elite end of the global field in category 1 is the "Global Super-league" (*The Economist* 2005) where knowledge power is concentrated: Harvard, Stanford, MIT, Yale, Princeton, Caltech, Chicago, Pennsylvania, Berkeley, and other leading lights of the University of California system, the large midwestern universities and others in the United States, plus a handful in the United Kingdom led by Cambridge and Oxford (category 1 in table 3.2). In a world in which every research university is visible to every other and ranked against one another on a global scale, knowledge flows freely across borders, and a growing number of students and faculty follow. Here Super-league universities have become the elite subfield of the global sector. Their brands are recognized around the world, are universal objects of desire, and draw talent from everywhere. Although the extent of global engagement varies, and some enhance their global position by being particularly active across borders, these universities derive their ultimate global importance from their presence in the subfield of elite universities in their own nations. Thus maintaining the vertical distinction between themselves and other nationally and locally based institutions is crucial to their global role. Some carry out very strenuous boundary work, in the manner that Bourdieu (1984) identifies, to sustain prestige. This work is particularly important to Oxford, Cambridge, Imperial, and London in the United Kingdom. While all American doctoral universities obtain a significant global status, simply by virtue of national identity, regardless of the extent of their global engagement, this is less true for universities in the United Kingdom. Minor British universities do not have a high global status. In the United States, however, institutions do not have this problem. They can play the national/local and global games almost as one and the same. As we will discuss, this is a key characteristic of hegemony.

At the opposite end of the field are institutions like commercial companies, focused on revenues, cost management, and expansion (Breneman et al. 2007 discuss U.S.-based for-profits). This group includes the University of Phoenix and global e-learning enterprises, as well nonprofit universities that provide international education on a revenue-raising commercial basis. In the intermediate zone between the two subfields, many research universities have become more heteronomous, their status logics often overdetermined by corporatization and commodification.[4] Their global research and status-building mission vary.

One example of these intermediate institutions is those British and Australian universities (category 2b) that compete in the global research stakes while also building high-volume concentrations of full-time fee-paying international students to plug the hole left by reductions in the government funding of teaching and basic research. Below that group in status are ostensibly teaching-research universities for which the research mission is decisively subordinated to chasing cross-border revenues (category 4b). Other leading national research universities (category 4a) operate as elite universities but fall below the Super-league in research and have no presence in the global market for students. Their assiduous boundary formation at home cannot deliver standing in the global market, in which they might be subordinated by institutions that have a lesser historical status at home but are more active across borders. Outside global operations altogether are institutions that are solely national with a local mission

Table 3.1 The Polar Field of Global Higher Education, After Bourdieu

(Horizontal axis maps autonomy/heteronomy; vertical axis maps degree of global engagement, numbers signify order of status in *global* field)

Autonomous Subfield of elite research universities, prestige-, not profit-driven.	1 The Global Super-league: many U.S. doctoral–sector and U.K. high-prestige universities. Prestige from stellar research reputation and global power of degrees. Autonomy from not just national system position but global power (e.g., Harvard, Cambridge, etc.)	2b Elite non-U.S. national research universities with strong cross-border role: prestige-driven, nonprofit research universities at national level. Global presence in research; cross-border students; some offer for-profit foreign degrees (e.g., Sydney, Warwick, Leiden. LSE UK on border between categories 1 & 2).	4b Teaching-focused export universities: lesser-status nonprofit universities, operating commercially in the global market, providing lower-cost / lower-quality foreign education at scale. Often have minor research role (e.g., Oxford Brookes, Central Queensland).	3 Elite and globally focused for-profits: fully for-profit institutions operating on global basis, global prestige, largely teaching focused, with some research. National exclusivity and global power enable greater autonomy than in for-profits in category 6 (very small category, e.g., Indian IITs, IMs).	6 Lesser prestige teaching only global for-profits: Fully commercial operators actively building export markets, low-cost mass production, no research (Phoenix, DeVry, various global e-Us).	Heteronomous Subfield of institutions providing commercial vocational cross-border education: teaching-focused exporters (includes for-profits and revenue-driven units of nonprofits).
Notes 1. Autonomy relative to global field. 2. Elite teaching-only liberal arts colleges are feeders for elite U.S. research universities.						

2a Less globally engaged U.S. doctoral universities. Retain global prestige and some research role though marginal interest in cross-border students and foreign engagement (e.g., some U.S. state universities).

4a Nationally bound elite research universities: prestige providers in a single nation, research intensive. Nationally competitive with segment 2, not 1. Varying global presence in research, (e.g., U Buenos Aires, many in Europe and Japan).

5 Teaching-focused national universities: largely teaching-focused institutions, marginally global in research and/or cross-border teaching (e.g., most Malaysian public universities, some Canadian community colleges).

7 Nonprofits without global agendas: teaching-focused, local demand orientation. No cross-border role (largest group, especially in importing nations).

8 For-profits with minor global functions: commercial operators focused on local market with some cross-border students (e.g., some private industry training in Australia).

9 For-profits without global agendas: local degree mills, no cross-border students (large category in some nations, e.g., Philippines).

Table 3.2 Coverage of the Field of Global Higher Education in the University Rankings by Shanghai Jiao Tong University (top 200/500) and the *Times Higher Education Supplement* (top 200)

Autonomous Sub-field: elite research universities						Heteronomous Subfield: commercial vocational cross-border education
	1 Global Super league dominates JTU from the top in status order; also leads TH along with some presence also from categories 2 and 4a. 2a Less globally engaged American doctoral universities; significant proportion of JTU top 500 due to research outputs, little role in TH.	2b National elite non–U.S. research universities with strong cross-border role; significant second-order presence in JTU top 200/500, after category 1; higher up in TH, driven by reputational survey, some in top 50 mixed with category 1	4b Teaching-focused export universities; no presence in JTU top 500; reputation and student internationalization indicators push some Australians into TH top 200.	3 Elite and globally focused for profits; Indian IITs appear in TH ranking at 57 but not in JTU ranking.	6a Lesser-prestige teaching-only global for profits; no presence in either ranking.	

4a Nationally bound elite research universities; some have enough research to appear in JTU top 200, many in top 500; in TH the survey ensures an erratic list of national leaders with weaker global connectivity in top 100 and 200.

5 Teaching-focused national universities; no presence in either ranking.

8 For-profits with minor global functions; no presence in either ranking.

(categories 7 and 9). Although these are outside global operations, they are not outside the global field. Whether or not they like it, regardless of the strength of their relations with local constituencies, such institutions are being devalued by global transformation.

The polar nature of global higher education reinforces the global hegemony of the doctoral universities in the United States that are predominantly located in the global subfield of elite university education and research. The Bourdieuian theorization of the field also helps explain why the American universities sustain a dominant global position without having to build their global operations as aggressively as others do, and why the institutions in the other English-speaking countries seem so much more frenetic in their pursuit of global strategic ambitions. Nevertheless, in global higher education, the polarity between the two principles of hierarchization works somewhat differently for the market, an art described by Bourdieu (1993). The elite end of the university field is more robust than elite cultural producers, more closely integrated with the centers of economic and political power. Super-league universities, particularly the U.S. Ivy League, are economically stronger than mass producers of higher education. This tension between Bourdieu's two principles is absorbed not just between the different types of university in the field but also inside elite universities, especially their research, which is alternately fundamental and commercial, for example, bioscience (Bok 2003). Nevertheless, Bourdieu is right to argue that the more autonomous that universities become, the less they will be commercial in temper. The ultimate rationale of the Super-league is not revenue but prestige. The driving forces of university prestige are the production of knowledge and of social position.

Bourdieu also discusses the strategic behavior of agents within the field of power. Agents within the field compete with one another for resources, status, or other objects of interest. In the field, "every position-taking is defined in relation to the *space of possibles* which is objectively realized as a *problematic* in the form of the actual or potential position-takings corresponding to the different positions" (Bourdieu 1993, 30, italics in original). Bourdieu refers to position-taking as the "space of creative works" (39), but only some position-takings and "trajectories" (the succession of positions occupied by an agent over time) are possible. Agents identify such positions as they respond strategically to changes in the settings and the moves in the game. Agents do not simply respond as automata to structured signals in the environment. "Although position helps to shape dispositions, the latter, in so far as they are the product of independent conditions, have an existence and efficacy of their own and can help shape positions" (Bourdieu 1993, 61–62). Bourdieu finds that the room for self-determination, "the scope allowed for dispositions," is variable, shaped by the autonomy of the field in relation to other fields, by the position of the agent in the field, and by the extent to which the position is a novel and emerging one, or path-dependency has been established (72).

Bourdieu's notion of interplay between "position" and "position-taking," between the structured starting position within the global field and the scope for autonomous action, is helpful. But there are questions about how much room he leaves for self-determining agency and about the assumption of universal competition. Bourdieu also fails to distinguish between hierarchy and the overwhelming power of the kind exercised by American film or American higher education. This brings us to Gramsci and his notion of *egemonia* (hegemony).

HEGEMONY IN HIGHER EDUCATION

The current discussion of hegemony in social organization starts with the work of Antonio Gramsci, who contrasts and also combines two different regimes of power. First is domination or coercion by the open state machine, the "State-as-force" (Gramsci 1971, 56). Second is the exercise of hegemony, which is secured primarily through civil society, including educational institutions (Gramsci 1971, 12). Hegemony is "the 'spontaneous' consent given by the great masses of the population to the general direction imposed on social life by the dominant fundamental group," which derives its prestige from "its position and function in the world of production" (Gramsci 1971, 12). Hegemony is a social construction in the realm of intellectual reason, ideas, and also popular culture. It is "an order in which a certain way of life and thought is dominant, in which one concept of reality is diffused throughout society in all its institutional and private manifestations" (Williams 1960, 587). The construction of hegemony is an active, complex process, a coherent integration of separate and, at times, contradictory belief systems, meanings, and practices into a single regime. The formal institutions of civil society such as universities are analytically distinct from the state (political society) but intertwined with it. "One might say that state = political society + civil society." "In other words," stated Gramsci, the state is "hegemony protected by the armour of coercion" (Gramsci 1971, 10). Rule by consent is underpinned by rule by force.

Hegemony is reproduced in and through *institutions* with their own autonomy and techniques. It is driven also by identifiable *social formations* or interests: "effective movements and tendencies, in intellectual and artistic life, which have significant and sometimes decisive influence on the active development of culture and which have a variable and often oblique relation to formal institutions" and provide "the link between culture and society" (Williams 1977, 117, 120). *Tradition* is also an active, shaping force in hegemony. Raymond Williams (1977) notes that in a culture, certain meanings and practices are selected while others are neglected or excluded. The hegemonic institutions sustain a "deliberately selective and connective process which offers a historical and cultural ratification of a contemporary order" (116). The selection becomes the common "tradition" (1977). But hegemony is more than the sum of top-down institutions, social formations, and traditions. It rests also on self-forming subjects (Rose 1999), people who identify voluntarily with it as its instruments. Here language and education are central to the formation of an active constituency for hegemony.

Gramsci's notion of hegemony originated in linguistics, and language plays a special role in his argument. Under conditions of cultural hegemony, a given population adopts linguistic forms and even an entire language from another group of people. Adoption is not triggered by coercion but relates to cultural prestige and economic, political, social, and, at times, military power (Ives 2004, 82, 47). Gramsci's theorization also places the university in a pivotal role in civil society and in hegemony as the institution that standardizes and inculcates the dominant language and authoritative knowledge, a site of cultural activity in its own right and the place where the next generation of social leaders is formed. In universities, people learn to construct themselves in the terms of hegemony, both questioning and remaking tradition. They are attached to the university not simply because of the intrinsic lure of science or culture—that is enough for some, but not for most—but because leading families use the university. In the university, powerful social groups are reproduced; their career paths are defined; and the initial momentum of their upward trajectories is secured. The lure of the leading universities, which draws the great volume of student applications, is the promise of social position. The lure of the leading global universities is the promise of mobile success that can be taken everywhere. Nevertheless, as David Forgacs puts it in *The Antonio Gramsci Reader*, this does not mean that everything that takes place in universities and the rest of civil society "is subservient to the state or reflects ruling class interests." By distinguishing between state and civil society, "Gramsci avoids on one hand a liberal reductionism, which sees civil society as the realm of free individuality entirely apart from the state, and on the other a statist and functional reductionism, which sees everything in society as belonging to the state and serving its interests" (Gramsci 2000, 224).

In higher education, nation-building is carried out both instrumentally and reflexively. From time to time, the state itself is criticized and thereby renewed, much as in Habermas's (1989) notion of the "public sphere" (Calhoun 1992; Marginson 2006c; Pusser 2006). In fact, universities are able to conduct scientific research and secure consent for the nation-state only because they are independent of the machinery of government. University autonomy is always relative but can be substantial and generative under specific historical conditions (Ordorika 2003). In inclusive Latin American public institutions, such as the Universidad nacional autónoma de México (UNAM), the university from time to time becomes a site in which political society itself is placed in continual question; the state machine can be directly challenged; and alternative hegemonic political projects and leadership can emerge. But there always are difficulties in the relationship between the universities and the government. This is "the weakest link of the public university, because the scientific and pedagogical autonomy of the university is based on its financial dependency on the state" (Santos 2006, 62).

Did Gramsci see hegemony, with its grounding in city-states and nations, as operational at the global level beyond the nation-state? Yes, he did, making the prescient statement that "every relationship of 'hegemony' is necessarily an educational relationship and occurs not only within a nation, between the various forces of which a nation is composed, but in the international and worldwide field, between the complexes of national and continental civilizations" (Gramsci 1971, 350).

In one respect, Gramsci's theorization seems dated. He argues that the potential for American hegemony is retarded by the later historical development of the United States vis-à-vis Europe. The United States "has not yet created a conception of the world or a group of great intellectuals to lead the people within the ambit of civil society" (1971, 272). The United States "lacks great historical and cultural traditions" (285). "Americanism," Gramsci states, is merely "an organic extension and intensification of European civilisation" (318). If Gramsci's observations were correct in the 1920s, the situation has now changed. Arguably the United States *has* created its own distinctive conception of the world; and it is there, not Europe, that the strongest universities lead global civil society and exercise hegemony in and through education and research.[5] Like the Gramscian institutions of hegemony in each nation, the Super-league embodies social formations and a tradition both national and global. It shapes worldwide knowledge formation and the idea of the university. However much university personnel might criticize particular imperial projects, such as the war in Iraq, the leading universities are animated by and reproductive of U.S. knowledge power worldwide. Given that education is central to all hegemonic projects, much is at stake in the building of global hegemony in higher education.

As Steven Lukes (2005) suggests, hegemonic relations of power in higher education are formed in three interrelated "Gramscian" domains. The first is the domain of institutional centrality, strength, and prestige. At the instrumental level, some institutions and national higher education systems exercise power over others through the accumulation of financial resources, the strength of faculty and student bodies, the potency of infrastructures, the global centrality and position of their base country, and their closeness to financial and political centers of national and global decision making. One manifestation of instrumental power within the global field is the participation of Super-league university personnel in elaborating higher education policies at agencies like the World Bank, OECD, Inter-American Development Bank, and UNESCO (United Nations Economic, Scientific, and Cultural Organization). The second domain is that of shaping and controlling higher education agendas. In decision making, institutions and systems exercise power through process rather than structural conditions and position. Power is expressed through the control of agendas as well in policy debates and policy design. At this level, power relationships are determined by direct instrumental power, coercion (threat of negative sanctions or use of positive incentives), and invocation of biases (norms, precedents, rules, or procedures). One example of agenda control in education is the worldwide spread of evaluation, standardization, and accreditation policies.

The third domain in which hegemony is exercised is that of framing the field and constructing dominant views of higher education, including accepted notions and discourses. Institutions in the strongest countries exercise power by forming widespread understandings of the nature and role of higher education, acceptable outcomes and processes, and the prevailing standards and norms. They frame the field itself, determining the conditions of interaction and the terms of competition. At the same time, the fact that Lukes provides a general theory of power rather than a theory of power in higher education should caution us against too readily applying these categories to the higher education sector without testing them empirically. Relations of power in higher education are situated in a larger space, articulated at many points through formal and cultural politics, government, sovereignty, and economic relations. It would be an illusion to suppose that these patterns of authority and hegemony could be undone and remade solely from within (Ordorika 2003).[6]

Gramsci also remarks that hegemony can vary in the degree of integration it facilitates. Hegemony normally presupposes that account is taken of the interests and tendencies of the groups over which the hegemony is exercised. But there is also the hegemony of the Italian Risorgimento, which does not feel the need to secure concordance between its interests and the dominated groups or to engage with their specificities such as languages and ways of life. "They wished to "dominate" and not to "lead" (Gramsci 1971, 104–5). As we shall see, the hegemony of the Risorgimento suggests the character of U.S. domination in higher education, inflected as it is with American exceptionalism and periodic American isolationism.

Mapping Global Hegemony

No empirical inquiry into global hegemony in higher education is completely satisfactory, owing to the multiple and heterogeneous nature of the observational tools and data sets. The most important sources are the global agencies, particularly the OECD (2006) and the World Bank (2007). Few data and analyses are constructed with hegemony in mind, and empirical coverage shows significant lacunae. On the whole, the existing data sets allow us to more readily compare worldwide higher education as a relational hierarchy using static markers of difference (e.g., expenditures on institutions and research) than to trace global flows of people, capital, communications, knowledge, and ideas in higher education. It is not yet possible to build the kinds of data sets that would allow us to comprehensively investigate flows on the bases of location of initiative and drive, intensity, direction, and reciprocity (Marginson and Sawir 2005). Castells (2001) has data on the intensity of Internet traffic by nation and city, the location of web page creation, and the languages in use in the Internet, data that point to the domination of English with some plurality at the edges. An equivalent set of data in relation to universities would be helpful. Information is available concerning cross-border student flows, faculty flows, publication and citation patterns, and language of use. Some nations collect data on foreign students, and others collect data on students crossing borders, and these do not always coincide (Kelo, Teichler, and Wachter 2005; OECD 2006, p. 303). Many nations collect information about outgoing short-term academic visits, and some, including the United States, track incoming short-term visits. Data on incoming academic personnel are more complete than the data on outgoing personnel and on return rates. Little information is available on cross-border postdoctoral appointments. Only some nations provide data on the proportion of foreign-born academic staff. Fortunately for the study of global hegemony, the United States provides more comprehensive information about people flows in higher education and research than do other nations (e.g., IIE 2006; NSB 2006).

Even so, more complete empirical data would still require interpretation and synthesis. Here, our investigation of hegemony is not data driven but theory driven. Bourdieu's theorization of fields of power, Gramsci on hegemony, and Lukes's domains of power relations enable us to begin to imagine (to "map") the complex global higher education environment. Drawing those theorizations into conjunction with the data allows us to (1) critically review the theorized mapping of that environment, and (2) test the data sets for coverage and clarity in a continuous and reciprocal process. For example, the data provide some insight into Bourdieu's polarity between elite and mass/commercial institutions on a global scale. They enable tracking publications' outputs (NSB 2006), institutional research performance (SJTUIHE 2007), and the locations of commercial institutional education. This exercise also demonstrates that data on the tuition market are not standardized and there is a lack of comparative data on student selectivity and on research in languages other than English. It also shows that in the global university sector, unlike the field of artistic production theorized by Bourdieu, status leadership coincides with the principal concentrations of economic resources.

Instrumental Conditions

Lukes (2005) identifies institutional centrality, strength, and prestige as the first domain of power relations. The instrumental or "structural" conditions of hegemony include the size and weight of national economies and university budgets, and the leading research universities' geospatial distribution. We emphasize three aspects of global stratification:

First is the worldwide hierarchy of national wealth as measured by (gross domestic product / gross national income) GDP/GNI per head. GDP/GNI per head is loosely correlated with tertiary education participation rates but more closely shadows research capacity. "Developed" nations dominate the list of the world's top 500 research universities in research outputs as measured by the Shanghai Jiao Ting Institute of Higher Education (SJTUIHE 2007). In total, 465 of the top 500 research universities are in nations with a per capita GDP of more than $20,000 per year and 193 of the top 200 research universities. In the middle group of nations, the infrastructure development and rates of student participation vary widely, with some nations approaching western European levels but with just a handful of research universities in the global top 500 (see table 3.3). China is in a special position. Per capita income is still relatively low, but GDP, higher education, and research are growing fast. Nations like Indonesia have both low rates of tertiary participation and relatively little science-based research. Some countries do not have any universities at all.

Table 3.3 Instrumental Conditions of Hegemony: U.S. GDP, per Capita GDP, Spending on Tertiary Education, and Number of Top Research Universities Compared with Eight Other Nations

	Population, 2005	GDP PPP, 2005	GDP per Head of Population PPP, 2005	Total Spending on Tertiary Education, PPP 2003/2005	Universities in SJTU Top 200, 2006	Universities in SJTU Top 500, 2006
	millions	*$US billions*	*$USD*	*$US billions*		
United States	296.5	12,409.5	41,854	359.9	84	167
Netherlands	16.3	537.7	32,929	7.0	7	12
United Kingdom	60.2	1,926.8	32,007	21.2	23	43
Australia	20.3	643.0	31,642	9.6	6	16
Japan	128.0	3,943.8	30,811	51.1	9	32
Singapore	4.4	116.8	26,844	n.a.	1	2
Mexico	103.1	1,052.4	10,209	13.7	1	1
China[a]	1,311.4	8,787.2	6,701	n.a.	2	14
Indonesia	220.6	847.4	3,842	5.1	0	0

Notes: PPP = Purchasing Power Parity; SJTU = Shanghai Jiao Tong University data (SJTUIHE 2007); spending on tertiary education is an approximation using 2005 GDP data and the 2003 proportion of GDP allocated to tertiary education.

[a] Includes Hong Kong but excludes five universities from Taiwan; n.a. = data not available.

Sources: Authors' elaboration based on authors' data; World Bank 2007: cols. 2–4 and part of 5; OECD 2006: part of col. 5; SJTUIHE 2007: cols. 6–7.

Second, as the example of China implies, national system size matters. All else being equal, larger nations have the capacity to sustain both greater autonomy and initiative within the global field. Larger nations have larger resource bases and greater resource flexibility, have more scope for a mission-based internal division of labor, have greater potential to self-reproduce a research infrastructure, and are less vulnerable to the outflow of skilled personnel. For example, in Germany and France, academic labor markets are more self-sufficient than elsewhere in Europe (Musselin 2005). Yet a paradox of large system size is that it can postpone the necessity for global engagement. Higher education is now globally referenced, and knowledge flows and people flows pour across the national border regardless. Ultimately, those national systems and research universities failing to pursue a global strategy will be left with less agency freedom at home and abroad. Smaller nations face a different set of strategic imperatives. They can scarcely afford to abstain from global engagement but struggle to maintain identity and autonomy vis-à-vis the larger players. This does not mean that smaller size signifies absolute global weakness or the absence of strategic options. Some small nations, such as Singapore, Switzerland, and the enclave of Hong Kong in China (Postiglione 2005), specialize in knowledge-intensive industries and cross-border services. They have positioned themselves as managers and brokers of global flows of finance, knowledge, and people.

Third, the United States' instrumental strength in higher education is massive compared with all other nations, whether "developed" or "underdeveloped." The strength of the United States begins with its scale as a nation, resources as measured by the level of per capita income, and the size of its national investment in higher education and research. The United States has the third largest population in the world; its GDP is much the largest; and its GDP per head exceeds $40,000. The next competitor, Japan, has less than half the population, one-third of the GDP, and a per capita income of just above $30,000. The United States also spends a higher proportion of its GDP (2.9 percent) on tertiary education than does any other nation. This amounted to approximately $360 billion in 2005 in PPP terms. The next largest, Japan, spent $51 billion. *The United States invests seven times as much on tertiary education as does Japan, the next nation.* This is almost on par with the American global supremacy in military weapons and the cinema industry. It is not surprising that the United States is overwhelmingly dominant in the Shanghai Jiao Tong University (SJTU) research university rankings based on publications, citations, and prizes for research performance. The United States houses eighty-four of the top 200 research universities.

The SJTU data also point to the secondary leadership role of the United Kingdom and hint that global power is not solely a function of resources. The United Kingdom's GDP per capita is about $32,000, and it spent $21 billion on tertiary education in 2005, 6 percent of the outlay of the United States. Yet the United Kingdom has twenty-three research universities in the top 200, 27 percent of the U.S. level. One reason is language.

Hegemony in and Through Language

The second and third domains of power identified by Lukes (2005) are shaping and controlling higher education agendas, and framing the field and constructing the dominant views of higher education. In higher education, an identifiable "way of life and thought," a "dominant tradition," operates globally. The global tradition is not all-pervasive. National traditions and localized practices persist, especially in teaching and professional preparation, but global tradition sets the agendas of research in research-intensive universities. This global tradition is created above all via the English language and the worldwide flows of research knowledge, especially in the sciences. It also is institutionalized in asymmetrical flows of students and faculty between countries.

English is one of two languages spoken by a billion people. The other is Pudonghua (Mandarin), or the standard dialect of China. In addition, two pairings of related and mutually intelligible languages are spoken by more than half a billion people: Hindi and Urdu, and Spanish and Portuguese. Three languages are spoken by more than 200 million people: Russian, Bengali, and Arabic, and four more are spoken by more than 100 million (Linguasphere Observatory 2006). Regardless of this plurality and the diversity of traditions of scholarship and inquiry, "it is English that stands at the very centre of the global knowledge system. It has become the lingua franca par excellence and continues to entrench that dominance in a self-reinforcing process" (Held et al. 1999, 346; Crystal 2003).

English is spreading as a medium of instruction in non-English-speaking nations, particularly in programs designed to attract foreign students. English is widely used in India and the Philippines. In Malaysia, it has been reintroduced into the schools and is dominant in the private tertiary colleges. In Europe, English is used especially in master's-level programs targeting foreign students and in doctoral education. Nations in which English is widely used include the Netherlands, Finland, Sweden, and Denmark. Another thirteen countries, including South Korea and Japan, provide some programs in English (OECD 2006, 291). As a second language, English is much more widely used throughout the academic world. A survey between 1998 and 1999 of European Region Action Scheme for the Mobility of University Students (ERASMUS) teachers and coordinators in Europe found that almost 90 percent of those from non-English-speaking countries spoke English. The next language, French, was spoken by fewer than half the respondents (Enders and Teichler 2005, 101). In global research, the use of Latin, French, German, and Russian are declining. French still is important in the Francophone countries; Arabic is a common medium of academic discussion in many nations; and Spanish is the regional language throughout Central and South America. Nevertheless, in many if not most nations, faculty receive financial or career incentives to publish in English. Linguistic diversity in higher education is often now expressed not in bilingual or multilingual practices but in the variation among different "Englishes," especially in Asia and Africa, in which English becomes inflected with elements from local or national language.

Even so, these trends do not quite capture the special status accorded to English, not just to the preferred use of English as a medium for the common intellectual conversation and the incidental neglect of conversations in other languages, but to a greater *direct and intrinsic* value placed on knowledge originating in English compared with other languages. Knowledge has somehow become more "true" if it begins in English, as indicated by the worldwide patterns of book translation. Books originating in English are much more likely to be translated into other languages than the other way round. The United States and the United Kingdom publish fewer translated books than do other large countries. For example, between 1983 and 1985, Spain had 7,711 book translations; Germany, 6,676; France, 3,979; and Japan, 2,696—in each case, more than half were from English to the national language—but just 1,139 in the United Kingdom and 606 in the United States (Held et al. 1999, 346). Much work in languages other than English, some of exceptional quality, never enters the one recognized global intellectual conversation. Work produced in English is much more likely to be used everywhere else. The articulation of power via linguistic origin is not confined wholly to native speakers, however. Professors from India or Singapore and teachers from Pakistan gain a referred global power and vocational mobility from the fluency in English that is endemic also to their education systems.

English has been taken up throughout the global field of higher education, not because of coercion exercised by Anglo-American universities, still less because of the intrinsic intellectual utility of their language, but because of the imperial economic, political, military, and cultural weight of the United Kingdom and then the United States in the last 250 years. Language translates Anglo-American domination in education into the fashioning of thought and communication in every other sphere of economic and social life. And so we have a worldwide academic monoculture in which the universities from all English language systems are complicit. For them, it is easy to set global agendas. How often are they challenged? Most principal academic journals are based in the United States, and few of their editors feel obliged to take into account any contributions not written in English. This asymmetrical and largely one-way exchange of knowledge is a taken-for-granted reality of academic life, a nonreflexive foundation against which academic reflexivities find their limit and are played out. In their noncoercive fashion, and seemingly (at least on the surface) with all the participants' consent, the civilities of academic life truncate human potential as surely as do poverty and war.

KNOWLEDGE CONCENTRATIONS AND FLOWS

The English-speaking nations constitute an extraordinary 71 percent of the Shanghai Jiao Tong University's top 100 research universities on the basis of measured research performance. Although the measure is biased in favor of research in English, the point is that this is the global mainstream. The United Kingdom has eleven of these universities, Canada four, Australia two, and the United States fifty-four. Another twenty-two of the top 100 are located in western Europe, six in Japan, and one each in Israel and Russia. The main western European nations are Germany (five), France and Sweden (four each), Switzerland (three), and Netherlands (two). Only one of the top 100 is in southern Europe, and none is in the Spanish-speaking countries, China, or India. India has three in the Shanghai Jiao Tong University's top 500, and China, excluding Taiwan, has fourteen (SJTUIHE 2007).

The Shanghai Jiao Tong ranking is configured in regard to globally comparable disciplines, which in practice means the science-based fields, with a minor role played by the more "scientistic" of the social sciences, economics/business, and psychology and its derivatives. Humanities are more nationally structured and correspondingly more centrally implicated in the formation of distinctive national, and sometimes more localized, identities. Until recently, in many nations, the humanities were often the medium for forming a significant sector of the national leadership, for example, classics and history in the training of the British and Indian civil servants. But now everywhere, the nation-bound nation-building project has been translated into the global competition state. There is a continuing demand for nationally grounded knowledge in many nations, for example, the role of Neo-Confucianism in China in the construction of Chinese identity in the world. But such national traditions cannot yield international rankings. Instead, it is in the sciences and the associated technologies that nations readily compete in both research and economy and can more readily measure their competitive standing in relation to one another. Thus the dominance of the research university as science university is entrenched. Besides an Anglo-American model, it is equally the model of western European higher education. But for western European universities, it is not enough to be in the historical vanguard of the science university; for in the construction of the global hierarchy, the globalization of science is overdetermined by the hegemony of language.

The leading universities keep for themselves prestige, financial resources, human talent, research infrastructure, and knowledge production, each of which produces the others. The principal criterion used in the Jiao Tong research rankings is the number of "Hi Ci" researchers, those in the top 250 to 300 scholars in their field as measured by citations (see table 3.4). Of these Hi Ci research-

Table 3.4 Concentrated Knowledge Power: "Hi Ci" Researchers, Selected Countries, 2007

United States	3,835
United Kingdom	443
Japan	246
Germany	242
Canada	174
France	157
Australia	105
Switzerland	102
Netherlands	92
Sweden	58
China	20
Spain	18
India	11
Singapore	4
Mexico	3
Indonesia	0

Source: Authors' elaboration based on data from ISI-Thomson 2007.

ers, no fewer than 3,835 are located in the United States, more than *eight* times the number in any other country. Among the U.S. universities, Harvard has 160 Hi Ci researchers, more than all the French universities together; Stanford 135; UC Berkeley 82; MIT 74; and Chicago 41. The University of Cambridge in the United Kingdom has forty-four. The Shanghai Jiao Tong rankings also measure the number of Nobel Prize winners associated with each university. Of the 736 Nobel Prizes awarded up to January 2003, 670 (91.0 percent) went to people from high-income countries, the majority to the United States, with 3.8 percent from Russia/Soviet Union/ eastern Europe and 5.2 percent from emerging and developing nations. The latter have by far their best prospect of winning a Nobel Prize in literature (10.1 percent) or peace (19.8 percent). These areas are excluded from the SJTU index of research performance (Bloom 2005).[7]

Where research capacity is concentrated, knowledge flows are generated and pushed outward to the rest of the world. In 2001, scientists and social scientists in the United States published 200,870 papers in major journals. The volume of papers from Japan was 57,420, the United Kingdom 47,660, Germany 43,623, and France 31,317. China had 20,978 papers in 2001, Australia 12,602, and India 11,076. Mexico produced 3,209 papers, an increase of 263 percent since 1988. Despite its size, Indonesia created just 207 papers in 2001 (NSB 2006). Not much knowledge is flowing from Indonesia to the United States. In the group of rising Asian science powers, between 1988 and 2001 the number of scientific papers produced per year increased sharply in South Korea (1,332 percent), Singapore (535 percent), Taiwan (472 percent), and China (354 percent). Mainstream research is more diverse in national origin than in linguistic medium, and the national diversity is increasing. The long lead of U.S. research universities and their continued domination of the material means of production—research infrastructure and personnel, electronic publishing, and journal production—and their capacity to co-opt talent from other nations via hirings and collaboration, ensures that U.S. universities will continue to dominate global knowledge flows for the foreseeable future.

The unevenness in the flows and the asymmetries in direction can be traced more precisely when moving from paper output to citation patterns. The United States produced less than a third of the world's scientific articles in 2001 but "accounted for 44 per cent of citations in the world scientific literature" (Vincent-Lancrin 2006, 16). On average, knowledge produced in the United States enjoys greater authority than knowledge from elsewhere, even good work by scholars from other nations working in English. This hierarchy in value, the special importance placed on knowledge from the United States, shows itself as or more strongly within the United States than it does outside it. To some American faculty, *nothing* is produced outside the United States. The external referencing of

U.S. phenomena becomes impossible, as the local is equated with the universal. The Carnegie survey found that while more than 90 percent of scholars from other nations believed it necessary to read foreign books and journals, only 62 percent of American scholars agreed, much the smallest number among the developed nations (Altbach 2005, 148–49). Philip Altbach stated that although U.S. scholars are "at the centre of the world academic system," "the American research system is remarkably insular, especially when compared to scientific communities in other countries. . . . The American system accepts scholars and scientists from abroad, but only if they conform to American academic and scientific norms" (Altbach 2005, 149–50). Academic faculty all over the world inhabit global fields in which they pursue the twin satisfactions of cultural production and social prestige. Outside the United States, many faculty have correspondingly ambivalent relations to their national and local contexts. Inside the United States, when faculty move between their local context to the larger academic world, they seem to be less conflicted. Many do not need to leave America.

Many exceptions to these generalizations can be found in U.S. universities, many instances of faculty with a cultural imagination, and some that evidence a profound determination to surmount insularity, which is the price that an imperial hegemony imposes on itself. In some respects, these faculty are the hope of the world, yet the generalizations hold. While the critics of hegemony struggle against its institutional logic, a more modest cosmopolitanism is compatible enough. Many U.S. faculty reject the raw edge of Huntington's (1996) thesis about the "clash of civilizations," but global exceptionalism, with its seductive sense of superiority, is hard to escape. Across borders, a confident American liberalism is manifested as a kind of missionary virtue: cross-border work too readily becomes a matter of what "we" can teach "them," not what we can learn or what we all can share. Ease of communication and global pedagogy are all too compatible with hegemony, which is cosmopolitan on the surface, but monolingual and culturally and technically superior at heart. To put it bluntly, no matter how much U.S. faculty might embrace tolerance and openness as virtues, the binary inside/outside logic of the global academic monoculture is not all that different from Huntington. Likewise, in the English-language countries, "diversity" has a more limited meaning than in western Europe or Latin America. It is understood in social rather than cultural terms or as a limited multiculturalism within the monoculture, for example, the access of nondominant groups to higher education. "This model values diversity as a function of competition and not the other way round" (Drache and Froese 2005, 26–27). In this framework, a global cultural diversity based on sovereign identities' equality of respect, which is the classic virtue of multilateralism, ceases to be seen as essential in itself as either a human right or a mutual benefit.

American public universities and faculty are being remade according to organizational blueprints that use business models grounded in the imagining of higher education as a market competition among firms. These models draw on performative protocols and systems of knowledge management that are not all that different from the organizational systems being imposed on universities outside the United States. In other words, U.S. public institutions, too, are victims of the reified models laid down by the New Public Management (NPM) and based on idealized versions of the Ivy League and the for-profit university. But the common fact of transformation does not eliminate the real cross-border differences in resources and power between American research universities and research universities in other countries. Even recognition of the common presence of the new public management is not enough to create in the eyes of American faculty, even most of those who are notable for liberal convictions, the kind of real solidarity that would flatten the global status hierarchy in their eyes. Beliefs in the intrinsic superiority of American higher education institutions over higher education in other nations are hard to shake. However problematized it might be within its own domain, beyond American shores the American public research university still shares with the Ivy League private university that all-pervasive sense of "American exceptionalism" that brings to each American research university a potent confidence in itself as bearer of a special global mission, albeit a mission that always seems to be less pressing than the all-important domestic U.S. agenda.

There is much that too many academic eyes in the United States cannot see. Still less do universities in the United States see themselves as others see them. But this partial blindness performs a useful function. Researchers and scholars inside the United States draw global authority from the binary inside/outside distinction and use it to perpetually remake the field in their own image. U.S. higher education draws the main benefit from the gift economy called academia, in which there is an unequal capacity to give. This is the essence of client relations. Notwithstanding the focus on commercial research in policy, the bulk of academic knowledge in the United States, as elsewhere, is produced as freely reproducible public goods, not privatized commodities (Stiglitz 1999). In that sense, it is part of a collective knowledge system offering benefits to all. But the coin of the benefactor has another side, as these benefits also are culturally loaded public goods. To the extent that they exclude knowledge produced in other nations and traditions, they constitute "public bads" in those locations (for more discussion of "public bads," which are the opposite of "public goods," see, among others, Kaul, Grunberg, and Stern 1999). The commons is diminished as well. To the extent that it reduces the overall diversity of knowledge, the hegemonic global system of knowledge constitutes a collective public bad (Marginson 2007c). This subtracts from the ultimate potentials of knowledge and thus from the potential goods accessible to U.S. faculty and English speakers as well as everyone else.

The inclusion/exclusion binary in the global knowledge system decisively overdetermines the free flow of knowledge goods imagined in global utopias. The universal circulation of all human knowledge is technically possible but does not happen. Some knowledge goods flow freely; others do not. Once a system of truth attains critical mass, it reproduces itself as true in circular fashion, relegating to the outer darkness, outside the circle, any viewpoint from which the system *qua* system could be objectified. To participate in the global knowledge system as self-determining agents, people outside the United States must accept these terms. Positioned within a global field framed by universal English and U.S. domination, they position-take on grounds only partly empathetic and familiar. They find themselves constantly oscillating between strategy and identity, knowing that by position-taking on these terms they are complicit in the very mechanisms that place them at a permanent disadvantage. No system of control is as effective as a system that is embraced voluntarily with a sense the inevitable has come.

Unequal People Flows

In worldwide higher education, short-term movement tends to be more a two-way (reciprocal) than a long-term movement, although some short- or medium-term movement does lead to permanent migration. Between 2000 and 2004, the number of mobile cross-border students rose by 41 percent (OECD 2006, 286), and in 2004, 2.7 million students were enrolled outside their country of citizenship. About half were students moving from China, India, and other Asian nations to English-speaking nations; another almost one-third was movement within Europe. In regard to country of destination, the largest group of students, 22 percent, entered the United States, followed by United Kingdom, 11 percent; Germany, 10 percent; France, 9 percent; and Australia, 6 percent (OECD 2006, 288). The surface appearance is one of multiple flows in all directions but a primary global flow within these flows. Research on student choice identifies a strong overall preference for the elite universities in the United States, especially among Asian families (e.g., Mazzarol et al. 2001). For their part, U.S. doctoral universities, unlike most universities in the United Kingdom, Australia, and New Zealand, do not set out to maximize the number of foreign students and the revenues they bring. Instead, U.S. doctoral universities want the best foreign students, not the most foreign students. One-third of their foreign intake is recruited at doctoral level. In 2003, the United Kingdom enrolled 23,871 foreign doctoral students, Spain 11,765, Australia 8,855, Switzerland 6,028 and Sweden 3,205 (OECD 2005). The role of these nations was dwarfed by that of the United States, which hosted 102,084 foreign doctoral students in 2004/2005. In addition, most of the foreign doctoral students enrolled in the United States receive scholarships or other subsidies from their American universities (IIE 2006). The United States has made itself the global graduate school.

Between 1977 and 1997, the foreign-born proportion of all American PhDs rose from 13.5 to 28.3 percent and, in engineering, from 32.1 to 45.8 percent (Guellec and Cervantes 2002, 77–78). As graduate assistants, foreign students are an important part of the U.S. national research effort, as many are later recruited into postdoctoral programs, and some build long-term careers. They find the U.S. labor market more flexible and open than the academic labor markets of most other nations. "Stay" rates vary by country of origin. Potential migration is high for students from China, Israel, Argentina, Peru, eastern Europe, and Iran; and some developed countries, including the United Kingdom, Canada, New Zealand, and Germany. In 2001, the stay rate for Chinese graduates in science and engineering was 96 percent, and for Indian graduates, 86 percent (Vincent-Lancrin 2004, 32). In 2003, three-quarters of EU citizens who obtained a U.S. doctorate said they had no plans to return to Europe (Tremblay 2005, 208). Conversely, stay rates are very low for South Korea, Japan, and Indonesia and relatively low for Mexico (Guellec and Cervantes 2002, 92). Even so, those graduates who do return to their country of origin or migrate elsewhere broadcast the norms of U.S. higher education throughout the world.

Although conclusive data are lacking, cross-border faculty recruitment seems to be growing relative to national labor markets at all career stages. But it has not subsumed national faculty labor markets into one worldwide set of regulations, salaries, and conditions (Musselin 2004, 2005). Nor does the globally mobile element constitute a single global labor market (Marginson 2009). Nevertheless, the scale of foreign doctoral education and the recruitment of foreign faculty into the United States have transformative implications for labor markets in other nations. For example, besides Germany's losing many doctoral graduates to the United States and United Kingdom, its own long standing as an attractor of foreign faculty and doctoral students has been diminished (Berning 2004). The most global element of faculty labor is the market for highly mobile researcher-scholars working at the top end of citation performance. This market is dominated by the Super-league universities (table 3.1), so that global salaries and conditions are an outgrowth of the American domestic system. For universities in other nations to compete effectively for high-value scientists, they must offer American salaries and something approaching American research infrastructure, as Singapore has done (Lee 2002).

Arguments that there is no such thing as "brain drain" and that we instead should talk about "brain circulation" are right in that mobility is frequently temporary and locations often unstable and that the research diasporas of South Korea, China, and India show an increasing tendency to move back from the United States, if not back and forth several times. But they are wrong in that they obscure the continuing asymmetries in people flows and hide the fact of U.S. hegemony. Few U.S. national doctoral graduates "brain drain" to the emerging and underdeveloped nations, and relatively few go to western Europe. The striking fact remains that just as every other nation has a balance-of-trade deficit with the United States in film and television, every other nation has a net brain drain of faculty labor in relation to the United States. The "brain circulation" concept provides cold comfort to those developing nations and university systems where the movement of talented scholars and researchers continues to be almost all one-way and permanent in character.

The pattern of global people flows in higher education clarifies the shape of global hegemony in higher education. A binary hierarchical model that imagines the world in terms of developed/underdeveloped is not sufficiently dynamic and creates the false impression that every nation is on the same developmental ladder. Rather, the structural logic of the global field is that of core/periphery, with the United States at the global core. Systems and universities are arranged at increasing distances from the relatively advanced national systems in the global semiperiphery (e.g., Australia or Finland) to emerging systems in the global periphery (e.g., Mexico or South Africa) to nations without research capacity at the global margins. The core exerts a magnetic effect on periphery and margins, continually drawing talented people and resources into itself. Some of these it holds permanently; others later move back to the periphery and the margins as its agents. In its alliance with hegemonic English, the attribute that all globally successful faculty share in full measure, the core/periphery dynamic more deeply entrenches the insider/outsider binary. But the beauty of the core/periphery model, its functional democratic ambiguity, is that it is never quite clear where the line between insider and outsider falls. Herein lies the deception at the heart of American global engagement. Who can quarrel with the provision of opportunities for upward mobility for the deserving poor? And talented people from all over the world *do* have significant personal opportunities in U.S. research universities, if they can reach those universities in the first place and if they are prepared to abandon their outsider identities once they get there. As they walk through the gate for the first time and begin the long and rocky journey to tenure, the Super-league is at its most cosmopolitan moment. Thus these selectively generous universities open themselves to the world, on one-way terms designed to accumulate their own human capital.

Unequal Capital Flows

We do not have global data on the cross-border flows of technological capital in the form of inventions and patents and research know-how. We do know that the characteristically Anglo-American insistence on intellectual property rights is played out in asymmetrical capital flows, in which the dominant powers absorb a range of know-how, discoveries, and ideas from other nations and return these as commodities for which full prices are charged. The only saving graces are the public good character of research knowledge and the technical and juridical impossibility of preventing the cost-price replication of cultural commodities, which undermines the imperial property regime (Drache and Froese 2005). We do have better data on the capital flows associated with the cross-border student markets. In 2001, the United States took in $11.5 billion from foreign students, and Australia took in $2.1 billion (see table 3.5). Comparatively few domestic students from either country went abroad (another sign of the English-language universities' indifference to plural encounters); outward mobility cost the United States $2.4 billion and Australia $0.4 billion. In net terms, the cross-border capital flows in favor of those nations were $9.1 billion in the United States and $1.6 billion in Australia (OECD 2004, 32).[8] Since 2001, Australian education exports have grown sharply, and the estimated revenues from student fees and expenditures is now $7.0 billion (ABS 2006; Marginson 2007a).[9]

Table 3.5 might suggest that capital accumulation is the driver of global educational activity in these two nations. While this is true of at least some Australian universities operating within the subfield of commercial cross-border education, it is not true of the U.S. doctoral sector. In the United States, both foreign policy goals and the needs of research dictate a focus on subsidizing and recruiting talent, not on commercial revenues. Both when it retains foreign students

Table 3.5 Unequal Global Capital Flows in Higher Education: Selected Nations and Selected Capital Flows, 2001

	Revenues from Foreign Students, 2001	Cost of National Students Abroad, 2001	Net Capital Flows, 2001
	$US million	*$US million*	*$US million*
United States	11,490	2,380	9,110
Australia	2,145	529	1,616
Canada	727	529	198
Mexico	31	81	-50
Greece	124	205	-81

Note: Does not include revenues from patents and research, publishing and consulting activities, or the governmental flows of foreign aid for tertiary education.

Source: Authors' elaboration based on data from OECD 2004, 32.

and when it sends them back, U.S. international education becomes one pillar of the imperial economic and political-military relationship between the United States and the world. Since Woodrow Wilson was president, the American foreign policy establishment has supported international education, and generations of benefactors have donated scholarships to incubate and Americanize foreign elites. Global hegemony is a much bigger prize than capital accumulation in higher education alone, and still bigger than the fiscal savings that have driven the Australian commercialization. Global hegemony opens the way to the maximum possible capital accumulation, political power, and cultural shaping across the full range of social and economic sectors.

The principal material constituent of global hegemony in higher education is not financial capital but the capacity to produce research and knowledge, in which the United States dominates the field. We emphasize again that this research is subsidized rather than based on the commercial market and that much of it is pure basic research. Likewise, the prime objective of the Asian science powers, those challengers of hegemony on the grounds of hegemony, is not export capacity but research capacity. That Australia and New Zealand leverage the positional advantage of an English-language system to chase down revenues, not research capacity, is a Bourdieuian sign that their position-taking strategies are being played out in the semiperiphery, not at the heart of the hegemony (Marginson 2007a). That despite its outlay on foreign talent, the United States has engineered it so that other nations provide $9 billion to fund the hegemonic project in higher education is yet another sign of remarkable global domination.

SUMMARIZING HEGEMONY

The global currencies are English-language research knowledge and positional advantage. The former signifies the latter while also providing the medium in which the leading universities shape and control agendas, frame the field, and construct the norms of the sector. Although the logic is a core/periphery model and an inclusion/exclusion dynamic, the normalizing effects of hegemony are felt everywhere. Meanwhile, the great American universities engineer the consent of elites from other nations who finish their education in the United States. Here we find the Gramscian sequence between the two regimes of power. Global consent engineered in civil society in the peaceful realms of the lecture hall and the research laboratory becomes an active condition of American global rule by financial weight and military force. The flows of people, knowledge, ideas, and resources in higher education, and their many fecund potentials, become harnessed for nationally specific global objectives, that is, for the fulfillment of the ends of empire.

To worldwide American power in higher education is joined the secondary global role of the United Kingdom in the spheres of culture and language, research, and elite university education and in the technologies of governmental neoliberalism. In the United Kingdom, it is nearly hegemony, and this brings with it an oscillation between a sense of helplessness in the face of brash American power, and the practical confidence and sense of cultural superiority, which, born of empire, are still deeply ingrained. To many in higher education outside the English-speaking world, the difference does not matter. To them, globalization appears simply as a single Anglo-American process. Yet "Americanization" is remarkably flexible: more various and innovative than British rule and far less planned and driven by the state, the province of autonomous institutions and faculty, and the sum of a multitude of spiels and deals. It rarely involves the U.S. government directly. Still, the nation supports its universities abroad despite the polemical sniping of faculty and the episodic problems in securing visas for scholars and students from countries under suspicion. The cross-border dealings of U.S. universities together reflect a surprising degree of cultural coherence in their interface with the rest of the world. In the last analysis, none can forget that they are American, and they have this in common with Washington. It is the kind of mutually supportive relationship between civil society and state that Gramsci imagined. Universities do not always relate to states in this way, but they do so in the context of hegemony.

The most remarkable thing is that the effects of U.S. universities on the higher education world are profound and continuous, sustained by many communications and engagements, yet U.S. universities largely protect themselves from contamination by foreign influences in a sector where multiple loyalties and hybrid identities are part of the stock in trade. Globalization in higher education is what the United States brings to the rest of the world, not what the world brings to U.S. universities. Hegemony in higher education is framed by American exceptionalism and the episodic American isolationism. Of course, it depends which agent is in play. Americanization at the World Bank is a missionary ideology for remaking the higher education world on quasi-American lines. But the Americanization of the Ivy League deals selectively and, in its own mind, occasionally across borders. It always retains the option of indifference. This is another sign of the university as aristocracy, as Bourdieu (1988) notes. When elite U.S. research universities consider foreign universities, when they look up briefly from their fascination with all things local (which also being imperial would normally be expected to subsume offshore matters), they do not waste time in loose fishing expeditions. They use the open global setting instrumentally, sending good American knowledge in one direction and drawing talented foreigners from the other. Otherwise, they largely ignore foreign universities. American universities take what they want from the rest of the world and junk the rest. They are not interested enough in engaging so closely with non-American institutions as to necessitate learning their languages of use, as in the classic British imperial strategy described in *Orientalism* (Said 1979). Nor are they much interested in converting foreign universities or in making money from them. Still less are they interested in taking continuing responsibility for capability building in emerging national systems. Foreign universities are left to benignly evolve toward U.S. templates according to their own capacity and "merit." This is a top-down globalization that marginalizes the cultural "other" rather than absorbing it and building hybrid fusions as, for example, the Asian science powers are doing. It is the classic hegemony of the nineteenth-century Italian Risorgimento. It does not lead, but it dominates.

Arjun Appadurai (1996) suggests that this kind of hegemonic relationship can be subverted from below in the hybrid cultural forms constructed by diasporic communities. Perhaps we can identify such forms in the academic spaces created by American exceptionalism and isolationism. The global university hegemony has more potential for hybridity in some domains than others. Organizational models are nested in historical conditions and culture, and this opens them to local self-determination and variation. Teaching has a plurality of languages of use, including the heterogeneous "Englishes." Despite the fluidity of intellectual discourse, research and knowledge formation are less open to hybridity on hegemonic grounds. They constitute a tight binary global logic of inclusion/exclusion that assigns worldwide academic labor to one of two categories: (1) part of the global research circuit, which means using the dominant language and publishing in the recognized outlets; or (2) not part of the global research circuit, the bearer of knowledge that is obsolete or meaningless and doomed to irrelevance. Global flows might have facilitated diverse cultural encounters, but in the more global era since 1990, knowledge building outside the English language has become less, rather than more, visible. To establish a genuine cultural plurality in research, it is necessary to move outside the terms of hegemony.

TRACING THE INSTITUTIONALIZATION OF GLOBAL HEGEMONY

We turn now to the "how" of the framing of the field, the construction of the dominant views of global higher education, and the shaping of higher education agendas. We identify two components of the hegemonic model: (1) the tradition of the American university or, rather, a particular reading of that tradition, and (2) the new public management in higher education, including reforms designed to simulate a commodity market in the sector.

Diverse Traditions and Models

There is no one single "Idea of a University" (Newman 1899/1996), but many different missions, structures, and organizational cultures, associated with distinctive traditions and models. All are nested in national contexts, historical identities, and conditions of possibility. The United States has the traditions of the Ivy league private research university and the liberal arts college, the flagship state university and the community college, and newer models such as for-profits trading on the equity market. The systems of the "Westminster" countries (United Kingdom, Australia, New Zealand) combine university autonomy with explicit state steering. The Nordic/Scandinavian university is characterized by high participation, research culture, and strong state investment (Valimaa 2004, 2005); the German-style university with elite participation, research culture, and state administration; the Latin American public university with high participation, scholarly culture, and a special social and political centrality; the emerging science university systems of East and Southeast Asia, including China, Taiwan, South Korea, and Singapore, this last fostered by its state investment, Singapore's uniquely global orientation; and the technology- and business-focused institutions of India. Beyond the research university are the highly regarded vocational sectors in Germany (the Fachhochschulen) and Finland, as well as many other vocational and community-based programs, including for-profit models and online institutions, as well as many examples of specialized institutions in teaching and research.

Some tendencies toward global standardization are inevitable and desirable, for example, protocols for recognition and accreditation, and forums for publication. When global systems slip from facilitating and communicating diverse national and regional identities into the suppression of diversity through the installation of hegemonic norms, something is lost. There is a cultural imbalance in the emerging global systems. Most of the non-American traditions face crises of legitimacy and material possibility, particularly those dependent on high state investment. But the choice is *not* between a standardizing one-world hegemony and the old national diversity. Instead, the choice is between Americanized systems across the world attuned to the conditions and needs of one nation, in which most universities look like weak imitations of the real thing, and a more plural environment with space for national and regional self-determination in which several regionally based norms of higher education could flourish. Traditions with potentially broad appeal already exist in embryo. One possibility is a European university grounded in a distinctive mix of public and private goods and freedoms and sustained mostly by state investment, as exemplified by the successful Nordic university systems. Another possibility is the "state-building university" (Ordorika and Pusser in press), a model of higher education linked to the development projects of postcolonial societies and the developmental state. Arguably, state-building universities are already prominent in Latin America, and something similar can be discerned in parts of Asia and Africa as well.

Hegemonic Norms

How is it that the non Anglo-American traditions are under assault? They are being problematized and subordinated by the New Public Management (NPM), by the normalization of reified NPM models of U.S. higher education, and by global ranking on the terms of the hegemony.

The NPM first emerged in the United Kingdom in the 1980s. Although it predates the communicative globalization of the 1990s, that medium has accelerated its policy diffusion.[10] For the most part, NPM perspectives on higher education have been adopted by the worldwide financial sectors, which closely influence government, and global policy agencies outside the United Nations, especially the International Monetary Fund (IMF) and World Bank. NPM reforms includes government-steered competition among institutions, executive-steered competition among academic units; modernized management and entrepreneurship; marketing of institutions; systems with a mixture of public and private institutions and institutions with a mixture of public and private funding, higher tuition, rhetorical emphasis on customer focus; research links with industry; performance measures and output-based funding; and relations with funding agencies based on contracts, accountability, and audit. NPM reforms are driven by desires for fiscal efficiency and global competitiveness and entail the reworking of control systems. In their full form, the NPM models national systems as economic markets and imagines universities as firms driven by economic revenues and market share, not teaching, research, and service. In the last two decades, the NPM has been the main policy conversation. Numerous studies, supportive and critical, attest to its impact (e.g., Clark 1998; Henkel 2005, 2007; Marginson and Considine 2000; Musselin 2005; Nowotny, Scott, and Gibbons 2001; Rhoads and Torres 2006). Bensimon and Ordorika (2006) note that in Mexico, performance management and individualizing faculty incentives have redirected the effort from the broader social mission of the public university to globally reputable "outputs." This is not to say that NPM reforms are uniform or uniformly applied, or inevitable. Except when conditions are set by World Bank loans, the implementation of NPM is essentially shaped by national politics, governmental culture, and local stakeholders, not global agents.

Although the NPM began life as the child of British neoliberalism, its ideal models of higher education were borrowed from the United States. It is inevitable that given the worldwide dominance of U.S. higher education, the American traditions would be closely watched. Nevertheless, imitation sometimes makes poor policy and poorer identity. Nor is isomorphism always possible. Even though policymakers everywhere seem to believe that if their universities imitate U.S. universities, they will succeed like them, the NPM cannot deliver U.S. outcomes without the national/global conditions that sustain the U.S. brand of "academic capitalism" (Slaughter and Leslie 1997; Slaughter and Rhoades 2004). Policies of imitation with insufficient regard for local context are likely only to confirm the dominance of the prototype American parent, thereby illuminating the vertical distinctions in the sharpest possible relief. There is more than one possible "American model" besides the Ivy League, however. Most U.S. enrolments are in the public sector, which includes the University of California system and land grant and other public flagship universities in different states. The diversity of the U.S. system is seen as one of its characteristic virtues and is spotlighted by the NPM for imitation elsewhere. This points to the fact that the hegemonic norms are based on a particular reification of U.S. practices. This has produced two global models, not so much blueprints as social imaginaries diffused across nations, institutions, and social agents; often in vague forms and imprecise notions; combining structures, technologies, behaviors, and values:

- The hegemonic norm of research university, the "entrepreneurial model" (Clark 1998), is centrally focused on knowledge production, emphasizing research and graduate studies, excellence and prestige, tied to business and the knowledge economy, competitive for students and funds, productive and efficient, internationally oriented, and achieving greater autonomy via financial diversity, including tuition and philanthropy. One set of this model's roots date before the twentieth century in Europe, especially in Germany and the United Kingdom. Its other set of roots, in the most specifically American evolution of massive educational and research empires after World War II, the "multi-versity" (Kerr 1963), is exemplified most closely in contemporary practices by the Ivy League private universities in the United States, such as Harvard and Stanford. These universities are not as responsive to markets as the norm promises, but they impart tremendous prestige to the model.

- The hegemonic norm of for-profit vocational university is centrally focused on vocational training for business; computing; perhaps mass professions such as health; accountable for immediate vocational relevance; business-like in organizational culture; expansionary in student numbers, sites, and market share; spare and efficient with few "frills" such as research, libraries, or academic freedoms; with teaching borrowed from the vocational field and curriculum packages; and "customer" focused, using performance management of staff and quality assurance. This form has a mixed record around the world but in the United States, it is embodied in corporations that raise significant equity funds (Ortmann 2002), including the Apollo Group, parent company of the University of Phoenix. Phoenix is the largest and fastest-growing private university in the United States and has spread to a dozen other countries.

By pushing institutions toward one of these norms, the NPM reform process draws them into two homogenous systems, in which all are readily compared with one other across borders and all appear as inferior to institutions in the global core in the United States. Yet here there is a double irony, two different slippages between the idealized models and the world of practice.

First, the Ivy League model does not travel across borders. No other nation has a sector like the Ivy League, at one time able to amass both public and private resources and to concentrate public and private prestige. The difference in other nations is that national research investments in the sciences are largely concentrated in public or national universities. Even in Japan, where private universities enroll the majority of students, and the most prestigious private institutions sometimes educate the majority of national cabinet members, within the university field itself the national imperial group led by Tokyo University tower over Keio University and Waseda University because of the accumulated state investments in research. This does not diminish the power of the U.S. Ivy League to compel the helpless admiration of the rest of the world. No doubt, a distant and unobtainable paradise secures an even more powerful hold on the imagination than one that can readily be seen and emulated; and no doubt also, the unobtainable model constitutes a firmer vertical barrier and hence a steeper, more powerful kind of global control.

Second, both of these models depart from actual American practice in significant ways. U.S. higher education is much more politicized than the NPM imagines: consider the complex interest-group politics played out around the accreditation agencies—which sit somewhere between state, civil society, business, and community—and the long role of congressional committees in shaping the national evolution of the higher education sector (Slaughter and Leslie 1997). In addition, U.S. private institutions are less the agents of market economy than the NPM imagines. They are heavily dependant on state support via student loans and, in the case of the Ivy League, public funding of research. Public funding is essential to the global strength of all U.S. institutions. Thus by encouraging other nations to withdraw from state support, comparative American global competitiveness is *directly* improved. The United States maintains its level of public subsidy of higher education while that same subsidization is reduced elsewhere. Further encouraging other nations to reduce the role of government in higher education, for example, via WTO/GATS (2005), opens their national policy systems to American profit making by Phoenix and others in the newly opened marketplace in those nations. Finally, neither model fits the comprehensive public research university and the four-year and two-year colleges. This the NPM exploits, however. Measured against these two norms, the actual existing public institutions look flawed. Here the American public sector is subject to many of the same normalizing pressures reshaping systems and institutions elsewhere. Compared with high-status private universities, public research universities are made to look overly democratic if they expand access rather than intensifying selectivity. Yet compared with the commercial sector, public research universities look inefficient, underfocused, and indifferent to the "customer"; and the commercial sector manages to claim democratic credentials somehow separated from governance, transparency, and accountability.

Rank Ordering the Field

The two norms of the entrepreneurial research university and the for-profit vocational university embody in an NPM form the subfields identified by Bourdieu: that of the autonomous and elite research university focused on knowledge and prestige, and that of the heteronomous mass training institution focused on economic volumes and revenues. The NPM has earmarked each subfield for organization as a specific global market. We see that global hegemony extends not just to normalization of a single ideal type but to the continuing reconstitution of the global field as a whole. In this process, non-elite institutions are subject to a reinforced heteronomy and the terms of all position-taking are altered. Universities and all other higher education institutions are positioned as quasi firms; competitive pressures become more determining; and economic imperatives bite more deeply, though again the last change shows itself mostly at the heteronomous end of the field. Higher education is moved closer to the positional war of all against all, the universal market imagined by Bourdieu.

Global university ranking makes a competitive field of global higher education more explicit and orders the two subfields (especially the elite research universities) along hegemonic lines. The Shanghai Jiao Tong University Institute of Higher Education (SJTUIHE) began ranking research universities in 2003, and the *Times Higher Education Supplement* began ranking its "world's best universities" in 2004. The two ranking systems differ in their framing of the field (see table 3.6). The SJTUIHE maps the subfield of research-intensive universities, focusing solely on research rather than status data. The *Times* attempts to draw both subfields into a single league table, incorporating research, status, and international marketing. Neither ranking system fully encompasses the global field, but both contribute to its formation.

The SJTUIHE rankings were welcomed by the Chinese government as a means of comparing Chinese universities to the top research performers world-

Table 3.6 Shanghai Jiao Tong University and *Times Higher Education Supplement–*
QS World University Rankings

Shanghai Jiao Tong University IHE Ranking, 2006	*Times Higher Education Suppelement* Ranking, 2006
1–100.0 Harvard, USA	1–100.0 Harvard, USA
2–72.6 Cambridge, UK	2–96.8 Cambridge, UK
3–72.5 Stanford, USA	3–92.7 Oxford, UK
4–72.1 UC Berkeley, USA	4–89.2 MIT, USA
5–69.7 MIT, USA	4–89.2 Yale, USA
6–66.0 Caltech, USA	6–85.4 Stanford, USA
7–61.8 Columbia, USA	7–83.8 Caltech, USA
8–58.6 Princeton, USA	8–80.4 UC Berkeley, USA
8–58.6 Chicago, USA	9–78.6 Imperial College, London, UK
10–57.6 Oxford, UK	10–74.2 Princeton, USA
Top 100 USA 54; UK 11; Japan 6; Germany 5; Canada, France, and Sweden, 4 each.	Top 100 USA 33; UK 15; Australia and Netherlands, 7 each; France and Switzerland, 5 each.
Top 200 USA 87; UK 22; Germany 15; Japan 9; Canada 8; Netherlands 7; France, Switzerland, Australia, and Italy, 6 each.	Top 200 USA 55; UK 29; Australia 13; Netherlands and Japan, 11 each; Germany 9; Canada 6; China 6; Belgium 5.
Top 500 USA 167; UK 43; Germany 40; Japan 32; Italy 23; Canada 22; France 21; China 19 (14);[a] Australia 16.	Top 500 (not listed)
Universities from less affluent countries[b] Seven (3.5%) of the top 200: China 3; Russia, Mexico, Argentina, and Brazil, 1 each. Some of these are very large.	Universities from less affluent countries[b] Fifteen (7.5%) of the top 200, including China 6; India 3; Russia and Malaysia 2 each; Mexico and Thailand 1 each. Reputational survey picks

35 (7.0%) of the top 500: China 14; Brazil and South Africa 4 each; Russia, Hungary, Poland, and India 2 each; Argentina, Mexico, Czech Republic, Chile, and Egypt 1 each.	up some leading national institutions in emerging countries that would not otherwise appear.
Vocational universities In general, vocationally focused research universities do much less well than basic research-focused universities; pure vocational sectors (e.g., Germany) do not appear.	**Vocational universities** Vocationally focused institutions in Netherlands and India rank ahead of basic research universities; some vocationally focused universities from Australia included in second 100.

Notes: [a] Includes 5 from Taiwan.

[b] Universities from countries with per capita incomes of less than $20,000 per year.

Source: SJTUIHE 2006; *Times Higher* 2006.

wide. The objective in establishing the competitive position of China's universities is to underpin the government's policies designed to catch up. The exercise requires realism, measurable outputs, and sound data. The SJTUIHE states that only research, meaning published research in English in the sciences, is sufficiently standardized to enable comparison on a quantitative basis across the world. Twenty percent of the SJTUIHE index is constituted by citation in leading journals, 20 percent by articles in *Science* and *Nature*, and 20 percent by the number of ISI-Thomson (2006) "HiCi" researchers in the institution are in mostly science-based fields. Another 30 percent derives from the distribution of the winners of Nobel Prizes and fields medals in mathematics according to university of training (10 percent) and current employment (20 percent). The remaining 10 percent is determined by taking the total from the preceding data and dividing by the number of staff.

The SJTUIHE rankings favor large, research-intensive universities with comprehensive research performance in a range of fields, universities and nations that invest in scientific infrastructure at scale, and English-language nations. Americans enjoy an additional advantage because of circular citation patterns: Americans tend to cite Americans (Altbach 2006). This league table creates a coherent mapping of the field consistent with prior assumptions about elite universities. It precisely orders the hierarchy of research universities while tightly coupling status with measured research outcomes and installing research capacity firmly as the principle of division between center/periphery/

margins, the fulcrum where global power and differentiation are turned. Being grounded in standardized research data, the rankings reinforce the authority of those data and of global standardization itself. In the process, the SJTUIHE rankings not only confirm the dominance of American and English-language universities and the prestige of the leading institutions, but they also confirm their idea of the university. Coherence is secured by ignoring the economic logic of the other subfield, that of commercial education. Institutions strong in the commercial market are not acknowledged for that. Only their research outputs, if any, are measured. In the SJTUIHE rankings the field is re-represented as a single league table in which only one principle of hierarchization, rather than both, is in operation.

The *Times* ranking was developed by Rupert Murdoch's *Times* in 2004 (*Times Higher* 2007). It is designed to secure a more plural definition of higher education than that used by SJTUIHE, and it tends to favor both high-status research-intensive universities and universities that are particularly strong in the market for international students. Forty percent of the *Times* index is an opinion survey of worldwide faculty ("peers"), and another 10 percent is a survey of "global employers." There are two "internationalization" indicators: the proportion of international students (5 percent) and staff (5 percent). Another 20 percent is determined by the student-staff ratio, a proxy for teaching "quality," and the remaining 20 percent is the number of research citations per staff member. Research standing is captured by the citation data and, more partially, the surveys of "peers." Economic clout in the global market for cross-border education is shown by the internationalization of students indicator, which rewards volume building in the mass market for cross-border education, and, more doubtfully and partially, by the surveys of peers and employers and the internationalization of faculty.

The outcome is a less coherent mapping of the field. Two subfields and two principles of hierarchization do not fit into one league table. The *Times* index credits elite research university status twice, once directly and one via the indicators of global reputation, while crediting economic status once. This produces a composite league table in which the research leaders are again dominant and the U.S. Ivy League heads the pack, modified by universities strong in the market for international students, with some universities with a vocational flavor (the *Times* includes the Indian IITs and promotes the Dutch technical universities), and leading universities in countries such as China that have been buoyed by the reputational surveys. British and Australian universities have the greatest presence in the commercial market for international students, and both nations do much better in the *Times* ranking than in the Shanghai Jiao Tong ranking. Australia has seven universities in the *Times* top 100, with six in the top 50, and is ranked as the third-strongest system in the world, ahead of Japan, Canada, and all the nations of western Europe. But Australia has none of the Shanghai Jiao Tong top 50 and only two of the top 100. Whereas the United States has fifty-four research universities in the Shanghai Jiao Tong top 100, the *Times* manages to reduce American world leadership to just thirty-three. The *Times* exercise can be understood as an attempt by a British publisher to assert an Anglo-American hegemony as distinct from American hegemony in higher education. The credibility of the *Times* data, however, are impaired by methodological weaknesses in the survey, by the fact that the survey data can be altered or interpreted to secure one or another outcome,[11] and by dramatic oscillations each year in the ranking of some universities (Marginson 2007b).

Like the SJTUIHE ranking, the *Times* ranking reinforces the presumed global hegemony overall. "The fact is that essentially all of the measures used to assess quality and construct rankings enhance the stature of the large universities in the major English-speaking centers of science and scholarship and especially the United States and the United Kingdom" (Altbach 2006, 1). The rankings elevate on the global scale especially the universities in the Super-league, which now loom larger over each national hierarchy. The rising Asian science powers, which for the first time are able to chart their own course in higher education, are told in no uncertain terms by the rankings that to succeed at the global level, they must confine themselves to the terms of an American domination that at this time seems unchallengeable. Whether they subordinate themselves to the hegemony is yet to be determined.

The potency of specifically global referencing and its norms is almost universal. Except in the United States, every university and its public know where that university stands in the Shanghai Jiao Tong and/or *Times* list, especially whether the university is inside or outside. It matters. The criteria for success are clear, and so rankings channel position-taking into a small number of steps enabling movement up the table. Innovations in curriculum, pedagogy, delivery, and organizational design that are distinctive to particular institutions, localities, or cultures are inhibited by the long lead time necessary before they come to fruition. The tyranny of rankings is the tyranny of equity prices. It enforces a short-term mind-set that cuts off the potential for investment in bold new strategies, especially outside the dominant norms. Furthermore, by narrowing the possible trajectories, rankings marginalize the heterogeneous traditions and models. Here the higher education status quo is protected by default. In the exceptional case of the United States, the global rankings do not matter much. Instead, in that nation the tyranny of the national ranking by *U.S. News & World Report* is almost complete. For American university presidents and publics, the national ranking might serve to compose a de facto global ranking, for the parochial horizon is sufficient to reach across more than half the world leaders.

Global referencing of the rankings creates greater heteronomy across the sector, except in the Super-league universities, whose freedoms are enhanced. This heteronomy is different from the assertion of government controls at the national level. As we have seen, when operating in the national field, universities exercise a reflexive autonomy vis-à-vis the nation-state. This is a two-sided, never-resolved process in which institutions are continually under pressure from the state to weaken their autonomy while from time to time the state itself is criticized and sometimes renewed. This nation-state reflexivity is disrupted by the pull toward global rankings, fragmenting the old role of universities in nation-building. But global rankings do not establish an equivalent reflexivity in the global dimension. There is no global state, and even though global hegemony is everywhere, it is also out of reach. The universities in the Super-league have an ongoing relationship with the global centers of power, but they usually use this as a U.S.-focused reflexivity that rarely acknowledges the global dimension except by default. Other universities lose their reflexive role once they look to the global level, as the rankings say they must. How can they interpolate themselves into a world-making project on terrain blocked out by the Super-league? Thus the university as an institution is diminished.

BEYOND GLOBAL HEGEMONY

Global educational hegemony is a fact. But no closure is ever complete; the imaginative possibilities are always open; and the longer term has potential for plural centers of power. The Internet, air travel, and research are not confined to English-speaking nations, and we can envisage a more diverse cultural environment with European, Spanish-speaking, Chinese, Islamic, and other globalizations. Drache and Froese (2005) noted that the film industry was exhibiting signs of pluralization that "nobody could have foreseen a few decades ago." In dollar terms, Hollywood is still supreme, generating $6.4 billion in international sales each year, compared with foreign earnings of $100 million in India (Drache and Froese 2005, 7–8, 24), but Bollywood produces more than eight hundred films in twenty-five different Indian languages each year from many regional centers. Selected Bollywood and "cross-over" products are breaking into mainstream global cinema markets. Other creative powers include animation in Japan, film in China and Iran, and television production in Mexico, Venezuela, and Brazil. That is film. Where and how could the remarkable global hegemony in higher education and research begin to fragment? What conditions and factors shape individuals' and institutions' potential within the global field? How ontologically open is the global field and the possible trajectories?

Global Agency and Ontology

Bourdieu's notion of the interdependency of position and position-taking strategy helps explain the actions of institutions and individuals within the field of power, for example, the decisions of university executives and the trajectories they envisage (Marginson and Considine 2000). The theorization is particularly relevant to studying orthodox, often mimetic, and predictable decisions premised on maintaining relative position. It is less relevant to the practices of university and disciplinary leaders when they reimagine their options, for example, by conceiving a change in field boundaries or a change in the products of higher education, or a break with competition as the norm of relations in the field. From time to time, off-the-wall innovations appear that cannot be adequately explained by positions and conditions. Such innovations are especially apparent in the global dimension, for example, the early initiatives in locating branches of foreign universities in importing nations. Here Bourdieu is open to question. First, he universalizes competition in the field of power. No respite from the relentless Hobbesian war of all against all that continually eats into our conditions of possibility seems likely. Second, Bourdieu argues that freedom— that is, the potential for self-determination—should be understood merely as freedom from material necessity. In *Distinction* (1984), Bourdieu talks about an opposition between "the tastes of luxury (or freedom) and the tastes of necessity" (177). The scope for action is confined by prior class relations and resource levels locking up the potential of self-determination itself. But while it is true that self-determination is conditioned by material resources and historical relations of power and that it is essential to understand those conditions, they do not foreclose all possibilities.

History suggests that freedom also is conditioned by agency itself, by the imagination and the capacity of agents to work on the limits. With his emphasis on the will and individual initiative, Gramsci understood this (Williams 1960).

Bourdieu did not see "strategy" as based on conscious imagining and deciding as much as on learned dispositions, the habitus. We move instinctively in response to a structured set of possibilities as they shift and change. The range of possible position-taking strategies, and the limits of that range appropriate to the position of each agent and to the state of the struggle, are burned into the agent's unconscious mind and conditions his or her every action. "Because position-takings arise quasi-mechanically—that is, almost independently of the agents' consciousnesses and wills—from the relationship between positions, they take relatively invariant forms" (Bourdieu 1993, 59). Arguably, with his attenuated vision of the scope for reflexive self-determination, Bourdieu has left insufficient space for the play of the conscious creative imagination in strategy making.

Amartya Sen (1985) finds that freedom as self-determination has two principal components. He calls these "agency freedom" and "freedom as power," or, in a later work (Sen 1992), "effective freedom." Agency freedom is where identity is located, the imagination is gathered, and the will is formed. Freedom as power is, roughly speaking, positive freedom, including the resource capacity to realize one's goals. Sen distinguishes both these forms of freedom from negative freedom, freedom from coercion, which is foundational to Hayek (1960), and neoliberalism (Marginson 1997). Sen explains that negative freedom is one condition of self-determination but less important than freedom as power, and it is presupposed by freedom as power. Positive freedom entails negative freedom, but the reverse is not the case. Sen argues that the range of choices available to us is an important element of freedom, again in contrast to Hayek, to whom the range of choice is not important and what matters is the absence of coercion, that is, who is doing the choosing (Sen 1992, 63). Sen also emphasizes that the extent of freedom should be distinguished from resources and other means to freedom. Two agents with the same resources and same negative freedom may have a different *freedom to achieve*. When resources are held constant, the primary source of variations in freedom is agency freedom. Here the range of choices can be expanded, in the first instance by thought. Thus to the long list of elements that might differentiate freedom to achieve in global higher education, including national GDP, investment in higher education, research capacity, language of use, the volume and intensity of cross-border engagements, and so on, we can add another quality crucial to establishing the boundaries of the possible in the global higher education environment. This quality is an aspect of agency freedom. It is the *imagination*: the possibilities imagined by universities, groups, and individuals.

But if we entertain a notion of agency that leaves more space than does Bourdieu for conscious positivity and acts of will, it will have implications for the notion of relational field. In his description of the global space, Arjun Appadurai (1996) foregrounds agency and is centrally interested in global imaginings while at the same time he describes the structure of the field as ontological openness, a world vectored by different cultural flows, the heterogeneous and disjunctive "scapes" with their uneven shapes and articulations. Appadurai's "scapes" are structures—this is not simply a description of the imagination floating free of the constraints of power, cultural categories, and economic materiality—but he emphasizes the changeability, volatility, and contingency of all categories and structures. The implication is that in the global setting, more so than in the national setting, even the structures of hegemony in higher education are provisional, partial, and contested. They are relativized by the other parts of the field and in continuous transformation. One element continuously at play within the field (and one of the principal sources of its ontological openness) is the imagination and will of agents. In the global setting, agents have more and more varied spaces in which to innovate than they do in the national field. The global environment is in continuous formation; the map of positions is continually being reworked; and novel positions are emerging.

Why is there greater ontological openness in the global setting? One factor is the growth, extension, openness, reciprocity, and dynamism of the global flows of people, knowledge, ideas, technologies, and capital in higher education and other sectors. As the fluid metaphor of "flows" implies, cross-border flows continually generate change and themselves undergo change. This tends to "loosen" the relations of power in worldwide higher education to some extent, thereby imparting a certain dynamism, instability, openness, and unpredictability, and more so than in national systems. Other factors are the exponential tendency in the expansion of networks described by Castells (2000); more permeable national borders and the flaky nature of both global networks and the borders of the global field; the volatility and vitality of the space for position-taking; the lacunae in formal governmental regulation of the cross-border of systems and institutions; and the space for spontaneous association this creates (Marginson and van der Wende 2009). Above all are the expanded potentials for agency freedom created by the global transformations in space and time: more multiple locations; faster passage between them; instantaneous, expanded, intensified, and multiassociating communications; more multiple *identities*; and multiple and variously articulated spheres of action.

The complication for analyzing relations of power in higher education—and for all those who theorize the mutual exclusivity of the modern and postmodern, and the national and the global—is that in the global setting, we can all too readily detect both Bourdieuian relations and Appaduraian relations at work. On the field of the global with its unevenness, alterity, and disjuncture, we nevertheless detect the Bourdieuian binary between elite and mass, between the principle of autonomous culture and the principle of heteronomy, together with vigorous boundary-making and hierarchy-forming activities, such as university rankings that are sustained by the principal beneficiaries. In essence, this is what the hegemonic project is: the imposition of form on flux, the bold attempt to stop time and center power in particular places, and the necessary blindness of reflexivity that this entails. How could any such project ever be anything but provisional? How can it not fail "in the long run"? But that does not mean that it is ephemeral, unable to secure potent effects, or incapable of immediate domination. It means only that the project must be continually made and remade, as Gramsci saw, until the capacity for renewal is undermined, fragmented, or exhausted.

Meanwhile, one of the continuous and immediate effects of hegemony in higher education is precisely to articulate and differentiate the agency freedoms themselves in the interest of the hegemonic project. The expanded and more open global ontology is experienced differentially. Some have greater freedoms of action than others. Bourdieu's point is that autonomy and capacity are located at the field's high-status academic subfield and, above all, in the Super-league universities. There the hypothetical scope for strategy is maximized (although it tends to be confined to strategies that reproduce hegemony or are at least consistent with it). Other institutions and agents in higher education can imagine more radical alternatives but have fewer means of implementation. Some are so overshadowed by hegemony as to have fewer, not more, options in the global environment. Here the differentiation of freedom as power—some systems conduct basic research and others not; some institutions are more globally connected than others—constrains the potential of agency freedom. It does not eliminate the desire for self-determination or the possible imaginings. But it does suggest the need for new approaches to identity and self-organization.

For national systems and institutions outside the United States and outside the Anglo-American dyad, which is the half-integrated extension of the American global project in higher education and research, one strategic way forward lies in regional (metanational) organization, to accumulate critical mass and perhaps to consolidate cultural identity. In the face of American global hegemony, larger units are required. In Europe, regionalization through the Bologna and Lisbon accords is fostering structural commonality, the intensive movement of people, and advanced research cooperation. Bologna walks a tightrope between fragmentation and homogenization. The latter poses dangers especially in the vulnerable post-Soviet nations, but the gains have been impressive. Latin America has potential for more advanced cooperation, as some higher education systems are benefiting from a prolonged period of democratic rule and the growth of civil institutions and governments with a social agenda beyond the Washington consensus. This is already happening in the nations of the "Southern Cone" via MERCUSOR.

A second way forward is intensified capacity building on a national scale to provide the basis for a more potent global intervention. Here capacity building has two aspects: material resources, and projects grounded in proactive national identity. China doubled its real per capita income the last decade and, according to some projections, will overtake the United States' PPP GDP by 2025. Higher education in China is undergoing a major state-driven development in extraordinarily rapid time. Between 1990/1991 and 2002/2003, the gross enrollment ratio rose from 3 to 13 percent (World Bank 2007). From 1998 to 2004, a period of only six years, the total number of undergraduate admissions in China multiplied by *four times* (Liu 2006). China now accounts for half the R&D expenditure of the non-OECD nations (Vincent-Lancrin 2006, 16) and is the second largest R&D investor in the world. This transformation has incalculable long-term consequences for worldwide provision, for the map of research and flows of knowledge and people, and for the pattern of alliances and networks. But equally important and the necessary corollary of this process of material stock piling and people building is the sense of national/global mission in Chinese higher education. As Zhang Xiaoming and Xu Haitao (2000) put it: "Many non-western societies are trying to evaluate themselves with western standards and then develop what they lack. The time seems ripe for change with regard to such an unwise approach" (103). Internationalization should emphasize "not the elimination of cultural differences but international exchange on an equal footing" (104). Differences in national power inevitably results in inequalities, but "no route to development, autonomy and power can be separated from international systems" (110). Openness to and open participation in the global dimension are essential. At the same time, maintaining a strong sense of both national tradition and national strategic project is equally important. In the face of cross-border flows, the national project should be not be one of adaptation to global normalization and standardization but one of "indigenization," in which foreign culture is "grafted onto the tree of indigenous culture" (104).

Taiwan, Singapore, and South Korea are on a similar path to China in higher education; Singapore has developed a particularly sophisticated capacity for global strategy that reflects a coherent national project, in which it seems that the gap between global identity and national/local identity, the duality that attends university work in most nations outside the United States, has largely been closed by a deliberate act of national will. Multiple identities create strategic flexibility, enabling freer movement among different spheres of operation, while a successful global strategy also requires that multiple identities cohere. Much hangs on how this is managed in nonhegemonic nations, whether they can sustain both multiplicity and coherence. How China manages biculturalism in higher education, and the extent to which Pudonghua (Mandarin) becomes a language of global communication and of research, will be a principal factor determining the extent of cultural plurality of knowledge. The Spanish language might also gain a greater global role, given the weight of Latin America and the growing importance of Spanish in the United States. Arabic, as well, has some prospects of consolidating a global role.

STRATEGIZING THE GLOBAL

The global field of higher education contains global markets but is more heterogeneous than the single "global market" coined by the NPM and university rankings. It is standardized not by the laws of motion of capital accumulation but by Anglo-American hegemony and the dominance of the autonomous subfield of research universities from the United States (primarily) and the United Kingdom. The instruments of domination are language and monoculture, research and publishing systems, knowledge flows, and the people flows that follow; even though global uniformity is incomplete and practiced at the expense of much diversity. Global market forces often are assumed to be enforcing the American hegemony and standardization in higher education, suppressing cultural diversity by the worldwide accumulation of capital in this industry sector as in others. But universities are not banks, mining companies, or computer manufacturers. Their social logic is different. In higher education, hegemonic language and knowledge are the prior and essential conditions for the evolution of global markets, not vice versa. The techniques of university ranking became possible only because of the previous universalization of English-language research in the sciences. Likewise, higher education is often assumed to be commodified at the behest of the state, but the global elite universities are not becoming knowledge commodity factories. Despite the commodification at their edges, their primary concern is to extract support from state and civil society for basic research in the classical form of a public good. (Below the level of the hegemonic institutions, heteronomy and commodity forms are more determining.) Like the Catholic Church and other organized religions that also predate finance capital, the Super-league university is essentially its own creature. Ironically, perhaps, the premodern origins of the elite university enable it to play a primary role in constructing global relations in this era.

The hegemonic higher education sector serves business and the imperial nation-state but does so from a condition of autonomous reflexivity. The Super-league is not an artifact of the state or the economy, despite the "knowledge economy" discourse. Civil society in the form of the Super-league research universities has moved beyond the Gramscian horizon of the national class structure and the sphere of the nation-state into a global space where it is accountable first to the one national power that spans the full planetary terrain (albeit accountable to it in national, not planetary, guise) and second to the globally mobile social elites that are now among its primary users. In this global space, the defining features of the leading universities remain specific to them: the production of knowledge and of the social status or positional goods (Hirsch 1976) attached to authoritative knowledge. Research capacity, not economic capital, is the primary material constituent of global hegemony in higher education.

Global relations of power in higher education are determined by the positioning and self-positioning of countries, universities, and individual agents by and toward the hegemonic project. Some agents in the global setting are central to that project and benefit from it; some agents are absorbed into it; and others marginalized or excluded from it. The Bourdieuian binary logic of the global sector, divided between elite research universities and mass/commercial education, is the divide between knowledge power and the commodity economy in higher education, and the ultimate divide between inclusion and exclusion. From where, then, can the challenge come? Given the weight of hegemony—and given also the more jagged and fluid Appadurain world on top of which the hegemony sits, a world held in place by the weight of categorical power but one always threatening to break the binds—how might we move to create space for local, national, and regional autonomy while preparing more democratic and pluralistic global relations in higher education?

The resource support of national governments is essential to global competence and autonomy. National investment continues to be crucial. At the same time, by itself it is not enough to secure the space for strategy beyond hegemony; and if the options are limited to enhancing national competitiveness, this will reproduce both hegemony and subordination to it. When global strategy is secured by dumbing down local contents, identity is negated. Here local and national revolts against the NPM and commodification can establish space for more generous social projects but are unlikely to be decisive vis-à-vis hegemony as long as the monoculture in language and research remains intact. Otherwise, the monocultural hegemony will continue to shape the desired outcomes and forms of higher education, and the Super-league will retain full authority, which is a function of global civil society rather than national policy or World Bank conditions. Policy will continue to be conducted in these terms, and sooner or later, recalcitrant local institutions and national systems will be pulled back (or will pull themselves back), becoming renormalized in the terms of hegemony. Regional and other cross-border alliances are necessary because they provide more room for alternative approaches and cultural identity building. Here the strategic problem is to break free of hegemonic global standards and standardization without losing the global. Local and national projects are needed that are "conceived in a non-nationalist way" (Santos 2006, 80) and that build forms of local and national autonomy that are part of a new kind of global civil society:

> From the perspective of the peripheral and semi-peripheral countries the new global context demands a total reinvention of the national project without which there can be no reinvention of the university. There is nothing nationalistic about this demand. There is only the need to invent a critical cosmopolitanism in a context of aggressive and exclusive globalization (Santos 2006, 78).

The essence of global civil society—analogous to the modern national societies built before it—is that agency, fluid within the common space, is irreducibly global and local/national at the same time. Building on these local and national initiatives while remaining subject to the factors that condition agency (including the imaginations of local leaders), parts of the higher education world *can* constitute an alternative globalism apart from that of the U.S.-dominated communications and entertainment sectors, the finance sector, and the Super-league universities. In doing so, individual universities may need to use the freedoms flowing from both their old autonomy and the new global agency and ontology, so as to strike out ahead of their national governments. Such an alternative globalization would have two principal elements. These are partly independent, partly dependent, and each is necessary to the other.

First, *diversity*. To establish a genuine cultural plurality in research, it is necessary to move beyond the current hegemony. Likewise, to move beyond the current hegemony, it is essential to establish genuine cultural plurality in research and knowledge. One condition for this process of pluralization is sustaining linguistic diversity in the global higher education sector, not as a substitute for global communication, which is inevitable and necessary, but alongside it and as part of it. A hopeful sign here is the potential for cultural plurality in the "belly of the beast" in the United States itself. Demographic and cultural Hispanization could provide favorable conditions for broadening U.S. perspectives in the larger global setting and might even lead to greater engagement with non Anglo-American models of higher education.[12]

Second, the *social agenda*. Individually and collaboratively, universities everywhere can bring their resources to bear on the diagnosis and solution of the many urgent problems that humanity faces. Global warming and climate change head the list, followed by poverty and illiteracy, civil and foreign warfare, human trafficking, and epidemic disease. Here the scope for cross-border cooperation beyond the terms of hegemony is vast. "The goal is to re-insert the public university in the collective solution of social problems, which are now insoluble unless considered globally" (Santos 2006, 79). At the same time, even though critical cosmopolitanism in the global dimension is necessary, it is not by itself sufficient. If the common global character of problems and solutions is configured so as to empty out the local and national specificities of those problems, the move to diversity will be ineffective, and a shallow difference will be all that is left. Cosmopolitanism will be played out as a set of predictable signifiers within a single game. The global starts to peel away from place and is vulnerable to capture by the agents of market power. Universities become divided between global players and those confined to what they can see. The social agenda's many points of purchase on egalitarian politics will be lost.

Finally, culture, language and alternative approaches to research and knowledge are right at the center of the problem of strategy in higher education. It is here, in the domain of research and knowledge, that the global hegemony in higher education is primarily sustained. Higher education is not permanently subordinated to the formation of global markets and inevitably complicit in its own normalization in the terms of hegemony. As long as they retain a role in knowledge formation, institutions have the potential for autonomous power on the global level. When higher education is reduced merely to producing and allocating positional goods, like a labor bureau, its historical potential is decisively limited. It becomes more Bourdieuian, more category bound, than it is at present. If knowledge formation is quintessentially global, it also constitutes an endless possibility for diverse identities, for local praxis and language maintenance and the reentry of local ideas into the common conversation. For universities, research groups, and faculty within the United States, the essence of counter-hegemony is to aid in building the capacity for knowledge formation in other places. It is when the role of the university in knowledge formation is at the fore that the fuller play of the imagination becomes possible, the larger promise that an Appadurian global order/disorder offers us.

NOTES

We express our grateful thanks to the anonymous reviewer of this chapter, whose insightful criticisms and positive suggestions added much value to the development and finalization of the text. We thank all the reviewers for their stimulating feedback while noting that several of them were uncomfortable with the portrayal of American power in the worldwide high education sector. No one actually disputed the facts of global hegemony as we have described them here. But some reviewers wanted us to be less clear and direct about the matter or to emphasize ways in which American universities and American faculty were similar to those in other nations, rather than to focus on ways in which the global roles of American universities and faculty differed from those of other nations.

1. Technically, the value of a network increases as the square of the number of nodes in the network:

   > When networks diffuse, their growth becomes exponential, as the benefits of being in the network grow exponentially, because of the greater number of connections, and the cost grows in linear patter. Besides, the penalty for being outside the network increases with the network's growth because of the declining number of opportunities in reaching other elements outside the network. (Castells 2000, 71)

2. Arguably, Pierre Bourdieu (1984, 1988, 1993, 1996) is the only major social theorist, and certainly the only one since 1960, who has devoted much of his total output to analyzing education and universities. His work, however, is bound to only one nation—he universalizes on the basis of the French case—and is not global in scope. In earlier periods, others such as Ortega y Gasset and Talcott Parsons focused on universities to some extent. Among the more contemporary theorists, Habermas, Lyotard (1984), and Derrida (2004) have produced works that bear directly or indirectly on universities and knowledge. While some of these works, such as Lyotard's famous essay on the postmodern condition and knowledge, are undoubtedly important, only Bourdieu made higher education a central feature of his life's work.

3. Although this issue deserves more attention, in the global setting, boundaries and membership in the field of higher education are not only contestable but also unstable, acquiring new permutations given the permeability of boundaries and multiplicity of identities.

4. Has the whole field has been pulled toward economic and political power so that the autonomy of higher education has generally been reduced? Some people advocate that position (e.g., Slaughter and Leslie 1997), but perhaps it is not so simple. Although the heteronomy of the mass and middling universities has increased, and commercial science has found its way into the Ivy League, the Super League seems to have more independent agency than before. Perhaps, as in economic and political life, the field of higher education is becoming more steeply hierarchical, with the Bourdieuian elite becoming more concentrated on a global scale.

5. Perhaps a case can be made for an Anglo-American hegemony in higher education, given the global leadership exercised alongside the Ivy League by the major British institutions—although lesser British institutions have less global clout than their American counterparts—and given the centrality of the English language to global hegemony, especially in research. But if there is an Anglo-American hegemony (Marginson 2006a), then the United Kingdom is a relatively subordinated partner, despite the global authority of Oxford and Cambridge.

6. The transformation of the university in the context of social relations is too large a topic to be explored in this chapter, which thus finds itself carrying a de facto "internalist" bias. But among others, see Ordorika 2003 and Santos 2006.

7. Of the nine scientists who came from emerging or developing countries and won Nobel Prizes in chemistry, physics, physiology, or medicine, four were working in universities in the United States and two in the United Kingdom and Europe (Bloom 2005).

8. Relative to the revenue flow in their favor, these two nations spent little on foreign aid for postsecondary education: United States US$111 million and Australia US$13 million (OECD 2004, 286).

9. This makes education one of Australia's four most valuable exports, along with coal, iron ore, and tourism.

10. It is not surprising that some analysts see the NPM, globalization, and an imperial Americanization or Anglo-Americanization as simply one process (Currie 2005).

11. At a conference in Brisbane, Australia, on February 12, 2008, a representative of QS Marketing, the marketing firm that conducted the two surveys for the *Times Higher,* stated that the return rate for the 2006 survey of academic "peers" was only 1 percent and the response group was loaded in favor of returns from the United Kingdom and Australia. The responses were not tested for representivity and/or weighted to correct for bias.

12. A plurality of models would enable greater diversity in global comparisons of institutions. At worst, this means university rankings based on several league tables rather than one. At best, it can lead to a move away altogether from the whole institution comparison toward assessments based on disaggregated disciplines and services, as developed by the Centre for Higher Education Development (CHE) in Germany. Lest this be considered utopian, the CHE system already is established as the principal mode of inter-institutional comparison in Germany, Austria, Netherlands, and Flanders and will spread further in Europe (Marginson 2007b). This development also underlines the salience of regional modes of organization in higher education and research in the face of the global hegemony.

REFERENCES

ABS (Australian Bureau of Statistics). 2006. *Balance of Payments and International Investment Position*. Australia, December, Catalogue 5302.0. Canberra: ABS.

Altbach, P. 2005. "Academic Challenges: The American Professoriate in Comparative Perspective." In *The Professoriate: Portrait of a Profession*, ed. A. Welch, 147–65. Dordrecht: Springer.

———. 2006. "The Dilemmas of Ranking." *International Higher Education*, no. 42: 13.

Appadurai, A. 1996. *Modernity at Large: Cultural Dimensions of Globalization*. Minneapolis: University of Minnesota Press.

Bensimon, E., and I. Ordorika. 2006. "Mexico's Estimulos: Faculty Compensation Based on Piecework." In *The University, State and Market: The Political Economy of Globalization*, ed. R. Rhoads and C. Torres, 250–74. Stanford, Calif.: Stanford University Press.

Berning, E. 2004. "Petrified Structures and Still Little Autonomy and Flexibility: Country Report Germany." In *The International Attractiveness of the Academic Workplace in Europe*, ed. J. Enders and E. de Weert, 160–82. Frankfurt: Herausgeber und Bestelladresse.

Bloom, D. 2005. "Raising the Pressure: Globalization and the Need for Higher Education Reform." In *Creating Knowledge: Strengthening Nations: The Changing Role of Higher Education*, ed. G. Jones, P. McCarney, and M. Skolnik, 21–41. Toronto: University of Toronto Press.

Bok, D. 2003. *Universities in the Marketplace: The Commercialization of Higher Education*. Princeton, N.J.: Princeton University Press.

Bourdieu, P. 1984. *Distinction: A Social Critique of the Judgment of Taste*. Trans. R. Nice. London: Routledge & Kegan Paul.

———. 1988. *Homo Academicus*. Cambridge: Polity Press.

——. 1993. *The Field of Cultural Production*. Ed. R. Johnson. New York: Columbia University Press.

——. 1996. *The State Nobility*. Trans. L. Clough. Cambridge: Polity Press.

Breneman, D., B. Pusser, and S. Turner. 2007. *Earnings from Learning: The Rise of For-Profit Universities*. Albany: State University of New York Press.

Calhoun, C. 1992. "Introduction: Habermas and the Public Sphere." In *Habermas and the Public Sphere*, ed. C. Calhoun, 1–48. Cambridge, Mass.: MIT Press.

Castells, M. 2000. *The Rise of the Network Society*. 2nd ed. Vol. 1, *The Information Age: Economy, Society and Culture*. Oxford: Blackwell.

——. 2001. *The Internet Galaxy: Reflections on the Internet, Business and Society*. Oxford: Oxford University Press.

Clark, B. 1998. *Creating Entrepreneurial Universities: Organizational Pathways of Transformation*. Oxford: Pergamon Press.

Crystal, D. 2003. *English as a Global Language*. 2nd ed. Cambridge: Cambridge University Press.

Currie, J. 2005. "Globalization's Impact on the Professoriate in Anglo-American Universities." In *The Professoriate: Portrait of a Profession*, ed. A. Welch, 21–34. Dordrecht: Springer.

Derrida, J. 2004. *Eyes of the University: Right to Philosophy 2*. Trans. J. Plug. Stanford, Calif.: Stanford University Press.

Drache, D., and M. Froese. 2005. "Globalization and the Cultural Commons: Identity, Citizenship and Pluralism After Cancun." Unpublished paper. Toronto: Department of Political Science, York University.

The Economist. 2005. "The Brain's Business." September 8.

Enders, J., and E. de Weert, eds. 2004. "The International Attractiveness of the Academic Workplace in Europe—Synopsis Report." In *The International Attractiveness of the Academic Workplace in Europe*, ed. J. Enders and E. de Weert, 11–31. Frankfurt: Herausgeber und Bestelladresse.

Enders, J., and U. Teichler. 2005. "Academics' View of Teaching Staff Mobility: The ERASMUS Experience Revisited." In *The Professoriate: Portrait of a Profession*, ed. A. Welch, 97–112. Dordrecht: Springer.

Gramsci, A. 1971. *Selections from the Prison Notebooks*. Trans. Q. Hoare and G. Nowell Smith. New York: International Publishers.

——. 2000. *The Antonio Gramsci Reader*. Ed. and trans. D. Forgacs. New York: New York University Press.

Guellec, D., and M. Cervantes. 2002. "International Mobility of Highly Skilled Workers: From Statistical Analysis to Policy Formulation." In *International Mobility of the Highly Skilled*, ed. 71–98. Paris: OECD.

Habermas, J. 1989. *The Structural Transformation of the Public Sphere: An Inquiry into a Category of Bourgeois Society*. Trans. T. Burger with the assistance of F. Lawrence. Cambridge, Mass.: MIT Press. First published in Germany in 1962.

Harvey, D. 1990. *The Condition of Postmodernity: An Enquiry into the Origins of Cultural Change*. Oxford: Blackwell.

——. 2006. *Spaces of Global Capitalism: Towards a Theory of Uneven Geographical Development*. London: Verso.

Hayek, F. 1960. *The Constitution of Liberty*. London: Routledge & Kegan Paul.

Held, D., A. McGrew, D. Goldblatt, and J. Perraton. 1999. *Global Transformations: Politics, Economics and Culture*. Stanford, Calif.: Stanford University Press.

Henkel, M. 2005. "Academic Identity and Autonomy in a Changing Policy Environment." *Higher Education* 49: 155–76.

——. 2007. "Can Academic Autonomy Survive in the Knowledge Society? A Perspective from Britain." *Higher Education Research and Development* 26 (1): 87–99.

Hirsch, F. 1976. *Social Limits to Growth*. Cambridge, Mass.: Harvard University Press.

Huntington, S. 1996. *The Clash of Civilizations and the Remaking of World Order*. New York: Simon & Schuster.

IIE (Institute for International Education). 2006. "Data on US International Education." Available at http://www.iie.org/ (accessed February 1, 2006).

(ISI) Institute for Scientific Information-Thomson. 2007. "Data on Highly Cited Researchers." Available at http://isihighlycited.com/ (accessed April 10, 2007).

Ives, P. 2004. *Language and Hegemony in Gramsci*. London: Pluto Press.

Johnson, R. 1993. Introduction to *The Field of Cultural Production*, by Pierre Bourdieu, 1–25 New York: Columbia University Press.

Kaul, I., I. Grunberg, and M. Stern, eds. 1999. *Global Public Goods: International Cooperation in the 21st Century*. New York: Oxford University Press.

Kelo, M., U. Teichler, and B. Wachter, eds. 2006. *Eurodata: Student Mobility in European Higher Education*. Bonn: Lemmens Verlags- and Mediengesellschaft.

Kerr, C. 1963. *The Uses of the University*. Cambridge, Mass.: Harvard University Press.

Lee, M. 2002. "The Academic Profession in Malaysia and Singapore: Between Bureaucratic and Corporate Cultures." In *The Decline of the Guru: The Academic Profession in Developing and Middle-Income Countries*, ed. P. Altbach, 141–72. Boston: Boston College Press.

Linguasphere Observatory. 2006. "Linguasphere Table of the World's Major Spoken Languages 1999–2000." Available at http://www.linguasphere.org/language.html (accessed April 2, 2006).

Liu, N. 2006. "The Differentiation and Classification of Chinese Universities and the Building of World-Class Universities in China." Seminar presentation, Leiden University,

February 16, 2006. Available at http://www.leidenslatest.leidenuniv.nl/content_docs/presentation_prof._liu.ppt#364,4,Dream of Chinese for WCU (accessed July 6, 2008).

Lukes, S. 2005. *Power: A Radical View*. 2nd ed. Houndmills: Palgrave Macmillan.

Lyotard, J-F. 1984. *The Postmodern Condition: A Report on Knowledge*. Trans. G. Bennington and B. Massumi. Minneapolis: University of Minnesota Press.

Mandel, E. 1975. *Late Capitalism*. Trans. J. de Bres. London: Verso.

Marginson, S. 1997. *Markets in Education*. Sydney: Allen & Unwin.

——. 2006a. "The Anglo-American University at Its Global High Tide." Review essay. *Minerva* 44: 65–87.

——. 2006b. "Dynamics of National and Global Competition in Higher Education." *Higher Education* 52: 1–39.

——. 2006c. "Putting 'Public' Back into the Public University." *Thesis Eleven* 84: 44–59.

——. 2007a. "Global Position and Position-Taking: The Case of Australia." *Studies in International Education* 11 (1): 5–32.

——. 2007b. "Global University Rankings: Where to from Here?" Paper presented to the Asia-Pacific Association for International Education conference, National of Singapore, March 7–9.

——. 2008a. "Global Field and Global Imagining: Bourdieu and Relations of Power in Worldwide Higher Education." *British Journal of Educational Sociology* 29 (3): 303–16.

——. 2008b. "Hayekian Neo-liberalism and Academic Self-Determination." *Educational Theory* 58 (3): 269–87.

——. 2009. "The Academic Professions in the Global Era." In *The Academic Profession and the Modernization of Higher Education: Analytical and Comparative Perspectives*, ed. J. Enders and E. de Weert, 96–113. Dordrecht: Springer.

Marginson, S., and M. Considine. 2000. *The Enterprise University: Power, Governance and Reinvention in Australia*. Cambridge: Cambridge University Press.

Marginson, S., and G. Rhoades. 2002. "Beyond National States, Markets, and Systems of Higher Education: A Glonacal Agency Heuristic." *Higher Education* 43:281–309.

Marginson, S., and E. Sawir. 2005. "Interrogating Global Flows in Higher Education." *Globalization, Societies and Education* 3 (3): 281–310.

Marginson, S.. and M. van der Wende. 2009. "The New Global Landscape of Nations and Institutions." In *Higher Education to 2030*. Vol. 2, *Globalization*, ed. OECD, 17–62. OECD: Paris.

Marx, K. 1970. *Grundrisse*. Trans. M. Nicolaus. Harmondsworth: Penguin.

Mazzarol, T., G. Soutar, D. Smart, and S. Choo. 2001. "Perceptions, Information and Choice: Understanding How Chinese Students Select a Country for Overseas Study." Canberra: Australian Education International, Commonwealth of Australia. Available at www.dest.gov.au (accessed December 18, 2004).

McLuhan, M. 1964. *Understanding Media*. London: Abacus.

Musselin, C. 2004. "Towards a European Academic Labour Market? Some Lessons Drawn from Empirical Studies on Academic Mobility." *Higher Education* 48: 55–78.

——. 2005. "European Academic Labour Markets in Transition." *Higher Education* 49: 135–54.

Naidoo, R. 2004. "Fields and Institutional Strategy: Bourdieu on the Relationship Between Higher Education, Inequality and Society." *British Journal of Sociology of Education* 25 (4): 446–72.

Newman, J. 1899/1996. *The Idea of a University*. Ed. F. Turner. New Haven, Conn.: Yale University Press.

Nowotny, H., P. Scott, and M. Gibbons. 2001. *Rethinking Science: Knowledge and the Public in an Age of Uncertainty*. Cambridge: Polity Press.

NSB (National Science Board). 2006. "Science and Engineering Indicators 2004." Available at http://www.nsf.gov/statistics/seind04/ (accessed April 9, 2006).

OECD (Organization for Economic Cooperation and Development). 2004. *Internationalization and Trade in Higher Education: Opportunities and Challenges*. Paris: OECD.

——. 2005. *Education at a Glance*. Paris: OECD.

——. 2006. *Education at a Glance*. Paris: OECD.

Ordorika, I. 2003. *Power and Politics in University Governance: Organization and Change at the Universidad Nacional Autonoma de Mexico*. New York: RoutledgeFalmer.

Ordorika, I., and B. Pusser. In press. "La máxima casa de estudios: The Universidad Nacional Autónoma de México as a State-Building University." In *Empires of Knowledge and Development: The Roles of Research Universities in Developing Countries*, ed. P. Altbach and J. Balan. Baltimore: Johns Hopkins University Press.

Ortmann, A. 2002. "Capital Romance: Why Wall Street Fell in Love with Higher Education." The For-Profit Higher Education Research Project at the Curry School of Education, University of Virginia. Available at http://curry.edschool.virginia.edu/forprofit/workingpapers.htm (accessed April 11, 2006).

Postiglione, G. 2005. "China's Global Bridging: The Transformation of University Mobility Between Hong Kong and the United States." *Journal of Studies in International Education* 9 (1): 5–25.

Pusser, B. 2006. "Reconsidering Higher Education and the Public Good: The Role of Public Spheres." In *Governance and the Public Good*, ed. W. Tierney, 11–28. Albany: State University of New York Press.

Rhoads, R., and C. Torres. 2006. *The University, State, and Market: The Political Economy of Globalization in the Americas*. Stanford, Calif.: Stanford University Press.

Rose, N. 1999. *Powers of Freedom: Reframing Political Thought*. Cambridge: Cambridge University Press.

Said, E. 1979. *Orientalism*. New York: Vintage Books.

Santos, B. de Sousa. 2006. "The University in the 21st Century: Towards a Democratic and Emancipatory University Reform." In *The University, State, and Market: The Political Economy of Globalization in the Americas*, ed. R. Rhoads and C. Torres, 60–100. Stanford, Calif.: Stanford University Press.

Sen, A. 1985. "Well-being, Agency and Freedom: The Dewey Lectures 1984." *Journal of Philosophy* 82 (4): 169–221.

——. 1992. *Inequality Reexamined*. Cambridge, Mass.: Harvard University Press.

——. 2000. *Development as Freedom*. New York: Anchor Books.

SJTUIHE (Shanghai Jiao Tong University Institute of Higher Education). 2007. "Academic Ranking of World Universities." Available at http://ed.sjtu.edu.cn/ranking .htm (accessed March 15, 2007).

Slaughter, S., and L. Leslie. 1997. *Academic Capitalism*. Baltimore: Johns Hopkins University Press.

Slaughter, S., and G. Rhoades. 2004. *Academic Capitalism and the New Economy: Markets, State and Higher Education*. Baltimore: Johns Hopkins University Press.

Stiglitz, J. 1999. "Knowledge as a Global Public Good." In *Global Public Goods: International Cooperation in the 21st Century*, ed. I. Kaul, I. Grunberg, and M. Stern, 308–25. New York: Oxford University Press.

Times Higher. 2007. "World University Rankings." *Times Higher Education Supplement*. Available at www.thes.co.uk (accessed March 15, 2007).

Tremblay, K. 2005. "Academic Mobility and Immigration." *Journal of Studies in International Education* 9 (3): 196–228.

UNESCO Institute for Statistics. 2007. "Data on Culture and Communications." Available at http://www.uis.unesco.org/ev.php?URL_ID=5208andURL_DO=DO_TOPI-CandURL_SECTION=201 (accessed February 26, 2007).

Valimaa, J. 2004. "Nationalization, Localization and Globalization in Finnish Higher Education." *Higher Education* 48: 27–54.

——. 2005. "Globalization in the Concept of Nordic Higher Education." In *Globalization and Higher Education*, ed. A. Arimoto, F. Huang, and K. Yokoyama. International Publications Series 9. Hiroshima: Research Institute for Higher Education, Hiroshima University. Available at http://en.rihe.hiroshima-u.ac.jp/pl_default _2.php?bid=63653 (accessed February 10, 2006).

Vincent-Lancrin, S. 2004. "Building Capacity Through Cross-Border Tertiary Education." Paper prepared for the UNESCO/OECD Australia Forum on Trade in Educational Services, October 11–12, 2004. Available at http://www.oecd.org/dataoecd/43/25/33784331 .pdf (accessed February 10, 2006).

——. 2006. "What Is Changing in Academic Research? Trends and Futures Scenarios." Draft paper, OECD-CERI, Paris.

Williams, G. 1960. "The Concept of 'Egemonia' in the Thought of Antonio Gramsci: Some Notes on Interpretation." *Journal of the History of Ideas* 21 (4): 586–99.

Williams, R. 1977. *Marxism and Literature*. Oxford: Oxford University Press.

World Bank. 2007. "World Bank Data and Statistics." Available at http://www.worldbank.org/data (accessed February 28, 2007).

WTO/GATS. 2005. World Trade Organization Website on Negotiations on the General Agreement on Trade in Services (GATS) in Relation to Educational Services. Available at http://www.wto.org/english/tratop_e/serv_e/education_e/education_e.htm (accessed September 11, 2005).

Zhang Xiaoming and Xu Haitao. 2000. "Internationalization: A Challenge for China's Higher Education." In *Current Issues in Chinese Higher Education*, 101–15. Paris: OECD.

FOUR

The State, the University, and Society in Soviet and Russian Higher Education

The Search for a New Public Mission

MARK S. JOHNSON
AND ANDREY V. KORTUNOV

Any analysis of the evolving relations between the state, the university, and society in contemporary Russia must situate that analysis in a historical understanding of how those relations have evolved since the late nineteenth century, especially how these relations have changed since the collapse of the Soviet Union in 1991. One aspect of those relations has been a consistent pattern of institutional differentiation in Russian higher education, a pattern that began well before 1917 and became apparent with the emergence of the Stalinist higher education "system" in 1928. This differentiation entailed often stark separations between Soviet universities and an array of more specialized higher education institutions (technical or polytechnical, pedagogical, agricultural, and medical institutes); as well as an even greater separation between the teaching mission of higher education institutions and the research function of the institutes of the Soviet Union's Academy of Sciences (with similar "academy" structures in agriculture and medicine, and in many of the union republics). That is, the very concept of the "comprehensive" public research university has been contested and complex in Russia throughout its modern history.

Since 1991, institutional leaders and policymakers in Russia have struggled to build, or rebuild, comprehensive research universities (comprehensive in both senses, with a full array of disciplines and professional schools as well as advanced research and education), with mixed success. Thus, an analysis of the search for a new public mission for the research university in Russia today must account for this unique historical and institutional "geography" and also for the reemergence of private universities. Such an analysis must also acknowledge that both Soviet and post-Soviet higher education expanded rapidly in ways that were popular with much of the public and that responded to social demands for upward mobility, career education, and entry to the professions. For all the political complexities and policy conflicts detailed in this chapter, these waves of rapid systemic expansion were perhaps, by default, the central element of the "public mission" in Soviet and post-Soviet higher education.

Higher education in the Soviet era (1917–1991) was also directly connected, often by state decree, to both basic and applied research, economic development, and civic socialization. Of course, all these "public" functions, along with the system's rapid expansion, were shaped by the political needs of the Communist Party and the economic interests of the Soviet state. In fact, this connection was made manifest and invested with legitimacy through the official designation of *state* university (*gosudarstvennyi universitet*) throughout the Soviet and post-Soviet years. Since the fall of the Soviet Union in 1991, yet another wave of systemic expansion appeared in profound curricular shifts toward economics, management, and law; in enthusiastic if often chaotic internationalization; and in the conversion of narrowly profiled Soviet-era institutes into self-styled "universities," both public and newly or partially privatized. To further complicate this analysis, even as the number of institutions and enrollments expanded throughout the Soviet period, the state and the higher education bureaucracy practiced gross political and social discrimination in admissions and promotions and involuntarily "assigned" many graduates to jobs in the planned economy. Even though professors at leading Soviet universities and the upper ranks of the academic profession enjoyed comparatively high prestige and relative autonomy in the later Soviet decades, the role of society as such—or, more precisely, of social groups as *active* participants in the formation of higher education policy—remained limited. In the post-Soviet period, even as new market forces again caused the system to expand and as Russian society differentiated into multiple "publics," the sharp decline in state funding and regulatory capacity led to the degradation of social equity and regional mobility, and measures of academic quality became extremely problematic. Thus, while many members of Russian society (or at least those able to afford the new tuition and other fees) have become more active since 1991 as *consumers* of higher education services, the role of organized social groups or of Russian civil society in the policy process or in university governance remains limited.

To summarize, the evolving relations between the Russian state, higher education, and society have arguably been generally consistent in the modern era, despite often radical and even violent changes in political economy and higher education policy. In part because the rapid expansion of the system channeled and deflected many social interests, or perhaps because other regional, religious, and national interests were repressed or assimilated, the basic relations of power in and around Russian higher education have remained remarkably stable. The Russian state has retained its dominant role, often in close partnership with powerful higher education institutional leaders and professional elites, even if state authority faltered temporarily during key turning points (during the revolutionary upheavals of 1917/1918 and again in the late 1980s and early 1990s). The direct role of Russian society and especially of Russian civil society (before 1917 and after its reemergence in 1987) has been limited, however, or at least carefully mediated and controlled, throughout this history.[1] Finally, we argue at the end of the chapter that the struggle today and the key issue in any new international or interdisciplinary research agenda should be precisely that: analyzing the social dimensions of the transformation of Russian higher education and then using this research to help revitalize the public mission of Russian universities.

To step back and consider all this from a more global and comparative perspective, all the most basic questions apply as we consider the social role of Soviet and Russian higher education, however distinctive it may be in other ways.[2] How and why has Russian state power shaped and regulated these relations with different social groups? What were the precise boundaries of institutional autonomy and the mechanisms of governance in Soviet and now in Russian higher education? What were the limits or contours of academic freedom, or at least of professional identities and practices, in the Soviet system? How and why have these policies and practices changed since the end of Soviet higher education in 1991? In regard to current European and U.S. policy debates, how might such a "new public agenda" for the transformation of Russian higher education be most successfully articulated and popularized? How can Russian society, possibly civil society or students themselves, contribute to these reform processes?[3] In a very real sense, knowledge was a "public good" in the Soviet higher education system, albeit one that was often harshly controlled and mobilized for specific tasks by party-state power. As Russian universities have come to embrace a distinctive if still chaotic and state-dominated form of "academic capitalism" and have struggled to build more "entrepreneurial" institutions, what has been gained and what has been lost in those transformations?[4] Given the distinctive historical background of all these questions in Soviet and post-Soviet Russia, this chapter first offers an historical analysis to better contextualize the policy choices since 1991 and to illuminate future prospects.

THE LEGACIES OF LATE IMPERIAL RUSSIAN HIGHER EDUCATION AND SCIENCE

The historical legacies of late Imperial Russian higher education are hard to disentangle from the public hopes that existed for its rapid expansion in the years before 1917, even if many of those plans remained unrealized at the time of the Russian Revolution. Some analysts have argued that the education system in czarist Russia had been "top heavy" since its origins in the early 1700s, with too much official attention and state funding lavished on elite training and the Academy of Sciences and far too little invested in mass education. One might just as reasonably argue that all levels of research and education suffered from too much official interference and far too little state or public investment. It also is clear that the overwhelming dominance of an ethos of "fundamental" or basic research and of a cluster of elite institutions in St. Petersburg and Moscow contributed to the chronic neglect of more prosaic educational needs, especially mass vocational and secondary education, and perhaps especially in the eastern and southern regions and the non-Russian provinces of the Russian Empire.

The politics of higher education in this period also were shaped by struggles to carve out greater institutional autonomy for the universities (partially enshrined in the Statute of 1863, which empowered faculty far more than students). These rights were then curtailed during later waves of official repression, intended to suppress student radicalism (as embodied in the more restrictive and authoritarian Statute of 1884). In anticipation of the Stalinist-era policies, the years after 1884 witnessed the creation of powerful state-appointed "curators," the appointment of university rectors, and an outright ban on student organizations, controls that were only partially relaxed in 1905 and then reimposed in 1910.[5] While some exceptionally talented individual Russian scholars and researchers emerged out of this system (especially in fields such as mathematics, chemistry, and physiology and also in the arts and literature), they often seemed to struggle amid institutionally weak universities, diffuse professional networks, a stultifying atmosphere of official repression, and strict limits on private-sector support or nonstate investment in advanced education or scholarly publications.

In perhaps the most significant anticipation of Soviet-era policies and practices, the limitations imposed on Russian higher education before 1917 also contributed to a pattern of institutional diversification and curricular specialization. Stymied by official restrictions on the growth and possible regional expansion of comprehensive state universities (in the grip of the politically conservative Ministry of Education), more innovative commercial and industrial interests worked through the Ministry of Finance and the Ministry of Trade and Industry, as well as directly with regional administrations and business leaders, to establish new commercial institutes (in fields such as banking, finance, management, and law); new technical institutes (in fields such as mining, metallurgy, engineering, and economics); and new specialized institutes in fields such as railway transportation, agriculture, and oil production. In contrast, the Russian public universities usually included faculties (*fakul'tety*, or divisions) in law, medicine, history and philology, and mathematics and natural sciences and were in theory committed to combining research and teaching, even if not all were comprehensive (or "multifaculty").

World War I then caused severe systemic crises for Russian higher education but also led to transformation in the relations between the state, the university, and society that carried over directly into the Soviet period.[6] The effects of rapid and often chaotic military and industrial mobilization in 1914 produced severe disruptions, as many state officials and educators realized just how much both Russian higher education and Russian industry depended on imports of advanced materials (in areas such as chemicals, optics, and synthetics, all vital to the war industry), industrial and military technologies, and trained scientific talent from Europe, especially from Germany.[7] This led directly to efforts to foster university-industry partnerships, as well as a pervasive (if at that time not yet fully realized) militarization of Russian university life and of state-sponsored scientific research. Equally significantly, World War I witnessed innovative efforts such as those of Vladimir I. Vernadskii (1863–1945) and the Commission for the Study of the Natural Productive Forces of Russia (KEPS), to integrate Russian science and research directly with the study of natural resources and their use in industrial and military development.[8] In an innovative policy that presaged—and directly helped inspire—the global emergence of state-sponsored "big science" in the middle of the century, Kliment A. Timiriazev (1843–1920), Vernadskii, and other leading Russian scientists aggressively advocated the principle of state-funded specialized research institutes that were to be separated from university teaching. While this policy connected Russian research institutions directly to state power and massive "public" investment, it also worked to detach researchers from the broader "social" world of university life, especially from undergraduate teaching.

During the war, many students volunteered for local relief efforts, but they were not conscripted en masse out of the universities and specialized institutes until 1916. In yet another portent of Soviet-era transformations, the czarist regime's attempt to limit admissions in 1916 inadvertently contributed to a "social opening" for lower-class and "unregulated" admissions, especially of women and national minorities and of Jewish and other students who had been excluded by imperial fiat. Clearly, there was an enormous pent-up public demand for higher education that began to transform the role of the university in Russian society even before the revolutionary upheavals of 1917. A new and more liberal university statute was drafted in 1915, which recognized the autonomy of institutions and their right to control their own governance, a measure that also approved the creation of new universities, although almost all this remained unimplemented amid the chaos of war.

In fact, this brief and tumultuous period between 1915 and about 1918 may well represent the point in this history at which Russian society and its educated and professional elites most openly expressed themselves on issues of higher education policy, even as their ability to influence events spun out of control, as state funding and regulatory capacity declined precipitously, and as the imperial system broke apart. Significantly, major universities and specialized institutes were evacuated away from the western regions and military fronts, which in time contributed to a major expansion of higher education in southern and eastern Russia as libraries, laboratories, and entire faculties were evacuated. After the fall of the Russian monarchy in early 1917, the provisional government granted sweeping autonomy to all higher education institutions, even as the ability of the Russian state to finance or regulate higher education and scientific research continued to collapse. For all the attempted radical policy reforms and ad hoc social transformations in Russian higher education during the war, the larger picture is one of deepening chaos and incipient systemic collapse.

When analyzing this period as a whole, several decades before 1917/1918 were characterized by a thwarted social demand for the rapid expansion of higher education and a growing consensus that precisely such an expansion was necessary for national development (whether that development was imagined as a capitalist or, more popularly, as a socialist project). The prewar era also witnessed the growing "internationalization" of Russian higher education as scholars and students circulated to European universities and began to contribute to international academic journals.[9] Bitter power struggles continued around university autonomy, the role of faculty and students in governance, the balance between state power and regional authority, admissions policies, and curricular priorities. The war years also saw the beginning of what would become an internationally unprecedented integration of Russian higher education and research with industrial production, pervasive militarization, and a legacy of institutional and disciplinary specialization. Following an exaggerated version of the German model, Russian academic elites embraced state power and a professional ethos that separated basic or "fundamental" research from university teaching. Significantly, a distinctive national turn in Russian intellectual life and the creation of new Russian-language academic serials and scholarly societies started during the war years, even if this necessary turn toward self-sufficiency later was ruthlessly maintained by Soviet state power and closed borders.[10]

EARLY SOVIET HIGHER EDUCATION: CONSOLIDATION AND UNSTABLE COMPROMISES

During the first years of Soviet power, many of these struggles and processes of transformation continued, but now within the radically changed economic and political context of Soviet state socialism characterized by the decline of the private economy, the dispersal of many members of the old elites, chaotic nationalization, and the often harsh ascendance of the Russian Communist Party and its working-class constituencies. All higher education and research were consolidated under state auspices by banning private higher education in 1918 and absorbing innovative private institutions and semi-independent women's courses into an array of new state universities and institutes.[11] Pedagogical and technical faculties (especially in various fields of engineering) were added to existing universities, and dozens of new higher education institutions were created in the 1920s, especially in national minority areas and around the periphery of the former empire. In fact, Russian higher education became the most radically inclusive in the world when admissions were thrown open by decree in 1918 and all limits on the admission of working-class students, women, and national minorities were ended, although all the inevitable problems with institutional capacity, academic performance, and retention inherent in such revolutionary expansion were quickly realized. These problems then led to the creation of workers' faculties (the *rabfak* system) in 1919, which was intended to provide remedial education and preparatory classes for students with incomplete secondary education or from disadvantaged backgrounds. These first years of Soviet higher education necessarily entailed many political and policy compromises as the regime struggled to "proletarianize" the student body, higher education faculties and administrative staffs, and research institutions. Communist youth groups agitated within institutions to expand admissions and to align curricula with the ideological goals of various factions of the Communist Party. Yet according to most contemporary accounts, middle-class or "bourgeois" students still held sway in many institutions, perhaps inevitably so in light of their elite secondary school backgrounds and perhaps especially from the advantages of the vast cultural and social capital to be gained from family and private tutoring, even in the midst of revolutionary social upheaval. From another perspective, the communist regime and its emergent elites were collaborating to create a new "state nobility" from a fusion of some members of the old elites (from the intelligentsia and managers) and new aspirants or the upwardly mobile (raised up from the working class).[12]

In fact, many "bourgeois" professors and scholars were retained and often continued to exercise real intellectual influence, even as others were singled out for repression, involuntary retirement, or foreign exile. These conflicts were especially bitter in academic fields like history, law, philosophy, and theology, precisely the curricular terrain where the Communist Party demanded exclusive dominance and ideological conformity. Bitter struggles continued over university governance, among some professors who fought to maintain their professional autonomy against communist student groups and against the regime that sought to extend its regulatory and ideological authority over all aspects of higher education. Significantly, many radical students and communist academics proudly rejected both the "bourgeois" autonomy of the university and the alleged myth of the objective or "pure" nature of science and scholarship. Of course, this rejection of corrupt "Western" knowledge was advanced in the name of a new, but more inclusive, proletarian and thus truly international conception of scholarship, even as at least some Soviet scholars and students renewed their contacts and collaboration with colleagues at European and American universities.

Thus, a historically unprecedented wave of rapid institutional expansion in Russian and Soviet higher education, an equally unprecedented "social opening" of admissions and educational opportunity, and the beginnings of what would become an utterly profound ideological transformation took place during the 1920s, but the compromises that were reached remained unstable. Furthermore, the perceived acute need to integrate state-funded higher education and research with industrial and agricultural production, which had begun during World War I, also remained unresolved, even as many technical specialists and scientists came to identify with the communist regime's modernizing agenda.[13] Acknowledging the limitations or unstable nature of the progress made in Soviet higher education in the 1920s does not mean, however, that the policy choices made in the 1930s were necessarily inevitable or, ultimately, either effective or sustainable, as almost all the Soviet literature argues.

In fact, the deeper pattern still prevailed: the Russian state reasserted its power over higher education, albeit in new and often revolutionary ways. In close coordination with its hybrid academic, scientific, and managerial elites, the role of Russian society as such remained limited or carefully controlled. More precisely, some elements of the new Soviet "public" were empowered by the self-consciously "socialist" higher education system (many young people, communists, working-class adults) as others suffered or were marginalized (the "old" class and business elites, religious believers, many established professors and researchers).

STALINIST HIGHER EDUCATION: RAPID EXPANSION AND INSTITUTIONAL FRAGMENTATION

Several dramatic phases of systemic transformation then occurred in 1928 and after, in ways that laid the foundations for Soviet higher education and research until the 1950s and that have continued to shape the system until the present. The ascendant Stalinist leadership of the Communist Party worked during the period of the "Great Break" and the self-styled Cultural Revolution (1928–1931) to forcibly combine communist higher education institutions with the state sector of regional universities, specialized institutes, and the Academy of Sciences; and it subjected all to centralized authority and harsh ideological controls[14] These interventions brought a new and intense emphasis on vocational and professional training, technical education, and applied research, with all of Soviet higher education connected tightly to the immediate needs of industrial expansion and agricultural collectivization. Communist Party cadres and working-class students were mobilized by the thousands into new technical training programs and, from there, directly into production and leading positions in the party and state bureaucracy. Almost all specialized secondary and postsecondary training and degree programs were abruptly shortened and accelerated. This also entailed the often chaotic structural transformation of the entire system, as multifaculty universities were broken up into hundreds of highly specialized institutes (in the arts and humanities, agriculture, various fields of science and industry, medicine and public health, and pedagogy or teacher training). These years also witnessed sometimes violent attempts to transform the universities and specialized institutes from within: the purging of "bourgeois" professors (in the "reelections" of 1929, 219 of 1,062 were fired) and the "Bolshevization" of the Academy of Sciences and its subsidiary research institutes. Party-state authority over higher education administration was locked into place and internal governance reoriented around a strict system of "one-man management" (*edinonachalie*).

This fragmentation and specialization, combined with the rapid expansion of the entire system of Soviet higher education in the 1930s, accounts for the historically and internationally unprecedented patterns of growth that followed. The number of higher education institutions (or VUZy, for *vysshye uchebnye zavedeniia,* a category that also included VTUZy, or technical institutions) in the Soviet Union grew from a base of seventeen universities and a total of eighty-seven VUZy in 1925 to about seven hundred institutions in 1932, a number that was later reduced to about five hundred as institutions were reconsolidated.[15] This rapid expansion and fragmentation was accompanied by radical attempts to foster "brigade" and other collectivist and "engaged" methods of instruction, with students "studying" through working in factories, collective farms, and political campaigns. During the 1930s, an array of new institutions were established, especially powerful industrial, technical, and scientific institutes across the eastern and southern regions of the Russian republic (RSFSR, or Russian Soviet Federated Socialist Republic), as well as new multifaculty universities in almost all the union republics of the USSR. This massive reorganization and sharp institutional differentiation may have been useful in the short term and when harnessed to the immediate needs of specific industries and regions. But arguably it also was extremely disruptive and bureaucratically arbitrary and inimical to long-term development.

The role of state power was also transformed in the 1930s and reshaped by two profound administrative separations. The first separation was between the system of general or school education and the realm of secondary specialized and higher education, with much of the latter moving under the authority of central economic planning agencies or "branch" (*otraslevoi*) commissariats in industry and agriculture. The second separation, which also built on earlier patterns, was between advanced research institutions (especially around the Academy of Sciences, which quickly recovered its power and relative autonomy) and the more specialized VUZy and VTUZy, with the latter focused more narrowly on career training and professional education. All this was accompanied by a powerful thrust toward centralization, with "all-Union" or central state agencies taking control of higher education and research across the USSR. Michael David-Fox has characterized this as constituting "the demise of the research university in Russia," in which public universities were forced into narrow vocational and professional roles, a uniquely "Soviet rather than Humboldtian mold," even as the higher education system expanded rapidly and became more socially inclusive.[16]

These radical changes predictably led to a sharp decline in academic quality and chronic instability in admissions and internal governance in the early 1930s, and the Communist Party and state then moved to "stabilize" the higher education system, but on its new "Soviet" foundation. This foundation included measures in 1932 to restore authority over grading to the faculty (and to minimize the influence of party activists); to strengthen more traditional entrance exams and admissions standards; to abolish all "brigade" and other "leftist" instructional methods; and to mandate that formal theses be required for all advanced degrees and faculty appointments. While political criteria (and, by many accounts, corruption) could still be used to circumvent these restored academic standards, the Soviet higher education system clearly stabilized around the economic needs of the Stalinist regime as well as the social interests of its managerial, technical, and academic elites. Subsequent measures in 1934 restored traditional academic degrees, the study of more traditional history and geography, lecture-based instructional methods, and the authority of the faculty, at least vis-à-vis students. A new vision of the Soviet university coalesced as occupying a middle ground (below the academies and their research institutes but above most of the more narrowly specialized postsecondary institutes), dedicated to training teaching staff for secondary schools and for other VUZy and VTUZy, as well as to training middle-rank researchers, lab assistants, engineers, and technical specialists. Led by the powerful Leningrad State University (LGU) and Moscow State University (MGU), as well as by some of the stronger regional universities such as Kazan, Saratov, Sverdlovsk (Ekaterinburg), Tomsk, and Irkutsk, state universities pushed away their "weak" pedagogical faculties and pulled back core faculties in mathematics and the sciences and in the arts and humanities.[17]

On the eve of World War II, a powerful new state intervention into specialized secondary and higher education was launched with the creation of state labor reserves and the imposition of up to three-year mandatory job assignments. Such a tight harnessing of an entire national system of vocational training and professional education to the immediate needs of production and military mobilization was internationally unprecedented, however chaotic or inefficient it may have been in its actual implementation. This entailed "drafting" up to a million secondary students per year directly into work, combined with draconian labor discipline and paramilitary and civil defense training for all students. Vocational and professional training programs were once again shortened and accelerated, and these new policies all combined to narrow eligibility and admissions into higher education. Fees were imposed for specialized secondary and higher education in 1940, which contributed to the stabilization of a new Stalinist social order and of a distinctively Soviet "class system" around access to higher education and entry into the professions.[18] Finally, by the 1940s, more than a third of all faculty members and researchers were members of the Communist Party, which represented the culmination of processes of professional "politicization" that had begun in the 1920s and accelerated in the 1930s. Of course, this also meant that during the terror of the late 1930s, this protected some academics while exposing others to repression, as patron-client networks in all spheres of Soviet life, especially among the Soviet elites, were consumed by brutal political violence. Even though innumerable professional careers and lives were destroyed by the terror, and Soviet education and intellectual life may have been permanently damaged, at least some leading researchers continued their scientific and technical work inside the gulag system.[19]

World War II resulted in the massive destruction of higher education facilities in the USSR's western regions, the catastrophic loss of life among young men, and the mobilization of thousands of faculty and hundreds of thousands of students. Yet the war also seemed to reinforce or consolidate the systemic transformations of the middle and late 1930s.[20] In a very real sense, as many universities and institutes were evacuated from the occupied areas, the war also accelerated ongoing processes, which included the expansion of higher education in the Urals and Siberian regions of the RSFSR and in the Central Asian union republics. The war also served to forge tighter links between training, research, and the immediate needs of industrial production and also the ever more pervasive militarization of Soviet higher education and science policy. After the war, the Stalinist academic order was triumphantly reconsolidated, with the Academy of Sciences of the USSR at its pinnacle, but with an added dimension of xenophobic (and often self-defeating) nationalism that worsened with the onset of the cold war in the late 1940s and early 1950s.[21] Tragically, in light of the massive needs for postwar reconstruction, the tentative intellectual and scientific connections with international colleagues that had been established or, in some cases, reestablished, during the war were closed off, and scientists and researchers were subjected to new waves of ideological scrutiny and repression.

In fact, one of the most destructive Stalinist interventions into Soviet intellectual life occurred during this period, the terror unleashed by Trofim D.

Lysenko (1898–1976) and his followers in the fields of plant biology and genetics. Arguments have continued whether the intensely destructive effects of "Lysenkoism" (in both science and agriculture) remained limited because of the strengths of Russian scholarship and the resiliency of the academy system, whether it demonstrated the inherent weaknesses of the entire Soviet system of science and research, or whether it was a relatively isolated or anomalous episode in an otherwise impressive era of "big science" and technical achievements.[22] The postwar years also were the time of the often brutal "Stalinization" of universities in the Baltic republics and western Ukraine. More positively, during these years the higher education system in eastern Ukraine, Belarus, and the western RSFSR was quickly reconstructed, and new, multifaculty universities were created across the USSR, so that by the early 1950s each of the fifteen union republics had at least one major university.[23] These efforts to create a new higher education infrastructure in the Soviet east and south affected developments in those regions for decades to come and helped create new "national" and professional elites in the republics, even as some of the new universities remained marginal or dependent in relation to the powerful academic complexes in the urban core of the RSFSR and eastern Ukraine. Again, while undeniably "popular" with emergent elites and the mass "publics," these new systems for higher education and research in the regions and union republics were both strengthened and constrained by the enforced emphasis on Russian-language instruction and the unionwide circulation of academic elites.

To step back and analyze this period as a whole, the Stalinist era from 1928 to 1953 in Soviet higher education and science created ambiguous legacies. On the one hand, massive state support and "public" investment in higher education and research created powerful instruments to force through party-state economic plans and political goals. This proved to be an attractive (or threatening but still compelling) model for other nations as they developed their own complexes for "big science" and state-sponsored technological and military research.[24] On the other hand, these impressive achievements were constrained by a highly bureaucratized administrative system. They remained locked into narrow and rigid vocational and professional curricula, were forced to operate within academic fields saturated by Stalinist ideology, were arbitrarily isolated from international scholarship, and were episodically torn apart by brutal political interventions and factional struggles. While political repression eased dramatically in the post-Stalinist era, the foundations of the Soviet higher education system remained in place.

In a very real sense, Soviet society itself was brought into being by this system, and the "public" demand for career education and upward mobility was served by its rapid expansion, even as the relations between state power, the university and Russian society remained dictated by the party-state and its elites. Ultimately, however, the system's intellectual constraints, organizational rigidities, and uniquely imbalanced spending priorities and power relations led to new systemic crises, especially as the Soviet system gradually opened back up to global influences in the post-Stalin era. From another perspective, as Russian society became more urbanized and differentiated, the rigid and inflexible official higher education system became increasingly seen as creating more obstacles than opportunities.

AFTER STALINISM: ATTEMPTED REFORMS AND SYSTEMIC STABILIZATION (OR STAGNATION)?

After the death of Josef Stalin in 1953, several attempts were made to loosen up this system, including a preliminary effort in 1954 to devolve some of the responsibilities of the all-Union Ministry of Higher Education down to the regions and union republics. These measures were intended to strengthen higher education and research in the regions where graduates were needed, as well as to cautiously foster the "nativization" (*korenizatsiia*, or indigenization, i.e., raising up more educated professionals from among the titular nationalities of the union republics) of higher education, at least in some fields. The nearly nine hundred narrow specializations of the Stalinist academic order were recast into fewer than three hundred in 1954, and the system was refocused on training "specialists of a broad profile."[25] Taken as a whole, it is clear that the party-state continued to dictate higher education and research policy but also that powerful academic elites and institutional interests had emerged within the "Stalinist academic order," even though the direct expression of broader social interests remained limited or carefully controlled.

The party-state leadership under Nikita Khrushchev then attempted several dramatic reforms in 1958 and after, especially to integrate (or to reintegrate) specialized secondary and higher education more closely with industrial and agricultural production, and to require a period of mandatory work before entry into higher education and research careers.[26] These attempted reforms seem to have essentially failed by the early 1960s, because of resistance from state enterprises (which resisted sharing the costs of such on-the-job training) but also, significantly, because of widespread passive resistance from parents, students, and educators. Khrushchev seems to have tried to "force down" students' and graduates' career expectations, as well as to forcibly "re-profile" many VUZy and VTUZy back toward the more narrow vocational and technical roles of the early 1930s. Yet these efforts were thwarted, perhaps by the rising class status and social expectations of the emerging Soviet middle class and by the institutional self-interest and academic aspirations of leading educators in the stronger VUZy and VTUZy. There were efforts, too, to revitalize political indoctrination, to intensify antireligious education among young people (yet again, seemingly with very limited success), and to expand correspondence (*zaochnyi*) or part-time and evening courses, which were intended to allow young people and young adults to work while studying and to foster social inclusion. The system had seemingly "stabilized" to the point that the authority of the party-state leadership was no longer absolute, but it did not allow any alternative networks of professional authority or mechanisms for social influence to emerge.

A new model of "science cities," most notably Akademgorodok (1959) was created at this time and was linked to the new Novosibirsk State University and various research institutes of the Academy of Sciences. New, multifaculty universities also were established with the goal of creating a network of "Soviet universities" in every union and autonomous republic of the USSR. A ring of such "science cities" steadily expanded around Moscow, often for military research, and similar research clusters (linked to regional branches of the Academy of Sciences) grew in the Urals, Siberia, and the Far East. Efforts were also made to draw international students to the USSR, most notably through the creation in 1960 of Patrice Lumumba University of People's Friendship in Moscow, efforts that later declined in the 1970s, seemingly because of constraints on funding.[27] The vast establishment of Soviet higher education and research, despite lingering questions about its effectiveness and concerns about its international competitiveness, flourished during this "golden age" at the same time that U.S. higher education grew rapidly and new "national" universities were created in many postcolonial nations. In fact, the real (or perhaps imagined) achievements of Soviet education helped exacerbate those cold war rivalries.

After 1964, less dramatic but significant changes were made under the leadership of Leonid Brezhnev, years characterized by efforts to roll back Khrushchev's attempted vocational reforms and to focus state resources on leading Soviet universities. Efforts were made to improve the research capacity of the leading VUZy and VTUZy, as well as to link them more closely to advanced research and training in academy institutes. Special efforts were undertaken throughout the 1970s to raise academic quality by encouraging students to enter full-time or day degree programs (which had risen to 60 percent of enrollments by the

1970s), and more money was poured into the preparation of graduate students and junior faculty, which was intended to improve the quality of university education.[28] Postsecondary curricula in all fields were modernized (especially in the sciences and technology), and ideological indoctrination was refocused through new courses on the history of the Communist Party and the "Soviet state and law." Interestingly, some nominal efforts were also made to foster "public" advisory bodies around higher education institutions, although the only enduring result of this seems to have been the emergence of councils of rectors in some regions (i.e., of powerful figures who were simultaneously party-state officials and institutional leaders and whose power endured in similar "professional" networks until today). Efforts were also made to refine governance, with more "open" competitions for academic posts, the election of deans, and the strengthening of university academic councils. A solid professional and academic core had thus emerged within the Soviet higher education system, especially within the leading state universities and the strongest specialized VUZy and VTUZy, and was linked, in at least some regions, to research institutes of the USSR's Academy of Sciences.

To step back once again and analyze this period as a whole, despite all the investments lavished on Soviet higher education and research during this "golden age" in the 1960s and early 1970s, neither the party-state leadership nor institutional leaders seemed willing or able to confront the chronic or systemic problems, especially those relating to managerial weakness and difficulties in applying research to new technologies and innovation.[29] The system of mandatory job placements was chronically inefficient, with severe mismatches between the needs of labor "markets" or enterprises and the skills of graduates, with many graduates evading their assignments. Existing policies for entrance exams and admissions remained rigid, with little flexibility across the system and little or no allowance for simultaneous applications to different institutions or for changes in career plans or professional interests. Serious concerns persisted about the motivation, skills, and academic performance of Soviet students, especially in the weaker or more narrowly profiled institutions. A rigid emphasis was maintained on quantitative indicators and inputs, with little or no attention or systemic capacity to focus on the qualitative dimensions of teaching and learning, much less on student learning or instructional "outcomes." Institutional "stability" and "trust in cadres" during the Brezhnev years seemingly meant little accountability for institutional leaders, for teaching or research faculty, or for many Soviet students, for whom promotion was often automatic. That is, for all its impressively high enrollments and real scientific achievements, this period also was marked by an "institutional automatism" and a growing recognition among experts that Soviet higher education was structurally inefficient and dysfunctional and that the "faults of the system tend(ed) to be strongly cumulative."[30] Even though the immediate vocational and career interests of many members of the Soviet public were arguably met by this system, little or no allowance was made for any flexibility or adaptability in the provision of higher education. Even more fatally, as the state system faltered, legal limits continued to be enforced on private tutoring, any manifestation of private or religious higher education, and international travel for education or research.

The last years of Soviet higher education during the leadership of Mikhail Gorbachev and the reforms of *perestroika* between 1985 and 1991 represented the culmination of all these trends, in that the chronic problems finally built to the breaking point and began to tip into severe systemic crisis, but also because Soviet higher education's intellectual and professional potential also finally began to be realized, if somewhat chaotically.[31] Limitations on international travel and study abroad were eased; bilateral scholarly exchanges began to proliferate; and the lifting of censorship allowed both popular and scholarly publications to flourish in the spirit of *glasnost'*. Measures promulgated in 1987 and 1988 sought to improve "coordination" within the system (the connections between higher education, research, and production), but now through new, more market-based mechanisms such as contract research. Other attempted reforms supported more practical career education and adult retraining tied to economic reforms in pursuit of gradual liberalization, and also greater institutional autonomy and responsibility. As the central authorities faltered, higher education and other leaders in the union republics (most notably in the Baltic region and the southern Caucasus) began to agitate for greater "national" autonomy. More active and participatory instructional methods were developed, drawing in part on the more progressive Soviet educational and psychological traditions of the 1920s, and curricula were modernized once again, especially in the humanities and social sciences. After a sixty-year hiatus, institutional governance in Soviet higher education expanded, too, to include student representatives and junior faculty.

Unfortunately, faced with demands for cost-accounting and efficiency, inefficient and unprofitable industrial and agricultural enterprises began to resist paying (much less expanding) their subsidies for higher education, vocational or professional training, and research. Mechanisms to link higher and professional education to economic planning and to control the "distribution" (*raspredelenie*) of graduates began to break down.[32] The increasingly frantic efforts to raise academic quality ran into the structural constraints of a system that had long separated research (in academy and military institutes) from teaching (in universities and specialized training institutes). Furthermore, the system only haphazardly punished student academic misconduct or poor performance and had only a few autonomous professional associations or vibrant scholarly networks to "scale up" new curricular and instructional innovations. The diverse Russian and Soviet "publics" that emerged amid the decentralization and democratization of *perestroika* were making new and increasingly vocal demands on the higher education system, but they seemed to lack any coherent associational or professional levers with which to press those demands or to directly influence either governance or policymaking.

Overall, almost all the attempted higher education reforms of the late 1980s were stymied by the deepening financial and political crises of the Soviet system as the budgetary and administrative capacity of the central government declined and the "all-Union" planned economy slowed down and then disintegrated. Even more tragically, besides all these long-simmering systemic problems, many members of the Soviet public saw their once robust higher education system inexplicably pulled out from under them, taking with it their class status, professional identities, and social capital.[33]

THE TRANSFORMATION OF RUSSIAN HIGHER EDUCATION SINCE 1991

The collapse of the Soviet Union in late 1991 and the emergence of fifteen independent post-Soviet nations represent a decisive break with these Soviet and state socialist legacies, and by the late 1990s Russia joined, or more accurately rejoined, the mainstream of global higher education development. In fact, the previously closed, or autarkic, system was exposed to the full force of globalization, new information technologies (however partially assimilated), and global policy trends. Yet at the same time, powerful institutional and professional legacies of the Soviet era persisted, perhaps especially the division between the academy institutes and their research mission (in the natural and physical sciences, agriculture, medicine, and pedagogy, even if they were much reduced in funding and policy influence) and the universities' teaching and training missions, with many specialized postsecondary institutes rapidly recasting themselves as "universities" in a bid for greater status and market share. This complicated pattern of simultaneously embracing and resisting global influences and policy trends at least complicates some of the central tenets of world culture theory and "neo-institutionalism." It suggests that even if some aspects of post-Soviet reform accord with global policy trends, the ways in which state power and professional relations work beneath the surface of this policy rhetoric remain historically conditioned and regionally particular.[34]

The Russian universities themselves initially proved to be very conservative in their internal governance and educational practices, and higher education institutions turned out to be much more "stable" (or stagnant) than other sectors of society (such as industry, banking, civil society, political parties, and the media). All the subsequent changes notwithstanding, the structural core of Russian higher education remained largely a product of the Soviet era. Even many of the newly emerging private universities and career education programs tended to copy the old model, though recast in more superficially "Western" terms. Even more important to our purposes here, another powerful enduring legacy of the Soviet era is the persistent weakness of public influences or of civil society in the reshaping of the system, and the enduring dominance of state interests as allied with key academic and professional elites in the making and remaking of university governance, curricular policies, and instructional practices. That is not to say that these changes were not contested, because they were, often bitterly so. Rather, the deeper patterns of power relations in higher education that we just described endured even amid the often drastic changes in Russia's liberalizing (or at least privatizing) economy and its chaotically democratizing (and then recentralizing) political order. In fact, there were clearly innovative and reform-minded institutional leaders and education managers, but their incentives to produce truly radical changes were limited at best as the sector simultaneously experienced plunging state funding and exploding social demand for higher education and career retraining. At the same time that the ability of the Russian state and federal policymakers to influence the system declined, at least temporarily, the universities themselves experienced an unexpected boom. That is, even as profound changes began to transform the social sciences and humanities as a whole, the need for massive retraining expanded and quality standards were so ambiguous that "universities" (both established and duly renamed) were able to rapidly expand enrollments and degree programs by adding newly "fashionable" disciplines such as economics and business, management, political science, law, and information technologies.[35] Many institutions also were able to make full use of Soviet-era investments in higher educational infrastructure, and leaders could often afford to neglect their campuses, student dormitories, libraries, lab equipment, and other assets they inherited from the Soviet past.

Thus, in the early 1990s (as arguably had also happened earlier between 1915 and 1918), the balance of power temporarily shifted from the state to its academic and managerial elites, but the essential institutional structures and professional networks that bound them together remained remarkably persistent.[36] Russian universities have long confronted two challenges in dealing with the "outside world": protecting their autonomy from the state without losing state investment and regulatory protection (their monopolistic advantages), and being socially relevant (and now competitive in the emerging higher education marketplace) without exposing themselves to overt political risks or unmanageable social demands. As in earlier periods, the primary response to social pressures and public demands was to throw open enrollments (if now accompanied by rising tuition and fees), but not to fundamentally democratize governance or policymaking (e.g., through the possible introduction of public boards of trustees or even of influential alumni associations). The Russian higher education sector undeniably gained unprecedented freedom, and there were sweeping changes in curricula and instructional methods, supposedly in response to the demands of new "publics" and market pressures. New private higher education institutions opened up to meet rising demand (especially in fields such as business, law, and economics, as well as in career and semiprofessional education), and this helped meet the surging public demand. But these new institutions also led to the rise of many low-quality "training" programs, commercial providers, and poorly regulated "affiliates" (*filialy*) of state universities.[37] Of course, this new freedom to respond to public demands also meant the equally unprecedented freedom to fail, and higher education institutions in Russia and throughout the region suffered grievously amid a policy environment in the 1990s that, in the name of often abstract approaches to privatization and decentralization, saw central authorities, regional administrations, and economic enterprises simply abdicate much of their responsibility to provide adequate funding, to maintain the infrastructure, and especially to offer social equity in and access to higher education.[38] In fact, despite all the new multilateral and bilateral assistance programs that sought to influence these processes, by the end of the 1990s there was a growing sense of "policy incoherence" and a growing realization that the Russian state had abdicated its fundamental responsibility for adequate investment and policy coordination in higher education.[39] All this was accompanied by rising concern about the "brain drain" and the inadvertent effects of international programs and market forces in draining academic talent out of the profession and away from the region.[40]

The evolving relations between Russian higher education institutions and the state created a struggle for greater autonomy that had several dimensions.

These included the quest to fix institutional autonomy in law and policy (through the election of rectors and deans, the right to determine university charters, attempts to secure financial flexibility, and the right to control their own property and possible endowments). This also encompassed the quest for academic and intellectual autonomy (the right of at least some faculty and students to dissent, and the relative scope of academic freedom) and the quest for professional autonomy (the right of faculty to set curricula and academic standards, to assert themselves in their long-standing rivalry with the Academy of Sciences for leadership in research and control of state research funding, and attempts to introduce locally relevant curricula and courses). These demands for autonomy seemed, however, seldom to lead to genuine or enduring innovation in university management or teaching methods. In most cases, these demands tended to lead more to a wide spectrum of commercial and semicommercial activities, from the introduction of tuition and fees, to leasing office space and university equipment, to contract research and corporate training programs. In their own particular ways, Russian universities struggled to redefine the balance between higher education as a public good (whether Soviet style or in the context of post-Soviet societies) and the new opportunities of "academic capitalism."[41]

But even during the turbulent 1990s, almost all Russian state universities continued to look to the state for core funding, political support, and legitimacy. They fought over shrinking budgets in order to gain recognition, policy guidance, and political protection, and many university elites remained closely connected to regional administrators and federal leaders. After the rise of Vladimir Putin in 1999/2000, a new policy trend emerged clearly in 2001 and after, which was characterized by a reassertion of the authority of the federal state and the Ministry of Education through its control of academic "standards," the approval of degree programs, and a more robust system of accreditation.[42] This new academic order also sought to support more effective institutional autonomy and entrepreneurial reforms, albeit balanced by a renewed emphasis on policy coordination within the federal "educational space" and the integrity of the national system of higher and professional education. Incentives for compliance included renewed financial support for Russian public universities, even as the state worked to close down low-quality public and many private providers (especially shady for-profit institutions and "degree mills") and to consolidate redundant or narrowly profiled institutions into massive new "federal" universities (initially in Rostov and Krasnoyarsk, and now in St. Petersburg, Moscow, and possibly other regions such as the Urals and the Far East).

The Russian state has sought to reassert its authority to regulate higher education and to harness state-funded research more closely to military needs and economic competitiveness, and it has pursued these goals through a renewed alliance with its academic, technical, and now its new business elites. A new element in this system is the role of the Russian public (and especially of an emerging or reemerging middle class) but, yet again, seemingly more as passive consumers of higher education services than as active participants in policymaking or institutional governance. In the absence of any meaningful systems of university "ratings" or quality assurance, or even of objective and reliable media evaluations of degree programs and policy trends, the Russian public remains woefully uninformed about precisely what they are buying in the new higher education marketplace. Other key reforms in recent years have included the creation of a new unified state exam system, in order to better regulate and open up admissions and limit corruption; efforts (yet again) to raise academic quality and international competitiveness through the integration of research and education; and efforts to foster (yet again) more systematic cooperation between academy research institutes and leading Russian universities.

These new policy frameworks were only part of the changing dynamic, combined with a growing recognition by at least some university leaders that they would have to embrace significant internal reforms in university management, especially involving strategic planning, fund-raising, and external partnerships, in order to adjust to the demands of the new environment.[43] One could also argue that this shift away from a more market-driven U.S. model (that was at least rhetorically dominant in the early and mid-1990s) toward a more structured or state-directed European model aligns more closely with Russian academic traditions and also reflects deeper trends in the development of European higher education, as projected for Russia by TEMPUS and other cooperative programs and as then consolidated and institutionalized by Russia's entry into the Bologna Process in 2003.[44] Of course, entry into Bologna signals a number of clear transnational goals and policies (such as a dual-degree system, credit transfer systems, transparency, and now the involvement of student unions in governance), but it remains unclear whether Russian universities will fully comply with all of this agenda or whether the Russian state can or will compel compliance.

At least some leading Russian federal policymakers seem to have agreed on an agenda for reform with at least some university leaders: finding new approaches to research management, fostering innovation in fund-raising and creating new government-university-business partnerships, building collaborative research projects and academic networks with international partners, and building capacity for professional development and institutional renewal. Their ability to overcome vested interests and implement these ambitious reforms remains an open question. Higher education is still quite detached from the labor market; teaching methods are often archaic; and research and teaching are not consistently integrated.[45] Furthermore, governance remains highly centralized and opaque, and corruption remains pervasive. Many factors might prevent the Russian state from fulfilling this new role, including opposition to consolidation from regional leaders and vested interests in archaic institutions, an acute lack of trained higher education managers and policy analysts, and opposition from powerful elected rectors and their client networks among university faculty. More positively, pressure for reform will continue to come from powerful business groups and employers, from global policy actors and the pressure of international ranking systems (in which Russian universities have done very poorly), and, one hopes, from the Russian public and especially the students themselves, not just as consumers, but as more engaged and active citizens. It is also possible, however, that state regulation and "public" investment are now flowing back into Russian higher education before the system was truly reformed, or at least before a new role for the diverse Russian publics and for the articulation of social demands had been consolidated or institutionalized.

In conclusion, we would argue that the weak link in the relations between the state, the university, and society in Russia remains society itself, whether that is understood to include parents and students, less powerful local and regional governments, small businesses, or, perhaps especially, Russian civil society and nonprofit organizations. As relations between the federal state and the leading universities have "restabilized," university governance and policy-making have clearly not adapted or expanded to include student and public voices. While some innovative programs (such as a new initiative between the New Eurasia Foundation and the Mott Foundation) are being encouraged to expand the role of universities in community development, and some efforts are being made to link universities more closely to school education, much more could be done to deepen and revitalize the public and civic mission of Russian research universities. In fact, perhaps the single most important issue for a new social science research agenda in Russia would be to encourage the rigorous analysis of Russian higher education itself. There remains an acute need to continue to build the professional capacity and scholarly networks to analyze precisely these evolving relationships and policy issues in and around newly revitalized Russian public universities, and to advocate from both within and without for an expanded public mission, for greater civic engagement, for the transformation of higher education governance, and for sustained attention to the issues of social equity and ethnic inclusion in Russia and in all of Eurasia.

NOTES

1. Alfred B. Evans, Laura A. Henry, and Lisa McIntosh Sundstrom, eds., *Russian Civil Society: A Critical Assessment* (Armonk, N.Y.: M. E. Sharpe, 2005).

2. Guy Neave, ed., *The Universities' Responsibilities to Society: International Perspectives* (Oxford: Elsevier Science for UNESCO and International Association of Universities, 2000); also Thomas Ehrlich, ed., *Civic Responsibility and Higher Education* (Phoenix: Oryx, 2000).

3. On innovative approaches to these issues in the United States., see Adrianna J. Kezar, Tony C. Chambers, and John C. Burkhardt, *Higher Education for the Public Good: Emerging Voices from a National Movement* (San Francisco: Jossey-Bass, 2005); and in Europe, see Sjur Bergan, ed., *The University as Res Publica: Higher Education Governance, Student Participation, and the University as a Site of Citizenship* (Strasbourg: Council of Europe, 2004).

4. Sheila Slaughter and Gary Rhoades, *Academic Capitalism and the New Economy: Markets, State and Higher Education* (Baltimore: Johns Hopkins University Press, 2004); also Burton R. Clark, *Creating Entrepreneurial Universities: Organizational Pathways of Transformation* (Oxford: Pergamon, 2001).

5. Samuel D. Kassow, *Students, Professors and the State in Tsarist Russia* (Berkeley: University of California Press, 1989); and A. I. Avrus, *Istoriia rossiiskikh universitetov: Ocherki* (Moscow: Moscow Public Science Foundation, 2001).

6. E. S. Liakhovich and A. S. Pevushkin, *Universitety Rossii v istorii i kul'ture dorevoliutsionnoi Rossii* (Tomsk: Tomsk State University, 1998).

7. Paul J. Novgorotsev, "Universities and Higher Technical Schools," in his *Russian Schools and Universities in the World War* (New Haven, Conn.: Yale University Press and the Carnegie Endowment for International Peace, 1929); and Alexei B. Kojevnikov, *Stalin's Great Science: The Times and Adventures of Soviet Physicists* (London: Imperial College Press, 2004).

Support for research on the historical sections of this chapter was provided to Mark Johnson through a major research grant from the Spencer Foundation, with thanks to Andrea Lucard.

8. Vladimir I. Vernadskii, *Ocherki I rechi* (Petrograd: NTO VSNKh RSFSR, 1922); and Kendall Bailes, *Science and Russian Culture in an Age of Revolutions: V. I. Vernadsky and His Scientific School, 1863–1945* (Bloomington: Indiana University Press, 1990).

9. Konrad Jarausch, ed., *The Transformation of Higher Learning, 1860–1930: Expansion, Diversification, Social Opening and Professionalization in England, Germany, Russia and the United States.* (Chicago: University of Chicago Press, 1983); also Hans de Wit, *Internationalization of Higher Education in the United States of America and Europe: A Historical, Comparative, and Conceptual Analysis* (Westport, Conn.: Greenwood Press, 2002).

10. Daniel A. Aleksandrov, "Pochemu sovetskie uchenye perestali pechatat'sia za rubezhom: stanovlenie samodostatochnosti i izolirvannosti otechestvennoi nauki, 1914–1940," *Voprosy Istorii Estestvoznaniia i Tekhniki* no. 3 (1996): 3–24.

11. Shikhulla Kh. Chanbarisov, *Formirovanie Sovetskoi universitetskoi sistemy* (Moscow: Vysshaia shkola, 1998); and Michael David-Fox, *Revolution of the Mind: Higher Learning Among the Bolsheviks, 1918–1929* (Ithaca, N.Y.: Cornell University Press, 1998).

12. Sheila L. Fitzpatrick, *Education and Social Mobility in the Soviet Union, 1921–1934* (Cambridge: Cambridge University Press, 1979); also Pierre Bourdieu, *The State Nobility: Elite Schools in the Field of Power*, trans. Lauretta C. Clough (Stanford, Calif.: Stanford University Press, 1996).

13. Iu. V. Kliuchkova, et al., *Smena vekh: sbornik statei* (Prague: Nasha rech', 1922); and Kendall Bailes, *Technology and Society Under Lenin and Stalin: Origins of the Soviet Technical Intelligentsia, 1917–1941* (Princeton, N.J.: Princeton University Press, 1978).

14. Loren R. Graham, *The Soviet Academy of Sciences and the Communist Party, 1927–1932* (Princeton, N.J.: Princeton University Press, 1967); also Michael David-Fox and Gyorgi Peteri, eds., *Academia in Upheaval: Origins, Transfers, and Transformation of the Communist Academic Regime in Russia and East Central Europe* (Westport, Conn.: Praeger, 2000).

15. *Kul'turnoe stroitel'stvo SSSR: statisticheskii sbornik* (Moscow: Gosplanizdat, 1940).

16. David-Fox, *Revolution of the Mind*, 265.

17. Evgenii V. Chutkerashvili, *Razvitie vysshego obrazovaniia v SSSR* (Moscow: Vysshaia shkola, 1961).

18. Nicholas Timasheff, *The Great Retreat: The Growth and Decline of Communism in Russia* (New York: Dutton, 1946); also David L. Hoffman, *Stalinist Values: The Cultural Norms of Soviet Modernity, 1917–1941* (Ithaca, N.Y.: Cornell University Press, 2003).

19. I. G. Aref'eva, ed., *Tragicheskie sud'by: Repressirovanie uchenye Akademii Nauk SSSR* (Moscow: Nauka, 1995); L. L. Kerber and V. Hardesty, *Stalin's Aviation Gulag: A*

Memoir of Andrei Tupolev and the Purge Era (Washington, D.C.: Smithsonian Institution Press, 1996).

20. Mikhail R. Kruglianskii, *Vysshaia shkola SSSR v gody Velikoi Otchestvennoi voiny* (Moscow: Vysshaia shkola, 1970); also Avrus, *Istoriia rossiiskikh universitetov*, chap. 7.

21. For a defense of the academy system and of the achievements of the system as a whole, see Sergei I. Vavilov, *Sovetskaia nauka na novom etape* (Moscow: Academy of Sciences of the U.S.S.R., 1946); for a more critical and yet still balanced perspective on this period, see Nikolai Krementsov, *Stalinist Science* (Princeton, N.J.: Princeton University Press, 1997).

22. Alexander Vucinich, *Empire of Knowledge: The Academy of Sciences of the USSR (1917–1970)* (Berkeley: University of California Press, 1970); as opposed to the more sweepingly critical perspective of Valery Soyfer, Leo Gruliow, and Rebecca Gruliow, *Lysenko and the Tragedy of Soviet Science* (New Brunswick, N.J.: Rutgers University Press, 1994).

23. Ivan G. Petrovskii, *Higher Education in the U.S.S.R.* (Moscow: Soviet News, 1953); also Jaan Pennar, Ivan I. Bakalo, and George Z. F. Bereday, *Modernization and Diversity in Soviet Education: With Special Reference to Nationality Groups* (New York: Praeger, 1971).

24. For the paradigmatic success, see Jeff A. Hughes, *The Manhattan Project: Big Science and the Atom Bomb* (New York: Columbia University Press, 2002); for alternative examples of policies constrained by national autarky and ideological dogmas, see Margit Szollosi-Janze, ed., *Science in the Third Reich* (Oxford: Berg, 2001); and the comparative analysis of Nazi, Soviet, and other scientific regimes in an international context by Paul R. Josephson, *Totalitarian Science and Technology*, 2nd ed. (Amherst, N.Y.: Humanity Books, 2005).

25. K. T. Galkin, *Vyshee obrazovanie i podgotovka nauchnykh kadrov v SSSR* (Moscow: Nauka, 1958).

26. Vyacheslav P. Yelyutin, *Higher Education in the USSR* (New York: International Arts and Sciences Press, 1959); and Seymour Rosen, *Higher Education in the U.S.S.R.: Curriculums, Schools, and Statistics* (Washington, D.C.: U.S. Department of Commerce, 1963).

27. Kurt Muller, *Foreign Aid Programs of the Soviet Bloc and Communist China: An Analysis*, trans. by Richard H. Weber and Michael Roloff (New York: Walker, 1967).

28. G. I. Ushakov and A. S. Shuruev, *Planirovanie i finansirovanie podgotovki spetsialistov* (Moscow: Vysshaia shkola, 1980); for a precise and penetrating analysis of these changes, see George Avis, "Soviet Union," in *International Higher Education: An Encyclopedia*, ed. Philip G. Altbach (New York: Garland, 1991), vol. 2, 781–98.

29. Thane Gustafson, "Why Doesn't Soviet Science Do Better Than It Does?" In *The Social Context of Soviet Science*, ed. Linda L. Lubrano and Susan G. Solomon (Boulder, Colo.: Westview Press, 1980), 31–67.

30. The quotation is from Mervyn Matthews, *Education in the Soviet Union: Policies and Institutions Since Stalin* (London: Allen & Unwin, 1982), 172; and the analysis of pervasive "institutional automatism" is from M. Buttgereit, "Higher Education and Its Relations to Employment in the USSR and in the Federal Republic of Germany—A Comparison," in *Higher Education and Employment in the USSR and in the Federal Republic of Germany*, ed. R. Avakov et al. (Paris: International Institute for Educational Planning, 1984), 231–326.

31. This issue remains bitterly contested by analysts. For a persuasively pessimistic argument, see Matthews, *Education in the Soviet Union*, who argued in 1982: "The Soviet educational system has been nurtured and molded to support the regime in every way possible. The political docility of the overwhelming majority of its participants is hardly open to question" (p. 204). For an influential and more optimistic argument, that Soviet higher education had successfully led to the liberalization of Soviet society, see Moshe Lewin, *The Gorbachev Phenomenon: A Historical Interpretation* (Berkeley: University of California Press, 1988).

32. Stephen L. Solnick, *Stealing the State: Control and Collapse in Soviet Institutions* (Cambridge, Mass.: Harvard University Press, 1998).

33. Alexei Yurchak, *Everything Was Forever Until It Was No More: The Last Soviet Generation* (Princeton, N.J.: Princeton University Press, 2006).

34. S. Gili Drori, John W. Meyer, Francisco O. Ramirez, and Evan Schofer, *Science in the Modern World Polity: Institutionalization and Globalization* (Stanford, Calif.: Stanford University Press, 2003); David John Frank and Jay Gabler, *Reconstructing the University: Worldwide Shifts in Academia in the 20th Century* (Stanford, Calif.: Stanford University Press, 2006).

35. Otto Latsis, *Transformatsiia gumanitarnogo obrazovaniia v Rossii* (Moscow: Interpraks, 1995); see also Iurii N. Afanas'ev, *Universitas Humana: Gumanitarnyi universitet tret'ego tysiacheletiia* (Moscow: Russian State Humanities University, 2000); Blair Ruble, Nancy Popson, and Susan Bronson, *The Humanities and Social Sciences in the Former Soviet Union: An Assessment of Need* (Washington, D.C.: Kennan Institute, 1999); and Voldemar Tomusk, *The Open World and Closed Societies: Essays on Higher Education Policies "In Transition"* (New York: Palgrave Macmillan, 2004).

36. Olga B. Bain, *University Autonomy in the Russian Federation Since Perestroika* (New York: Routledge Falmer, 2003). On the larger patterns of post-Soviet elite "reformation," see also Olga V. Kryshtanovskaia, *Anatomiia rossiiskoi elity* (Moscow: Zakharov, 2005).

37. On the broader global dimensions of these processes, including the rise of transnational and corporate providers, see Philip G. Altbach and Daniel C. Levy, eds., *Private Higher Education: A Global Revolution* (Rotterdam: Sense Publishers, 2005).

38. Sergei V. Shishkin et al., *Dostupnost' vysshego obrazovaniia v Rossii* (Moscow: Independent Institute for Social Policy, 2004); also Alina S. Zaborovskaia, Tatiana L. Kliachko, and Sergei V. Shishkin, *Vysshee obrazovanie v Rossii: Pravila i real'nost'* (Moscow: Independent Institute of Social Policy, 2004); and on larger trends in social inequality and stratification, Theodore P. Gerber, "Russia: Stratification in Postsecondary Education Since the Second World War," in *Stratification in Higher Education: A Comparative Study*, ed. Yossi Shavit, Richard Arum, and Adam Gamoran (Stanford, Calif.: Stanford University Press, 2007), 294–320.

39. Ian Whitman et al., *Tertiary Education and Research in the Russian Federation* (Paris: OECD, 1999)

40. A. Iurevich and I. Tsapenko, *Nuzhny li Rossii uchenye?* (Moscow: Editorial URSS, 2001).

41. See also Gilles Breton and Michel Lambert, eds., *Universities and Globalization: Private Linkages, Public Trust* (Paris: UNESCO Publishing and Economica, 2003); also Slaughter and Rhoades, *Academic Capitalism*; and Roger L. Geiger, *Knowledge and Money: Research Universities and the Paradox of the Marketplace* (Stanford, Calif.: Stanford University Press, 2004).

42. Ministry of Education of the Russian Federation, *O kontseptsii modernizatsii rossiiskogo obrazovaniia na period do 2010 goda* (Moscow: Ministry of Education, 2001); also Carole Sigman, "The Impact of 'New Public Management' on Russian Higher Education," *Russie.Nei.Visions*, no. 30 (French Institute of International Relations, April 2008).

43. Michael Shattock, ed., *Entpreneurialism and the Transformation of Russian Universities* (Paris: International Institute for Educational Planning / UNESCO, 2004); also V. M. Filippov et al., *Upravlenie v vysshei shkole: opyt', tendentsii, perspektivy* (Moscow: Logos, 2006).

44. V. D. Shadrikov et al., *Formirovanie obshcheevropeiskogo prostranstva vysshego obrazovaniia* (Moscow: Ministry of Education and Science of the Russian Federation and the Higher School of Economics, 2004); also Andrei Iu. Melville, ed., *"Myagkii put'" vkhozhdeniia Rossiiskikh vuzov v Bolonskii Protsess* (Moscow: OLMA Press for the National Training Foundation and Information-Scholarship-Education Center, 2005); for a more critical perspective on the Bologna Process, see also Voldemar Tomusk, ed., *Creating the European Area of Higher Education: Voices from the Periphery* (Dordrecht: Springer, 2006).

45. Erik Livin and Leonid Polishchuk, *Problema kachestva vysshego obrazovaniia: rol' gosudarstva, konkurentsii i rynka truda* (Moscow: National Training Foundation, 2006); also Tatiana Kastueva-Jean, "The 'Greatness and Misery' of Russian Higher Education," *Russie.Nei.Visions*, no. 14 (French Institute of International Relations, September 2006); and Tatiana Kastueva-Jean, "Higher Education, the Key to Russia's Competitiveness," *Russia.Nei.Visions*, no. 28 (French Institute of International Relations, April 2008).

Public Research Universities in
Latin America and Their Relation
to Economic Development

FIVE

JUAN CARLOS MORENO-BRID
AND PABLO RUIZ-NÁPOLES

In 1990, the average incidence of poverty and extreme poverty[1] in Latin America was 48.3 percent and 22.5 percent, respectively. The slow economic expansion experienced since then plus the reorientation of public spending on social needs managed to only partially alleviate this situation but was far from sufficient. Indeed, in 2005, 38.5 percent of Latin America's total population of 556 million was still poor.[2] This percentage is similar to the one recorded in 1980, thus implying that the absolute number of poor people in this region is much higher today than it was twenty-five years ago. This impoverishment has been accompanied by the deterioration of labor market conditions, with informality and open unemployment reaching historical peaks.

Given this pressing social context, it is evident that Latin America faces the urgent challenge of achieving high and sustained rates of economic expansion and employment to alleviate poverty. To meet this challenge, it will have

A preliminary version of this chapter was published as Working Paper no. 07/08–1 of the David Rockefeller Center for Latin American Studies, Harvard University.

to modernize its productive structure and its machinery and capital equipment to be able to compete in world markets on the basis of not low wages but increased value added and technological sophistication. Such transformation requires an increasingly qualified labor force combined with a dynamic entrepreneurial sector that has a strong commitment to innovate. Such combination is indispensable to reduce the gap between the region's pace of technological and scientific progress, and ultimately its economic development and that of industrialized nations.

The challenge is daunting given Latin America's rather disappointing economic performance since the early 1980s and the constraints imposed on the region's policy options by global markets and international capital flows. The situation has been further complicated in Latin America by the Washington Consensus–based reforms that weakened the state's capacity to intervene in the economy and reduced the public investment that was far from fully compensated by the private sector.

As we argue here, strengthening Latin America's public universities and, in general, its institutions of higher learning and research is necessary to increase its international competitiveness and begin long-term economic expansion. Indeed, in the region, public universities are the principal institutions that keep pace with advances in science and technology. Without these advances, the region is unlikely to succeed in its quest for economic development. What is the economic impact of the public universities? How do public research universities support technological innovation in Latin America? How can they be made more efficient and effective to promote economic development? What are their main obstacles in this regard?

Before addressing some of these issues, two important caveats are necessary. The first is that the economic impact of universities in developing countries is not often assessed. For example, although since the 1990s there has been a rapidly growing literature on this issue for developed economies,[3] just a few months ago the first ever study to quantify the economic effect of Cambridge University was completed. According to its results, its impact on the British economy amounted to a total of £58 billion over a ten-year period.[4] A similar study of Latin American universities has yet to be carried out, partly because of the lack of some of the data necessary to apply the methodologies designed for developed nations.

We should stress that by addressing their economic effect, our research focuses on only one aspect of the diverse roles and responsibilities of public universities. Moreover, in our view, their economic impact is just one aspect of their social influence in developing countries and not necessarily the most relevant one. In fact, we tend to agree with the view that in Latin America, public universities are the *conscience* of the society in which they emerge.[5] Indeed, these institutions have been fundamental influences in building citizenship and strengthening democratic values in this region. To illustrate, recall that in Latin America's not too distant undemocratic past, troops or paramilitary groups commonly entered public universities to violently repress professors' or students' organizations and imprison or murder their leaders.

In addition, in our region, public universities still have a key role in teaching and research in philosophy and many of the arts and sciences, some of which typically tend to be inadequately funded or covered by private institutions. Because their fees usually are much lower, public universities traditionally have been the entry to higher education for the middle classes and, to a certain extent, the lower classes not able to afford private graduate training. These functions strengthen social cohesion, the creation of human capital, and the diffusion of knowledge.

The contribution of public universities to Latin America's development covers a series of social, cultural, and political functions that cannot be assessed exclusively in regard to their economic impact. In particular, we believe that public universities in Latin America play a key role in preserving and expanding its culture and historical heritage, a role important to globalization.

The second caveat is that talking about the region as a whole always risks ignoring major differences and key peculiarities or traits of individual countries regarding their economic and social performance and the role of universities. Certainly, the diversity of some groups of Latin American countries in their economic size, degree of industrialization, basic indicators of health, and primary and advanced education, as well as their population's human capital formation and their overall technological capacities, points to the need for in-depth case studies of the cross-national variations in the universities' roles and potential impacts on economic development. But while acknowledging these differences, we believe that the issues identified in this chapter are important to most, and perhaps all, countries in Latin America.

An immediate task to extend our work presented here is conducting in-depth studies of national cases in order to create a typology of countries and public universities. Such a typology would identify the elements and institutional aspects that help ensure the universities' favorable and significant impact on economic development. Perhaps even more important are the factors impeding the creation of such positive links.

This chapter will not offer a list of merit or an honor roll of universities in Latin America. For this, readers should consult the annual rankings calculated by various institutions, such as the *Academic Ranking of World Universities* published by the Institute of Higher Education of Shanghai Jiao Tong University and the *Higher Education Supplement* published by the *Times* of London.

HUMAN CAPITAL FORMATION, ECONOMIC GROWTH, AND ECONOMIC THEORY

A main tenet of our analysis is that Latin America's economic growth[6] depends on investment and the application of technological and scientific progress to modernize the region's production processes. To achieve this, it must devote more resources to expanding and improving three elements of the region's innovation systems: (1) scientific infrastructure, (2) supply of highly qualified research personnel, and (3) working links between research centers and productive firms. Those governments interested in enhancing the growth potential of their economies must try to improve the local physical and human capital needed for research and development (i.e., the supply side). At the same time, they must create the conditions to ensure that the national science and technology centers have relevant, effective, and efficient links with the domestic business sector. That is, they must create a demand for science and technological innovation from the local business sector. Failing to pay attention to this leads to the paradoxical situation in which many countries in Latin America and other developing economies are using precious public resources to send some of their brightest young people to obtain graduate training abroad in high-tech areas, only to have many of them not return because there is no demand for their skills!

In Latin America, public universities are the institutions where most of the local scientific and technological research and development is carried out and where most students in these fields receive their formal training. Some of these institutions, though certainly not the majority, are internationally renowned. In fully industrialized countries, research and development are conducted mainly by private universities and the technological departments of private and public firms. Perhaps the major difference between developed and developing nations is the weak links between the universities and the local business sector. Indeed, in the region, the universities' research agenda has very limited relevance to private businesses' needs and pressures to reduce costs or innovate its technology. Correcting this deficiency would require government intervention to create a collaborative working agenda between academic institutions and local private or public firms, beyond the state's financing of science and technology (including the professional training).

From kindergarten to graduate and postgraduate school, widespread access to quality education has a high social value, reflected in a better-educated population, a richer material well-being, and stronger social cohesion. In fact, the average educational achievement is typically considered a key indicator of a country's human development. In countries on the road to development, education is critical to improving skills and productive capacities as well as promoting social integration and upward mobility. Technological progress is directly linked to scientific research and thus to the training of scientists and engineers. In general, it is universities and technological institutes that provide such training. Public universities and academic centers are the source of most of the research done in developing countries. In Latin America, most research and development projects are financed or carried out by state institutions. More than 75 percent of all graduate students are enrolled in public universities, and on average, approximately 80 percent of all researchers are employed in public entities.[7]

Besides the impact of education on each nation's economic development through the advances in science and technology, higher levels of education are associated with higher incomes. Education also affects economic equality. In the medium term, the less educated a country's population is, on average, the lower its per capita income will be, and perhaps the more concentrated its income distribution will be.

Paradoxically, the undeniable and conspicuous relationship between, on the one hand, education—particularly tertiary and graduate—and, on the other hand, technological change and economic growth, had not been well captured until a few decades ago, by the standard theoretical models used by the mainstream economics profession. In fact, not long ago, such literature saw technological change merely as the residual from growth accounting exercises, determined in an exogenous and independent way of investment.[8] A notable exception was Nicholas Kaldor's theoretical work on economic growth,[9] which pointed out that technology changes are incorporated in new investments. According to him, research universities have a direct economic effect associated with the diffusion of scientific and technological changes, in addition to their impact on human capital formation. Not until the advent of the so-called new growth theory was this shortcoming of mainstream economics corrected, and technological change was recognized as an endogenously determined influence on structural change and economic growth at the micro- and the macroeconomic level.

Today, the literature on growth economics recognizes the relevance of human capital formation and technological advancement to development. Among the main contributions from the neoclassical school are those by Paul Romer[10] and Robert Lucas;[11] with a neo-Schumpeterian view, Philippe Aghion and Peter Howitt;[12] from the structuralist/evolutionist school, Giovanni Dosi[13] and Stan Metcalfe.[14] Whether through their effects on the surge of new products or processes, on the increased competitiveness of firms, or on the expansion of their markets, for instance, these scholars recognize research and education as essential to a dynamic and internationally competitive economy.[15]

But independently of when mainstream economic theory formally incorporated knowledge embodied in the notion of human capital and technology as a main determinant of economic growth, it was recognized as an important, new factor of production based on innovation.[16] This chain of influence of knowledge from higher education to economic growth is illustrated in figure 5.1.

Two relations in this diagram pertain to developing countries. The first shows how scientific activities are related, through innovation, to the production of wealth and income, and job generation. The second relation is the link, here called the technology transfer office (TTO), between the university and the business sector. The weakness or absence of this link is significant and is a phenomenon that worries both developing and developed economies. Indeed, in no country are scientific research and technological innovation linked auto-

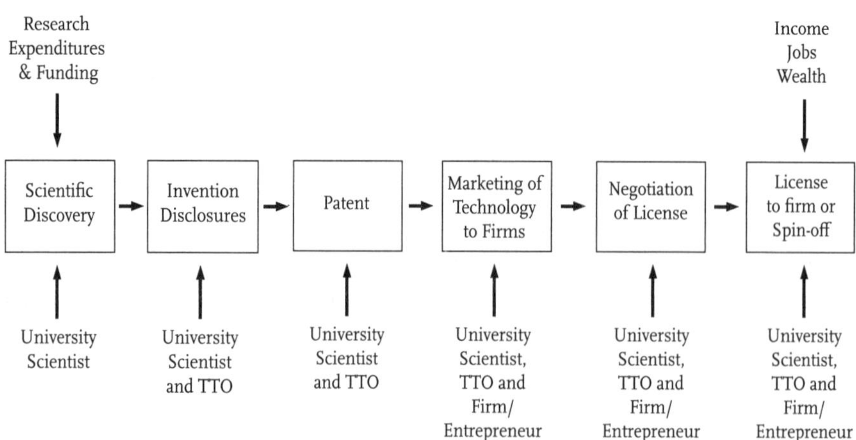

Figure 5.1 Scientific Activities and the Link Between the University and the Business Sector

Source: Authors' elaboration on Feldman and Stewart 2007, 26.

matically to the production process, unless there is an agent or institution (here named the TTO) responsible for building such links. The institutional expression of this transfer unit depends partly on government policies and partly on the participation of the local business sector.[17] In any case, the absence or fragility of such institutions is worse in Latin America than in western Europe or the developed world.

TECHNOLOGICAL PROGRESS AND LATIN AMERICA'S CURRENT QUEST FOR GROWTH IN THE GLOBAL ECONOMY

Together with this advance in economic theory regarding the contribution of innovation and research to development, the world's economic structure and political scene changed dramatically, marked by the swift pace of technological progress, especially the intense and rapid advance of science and technology. Areas like computers, microelectronics, robotics, and biotechnology and their applications to communications, production, and services have flourished. This in turn has modified the demand and consumption patterns in most countries and industrial processes and is remapping the world's trade and production of goods and services.

Both developing and developed nations are finding that their international competitiveness and economic growth potential are based more and more on their technological prowess and ability to adapt and to innovate in niches or across the board in different industries. New competitors like China and India now are prominent on the international trade scene, putting pressure on Latin America to transform and modernize its own productive structure. To meet this challenge, Latin America will have to raise the quality of its teaching, training, and research capacity to innovate in order to create a sustained and robust long-term economic expansion.

To better gauge the ability of public universities to promote Latin America's economic development today, we start with a brief overview of the area's recent growth performance and economic outlook, particularly its research and technical progress.

Economic Liberalization and Growth in Latin America: 1980–2006

In the 1990s, in the aftermath of the debt crisis, Latin American governments instituted radical reforms to eliminate trade protection, liberalize financial markets, and reduce the state's intervention in the economy, using a new, neoliberal strategy. The public sector was downsized, and state enterprises were either shut down or privatized. Most subsidies and industrial policies were canceled. Development banks and other public institutions aimed at fostering planning and development were weakened. Trade protectionism was eliminated, and financial and other markets were deregulated and opened to international competition, thereby increasing the role of private capital, particularly foreign capital, in allocating investments.

The reforms' results, however, were frustrating. They did reduce inflation and fiscal deficit and brought about an export boom in Latin America. But they were unable to trigger high and sustained economic growth or job creation. For most of the region's countries, investment has been laggard, and the pace of economic expansion has been far from dynamic. In fact, the average rate of growth of real GDP per capita and of labor productivity has since then been much lower than it was between 1950 and 1980, before the neoliberal, macroeconomic reforms were launched. Poverty still afflicts a vast proportion of the population; the region is not catching up with the developed world; and the gap between the haves and the have-nots is widening.

Why did the reforms fail? First, private investment did not compensate for the drop in public investment. After years of decline during the debt crisis, the lack of investment impeded the modernization of domestic machinery and equipment, thereby slowing the rise in productivity and international competitiveness. Second, although exports certainly have risen, they have been not been linked closely enough to the domestic economy and have tended to be based on either low-tech assembling activities (*maquiladoras*) or natural-resource based manufactures with rather low or intermediate technological content. Thus the reforms have failed to act as an engine of growth for the region. Nonetheless, between 2003 and 2006, the region experienced a substantial economic recovery boosted by foreign demand, mainly for mineral inputs and natural resource–based products, improvements in trade, and a massive flow of family remittances from abroad. For most countries in the region, however, this recovery has not been accompanied by a surge in investment to ensure annual rates of economic expansion over and above the 6 percent needed to generate sufficient jobs and alleviate poverty.

The consensus is that Latin America is at a crossroads. On the one hand, the region cannot continue competing internationally on the basis of low wages, now that China and other East Asian economies offer substantially lower unit labor costs. On the other hand, with few exceptions, Latin America's economies do not yet have the technological capacity or specialized human capital to successfully compete internationally at a large scale on high-tech products. Certainly, there is no one strategy for development best for every country at all times. In particular, the recommendations that the state should refrain from directly intervening in the economy and that the free interplay of market forces was the only road to be followed—as argued by the Washington Consensus— proved to be incorrect.[18]

In any case, in order for Latin America to succeed in its quest for high economic growth based on international trade in knowledge-intensive goods and services, it must strengthen its capacity to innovate and conduct research and development, recognizing that public research universities are a mainstay of the national innovation systems. Because of their role in training human resources and carrying out research, they can help the economy and society adapt to the globalized market and, ultimately, to join the ranks of developed nations. A key element in this regard is translating such research and human capital formation into innovation and thus into faster productivity growth. This outcome, however, depends not only on the isolated efforts of such universities but also on the overall institutional commitment to innovation. In particular, it depends on how innovation is linked with financial and productive capital so that it may be locally exploited efficiently and effectively.

One important function of universities is to create a critical mass of scientists and engineers to work directly in industry, business, and government. The developed countries' universities and technological institutes have been doing this for a long time. In these countries, large corporations have R&D departments that hire university graduates. These companies, together with government agencies, finance scientific and technological research projects in universities and research institutes. In addition, the private sector supplies funds for higher education and research through different mechanisms (see tables 5.1 and 5.2). Finally, in such countries, corporations tend to prefer using technology produced by their own national system of innovation, allowing them to "own" knowledge generated both in their own country as well as elsewhere and apply it to local production.

OBSTACLES TO THE DEVELOPMENT OF SCIENCE AND TECHNOLOGY IN LATIN AMERICA

Latin America's achievements, and perhaps capabilities, in creating innovative technology have been few.[19] The region contributes less than 1.5 percent of

Table 5.1 Human Resources in Research and Development

Country	Year	Researchers				Researchers by Sector of Employment			
		Full-time Equivalent	Researchers per Million Inhabitants	Head Count	Researchers per Million Inhabitants	Business Enterprise	Government	Higher Education	Private Nonprofit
Latin America									
Argentina	2003	27,367	720.1	43,609	1,147.4	3,101	10,201	13,485	580
Chile	2003	7,085	444.2	8,658	542.8	985	471	5,225	404
Uruguay	2002	1,242	366.3	3,839	1,132.1	12	166	1,064	n.a.
Cuba	2003	n.a.	n.a.	6,027	537.2	n.a.	n.a.	n.a.	n.a.
Costa Rica	1999	n.a.	n.a.	1,412	367.7	n.a.	n.a.	n.a.	n.a.
Venezuela	2003	n.a.	n.a.	6,100	236.3	n.a.	n.a.	n.a.	n.a.
Brazil	2000	59,838	344.2	n.a.	n.a.	15,989	4,736	38,701	412
Mexico	2002	27,626	268.4	n.a.	n.a.	n.a.	n.a.	n.a.	n.a.
Peru	1997	5,576	225.9	n.a.	n.a.	n.a.	n.a.	n.a.	n.a.
Bolivia	2002	1,040	120.1	n.a.	n.a.	52	156	728	104
Colombia	2003	4,829	109.2	10,851	245.4	417	500	3,707	206
Ecuador	2003	645	50.2	845	65.7	n.a.	n.a.	n.a.	n.a.

Other Countries

Japan	2003	675,330	5,286.9	830,545	6,502.0	458,845	33,711	172,396	10,378
United States	2002	1,334,628	4,605.0	n.a.	n.a.	1,066,000	47,822	208,806	12,000
Australia	2002	73,344	3,758.9	n.a.	n.a.	20,622	8,036	42,780	1,906
Canada	2002	112,624	3,596.9	n.a.	n.a.	69,634	7,820	34,910	260
Russia	2004	477,647	3,319.3	401,425	2,789.6	257,621	147,896	70,844	1,286
Germany	2004	269,500	3,260.9	n.a.	n.a.	162,000	40,000	67,500	n.a.
France	2003	192,790	3,212.7	240,186	4,002.6	100,646	24,541	64,403	3,200
Korea	2003	151,254	3,186.7	198,171	4,175.2	111,388	11,974	26,419	1,473
United Kingdom	2003	165,460	2,712.0	n.a.	n.a.	102,684	9,278	49,000	4,498
Spain	2003	92,523	2,195.4	158,566	3,762.5	27,581	15,489	49,196	258
Hong Kong	2002	10,639	1,563.8	n.a.	n.a.	3,142	212	7,285	n.a.
Italy	2003	70,332	1,213.5	107,454	1,853.9	26,866	13,976	27,774	1,716
China	2004	926,252	708.1	n.a.	n.a.	484,164	191,957	185,987	n.a.
India	1998	117,528	119.1	n.a.	n.a.	34,973	60,455	22,100	n.a.

Source: Authors' elaboration based on data from UNESCO, 2006.

Table 5.2 Gross Expenditure on Research and Development (GERD)

Selected Countries	Year	Gross Expenditure on R&D			GERD by Sector (%)				GERD by Source (%)				
		PPP Dollars (millions)	As Percentage of GDP	Per Capita PPP Dls	Business Enterprise	Govern-ment	Higher Education	Private Nonprofit	Business Enterprise	Govern-ment	Higher Education	Private Nonprofit	Abroad
Latin America													
Brazil	2003	13,487.0	0.98	74.35	n.a.	n.a.	n.a.	n.a.	41.0	30.4	28.6	n.a.	n.a.
Cuba	2003	n.a.	0.65	n.d.	0.0	0.0	0.0	0.0	35.0	60.0	0.0	0.0	5.0
Chile	2003	980.8	0.61	61.49	37.8	12.7	33.8	15.8	35.2	50.5	0.0	0.5	13.3
Argentina	2003	1,825.7	0.41	48.04	29.0	41.1	27.4	2.5	26.1	44.2	25.9	2.3	1.4
Mexico	2002	3,604.7	0.40	35.02	29.8	41.4	28.6	0.3	30.6	61.0	7.1	0.3	1.0
Costa Rica	2000	131.2	0.39	33.40	23.3	19.5	36.2	21.0	n.a.	n.a.	n.a.	n.a.	n.a.
Uruguay	2002	68.9	0.26	20.33	49.0	19.4	31.6	0.0	46.7	17.1	31.4	0.1	4.7
Venezuela	2003	359.0	0.28	13.91	0.0	0.0	0.0	0.0	1.0	71.6	27.4	0.0	0.0
Bolivia	2002	60.5	0.28	6.99	25.0	21.0	41.0	13.0	16.0	20.0	31.0	19.0	14.0
Peru	2003	149.7	0.10	5.51	9.8	35.4	44.7	10.1	n.a.	n.a.	n.a.	n.a.	n.a.
Ecuador	2003	32.4	0.07	2.52	12.9	34.9	10.8	41.4	n.a.	n.a.	n.a.	n.a.	n.a.

Other areas

Japan	2003	112,221.8	3.15	878.54	75.0	9.3	13.7	2.1	74.5	17.7	6.3	1.2	0.3
United States	2003	291,765.1	2.67	997.09	69.8	12.4	13.7	4.1	63.8	30.8	2.8	2.9	0.0
Korea	2003	22,761.5	2.64	479.56	76.1	12.6	10.1	1.2	74.0	23.9	1.7		0.4
Germany	2003	58,683.0	2.56	710.60	69.7	13.4	16.8	0.1	66.3	31.2	0.3	0.0	2.3
France	2003	36,717.4	2.22	611.87	62.6	16.7	19.4	1.3	50.8	39.0	1.9	0.0	8.4
Canada	2003	19,398.9	2.00	613.18	55.8	10.0	33.9	0.3	49.3	24.5	14.9	2.6	8.6
U.K.	2003	30,503.6	1.89	514.55	65.7	9.7	21.4	3.2	43.9	31.3	1.0	4.5	19.4
Australia	2002	9,499.2	1.70	486.84	51.2	19.3	26.7	2.8	48.8	42.4	4.7		4.1
China	2003	84,618.3	1.31	65.09	62.4	27.1	10.5	0.0	60.1	29.9	0.0	0.0	2.0
Russia	2003	16,926.4	1.28	117.04	68.4	25.3	6.1	0.2	30.8	59.6	0.5	0.2	9.0
Italy	2003	17,748.0	1.14	306.21	n.a.	n.a.	n.a.	n.a.	n.a.	n.a.	n.a.	n.a.	n.a.
Spain	2003	10,172.2	1.11	241.37	54.1	15.4	30.3	0.2	48.4	40.1	5.4	0.4	5.7
Hong Kong	2002	1,089.8	0.60	160.19	33.2	3.1	63.6	0.0	35.3	62.8	0.2	0.0	1.7

Source: Authors' elaboration based on data from UNESCO, 2006.

the world's scientific output[20] but accounts for 8.5 percent of the world's total population. Part of the reason is that in Latin America, the conditions to put in place an efficient system of science, technology, and innovation have been difficult, facing major obstacles. One is the paucity or lack of private businesses funding and collaboration with universities and institutes for research and development. The situation is worsened by the fact that in Latin America, as in many semi-industrialized, developing economies, private firms have no R&D departments and tend to spend relatively little overall on R&D. In general, they acquire their technology directly from abroad and devote few resources to technical innovation beyond that concerning administrative or marketing processes. Moreover, local scientists, technological experts, and researchers tend not to be fully recognized as relevant to production in national industries or as having interesting or lucrative career options.

Recent data available for Latin America estimate the number of researchers at around 150,000, including personnel working in production and education. The ratio of researchers to the total population is between 50 researchers per million inhabitants in Ecuador and 720 in Brazil, whereas Japan has 5,300 researchers per million inhabitants, the United States 4,600, and Spain 2,200 (see table 5.1). Latin America's numbers are low by international standards (see tables 5.3 and 5.4).

Besides offering undergraduate and graduate programs in a wide variety of disciplines, modern universities in the Western world systematically carry out theoretical and applied research. In Latin America, in contrast, only a minority of the more than 2,500 academic institutions (private or public) defined as universities go beyond undergraduate teaching and offer graduate programs in science and technology. The even smaller number of academic institutions that are engaged in scientific research and technology development are typically public universities.[21] Moreover, close to 80 percent of these 2,500 universities are concentrated in only six countries, and at most, only an estimated 15 percent of the institutions are able to carry out research and development that meets internationally competitive standards.[22]

There is no reason to believe that this situation has improved significantly in the last decade. Most Latin American countries spend less than 0.5 percent of the gross domestic product (GDP) on science and technology. None of them spends more than 1 percent of GDP, the minimum proportion recommended by a number of international organizations. For example, Mexico spent an average of 0.4 percent of its GDP over the last ten years. In contrast, Japan, the United States, South Korea, Germany, France, and Canada spent between 2 and 3 percent of their GDP on science and technology (see table 5.3). Also, in Latin

Table 5.3 Tertiary Education Graduates by Field, 2004

| Selected Countries | Total Number of Graduates | Graduates by Field of Education as a Percentage of Total | | | | | | | | | | Not Known |
| | | Science and Technology Fields | | | Other Fields | | | | | | | |
		Total	Science	Engin. M. & C.	Total	Education	Humanities and Arts	Social Sciences	Agriculture	Health and Welfare	Services	
Latin America												
Brazil	497,598	12.8	7.2	5.6	80.9	27.0	3.2	35.0	1.8	12.1	1.8	6.3
Mexico	339,450	28.7	11.2	17.5	71.3	15.8	1.4	41.2	2.1	10.4	0.4	n.a.
Venezuela	101,112	n.a.	n.a.	n.a.	n.a.	n.a.	n.a.	n.a.	n.a.	n.a.	n.a.	n.a.
Colombia	65,720	24.7	2.3	22.4	75.3	17.3	2.3	46.3	0.7	8.8	n.a.	n.a.
Chile	64,364	26.3	0.9	25.3	73.7	12.5	6.0	40.9	4.3	10.0	n.a.	n.a.
Costa Rica	26,463	11.9	6.0	6.0	88.1	34.5	3.3	38.6	1.3	9.5	1.0	0.0
Bolivia	19,326	n.a.	n.a.	n.a.	n.a.	n.a.	n.a.	n.a.	n.a.	n.a.	n.a.	n.a.
Uruguay	7,476	n.a.	n.a.	n.a.	n.a.	n.a.	n.a.	n.a.	n.a.	n.a.	n.a.	n.a.

(continued on next page)

Table 5.3 Tertiary Education Graduates by Field, 2004 *(continued)*

Selected Countries	Total Number of Graduates	Graduates by Field of Education as a Percentage of Total										
		Science and Technology Fields						*Other Fields*				*Not Known*
		Total	Science	Engin. M. & C.	Total	Education	Humanities and Arts	Social Sciences	Agriculture	Health and Welfare	Services	
Other areas												
United States	2,473,299	12.4	7.0	5.4	72.1	11.1	13.1	36.5	0.9	6.4	4.0	15.5
China	1,948,080	n.a.	n.a.	n.a.	n.a.	n.a.	n.a.	n.a.	n.a.	n.a.	n.a.	n.a.
Russia	1,706,156	25.6	5.9	19.7	70.7	7.6	5.2	44.9	4.3	6.0	2.7	3.8
Japan	1,051,262	21.5	3.0	18.6	73.1	6.9	15.8	24.9	2.2	12.3	11.0	5.3
U.K.	595,641	22.7	14.6	8.1	75.5	9.9	15.3	30.9	1.0	17.8	0.7	1.8
France	584,849	29.3	13.0	16.3	70.6	6.6	12.4	39.7	0.3	7.6	4.1	n.a.
Germany	319,791	26.9	10.1	16.8	72.9	7.5	10.4	23.5	2.4	25.2	3.9	n.a.
Spain	298,448	27.9	11.0	16.9	72.1	11.2	9.3	29.3	2.1	12.9	7.2	n.a.
Italy	248,710	22.7	7.5	15.2	76.7	8.7	13.2	33.6	2.2	16.0	3.0	0.5
Australia	233,488	23.1	14.7	8.4	84.8	10.8	11.6	43.3	1.3	14.4	3.4	0.1
Hong Kong	53,104	28.0	12.4	15.6	47.1	9.4	7.5	26.5	n.a.	3.3	0.4	24.8

Source: Authors' elaboration based on data from UNESCO, 2006..

Table 5.4 Education Expenditure by Different Sources as a Percentage of GDP, 2004

	All Sources		Public Sources		Private Sources		International
	Total	Tertiary	Total	Tertiary	Total	Tertiary	
Latin America							
Mexico	6.25	1.39	5.06	0.99	1.18	0.40	n.a.
Colombia	7.84	n.a.	4.90	n.a.	2.93	n.a.	n.a.
Costa Rica	4.78	0.93	4.73	0.93	n.a.	n.a.	0.05
Chile	7.23	2.20	3.97	0.38	3.26	1.83	n.a.
Argentina	4.74	1.09	3.94	0.70	0.80	0.39	n.a.
Peru	n.a.	n.a.	2.99	n.a.	n.a.	n.a.	n.a.
Uruguay	2.84	0.58	2.57	0.55	0.21	n.a.	0.06
Other areas							
United States	7.44	2.70	5.49	1.22	1.95	1.48	n.a.
France	5.88	1.06	5.41	0.91	0.46	0.15	n.a.
U.K.	5.98	1.16	5.05	0.83	0.93	0.33	n.a.
Germany	5.30	1.08	4.42	0.98	0.87	0.09	0.01
Hong Kong	n.a.	n.a.	4.36	n.a.	n.a.	n.a.	n.a.
Spain	n.a.	n.a.	4.33	0.94	n.a.	n.a.	n.a.
Australia	5.83	1.57	4.33	0.76	1.51	0.81	n.a.
Korea	7.06	n.a.	4.12	n.a.	2.95	1.88	n.a.
Russia	n.a.	n.a.	3.84	0.65	n.a.	n.a.	n.a.
Japan	4.67	n.a.	3.48	n.a.	1.19	0.63	n.a.

Source: Authors' elaboration based on data from UNESCO, 2006.

America, between 60 and 90 percent of most science and technology expenditures are made by the state, either directly or through public institutions. The rest of the funding comes from either the private sector or external sources. In contrast, in most developed countries, government financing makes up less than 50 percent of the total funding for R&D.

Another element in the region that weakens its capacity to innovate and the potential impact of universities on economic growth is that generally the

Table 5.5 Tertiary Education Enrollment and Teaching Staff, 2004

Selected Countries	Total Enrollment			Gross Enrollment Ratio	Distribution of Students by ISCED Level (%)			Gross Graduation Ratio 5A	Teaching Staff	Student/Teacher Ratio
		Public	Private		5A	5B	6			
World	131,999,450			23.7	79.0	19.2	1.7		8,475,673	15.6
Latin America	12,099,953	62.7	37.3	34.1	79.1	22.7		12.4		13.2
Argentina	2,026,735	78.9	21.1	61.1	74.0	25.7	n.a.	7.7	127,077	15.9
Chile	567,114	25.8	74.2	43.2	83.0	16.7	n.a.	15.8	n.a.	n.a.
Bolivia	346,056	n.a.	n.a.	40.6	n.a.	n.a.	n.a.	n.a.	17,759	19.5
Venezuela	983,217	72.9	27.1	39.3	61.6	34.3	4.1	11.5	n.a.	n.a.
Uruguay	98,520	89.8	10.2	37.8	76.3	23.6	n.a.	9.0	11,989	8.2
Cuba	235,997	100.0	0.0	33.0	98.9	n.a.	1.1	13.6	44,669	5.3
Peru	831,345	53.1	46.9	31.5	54.1	45.8	n.a.	n.a.	56,070	14.8
Colombia	1,112,574	45.0	55.0	26.9	81.8	18.1	n.a.	5.9	87,544	12.7
Mexico	2,236,791	66.8	33.2	22.5	96.6	2.9	n.a.	14.4	231,558	9.7
Brazil	3,582,105	31.7	68.3	20.1	n.a.	n.a.	n.a.	13.2	242,475	14.8
Costa Rica	79,499	n.a.	n.a.	19.0	85.2	14.6	n.a.	20.8	4,494	17.7

Other areas	62,780,117	66.7	33.3	59.9	72.2	25.2		35.4		15.8
Korea	3,223,431	19.4	80.6	88.5	58.8	40.0	1.1	34.4	172,572	18.7
United States	16,900,471	76.1	23.9	82.4	76.6	21.1	2.2	34.5	1,174,831	14.4
Australia	1,002,998	99.2	0.8	72.2	79.9	16.4	3.7	46.9	n.a.	n.a.
Russia	8,622,097	88.8	11.2	68.2	74.9	23.3	n.a.	37.1	601,354	14.3
Spain	1,839,903	86.4	13.6	65.7	81.9	13.9	4.2	36.1	140,740	13.1
Italy	1,986,497	93.6	6.4	63.1	97.0	1.1	1.9	31.3	91,978	21.6
U.K.	2,247,441	0.0	100.0	60.1	73.2	22.8	4.0	39.1	111,830	20.1
Canada	1,192,570	n.a.	n.a.	57.2	72.5	25.4	2.2	32.9	131,320	9.1
France	2,160,300	83.6	16.4	56.0	71.5	23.8	4.7	42.7	135,783	15.9
Japan	4,031,604	23.0	77.0	54.0	73.8	24.4	1.8	36.8	496,370	8.1
Hong Kong	155,761	96.6	3.4	32.1	54.4	42.3	3.4	17.8	n.a.	n.a.
China	19,417,044	n.a.	n.a.	19.1	51.6	47.7	0.7	n.a.	850,227	22.8

Notes: ISCED International Standard Classification of Education.
 5A= BA and MA programs; 5B = technical education ; 6 = doctorate.
n.a. = not available
Source: Authors' elaboration based on data from UNESCO, 2006.

distribution of expenditures on science and technology does not favor engineering. It receives only 10 percent of the total, thus greatly limiting the region's technological capability.[23] Moreover, no more than an average of 30 percent of graduates choose science and engineering careers (see table 5.5).

Another obstacle that the region and its research universities face is the lack of interaction and collaboration among Latin American scientists and between them and the local industry.[24] As the data show, Latin American industrialists prefer to base their technological advancement on buying imported machinery, equipment, and know-how from developed countries. This reliance on imported capital goods and know-how is evidenced by the sharp deterioration of the trade balance during economic upswings when new investments are put in place.

As mentioned, public universities and research institutions in Latin America are responsible for undergraduate/graduate programs as well as for the vast majority of local research in science and technology. We therefore must differentiate state spending on science and technology from that on higher education. According to the data presented here, public expenditure in Latin America to promote science and technology is very low in relation to its GDP compared with that of developed countries.

More effort is needed to augment public and private spending in these areas.[25] In addition, we must define those developments in science and technology that in the long run could serve as engines of growth in their impact on competitiveness and economic growth. The challenge is "picking winners" that provide timely policy support tied to clearly defined performance criteria and, at the same time, that can withdraw this support from sectors or firms that are not performing as expected. In other words, the challenge is to "let losers go."[26] The policy for developing key sectors should rely on transparent and temporary incentives that are tightly linked to a given set of performance indicators and are granted in such a way that firms or activities that fail to meet the performance criteria are quickly removed from the list of beneficiaries.

HIGHER EDUCATION AND GRADUATE PROGRAMS IN LATIN AMERICA

For a number of reasons, in Latin America, public universities are responsible for most postgraduate training, including that in science and technology. Most of the qualified researchers working in these fields in Latin America have been trained and/or are at work in public universities. To the extent that a critical mass for research in science and technology has been established in different countries in our region, it has been trained in public universities and supported by government funds.

In most countries of Latin America, higher education is in the hands of public institutions (see table 5.5). For different reasons, over the last two decades the number of private institutions competing in some fields with public universities has significantly increased. Surprisingly, two-thirds of higher education also is provided by public institutions in the developed countries selected for comparison (see again table 5.5). This is where the highly qualified human resources are trained and employed and the main research laboratories and facilities have been built. Without public research universities, the region would have only a very few professionals with a solid education in specific branches of knowledge and the ability to constantly adapt and stay up to date in their fields. These professionals include the high-level scientists or engineers who either can go into production or concentrate on research and teaching.

According to UNESCO estimates, just over 13 million students are enrolled in Latin America in what is defined as *tertiary* education (see table 5.6). As with other indicators, 86 percent of this enrollment is concentrated in only seven countries in the region (Argentina, Brazil, Chile, Colombia, Mexico, Peru, and Venezuela). In almost every country, one single major—business administration—is chosen by 33 percent of all students, a percentage close to that of science, engineering, and health combined. Note, too, that the average gross enrollment ratio (20 to 40 percent)[27] in most Latin American countries, except Argentina, is less than half that in most developed countries (50 to 90 percent), (see table 5.5). The graduation ratio also is less than half in Latin America (12.4 percent) than in the developed countries (35.4 percent), even though the ratio of teaching staff per student is similar, reflecting the lower efficiency in Latin America. U.S. and European universities are preferred by master's and doctoral candidates from several countries over the institutions in their own countries or regions. The Latin American demand for studying in the United States is about 10 percent of the total, including undergraduate studies.[28]

For different reasons, the demand for graduate studies in some Latin American countries increased significantly in the 1990s, mainly for master's programs, which accounted for 65 percent of all graduate students. By field, this increase was mainly in the social and administrative sciences, the largest area of all.[29] These trends appear to have continued in the last ten years, and thus Latin America's graduate systems tend to favor master's programs, especially in business administration, law, psychology, economics, and social sciences.

Table 5.6 Education Expenditure, Percentage of GDP, 2004

Selected Countries	Total Public Expenditure on Education		Public Expenditure per Tertiary Student as a Percentage of GDP per Capita	Educational Expenditure in Tertiary as a Percentage of Total Educational Expenditure in Public Institution			
	As a % of GDP	As a % of Total G. exp.		Salaries, All Staff	Other Current	Total Current	Capital
Latin America							
Bolivia	6.4	18.1	35.9	n.a.	n.a.	100.0	n.a.
Mexico	5.3	n.a.	49.8	75.2	22.1	97.3	2.7
Costa Rica	4.9	18.5	n.a.	n.a.	n.a.	n.a.	n.a.
Colombia	4.9	11.7	26.3	49.7	37.5	87.2	12.8
Chile	4.1	19.1	15.3	61.7	31.4	93.2	6.8
Argentina	4.0	13.8	13.1	88.4	10.6	99.1	0.9
Peru	3.0	17.1	14.0	61.3	35.3	96.6	3.4
Uruguay	2.6	9.6	19.0	77.0	17.2	94.3	5.7
Cuba	n.a	19.4	n.a.	37.7	43.7	81.4	18.6
Other areas							
United States	5.7	n.a.	25.9	53.5	37.2	90.7	9.3
France	5.6	n.a.	29.3	65.7	23.6	89.3	10.7
U.K.	5.3	11.5	28.8	n.a.	n.a.	n.a.	n.a.
Australia	4.9	n.a.	22.6	53.9	36.5	90.4	9.6
Germany	4.8	n.a.	n.a.	65.0	25.4	90.3	9.7
Italy	4.7	n.a.	27.4	52.7	30.7	83.4	16.6
Hong Kong	4.7	23.3	67.1	74.6	21.4	95.9	4.1
Spain	4.5	n.a.	23.1	64.4	16.1	80.5	19.5
Korea	4.2	15.5	n.a.	n.a.	n.a.	n.a.	n.a.
Russia	3.8	10.7	n.a.	n.a.	n.a.	n.a.	n.a.
Japan	3.6	n.a	17.1	56.5	27.9	84.4	15.6

Source: Authors' elaboration based on data from UNESCO, 2006.

Globalization and stabilization plus structural adjustment programs have imposed new demands on Latin America's public universities. In addition, the urgent need to transform and modernize its industrial apparatus and direct it to more knowledge-intensive activities has put additional pressure on them and national or regional innovation.

More specifically, globalization, and the increased international competition that it has engendered, challenges public universities to meet world standards. As students, professors, researchers, and funds acquire greater international mobility, both public and private universities must modernize and become competitive. For some universities, the only effective response may be to concentrate their research and teaching on only a few fields, thereby closing down or trimming their curricula, departments, and campuses. This option, however, risks eliminating or weakening the capacity for interdisciplinary or multidisciplinary studies, a much-valued trait that is the essence of a university as originally conceived. Other universities may choose to form alliances with top-level universities and research centers in developed economies. Table 5.7 lists the top ten universities in Latin America, ranked according to the Institute of Higher Education of Shanghai Jiao Tong University. The table shows that only ten universities in the region ranked among the top 500 on the world. Six of them are in Brazil, two in Chile, one in Argentina, and one in Mexico.

Gearing up Latin American universities to meet international standards has many advantages, no doubt. But it also has risks and costs. One of the risks is that the public universities' research agendas may echo more and more the international one, with global concerns taking precedence over national problems. That is, the public universities must become more internationally competitive while at the same time preserving their national and regional relevance to economic and social issues.

The financial costs are evident, too, as modernizing and improving research equipment and human capital will certainly require additional funds. In this regard, we recall the backlash against public institutions, including universities, from the intellectual climate that flourished in many Latin American countries. It began in the mid-1980s and, until rather recently, was directed against the interventions by the public sector combined with the region's structural fiscal weakness that led many governments to cut the funds to public universities. Such cuts, having more an ideological than a scientific basis, were rationalized on two grounds. The first one was that the subsidies for graduate education were seen as regressive, as they tended to benefit the middle class. The second was that following the neoliberal mantra, public universities, like other public

Table 5.7 Latin American Universities Ranked in World's Top 500, 2008

Rank 2008	University	Country
1 (101–151)	Universidad de São Paulo	Brazil
2 (152–200)	Universidad de Buenos Aires	Argentina
2 (152–200)	UNAM	México
3 (201-302)	Universidad estatal de campinas	Brazil
4 (303–401)	Universidad federal de minas gerais	Brazil
4 (303–401)	Universidad federal de Rio de Janeiro	Brazil
5 (402–503)	Pontificia universidad católica	Chile
5 (402–503)	Universidad de Chile	Chile
5 (402–503)	Universidad estatal paulista	Brazil
5 (402–503)	Universidad federal de Rio Grande do sul	Brazil

Source: Authors' elaboration based on data from University Rankings, Institute of Higher Education, Shanghai Jiao Tong University, China, as reported in: http://es.wikipedia.org/wiki/Clasificaci%C3%B3n_acad%C3%A9mica_de_universidades_de_Latinoam%C3%A9rica.

entities, were inefficient and thus needed to be disciplined by market forces. In any case, the funds for public universities drastically dropped in real terms. This reduction, coupled with the trend to put in place performance-linked criteria and incentives for wages and salaries settlements, has changed the working environment and capabilities in many Latin American public universities. Whether such changes will strengthen or weaken their research capabilities must be determined case by case.

Another challenge for public research universities is the need to absorb the increased demand of the area's rapidly growing population for graduate and postgraduate education. This challenge can be adequately met only if standards of quality are maintained or raised. Finally, there is the issue of strengthening the relation between public universities and the business community in regard to training, research innovation, and national economic performance and competitiveness. How the public universities in Latin America meet these challenges will likely determine the future development path of the region.

In regard to public spending in higher education in Latin America, the main problem in some leading countries lies not so much in the relative spending in terms of GDP, as compared with that of the developed countries (e.g., Mexico is very close to the United States, above 5 percent), but where it is concentrated.

Without reducing the absolute amount of public spending in social sciences and the humanities, more money should be spent on engineering and natural and exact sciences, areas in which Latin America is far behind the developed countries. Moreover, it is clear that to grow in the long run at a high and constant rate, these economies need a highly qualified professional and labor force in science and technology.

THE MISSING LINK IN LATIN AMERICA: UNIVERSITY-INDUSTRY

Despite the wave of privatization-oriented policies in Latin America over the last twenty years, higher education institutions and research centers are still mostly public institutions funded by the state. These institutions provide most of the highest levels of training of human resources in science and technology and almost all the scientific and technological research done in the region.[30] In Latin America, these public universities conduct the research and training in the fields currently crucial to innovation-led growth.

If the links between university research and industrial activities and performance are weak in most countries of the world, in Latin America they are even weaker. To tighten them and make them more conducive to growth, an effective national innovation system is required that contains (1) human resources (research and technical personnel), (2) an adequate infrastructure (laboratories, workshops, computers, libraries), and (3) institutions that link the academic research groups in the universities with the firms producing goods and services for the market. This institutional framework would include a wide variety of alliances between government agencies, firms, and academic institutions that create an "innovation environment."[31]

This last element, the "missing link," is a fundamental weakness in developing countries, given that with notable exceptions, their local private and public firms typically do not have R&D departments. Latin American countries in general have a weak basis on which to establish a strong innovation system with a potentially significant impact on economic growth. In particular, intellectual property rights and funding sources for science and technological innovation are very scarce in most of the region.

In our view, the greatest limitation, or constraint, is the lack of university-business links. In fact, except for some policy efforts in Argentina, Brazil, Chile, Mexico and Venezuela, which are not necessarily coordinated with corresponding industrial or sectoral policies, few government policies are oriented to link the research and training agendas of public and private universities with local firms' innovation needs. The university-industry links in developed countries were not established by chance or by market forces alone. Many countries consciously promoted a mutually beneficial relation between research centers (usually universities) and private (as well as public) firms in many industries. This was a matter of state policy.[32] In Latin America, though, these links are generally weak and, in many cases, virtually nonexistent. This is, in our view, the fundamental missing element in the chain that runs from research to innovation and to economic growth. Action by the state will be required to overcome this constraint, that is, to transform this missing university-firm link into a university-government-industry.

How should the region move to meet these challenges? [33] In principle, one way would be to increase public investment in public higher education and research training across the board. But the fragility and paucity of Latin America's fiscal resources will limit this option unless radical fiscal reforms are implemented. Another way, perhaps with more impact, is to pursue university-industry-government initiatives of research, innovation, and development. Still another way is to use specific targeted models, including international collaborations. These options are not mutually exclusive. Comparative research on estimating the viability and potential costs/benefits of the different approaches based on international comparisons is urgently needed. This research could greatly advance Latin America's policies to give public universities a greater role in the research-innovation-production process.

We must stop looking at innovation as the result of technological research in laboratories of big manufacturing firms in industrialized economies. This view, albeit usually correct for most of the twentieth century, is now questioned. As Vijay Vaitheeswaran pointed out, the advantage of the big laboratories is reduced by the spread of information technologies that are speeding and easing the access to knowledge by smaller players in developing countries.[34] Moreover, as he stated, much innovation today is in services and processes.

It is not yet clear what the ideal university-business firm links would be to strengthen innovation in Latin American countries. One reason is that innovation has many phases and forms. It can apply to production processes, services, or management, with changes that raise productivity and increase wealth. Incidentally, it may or may not involve new products or new ways of doing things. Or it may simply be achieved by applying old techniques to fulfill different needs.

In any case, given the diverse nature and expression of innovation, even measuring it is difficult. Its manifestations in manufacturing or production processes are usually assessed by the number of patents or the introduction of new techniques. This practice, although standard, may be inaccurate because for many firms and countries, particularly developing countries, the costs of patenting may outweigh its benefits. Moreover, in management and in many services, patenting is simply not applicable as a measure of innovation. This is important if one recalls that services account for a vast proportion of the economic activity in many developing countries.

Thus, fostering innovation certainly requires funds and human capital but also specific institutional arrangements tailored to the different countries or branches of productive activity concerned. The one-size-fits-all approach to innovation is simply not relevant. In this matter it is useful to point out that *at the level of the firm*, there is no evidence of a strong correlation between higher spending on research and development and the usual indicators of business performance: growth, profitability, and return to shareholders.

Without a specific long-run strategy in which both the state and the private sector are committed to promoting innovation, Latin America will not likely experience the significant and persistent boost in its productivity needed to enter a sustained path of high rates of economic growth.

CONCLUSIONS

Latin America's economic development urgently needs top-level institutions capable of teaching and conducting relevant and high-quality research in science and technology. The innovation system now in place—in which public universities play a key role—is insufficient and ineffective to meet this challenge, and the institutional, financial, and human resource bases for such systems are deficient. The number of active and researchers being trained in the various areas is low, in both absolute and relative terms. As important as they are to Latin America, public universities generally do not have adequate infrastructure, human resources, or functional links with the industrial or service sector, preventing them from becoming a major force in local technological progress and innovation. There is little real collaboration between the research community, including the public universities, and the industrial or service producers.

These weaknesses can perhaps be seen best in the graduate programs, the basis for training high-level scientists and technicians. Both the absolute and relative enrollment sizes are low. The structure of graduate programs and higher education in general is uneven, to the detriment of the sciences and engineering.

This has forced Latin Americans to continue to obtain their graduate training in other countries. While some Latin American countries have what we could call the minimal basis for carrying out scientific-technological activities (infrastructure, researchers, basic and applied scientific production, and graduate programs), it is not sufficient in either quantity or quality.[35]

Substantial political efforts and investments are needed, particularly in the short term, to train *human resources* better and in the numbers required by the demand. The costs to public universities of training scientists or high-level technicians and creating the conditions for cutting-edge research are high and growing. This makes creating, maintaining, and developing science and technology systems a regional and national necessity for the scientific communities and institutions of different Latin American countries and for each country's governments, scientific communities, and industrial representatives and groups. Although mechanisms for inter-American collaboration do exist, scientific collaboration has not often been used to strengthen national innovation systems until now.[36]

These investments' profitability is not immediately visible. Moreover, its social benefit is greater than its individual benefit. If based solely on market criteria, these efforts and investments may not take place. The positive benefits of research and development justify having public research universities in Latin America. Public universities and other institutions of higher learning have the capacity to meet the demand by society for educational services as well the demand by local corporations, governments, and academic institutions for qualified human resources. If institutions of higher learning operated exclusively on the criterion of profitability, they would offer majors in those professions with the greatest market demand, in order to generate short-term profits. Public universities ensure that research and teaching in disciplines that, although not currently in demand by the private sector, are crucial to long-term economic growth and development.

Scientific disciplines are the most expensive and those seemingly least in demand today. That is why public universities must implement policies and operating criteria to raise this demand. Higher education should be supported with resources from different sources as well as the state. Under current conditions, it would be desirable for the private sector to contribute as well, though without endangering educational institutions' autonomy. They must able to plan for, finance, and provide high-quality training and research in disciplines that might not seem very profitable right now but that will be in demand and be important in the near future.

Economic growth requires specific numbers of technicians, professionals, and scientists in different areas of the economy and society in order to achieve balanced development. Public research universities in Latin American, as well as other institutions of higher learning, face important challenges today. Perhaps the most crucial is satisfying the demand for research and training high-level human resources in science and technology in sufficiently high numbers to promote economic growth based on comparative advantages rooted in knowledge-intensive activities and not on unskilled, poorly paid workers. Furthermore, this challenge must be met while complying with the efficiency and quality expected by the national and world economy.

Public universities must have the coordinated support of both the state and the private sector. Without such support, they cannot modernize and strengthen their teaching and research capabilities. In each country, how this support is obtained and guaranteed over the long term fashion depends on the position of public universities and higher education in the national polities. In Latin America, especially in countries where democratic governance is rather new, if the establishment and ruling classes are not identified with the, say, philosophy and practice of public universities, these institutions will probably face acute difficulties and pressures—financial, political, and otherwise—that will block their research and development agenda as well as growth possibilities.

In any case, as long as the missing link here identified persists—the gap between the research agenda and the local business sectors' needs—the economies will find it increasingly difficult to compete internationally based on something besides mineral or natural resources or activities marked by the intensive use of cheap, unqualified labor. If the status quo continues, economic development will be more and more a chimera than a concrete reality.

NOTES

1. See the definition of poverty and extreme poverty in World Bank, *World Development Report 2000/2001, Attacking Poverty* (Washington, D.C.: World Bank, 2001), 15–17.

2. United Nations Economic Commission for Latin America and the Caribbean, *Social Panorama 2006* (Santiago de Chile: United Nations, 2006).

3. See, in particular, the excellent review by Joshua Drucker and Harvey Golstein, "Assessing the Regional Economic Impacts of Universities: A Review of Current Approaches," *International Regional Science Review* 30 (2007): 20–46.

4. CAM, *Cambridge News*, no. 49 (Cambridge: Cambridge University, 2006). This pioneering research by the East Development Agency also indicates that the university "contributes 961 million pounds to the economy in direct expenditure. It employs 11,700 people, and in total supports more than 77,000 jobs."

5. Javier Palencia, *La universidad latinoamericana como conciencia* (Mexico City: UNAM, 1982).

6. Economic growth is conventionally identified with the rate of change of gross domestic product (GDP) per capita at constant prices. This indicator, however, does not consider the distribution of the benefits of such growth or its environmental impact. For an alternative measure of economic progress, see the UNDP's human development index, prompted by Amartya Sen.

7. Carlos Tunnermann, *La universidad latinoamericana ante los retos del siglo XXI* (Mexico City: Unión de universidades de América Latina, 2003).

8. Xavier Sala-i-Martin, *Apuntes de crecimiento económico* (Barcelona: Antoni Bosch, 2000).

9. Nicholas Kaldor, "A Model of Economic Growth," *Economic Journal* 268 (1957): 591–624.

10. Paul M. Romer, "Increasing Returns and Long Run Growth," *Journal of Political Economy* 94 (1986): 1002–37; and Paul M. Romer, "Endogenous Technological Change," *Journal of Political Economy* 98 (1990): 71–102.

11. Robert, E. Lucas, "On the Mechanism of Economic Development," *Journal of Monetary Economics* 22 (1988): 3–42.

12. Philippe Aghion and Peter Howitt, "A Model of Growth Through Creative Destruction," *Econometrica* 60 (1992): 323–51.

13. Giovanni Dosi, *Technical Change and Industrial Transformation* (New York: Macmillan, 1984).

14. Stan Metcalfe, "The Economic Foundations of Technology Policy," in *Handbook of the Economics of Innovation and Technical Change*, ed. Paul Stoneman (Oxford: Blackwell, 1995), 409–512.

15. In this chapter, it is important to stress the strand of research produced in Latin America in the last ten years, focusing on the links between universities, science/technology, and human capital formation and their impact on economic growth. See Mario Cimoli et al., *Growth, Structural Change and Technological Capabilities: Latin America in a Comparative Perspective*, Working Paper Series no. 11 (Pisa: Laboratory of Economics and Management, Santa Ana School of Advanced Studies, May 2006); Mario Cimoli, Joâo Carlos Ferraz, and Annalisa Primi, *Science and Technology Policies in Open Economies: The Case of Latin America and the Caribbean*, Serie desarrollo productivo no. 165, ECLAC (Santiago de Chile: United Na-

tions, 2005); Carlos Tunnermann, *La universidad latinoamericana ante los retos del siglo XXI* (Mexico City: Unión de universidades de América Latina, 2003); Salvador Malo, "El Proceso Bolonia y la educación superior en América Latina," *Foreign Affairs en español* 2 (2005): 21–33. For a more global perspective, see Shahid Yusuf and Kaoru Nabeshina, eds., *How Universities Promote Economic Growth* (Washington, D.C.: World Bank, 2007).

16. Tatyana Soubbotina, *Beyond Economic Growth, an Introduction to Sustainable Development* (Washington, D.C.: World Bank, 2004); Alfred Watkins, "Education, Science, Technology and Innovation" (paper presented at the Workshop on Technology Innovation, Private Sector Development and Economic Growth, Hangzhou, China, May 25–27, 2005); Jean Guinet, "Connecting Science to Innovation: A Key Task for Achieving Sustainable Growth" (paper presented at the Workshop on Technology, Innovation, Private Sector Development, and Economic Growth, May 25–27, 2005, Hangzhou, China); Maryann Feldman and Ian Stewart, "Well-springs of Modern Economic Growth: Higher Education, Innovation and Local Economic Development" (unpublished manuscript, University of Georgia and University of Toronto, 2007); Shahid Yusuf and Kaoru Nabeshina, eds., *How Universities Promote Economic Growth* (Washington, D.C.: World Bank, 2007).

17. Shahid Yusuf, "University-Industry Links, Policy Dimensions," in *How Universities Promote Economic Growth*, ed. Shahid Yusuf and Keroe Nabeshima, 1–23 (Washington, D.C.: World Bank, 2007).

18. For an excellent analysis of the obstacles to Latin America's economic and social development and the elements to be taken into account in the design and implementation of strategies to overcome them, see UN ECLAC, *Globalization and Development* (Santiago de Chile: United Nations, 2002). Interesting contributions to the literature on economic growth and development strategies can be found in the works by José Antonio Ocampo, K. S. Jomo, and Sarbuland Khan, eds., *Policy Matters: Economic and Social Policies to Sustain Equitable Development* (London: Zed, 2007); Dani Rodrik, *One Economics, Many Recipes: Globalization, Institutions, and Economic Growth* (Princeton, N.J.: Princeton University Press, 2007); and Ha-Joon Chang, *Kicking Away the Ladder: Policies and Institutions for Economic Development in Historical Perspective* (London: Anthem Press, 2003).

19. Enrique Martín Del Campo, "La cooperación científico-tecnológica en América Latina y el Caribe," in *La Ciencia en la integración latinoamericana, memoria, ciencia y desarrollo*, Serie encuentros, 32–37 (Mexico City: CONACYT, 1998); and Mario Cimoli et al., *Growth, Structural Change and Technological Capabilities: Latin America in a Comparative Perspective* (Pisa: Santa Ana School of Advanced Studies, 2006).

20. Carlos Tunnermann, *La universidad latinoamericana ante los retos del siglo XXI* (Mexico City: Unión de universidades de América Latina, 2003).

21. In Latin America, most public universities engage in research. Thus, the distinction between public research universities and other public universities that is relevant in the United States is not so there. Note, however, that *private* universities in Latin America generally carry out little or no research. For a study of the macro universities (largest) in Latin America, see Axel Didriksson, "Las macrouniversidades de América Latina y el Caribe" (paper presented at the Reunión de macrouniversidades de América Latina y el Caribe, Universidad central de Venezuela, Caracas, Venezuela, June 13–14, 2002).

22. Martín Del Campo, "La cooperación científico-tecnológica," 32–37.

23. Ibid.

24. See Hugo Aréchiga, "La ciencia como factor de integración en Latinoamérica," in *La ciencia en la integración latinoamericana, memoria, ciencia y desarrollo*, Serie Encuentros (Mexico City: CONACYT, 1998), 11–12; Judith Zubieta, Gerardo Suárez, and Ana Hilda Gómez, "Problemática del desarrollo científico y tecnológico en México," *Mexican Studies / Estudios mexicanos* 15 (1999): 193–211; Martín Puchet-Anyul and Pablo Ruiz-Nápoles, "Aspectos económico institucionales del marco regulatorio mexicano del sistema nacional de innovación"(México: Facultad de Economía, UNAM, 2005).

25. For recent contributions to the study of scientific, technological, and innovation policies in Mexico, see Gabriela Dutrenit, coord., *Bases y mecanismos para una política de ciencia, tecnología e innovación en México* (Mexico City: Foro consultivo científico y tecnológico, 2006).

26. Since the late 1990s, there has been a revival of industrial policy both in the developed world as well as in semi-industrialized economies. For an analysis of the causes of this phenomenon, see Dani Rodrik, "Industrial Policy for the Twenty-first Century," KSG Working Paper (2004), available at http://ssrn.com/abstract=617544 (accessed May 20, 2007).

27. The number of students currently enrolled, independent of their ages, divided by the age group population they should belong.

28. UNESCO, *Education Trends in Perspective Analysis of the World Education Indicators* (Paris: UNESCO and OECD, 2005).

29. Rocío Santa María, *Los desafíos del posgrado en América Latina* (Mexico City: UDUAL, 1995).

30. A particular and, to some extent, representative case is that of the National Autonomous University of Mexico (UNAM), ranked worldwide by the *Times Higher Education Supplement* as number 74.

31. Shahid Yusuf, "University-Industry Links, Policy Dimensions," in *How Universities Promote Economic Growth*, ed. Shahid Yusuf and Kaoru Nabeshima, 1–23 (Washington, D.C.: World Bank, 2007).

32. Ibid.

33. We acknowledge and sincerely thank Prof. Diana Rothen for sharing with us her ideas, expressed here in the last paragraph of this section.

34. Vijay Vaitheeswaran, "Something New Under the Sun: A Special Report on Innovation," *The Economist*, October 13, 2007.

35. The approximately 150,000 working researchers in Latin America produce only 1.5 percent of the articles published in internationally circulating peer-reviewed journals. See Martín Del Campo, "La cooperación científico-tecnológica," 32–37.

36. Silvia Ortega, "La acción internacional del Conacyt: Una referencia a la cooperación internacional," in *La ciencia en la integración latinoamericana, memoria, ciencia y desarrollo*, Serie encuentros (Mexico City: CONACYT, 1998).

REFERENCES

Aghion, Philippe, and Peter Howitt. "A Model of Growth Through Creative Destruction." *Econometrica* 60 (1992): 323–51.

Aréchiga, Hugo. "La ciencia como factor de integración en Latinoamérica." In *La Ciencia en la integración latinoamericana, memoria, ciencia y desarrollo*. Serie encuentros, 11–12. Mexico City: CONACYT, 1998.

Asociación nacional de universidades e instituciones de educación superior. *Anuario estadístico, posgrado*. Mexico City: ANUIES, various years.

CAM, *Cambridge News*, no. 49, Cambridge: University of Cambridge, 2006.

Chang, Ha-Joon. *Kicking Away the Ladder: Policies and Institutions for Economic Development in Historical Perspective*. London: Anthem Press, 2003.

Cimoli, Mario, and Giovanni Dosi. "Technological Gaps and Institutional Asymmetries in a North-South Model with a Continuum of Goods." *Metroeconomica,* 39 (1994): 245–74.

Cimoli, Mario, Joâo Carlos Ferraz, and Annalisa Primi. *Science and Technology Policies in Open Economies: The Case of Latin America and the Caribbean*. Serie desarrollo productivo no. 165, ECLAC. Santiago de Chile: United Nations, October 2005.

Cimoli, Mario, Marcio Holland, Gabriel Porcile, Annalisa Primi, and Sebastian Vergara. *Growth, Structural Change and Technological Capabilities: Latin America in a Comparative Perspective*. Working Paper Series no. 11. Pisa: Laboratory of Economics and Management, Santa Ana School of Advanced Studies, May 2006.

Didriksson, Axel. "Las Macrouniversidades de América Latina y el Caribe." Paper presented at the Reunión de macrouniversidades de América Latina y el Caribe, Universidad central de Venezuela, Caracas, Venezuela, June 13–14, 2002.

Dosi, Giovanni. *Technical Change and Industrial Transformation.* New York: Macmillan, 1984.

Drucker, Joshua, and Harvey Golstein. "Assesing the Regional Economic Impacts of Universities: A Review of Current Approaches." *International Regional Science Review* 30 (2007): 20–46.

Dutrenit, Gabriela, coord. *Bases y mecanismos para una política de ciencia, tecnología e innovación en México.* Mexico City: Foro consultivo científico y tecnológico, 2006.

Feldman, Maryann, and Ian Stewart. "Well-springs of Modern Economic Growth: Higher Education, Innovation and Local Economic Development." Unpublished manuscript, University of Georgia and University of Toronto, 2007.

Guinet, Jean. "Connecting Science to Innovation. A Key Task for Achieving Sustainable Growth." Presentation at the Workshop on Technology, Innovation, Private Sector Development, and Economic Growth, Hangzhou, China, May 25–27, 2005.

Institute of Higher Education. "Academic Ranking of World Universities," Shanghai Jiao Tong University, Shanghai, China, 2008.

Kaldor, Nicholas. "A Model of Economic Growth." *Economic Journal* 268 (1957): 591–624.

Lucas, Robert E. "On the Mechanism of Economic Development." *Journal of Monetary Economics* 22 (1988): 3–42.

Malo, Salvador. "El Proceso Bolonia y la educación superior en América Latina." *Foreign Affairs en español* 2 (2005): 21–33.

Martín Del Campo, Enrique. "La cooperación científico-tecnológica en América Latina y el Caribe." In *La Ciencia en la integración latinoamericana, memoria, ciencia y desarrollo.* Serie encuentros, 32–37. Mexico City: CONACYT, 1998.

Metcalfe, Stan. "The Economic Foundations of Technology Policy." In *Handbook of the Economics of Innovation and Technical Change,* ed. Paul Stoneman, 409–512. Oxford: Blackwell, 1995.

Ocampo, José Antonio, K. S. Jomo, and Sarbuland Khan, eds., *Policy Matters: Economic and Social Policies to Sustain Equitable Development.* London: Zed, 2007.

Ortega, Silvia. "La acción internacional del Conacyt: Una referencia a la cooperación internacional." In *La Ciencia en la integración latinoamericana, memoria, ciencia y desarrollo.* Serie encuentros, 54–63. Mexico City: CONACYT, 1998.

Palencia, Javier. *La universidad latinoamericana como conciencia.* Mexico City: UNAM, 1982.

Puchet-Anyul, Martín, and Pablo Ruiz-Nápoles. "Aspectos económico institucionales del marco regulatorio mexicano del sistema nacional de innovación." Unpublished manuscript, Facultad de economía, UNAM, Mexico, 2005.

Rodrik, Dani. "Industrial Policy for the Twenty-first Century." KSG Working Paper no. RWP04–047, November 2004. Available at http://ssrn.com/abstract=617544 (accessed May 20, 2007).

——. *One Economics, Many Recipes: Globalization, Institutions, and Economic Growth.* Princeton, N.J.: Princeton University Press, 2007.

Romer, Paul M. "Increasing Returns and Long Run Growth." *Journal of Political Economy* 94 (1986): 1002–37.

——. "Endogenous Technological Change." *Journal of Political Economy* 98 (1990): 71–102.

Sala-i-Martin, Xavier. *Apuntes de crecimiento económico.* 2nd ed. Barcelona: Antoni Bosch, 2000.

Santa María, Rocío. *Los desafíos del posgrado en América Latina.* Colección UDUAL no. 6. Mexico City: Unión de universidades de América Latina, 1995.

Soubbotina, Tatyana P. *Beyond Economic Growth. An Introduction to Sustainable Development.* 2nd ed. WBI Learning Resources Series. Washington, D.C.: World Bank, 2004.

Times. Higher Education Supplement. London, 2008.

Tunnermann, Carlos. *La universidad latinoamericana ante los retos del siglo XXI.* Colección UDUAL, no.13. Mexico City: Unión de universidades de América Latina, 2003.

UN ECLAC (United Nations Economic Commission for Latin America and the Caribbean). *Education and Knowledge: Basic Pillars of Changing Production Patterns with Social Equity.* Santiago de Chile: United Nations, 1992

——. *Globalization and Development.* Santiago de Chile: United Nations, 2002.

——. *Social Panorama 2006.* Santiago de Chile: United Nations, 2006.

UNESCO (United Nations Organization for Education, Science and Culture). *Anuario estadístico,* Paris: UNESCO, 1998.

——. *Education Trends in Perspective Analysis of the World Education Indicators.* 2005 ed. UNESCO Institute for Statistics and Organization for Economic Cooperation and Development, 2005.

——. *Global Education Digest 2006.* Paris: UNESCO / Institute for Statistics, 2006.

——. *Informe mundial de la ciencia.* Paris: UNESCO, 1996.

Vaitheeswaran, Vijay. "Something New Under the Sun: A Special Report on Innovation." *The Economist,* October 13, 2007.

Watkins, Alfred. "Education, Science, Technology and Innovation." Paper presented at the Workshop on Technology Innovation, Private Sector Development and Economic Growth, Hangzhou, China, May 25–27, 2005.

World Bank. *World Development Report 2000/2001: Attacking Poverty.* Washington, D.C.: World Bank, 2001.

Yusuf, Shahid. "University-Industry Links, Policy Dimensions." In *How Universities Promote Economic Growth*, ed. Shahid Yusuf and Kaoru Nabeshima, 1–23. Washington, D.C.: World Bank, 2007.

Yusuf, Shahid, and Kaoru Nabeshina, eds. *How Universities Promote Economic Growth.* Washington, D.C.: World Bank, 2007.

Zubieta, Judith, Gerardo Suárez, and Ana Hilda Gómez. "Problemática del desarrollo científico y tecnológico en México." *Mexican Studies/Estudios Mexicanos* 15 (1999): 193–211.

When Neoliberalism Colonizes
Higher Education in Asia

SIX

*Bringing the "Public" Back
to the Contemporary University*

KA HO MOK

EAST MEETS WEST MEETS NEOLIBERALISM

Despite the debates on whether the impacts of globalization on social, economic, political, and cultural developments of the contemporary world are true, we cannot deny that neoliberalism and marketization have significantly transformed our daily lives, no matter where we live in the East or West. The ideas and practices of neoliberalism dominate the economic and also the social, cultural, and political spheres (Giroux 2002; Mok and Welch 2003; Painter and Wong 2005). Critical analysts have repeatedly argued that neoliberalism is the most dangerous ideology of the moment. Henry Giroux, for example, believes that "civic discourse has given way to the language of commercialization, privatization, and deregulation and that, within the language and impacts of corporate culture, citizenship is portrayed as an utterly privatized affair that produces self-interested individuals" (2002, 1). Even those market fundamentalists like Milton Friedman, Robert Nozick, and Francis Fukuyama contend that "neo-liberalism attempts to eliminate an engaged critique about its most basic principles and social consequences by embracing 'the market as the arbiter of social destiny'" (Rule 1998, 31).

Despite the invaluable role of noncommodified public spheres in history (Herman and McChesney 1997), corporate culture extends even deeper into basic institutions of civil and political society. Against the growing prominence of neoliberalism, corporate culture and neoliberalism are a simultaneous diminishment of noncommodified public spheres; organizations such as public schools, churches, noncommercial public broadcasting, libraries, trade unions, and various voluntary institutions have been reduced in importance, becoming less engaged in addressing the relationship of the self to public life and social responsibility to the broader demands of citizenship (Giroux 2002, 4). To eliminate the cost of public services like housing, education, transport, care and other social protection services, policy tools such as privatization, marketization, commodification, and corporatization strategies are increasingly adopted to transform public-sector management and social service delivery. Citizens then must buy these services at market value rather than have them provided by the state. The growing prominence of neoliberalism and the popular practices of marketization, commodification, and privatization in the public sector have significantly changed cultures and beliefs, possibly threatening critical voices and undermining the social and public functions performed by public institutions (Harkavy 2006; W. Lee 2007; Lynch 2006; Marginson 2006).

This chapter examines how and what strategies that governments in Asia have adopted to restructure and transform their higher education systems to cope with the challenges of marketization and commodification in education.[1]

THE QUEST FOR RESTRUCTURING THE COMPETITION STATE AND HIGHER EDUCATION

In order to enhance their global competitiveness, governments in different parts of the world have started to conduct comprehensive reviews of and implement plans to restructure their higher education systems (Mok and Welch 2003). In response to the growing pressures of globalization forces, modern states have attempted to reinvent themselves by moving beyond the welfare state to the so-called competition state (Gill 1995; Jordana and Levi-Faur 2005; Moran 2002). Facing similar competitive pressures, governments across different parts of the globe have undertaken regulatory reforms such as the privatization or corporatization of state-owned industries or publicly owned organizations like the post office and the universities, opening up new markets to multiple providers and introducing new regulatory regimes under the control of independent regulators

(Drahos and Jospeh 1995; Levi-Faur 1998; Scott 2004). To enhance the efficiency of public policy and public management, some modern states deregulate some areas while enforcing competition in others, hence becoming a facilitator or even a generator of markets. Thus, the extent and the role of reregulation or re-centralization in the processes of market restructuring are often accompanied by the emergence of strong regulatory states and by the entrepreneurial role states play (Chan and Tan 2006; Ng and Chan 2006). Unlike Cerny's (1997) character-ization of the competition state as a basically liberal state, Levi-Faur argues that the state (particularly in the intensified global competitive environment) faces a paradox: "*the greater the commitment of the competition state to the promotion of competition, the deeper its regulation will be*" (Levi-Faur 1998, 676, italics added). The actions and missions of the competition state do not necessarily cause the state to retreat from the market but, rather, to be reasserted under changing so-cial and economic circumstances (Levi-Faur 1998, 676).

To promote basic national interests through the creation and enforcement of competition, the developing states in Asia have taken the opportunity of-fered by the economic restructuring processes to transform them into "mar-ket accelerationist states" by shaping the market institutions for the benefits of market creation (M. Lee 2004; Mok 2006a). Unlike the regulatory state in America, which evolved against a liberal market economy, the regulatory state in Asia emerged from a combined strong state and a free-market economy, in which the state commits ideologically to an "authoritarian mode of liberalism." As Kanishka Jayasuriya pointed out, "This authoritarian liberalism presupposes the existence of a strong (or better described as politically illiberal) state with a capacity to regulate the economy" (2000, 329). To promote competition in the markets against authoritarian liberalism, a *market accelerationist state* is forming (Mok 2006b, italics in original). The market accelerationist state has the features of the "dualistic state" that Fraenkel (1941) described: a strong state combined with a liberal market economy. With this state architecture in place, the suc-cess of the markets rests on the presence of strong regulatory institutions. It is against this wider sociopolitical context that far more procompetition policy in-struments are adopted by modern states to transform the way that the public sector is governed. Hence, the higher education sector, like other public policy domains, has become "private." Ideas and strategies based on neoliberalism and economic rationalism also are increasingly influencing the way that public pol-icy is managed (Brehony and Deem 2005a; Neubauer 2006). Similar to their Western counterparts, governments and universities in Asia also have adopted far more procompetition policy instruments to transform university education, research, and governance, whose development has drastically changed the university sector in Asia. Next we focus on three aspects of change resulting from the implementation of the practices of neoliberalism: first, the incorporation and corporatization of public universities; second, the quest for becoming entrepreneurial universities; and third, the growing importance of the "world-class" university movement.

NEOLIBERALISM AND UNIVERSITY RESTRUCTURING IN ASIA

Incorporation and Corporatization of Public Universities

Influenced by the popular tide of neoliberalism, especially by the U.S. university models, higher education systems in Asia have started restructuring and reforming exercises to "displace political sovereignty with the sovereignty of 'the market'" (Comaroff, cited in Giroux 2002, 5). When examining how the ideas and practices of neoliberalism have restructured Asian higher education systems, we are interested more in the process by which higher education has been transformed as a neoliberalist tradition than in interpreting "neoliberalism" as an actor for causing changes. Not being satisfied with the conventional model based on "state-oriented" and "highly centralized" approaches to higher education, Asian governments have recently tried to "incorporate" or introduce "corporatization" and "privatization" measures to run their state and national universities, believing that their transformation could make national universities more flexible and responsive to socioeconomic changes (Mok 2006c; Oba 2006). Accordingly, state universities in Asia are now required to become more proactive and dynamic when looking for their own financial resources.

By adhering more to market and corporate principles and practices, Hong Kong's universities are now based on a market-oriented and business corporation model. This city-state's universities have undergone corporatization and privatization, by which Hong Kong's higher education institutions have encouraged entrepreneurship to search for additional revenue from the market (Lee and Gopinathan 2005; Mok 2005a). To enhance the efficiency of university governance, the University Grant Committee (UGC), the organization shaping the direction of higher education development in Hong Kong, recently subscribed to the notion of "deep collaboration" among universities, believing that universities in the city-state would be more successful if they worked together. The UGC even supports universities' merging or restructuring in other ways to further establish Hong Kong as a regional center for excellence in research and scholarship (Chan 2007; H. Lee 2005).

Similarly, Taiwan's Ministry of Education decided to change the statutory position of state universities to an independent judicial entity, by adopting the principles and practices of corporatization. To reduce the state's burdens in higher education financing, all national universities in Taiwan must generate additional funds from nonstate sectors such as the market and business enterprises. The universities have experimented with various kinds of market-driven strategies. The Taiwan government also has tried to restructure its state universities by passing a new university bill to make state universities into independent legal entities. Influenced by the Japanese model, Taiwan's state universities have to establish new governance structures and are under immense pressure to obtain additional financial support from nonstate resources, especially since the Taiwan government has significantly reduced its funding for them (Lo and Weng 2005; Tien 2006).

The government of the People's Republic of China (PRC) has found only the old way of "centralized governance" in education inappropriate to the new market economy (Yang 2002). Acknowledging that overcentralization and stringent rules would kill the initiatives and enthusiasm of local educational institutions, the Chinese Communist Party (CCP) called for streamlining the administration, devolving power to lower-level units so as to allow them more flexibility. In the last decade or so, higher education in the post–Mao Zedong era has instituted structural reforms ranging from curricular design, financing, promotion of the private/*minban* sectors in providing higher education, to strategies to develop "world-class" universities. To promote the competitiveness of its higher education in the global marketplace, the Chinese government has introduced various restructuring exercises to merge universities or to streamline the stubbornly sustained bureaucratic university systems (Min 2004). In 1995, the central government issued a policy document entitled "Suggestions for Deepening Higher Education Structural reform," which recommended four major restructuring strategies: "joint development" (*gongjian*), "restructuring" (*huazhuan*), "merging" (*hebing*), and "cooperation" (*hezuo*) to reform its higher education systems (Chou 2006; Lo and Chan 2006; Mok 2005d).

Like China, Japan is not immune from the impact of neoliberalism, managerialism, and economic rationalism, the three ideologies underlying public-sector reforms and reinventing government projects across the world. With the intention of making its state university system more responsive and flexible in coping with the intensified pressures of the growing impacts of globalization, since 2004 the Japanese government has incorporated all state universities. Central to the transformation of the existing national universities into "national university corporations" are three aspects of reform: increased competitiveness in research and education, enhanced accountability together with the introduction of competition; and the strategic and functional management of national universities (Oba 2006).

Higher education restructuring is popular not only in East Asia but also in Southeast Asia. Having reflected on the changing university governance models and evaluated the recent experiences of Singapore Management University running on a corporate model, Singapore's Ministry of Education decided to change the governance models of the existing state universities, the National University of Singapore and the Nanyang Technological University, by making them independent legal entities through the process of "corporatization" (Mok 2005b, 2006b). By incorporatizing these state universities, the Singapore government hopes that its universities can become more entrepreneurial. Similarly, public universities in Malaysia began in 1998 a similar project to "corporatize" its national universities. In the last few years, Malaysia's private universities have grown in number, and its public universities are run like as corporations. According to Molly Lee (2004), "The structural changes in the corporatized universities show that collegial forms of governance has been sidelined, entrepreneurial activities have increased, and corporate managerial practices have been institutionalised" (M. Lee 2004, 15). The influence of neoliberalism and market forces on higher education becomes clear when universities begin to try to become more entrepreneurial.

The Quest for "Entrepreneurial University" and Corporate Influences

Similar to their American, Australian, and British counterparts, Asian universities are now under constant pressure to become more "entrepreneurial" in looking for alternative funding sources from the market and strengthening their partnerships with industry and business (Marginson and Considine 2000; Olsen and Gornitzka 2006). The pressure to transform education from a public service to a tradable service is part of the ideology of the World Trade Organization (WTO)'s General Agreement on Trade and Services (GATS), which is to liberalize services in all sectors of the global economy (Robertson, Bonal, and Dale 2002). After GATS deemed higher education an important trade service, the universities' performance now is assessed by their profitable return on investment to shareholders, and they are "operated in a business-like fashion with small boards, recruitment of financial and commercial expertise, strong professional management, and leaders as market entrepreneurs" (Olsen and Gornitzka 2006, 2). Attaching so much more weight to entrepreneurial efficiency and effectiveness, the identity of contemporary universities has been challenged by market forces, and they are being forced to adapt quickly to socioeconomic and sociopolitical changes. Besides the traditional missions of teaching and research, contemporary universities are having to expand the third mission, becoming more entrepreneurial in their social and economic development (Etzkowitz 2003). In the last decade or so, Asian universities have increasingly become powerful, consumer-oriented corporate networks, owing to the growing corporate influence on education, research, and governance. With less financial support from the state, coupled with the adverse impact of the financial crisis on East Asia, universities are trying to become more "entrepreneurial" by developing closer links with the business and industrial sectors, collaborating on research projects or offering more self-financing and fee-paying academic programs to generate additional income (Mok 2005a). One of the major tasks confronting Asian university presidents or vice-chancellors, like their counterparts in the United States, Australia, and the United Kingdom, is fund-raising.

Believing that universities should work closely with business and industry, Hong Kong encourages all public universities to strengthen their links with the local businesses and industries, by forming partnerships and collaborating on research. In the last ten years, university-run enterprises and business partnerships have become more popular in the city-state. To promote fund-raising in public universities, the Hong Kong government introduced in 2003 a plan for matching grants for eight public universities, offering HK$1 billion in matching grants on a dollar-for-dollar matching basis. When it proved successful, the government provided two more rounds of grants. Although some established universities like the University of Hong Kong (the oldest university in Hong Kong) and the Chinese University of Hong Kong, founded in 1963, have been able to obtain donations and funds from local businesses and the community, the newly established and/or small public universities have had difficulty raising much money (H. Lee 2005).

Like Hong Kong, higher education institutions in Taiwan are under great pressure to become entrepreneurial, especially when Taiwan's Ministry of Education reduced its financial support to the national universities. Recent studies of organizing technovation and technological dynamism in Taiwan suggest that the state's role in R&D policies has fundamentally changed. Changing from acting as a "market-constructing state" to a "market-facilitating state," the Taiwan government now encourages various actors to collaborate and compete. In promoting R&D and entrepreneurial activities, government policymakers now interact more with other actors from the scientific community and the market to develop projects promoting entrepreneurialism. Instead of being involved in directing R&D and other entrepreneurial activities, the Taiwan government entrusts other public organizations such as the National Science Council (NSC), one of Taiwan's government organizations, to oversee biotech development. Working closely with the Science and Technology Advisory Group and the Biotechnology Strategic Review Board, the NSC is responsible for implementing key national science and technology projects. Many more biotech projects are directly run by commercial firms. Even though the Taiwan government still makes the rules for introducing competition in R&D and entrepreneurial activities, nonstate players like those working in the scientific community and the market actually oversee them (Chen 1997; Hsu and Chiang 2001). Since the 1990s, Taiwan has formed an increasing number of alliances, "bringing together firms, and public sector research institutions, with the added organizational input of trade associations, and catalytic financial assistance from government" (Mathews 2002, 633).

Like Hong Kong and Taiwan, the Singapore government has tried to withdraw partially from directly managing economic affairs and R&D by empowering the National Science and Technology Board (NSTB) to oversee and coordinate R&D activities (Lai 2003). Realizing that the conventional university governance model (i.e., a state-directed and centralized model) can never make Singapore's state universities entrepreneurial, the Singapore government has created the Singapore Management University (SMU), which uses an entirely new governance model. Intending to make SMU more flexible in governance and more responsive to the changing education needs of the business and commercial sectors, the Singapore government made SMU a publicly funded but privately run university. The government provided the set-up fund for SMU and established an endowment to finance its future development. According to Professor Tan Chin Tiong, SMU's provost, the newly established university has been successful in developing close relationships with the business and commercial sectors not only in Singapore but also overseas. In response to the Singapore government's university matching grant plan, SMU has been able to match the fund-raising targets set by the government. Dr. Lee Ka Shing, a famous Chinese businessman in Hong Kong, donated $HK 1 billion to SMU's endowment fund. In addition to fund-raising, SMU has maintained a close relationship with business and commercial sectors (interview, February 2005, Singapore).

In my recent fieldwork in Malaysia, I found that the Malaysian government also has recognized the importance of using neoliberal ideas and practices to reform its universities. Believing that market forces and corporate doctrines will promote good governance in higher education, university professors are strongly encouraged to move beyond their "comfort zone" to strengthen the partnerships between universities and the business and industrial sectors (interviews, April 2006, Malaysia).

Since the 1990s in China, several university academics have entered the business and industrial sectors, known as the "jumping into the sea" (venturing into the business sector) phenomenon (Mok 2000). With the strong encouragement of the state to form public-public and university-business-industry partnerships, science parks have become increasingly popular in some economically advanced areas like Shenzhen and Jiangsu. Because of the proximity of Hong Kong to Shenzhen, universities from Hong Kong have opened campuses or set up research and business operations in Shenzhen. To take advantage of China's economic opportunities, the Singapore government launched an R&D project with a local government in Suzhou. In Beijing, university-led companies have flourished in the last two decades and Zhongguan chuen, a center for university and business collaboration, has developed rapidly, becoming known as China's Silicon Valley. Similar developments can be found elsewhere in East and Southeast Asia (Morshidi 2006; Tsuruta 2006; Varghese 2004). Clearly, universities in East Asia, like their counterparts in Australia, the United States, and the United Kingdom, have begun to shift from the mission of research and teaching to the promotion of economic and social development. East Asia has begun its transformation into the "entrepreneurial university." In addition to the transformation of the universities' management and governance, the growing popularity of the global university rankings has significantly altered their research and the academic culture.

The Quest for "World-Class" Status: Climbing the World University League

Hoping to enhance their global competitiveness and catch up as "late comers" in their development, governments and universities in Asia take university rankings very seriously (Mok 2006c). Recent studies have repeatedly shown that universities in East Asia are increasingly being urged to compete internationally, and research is one of the measurements of a university's performance. Various Asian university systems also have ranked their own universities (Liu and Cheng 2005; Research Center 2005; Zhejiang University 2006). As Kathleen Lynch suggested, "Commercial rankings or league tables [can be found] not only within countries, they have also started to operate between countries" (2006, 5). These global university rankings show how market values affect how universities are assessed.

Positioning itself as a regional hub of higher education, Hong Kong stresses research, as reflected in the government's research performance–led funding formula. Since the 1990s, Hong Kong higher education has tried several research assessment exercises (RAEs), modeled on the British approach to monitoring research performance. Universities in Hong Kong have been asked to adopt different roles and missions, identify their major strengths, and develop their centers of excellence. Academics currently working in Hong Kong are urged by the government to engage in international research, to improve their teaching, and to contribute to professional and community services. In their competition with the world's top universities, Hong Kong's universities have struggled to compete for limited resources, just as universities in central Europe are having to do (Kwiek 2004). Under the threat of "publish or perish," academics in Hong Kong are choosing more carefully the journals to publish in, with international Social Science (SSCI) and Science Citation (SCI) indexed journals being popular. In the meantime, Hong Kong's university presidents and vice-chancellors are concerned with their institutions' global ranking (Chan 2007; Mok 2005e).

The Taiwan government has realized that globalization has accelerated competition among higher education institutions globally. To improve the global competitiveness of Taiwanese institutions, the Executive Yuan (the executive branch) set a policy target of making at least one university in Taiwan one of the top 100 universities in the world and making at least fifteen departments or cross-university research centers the top in Asia within the next five years (Lu 2004). With these policy objectives, the Ministry of Education and the National Science Council have jointly launched the "Programme for Promoting Academic Excellence of Universities" to improve the universities' infrastructure and encouraging research (MOE 2000). Well aware of the importance of its international position, Taiwan's higher education institutions now attach far more weight to university rankings. For instance, in the last few years, the Research Institute of Higher Education at Tamkang University has conducted university assessment studies. University league tables have been produced and subsequent reports have aroused much debate in Taiwan (Lo and Chan 2006; Lo and Weng 2005; Research Institute 2005). As in Hong Kong, research assessment has dominated academic life in Taiwan. Even though its universities established the Taiwan Social Science Citation Index (TSSCI) in order to counterbalance the pressure to publish only in SSCI journals, academics know that publishing in international journals has special weight in promotion and research evaluations (Chen and Lo 2007).

To enhance the international competitiveness of Chinese universities, the Chinese government has begun a few major projects, such as the 211 Project and the 985 Program, to enable some higher education institutions to become world-class universities. For the 211 Project, the government is attempting to one hundred universities and disciplines in the twenty-first century, with additional funding allocated to institutions of higher education to improve their teaching and research facilities. The 985 Program is intended to transform Beijing University and Tsinghua University into world-class universities by 2015 and 2011, respectively. Realizing the intensified global competition among leading universities and desiring higher rankings in global university league, the Chinese government has identified key national bases for humanities and social sciences research and established national laboratories to promote scientific research (Huang 2006). A research institute of higher education based in Shanghai recently published a report, "The Academic Ranking of World Universities," which has attracted a great deal of attention and sparked considerable debate among academics in China (Liu and Cheng 2005). In the quest for world-class universities in China, other research institutions there, like the Research Center of Chinese Scientific Evaluation of Wuhan University and Zhejiang University's College of Education, have also conducted similar kinds of research to promote university assessment and performance (Research Center 2005; Zhejiang University 2006). King-lun Ngok and Weiqing Guo (2007) critically reviewed the quest for world-class universities in China, pointing o the gap between the government's policy goals and what actually can be accomplished. They also discovered some bad practices and even corruption by academics, resulting from the strong drive to obtain world-class status.

In Japan, academics are becoming increasingly aware of global university rankings and have begun their Flagship Universities project to identify those Japanese universities that could become "world-class universities." According to Akiyoshi Yonezawa (2006), since the nineteenth century, the consistent and protracted development of Japan's higher education system has long been driven by strong national initiatives. Heavily invested in its university systems, Japanese universities dominated the top echelons in *Asia Week*'s annual "Asian University Ranking." Nonetheless, Japanese universities have fallen in only the regional and world rankings. The Japanese government has thus become very concerned about repositioning the country's universities in the rapidly changing global environment. Accordingly, the government has allocated additional resources to promote internationalization and has strongly encouraged students and academics to engage in international collaborations and exchanges (Furushiro 2006; Yonezawa 2006).

Similarly, universities in Singapore are becoming increasingly aware of their international standing. To strengthen Singapore as a regional hub of higher education, the government invited some of the world's top universities to open branch campuses in the city-state. In addition, the government has attracted leading academics to collaborate with local scholars (Mok and Tan 2004). Other Southeast Asian countries, like Malaysia, are doing the same, especially when the university system has restructured in accordance with neoliberalism. The current government in Malaysia is anxious to make its country a regional hub of higher education. The government is appointing more academics from abroad and is supporting research and teaching collaborations with overseas institutions (interviews with Professor S. Morshidi and Mr. Abdul Razak, April 2006, Malaysia).

The quest for the world class university status has a cost. Academics in Asia are pressured to publish in international peer-reviewed journals, especially when the assessment of their performance is closely linked to their publication in Science Citation Index (SCI), Social Science Citation Index (SSCI), Engineering Index (EI), and the like, all English-language journals. A growing number of Asian academics, therefore, are concerned whether it is better to publish their research findings in international or local journals. Because publishing their research findings locally would have more impact on local social and economic developments or more influence on local policy formation, some Asian academics decide to conduct more locally relevant research. Nonetheless, they may have difficulty, especially when their performance is based on international ranking. For this reason, some Asian scholars have criticized their governments for basing their performance on publishing in English-language journals while undervaluing local publications. Some scholars in China even see themselves as being prostituted by being forced to publish in international journals. Other Asian academics consider their academic freedom as being threatened by the corporate values and cultures increasingly affecting how academic research is managed (Chen and Lo 2007; Kim 2007; Petersen and Currie 2007; Vidovich, Yang, and Currie 2007). Some Asian scholars have even begun to be concerned about the rise of neoimperialism in education, while many others

Table 6.1 Number of Patents Granted by U.S. Patent Office to the Southeast Asia Region, Selected Southeast Asian Countries, and Developed Countries

	Number of Patents		Patents per 100,000 People		
	1990–1994	*2000–2004*	*1990–1994*	*2000–2004*	*% Change*
SE Asia	31	140	0.01	0.04	15.3
Indonesia	6	15	0.00	0.01	8.8
Malaysia	13	64	0.07	0.28	15.3
Philippines	6	18	0.01	0.02	10.4
Thailand	6	43	0.01	0.07	20.9
Developed countries (average)	104,170	168,017	12.88	19.58	4.3

Source: Authors' elaboration based on data from World Bank 2007, 155.

are concerned with the university's restructuring using managerialist ideas and practices, which have not empowered but constrained their academic freedom (Currie, Petersen, and Mok 2006; Lee and Gopinathan 2007; Mok 2007; Ngok and Guo 2007; Yang 2007).

Most sociologically significant, those university performance indicators skewed in favor of the Anglo-Saxon paradigm could intensify the disparities between the North and the South (Welch and Mok 2003). According to a report by the World Bank (2006), the gap between the developed economies in the West and countries in Southeast Asia widens when comparing the number of patents in the developed countries in the West with those in the developing countries in the East. Table 6.1 shows the vast disparity in patents granted to developed countries compared to those granted to Southeast Asian countries. Together with the newly industrializing countries in East Asia, the developed economies in the Northern Hemisphere account for 84 percent of all scientific articles published (World Bank 2000, 69).

Even though a growing number of academics in East Asia and Australia have managed to publish in SCI, SSCI, and EI listed journals, recent data show that higher education in Southeast Asia contributes much less to total R&D than do developed nations in the Northern Hemisphere (see tables 6.2 and 6.3).

After comparing and contrasting the scientific impact of nations, Lisa Lucas (2007) described the wide gap between the developed countries in the West

Table 6.2 Papers and Citations by Country, 1980s and 1990s

Country	Number of Papers, 1981	Number of Papers, 1995	Number of Citations, 1981–85	Number of Citations, 1993–97
Indonesia	89	310	694	3,364
Malaysia	229	587	1,332	3,450
Philippines	243	294	1,379	2,893
Thailand	373	648	2,419	8,398
Vietnam	49	192	203	1,657

Source: Authors' elaboration based on data from World Bank 2000, 125–27.

and countries in Asia according to the top 1 percent of highly cited publications between 1997 and 2001. Not surprisingly, in 2004, the top three in the global ranking went to the United States, the fifteen countries of the European Union, and the United Kingdom, with Australia and China ranking eleventh and twentieth, respectively (see table 6.4). It is clear that the gap between the Northern and Southern hemispheres will widen if we adopt the criteria determined by the Anglo-Saxon paradigm in ranking university performance worldwide (Welch 2007). More detrimentally, the overemphasis on international ranking and the quest for the world-class university status have led to shifting agendas favoring an international reputation instead of local research contributing to domestic development.

Table 6.3 Research and Development Performance by Sector

	Business	Government	Higher Education
SE Asia	51.3	22.1	15.7
Indonesia	14.3	81.1	4.6
Malaysia	65.3	20.3	14.4
Philippines	58.6	21.7	17.0
Thailand	43.9	22.5	31.0
Developed countries (average)	62.9	13.3	27.0

Source: Authors' elaboration based on data from World Bank 2007, 151.

Table 6.4 Comparing the Scientific Impact of Selected Nations

Rank	Country	Top 1 % of Highly Cited Publications, 1997–2001
1	United States	23,723
2	European Union 15	14,099
3	United Kingdom	4,831
7	Canada	2,195
10	Netherlands	1,435
11	Australia	1,049
20	China	375

Source: Authors' elaboration based on data from Lucas 2007, 3.

In sum, the restructuring of higher education toward incorporation and corporatization, coupled with the quest to become entrepreneurial and world-class universities, indicates that higher education in Asia has been transformed with a strong corporate influence, especially when neoliberal ideas and practices are increasingly dominating the higher education discourse. One point that deserves special attention is that when analyzing the impact of neoliberalism on higher education in Asia, the transformation has been driven not only by the global marketization of higher education but also by local forces. To improve the global competitiveness of their higher education systems, most universities in Asia have been restructured in a highly interventionist manner. Hence, it is not surprising that these state-run projects are aimed at improving national economic competitiveness (partly by making the universities that remain nonmarket actors competitive in quasi-market rankings and reputational arenas) (Kim 2007; Mok 2007; Tien 2006).

INTERNATIONALIZING STUDENTS' LEARNING EXPERIENCES

In addition to the international ranking of research and publications, many universities in Asia have adopted different strategies to internationalize their students' learning experiences. As a result, international student exchanges have become increasingly popular, and some Asian governments and universities offer financial assistance to students to study overseas. For instance, the governments of the PRC and Taiwan offer scholarships to graduate students to study abroad for either one semester or an entire academic year. Similarly, the Hong Kong government's University Grant Committee has designated a special fund to promote international student exchanges. Other Asian countries, such as Singapore, Malaysia, Japan, and South Korea, have similar programs. In South Korea, the Brian 21 program, a project promoting international ranking, puts much weight on students' international learning experiences (Mok 2007; Tin et al. 2005).

Reforming curricula and adopting English as the language of instruction also are part of the internationalization of Asian universities. Many Asian universities also have begun to recruit faculty members from other countries. For example, China, Hong Kong, South Korea, and Singapore offer highly competitive salaries to attract foreign professors to teach in their university systems, and some university systems, like those in the PRC, South Korea, and Taiwan have adopted English as the language of instruction in order to attract foreign students (Altbach 2004). Asian universities' curricula also have features such as internationalization, whole-person development, problem-based learning, internships, and co-op programs (Tin et al. 2005).

NEOLIBERALISM COLONIZING UNIVERSITY RESEARCH, EDUCATION, AND GOVERNANCE

The Quest for a World-Class University and Research Culture

What will be the consequences of this drive to restructure and to gain world-class status, which can be achieved by only a very few institutions in each country, as Altbach (2004) points out? There inevitably will be many losers. The United Kingdom has closed departments in different disciplines (particularly, but not exclusively, in laboratory-based disciplines) at various universities as a consequence of low research assessment exercise (RAE) grades or the loss of funds to maintain them (Jobbins 2005). In the Netherlands, the lower-tier higher education institutions responsible for professional education have struggled to keep pace with the reforms of the higher education institutions (Litjens 2005). It seems inevitable that students in publicly funded institutions in countries like Germany will lose their right to free tuition, as they already have in many other countries (European Commission Representation 2006). In Europe as a whole, the European Commission has been discussing ways in which European universities can compete worldwide collectively as well as individually to raise their overall profile. In East Asia, several countries have restructured their higher education systems to achieve world-class positioning and have used a series of internal ranking exercises to strengthen their global position.

Concentrating funds on research (as a means of ensuring "world class status" for the few) affects the development of national higher education systems in many ways. The national role of universities may be ignored in favor of an international role (as in East Asia where publication in English-language journals has taken precedence over publication in other languages). In regard to the related quest for an international academic labor market, Marek Kwiek noted the problems faced by the central European universities in funding these larger public higher education systems (Kwiek 2004). A report for Universities UK, "Funding Research Diversity," compares regional differences in England, Wales, Scotland, and Northern Ireland (Adams and Smith 2003). Using research assessment exercise grades, citation indexes, publication rates, and rates of staffing, the report demonstrates the disparities and also how the further concentration of research resources might affect levels of research achievement. The report found overwhelmingly that three regions in southeast England, including London, had the highest number of departments rated 5/5 in the RAE. If research resources from the RAE continue to be devoted to them, then the universities in these areas will be able to obtain more funding, whereas places like Wales and the East Midlands would lose dramatically, and places in the West Midlands and northeastern England would suffer fewer losses (Adams and Smith 2003). The substantial losses of some regions would result, they argue, in "reduced regional research capacity [that] will have knock-on effects for regional economic performance and the capacity for technology innovation" (Adams and Smith 2004, 23). The negative effects of the further concentration of research resources cannot be overstated (Adams and Smith 2004; Association of University Teachers 2003).

This also is likely to be the case for other countries. Even though the governments of many European and East Asian countries may believe that only their quest for world-class status matters, some of the institutions may disagree. At the same time, it is often difficult or impossible for institutions in any one country to opt out of the quest altogether, as "at some stage and for some important purpose, every institution is going to rely on the strength and reputation of the system as a whole" (Watson 2006, 15). Each country restructuring its higher education systems also must consider where such ideas come from and how well they work in different contexts. Opposing the quest for "world-class" universities, some academics in China not surprisingly feel forced into "prostitution," especially when they are being ranked by the internationally refereed publications while local or national publications are getting less recognition (Vidovich, Yang, and Currie 2007).

The most damaging part of the quest for world-class university movement is the creation of a research culture that promotes "instrumental" and "short-sighted" values. Under the pressure to publish in internationally recognized venues such as SCI and SSCI journal articles, many academics in Asia now pay no attention to the university's public functions. Believing that it is important to be published only in internationally leading journals or by major university presses in the United States and the United Kingdom, academics in Asia are becoming less interested in domestic affairs and social issues. With the emphasis on corporate values in research, the role of public universities in developing the civil, political, social, and cultural institutions of the local or global society has been neglected. Similar to the experiences in the United States or in Europe, the disincentives to being public intellectuals and sharing ideas with the public in one's society or outside the universities have been growing. And since the engagement in public debate in newspapers and in community actions and movements, policy research is no longer considered important (Baker et al. 2004; Brock-Utne 2005; Bruce 2006; Giroux 2002). Therefore, the public university has systematically devalued dialogue with nonacademic persons and bodies; and academics no longer value policy-relevant and applied research, as it cannot give them international recognition.

Still worse, many Asian scholars whom I have met and worked with in the last decade have continued to complain about the difficulty in finding colleagues even for engaging in social activities, simply because most of them prefer concentrating on their research. Ironically, many of them see one another only at international conferences. Indeed, many of the core Asian values related to social harmony, mutual respect, and the emphasis on collective interests are being threatened by this more individualistic and instrumental research culture. Therefore, we need to ask the following questions: Can the standards and practices commonly available in the West be adapted to Asian traditions and cultures? Would the adoption of these Western practices be distorted outside their usual context? Most important, would there be only one "international standard" as defined solely by, or even dominated by, the Anglo-Saxon paradigm? Who should be involved in defining these "international standards"? Outside their usual context, the adoption of such global strategies or global reform measures may prove to be counterproductive.

After all, the universities' existing assessment criteria are narrow and selective in focus. They are driven primarily by corporate and commercial interests but fail to provide comprehensive reviews of university performance. Moreover, the students studying in these universities may not really receive a "world-class" education. As Jeanette Taylor (2001), David Dill (2003) and Maarja Soo (2003), and Rosemary Deem, Ka-ho Mok, and Lisa Lucas (2006) have pointed out, although rankings of universities are proliferating, they do more harm than good to university research, since these rankings direct academics away from many of the core values that are central to university work, such as quality teaching, outreach, inclusion, and research that enhances humanity and social development.

THE INTERNATIONALIZATION OF UNIVERSITY EDUCATION AND NEOIMPERIALISM IN EDUCATION

The globalizing economy and the ascendancy of neoliberalism have significantly shaped the design of university curricula. In addition to the university education's being oriented toward a market-driven curriculum and an emphasis on vocation, many higher education institutions have either enlarged their class size or adopted new technologies to promote online learning to reduce costs but maximize profits. Thus, interactions between staff and students are becoming less important, particularly with the introduction of more corporate principles and practices. The increasing criticism of digital diploma mills and distance education is not surprising (Arnone 2002; Noble 2001; Trend 2001; Young 2002). Substituting technology for pedagogy not only standardizes and rationalizes course materials but also contributes to the problems of "instrumental rationality," which leads to "forms of social engineering that authorize actions that become increasingly 'reasonable' and dehumanizing at the same time" (Zygmunt Bauman, cited in Giroux, 2002, 29). Another trend in the "standardization" of the university education is the internationalization of higher education. In the last decade, international student and staff exchanges, the recruitment of more foreign students, and the adoption of English as the language of instruction also have become popular in universities in both the East and West (de Wit 2006; Mok 2007). Comparing the internationalization of universities in the West and the East, I would argue that the major drive for internationalizing universities in Australia, the United Kingdom, and the United States is to recruit foreign students in order to generate more income. But the quest for the internationalization of Asian universities is different, as it is to catch up with international trends in order to obtain a better position in the global university rankings (Mok 2006c).

Believing that international perspectives are important to a university education, higher education institutions in Asia have actively promoted the internationalization of universities. For example, in 2003, after Hong Kong's universities completed another Teaching and Learning Quality Processes Review, the assessment panel began emphasizing a "student-learning culture," which makes "problem-based learning" central to teaching and learning. Then, beyond educating students as good learners, the panel began stressing the development of the whole person. Instead of requiring students to acquire more information, they should engage in self-directed learning, working in teams, and becoming more independent. Students' international outlook and problem-solving skills are being enhanced through international exchanges, internships, work placements, and practicum (Mok 2005c).

To prepare and equip students for globalization, the Singapore government has reviewed the design of its universities' curricula and now emphasizes a broad-based cross-disciplinary university education (*Straits Times*, August 13, 1999). More innovative ways of teaching and assessment have been introduced, with a focus on creative and critical thinking. Meanwhile, the role of universities in knowledge creation has been strengthened in postgraduate and research education. By enhancing their research capabilities and engaging in more multidisciplinary research initiatives, universities can be a significant resource of new ideas and inventions with the potential for commercial applications (Lee and Gopinathan 2001). Because "internationalization" is one of the major agendas adopted by higher education systems in Asia, universities in not only Hong Kong and Singapore but also Taiwan, South Korea, Japan, and even the PRC are anxious to expand their international student exchange programs (Tin et al. 2005). In addition, they are admitting foreign students or sending their own students abroad. Some scholars believe that study abroad and student exchanges are powerful internationalizers of higher education (Burn 2002) and that combining education and work in another country greatly enriches students' learning experiences.

Japan has actively promoted the internationalization of higher education through exchanges of students and staff. According to the Japan Association for Student Support Organization (JASSO), 121,812 international students studied at Japanese universities and colleges in 2005, and 35,379 students studied at Japanese-language educational institutions in 2004 (JASSO 2005). According to a report entitled "Development of New Policies for International Student Exchanges" published by the Central Council of Education, the Japanese government will promote more international student exchanges in the future. Universities in

Japan have also taken international ranking very seriously. In the last two years, I have been involved in "developing evaluation criteria to assess the internationalization of universities." Foreign advisers were invited to join the research team in Japan in an international symposium to draw up criteria for evaluating the international dimension of Japanese universities (Osaka University Report 2006). Despite its rich cultural foundation, Japan is now trying to find an appropriate policy for using English in teaching and learning.

Many Chinese universities now collaborate with foreign institutions for research and joint programs. International exchanges of students and staff are popular as well. For example, Chinese account for the largest number of foreign students in the United Kingdom. Some of the leading Chinese universities have begun to adopt English as one of the languages of instruction. For instance, in 2004, of the 4,000 undergraduate programs at Zhejing University, one of China's top universities in China, more than 160 were taught in two languages (Gu, cited in Huang 2006, 5), and other universities have started teaching biology, information science, new materials, and international trade and law in English (Huang 2006). In Taiwan and Hong Kong, too, teaching courses in English, sending students abroad, and transnational education are becoming increasingly popular (Lo and Weng 2005; Song and Tai 2006; Yang 2006).

It is clear that in Asia, internationalizing higher education has considerably shaped both the universities' curricula and the students' learning experiences. Nonetheless, "internationalization" in Asia is not merely following American or Anglo-Saxon standards and practices. Although the academic communities in Europe and the United States have been regarded as more "advanced" than the Asian counterparts, higher education institutions in general and academics in particular must determine to what extent and in what way the so-called good practices of the West can really be adapted to non-Western education systems. Even though many of the Asian societies discussed here that were colonies before World War II and, after the war, gained independence, many of them still act like colonies in practice, since most of them were strongly influenced by Anglo-Saxon standards or ideologies. Similar to the debates regarding the use of English for publication purposes in foreign journals, Asian scholars and students find it difficult to accept that the publications written in their own language are worth less (Chen and Lo 2007). I am not belittling the importance of English as an international language that can enhance communication in the international community. Instead, the issue is undermining the importance of local languages. As Kathleen Lynch observed,

> If public interests are to be saved, academics need to publish in their own countries and in their own languages, especially in fields like the humanities and social sciences where so much of what needs to be understood is local as well as global. For this to happen, such work needs to be rewarded not sanctions. (2006, 9)

Using English as the language of instruction should be determined by academics. But I have observed that an increasing number of universities have opted to make English the language for teaching and learning and that those academics and students who do not use it will be penalized.

The problems that Asian university systems are confronting today are the introduction of English as the language of instruction; the adoption of curricula from Australia, the United Kingdom, and the United States; study abroad programs and international exchanges; and the quest for the world-class universities as defined by the Anglo-Saxon world. These problems have not only created a new "dependency culture" but also reinforced the American-dominated "hegemony," particularly in regard to university rankings, citation indexes, and the kinds of research that count as high status. Since the nineteenth century, Asian societies seem to have treated "internationalization" as "Westernization" and "modernization" as "Americanization" (Mok 2007). Analyzing such "internationalization experiences" in light of Kazuhiro Ebuchi's (1997) framework, "internationalization" could be interpreted as an "intransitive verb" or a "transitive verb." The concept of "internationalization as a transitive verb" in English "is a historical concept, which emerged from a nation with 'hegemony' in the international order, while that of 'internationalization as an intransitive verb' is one from a 'smaller nation' which was forced to follow a 'larger nation'" (Ebuchi 1997, 7). Thus not only European but also Asian states should be aware of the differences between policy learning and policy copying. If we copy policy practices without proper adaptation and careful contextualization, we may encounter problems. In Asia, these may be a process of recolonization or neoimperialism, resulting in reproducing learning experiences that do not fit into the specific cultural and political environment.

CORPORATE GOVERNANCE AND THE UNDERMINING OF ACADEMIC FREEDOM

The forces of neoliberalism and corporate culture have gained ascendancy in transforming university governance in the United States, the United Kingdom,

Australia, Europe, and Asia (Brehony and Deem 2005a; 2005b; Bruce 2006; Chan 2007; Marginson 2006; Marginson and Considine 2000). Although the strategies of incorporation and corporatization used by universities to improve their governance and management efficiency have not been used often by universities in the West, they have become far more common in the East. Even the governments of socialist countries like China and Vietnam have adopted similar strategies to streamline university administration and promote a corporate culture in the university's governance. With this mind, Michael Crow, president of Arizona State University, declared that the professors now should be labeled "academic entrepreneurs." Believing that the university is a knowledge enterprise, he called on his fellow professors to expand what it means to be a knowledge enterprise by using knowledge as a form of venture capital (Blumenstyk 2001, A29). As universities rely more on financial support from the business and commercial sectors, commercial interests and corporate influences in turn affect how the universities are governed. Therefore, "academic titles not only signal wealthy corporate donors' influence on universities, but have also served as billboards for corporations" (Giroux 2002, 14) while universities are increasingly governed and managed by managers with corporate leadership experience rather than by academics displaying intellectual reach and civic courage.

With such a corporate governance culture in place, broader considerations of ethics, equity, and justice will no longer be important. When the ideas of economic rationalism and managerialism are transformed into practices, the cost accounting principles of efficiency, calculability, predictability, and control of the corporate order will undermine the academic traditions that value collegial leadership and academic freedom. After the appointment of James Carlin, a multimillionaire and former successful insurance executive, as the chairman of the Massachusetts State Board of Education, he gave a speech to the Greater Boston Chamber of Commerce attacking the academic professoriate. He argued that colleges and universities should be downsized and follow successful corporations in their management. In addition, he called for the end of the tenure system and openly declared that democratic governance was not appropriate to the university. Finally, he emphasized the commercialization of knowledge production and research in universities (Carlin, cited in Honan 1998, 4A33).

Carlin's anti-intellectualism is popular in Asia, where university presidents and vice-chancellors act like CEOs, and university governance emphasizes efficiency and "accountancy." My study of academic freedom in Hong Kong clearly shows that university academics feel their academic autonomy being threatened by the growing influences of marketization of higher education and the prominence of corporate governance in universities (Currie, Petersen, and Mok 2006). Similarly, the "empowerment" of public universities' financial flexibility in Singapore, China, and Taiwan through the policy of decentralization has not made academics feel more "liberated" and "emancipated." Instead, Asian academics complain about "recentralization" and "reregulation" through various forms of quality assurance and accountability exercises, and they regard the kind of decentralization policy implemented in the university sector as a form of "centralized decentralization" (Chan 2002; Chen and Lo 2007; Lee and Gopinathan 2007; Mok 2003; Mok and Tan 2004). In short, the ascendancy of neoliberalism and the growing prominence of corporate culture in university governance have undermined academic freedom and muted academia's critical voices. To uphold the ideals of public universities, we should challenge the discourse dominated by neoliberalism, by bringing the "public" back to the university education, research and governance.

BRINGING THE "PUBLIC" BACK TO THE PUBLIC UNIVERSITIES

Redefining the Regime of Truth and Connecting to the Broader Public Sphere

As academics working in the university sector, we should be the most knowledgeable and qualified people to determine the way that the university's research, education, and administration are managed. To turn back the excessive market forces and corporate influences on higher education, academics should organize as a united community to redefine the regime of truth. Since "the university is no longer a quiet place to teach and do scholarly work at a measured pace and contemplate the universe as in centuries past" (Skilbeck 2001, 6), academics should bear the social responsibility of transforming the sector by revitalizing the "publicness" of contemporary universities. We have sent out clear warning signals that public universities are in deep crisis with the corporate culture and neoliberal practices continuing to capture the hearts and minds of academics and students, especially when higher education has become "commodified." In his 2005 article entitled "Knowledge Commons or Economic Engine—What's a University For?" Bryn Williams-Jones raises a self-reflective question. By embracing the notion of the entrepreneurial university, the knowledge commons has been seriously threatened. Since the true "soul of the university" lies in "communities of scholars," academics should extend their mission beyond their individual private good (Kirp 2004).

Because many university presidents have been fatally compromised by business, "faculty members are in the best position to appreciate academic values and insist on their observance" (Bok 2003, 189). As academics, we should guard against the growing commercialization of higher education by promoting students' idealism and enhancing their engagement in society and politics. To prevent students from believing that universities are continuing to abandon academic values and scholarly pursuits to openly and enthusiastically function as entrepreneurial, ferociously competitive, profit-making corporations, faculty members should actively engage in caring public affairs and social issues (Harkavy 2006). According to Calhoun (1992), contemporary universities should be working on behalf of humankind, and therefore he emphasizes the importance of producing public goods. Following Habermas, Calhoun calls for public universities to communicate with the broader public sphere beyond the university. Beyond the agendas dominated by corporate interests, public academic work is shaped by both a broad public discourse and more specialized policymaking by public agencies. To Calhoun, "the university has a viable credentialing system ensuring that those inside the public conversation are qualified to contribute" (Bruce 2006, 52).

Like Calhoun, Brian Pusser (2005) proposes that the university itself is a public sphere that provides institutional space for reasoned argument and differing values. Similarly, Ellen Willis notes that the university "is the only institution of any size that still provides cultural dissidents with a platform" (1999, 27). Henry Giroux argues that higher education must be embraced as a democratic sphere because it enables students to learn the power of questioning authority, thereby recovering the ideals of engaged citizenship, reaffirming the importance of the public good, and expanding their capacities to make a difference (2002, 31). Following the ideas of Noam Chomsky, Edward Said, and Pierre Bourdieu in regard to public intellectuals, academics should engage in a permanent critique of all abuses of power and authority, in order "to create the social conditions for the collective production of realist utopias" (Bourdieu 2000, 42–43). As the famous scholar-official Fan Zhongyan (989–1052) suggested, the important responsibility of intellectuals is "to be the first to worry about the worries of the world, the last to take pleasure in its pleasures." This quotation demonstrates the strong conviction of the Chinese intelligentsia, who were both highly educated and often concerned themselves with ideas and new developments, especially in the arts and politics. Following the Confucian literati tradition, intellectuals in contemporary China still act as the country's social conscience, and therefore many of them continue to question the ruling class and openly criticize the corruption and graft of their times. Instead of being colonized by the ideas and practices of neoliberalism, Asian scholars must revive such traditions by revitalizing the public functions and critical roles of intellectuals (Marinelli 2007). Only by engaging with the wider society by offering policy alternatives based on solid and relevant local research can academics shape local economic, social and political debates and eventually influence policymaking.

Shaping Knowledge Commons and Promoting Civic Responsibility

Fighting against the dominance of neoliberalism, the university and the academia should redesign their curricula and pedagogy. In his comparative study of lifelong learning in Asia, Wing-on Lee (2007) argues that although the lifelong learning slogan demonstrates rhetorical ideals, a closer scrutiny of the curricula promoting lifelong learning reveals simply an economic agenda. According to Lee, "the liberalisation ideals and values related to lifelong learning are only seen as an instrumental means to achieve economic ends" (W. Lee 2007, 11). Like Williams-Jones, Lee therefore calls for academics to bring back to curricula the missing values such as democracy and active citizenship and to make higher education part of a broader battle over the defense of public goods and social justice. As Lee Shulman, president of the Carnegie Foundation for the Advancement of teaching, argues in his *Educating Citizens*, a democratic society requires an "educated citizenry blessed with virtue as well as wisdom" (Shulman 2003, viii).

As social research has clearly suggested, the marketization of education has resulted in declining education standards and widened social and educational inequalities (Bok 2003; Dill 2003; Lauder et al. 1999; Mok and Lo 2007). Academics and universities have a moral obligation to question the hegemony of the market and to stand outside the market mechanism (Gibbs 2001). Instead of adhering to the WTO's directive to make higher education a tradable service, the international academic community should encourage individuals and groups to participate in democratic, civil, and cultural life; to combat racism and xenophobia; to expand diversity; and to build social cohesion as proposed by the European Association for the Education of Adults (EAEA 2001). As "change agents," academics have the ability and responsibility to reveal the dangers of corporate marketing and communicate to students and the wider community about the ideals of universities and the importance of universities' public functions (Bruce

2006; Doring 2002). To realize Dewey's proposal for a participatory democracy as the Good Society (Dewey 1969), the university can never deny its role as the agency to implement it (Harper 1905 cited in Harkavy 2006, 7).

In view of the growing impact of globalization, some Asian university systems have started reforming their curricula by encouraging their university students to become responsible global citizens. For instance, the Faculty of Social Sciences of the University of Hong Kong (HKU) has taken the ideas of "social entrepreneurship" and "global citizenship" very seriously. It now encourages its students to participate in international student exchange programs so as to have more exposure to other cultures and to develop a better understanding of the world. In addition, they also should serve the local community. Teaching university students to become responsible global citizens is not unique to Hong Kong. Other higher education systems such as Singapore's put more weight on "whole-person development" in university education.

THE BALANCE BETWEEN MARKET FUNDAMENTALISM AND DEMOCRATIC VALUES

This chapter examined how neoliberalism has penetrated the higher education institutions in Asia by influencing the way that university education, research, and governance is managed. Like universities in the West, Asian universities are undergoing significant transformations, particularly since corporate values and market-driven practices began dominating higher education. I also discussed the roles of academics and public universities in engaging in the wider society by shaping the public discourse and challenging the existing arrangements, which are primarily determined by the principles and practices of neoliberalism. The university sector and academia should work closely together to expand the public sphere in upholding social justice and other related values. As academics, we should protect and advance the traditions of critical intellectuals, as Bourdieu proposed. Our success will depend on the relationship between intellectuals and their social connections in the field. Although the field is influenced by the concerns and conflicts of the larger society, its logic is its own (Bourdieu 1971, 1985). Ideas can never be totally separated from their place in institutions, so their practices and social relations must be closely related to a broader academic background. Following this reasoning, I see belief systems as mixtures of good reasoning, inherited conventions, and the orientations perpetuated by institutions, practices, and social relations, along with rational, traditional, and ideological elements. Extending intellectual influences to the wider public sphere, academics should preserve their critical intellectual tradition by forming a cohesive social group to engage with the broader society. Even though it will be difficult to turn away entirely from marketization and corporate influences, the university sector in general and the academic community in particular should guard against the continual colonization of the higher education sector by neoliberalism. Most important, the university should strike "a balance between democratic values and market fundamentalism, between identities founded on democratic principles and identities steeped in forms of competitive, self- interested individualism that celebrate their own material and ideological advantages" (Giroux 2002, 33).

NOTES

Some of the materials used in this chapter are based on another paper by the author presented at the Consortium of Higher Education Researchers Conference, Kassel, Germany, September 7–9, 2006.

1. When talking about "Asia" in this chapter, I am referring to Asian countries and societies that have tried to transform their higher education systems in accordance with neoliberalist doctrines and practices. Some of the Asian societies reviewed in this chapter are city-states like Hong Kong and Singapore, and others are nation-states. The following discussion focuses on more economically and socially developed as well as developing countries. One criterion for selecting these case studies is related to a similar approach that these Asian states and societies, of both socialist/communist and countries, adopted to change their higher education systems based on neoliberalism.

REFERENCES

Adams, J., and D. Smith. 2003. "Funding Research Diversity: The Impact of Further Concentration on University Research Performance and Regional Research Capacity." Available at bookshop.universitiesuk.ac.uk/downloads/ funding_tech.pdf (accessed July 7, 2007).

——. 2004. *Research and the Regions: An Overview of the Distribution of Research in UK Regions, Regional Research Capacity and Links Between Strategic Research Partners.* Oxford: Higher Education Policy Institute.

Altbach, P. 2004. "The Costs and Benefits of World Class Universities." *Academe*, January/February. Available at http://www.aaup.org/publications/Academe/2004/04jf/04jfaltb.htm (accessed March 17, 2007).

Arnone, M. 2002. "Army's Huge Distance-Education Effort Wins Many Supporters in Its First Year." *Chronicle of Higher Education*, February 8, 2002, A33–A35.

Association of University Teachers. 2003. "The Risk to Research in Higher Education in England." Available at http://www.aut.org.uk/index.cfm?articleid =591 (accessed July 7, 2007).

Baker, J., K. Lynch, S. Cantillon, and J. Walsh. 2004. *Equality: From Theory to Action*. London: Palgrave Macmillan.

Blumenstyk, G. 2001. "Chasing the Rainbow: A Venture Capitalist on the Trail of University-Based Companies." *Chronicle of Higher Education*, March 15, 2002, A28–A32.

Bok, D. 2003. *Universities in the Marketplace: The Commercialization of Higher Education*. Princeton, N.J.: Princeton University Press.

Bourdieu, P. 1971. "Intellectual Field and Creative Project." In *Knowledge and Control: New Directions for the Sociology of Education*, ed. M. F. D. Young, 161–88. London: Collin-Macmillan.

——. 1985. "The Genesis of the Concepts of Habitas and of Field." *Sociocriticism* 2: 11–24.

——. 2000. "For a Scholarship of Commitment." *Profession* 42: 43.

Brehony, K., and R. Deem. 2005a. "Challenging the Post-Fordist / Flexible Organisation Thesis: The Case of Reformed Educational Organizations." *British Journal of Sociology of Education* 26(3): 395–414.

——. 2005b. "Management as Ideology: The Case of 'New Managerialism' in Higher Education." *Oxford Review of Education* 31(2): 213–31.

Brock-Utne, B. 2005. "In Whose Language Is Whose Knowledge Presented in Africa and in Europe?" Paper presented to the GENIE Summer Institute, Aalborg, Denmark, July 5–7.

Bruce, V. 2006. "Markets and Higher Education: A Regime of Truth?" *Irish Educational Studies* 25(2): 141–54.

Burn, B. 2002. "The Curriculum as a Global Domain." *Journal of Studies in International Education* 6(3): 253–61.

Calhoun, C. 1992. "Introduction: Habermas and the Public Sphere." In *Habermas and the Public Sphere*, ed. Craig Calhoun, 359–76. Cambridge, Mass.: MIT Press.

Cerny, P. 1997. "Paradoxes of the Competition State: The Dynamics of Political Globalization." *Government and Opposition* 32: 251–74.

Chan, D. 2002. "Policy Implications of Adopting a Managerial Approach in Education." In *Globalization and Education: The Quest for Quality Education in Hong Kong*, ed. K. Mok and D. Chan, 243–58. Hong Kong: Hong Kong University Press.

——. 2007. "Global Agenda, Local Response: Changing Education Governance in Hong Kong's Higher Education." *Globalization, Societies & Education* 5 (1): 109–24.

Chan, D., and J. Tan. 2006. "Privatization and the Rise of Direct Subsidy Scheme Schools and Independent Schools in Hong Kong and Singapore." Paper presented at the Asia Pacific Educational Research Association 2006 International Conference, Hong Kong, November 28–30.

Chen, D., and Y. Lo 2007. "Critical Reflections of the Approaches to Quality in Taiwan's Higher Education." *Journal of Comparative Asian Development* 6 (1): 165–86.

Chen, S. H. 1997. "Decision-Making in Research and Development Collaboration." *Research Policy* 26(1): 121–35.

Chou, P. 2006. "Taiwan's Higher Education at the Crossroad: Implications for China." Paper presented at the senior seminar, Education for 2020 Project of East-West Center, Honolulu, September 6–12.

Currie, J., C. Petersen, and K. Mok. 2006. *Academic Freedom in Hong Kong*. Lanham, Md.: Lexington Books.

Deem, R., K. Mok and L. Lucas. 2006. "East Meets West Meets 'World-Class': What Is a 'World-Class' University in the Context of Europe and Asia and Does It Matter?" Paper presented at the Consortium of Higher Education Researchers Conference, Kassel, Germany, September 7–9.

Dewey, J. 1969. "The Ethics of Democracy." In *The Early Works of John Dewey, 1882–1898*, vol. 1. Carbondale: Southern Illinois University Press.

de Wit, H. 2006. "Quality Assurance of Internationalization." Paper presented at the Osaka Conference on Internationalization of Universities, Osaka, January 13–14.

Dill, D. D. 2003. "Allowing the Market to Rule: The Case for the United States." *Higher Education Quarterly* 57 (2): 136–57.

Dill, D. D., and M. Soo. 2005. "Academic Quality, League Tables and Public Policy: A Cross-national Analysis of University Ranking Systems." *Higher Education* 49: 495–533.

Doring, A. 2002. "Challenges to the Academic Role of Change." *Journal of Further and Higher Education* 26(2): 139–57.

Drahos, P., and R. Jospeh. 1995. "The Telecommunications and Investment in the Great Supranational Regulatory Game." *Telecommunications Policy* 188: 619–35.

Ebuchi, K. 1997. *Study of the Internationalization of Universities*. Tokyo: Tamagawa University Press.

Etzkowitz, H. 2003. "Research Groups as 'Quasi-Firms': The Invention of the Entrepreneurial University." *Research Policy* 21: 109–21.

EAEA (European Association for the Education of Adults). 2001. "EAEA's Policy Statement About Lifelong Learning in Europe." Available at http://www.kaapeli-fi/~vsy/eaea/doc/memppol.html (accessed January 12, 2007).

European Commission Representation in the United Kingdom. 2006. Report on Seminar "Delivering on the Modernisation Agenda for Universities; Education, Research and Innovation." London: European Commission Representation in the United Kingdom.

Fraenkel, E. 1941. *The Dual State.* Trans. from German by E. A. Shils, in collaboration with E. Lowenstein and K. Knorr. Oxford: Oxford University Press.

Furushiro, N., ed. 2006. *Final Report of Developing Evaluation Criteria to Assess the Internationalization of Universities.* Osaka: Osaka University.

Gibbs, P. 2001. "Higher Education as a Market: A Problem or Solution?" *Studies in Higher Education* 26 (1): 85–94.

Gill, S. 1995. "Globalization, Market Civilization and Disciplinary Neoliberalism." *Millennium* 24 (3): 399–423.

Giroux, H. 2002. "Neoliberalism, Corporate Culture. And the Promise of Higher Education: The University as a Democratic Public Sphere." *Harvard Educational Review* 72 (4): 1–52.

Gueno, A. 1998. "The Internationalisation of European Universities: A Return to Medieval Roots." *Minerva* 36 (3): 253–70.

Harkavy, I. 2006. "The Role of Universities in Advancing Citizenship and Social Justice in the 21st Century." *Education, Citizenship and Social Justice* 1 (1): 5–37.

Herman, E., and R. McChesney. 1997. *The Global Media: The New Missionaries of Global Capitalism.* Washington, D.C.: Cassell.

Honan, W. 1998. "The Ivory Tower Under Siege." *New York Times,* January 4, 1998, 4A33.

Hsu, C-W., and H-C. Chiang. 2001. "The Government Strategy for the Upgrading of Industrial Technology in Taiwan." *Technovation* 21 (2): 123–32.

Huang, F. 2006. "Difference in the Context of Internationalization by Region: China." In *Final Report of Developing Evaluation Criteria to Assess the Internationalization of Universities,* ed. N. Furushiro, 15–23. Osaka: Osaka University.

JASSO (Japan Student Services Organization). 2005. *International Students in Japan at a Glance in 2005.* Tokyo: JASSO.

Jayasuriya, K. 2000. "Authoritarian Liberalism, Governance and the Emergence of the Regulatory State in Post-Crisis East Asia." In *Politics and Markets in the Wake of the Asian Crisis,* ed., R. Robertson et al., 99–115. London: Routledge.

Jobbins, D. 2005. "Moving to a Global Stage: A Media View." *Higher Education in Europe* 30 (2): 137–45.

Jordana, J., and D. Levi-Faur. 2005. "Preface: The Making of a New Regulatory Order." *Annuals of the American Academy of Political and Social Science* 598: 1–6.

Kim, T. 2007. Restructuring Higher Education in South Korea: Policy and Practice—The Public-Private Problem." *Journal of Comparative Asian Development* 6 (1): 87–106.

Kirp, D. L. 2004. *Shakespeare, Einstein, and the Bottom Line: The Marketing of Higher Education*. Cambridge, Mass.: Harvard University Press.

Kwiek, M. 2004. "The Emergent Educational Policies Under Scrutiny. The Bologna Process from a Central European Perspective." *European Educational Research Journal* 3 (4): 759–76.

Lai, P. S. 2003. "Report on Entrepreneurship Environment in Singapore." Available at http://www.mit.edu (accessed September 10, 2007).

Lauder, H., et al. 1999. *Trading in Futures—Why Markets in Education Don't Work*. Buckingham: University of Dublin.

Lee, H. 2005. "Major Issues of University Education Policy in Hong Kong." *Asia Pacific Education Review* 6 (2): 103–12.

Lee, H., and S. Gopinathan. 2001. "Centralized Decentralization of Higher Education in Singapore." *Education and Society* 19 (3): 79–96.

——. 2005. "Reforming University Education in Hong Kong and Singapore." In *Globalization and Higher Education in East Asia*, ed. K. Mok and R. James, 56–98. New York: Marshall Cavendish Academic.

——. 2007. "University Restructuring in Singapore: Amazing or a Maze." *Journal of Comparative Asian Development* 6 (1): 107–42.

Lee, M. N. N. 2004. *Restructuring Higher Education in Malaysia*. Penang: School of Educational Studies, Universiti Sains Malaysia.

Lee, W. 2007. "Lifelong Learning in Asia: Eclectic Concepts, Rhetorical Ideals, and Missing Values: Implications for Values Education." Paper presented at the Biannual Conference of Comparative Education Society of Asia, Hong Kong, January 8–10.

Levi-Faur, D. 1998. "The Competition State as a Neo-Mercantilist State: Understanding the Restructuring of National and Global Telecommunications." *Journal of Socio-Economics* 27 (6): 655–86.

Litjens, J. 2005. "The Europeanisation of Higher Education in the Netherlands." *European Educational Research Journal* 4 (3): 208–18.

Liu, N., and Ying Cheng. 2005. "Academic Ranking of World Universities." *Higher Education in Europe* 30 (2): 127–36.

Lo, Y., and D. Chan. 2006. "The Impact of Globalization on Higher Education in Taiwan and Mainland China." Paper presented at the International Conference on GDPism and Risk: Challenges for Social Development and Governance in East Asia, Bristol, UK, July 12–13.

Lo, Y. W., and F. Weng. 2005. "Taiwan's Responses to Globalization: Decentralization and Internationalization of Higher Education." In *Globalization and Higher Education in East Asia*, ed. K. Mok and R. James, 137–56. New York: Marshall Cavendish Academic.

Lu, M. L. 2004. "The Blueprint and Competitiveness of Taiwan's Higher Education." Paper presented at Cross Strait Seminar on Review and Prospect of the Policy of University Excellence, Taiwan, March 25–26.

Lucas, L. 2007. "Academic Freedom and Research Evaluation and Funding Policies: Comparative Perspectives." Paper presented at the Symposium on Academic Freedom, Bristol, UK, June 13.

Lynch, K. 2006. "Neo-liberalism and Marketisation: The Implications for Higher Education." *European Educational Research Journal* 5 (1): 1–17.

Marginson, S. 2006. "Putting 'Public' Back into the Public University." *Thesis Eleven* 84: 44–59.

Marginson, S., and M. Considine. 2000. *The Enterprise University: Power, Governance and Reinvention in Australia.* Cambridge: Cambridge University Press.

Marinelli, M. 2007. "Intellectual Intersections: Negotiating Identity and Autonomy Between the State and the Public." Paper presented at the Symposium on Academic Freedom, Bristol, UK, June 13.

Mathews, J. A. 2002. "The Origins and Dynamics of Taiwan's R&D Consortia." *Research Policy* 31 (4): 633–51.

Min, W. 2004. "Chinese Higher Education: The Legacy of the Past and the Context of the Future." In *Asian Universities: Historical Perspectives and Contemporary Challenges,* ed. P. Altbach and T. Umakoshi, 53–84. Baltimore: Johns Hopkins University Press.

MOE (Ministry of Education), Taiwan. 2000. *List of Projects for the First Round of the Program for Promoting Academic Excellence of Universities.* Taipei: Ministry of Education.

Mok, K. 2000. *Social and Political Development in Post-Reform China.* Basingstoke: Palgrave Macmillan.

——, ed. 2003. *Centralization and Decentralization: Educational Reforms and Changing Governance in Chinese Societies.* Dordrecht: Kluwer Academic Publishers, and Hong Kong: Comparative Education Research Centre, University of Hong Kong.

——. 2005a. "Fostering Entrepreneurship: Changing Role of Government and Higher Education Governance in Hong Kong." *Research Policy* 34: 537–54.

——. 2005b. "Globalization and Educational Restructuring: University Merging and Changing Governance in China." *Higher Education* 50: 57–88.

——. 2005c. "Globalization, Internationalization and Academic Exchange: Experience of Higher Education in Hong Kong." In *Academic Exchange and Educational Modernization,* ed. Z. P. Tin et al., 15–26. Hangzhou: Zhejiang University Press.

——. 2005d. "Pro-Competition Policy Tools and State Capacity: Corporatization of Public Universities in Hong Kong and Singapore." *Policy & Society* 24 (3): 1–26.

——. 2005e. "The Quest for World Class University: Quality Assurance and International Benchmarking." *Quality Assurance in Education* 13 (4): 277–304.

——. 2006a. *Education Reform and Education Policy in East Asia*. London: Routledge.

——. 2006b. "Varieties of Regulatory Regimes in Asia: The Liberalization of the Higher Education Market in Hong Kong, Singapore and Malaysia." Paper presented at the Asia Pacific Educational Research Association 2006 International Conference, Hong Kong, November 28–30.

——. 2006c. "When Domestic Forces Meet the Global Trends: The Liberalization of the Privateness in East Asian Higher Education." Paper presented at the International Workshop on "Frontier of Private Higher Education Research in East Asia," Tokyo, December 14–15.

——. 2007. "Questing for Internationalization of Universities in Asia: Critical Reflections." *Journal of Studies in International Education* 11: 433–54.

Mok, K., and Y. Lo. 2007. "Embracing the Market: The Impacts of Neo-Liberalism on China's higher education." *Journal for Critical Education Policy Studies* 5 (1). Available at http://www.jceps.com/index.php?pageID=article&articleID=93 (accessed July 7, 2007).

Mok, K., and J. Tan. 2004. *Globalization and Marketisation in Education: A Comparative Analysis of Hong Kong and Singapore*. Cheltenham: Edward Elgar.

Mok, K., and A. Welch, eds. 2003. *Globalization and Educational Restructuring in the Asia Pacific Region*. Basingstoke: Palgrave Macmillan.

Moran, M. 2002. "Understanding the Regulatory State" (review). *British Journal of Political Science* 32: 391–413.

Morshidi, S. 2006. *Transnational Higher Education in Malaysia: Balancing Benefits and Concerns Through Regulations*. RIHE International Publication Series 10: 109–26.

Neubauer, D. 2006. "On the Public Good." Paper presented at the senior seminar, Education for 2020 Project of East-West Center, Honolulu, September 6–12.

Ng, P., and D. Chan. 2006. "A Comparative Study of Singapore's School Excellence Model with Hong Kong's School-Based Management." Paper presented at the Asia Pacific Educational Research Association 2006 International Conference, Hong Kong, November 28–30.

Ngok, K., and W. Guo. 2007. "The Quest for World-Class Universities in China: Critical Reflections." *Journal of Comparative Asian Development* 6 (1): 21–44.

Noble, D. 2001. "The Future of the Digital Diploma Mill." *Academe* 87 (5): 29.

Oba, J. 2006. "Incorporation of National Universities in Japan and Its Impact upon Institutional Governance." Paper presented at the International Workshop on University Restructuring in Asia, Hiroshima, January 16.

Olsen, J. P., and A. Gornitzka. 2006. "Making Sense of Change in University Governance." *IAU Horizons* 11.4 and 12.1: 1–3.

Osaka University Report. 2006. *A Final Report on Developing Evaluation Criteria to Assess the Internationalization of Universities*. Osaka: Osaka University.

Painter, M., and S. Wong. 2005. "Varieties of Regulatory State? Government-Business Relations and Telecommunications Reforms in Malaysia and Thailand." *Policy and Society* 24 (3): 27–52.

Petersen, C., and J. Currie. 2007. Higher Education Restructuring and Academic Freedom in Hong Kong." *Journal of Comparative Asian Development* 6 (1): 143–64.

Pusser, B. 2005. "Reconsidering Higher Education and the Public Good: The Role of Public Spheres." Unpublished manuscript, Curry School of Education, University of Virginia, Charlottesville.

Research Center of Chinese Scientific Evaluation of Wuhan University. 2005. *How Do We Rank the Scientific Research Competition of the World Universities?* Wuhan: Research Center of Chinese Scientific Evaluation, Wuhan University.

Research Institute of Higher Education and University Evaluation. 2005. *University Rankings in Taiwan*. Taipei: Tamkang University.

Robertson, S., X. Bonal, and R. Dale. 2002. "GATS and the Education Service Industry: The Politics of Scale and Global Restructuring." *Comparative Education Review* 56 (4): 472–96.

Rule, J. 1998. "Markets, in Their Place." *Dissent* (winter): 31.

Scott, C. 2004. "Regulation in the Age of Governance: The Rise of the Post-Regulatory State." In *The Politics of Regulation: Institutions and Regulatory Reforms for the Age of Governance*, ed. J. Jordana and D. Levi-Faur, 145–74. Cheltenham: Edward Elgar.

Shulman, L. S. 2003. Foreword to *Educating Citizens: Preparing America's Undergraduates for Lives of Moral and Civic Responsibility*, ed. A. Colby, T. Ehrlich, and E. Beaumont. San Francisco: Jossey-Bass.

Skilbeck, M. 2001. *The University Challenged: A Review of International Trends and Issues with Particular Reference to Ireland*. Dublin: Higher Education Authority.

Song, M., and H. Tai. 2006. *Transnational Higher Education in Taiwan*. RIHE International Publication Series 10: 151–69.

Taylor, J. 2001. "The Impact of Performance Indicators on the Work of University Academics: Evidence from Australian Universities." *Higher Education Quarterly* 55 (1): 42–61.

Tien, F. 2006. "Incorporation of National University in Taiwan: Challenges for the Government and the Academics." Paper presented at the International Workshop on University Restructuring in Asia, Hiroshima, January 16.

Tin, Z. P., et al., eds. 2005. *Academic Exchange and Educational Modernization*. Hangzhou: Zhejiang University Press.

Trend, D. 2001. *Welcome to Cyberschool: Education at the Crossroads in the Information Age*. Lanham, Md.: Rowman & Littlefield.

Tsuruta, Y. 2006. *Transnational Higher Education in Japan*. RIHE International Publication Series 10: 59–90.

Varghese, N. V. 2004. "Institutional Restructuring in Higher Education in Asia: Trends and Patterns." Theme paper prepared for the Policy Forum on Institutional Restructuring in Higher Education in Asia, Hue City, Vietnam, August 23–24.

Vidovich, L., R. Yang, and J. Currie. 2007. "Changing Accountabilities in Higher Education: Education as China 'Opens Up' to Globalization." *Globalization, Societies & Education*, 5 (1): 85–107.

Watson, D. 2006. "UK Higher Education: The Truth About the Student Market." *Higher Education Review* 38 (3): 3–16.

Welch, A. 2007. "Governance and Higher Education in South East Asia: Finance, Devolution and Transparency in the Global Era" *Asia Pacific Journal of Education* 27 (3): 237–53.

Welch, A., and K. Mok. 2003. "Conclusion: Deep Development of Deep Division." In *Globalization and Educational Restructuring in the Asia Pacific Region*, ed. K. Mok and A. Welch, 333–56. Basingstoke: Palgrave Macmillan.

Williams-Jones, B. 2005. "Knowledge Commons or Economic Engine—What's a University For?" *Journal of Medical Ethics* 31: 249–50.

Willis, E. 1999. *Don't Think, Smile: Notes on a Decade of Denial.* Boston: Beacon Press.

World Bank. 2000. *Higher Education in Developing Countries: Peril and Promise.* Washington, D.C.: World Bank.

——. 2007. *An East Asian Renaissance: Ideas for Economic Growth.* Washington, D.C.: World Bank.

Yang, R. 2002. *The Third Delight: Internationalization of Higher Education in China.* London: Routledge.

——. 2006. *Transnational Higher Education in Hong Kong: An Analysis.* RIHE International Publication Series 10: 35–58.

——. 2007. "Incorporation and University Governance: The Chinese Experience Using University Enrolment Expansion Policy as an Example." *Asia Pacific Journal of Education* 27 (3): 255–69.

Yonezawa, A. 2006. "Japanese Flagship Universities at a Crossroads." In *Final Report of Developing Evaluation Criteria to Assess the Internationalization of Universities*, ed. N. Furushiro, 85–102. Osaka: Osaka University.

Young, J. 2002. "Distance-Education Critic's Book Takes Aim at Army's Efforts." *Chronicle of Higher Education*, February 8, A34.

Zhejiang University. 2006. *A Report on the First Session of the International Academic Advisory Committee for University Evaluation.* Hangzhou: Zhejiang University.

Challenges for Higher Education
in Africa, *Ubuntu,*
and Democratic Justice

SEVEN

YUSEF WAGHID

This chapter explores the public mission of universities in Africa in relation to the challenges faced by higher education on the continent. As N'Dri Assié-Lumumba pointed out, from the late 1970s to the 1990s, higher education, especially universities in Africa, was characterized by great instability, as indicated by numerous confrontations between students, faculties, administrations, and governments.[1] This instability was further compounded by economic failures, stagnation, and regression, which slowed the advancement of higher education on the continent.[2] Some of the reasons that African universities were unprepared to satisfy societal needs are their alienation from the broader society and the business community and the inefficiency of university administration, organization, and management.[3] Agreeing with this view, David John Frank and John Meyer argue that the public mission of the modern university is to help with social problems such as improving business organizations and capital investments, protecting the natural environment, preserving human rights and cultural diversity, resolving crises of governance, and promoting democracy.[4] In this chapter I offer an account of Africanization that builds on earlier conceptions of *ubuntu* and nonbelligerent forms of deliberative democracy. I agree with Frank and Meyer that the university should be accountable to immediate problems at hand,[5] in particular preserving local cultures (in this case, *ubuntu*) in light of general norms (like the concept of deliberative democracy that I discuss here).

This chapter consists of two parts: the first is a general overview of higher education systems in Africa that describes some of the practices of some African university systems, and the second discusses how the practice of *ubuntu* (African humanism), coupled with deliberative democracy, can minimize the challenges to higher education in Africa, by proposing what higher education institutions should do to move away from their colonial past.

First I discuss some of the influences of colonialism on African higher education, emphasizing state intervention in higher education. Some countries seem to restrict institutions' autonomy and academic freedom, moderately in some countries and excessively in others. Next I argue for cultivating *ubuntu* and deliberative democracy, focusing on the implications of *ubuntu* and its link with narrativism as a way to achieve democratic justice on the African continent.

MAPPING SOME OF THE CHALLENGES TO AFRICAN HIGHER EDUCATION INSTITUTIONS

The colonization of most of the countries on the African continent introduced systems of higher education modeled on the colonizer's education systems. Indeed, for a long time, some African universities depended on their sister universities for resources such as staff and curricula. In those countries previously colonized by the British, examinations continued to be prepared in Britain. In addition, the Anglophone, Francophone, and Islamic universities in Africa all differed. Damtew Teferra and Philip Altbach contend that although many European countries colonized Africa, it was the British and the French who left the most lasting impact on Africa's higher education system.[6] William Saint notes that the Francophone and Anglophone universities continue to differ widely.[7] For instance, the Anglophone universities believe that a head of state can also be a university chancellor, whereas in the Francophone universities, the rector is given an open-ended appointment by the head of state in a centralized system. Besides influencing the universities' organization, the colonizers also determined the universities' language of instruction and communication. Egypt's Al-Azhar University is currently the only major academic institution in the world that is organized according to its original Islamic model.[8] Other universities on the African continent have followed a Western model of university organization.

From the beginning, universities in Africa were considered to be places for training elite members of society, which often limited many students' access to them. To an extent, this was because the colonizers needed to create workforce that could work with the colonial administrators. Accordingly, Africa's university system for a long time has focused on training a workforce for the government. This view of the university, however, is not the purpose of modern higher education, which generally is to train people not for existing jobs but for a progressive and expansionist future—for activities that may not exist or may be transformed in new ways.[9] This also explains why until recently, universities on the continent did not have high student enrollments. Compared with other continents, this low enrollment rate reflects students' limited access to universities. Richard Fehnel reports that "at the tertiary education level, only 3 percent of the college-age cohort in sub-Saharan Africa was educationally active in 1995, compared with 32 percent in Europe and central Asia."[10] He then explains that even in relation to other parts of Africa, sub-Saharan Africa lags far behind in its participation rates. Although by 1995, Africa had 1.8 million higher education students, 1 million of these were in Nigeria and South Africa,[11] with only 0.8 million in the rest of Africa. In addition to students' limited access to higher education in Africa, enrollment rates vary in the different countries, partly because the university is now perceived as a cultural center and not a place to learn technical skills.[12]

Teferra and Altbach note, too, that the influence of colonialism on African higher education helped restrict students' access, discouraged teaching students in indigenous languages, limited academic freedom, and prevented the Africanization of the curriculum.[13] Although France used to send people from its colonies to France for higher education, Zaire (now the Democratic Republic of Congo) did not have a single native engineer, lawyer, or doctor at the time of its independence.[14] Furthermore, the colonies' higher education systems also used the colonizer's language for instruction, coupled with limited academic freedom. Then, when the colonies gained independence, they dramatically restructured the curricula of their universities.[15] The colonizers had tended to favor law because it helped the colonial administrators, and gave short shrift to other disciplines such as science. Although the curricula of African universities today include almost all subject areas, their ties to their former colonizers remain strong, and no countries in Africa have changed their language of instruction.

Fehnel's emphasis, however, is not on the distribution of higher education or the legacy of colonialism. Rather, his point is that compared with other regions, Africa could enhance its development if it increased its enrollment and graduation rates at the tertiary level of education. Fehnel bases his argument on the demands of the global economy, contending that at least 12 to 15 percent of a nation's workforce must have a higher education to enable it to compete in the new global economy and that a constant effort must be made to keep this workforce abreast of changes.[16] Unfortunately, only 3 percent of the sub-Saharan population has received a higher education. This imbalance between the required number of highly educated personnel and the actual number of potential students means that Africa's higher education systems must make higher education available to more people in order to meet the growing demands of their economies. But these demands in turn pose challenges of capacity building.

In addition, war and conflict also have affected postsecondary education in some African countries. For instance, war and national strife brought the higher education system to a virtual standstill in countries such as Somalia, Angola and the Democratic Republic of Congo.[17] Likewise, as Teferra and Altbach explained, "Inadequate financial resources compounded with unprecedented demand for access, the legacy of colonialism, long-standing economic and social crises in many countries and the challenges of HIV/AIDS in many parts of the continent present the higher education sector with a bigger challenge."[18] According to them, the declining economies of African states have made it difficult for universities to train staff who can manage their systems. This is compounded by the high prevalence of HIV/AIDS on the continent, which has affected Africa's workforce in general. Furthermore, James Mittelman claims that the governance of higher education in Africa is driven by three forces, which he refers to as "pressure points."[19] These are the forces of globalization, the state, and the universities themselves. Of these three, Mittelman concedes that global forces play the biggest role in controlling how higher education systems are governed on the continent. These forces can be found in three dimensions: global finance, development assistance, and philanthropic activities.[20] Mittelman argues that Africa's economies are structurally weak, as they are subject to declining terms of trade and fluctuations in primary commodity prices. This forces African nations to depend on international financial organizations such as the International Monetary Fund and the World Bank. Furthermore, this involvement of international funders brings with it conditions to be fulfilled by the higher education system. These conditions include the type of education to be funded and where and how that education will be offered. In practice, every fund affects how an institution's governance structure is arranged. In many cases, the funds for higher education are spent on training primary school teachers, since higher education has been erroneously considered as not directly affecting the lives of ordinary citizens in Third World countries, particularly in Africa.

Global welfare or developmental assistance is supposed to strengthen the universities' capacity or output. In practice, however, developmental assistance seldom is spread throughout all areas of the higher education sector. That is, the very selective nature of development assistance determines how the higher education systems will be governed. Today, the term "development-related training program(s)" is used to determine whether or not a higher education institution program will be funded. I believe that it also fundamentally affects what that higher education institution will offer, how it will offer it, and to whom. I realize that most African universities and their research centers depend on foreign assistance.

Mittelman found as well that philanthropy has also determined the nature of governance in higher education, although to a smaller extent compared with economic forces. That is, philanthropic institutions tend to promote their own values. For instance, an arts foundation of a wealthy country might collaborate with an African art department only to promote the arts. Because philanthropic institutions are selective, the higher education institution's economic dependence on them may determine the scope of its operations.

In sum, globalization on the African continent affects the way that higher education systems are managed, because along with globalization comes global financial arrangements and conditionalities. The availability of financial resources affects the recruitment and retention of staff and the material resources available for teaching and learning. Teferra and Altbach further indicate that in the last decade, local governments have pressured the administrators of higher education institutions to find alternative sources of funding.[21] Universities thus have been forced by diminishing financial resources to charge fees to expand and extend their services, which has compromised the quality of higher education.[22] I agree with Akilagpa Sawyerr and William Saint that an overemphasis on student throughputs, for example, which determines an institution's financial income, could lead institutions to accept less-qualified students. According to Sawyerr and Saint, globalization seems to be the major factor driving the particular ways in which higher education operates today. Higher education is repositioned in relation to economic forces. Sawyerr and Saint state that the increasing pace of globalization is pushing Africa's higher education system toward the commodification of knowledge that can be used for the continent's social and economic development. That is, the higher education system should teach skills that are relevant to the labor market, which in turn has an enormous influence on the university's internal dynamics.[23] Today, the global market demands that for the most part, universities in Africa should fend for themselves and not rely on their country's government, a view that has led to higher fees, which is further proof of the commodification of knowledge. Science and economics have, however, received more funding from government and even from donors, which influences all of higher education. It is no wonder that a majority of privately funded higher education systems on the continent also tend to promote the money-generating degrees at the expense of a broader framework of knowledge promotion.

In almost every higher education system in Africa, the nature of each country's government varies. For instance, in Ghana, Uganda, and South Africa, the national government allows higher education institutions to be managed relatively freely. In other words, agreed-on policy frameworks adhere to national goals and the goals of higher education, and the institutions are expected to fulfill them without much interference. Within the statutes of these systems, normally referred to as "cooperative governance systems," the government intervenes only when these agreed-on goals are not met or the institutions are being mismanaged. In other African countries, the governance of higher education institutions range from moderate to heavy state control or interference. For instance, Egypt does not distinguish between the government/state and the university system. In addition, with the exception of South Africa, Ghana, and Uganda, it is common to make the heads of state also the chancellor of the nation's universities, as in Kenya, Malawi, Namibia, Zimbabwe, and many others. Sometimes the presidents are not just symbolic heads but wield enormous power, and other countries have special statutes giving the government control over the universities.

African governments today expect their universities to engage in more economic activity to compensate for the government's reduced funding. Students who now pay more for their university education could be regarded as economic stakeholders in the universities. Nonetheless, most of the universities' policies remain unchanged from those inherited from their colonializers, as is the case in Malawi and other countries, or have been changed to give the state more authority than other stakeholders in the system, as is the case in South Africa. As a result of their colonial past, some university systems still maintain a federal styles of management. For instance, Nigeria and Lesotho are similar in the way that their higher education systems are managed. Their systems are highly centralized, with a number of satellite colleges or institutions receiving structural and governance orders from a central office, which itself is under the control of the state government.

Some people think that the stable systems of higher education on the African continent indicate that the systems are under the sway of the demands and dictates of the state. As Teferra and Altbach explained, "Most African governments are intolerant of dissent, criticism, nonconformity and free expression of controversial, new, or unconventional ideas," hence the need to keep higher education systems under state control in order to avoid havoc.[24] This can be attributed partly to the continent's long history of colonial rule and colonial ties. Kelemi Mwiria argues that apart from the historical origin justifying the high level of government presence in higher education systems, universities also have been perceived as centers for national development.[25] Hence, African leaders find universities too visible and prestigious to be given complete autonomy and thus oversee or control most important stages or sections of the higher education system. They influence the selection of most officials and control the universities' agendas. The university and its chancellor (who in most cases happens to be the country's president as well) are closely linked to the country's Ministry of Education. Because most high officials are nominated, the chancellor probably sends "directives to council through their key nominees, such as the minister of education or the vice-chancellor."[26] This general trend affects the university's operations in such a way that instead of becoming academic sites, universities in most African countries often end up being the political playgrounds of the dominant forces in society.

In many African countries, the government and its ideology still determine higher education policy. For instance, in South Africa, higher education policies have largely been shaped by the African National Congress's (ANC) National Education Policy Investigation's findings, which clearly are biased toward the establishment of a single coordinated system of higher education. Similarly, the new system of outcomes-based education in South Africa shows the ANC's conceptual connection between acquiring knowledge competences and skills in order to produce students who are globally competitive and who can function in a global economy. Eugene Amonoo-Neizer argues that African universities were forced into financial diversification toward the end of the twentieth century.[27] International financial organizations forced governments to reduce their spending on public higher education. This pressure came in the form of reducing student-teacher ratios and the adaptation of more efficient means of running the institutions. Apart from this pressure, universities also must become more relevant as their costs rise. The idea of value for money has clearly changed the way that universities run their affairs.

Paul Zeleza argues that globalization in Africa has been "articulated primarily through structural adjustment programmes, and that globalization through its projects has accelerated the corporatisation of university management, commercialisation of learning and commoditisation of knowledge."[28]

Owing to globalization, the nature of university governance and the identity of scholarly discourse have changed as well. Zeleza traces the impact of globalization on higher education on the African continent through what he calls the "six Cs":

> Corporatisation of management (the adoption of business models for the organisation and administration of universities; collectivisation of access (growing massification of higher education, continuing education or lifelong learning, and accountability to outside stakeholders); commercialisation of learning (expansion of private universities, privatised programmes in public universities and vocational training); commodification of knowledge (increased production, sponsorship, and dissemination of research by commercial enterprises, applied research, and intellectual property norms); computerisation of education (incorporation of new information technologies into the knowledge activities of teaching, research, and publication); and connectivity of institutions (rising emphasis on institutional cooperation and coordination within and across countries).[29]

Globalization forces on universities a mind-set that affects most of the university's operations. In effect, higher education becomes an economic investment rather than a common good. Similarly, this trend introduces an instrumental mentality into learning as more emphasis is placed on the technical and professional fields at the expense of humanities and basic sciences.[30]

Globalization has also affected the way that property rights are understood and exercised in the universities. For example, the concept of property rights causes publishers to charge exorbitant prices for journal subscriptions, thereby preventing the Third World countries that cannot afford a subscription from benefiting from the expanding knowledge society.

In essence, the relationship between the state and the university affects how the university does what it does, where it does it, and with whom and for how long. For instance, in South Africa, the state favors an outcomes-based approach to education and, in fact, mandates universities to ensure its implementation through their academic programs. The strong relations between governments and universities have resulted in the universities' being run financially as state institutions. The better the relationship is between the government and the university, the more assistance the university will receive, thereby giving it more leverage over what it wants to do.

Higher education in Africa has been largely sustained by funding from national governments. When these institutions were established, the governments saw it as their mandate to provide for them completely. But with the growing demands for public money in other sectors, national governments have begun to encourage universities to find other financing. South African universities rely less on state funding than do other universities on the continent. African countries generally seem to expect that when the government funds higher education, the higher education system should promote its goals and aims. For instance, Mala Singh proposes that we look at universities in Africa from the functional perspective of the common good that higher education is meant to promote.[31] What is clear in Singh's perspective is the idea that no university exists just for itself or pursues knowledge for its own sake. The university's core functions of teaching, research, and community engagement are interrelated, and one function by itself cannot fully represent the others. This thinking is the basis of the view that all universities should respond to and enhance the social good.

One of the challenges facing higher education in Africa is quality education. Owing to dwindling state resources, Sawyerr and Saint observe that African universities have been forced to increase their student enrollments in order to bring in more student fees.[32] But in the case of Uganda, the country that they were analyzing, and many other African countries, the greater number of students opting for a public higher education has not been balanced by increased resources and staffing in the university. Thus, the dwindling numbers of academic staff in African universities are made to work with more students and fewer resources. As a result, the academic standards for the university have been compromised, because there does not seem to be enough time to prepare for classes and advise students.

Higher education in Africa also is dogged by the imbalance between academic staff and administrative/support staff. Countries like Lesotho, Madagascar, and Togo have fewer academic than nonacademic staff. For example, Lesotho has twice as many nonacademic as academic staff.[33] As a result, most of the resources for higher education are used for nonacademic matters such as staff salaries, so academic activities have fewer resources. Teferra and Altbach observe that "poorly trained and poorly qualified personnel; inefficient, ineffective, and out-of-date management and administrative infrastructure; and poorly remunerated staff are the norm throughout many systems on the continent."[34]

Why should higher education institutions be concerned about the Africanization (a matter of exercising *ubuntu*) of its governance structures, which could lead to academic practices such as institutional autonomy and academic freedom, critical research inquiry, and deliberative forms of teaching and learning?

AFRICANIZATION AND PLAUSIBLE FORMS OF
ACADEMIC PRACTICE

The idea of *ubuntu* (a form of communal engagement that allows criticality, does not dominate, and ensures that human relationships flourish) is found in almost all African languages, although not necessarily under the same name, which suggests that the notion must have been familiar to Africa's people in the past. For example, in Kenyan languages such as Kikuyu and Kimeru, *ubuntu* is referred to as *umundu* and *umuntu*; in kiSukuma and kiHaya of Tanzania, *ubuntu* is referred to as *bumuntu*; in shiTsonga and shiTswa of Mozambique, *ubuntu* is referred to as *vumuntu*; in Bobangi, spoken in the Democratic Republic of the Congo, *ubuntu* is referred to as *bomoto*; and in kiKongo of Angola, *ubuntu* is referred to is referred to as *gimuntu*.[35] How can the challenges posed by different higher education institutions in Africa be addressed by the notion of *ubuntu*; more specifically, how can *ubuntu* be interpreted differently in public universities in Africa? Most public universities in Africa seem to be subjected to overwhelming interference by the state, particularly regarding its governance, which is further challenged by its dependence on state funding. *Ubuntu* can be applied to the excessive state intervention in African higher education institutions. *Ubuntu* is relevant to African societies because of their history of colonization; racial oppression and segregation; and economic, political, and social instabilities; insecurities; and complexities.

Here I draw on the views of Moeketsi Letseka, who sees the "notion of *botho* or *ubuntu* (humanism) . . . as pervasive and fundamental to African socioethical thought, as illuminating the communal rootedness and interdependence of persons, and highlighting the importance of human relationships, . . . as an important measure of human wellbeing or human flourishing in traditional African life." He treats *botho* or *ubuntu* "as normative in that it encapsulates moral norms and virtues such as kindness, generosity, compassion, benevolence, courtesy, and respect and concern for others." Finally, he suggests "that educating for *botho* or *ubuntu*, for interpersonal and cooperative skills, and for human wellbeing or human flourishing, ought to be major concerns of an African philosophy of education"—more specifically Africanisation.[36] The question arises: What is the particular standing of *ubuntu* in Africa? My reading of the concept is that it offers both a general philosophical position as to how people should coexist organically and a way that Africa can contribute to the global culture, that is, a matter of reconciling the local (*ubuntu*) with the global (deliberative democracy).

As a philosophical position, *ubuntu* refers to the coexistence of people by having respect for one another and recognizing their vulnerabilities whenever they try to change their situation. When people have respect, they allow one another to live their lives according to what might be best for them. They do not impose their understanding of the world and what is best for them on others. Therefore, the Hutus and Tutsis from Rwanda or the Zulus and Xhosas from South Africa respect each other without imposing on the other their understanding of reality and what constitutes the good life. Tribal rivalries, which in many regions of the African continent often result in violent clashes (Kenya is a recent example), show that *ubuntu* is not always followed, yet it is a philosophical position with roots in African culture. In some places, such as in Nambia and South Africa, people peacefully coexist. In fact, *ubuntu* evolved over many centuries in traditional African culture and was expressed in songs, stories, customs, and institutions.[37] Some instances in which *ubuntu* was practiced in Africa are reflected in Julius Nyerere's concept of *ujaama* (that a person becomes a person through cooperation with others) and *unhu* (a way of confirming one's humanity in one's relations with others).

Critics of *ubuntu* might argue that the practice is not unique to Africa because in Western societies, communality and human interdependence have been practiced for a long time and that respect for others, generosity, kindness, and compassion are not new. I agree. But acting with regard to others also has a contextual dimension. That is, engaging with one another in postcolonial African societies will invariably be different from human interactions in non-African societies. For instance, having compassion for people suffering from famine and poverty in the Darfur region of Sudan is different from showing compassion to working-class European families who might be temporarily unemployed. The point is, on the one hand, that compassion in the sense advocated by *ubuntu* requires that people recognize the vulnerabilities of others brought about by ethnic conflict and political struggle in postcolonial societies and actually do something to help them. On the other hand, having compassion for unemployed working-class families because of insufficient job opportunities in perhaps highly flourishing economies that have never been subjected to pernicious forms of colonialism is different from exercising *ubuntu*. Put differently, *ubuntu* is exclusively linked to cultivating human cooperation and interdependence in postcolonial Africa in order to mitigate the effects of racism, exploitation, and domination. It is in this regard that I share Barney Pityana's[38] view that *ubuntu* is logically connected to the preservation of human dignity, the achievement of equality, the enhancement of human rights and freedoms, and the enhancement of the common good (more specifically, the subversion of racism, exploitation, and domination).

How, then, can this view of Africanization (more specifically the exercise of *ubuntu*) help create institutional autonomy and academic freedom, critical research inquiry, and deliberative forms of teaching and learning at African universities? First, *ubuntu*, with its emphasis on cooperation free from the domination of others (in this instance, the university by the state), is an idea that the university in Africa should not have absolute autonomy but, rather, "conditional autonomy." This view of autonomy recognizes the state's role in ensuring the effective use of public funds and the substantive rights of the university to academic freedom in teaching and research. In this regard I agree with Martin Hall that such a view of "conditional autonomy" could minimize state control or interference in the academic domain of higher education institutions. In his words, "conditional autonomy recognises the role of the state in steering the system and its outcomes through procedural controls, while respecting the autonomy of individual institutions in the substantive fields of their intellectual work."[39] This implies that individual institutions would assert their right to

> pursue research objectives on their own terms, to interpret their social responsibilities, to determine the content of the curriculum and to think in the manner that they think best . . . [while] the democratic state would always have a legitimate, overarching accountability for the disbursement of public funds and for the authentication of academic qualifications.[40]

Second, practicing *ubuntu*, with its view of humans' flourishing, can mean that the university does not have to relinquish its pursuit of criticality and democratic participation if "steered by the requirements of the labour market." Why not? Elsewhere I have argued for achieving democracy in a sphere of marketization if higher education is considered as a public good that allows space for the development of relations of trust, individual autonomy, and democratic dialogue.[41] Similarly, even if the university needs to develop human capital for global competitiveness and the establishment of a democratic citizenry (which are neoliberal concerns), higher education institutions need to restructure according to an organizational discourse that resonates with the "language of inclusion, social cohesion and increased participation"[42]—and, in Africa, a discourse of human interdependence devoid of exploitation and domination of the other. For instance, when a faculty must develop an academic program to prepare students for participation in a global economy and a democratic society, I cannot imagine how they can do this without the engagement of both the academic and the students.

Third, *ubuntu* does not abandon the idea that human relationships should be subjected to deliberation. Many African cultures accept that the authority of people in leadership positions should not be challenged, a practice that, in any case, seems very unlikely in countries such as Sudan, Ghana, and Malawi where university governance is subjected to state intrusion. Moreover, as a mark of respect for academic authority, several of my students from southern African countries are hesitant to challenge university professors. One student told me that she once wanted to question the chieftain of her tribe but refrained from doing so as a mark of respect for his leadership. This, she claimed, was because *ubuntu* implies respect for the human dignity of others. Such a view of *ubuntu* is restricted in that challenging someone else cannot be associated with disrespect. *Ubuntu* also assumes that human beings do not have differences and that they constitute a homogenous society. My contention is that human relations are full of ambivalence and conflict, and deliberation comes about when one person wants to justify his points of view to another person who may disagree with him. Moreover, following Kwame Gyekye[43] and considering Africa's history and culture, people should have less formal deliberative conversations. If my reading of Gyekye is correct, he means that conversations should be confined to articulating points of view in a logically defensible way through rigorous argumentation and debate in which points of view are challenged and undermined or persuasion and the quest for the better argument become necessary conditions for deliberative inquiry to unfold. I agree, since illiteracy and the lack of eloquence of ordinary citizens would exclude them from a deliberative conversation. Gyekye contends that Africa's colonial and postcolonial experience has had enduring effects on many Africans' mentality,[44] a colonial mentality that leads to "apism," the idea that people should look for answers to Africa's problems outside Africa, specifically in Europe. It is this same "apist" attitude by most of Africa's people that leads them to suppress their own opinions in favor of the wisdom of sages. I do not think that Gyekye would dismiss the wisdom of sagacity in deliberative discourse, since the individual's inclinations, orientations, intuitions, and outlooks are important to philosophical inquiry.[45] However, Gyekye's view suggests that ways should be found to make the less eloquent, illiterate, and seemingly inarticulate person express his or her thoughts. For this reason, his call for the application of less formal rules to deliberative conversation seems to be valid. In this regard, I suspect that Gyekye's emphasis on the application of a minimalist logic to deliberative conversation has some connection with allowing Africa's people to recite their oral narratives about their beliefs, values, folktales, drama, and cultural traditions without having to convince others of their orientations. This makes sense because many Africans do not necessarily know the logical reasons for their beliefs and values handed down to them by their ancestors. When I asked a master's degree candidate, who belonged to Nambia's Ovambu tribe, about his father's polygamist marriages, he did not entirely convince me when he told me that his father treated all his wives equally. However, if I had lectured him on the evils of polygamy, our conversation would not have continued for long. So, the idea of asking for a minimalist logic would establish conditions to include, rather than exclude, people from the deliberative conversation. In fact, including them in the conversation might give them an opportunity to challenge and question their own positions.

In essence, practicing *ubuntu* can lead to institutional autonomy and academic freedom, critical research inquiry, and deliberative forms of teaching and learning at African universities. For me, the Africanization of higher education institutions means that deliberations may lead to the questioning of academic authority. Conversely, *ubuntu* means having respect for the human dignity of others through deliberation, which invariably involves questioning and challenging academic authority. If higher education institutions are serious about Africanizing, they should restore deliberation and thereby create opportunities for people to engage with one another and, at the same time, develop respect for others' views. Indeed, it is a sign of disrespect for the other person if his or her views are not subjected to critical scrutiny.

One of the limitations of *ubuntu* is that it assumes that people need to take collective responsibility for one another's actions. But this is not always forthcoming, as is evident from the HIV/AIDS epidemic and the escalating levels of crime in (South) Africa, for which, it seems, no one really wants to assume responsibility because it is erroneously thought that individual responsibility is not possible, since "a person is only a person through other persons." Similarly, overextending *ubuntu* through deliberative democracy to invoke belligerence and distress can alienate people because their collectivity through *ubuntu* might be undermined and some people even excluded. For instance, students at the Durban Institute of Technology (in South Africa) who turned violent because of their refusal to pay their debts felt alienated and excluded because of management's unsympathetic attitude toward them. In Chad and Kenya, mistrust and refusal to engage with one another have demonstrated that *ubuntu* alone cannot resolve the political crises in these countries unless people can be made to feel the need to coexist through *ubuntu* and deliberative democracy. Simply put, the local value of *ubuntu* can have currency only if people see the need to peacefully cooperate and coexist.

In regard to universities, *ubuntu* (local) and its associated practices of non-belligerent deliberative democracy (global) can help improve institutions' governance, providing that conditions are cultivated that enable *ubuntu* and deliberative democracy to flourish. One of these conditions would be for people to acknowledge that something is wrong and needs to be remedied.

UBUNTU, DEMOCRATIC JUSTICE, AND THE AFRICAN UNIVERSITY

The fact that *ubuntu* is connected to human interdependence and well-being also suggests that the practice encompasses what Archbishop Desmond Tutu refers to as "going beyond justice toward forgiveness and reconciliation."[46] Thus, *ubuntu* implies both "compassion" and "recognition of the humanity of the other."[47] In Africa, at least three major injustices are evident that subvert human dignity, social/economic security, and peaceful coexistence: religious fundamentalism, famine, and political autocracy. First, the religious fundamentalism exercised by Muslim and Christian extremists in parts of eastern Africa clearly threatens the peaceful coexistence of people of diverse religions. The unacceptable intolerance shown by these religious groups in the name of their faith is evident in their burning of mosques and churches and the public executions of people, which cry out for the teaching of "respect for persons" in higher education institutions. This means that Africa's culturally diverse societies should demand that their universities make a concerted effort to understand and appreciate those features of their different cultures that others cherish and deem as important to their particular identity (such as through their literature, histories, and folklore). For instance, today it is not uncommon to find Muslims, Christians, and Jews attending the same educational institution. It would be an expression of *ubuntu* if students and educators from these groups learned (even through argument and debate) about one another's cultures. "Respect is blind if uninformed about relevant values and the reasons they provide; and it inevitably remains uninformed if nothing shakes us from our habits of seeing everything exclusively from our primary cultures' perspective."[48] If Africa's people can learn by discussing their cultural diversity and developing an appreciation of one another's cultures (even if they do not always agree with some aspects of their own or others' cultures), then the potential for religious extremism might be thwarted. Put differently, when people are engaged in a conversation underpinned by interdependence and disagreement (*ubuntu*), they engage with a collective identity—they find their commonalities. And educating people to become democratically just citizens means creating civil spaces in which they can learn to find commonalities and to respect the differences of others, that is, a matter of cultivating *ubuntu*.

Second, in parts of northern Africa, famine and hunger have risen to intolerable levels as a result of political exclusion. Universities must teach people how to confront their biases and control their arrogant preconceptions of others whom they may hardly understand. That is, people need to be taught how to openly confront other cultures and restrain their moral arrogance. After all, no single group can claim with confidence that it possesses the best, or the most humane and just, moral system.[49] *Ubuntu* comes into play when we stop looking at ourselves as more privileged than others.

Third, Africa's political autocracies have persisted despite the formation of the African Union and its New Economic Path to Africa's Development (NEPAD) project, whose purpose is to foster a culture of democratic governance. More specifically, NEPAD holds that the socioeconomic recovery and development of the African continent is impossible without true democracy, respect for human rights, peace, and good governance.[50] This vision on the part of African leaders sounds noble, and there is every justification for supporting such a view, since peace, security, good governance, respect for human rights, and sound economic management are preconditions for democracies to flourish. I want to support this view, since the hope of attaining international competitiveness, reintegration into the global economy, and building capacity on the African continent cannot be achieved without consolidating democracy. But it is at the level of democratic discourse that NEPAD's biggest challenge lies. How do NEPAD's partners sustain and cultivate spheres of communication and negotiation, which are not only central to the success of the alliance but also necessary in order to consolidate and enhance democratic discourse? It is not simply a matter of strengthening the mechanisms to resolve conflicts, promote human rights, and restore and maintain macroeconomic stability. Rather, it is a matter of NEPAD's partners' taking seriously the principles of deliberative democracy to enable their conversation to continue.

This brings me back to the claim I made earlier that political dictatorships (in the presence of NEPAD) not only undermine the voices of the majority of people but also exacerbate the already volatile climate of political instability and marginalization of the vulnerable others. Africa's universities must consolidate and advance an appreciation of listening. Only by listening to others subjected to political exclusion can political, economic, and cultural instability be rectified. In other words, cultivating *ubuntu* requires that we create a culture of listening to many voices that we might like or dislike and even deplore, that is, listening through active engagement with the aim of preventing any form of injustice. Here I agree with Amy Gutmann, who claims that respect for persons does not require that we "treat other people as if their lives were not worth living, a perspective that is antithetical to any plausible conception of democratic justice."[51]

Finally, the question arises: How can *ubuntu* be cultivated in higher education institutions? First, a liberal conception of democratic citizenship education requires that we find a space to discuss linguistic, cultural, ethnic, and religious differences, based on the understanding that people need to learn to live with others whose lifestyle may be deeply threatening to our own.[52] And by creating a space in which people can discover what they have in common and, at the same time, acknowledge their competing narratives and significations, they might create an opportunity to coexist. In this way, they would establish a community of conversation and interdependence and also one of disagreement, without disrespecting others.[53] Put differently, when people are engaged in a conversation underpinned by interdependence and disagreement, they engage in a dialogue with a collective identity. Educating people to become democratically just citizens requires creating spaces where they can learn what they share and respect the differences of others, that is, cultivate a democratic citizenship. Such a view of democratic citizenship education can be enhanced by the practice of *ubuntu* because it allows space for nonbelligerent deliberative engagement. Whereas Western (liberal) conceptions of democratic citizenship education seem to be biased toward rational argumentation and belligerent persuasion by offering the "better argument," *ubuntu* considers people's cultural lifestyles, especially of those who are not eloquent. *Ubuntu* demands that those who listen to people's often inarticulate narratives should construct them in a defensible way as if they would experience what others want to say. For example, university students who might not be capable of articulating their arguments in a defensible way should be offered an opportunity to recite their narratives. In turn, academics should construct the students' narratives in defensible ways as if the students are in fact articulating the narratives as justifiable arguments. In other words, *ubuntu* offers the possibility of experiencing others through deliberative engagement and the (re)construction of the thoughts of the inarticulate or otherwise muted other. This is an idea that might be able to cultivate Africanization at higher education institutions.

In conclusion, I have argued that African universities could limit some of the daunting challenges they currently face and that their public mission should seriously consider *ubuntu* and nonbelligerent forms of deliberative democracy. Only then can governance, teaching, and learning at these higher education institutions legitimately respond to alleviating some of the "crises" that confront them.

NOTES

1. N'Dri Assié-Lumumba, *Higher Education in Africa: Crises, Reforms, and Transformation* (Dakar: Council for the Development of Social Science Research in Africa, 2006), 71.
2. Ibid., 75.
3. Ibid., 78.
4. David John Frank and John Meyer, "University Expansion and the Knowledge Society," *Theory and Society* 36, no. 1 (2007): 290.
5. Ibid.
6. Damtew Teferra and Philip Altbach, "Trends and Perspectives in African Higher Education," in *African Higher Education: An International Reference Handbook,* ed. Damtew Teferra and Philip Altbach (Bloomington: Indiana University Press, 2003). 4.
7. William Saint, "Universities in Africa: Strategies for Stabilization and Revitalisation," World Bank Technical Report 194 (Washington, D.C.: World Bank, 1992), 72.
8. Teferra and Altbach, "Trends and Perspectives," 4.
9. David John Frank and Jay Gabler, *Reconstructing the University* (Stanford, Calif.: Stanford University Press, 2006), xii.
10. Richard Fehnel, "Massification and Future Trends in Higher Education," in *African Higher Education: An International Reference Handbook*, ed. Damtew Teferra and Philip Altbach (Bloomington: Indiana University Press, 2003), 73–81.
11. Ibid., 74.
12. Frank and Gabler, *Reconstructing the University*, ix.
13. Teferra and Altbach, "Trends and Perspectives," 4.
14. Ibid.
15. Ibid.
16. Fehnel, "Massification and Future Trends in Higher Education," 74.
17. Teferra and Altbach, "Trends and Perspectives," 3.
18. Ibid.
19. James Mittelman, "Academic Freedom: The State and Globalization," in *Academic Freedom in Africa,* ed. Mamadou Diouf and Mahmood Mamdani (Dakar: CODESRIA Book Series, 1994), 144–49.

20. Ibid., 144.

21. Teferra and Altbach, "Trends and Perspectives," 4. For example, at the institution where I work, Stellenbosch University in South Africa, less than 35 percent of its annual income comes from government subsidies. Other sources of income include student fees and funds from donors, patents, and research contracts. What makes it challenging is that the state subsidy per institution (twenty-three universities in all) is based on a funding formula that gives preference to research (publications and student throughputs). Therefore, universities in South Africa that do not conduct much research receive less in subsidies.

22. Akilagpa Sawyerr and William Saint, "Challenges Facing African Universities: Selected Issues," *African Studies Review*, 47, no. 1 (2004): 10.

23. Although South Africa's higher education system is geared toward achieving equitable redress after decades of apartheid rule, it also emphasizes that graduates should be equipped with the skills and qualities required for participation as citizens in a democratic society and as workers and professionals in the world labor market economy.

24. Teferra and Altbach, "Trends and Perspectives," 11.

25. Kelemi Mwiria, "University Governance and University-State Relations," in *African Higher Education: An International Reference Handbook*, ed. Damtew Teferra and Philip Altbach (Bloomington: Indiana University Press, 2003), 33.

26. Ibid., 34.

27. Eugene Amonoo-Neizer, "Universities in Africa: The Need for Adaptation, Transformation, Reform and Revitalization," *Higher Education Policy*, 11 no. 1 (1998): 305.

28. Paul Zeleza, "Neoliberalism and Academic Freedom," in *Africa Universities in the Twenty-first Century*, vol. 1, *Liberalism and Internationalisation*, ed. Adebayo Olukoshi and Paul Zeleza (Dakar: Council for the Development of Social Research in Africa, 2004), 42.

29. Ibid., 52.

30. Ibid., 53.

31. Mala Singh, *Re-inserting the "Public Good" into Higher Education Transformation*, Kagisano Higher Education Discussion Series 1 (Pretoria: Kagiso, 2001), 8.

32. Sawyerr and Saint, "Challenges Facing African Universities," 12.

33. Teferra and Altbach, "Trends and Perspectives," 6–7.

34. Ibid., 7.

35. Nkonko M. Kamwangamalu, "Ubuntu in South Africa: A Sociological Perspective to a Pan-African Concept," *Critical Arts* 13, no. 1 (1999): 26.

36. Moeketsi Letseka, "African Philosophy and Educational Discourse," in *African Voices in Education*, ed. Philip Higgs, Zola Vakalisa, Tatobeka Mda, and N'Dri Assié-Lumumba (Lansdowne: Juta, 2000), 179, 180.

37. Augustine Shutte, *Ubuntu: An Ethic for a New South Africa* (Cape Town: Cluster Publications, 2001), 9.

38. Barney Pityana, "The Renewal of African Moral Values," in *African Renaissance: The New Struggle*, ed. William Makgoba (Cape Town: Mafube & Tafelberg, 1999), 148.

39. Martin Hall and Ashley Symes, "South African Higher Education in the First Decade of Democracy: From Cooperative Governance to Conditional Autonomy," *Studies in Higher Education* 30 (2005): 199.

40. Martin Hall, "Academic Freedom and the University: Fifty Years of Debate" (paper presented to the Forum on Government Involvement in Higher Education, Institutional Autonomy and Academic Freedom, Council on Higher Education, University of the Western Cape, 2006), 5.

41. Yusef Waghid, "Globalisation and Higher Restructuring in South Africa: Is Democracy Under Threat?" *Journal of Education Policy* 16, no. 5 (2001): 455.

42. James Avis, "Policy Talk: Reflexive Modernization and the Construction of Teaching and Learning Within Post-compulsory Education and Lifelong Learning in England," *Journal of Education Policy* 15, no. 2 (2000): 196.

43. Kwame Gyekye, *Tradition and Modernity: Philosophical Reflections on the African Experience* (New York: Oxford University Press, 1997).

44. Ibid., 27.

45. Ibid., 12.

46. Robert Wilson, *The Politics of Truth and Reconciliation. Legitimizing the Post-Apartheid State* (Cambridge: Cambridge University Press, 2001).

47. Kader Asmal, Louise Asmal, and Ronald Roberts, *Reconciliation Through Truth. A Reckoning of Apartheid's Criminal Governance* (Cape Town: David Philip Publishers, 1996), 21.

48. Tony Hill, *Respect, Pluralism, and Justice* (Oxford: Oxford University Press, 2000), 83.

49. Ibid.

50. African Union, *The New Partnership for Africa's Development (NEPAD)*, 17, available at http://www.polity.org.za/govdocs/misc/nepad.pdf (2001).

51. Amy Gutmann, *Identity in Democracy* (Princeton, N.J.: Princeton University Press, 2003), 158.

52. Seyla Benhabib, *The Claims of Culture: Equality and Diversity in the Global Era* (Princeton, N.J.: Princeton University Press, 2002), 130.

53. Ibid., 35–41.

EIGHT

The Idea of the Public University and the National Project in Africa

Toward a Full Circle, from the 1960s to the Present

N'DRI T. ASSIÉ-LUMUMBA

AND TUKUMBI LUMUMBA-KASONGO

OBJECTIVES, ISSUES, AND PERSPECTIVES

The African public university is at a historic juncture in the mid-twentieth century while moving from formal colonial rule to political independence and cannot be fully understood if it is analyzed as merely a technical industrial unit geared toward processing and producing graduates.[1] This observation applies to all the political transitions in African countries that acquired their independence from a few in the late 1950s and then a majority in the 1960s and still more between the 1970s and 1990s. Irrespective of the means by which independence was acquired, because it was driven by a strong nationalist sentiment, it was expected to be more than nominal. In this context, the public university was conceptualized as a central and vital philosophical component of the essence and efforts of nation-building and the national and continental agendas for socioeconomic development. Thus, the analysis of the changes and the crises that the institutions of higher learning, primarily the university, have experienced to date and their possible transformation to respond to these crises must be contextualized broadly, even though in this chapter, we cannot fully address all the dimensions' complexities. These complexities are the reflections of national specificities, legacies of different colonial policies and Western higher education traditions, different stages in postcolonial African and global economic challenges, and their impact on the evolution of higher education.

The idea of the public university in Africa is a contemporary African state project. It is built on four complex characteristics: sovereignty, control over its territoriality, a loyal population, and international legitimacy or recognition by other states. The colonial African state as a social phenomenon was a historically constructed entity whose main objective to advance the interests and the agenda of the European colonial powers in the international political economy. As Tukumbi Lumumba-Kasongo stated, "Colonial Africa was created essentially as states and not as nations, and the neocolonial political elites inherited African states as central agencies in defining the parameters of the dynamics of economy, culture, and people or citizens" (Lumumba-Kasongo 2002). Thus, in the postcolonial period, the Africans expected and demanded that the executive power of the state, the government, or the administration be able to deconstruct what the colonial powers built in their interest and redefine the state differently through national projects. Despite its structural weaknesses, as reflected in the discussion about the concept of the national project, the African state is still the most visible African actor in world politics. Thus, the state's project cannot be carefully examined and fully understood outside the statist paradigms, structures, and politics.

If African political elites and their national projects could claim a sector that had been successful in its numeric expansion, demographics, and promotion of pride and creation of hope among the African people, it would clearly be the creation of public universities. These hopes and aspirations have had a powerful impact on the youth in general, particularly the socially disadvantaged. At the time of independence, many countries, especially small ones such as Togo, Equatorial Guinea, and Cape Verde, had no national universities of their own. By 2010, however, with very few exceptions, such as São Tomé, and Príncipe, every African country had at least one national public university with at least one campus. Arguably, the country with the most postindependence public institutions of higher learning is Nigeria, with more than fifty public universities, including twenty-four federal universities and thirty state universities in the Nigerian national university system.

Why and how has this seemingly tangible success not produced, in most cases, any sustained positive impact in qualitatively and continuously improving the socioeconomic conditions of the majority of the African people in most parts of the continent? Human capital theory, its inspired educational planning for the production of the needed human resources, and the United Nations development decade of the 1960s were firmly grounded on the development capacity of higher education. At the beginning of twenty-first century, despite the new and similar expectations set in the millennium development goals (MDGs), whose term will expire in 2015, there is a conspicuous absence of higher education in the MDGs' documents and activities. These issues are critical, considering the official mission assigned to the public universities in Africa at their inception and their current state.

The next questions are, What kind of public university can produce the necessary relevant, appropriate, and innovative scientific, artistic, and humanistic knowledge; modes of critical thinking and paradigms; and methodologies that should be used for social progress and national development in Africa in the context of the dominant liberal globalization or the world system and the objective conditions of the African states and societies? What kinds of political regimes and systems of governance and economic models can sustain the development of institutions of higher learning conceived as public and for the common good?

About fifty years ago, African scholars asked these questions when the then emerging African elites and people were struggling to find the formulas and means to gain their political independence from the European colonial powers. In Africa, the debate about higher education, and more specifically the university in the postcolonial context, was framed in terms of the university as a public institution dedicated to the public good, with the mission to fulfill the functions of teaching, research, and service to the broader society.

No single system of governance was able to adequately and comprehensively respond to these questions to the satisfaction of all the societal constituencies and national contexts. Various types of policies were formulated within historical and cultural realities and claims, geopolitical imperatives, ideological dispositions of political parties and elites, and expectations and demands from the general population. Thus, some of the answers could be found in the ways that various national agendas were set up and how policies based on these agendas were formulated and implemented.

It is significant that these questions were addressed through the national projects under the broad framework of national agendas. Africa in the twenty-first century, and the world for that matter, is obviously in a different era compared with that when most African countries achieved independence. Nevertheless, the issues raised at the time of independence are still important precisely because there have not been any comprehensive solutions to the African puzzles, as reflected in the worsening of Africa's economic and social conditions, as well as political deception despite some recent changes reflected in the rise of "autocratic multipartyism" (Lumumba-Kasongo 1998). It is important to factor in the nature of the world in a "hybrid transition." The multidimensionality of Africa's crisis necessitates critical thinking about the role of the comprehensive African university in this century and beyond.

Is the idea of the public university and national policies part of the African problems, or is the conception of the public university part of the African solution to the need for relevant human resources to engineer transformative social change? This chapter is essentially a general reflective inquiry, whose arguments, philosophical assumptions, and policy implications are clarified by comparative illustrations based on the authors' cumulative practical experiences. Our arguments and conclusions do not derive from empirically based generalizations about how the idea of the public university in nearly all of the fifty-three different countries (without counting Saharawi Republic) has been functioning in Africa. Rather, this work deals more with the question of its genuine or contested relevance to the challenging and failing paradigms of development in Africa and their policy implications and lessons.

How can we formulate and actualize the idea of public university within the existing context of generally embattled, very weak, failed, disappearing, collapsing, or timidly recovering states, with the further deterioration of social and human conditions in Africa owing to the hegemony of global liberalism and American unilateralism? As African people have struggled or demanded to directly or indirectly convert electoral democracies into social democracies for social change, is the public university still philosophically and functionally relevant in Africa?

With no exceptions, Africans in all walks of life have never perceived as controversial the idea of the public university in contemporary Africa. In fact, it has been one of the areas of consistent consensus among the various interest groups: families, students/youth, civil society, and governments. The public university has been politically and sociologically appealing to the African political elites from the first generation of graduates who achieved the highest levels of European formal education. The correlation between their respective formal educational achievements (albeit limited due to discriminatory colonial policies) and their accrued socioeconomic and political attainment inspired young people to work hard, to have hopes for the future, and to gain the skills needed for socioeconomic attainment. Thus, this idea has been popular. At the creation of the first wave of African universities, there were no national debates by African stakeholders, about whether any serious consideration should be given to private universities, be they owned by individuals, religious institutions, or private corporations. Indeed, African societies expected their younger members to attend the public schools without any major constraints or impediments from state and/or from the national and global economies. Access to a public university was generally considered a right, not a privilege. The public university was considered capable of providing the highest standards of higher education knowledge.

Attending the university was even considered a patriotic duty, a contribution to building prosperous postcolonial societies. In the immediate postcolonial era, the reality was that only those qualified in cognitive achievement in the required examinations at the end of secondary school could, in principle, enroll in universities in Africa or abroad. Those who were selected attended the public university and went through the process and the system with the hope of reaching the highest levels. From the youths' and families' standpoint, however, there was a difference between aspirations, expectations, and evolving realities.

Since the 1980s, many factors have hindered access to the university: stagnant or downward economic trends, global liberal economic reforms, and the introduction of the user fee, even at the primary and secondary levels, irrespective of ability to pay. These are the schools that feed higher education and that stagnated and whose enrollment even declined in nearly twenty countries. In addition to the already selective and elitist process, new proposed policies and additional mechanisms were set up for competitive admissions tests, an effective means to establish a less democratic system. The application of these policies resulted in limiting access to the university and, more generally, postsecondary education. The phenomenon of overcrowded classes commonly observed in numerous institutions in different African countries is thus not the result of the assumed "massification" but, rather, of the lack of new infrastructures to accommodate even only slightly more students.

The new process of selection is partly based on the ability to secure economic means to bear the cost. This raises some pertinent issues related to the notion of "public," "public good," or "public interest," which imply philosophically some kind of generally agreed-on common or collective social good. Politically, it implies national interest and a right and an idea of what belongs to all citizens in a given country. In Liberia, for instance, the notion of public is referred to by the euphemism of "our elephant." Everyone should have access to it. Do the national interests in Africa, as defined by various political regimes and external agencies, necessarily or always reflect those of the public arena?

The role and the functions of a university in Africa and/or an African university have generally been well documented by many scholars and students of higher education in Africa. The centrality of the university in dealing with the issues related to development and social progress cannot be overstated, as articulated in many publications since the 1960s (Abdalla 1977; Abegaz 1995; Aina 1995; Ajayi et al. 1996; Ashby 1964, 1966; Assié-Lumumba 1995a; Gaidzanwa 1995; Mohamedbhai 1995; Mwiria 1995; Negrao 1995; Sawadogo 1995).

For the first generations of African students studying in the European type of formal education, attending the university was perceived as a critical step in the normal progression on the ladder of learning. Indeed, the mere fact of attending the university was generally associated with a linear direction in the social process.

Until the 1990s, in most African systems of education, attending a university with all the costs fully covered, including substantial stipends, was not considered exceptional. This was the experience of those able to succeed in all the general cognitive requirements from primary to secondary schools in a given educational system under a specific political system. It was viewed as an automatic process as long as the secondary school terminal degree was acquired. A reflection on the particular idea of the public university has been taken for granted. At the time of struggles for political independence in Africa, it was believed that creating a public university was part of the citizen's right and the state's duty to actualize it. It also was thought that only a state with its resources could tackle the monumental task of setting in motion the developmental process with higher education as its central engine.

Regardless of the economic and financial problems associated with the creation of any institution of higher learning, especially a public university that is fully equipped to fulfill its mission, the African state has viewed the public university generally as a national symbol of honor and sovereignty in the quest for producing and using the highest level of knowledge and human resources as its active national treasure. It is associated with the principle of sovereignty of each state to articulate its autonomy through the creation of a public university not for its own sake but for planning and meeting critical human resource needs. Philosophical and constitutional questions such as what kind of right it is and what kind of obligation it carries have not been fully examined.

Since the 1960s, when most African countries won their nominal political independence, the discourse on and policy analysis of the place and the role of an African university have been central. An African university has been conceived by the African state as a national institution for social progress. At the individual and societal levels, it has been perceived as a symbol of expression of national pride and a personal channel for upward social mobility and the attainment of social power. It has been articulated as an institutional base to prepare youth for prestigious and high-paying jobs in the public administrations and private corporations as technocrats, bureaucrats, managers, and decision makers.

The arguments can be summarized as follows: Public African universities were created as part of the core ideas, thoughts, desires, and hopes of the African peoples as central instruments of social progress and policy discourse regarding the advancement of nation-building, regardless of people's social classes; gender, ethnic, and/or religious affiliations; and the political agenda of the state. The consensus that emerged without any systematic public debates was generalized across all social categories and states. Universities were intended to quickly produce the necessary human capacities in teaching and producing new knowledge, providing new skills, conducting research, and managing and distributing knowledge. The universities were both the mirrors of the new societies and the microcosms of the new elite with the tasks and the mission of leading African societies toward development. This was a gigantic responsibility.

The public universities face huge obstacles: extremely unsatisfied high expectations, fragile administrative and political structures, weak African political economies, the lack of serious reforms within the education systems at large, and the role of external agencies, including former colonial powers, private foundations, and the transnational financial institutions. Thus, African universities faced problems similar to those faced by other institutions toward the end of the 1970s in most countries. The decline of most African universities in the 1980s and 1990s had a more negative impact on the African societies than did any other institutions because of their imagined and/or real centrality and also because the direct "consumers" of the university education were the intellectuals and the youth—a social segment with new energies, high hopes, and a desire for change, growth, development, and social progress.

THE NATIONAL PROJECT AS A CONCEPT OF NATION-BUILDING: THE STATE'S OBLIGATIONS AND THE PEOPLE'S RIGHTS

The idea of the public university in Africa developed from the national project. This university was intended to be fully supported by public funds under the supervision of the public administration, with the assumption that this administration would be at the service of the greater society. It was designed to respond to the imperatives of scientific research, inquiries, learning, and possibilities in all sectors of life, covering all possible disciplines as articulated by the national government.

Depending on the structures of the government and colonial traditions, the public university has been directed by either the Ministry of Higher Education (and Scientific Research) or the Ministry of Education as a state agency. In the 1970s, Côte d'Ivoire, for instance, had a Ministry of Scientific Research, in addition to the Ministries of National Education and Higher Education, to emphasize research as one of the key functions of higher education. These ministries were aimed at producing knowledge to be integrated into policy. An impressive set of research centers and institutes in all the academic disciplines, from the humanities to the social and hard sciences, were established within the university. In addition to the teaching profession, the Ivorian government established a professional track for researchers in the university system, with a promotional ladder parallel to that of the teaching track, in order to promote scientific research for development. The Ministry of Higher Education and Scientific Research and these centers and institutes of research were fully funded by the state. Although many other African governments did not allocate as much financial and human resources to various units of research and teaching as Côte d'Ivoire did, this country was not exceptional in the general agenda and direction that many other governments were considering.

It is true that regardless of the ideological differences of the African political elites who inherited the state powers from the colonial states, they were genuinely committed to consolidating state power and building a nation. In their own ways, even the most brutal and destructive dictators ironically claimed to govern in pursuit of this mission as well. The postcolonial states were intended to create new nations, which would have similar rules, norms, and laws defined by other states and international organizations such as the League of Nations first and then the United Nations. From the state's point of view, postcolonial Africa would be invented through the nation-building processes.

Despite differences in the processes and mechanisms used to advance this mission, all new African regimes produced some national projects through which the issues of development, national identity, education, welfare programs, ethnicity, and territoriality were to be redefined. Various political regimes and struggles for independence produced different claims about their national projects or agendas. Some of these claims were real, as they were based on history, while others were imagined, as they were based on hope and ideology. Idealism and realism constituted the foundation of these projects, depending on the contexts in which they arose. In addition, the forms of colonial administration also shaped the character of the postcolonial national agendas.

World politics and history have produced different varieties of nationalism at the state, regional, and international levels. Some of the well-known nationalisms are fascism, religious extremism, separatism, individual ethnic or country reform, revolution, and political nationalism (Breuilly 1985). Despite their differences, they share some characteristics. Generally, nationalism has been defined in Western literature as emotional feelings of belonging to a cohesive social group that shares linguistic, political, religious, ethnic, and geographic characteristics. These characteristics create a consensus on the community's goals and purposes. There cannot be a nationalist movement without a national consciousness (Lumumba-Kasongo 1991, 21). The claims for advancing nationalism can use universalistic themes such as universal human rights and self-determination. But the ontology of nationalism itself or its ultimate end is about constructing some kind of particularism often expressed in cultural, religious, geographic, economic, or political terms. It is about the search for a particular identity around which rights and obligations are articulated. It is also the pursuit and elevation of phenomena like "I versus she/he," "we versus they." But nationalist meanings are more complex than the content of "I," "we," "they," or "us" (Gellner 1994, 280).

Political nationalism is associated with the feeling of inadequacy, dislocation, and dysfunctionality (Lumumba-Kasongo 2000, 104). From this perspective, a national project can be perceived as a state policy to address political inadequacy, citizenship dislocation, and social and structural dysfunctionality. In more positive terms, it can be articulated as the search for an optimal situation or at least for the improvement of an already satisfactory situation. Thus, political nationalism is about attempting to solve national problems or improve existing situations. The specific content and the ideology behind Africa's national projects vary from one political regime to another.

Three forms of nationalism help identify the variety or at least some major characteristics of the political regimes and their respective national projects. This categorization is far from historically and sociologically exhaustive. Instead, it is an effort to construct a framework of analysis for this work. Furthermore, this "categorization can be challenged, in that small and spontaneous movements that may not fit into its logic may be denied their authenticity and their claims and vitality" (Lumumba-Kasongo 1994, 88). The comparative dimension of this categorization is relevant, as it provides a scheme for contrasting ideas and assumptions behind the notion of a national project.

Three broad forms of nationalism have been produced in Africa. (1) The nationalism associated with the state's reforms, the reforms made by the colonial and postcolonial states in an attempt to make themselves adequate and useful. (2) Nationalism inspired by the contradictions and the imperatives of global capitalism articulated by local and international working classes and popular movements. This nationalism at the local level was essentially ideological, with a strong base for power and class struggles. (3) Separatist nationalisms, which were inspired by the local African traditions / precolonial political entities and fused with European values such as those in the Bible or religion in general. This nationalism can be defined as projecting a strong syncretism, an eclectic type of nationalism.

Through the state's nationalism, the reforms were generally intended to maintain the status quo or what can also be viewed as "the immorality of the state." Depending on the period and history of each country and its people, the state's nationalism can be characterized by the state's control of the negotiation processes between its elites and other members of civil society. These political elites made sure that the main objective would be to build state institutions, including educational institutions, with the university at the center and to produce and maintain some controlled social and cultural cohesion through a common political objective. Any attempt to have a different discourse or to disagree with the definitions of nation-building was considered as anathema, betrayal, political aberration, or abnormality.

During and after the cold war, the combination of all these three forms of nationalism produced various political regimes, such as African socialism, Afro-Marxism-Leninism, socialism, populist-nationalism, semi- to full-multiparty democracy, and monarchies. Even most military regimes that, with a few exceptions such as Algeria in the period of the liberation struggle and Burkina Faso under Thomas Sankara, did not stem directly from nationalist movements have claimed to produce some forms or elements of national projects. These were, for instance, the cases of Mobutu Sese Seko in the Democratic Republic of Congo (then Zaïre), François Tombalbaye of Chad, Samuel Doe of Liberia, Muammar Gaddafi of Libya, and Gnassingbé Eyadéma of Togo. In order to advance the mission of building unified states and subsequently the new nations, most of these regimes, even the enlightened ones like the African socialism of Julius Nyerere in Tanzania or the nationalist regime of Kwame Nkrumah in Ghana, tended toward authoritarianism and totalitarianism.

National projects have different cultural specificities, ideologies, supportive communities, and social classes. Some of the national projects served as masks for neocolonialism, while others were based on the conviction that Africa could produce its own capitalism (in spite of the neocolonial context) or "domesticated" capitalism, such as that of Félix Houphouët-Boigny of Côte d'Ivoire and Jomo Kenyatta of Kenya, or the homegrown socialism of Modibo Kéïta of Mali and especially Julius Nyerere of Tanzania. As Irving Leonard Markovitz noted,

> At the time of Africa's "nationalist movement," every regime, no matter how conservative, seemed bound to do something, if not about the misery of the mass of the population then at least about the fact that fewer and fewer people seemed willing to accept their "historical lot" and threaten to rise in rebellion. However, prediction of progressive policies did not in most cases turn out to be true. Organizations and bureaucracies designed in the interest of the poor serviced only the technicians and civil servants. These new organizations did, however, strengthen the state; they buttressed, reinforced, and institutionalized the power of the organizational bourgeoisie. They co-opted the most vocal critics and expanded the intermediary layers of well-paid allies into the cities, towns, and villages. (Markovitz 1987, 13)

The debates about the national project included the dilemma of reconciling nation-building and Pan-African unity as a necessary step in implementing the grand project for sustainable social progress in global Africa, with the university as a central institution. Ideologically, nation-state building has exclusionist tendencies that conflicted with the vision and effort of African-centered postcolonial reconstruction projects to which cross-border/regional universities were initially expected to contribute significantly.

For instance, institutions that started under the colonial rule were developed into subregional public universities, such as Makerere for East Africa with British colonial experience, and Université de Dakar or Université d'Abidjan, for French West Africa. Other cross-border institutions were conceived after the colonial era. For instance, Université nationale du Bénin in Bénin and Université du Bénin in Togo decided to build complementary institutional units. This was done to avoid costly duplications, given the scarcity of resources that would not allow two small countries to create full universities offering quality education in all the academic disciplines. Economies of scale were not the only important factors that led to the decision to offer university programs across their border. The project of using the state-run university as a pragmatic and more effective means to build a Pan-African nation—despite differences in ideology and political regimes and the obstacles of the artificial borders between states—was considered a viable alternative to the grand idea of policy reforms for Pan-Africanism.

As Julius Nyerere stated in his address, entitled "The Dilemma of the Pan-Africanist," delivered at the inauguration of the University of Zambia,

> The question we now have to answer is whether Africa shall maintain this internal separation as we defeat colonialism, or whether our earlier proud boast: "I am an African" shall become a reality. . . . [E]ach state has a government which is responsible to the people of its own area and to them only. It must work for their particular well-being or invite chaos in its territory. . . . On the one hand is the fact that Pan-Africanism demands an African consciousness and an African loyalty; on the other hand is the fact that each Pan-Africanist must also concern himself with the freedom and development of one of the nations of Africa. These things can conflict. (Nyerere, Nichol, and Pratt 1967, 1–2)

As already indicated, at independence, within the logic and imperatives of nation-state building, African countries without exception created their own apparatuses. The "nation-building" endeavor meant creating a nation from groups of people with a common African civilization and ethos, but subcultural specificities and differences in access to state resources from a common national treasury. This was while these people were trying to conform to a new common national reference, of which formal education was the principal instrument. Nyerere argued that because African leaders had failed to decisively opt for the political unity of Africa when the individual states became independent, they had the responsibility to commit themselves to the development of their respective nations to ensure social advancement on the continent, with a central role to be played by the university.

In state agendas for national and continental advancement, the public university loomed large as the one institution that had the power and support to foster national progress and cement the unity needed for collective well-being.

The postcolonial era has had three main waves of university creation. The first wave came immediately after independence. This university was modeled on the oldest European traditions (e.g., Oxbridge model in former British colonies, the Sorbonne model in former French colonies, and the Louvain model in the Belgian tradition). The Sorbonne model, for instance, was a public university, while the Louvain model was a Catholic university with a public mission. Regardless of the specifics of each model, the African university was intended to be academic and universalistic while also capable of responding effectively to the specific and immense needs of nation-building and socioeconomic development in a postcolonial context. As Burton Clark explains, "In developing countries, the state wants from the higher education system: socioeconomic relevance defined in terms of practicality and professionalization, cultural relevance referring to cultural revival and national identity, and political relevance defined as good citizenship and commitment to political goals" (Clark 1983, 250).

The debate over the university in the development process of the African continent in the context of the colonial and postcolonial sociopolitical dynamics was new,[2] but the intellectual and political discourse questioning or acclaiming the effective or even indispensable role of the university to sustain modernity, development, or social progress was not new. Indeed, in western European countries, especially France, which was one of the two countries that shared the university's Western tradition, and also in the United States, the university did not enjoy a linear progression.[3] As John Meyer and colleagues observed:

> Over the last two centuries, there have been so many clear practical and theoretical reasons why it [the university] should have lost out in the long-term expansion of higher education. Around the turn of the nineteenth century, critics accused the university of being archaic, linked to the old regime and its culture, and in need of replacement by specialized education in emergent sciences and technologies. In more radical countries [i.e., France and the United States], the university was partially replaced. . . . And in other countries such as Germany and Spain, a wave of university deaths also occurred. . . . By the end of the nineteenth century, however, the university was back everywhere. (Meyer et al. 2007, 198–99)

During the years of the doubt about the university while the institutional innovations have remained (e.g., *les grandes écoles* in France, the college system in the United States), in countries of the West and other regions, the role of the university as an agent in the modernization process has been paramount (Meyer et al. 2007, 198–99). Other examples include Japan during the Meiji Restoration and its emphasis on both mass education and the development of higher education as an investment in the consolidation of the state and development (Roesgaard 1998).

In the case of Africa, the university and its various interest groups were expected to have a central role in socioeconomic, sociopolitical, and sociocultural progress. From the African-socialist Nyerere to the Francophile and pro-Western capitalist Houphouët-Boigny, the arguments varied in form but very little in substance. Thus Nyerere stated:

> Schools and universities are part of an educational system: a national education system. They promote, and they must promote, a national outlook among the students. . . .

> Loyalty to the national constitution, to the elected leaders, to the symbols of nation-hood all these things are encouraged by every device. This is not only inevitable; it is also right. . . . If the present states are not to disintegrate, it is essential that deliberate steps be taken to foster a feeling of nationhood. Otherwise our present multitude of small countries, almost all of us too small to sustain a self-sufficient modern economy, could break into even smaller units perhaps based on tribalism. Then further period of foreign domination would be inevitable. . . . Let me repeat: in order to avoid internal conflict and further disunity, each nation state is forced to promote its own nation-hood. (Nyerere, Nicol, and Pratt 1967, 2)

Nyerere went on to point out that each well-organized and strong nation with a successful social and constitutional organization and economic output would make a needed contribution to lay the foundation of real African unity within a Pan-Africanist vision of a nation for global development in Africa. Teleologically, this process should be gradual and comprehensive.

Unlike in Europe and the United States, in Africa the dominant class that consolidated higher education for the advancement of society was internal. This is different from the colonial and postcolonial framework of external domination with a direct impact on domestic education, especially at higher education level, and an even more direct influence on the university.

In Africa, the initial reference of the postcolonial university to external powers' models led to extreme dependence and hence the characterization of the universities as multinational cultural subdivisions of these metropolitan institutions. Thus, paradoxically, "the same education which has produced nationalists eager to end colonial rule and to establish African self-government has also perpetuated cultural colonialism" (Mazrui 1975, 194) was further reinforced in the "new international cultural order" (Mazrui 1992, 96).

After the adoption of SAPs (structural adjustment programs) policies, the nature and mission of the second wave of universities were characterized by various, at times contradictory, factors and forces. These forces are the pressing need to respond to the high demand for higher education from the increasing number of graduates of secondary schools, to the need to be relevant and practical. Of particular importance is the quest for diversified sources of funding to relieve the state of its financial obligations that it could no longer meet during the economic crisis and disengagement programs prescribed by the Bretton Woods institutions. With the increasing global power of liberalization and the pressure to promote privatization, the result expected by these global institutions was to privatize the public university, starting with its resources. The high demand, unmatched by supply, and the liberalization contact set the stage for the third generation of universities.

The leaders of the new inherited postcolonial states generally felt the need to create new channels for training and recruiting politicians. The university community, composed of professors, researchers, and, most important, students, represented the potential political elite. With the largest proportion of the populations of the African countries composed of youth, it has been suggested that in these "transitional societies, the socialization and training must focus on youth groups" (Zolberg 1969, 105).

Thus, at the juncture of political independence, African political leaders and a small but powerful and growing intellectual elite, including the teaching staff and students, as well as the general populations, put their faith in education and ultimately higher education, especially the university, in the battle for development.

EVOLUTION OF THE MISSION AND FUNCTIONS OF THE UNIVERSITY IN AFRICA

A workshop organized by the Association of African Universities (AAU), entitled "Creating the African University: Emerging Issues of the 1970s" (Yesufu 1973), led to the publication of a seminal book with the same title. In this meeting, African scholars and top education administrators and chief academic officers addressed critical issues pertaining to the "development university." The five topics for reflection and discussion in this workshop were setting the priorities, defining the programs and curricula, Africanizing the university faculty and staff, and designing research, lifelong learning, and other innovative functions considered important to the university to be designated as a research university.

All these topics were defined as critical areas for the conceptualization, design, adjustment, and reform of the African university. They conceived of and projected the university as the state's institutional apparatus for learning and knowledge production geared toward improving the living standards of the African people and, more generally, promoting and accelerating the development of African societies. The idea of the African university and the conception of the development of African societies were intertwined. A major problem of the African university discussed in this workshop was the "the inability of the local university graduate to display the type of knowledge, initiative, maturity and capacity that is so vital for the modernization of Africa" (Yesufu 1973, 41). Thus, Yesufu further stated that a truly African university . . . must be one which, while acknowledging the need to transform Africa into the twentieth century, must yet realize that it can best achieve this result by completely identifying itself with the realities of a predominantly rural "sixteenth century" setting, and the aspirations of an unsophisticated, but highly expectant, people. It follows that the emergent African university must, henceforth, be much more than an institution for teaching, research and dissemination of higher learning. It must be accountable to, and serve, the vast majority of the African people who live in rural areas. The African university must be committed to active participation in social transformation, economic modernization, and the training and upgrading of the total human resources of the nation, not just a small elite. (Yesufu 1973, 41–42)

There was a high level of optimism in this workshop, in which major functions were identified and debated: "production and dissemination of knowledge specifically research," "intellectual leadership," human resource development, achievement of "social and economic modernization," and fostering "inter-continental unity and international understanding" (Yesufu 1973, 42–43).

At the lower levels of the educational system, families and communities have been contributing significantly to the cost. To these families, especially the poorest ones that were concentrated in mostly rural areas, the state was expected to be responsible for covering the full cost at the higher education level. Because of their limited national budgets, for these African countries, creating and securing human and physical resources for functioning public universities for development was an epic undertaking. It is worth recalling that in the colonial logic of domination, when African countries acquired their nominal political independence, higher education, particularly the university, was either at the initial stage or simply nonexistent. Thus, most countries had to create their universities from scratch.

In Africa, the state was nearly the sole provider of higher education revenues. In the Francophone countries, for instance, even in the 1990s after the pressure to privatize or, at least, increase the private contribution to the cost of education, public contribution still constituted up to 93 percent of the budget (Negrao 1995, 9–10). While African higher education received contributions from international organizations and industrial countries through bilateral and multilateral cooperation, and private foundations, the budgetary needs of African universities rested squarely on the public revenues. In the absence of domestic private contributions either from private industries and/or individual donors and foundations, public funding has been indispensable to the universities' functioning. Public funding has also philosophical and ethical dimensions in regard to the state's responsibility and the people's rights.

Based on a comparison of international statistics of education finance, Jose Negrao also demonstrated that in many industrial countries, mainly in Europe but also in Japan, public funding of higher education has been quite high, reaching an average of 84 percent of the higher education/university budget. Even in the United States, which has many private institutions of higher learning, especially the leading major research universities, the local administrative unit (school district) and the state and federal governments contribute considerable value. These funds flow through various channels, ranging from tax exemptions to various grants, including the states' and especially the federal government's huge grants. The major difference is that in Africa, state funding was the sole domestic source. This has been, and still is, problematic, given the shaky economic base of African states, which are basically suppliers of cheap raw materials with unstable and generally declining prices, and their citizens act simply as consumers of the made-in-foreign countries.

Another important feature of the African universities' financial base, at least in the first two postindependence decades, was the fact that African countries devoted to education a large proportion of their revenues in terms of the percentage of their GDP and public expenditures. In the 1960s and 1970s, they routinely allocated at least a quarter of their GDP to education. During this period, Côte d'Ivoire, for instance, was identified as allocating the largest proportion of its GDP and public expenditures to education of any country in the world. This was 7.4 percent of the GDP and 32.6 percent of public expenditures in 1973 and up to 10.0 percent and 45.0 percent, respectively, in 1981 (Assié-Lumumba 1995b, 333; Tuinder 1978, 281–82).

Furthermore, higher education received the largest share of the funds that governments allocated to education. Owing to the scarcity of national financial resources and increasing foreign debts, the allocation of large shares of small national budgets was an eloquent statement of the value of higher education in general and especially the university.

By any standards, African countries made major achievements in institutional building and enrollment in the immediate postindependence period. Compared with the initial numbers of students enrolled, the raw numbers, and especially the rates of increase were impressive.

Nevertheless, even with the continued rise in raw numbers, Africa as a world region had, and still has, the lowest proportion of its university-age population enrolled (see table 8.1).

Table 8.1 Gross Enrollment Ratio as a Percentage of Total Eligible for
Higher Education

Year	Gross Enrollment Ratio, Higher Education (%)
1965	0.8
1970	1.0
1975	1.7
1980	2.4
1985	2.9
1990	3.8
1995	4.8
1996	3.8
1997	2.3
2000	2.5

Source: Authors' elaboration based on data from World Bank, 2002.

As Keith Hinchliffe argues,

With a growth rate of over 11 percent a year since 1960, higher education enrollments in African countries average around one percent of the relevant age group. As a proportion of the total population, they are less than a quarter of those in Asian countries. Despite its small size, however, expenditure on the higher education sector averages one fifth of total educational expenditure which in turn accounts for one fifth of all central government expenditures. (Hinchliffe 1985, 2)

Decades later, the situation has not improved significantly. Thus, it is erroneous to apply the notion of "massification" instead of a more accurate reference to "overcrowding" to capture the consequence of the insufficient expansion of the existing infrastructure and the building of new facilities to respond to demand. Indeed, as David Bloom, David Canning, and Kevin Chan point out,

Enrollment rates in higher education in sub-Saharan Africa are by far the lowest in the world. Although the gross enrolment ratio (GER) has increased in the past 40 years—it was just 1 per cent in 1965—it still stands at only 5 per cent. . . . [Statistical evidence] shows that . . . the absolute gap by which it lags behind other regions has increased rapidly. The region's present enrolment ratio is in the same range as that of other developing regions 40 years ago. Moreover, gender disparities have traditionally been wide and remain so. (Bloom, Canning, and Chan 2005, 5)

Thus, human capital theory argues that there is a positive, linear, and causal relationship between education and development, so from the perspective of the rights of citizens to education, African countries would need even more financial resources to expand higher education. The main goals of the expansion were to increase the number of students so as to produce graduates with the skills and knowledge for the productive sectors and to promote their socioeconomic attainment. This was why some of the goals that were targeted for the 1980s by the African leaders at the historic Addis Ababa Conference of 1961 included universal primary and increased secondary enrollments as well as the production of significantly higher numbers of university graduates. As indicated earlier, since there have not been other national sources for substantial contributions to the cost of higher education, public funds are considered as necessary for the postindependence development agendas.

Ironically, a major economic crisis and parallel or subsequent educational crisis began unfolding in the 1970s, reaching a peak in the 1980s. The formulation and the implementation of the structural adjustment programs (SAPs) of the World Bank and the stabilization program of the International Monetary Fund (IMF) that started in the early 1980s exacerbated the crisis and the implications for the various aspects of SAPs for African universities. The affected areas included no expansion of general facilities and the privatization and/or no expansion of social services such as health care, early retirement, freezes in hiring and salary, and preference for funding basic education (although user fees were introduced at the lower levels as well).

Thus, a major issue related to funding of higher education as a national development project was the linkage between financial provision and the source of power and authority. In recent African history, the use of the state's legitimized power in organizing the university that was acquired through its funding of higher education has not been entirely positive. The state's infringement on academic freedom and the political appointment of high-level administrators and chief academic officers of universities were among the major shortcomings of state control over the universities from the 1960s to the 1980s. On a continent characterized by predominantly one-party political systems, until the development of multipartyism in the 1990s, movements and organizations such as unions made up of large proportions of the university community (students and faculty members) critical of the systems in power, constituted de facto opposition parties. Accordingly, they were treated as such, with notorious state brutality, by the one-party governments.[4] Arguably, such an exercise of power was at least due in part to the lack of financial and basic autonomy of education.

As we argued earlier, the state was also committed to using the same power to advance the key educational and broader societal goals of development. In fact, there is a need for the equitable allocation of resources to promote equality of educational opportunity across different regions, ethnic and religious groups, new emerging social classes, and gender. This need can be more decisively addressed by the state if it has direct control of the resources that must be distributed equitably to education and different social groups, especially the needy farmers and rural dwellers in general. Thus, a considerable proportion of the first waves of university students and graduates of modest social origins were able to attend universities because of the state funding that covered not only tuition but also the cost of social services, including lodging, boarding, health care, transportation, and stipends, in the form of scholarships for study at home and abroad. University students almost acquired the status of privileged group members within the public administration. These actual or perceived privileges also were treated as an investment in the future of the emerging nations.

In part based on considerable pressure from the populations, the second and third waves of universities were built after the 1980s amid the severe economic crisis and strong opposition of the international financial institutions, especially the World Bank. As Geremie Sawadogo points out, one of the greatest achievements of the African universities since the 1980s is the high rate of student enrollment in almost all the universities, despite the policies promoted by the SAPs aimed at restricting the number of new students (Sawadogo 1995).

As indicated earlier, the initial universities were designated as institutions for development and nation-building, to produce basic and scientific knowledge and form critical minds. But given increasing unemployment, the "brain drain" phenomenon, and the persistent call to combat poverty and promote well-being, the second and third waves of universities, especially those created in the 1990s and thereafter, were geared toward the attainment of perceived development. This pragmatism is reflected in the curricular emphasis on science and technology, corresponding more to the preference of the global liberal economy for these disciplines.

Even though the demand on the universities to perform has increased, since the 1980s, the government allocation of resources for higher education and especially for the universities has decreased. The dictates of global financial institutions with their direct involvement in the design of African domestic policies also started to alter the notion of national sovereignty and autonomy, the definition of national priorities, as well as the respective resource allocation. The neocolonial global frameworks—the dominance of the liberal global institutions on the national policy guidelines—did not really give a chance to African countries, their institutions, and their political forces to consistently exert autonomous power and authority. The SAPs, however, revealed a new form of aggressive and brutal intervention that restricted the funding of basic social services such as primary health care, even minimal agricultural subsidies, and basic education. Their influence also downgraded and labeled the university as unworthy of full public funding.

These policies weakened the commitment to support existing institutions and prevented the creation of new universities when the emphasis shifted to basic education. Thus, with this interference, the SAPs contained a major flaw that was reflected in the failure to anticipate the placements of the graduates of basic education in the secondary schools and subsequently in higher education, especially the university. Indeed, they did not take into account that the number of newly qualified candidates for higher education would be growing. Even the World Bank acknowledged that "in Sub-Saharan Africa, during the 1980s average public expenditure per student declined from $6,300 to $1,500 in real terms" (World Bank 1994a, 14). The 1990s witnessed a further decline of an estimated 30 percent. For many African countries, this means that the public expenditure per student in higher education is nearing or falling below the level, estimated at US$1,000 per student, which is believed necessary to provide a minimally acceptable level of higher education in today's world (Partnership for Capacity Building in Africa 1997, 9). With many African nations already spending a significant portion of their GDP on education, the additional resources required to simply maintain current levels of enrollments in higher education using the traditional residential campus model will not be available (Saint 1999, 4).

In the context of the liberal economic policies, African higher education was besieged by the Bretton Woods institutions. African university constituencies rightly viewed them as modern proxies of the old colonial power system. This is because they have been, in the name of "efficiency," "growth," and "free market," the vanguards in prescribing policies and formulas for curtailing the number of students to be admitted to the university and reducing the proportion of educational expenditure for the universities. They failed to even think of, and/or anticipate, the future educational needs and demands of the youth completing the basic education that they had been promoting. They lacked or did not feel compelled to adopt a holistic approach to the education sector and national development.

Yet as a proportion of the total or school-age population, higher education students still remained the lowest, compared with other regions of the developing world, while social demand had not abated. Furthermore, to date the opportunities have not been distributed equitably, and the needy segments of the general populations have grown larger.

When analyzing the role of African states in public engagement, it is important to revisit the global call for renewed support for Africa's development agenda, especially the MDGs. When most African countries acquired their nominal independence and some were still engaged in liberation struggles, the United Nations took the lead for global support for Africa. Thus, for instance, during the sixteenth session of its General Assembly, on December 19, 1961, the United Nations adopted several resolutions that directly focused on Africa's educational and socioeconomic development. They included Resolutions 1710 (XVI) on the "United Nations Development Decade," 1717 (XVI) on "African Educational Development," and 1718 (XVI) on "Economic Development of Africa."

That same year, African leaders met for the Addis Ababa Conference, at which they defined their educational needs for development. Subsequently, African countries declared education the "priority of all priorities" in their struggle to eradicate poverty and promote development. It was with the international backing and domestic popular contribution at the lower levels of education and the high demand for higher education that African governments embarked on their major projects of national development. This meant setting up higher education, especially creating the university, as a cornerstone. In fact, with the renewed popularity of human capital theory and its application to the foreign policy and development cooperation assistance of industrial countries and international organizations, the university, and generally higher education, was recommended to be treated globally as *l'enfant chéri* (beloved child) in the 1960s and 1970s (Schultz 1977).

The expected role and status of higher education were in sharp contrast to the new treatment that the universities received through the implementation of SAPs. From the perspective of the SAPs, the African university was the culprit of African predicaments that unfolded in the 1980s and hence justified the prescribed interventionist policies of deliberately underfunding African universities.

As in the 1960s, at the turn of the twenty-first century several official statements have been made about the concerns and engagement of the global community toward social progress in developing countries, especially Africa.

In the MDGs referred to earlier there, once again, has been a call for a global commitment to foster social progress in developing countries, especially in Africa. Also as previously indicated, the UN MDGs are reminiscent of the development decade of the 1960s, although the global context has changed considerably. The global optimistic outlook of the 1960s and 1970s has now generally disappeared. In fact, some have referred to the emergence of Afro-pessimism. Despite some continuing contributions, however, the onset of "aid" fatigue is clear, as reflected in the "international donor" community's nearly empty promises and additional conditions, ironically coupled with the increased interference of the Bretton Woods institutions reinforcing their role in defining African domestic policies. Thus, despite Africa's higher education needs, it is worth noting the conspicuous absence of higher education in the MDGs. From the African perspective, the mask of international support for development fell off with the crude realities of the economic crises and the intent and brutality of SAPs in disempowering the African states by prescribing the end of the states' sponsorship of social programs. The naïve expectation that African national development agendas could substantively depend on external approval and sponsorship ended. Merciless global liberalism, with its relentless privatization promotion motto and its dogma of "growth," has instead taken over.

Thus, the World Education Forum held in April 2000 in Dakar and the United Nations MDGs constitute the new statements for global commitments to achieve specified targets by the year 2015, and the spirit of mutual trust has been seriously undermined. Higher education, quality and relevant education, and research are indispensable to the attainment of the eight MDGs (i.e., eradicating extreme poverty and hunger; achieving universal primary education; promoting gender equality and empowering women; reducing child mortality; improving maternal health; combating HIV/AIDS, malaria, and other diseases; ensuring environmental sustainability; and setting up a Global Partnership for Development) and the EFA (Education for All). Yet the April 2000 Dakar Declaration did not mention "higher education" and "university" of any kind, nor are they referred to explicitly in the eight MDGs.

The universities need to produce relevant and critical knowledge and human resources to tackle old and new challenges, as it is precisely in the context of increased poverty that a socially responsible and caring state is needed. The model of higher education that most African states inherited from the European colonial rule is still structurally in place in European countries. There, higher education depends on public funding while pursuing policies for continued expansion and increased access, at both the national and, to a lesser extent, regional levels in the European Union.[5]

Public funding of the university is necessary in African countries, as this model corresponds precisely to Africa's needs for social services, since a still overwhelmingly impoverished population is struggling to set itself free from the poverty trap. Furthermore, many of these populations provide revenues for the states, for example, through their labor and production of commodities in cash-crop economies based on small, family-owned farms. This is in contrast to southern Africa, where European settlers control the large commercial farms. Unlike European and other industrial countries, most African countries do not yet have an industrial base or major alternative funding sources to provide a quality university education. This is particularly the case in South Africa, which has an advanced industrial economy, given the width of the gap from its past policy of apartheid and the legacy of inequality, state leadership, and commitment.

Furthermore, throughout Africa, poverty in the twenty-first century has new faces and new locations. Indeed, large numbers of rural populations have moved to the cities, pushed by harder living conditions and pulled by the actual or imagined opportunities in urban areas. These slums, with living conditions that are often even more precarious and appalling than those in the rural communities, are expanding in the numbers of residents and the area they occupy. This includes a growing proportion of youths with aspirations to better life experiences than their parents. They cannot be ignored, and their potential must be harnessed. The hard reality, though, is that while these populations around the major cities are closer to the physical locations of the universities, which are clustered in urban areas, the majority of their youth are sociologically much further away from the universities than the students of rural origin who in the 1960s and 1970s attended the new universities with full state support. As Birgit Brock-Utne observed,

> Even World Bank figures are unequivocal in showing that the majority of students in Africa—an average of about 60%—used to come from the ranks of the peasantry, workers, and small traders. These people are not likely to have the means [to] meet [the] increasing cost of university education. The natural outcome will be a decrease in enrolments and increase in dropout rates among students from poorer family backgrounds. (Brock-Utne 2003, 34)

Therefore, the state has an even greater role and responsibility to provide the necessary educational services, whether education is treated as a right or an investment. By themselves, the neoliberal policies are ontologically incapable of promoting these services for the development of the students' capabilities and the states' agendas for social progress.

Despite the increasing globalization, development policies are still mainly conceptualized, designed, and implemented at the level of nation-states in developing and industrial countries, even where multistate regional organizations have been established and are relatively functional. Therefore, African governments deserve and require national autonomy for the assessment of their priorities, their real needs, and the adoption of relevant policies to address them.

Certain dimensions of the university's functions—teaching, research, and services—only public universities or universities with a clearly articulated public mission can provide for African societies and people.

In several countries, private universities in both brick-and-mortar or distance-learning mode have emerged. Reasons for the emergence of private universities include, besides the global liberal model of promoting the private sector, the lack of efficiency or the generally dysfunctional nature of the public institutions, overcrowded facilities, excessively high student/professor ratios, and irregular academic years. This is a self-fulfilling prophecy, as the lack of funding of the public universities has led to their continued deterioration. The decline in quality erodes confidence.

Each national context for the emergence and evolution of these private universities is different. All these private institutions present the same challenges regarding the questions about the extent to which they consider the university's public mission important, for example, taking into account issues of inequality and state development agenda.

Nevertheless, their absence, emergence, and expansion reflect state policy. In Nigeria, for instance, at independence the university was conceived as public. Although the current number of federal and state institutions suggests a dominance of public universities, Nigeria currently has the largest number, twenty, of private universities.[6]

Some of these private institutions are based on distance learning enabled by information and communication technologies (ICTs), with alternative programs in dual- or single-mode institutions. Whether they are brick-and-mortar or distance-learning institutions, most of them are motivated by moneymaking possibilities or opportunities, with domestic and/or foreign origin. Because the users' ability to pay is critical, those segments of the population that need to benefit from publicly funded programs are likely to be excluded by these institutions.

In a few countries (e.g., Zimbabwe), the distance-learning university is part of the national/public higher education system. Nevertheless, even in such cases, the distance-learning institutions cannot duplicate many aspects of the functions of the classic university with a public mission, including research. More generally, the private universities in African countries are not bound by the responsibilities expected from public universities.

On the whole, then, the current state of African higher education indicates that without vigorous policy leadership and a funding commitment from the state, reconceptualizing an invigorated university with other, comprehensive, higher education institutions will not be addressed productively and holistically. The need for research on and solutions to social problems, including the question of social inequality with a particular emphasis on gender, can be effectively addressed only with strong state commitment.

Compared with the first two decades of the postcolonial era, women in higher education received less money, starting with the SAPs, even though the official national and international discourses continued to claim otherwise. The actual policies and discourses contradicted each other, especially during the second half of the Women's Decade that ended with the Nairobi Conference in 1985. For instance,

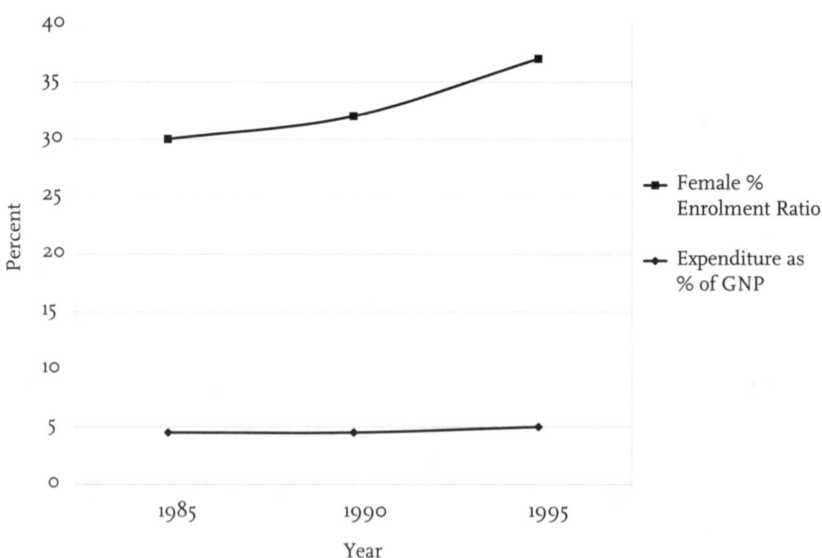

Figure 8.1 Public Expenditures for Education as Percentages of Female Enrollment and GNP

Source: Assié-Lumumba, 2000.

during this period, the proportion of the World Bank's education projects acknowledging gender was 28 percent between 1972 and 1981, while the proportion of total investment in education projects acknowledging gender was 16 percent during the same period. It is significant that in contrast, from the 1980s to the early 1990s, there was a clear "regional shift" in favor of South Asia, where the number of projects acknowledging gender increased from 12 to 38 percent, and the investment in the projects acknowledging gender importance also increased, from 8 to 65 percent. On the whole, the "total investment in higher education projects acknowledging gender in the Sub-Saharan African region during the 1980s decreased to a mere 6 percent from 16 percent in the 1970s" (Subbarao et al. 1994, 32).

The decade from 1985 to 1995 shown in figures 8.1 and 8.2 also corresponds to the worst phase of the economic crisis and the SAPs prescriptions and applications. Figure 8.1 indicates that during the economic crisis and the implementation of SAPs, there was an increase of 5 percent in the ratio of female enrollment in higher education institutions when public expenditures in education as a percentage of GDP rose by just 0.5 percent. Figure 8.2 shows that over the same decade, public expenditures for education as a percentage of government expenditure rose by an equivalent of 3.5 percent. Thus, there clearly is a positive

Figure 8.2 Public Expenditures for Education as a Percentage of Government
Expenditure
Source: Assié-Lumumba, 2000.

correlation between public expenditure on education as a percentage of government expenditure and the percentage ratio of female enrollment.

The role of the state in guaranteeing a consistent policy of opening access to underrepresented groups, in this case women, is necessary until the imbalance in Africa's development paradigms is corrected, especially with the capricious and contradictory positions and policies of some of powerful external agencies (Lumumba-Kasongo 2007).

IS THE IDEA OF PUBLIC UNIVERSITY STILL RELEVANT?

To answer this question adequately, we also should ask, To whom should this idea of the public university be relevant? In the way it was worded, the national project was supposed to benefit both the state and the people. The African state, though, has a higher responsibility, as it has to advance its agenda toward the creation of the nation, and the nation is ranked higher than the individual. The relevance of the public university has had this dual mission. The argument in this chapter is that there are persistent contradictions related to the evolution of the African states within the world of the states as reflected in their dependency syndrome, their antidemocratic practices, and their inability to actualize positively and consistently people's demands through effective policies. Nevertheless, both the state and society conceived the university to be essentially an instrument of social progress, a forum of social changes and higher ideas and thoughts. The idea of the classic university's mission has not disappeared or become irrelevant with poverty, malnutrition, conflicts, and insecurity.

The public university exists as a development institution for various reasons, including extreme poverty and other related challenges. With about 45 percent of the African population living in poverty, 300 million people living in absolute poverty, more than 30 million people infected with HIV AIDS, life expectancy declining in some countries from fifty-six years in the 1980s to forty-eight years in 2003, a rampant unemployment rate, major regional wars, and a massive displacement of people, Africa is economically the poorest region of the world, despite its abundance of natural and human resources (Mbaya et al. 2001). As of 1998, Africa comprised thirty-two of the world's forty-eight least developed countries (LDC) and thirty-four of the forty-five lowest-ranked countries for human development (UNDP 1998). At the end of the 1990s, Africa's share of world trade was 2 percent, and its share of world investment was 1 percent, neither of which had changed significantly in 2008.

Various entities are affected differently by poverty, which in turn impacts the trends and severity of poverty. The most common unit of analysis when dealing with poverty is the individual, but in a more refined analysis, the family, the community, the region, and the state must be accounted for as well. Since the 1990s, on the domestic front, various interest groups, such as students and families, teaching staff, administrators, and the state/government, have experienced increased poverty.

After African countries gained independence, the majority of the population was commonly understood as being poor. Hence, the state was expected to ensure that the children of poor farmers in remote villages who graduated from secondary schools would receive full support to study at the university. This was considered an investment for uplifting individuals and extended families and for broader social progress.

The eradication of poverty, gender inequality, and deadly but curable diseases and the promotion of social progress require the positive and vigorous intervention of a strong and caring African state providing services, especially to the neediest segments of the population. These services include not only equitable access to education with increased chances for the children of the poor to attain upward mobility, but also the diffusion of, and access to, knowledge produced through quality higher education for the benefits of society.

As already indicated, the African public university was established with the classic mission of universities everywhere, especially those with Western traditions. This mandate is to conduct research, to produce theories used to explain the world, to transmit old and new knowledge to the young generations, and to provide them with tools to be part of a relevant and legitimate critical community. With this specific mission, the African university was not intended to become a microcosm of African society. Even though many African political regimes have, during various periods, ignored academic freedom, temporarily closed the universities, and severely punished students and professors who have disagreed with their policies and practices, no regimes so far have succeeded in closing the universities permanently.[7] Part of the reason is that African universities are part of the international communities of reason and researchers, and also because these universities are a prominent part of the African communities. No power is able to permanently destroy or halt the enlightened ideas and thoughts of a people. Ironically, even when the governments were cracking down on protestors and ignoring basic academic freedom, they still respected the students and professors who dared challenge the SAPs. Generally, as expected by Africans, the community of enlightened people must advance the human cause.

Criticizing what he referred to as the ambivalent definition of what the university ought to do and what it should not be expected or forced to do in "meeting the needs of society," Yusef Waghid contends that it is possible for the university to retain its character as "a community of reason" while fulfilling its social mission in the process of nation building (Waghid 2002). He believes that the social role of the modern university must be framed by a complementary knowledge base, including what he calls both "disciplinary knowledge" and "socially distributed knowledge." Social justice in access to the totality of knowledge must guide public policy. The public university has a role to play in the production of knowledge, not only for its own sake and to assert membership in the global intellectual community, but also to provide knowledge of immediate relevance to social needs.

The idea of social justice in this context is closely related to the notion of "truth" and "social objectivity." Paulo Freire's *Pedagogy of the Oppressed* (1970) shows the dialogical relations between what is taught at the university and what should be practiced in society. The public university must advance the truth through its holistic perspective. This can be done if the university addresses pragmatically and theoretically the issues that most African people have been facing over the past twenty-five to thirty years. The legitimacy of the public university should be based on this dialogical relation between the state and society and between teacher and student. In relation to the current conditions in Africa, the mission of the African university can be a challenge, as it must participate in finding solutions to Africa's maladies. New theories and methods/approaches still are needed to understand Africa structurally and historically, its conditions, leaders, people, and complex university systems.

As African countries gained independence over a period of more than thirty years, the development of their institutions of higher learning underwent different evolutionary processes. Therefore, a typology of the broader and specific historical contingencies of postcolonial higher education, specifically the university, applies differently to the various national contexts and experiences. Even the countries that acquired their independence in the same period with relatively similar departing points had relatively different trajectories and experienced different progressions. That is, the typology and sequences of the institutions' evolution have been neither uniform nor exhaustive.

From the 1950s to the first decade of the twenty-first century, the various types of universities can be classified according to their status and mission as either public or private universities. Within each of these categories are reflected historical moments, national and local dynamics, and the global international context.

The majority of African countries have had about three waves of institutions, with the first generation of public universities created in the 1960s and 1970s. This was the period of human capital theory application and popular support at home and from the international partners. Despite the economic crisis, by the late 1980s and early 1990s, even countries that had already expanded their higher education systems were still under considerable pressure to open the systems further. Thus, a second wave of universities, composed of mostly public universities, was established between the 1980s and the early 1990s. A third wave has emerged since then and is mainly characterized by the greater number of private universities and the importance of the commercial motive.

The first generation of these universities usually were single-campus national universities, with teaching and research in all disciplines and fields of study. The second generation of universities tended to focus on specific disciplinary areas, mainly medicine, science, technology, and agriculture. These first two waves tended to be guided by the idea of the public university for the realization of the national development project. The third group of universities was more influenced by the increasing impact of globalization and liberalization and the consequences of the economic crisis. This third generation is characterized by the emergence of private institutions, both traditional brick-and-mortar institutions and distance-learning universities. A common factor in this latest wave is the centrality of the financial base of the institutions, whether public or private, with the public mission of the development university only a remnant. The ability to generate financial resources to survive (public) or to make a profit (most private institutions) is a driving force of the curricula. Indeed, these new institutions tend to offer courses in those disciplines considered to be of greater value to the global economy and also most likely to attract students with the greatest ability to pay.

In the specific case of Nigeria, I. A. Ajayi and Haastrup T. Ekundayo identified four generations of universities, from 1960 to the present (Ajayi and Ekundayo 2008). The first three generations are composed of federal and state public universities, and the fourth generation includes, beside public universities at the state level, distance-learning institutions and private universities as a new and salient feature.

Throughout the African continent, the latest wave includes distance-learning and/or private universities. The relative numerical or social importance of the private universities' secular or sectarian components varies according to past and recent history and current situations. On the sectarian front, it is striking that different Christian and Islamic denominations, with their respective global and geopolitical locations, alliances, ideological stands, and financial powers, are engaged in creating institutions of higher learning, including universities. While they appear to be able to attract students, given the overall high demand for higher education, they cannot take the place of the state in planning and executing national development agendas.

THE FUTURE OF THE PUBLIC UNIVERSITY IN AFRICA

The role and the function of universities in Africa are related to the broader socioeconomic development agenda. Moreover, the role of the state is in need of reconstruction. The state is required to guarantee the equal distribution of resources, service to the needy, and renewed investments in higher education. Only benevolent and caring states or some forms of the welfare states can do this. Private corporations or agencies, which are motivated by instant and sustained profit-making ventures, are ontologically unable to work toward this broader objective.

A new concept of the common good or social good in Africa is needed to rebuild the African university in order to reaffirm its mission and functions and, as a necessary support, its infrastructure and human-resource base. The university can help begin the process of halting and reversing the loss of its own graduates. It needs to devise ways to gain from the human resources already dispersed and transform the initial loss through "brain drain" into "brain gain." Within this framework, the African diaspora can also help the public university remain relevant.

Rethinking the structures of the African public university should include the cost of its own maintenance, its relation to ideas and social reproduction, its classic mission of producing educated citizens, and its relationship to the state. The African university is suffering from the same weaknesses as are the African states. African political leaders and educational authorities have depended heavily on "external donors" to support their national projects. Having learned from the past, it is time to adopt policies to abolish this dependence. Ali A. Mazrui argued that "in terms of culture, reliance on one external reference group is outright dependency; reliance on a diversity of external civilizations may be the beginning of autonomy" (Mazrui 1975, 206). In the search for solutions, it is worth revisiting his proposed three strategies for social progress in Africa through policies of domestication, diversification, and counterpenetration.

Programs such as the Lagos Plan of Action (1980), formulated by African political leaders, envisioned self-reliance, self-sustaining development, economic growth, and equal distribution of national resources. Having learned from the SAPs, instead of advancing the New Partnership for Africa's Development (NEPAD), for instance, which is part of the foreign aid scheme of increased dependency, the Lagos Plan of Action should be revisited to reconstruct higher education, especially the public university, as a central component of the African development agenda for the twenty-first century and beyond. Genuine democratic processes can help advance this mission of redefining the role and the structure of the public university.

The African state also needs to resume a serious dialogue with society, its institutions, and the nascent African private sector. Compared with countries in other regions of the world, African countries have not produced a significant nonnational agenda for universities. Nonnational projects are generally designed for potential exploitation, the advancement of individualism, and the protection of greed. Yet this generalization has not provided space to explore the creation of new partnerships between national and nonnational project agencies and agents. Without developing some notion of the social or common good and without agreeing on its philosophical and political content, the objectives of the national and nonnational projects in Africa are likely to remain divergent or even contradictory.

The African public university should claim its legitimacy in working to educate all the people and, at the same time, conduct research to be used for the current or future economy. In short, the new African public university examined in this chapter should have in its curriculum the core aspects of advancing scientific knowledge for peace, human security, the environment, critical comparative and historical studies, social and gender equality, individual and collective freedom, and rigorous research agendas for social progress. People are demanding peace, development, and genuine democracy beyond elections. This public university must pursue scientific, artistic, and humanistic endeavors within the framework of both human- and society-centered development paradigms and social progress in African countries and the global Pan-African community.

NOTES

1. There are institutions of higher learning on the African continent that can be referred to as universities, which date centuries back. They include the Alexandria

model, the monastic system, and the renowned institutions of higher learning of Islamic origin such as Karawiyyinn in Fez (Morocco) in 859 CE, Al-Azhar created in Cairo (Egypt) in 970 CE, and Sankore in Timbuktu from the twelfth century. This chapter focuses on the university of Western origin that was based on colonial experiences and considered an instrument for social progress at the time of independence in the mid-twentieth century.

2. In the early 1870s, both Edward Wilmot Blyden and James Johnson provided able intellectual leadership in the "Freetown debate," in which they advocated the idea of an African university for the advancement of Africans. The university they envisioned would teach a liberal arts–classical education and use African languages, linking contemporary Africa with the ancient civilization that eloquently testified to Africa's great achievements on the world scale. At that time, the Berlin Conference (1884–1885) and the scramble and subsequent formal colonization of the African continent that justified the postcolonial quest for development in the mid-twentieth century had not yet taken place.

3. The other country is Italy. With the Paris and Bologna models in the Middle Ages, these two countries created the Western tradition of university, which underwent various transformations in other periods and countries, for instance, in the nineteenth and twentieth centuries in Germany and the United States.

4. Ironically, some of the groups that have taken power since the 1990s, mainly through multiparty/democratic elections, have evolved to adopt the same behaviors as those of the governments they once criticized.

5. However, it is worth noting that even in these European countries, equality of opportunity has not been achieved. The 2005 uprising and violent protests of desperate youth with little education and few prospects for jobs in France's impoverished suburbs are an eloquent reminder of the structurally embedded inequality.

6. The process for arriving at such a large number was a nonlinear evolution from the supportive civilian and democratic administration of Shehu Shagari (1979–1983) to the abolition under one military regime (Muhammadu Buhari, 1983–1985), again a favorable climate under another (Ibrahim Babangida, 1985–1993). This was followed by the regime of a ruthless military ruler (Sani Abacha, 1993–1998). The decisive takeoff was under the second and civilian eight-year presidency of Olusegun Obasanjo that started in 1999. For more details on this evolution, see *Obasi 2007, 40.

7. As a matter of fact, with the exception of President Nyerere who resigned in his refusal to accept the SAPs' conditionalities, other leaders accepted different schemes of the SAPs. However, the educational and political leaders strongly criticized the Bretton Woods institutions and their policies that were considered a way to dis-

mantle the African universities by deliberately underfunding them. In interviews conducted for various studies, including Assié-Lumumba *1993 and *1995, critical views of African leaders in different regimes were unequivocally expressed.

REFERENCES

Abdalla, A. 1977. *Differing Types of Higher Education*. Paris: International Association of Universities.

Abegaz, B. M. 1995. *Universities in Africa: Challenges and Opportunities of International Cooperation, African Universities*. Accra: Association of African Universities.

Aina, T. A. 1995. *Quality and Relevance: African Universities in the 21st Century*. Accra: Association of African Universities.

Ajayi, I. A., and H. T. Ekundayo. 2008. "The Deregulation of University Education in Nigeria: Implications for Quality Assurance." *Nebula* 5, December.

Ajayi, J. E. A., L. K. H. Goma, and G. A. Johnson, with a contribution by W. Mwotia. 1966. *The African Experience with Higher Education*. Accra: Association of African Universities; London: James Currey; Athens: Ohio University Press.

Ake, C. 1982. *Social Science as Imperialism: The Theory of Political Development*. Ibadan: Ibadan University Press.

——. 1996. *Democracy and Development in Africa*. Washington, D.C.: Brookings Institution.

Altbach, P. 1982a. "Reform and Innovation in Higher Education." *Educational-Documentation and Information* 223: 5–55.

——. 1982b. "Servitude of the Mind? Education, Dependency, and Neocolonialism." In *Comparative Education*, ed. P. Altbach and G. Kelly, 469–84. New York: Macmillan.

Amin, S. 1990. *Maldevelopment: Anatomy of a Global Failure*. London: Zed.

——. 1997. *Capitalism in the Age of Globalization: The Management of Contemporary Society*. London: Zed.

Ashby, E. 1964. *African Universities and Western Tradition*. Cambridge, Mass.: Harvard University Press.

Ashby, E., in association with M. Anderson. 1966. *Universities: British, Indian, African; a Study in the Ecology of Higher Education*. Cambridge, Mass.: Harvard University Press.

Assié-Lumumba, N. T. 1993. *Higher Education in Francophone Africa: Assessment of the Potential of the Traditional Universities and Alternatives for Development*. Washington, D.C.: World Bank.

——. 1995a. *Demand, Access, and Equity Issues in African Higher Education: Past Policies, Current Practices, and Readiness for the 21st Century*. Accra: Association of African Universities.

———. 1995b. "Public Academic School Finance Allocation in Côte d'Ivoire." *Journal of Education Finance* 20 (winter): 332–50.

———. 2000. "Educational and Economic Reforms, Gender Equity, and Access to Schooling in Africa." *International Journal of Comparative Sociology* 41 (1): 89–120.

———. 2006. *Higher Education in Africa: Crises, Reform and Transformation*. Dakar: CODESRIA.

———, ed. 2007. *Women and Higher Education in Africa: Reconceptualizing Gender-Based Human Capabilities and Upgrading Human Rights to Knowledge*. Abidjan: CEPARRED Publications.

Assié-Lumumba, N. T., and T. Lumumba-Kasongo. 1991. "Economic Crisis, State and Educational Reforms in Africa: The Case of Côte d'Ivoire." In *Educational Reform in International Context: Ideology, Economy and the State*, ed. M. B. Ginsburg, 257–84. New York: Garland.

———. 1994. *Dependency and Higher Education Organization in Africa: The Case of the National University of Côte d'Ivoire*. Houston: Institute for Higher Education Law and Governance, University of Houston, Monograph Series, 93/2.

Bloom, D., D. Canning, and K. Chan. 2005. "Higher Education and Economic Development in Africa." Report to the World Bank. Cambridge, Mass.: Harvard University. Available at http://www.aau.org/wghe/publications/HE&Economic_Growth_in_Africa.pdf (accessed June 25, 2007).

Breuilly, J. 1985. *Nationalism and the State*. Chicago: University of Chicago Press.

Brock, A. 1996. "Budgeting Models and University Efficiency: A Ghanaian Case Study." *Higher Education* 32, (2): 113–27.

Brock-Utne, B. 1999. "African Universities and the African Heritage." *International Review of Education* 45 (1): 87–104.

———. 2003. "Formulating Higher Education Policies in Africa: The Pressure form External Forces and the Neoliberal Agenda." *Journal of Higher Education in Africa* 1 (1): 24–56.

Clark, B. 1983. *The Higher Education System: Academic Organization in a Cross-national Perspective*. Berkeley: University of California Press.

Crawley, F. P. 2000. "The Myth of a European Identity: The Role of the Universities in the Formation of European Citizens." In *Universities Remembering Europe: Nations, Culture, and Higher Education*, ed. F. P. Crawley, P. Smeyers, and P. Standish, 27–46. New York: Berghahn Books.

Freire, P. 1970. *Pedagogy of the Oppressed*. Trans. Myra Bergman Ramos. New York: Herder and Herder.

Gaidzanwa, R. B. 1995. *Governance Issues in African Universities: Improving Management and Governance to Make African Universities Viable in the 1990s and Beyond*. Accra: Association of African Universities.

Gellner, E. 1994. "Nations and Nationalism." In *Conflict After the Cold War: Arguments on Causes of War and Peace*, ed. R. K. Betts, 280–92. New York: Macmillan.

Ginsburg, M., ed. 1991. *Understanding Educational Reform in Global Context: Economy, Ideology, and the State*. New York: Garland.

Harbison, F. H., and C. A. Myers. 1964. *Education, Manpower, and Economic Growth; Strategies of Human Resource Development*. New York: McGraw-Hill.

Higgs, P. 2002. "Nation Building and the Role of the University: A Critical Reflection." *South Africa Journal of Higher Education* 16 (2): 11–17.

Hinchliffe, K. 1985. *Issues Related to Higher Education in Sub-Saharan Africa*. Washington, D.C.: World Bank.

Kwesiga, J. C. 2003. *Women's Access to Higher Education in Africa: Uganda's Experience*. Kampala: Fountain Publishers.

Lulat, Y. G-M. 2003. "Confronting the Burden of the Past: The Historical Antecedents of the Present Predicament of African Universities." In *Higher Education: Handbook of Theory and Research*, ed. J. C. Smart, vol. 18, 595–667. Dordrecht: Kluwer Academic.

Lumumba-Kasongo, T. 1986. *The Nature and the Role of Higher Education in Africa and Its U.S. Influence: The Case of the University of Liberia*. Monograph 86–7. Houston: University of Houston, Central Campus: Institute for Higher Education Law and Governance.

——. 1991. *Nationalistic Ideologies, Their Policy Implications and the Struggle for Democracy in African Politics*. Lewiston, N.Y.: E. Mellen Press.

——. 1994. *Political Re-mapping of Africa: Transnational Ideology and the Re-definition of Africa in World Politics*. Lanham, Md.: University Press of America.

——. 1998. *Rise of Multipartyism and Democracy in the Global Context: The Case of Africa*. Westport, Conn.: Praeger.

——. 2000. "Reflection on Nationalistic Discourses and Ethnonationalism in the Struggles for Democracy in Africa." In *The Political Economy of Peace and Security in Africa: Ethnocultural and Economic Perspectives*, ed. L. Adele Jinadu, 92–119. Harare: AAPS Books.

——. 2002. "Reconceptualizing the State as the Leading Agent of Development in the Context of Globalization in Africa." *African Journal of Political Science / Revue africaine de science politique* 7 (1): 79–108.

——. 2007. "A Theoretical Perspective on Capitalism and Welfare States and Their Responses to Inequality with a Focus on Gender: What Lessons for Africa?" In *Women and Higher Education in Africa: Reconceptualizing Gender-Based Human Capabilities and Upgrading Human Rights to Knowledge*, ed. N'D. T. Assié-Lumumba, 443–70. Abidjan: CEPARRED.

Markovitz, I. L. 1987. *Studies in Power and Class in Africa*. New York: Oxford University Press.

Mazrui, A. A. 1975. "The African University as a Multinational Corporation: Problems of Penetration and Dependency." *Harvard Educational Review* 45 (2): 191–210.

———. 1992. "Towards Diagnosing and Treating Cultural Dependency: The Case of the African University." *International Journal of Educational Development* 12 (2): 96.

Mbaya, K., M. Gregoire, L. Legros, and H. Ouedraogo. 2001. *Poverty Eradication: Where Stands Africa?* New York: United Nations Development Program.

Meyer, J. W., F. O. Ramirez, D. J. Franck, and E. Schofer. 2007. "Higher Education as an Institution." In *Sociology of Higher Education: Contributions and Their Contexts*, ed. P. J. Gumport, 187–221. Baltimore: Johns Hopkins University Press.

Mkandawire, T., and C. C. Soludo. 1999. *Our Continent, Our Future: African Perspectives on Structural Adjustment*. Dakar: Council for the Development of Social Science Research in Africa, CODESRIA.

Mohamedbhai, G. T. G. 1995. *The Emerging Role of African Universities in the Development of Science and Technology*. Accra: Association of African Universities.

Moyo, S. 2003. "Distance Learning and Virtual Education for Higher Education in Africa: Evaluation of Options and Strategies." *African and Asian Studies* 2 (4): 497–521.

Mudimbe, V. Y. 1988. *The Invention of Africa: Gnosis, Philosophy, and the Order of Knowledge*. Bloomington: Indiana University Press.

Mwiria, K. 1995. *Enhancing Linkages Between African Universities/the Wider Society/the Business Community and Governments*. Accra: Association of African Universities.

Negrao, J. 1995. *Adequate and Sustainable Funding of African Universities*. Accra: Association of African Universities.

Nyerere, J. K. 1967. *Education for Self-Reliance*. Dar es Salaam: Ministry of Information and Tourism.

———. 1968. *Ujamaa—Essays on Socialism*. Dar es Salaam: Oxford University Press.

———. 1973. *Freedom and Development. Uhuru na Maendeleo. A Selection from Writings and Speeches 1968–1973*. Oxford: Oxford University Press.

———. 1977. *The Arusha Declaration Ten Years After*. Dar es Salaam: Government Printer.

———. 1999. "Governance in Africa." *African Association of Political Science Newsletter*. New Series 4, no. 2 (May–August): 2–3.

Nyerere, J. K., D. Nicol, and R. C. Pratt. 1967. *The Inaugural Lectures of the University of Zambia*. Manchester: Manchester University Press.

Obasi, I. N. 2007. "Analysis of the Emergence and Development of Private Universities in Nigeria (1999–2006)." *Journal of Higher Education in Africa* 5 (2 and 3): 39–66.

Partnership for Capacity Building in Africa. 1997. *Revitalizing Universities in Africa: Strategy and Guidelines*. Washington D.C.: World Bank.

Roesgaard, M. H. 1998. *Moving Mountains: Japanese Education Reform.* Aarhus: Aarhus University Press.

Saint, W. S. 1999. *Tertiary Distance Education and Technology in Sub-Saharan Africa.* Washington, D.C.: World Bank.

Sawadogo, G. 1995. *The Future Missions and Roles of the African Universities.* Accra: Association of African Universities.

Schultz, T. W. 1977. "Investment in Human Capital." In *Power and Ideology in Education,* ed. J. Karabel and A. H. Halsey, 313–24. New York: Oxford University Press.

Subbarao, K., L. Raney, H. Dundar, and J. Haworth 1994. *Women in Higher Education: Progress, Constraints, and Promising Initiatives.* Washington, D.C.: World Bank.

Teferra, D., and P. G. Altbach, eds. 2003. *African Higher Education: An International Reference Handbook.* Bloomington: Indiana University Press.

Tuinder, B. A. den. 1978. *Ivory Coast, the Challenge of Success: Report of a Mission Sent to the Ivory Coast by the World Bank.* Baltimore: Johns Hopkins University Press.

UNDP (United Nations Development Program). 1998. *Human Development Report.* New York: Oxford University Press.

Waghid, Y. 2002. "Rationality and the Role of the University: A Response to Philip Higgs." *South Africa Journal of Higher Education* 16 (2): 18–24.

World Bank. 1991. *The African Capacity Building Initiative: Toward Improved Policy Analysis and Development Management in Sub-Saharan Africa.* Washington, D.C.: World Bank.

——. 1994a. *Higher Education: The Lessons of Experience.* Washington, D.C.: World Bank.

——. 1994b. *World Development Report: Infrastructure for Development.* Washington, D.C.: World Bank.

Yesufu, T. M., ed. 1973. *Creating the African University: Emerging Issues of the 1970s.* Ibadan: Oxford University Press.

Zeleza, P. T., and A. O. Olukoshi, eds. 2004. *African Universities in the 21st Century.* Vol. 1, *Liberalisation and International.* Dakar: CODESRIA.

Zolberg, A. R. 1969. *One-Party Government in the Ivory Coast.* Princeton, N.J.: Princeton University Press.

Rethinking What Is Made *Public*
in the University's Public Mission

NINE

JOHN WILLINSKY

Higher education recently has been trading on a long-standing image of itself as dedicated to a new-economy vision of itself as "a knowledge factory capable of spawning cutting-edge ideas, high-tech corridors, spin-off companies, and jobs," according to Jennifer Washburn's warning in *University Inc.*[1] Although this sort of commercialization is driven in part by reduced public funding and support for universities, it is leading to a spiral of public disengagement.[2] Each step down this knowledge-factory road leads to a further loss of the university's position in the community as a protected center of learning, operating at a remove from the larger, profit-driven knowledge economy. What is placed at risk is reflected in Roger L. Geiger's concern that the university's involvement in the marketplace "has diminished the sovereignty of universities over their own activities, weakened their mission of serving the public, and created through growing commercial entanglements at least the potential for undermining its privileged role as disinterested arbiters of knowledge."[3] Signs of the university's vulnerability are not hard to find. The U.S. Congress recently held hearings into whether universities are giving enough back to the larger community to warrant their endowment's tax-exempt status.[4]

It is Geiger's sense of the university's weakened "mission of serving the public" that I address in this chapter by offering what I hold to be a practical, realistic proposal for universities to provide greater institutional support for *open-access* initiatives in scholarly publishing.[5] This would mean reasserting a balance between public and private interests in the ownership of, and control over, the universities' published record of research and scholarship. At the center of this proposal is the use of new digital technologies to accelerate a long-standing historical process, namely, a gradual opening of science that increased the circulation of ideas and resources, and the standards by which work was made public.[6] The spirit of technologically enabled openness within the academic community today has led to an open-data movement,[7] forms of open-notebook science,[8] and researchers' increasing use of blogs and wikis.[9] Since 2002, the Massachusetts Institute of Technology (MIT) has been putting course outlines and slides online through its MIT OpenCourseWare, and dozens of universities are now offering free recordings of lectures through iTunes U.

In this chapter, I focus on the critical area of scholarly publishing, critical because for some years now the research library community has sensed that the rising price tag for access to the published literature is unsustainable.[10] At the same time, networked technologies have given rise to an open-access initiative that has made available a small proportion of the published record of research and scholarship free to readers online. I review a number of relatively simple and inexpensive steps by which universities can provide more support for open-access initiatives and propose that this support can only strengthen and extend their public mission.

For the universities to ignore this opportunity—that is, to treat open access to research as simply a publishing issue outside the university's public mission—is, first, to see their own access to the published literature restricted by the increasingly expensive business practices of commercial and nonprofit interests in scholarly publishing. Second, the universities would miss an opportunity to extend their public mission—which already includes making sure that knowledge important to the progress of humankind is made public by the best means possible—to include far greater public access to this knowledge. Scholarly publishing's embrace of digital technologies has indeed expanded the circulation of knowledge well beyond what was achieved by print, but that circulation is unduly limited, I argue, because it is bound by the legacy of print economies and revenue models. These publishers, who hold the copyright for a growing share of the published record, face few objections, even in principle, to working against what might otherwise seem to be a reasonable use of new technologies to extend the reach of the research library to a greater part of an interested community.

At the same time, a small, but significant, number of journals, researchers, and publishing projects are demonstrating that traditional subscription-based publishing models need not hold, given the available resources for managing, reviewing, and publishing this literature. The university thus has an opportunity to reassert its public mission as a beacon of learning by taking advantage of the many successful demonstrations over the last decade of how research and scholarship can be made available online free to other scholars and interested readers worldwide.

The public that is best served by open-access models of scholarly publishing is the academic community. Rapidly escalating prices in scholarly publishing over the last half century, especially for commercially published journals, has meant that researchers and scholars today, even at very good institutions, are limited to reading only some of the current literature in their area, which cannot be good for the quality of knowledge as a whole. Because the university's mission has always included circulating and reviewing knowledge, its public quality is a critical function. The university, then, has a responsibility to look for ways of extending access to the whole academic community, which in this digital era also means greatly extending public access to this body of knowledge.

For university extension courses, public lectures, and scholarly paperbacks, open access to research and scholarship means that this knowledge might circulate among a community that goes well beyond the academy. Professionals in medical offices and hospitals, classrooms and legal offices, factories and farms are now going online to look for research studies relevant to their work. Policymakers, politicians, amateur astronomers, and ornithologists are finding earlier studies of interest as well as recent discoveries. Even the public at large are discovering studies of interest in their roles as patients, parents, voters, bloggers, *Wikipedia* contributors, and simply curious readers.[11] The public's encounters with freely available research may be infrequent, perhaps before a visit to a physician, a particularly contentious school board meeting, a serendipitous Googling of a line of Shakespeare, or the discovery of a *Wikipedia* article. But because open-access research will not often be immediately accessible to a lay audience, such public encounters with research may lead to misunderstandings, frustrating searches for clarification, and exasperating discoveries of indecisive or contradictory findings.

I am not contending that the university's public mission is to provide a layperson's guide to knowledge, but to share what has been learned in the pursuit of knowledge. It also is part of that mission to make clear that the university is not the home of absolute and unequivocal truths, but of a much more dynamic, subtle and nuanced approach to knowledge. Whereas some of us are experimenting with ways of publishing research in more supportive reading environments, the public mission of the university at issue here is to share, as widely as possible, the fruits of its efforts. In doing so, it need not divert resources or energy—in a "popular science" tradition—from the rigorous pursuit of scholarly inquiry.[12] In that sense, open access is closer to the scholarly paperback than to the public lecture or the extension course. At the same time, the university needs to recognize that in this digital era, the standard for making something public is radically changing. It is not enough simply to move expensive journals online while continuing to raise the price of admission.

A NEW PUBLIC STANDARD

Today when government-funded work is made public, people expect to be able to find it available free online. If once it was enough to make such work public by printing it in a newspaper or selling it in bookstores, like research published in a journal, that standard no longer holds. *The Pentagon Papers* is a good example, which was excerpted in the *New York Times* in 1971 and sold in bookstores not long after.[13] Now, government documents, agency reports, court decisions, foundation-funded studies, as well as scandalous photos from the Abu Ghraib prison and the fabricated Vietnam war records of former President George W. Bush, all are part of the web's public sphere.

This shift in what it means to make something public also is at least beginning to set a new standard for academic work, as in the Social Science Research Council (SSRC)'s mission to "mobilize existing knowledge for new problems . . . and enhance public access to information." The SSRC now supplements its book-publishing program with a series of online forums and essays that make freely available the work of scholars who have come together to address such themes as "Is 'Race' Real?" It now seems that anything less than affording the public some, if not complete, access to research and scholarship diminishes, or so goes my case, the university's claim to be concerned about updating its public mission.

Here, then, is an opportunity for the university to raise the level of evidence and analysis, the quality of reflection and critique, in enabling its mission to bring knowledge to this newly enfranchised public sphere. At issue is not whether faculty members should abandon their research in favor of the blogs, wikis, bulletin boards, and social networks that make up a good portion of this public sphere. Indeed, what is most valuable about their contribution is the scholarly quality of their research and scholarship. In this new public sense, greater availability of that knowledge has already begun to have a salutary influence, judging by how this work has been cited and used.[14]

Until now, a number of faculty members, scholarly societies, research libraries, and entrepreneurs have taken advantage of this communication revolution. At best, perhaps 15 to 20 percent of the work produced and published each year is made open access.[15] The universities have been slow to take advantage of these systems' capacities for sharing knowledge, given how involved they have been in establishing more open forms of communication, beginning with the original ARPANET and continuing with their involvement in the production of open-source software for educational and research purposes.

All this activity points to the question of why so much of what is published in peer-reviewed journals is available to the public, professionals, and policymakers only if they are able to visit a research library with public-access terminals, afford an annual subscription, or pay up to $40 to view a single article. The system of journal publishing that has evolved since the seventeenth century has indeed proved to be an effective way of maximizing the distribution and circulation of knowledge in the world of print. By the late twentieth century, however, it had stopped being a very efficient economic system, judging by the vast differences in subscription fees, which, economist Ted Bergstrom has shown, bear no relation to the quantity or quality of work published but are the result of price increases related to corporate concentration among commercial scholarly publishers over the last four decades.[16] The idea of publishing an article in a journal to make the work public in a financially responsible and accessible way already was in a state of serious decline in the years leading up to the introduction of the World Wide Web.[17] The discrepancies, if not the inefficiencies, in this publishing economy have only been made worse by the introduction of online publishing. Although the proportion of the literature controlled by corporate publishing interests continues to grow, currently standing at 30 percent of journal titles, a new generation of independent open-access journals, accounting for perhaps 5 percent, are demonstrating that this knowledge can be made public in a whole new way.[18] What should be clear is that something is amiss in how scholarly publishing makes public this body of work.

In this chapter, I suggest how universities, scholarly societies, research libraries, faculty, and students can help speed this new public element into the flow of scholarly communication and bring more of this public good to an otherwise revitalized public sphere. The public and professionals have a good deal of interest in the latest research, whether out of personal concerns in the area of health or through broader interests with *Wikipedia*.[19]

WHAT IS *PUBLIC* IN THE UNIVERSITY'S MISSION

Research and scholarship contribute a great deal to the public good without ever finding their way outside the university libraries that subscribe to the requisite journals. Research does lead to public benefits and contributes to human understanding without public access beyond its publication in a scholarly journal of whatever cost. But in that sense as well, greater public access also means greater scholarly access. The work being made available free is, for example, being cited by researchers more often than articles that have not (yet) been given open access.[20] This global circulation of knowledge is no less basic to the advancement of research and thus essential to the university's public mission. But much of what is said about the university's public mission pertains just as much to this question of direct public access to knowledge as it does to the indirect public benefits of research and scholarship.

In his 1835 book *On the Origin of Universities and Academic Degrees*, which had been commissioned by the Privy Council of the British government (in response to petitions granting the University of London a charter), Henry Malden conveys this public mission's legendary standing in the "spontaneous" formation of these bodies: "The oldest universities of Europe sprung up in the twelfth century, and were formed by the zeal and enterprise of learned men, who undertook to deliver public instruction to all who were desirous of hearing them."[21] Today, nine centuries later, those who serve as the public figureheads of institutions, particularly the presidents of elite institutions, that undertake public instruction miss few opportunities to refer to the university's public service and mission.

Among recent university leaders, Harold T. Shapiro, the former president of both Princeton University and the University of Michigan, stated in the 2003 Clark Kerr Lectures that "private and public universities . . . serve society as both a responsive servant and a thoughtful critic" and referred to this service as "the university's public trust."[22] On the specific point of public access to knowledge, Shapiro cited Harvard president Josiah Quincy, whose 1833 appeal to the Massachusetts legislature reminded that public body of, in Shapiro's words, "the public character of Harvard's library assets."[23] Shapiro, in turn, asserted that Princeton is "not some kind of private social club," as all of its assets also "exist to serve a public purpose."[24] This service also connects "our rapidly accumulating new knowledge" with "the appropriate response of public policy" while recognizing that "the application of science is a social decision."[25] Shapiro recommended creating "venues for serious conversations" between scholars and the public.[26] Having greater access to the scholar's work in its published form would seem to be conducive to such conversations, not as a requirement, but as a courtesy and point of openness and respect for those with whom one is inviting such conversation.

Whereas Shapiro affirms what is public in the university's public mission, Derek Bok, a former president of Harvard University, sees that mission threatened by commercialization in many areas of university practice, pointing out that "in the past twenty-five years, the number and variety of commercial activities on the campuses of research universities have reached proportions never dreamed of in earlier periods."[27] On the one hand, "the profusion of these commercial ventures reflects the critical importance of research and advanced education to contemporary society."[28] On the other hand, these ventures have led to more than a few research scandals and faculty conflicts of interest, or what he politely refers to as "unwise compromises with basic academic values."[29] Bok considers the undue educational influence of athletic programs, overpriced professional programs, and pharmaceutical research funding, but he does not look at the increasing commercialization of scholarly publishing and the relative decline in the "public" nature of access to this knowledge as contributing to this breach in public trust.

If the leaders of higher education commonly overlook the potential for increasing public access to knowledge, so do, unfortunately, those who study higher education.[30] For example, in their recent collection *Higher Education for the Public Good: Emerging Voices from a National Movement*, Adrianna J. Kezar, Tony C. Chambers, and John C. Burkhardt express a deep concern with "a shift, and perhaps loss, in the role higher education plays in serving the public good."[31] They are encouraged, as I am, by "an emerging movement in higher education related to the public good" that has arisen in response to this loss.[32] The purpose of this movement is to "examine and build the role" that universities "play in the larger public good," as it devises "strategies to craft organizational cultures and environments that contribute to the public good."[33] I believe that far greater university and faculty involvement in open-access approaches to publishing is just such a strategy that would contribute to the public good.

Higher Education for the Public Good includes one chapter that deals directly with access to research: Judith A. Ramaley's "Scholarship for the Public Good."[34] Arguing for the "engaged university," Ramaley focuses on "the appropriate goals of scholarship" by calling for a greater balance between "theoretical and analytical conceptions" of research and "addressing very practical problems for which new knowledge or the integration of knowledge is needed."[35] She would include students in this process "and thus prepare them for citizenship and for the professional responsibilities that they will later assume," which, I add, they will assume after they have lost any right or ready ability to access the new knowledge or the integration of needed knowledge. Ramaley goes on to speak of creating "a student for life"; of the importance of fostering "communities of learning" in relation to industry, schools, health services, and other areas of modern life; and of "collaborative learning" in which knowledge is generated, applied, and interpreted.[36]

Although I think Ramaley's vision of research is encompassing and open, my question here is about access.[37] That is, how can we reasonably expect such learning to continue when access to the most vital sources of knowledge—with universities working to foster, in Ramaley's words, "a thirst for knowledge and a desire for practical outcomes"—are effectively cut off for those lifelong students and communities of learning?[38] Graduating students are needlessly being cut off today for no other reason than some universities do not realize how easily they could take advantage of current opportunities to make this knowledge a far greater part of the public sphere.[39]

My final example of contemporary calls for improving scholarship's public reach is from the American Sociological Association (ASA). Scholarly societies focus on the research side of academic life, and so they often are responsible for the leading journals in their field. The ASA recently sponsored a collection pertaining to "public sociology," after its 2004 annual conference on this theme (which was its best attended and most widely discussed annual meeting). In his presidential speech to the meeting, Michael Burawoy made clear that he saw public sociology as revitalizing the discipline, repositioning it once more as "the angel of history," as sociology "represents the interests of humanity—interests in keeping at bay both despotism and market tyranny."[40] In regard to the active defense of humanity, to beginning a public conversation based on public sociology and to "making the invisible visible and the private public," he pointed to the ASA's public work, which includes "congressional briefings and its regular press releases . . . [and] the column of our newsletter, *Footnotes*."[41] I suggest that in addition to these pieces, as well as op-ed articles in newspapers and the few popular books written by public sociologists, much more can be done to advance the ASA's newfound public mission, which would indeed enable the public and sociologists, working together or independently, "to draw on a century of extensive research, elaborate theories, practical interventions, and critical thinking."[42]

THE OPEN-ACCESS ARCHIVE

To extend their public mission, research universities should make more research and scholarship available to more people. Or rather, to prevent sociology and botany, for instance, from becoming relatively less public and less a part of the public sphere, given the current growth in access to information through other channels, the universities should explore how the new technologies of openness to which they are contributing can be used to make public more of what researchers are doing and have long done. To do this, university leaders, research librarians, authors, editors, scholarly societies, and anyone else who is concerned with the commercialization of higher education and who cares about restoring, if not extending, the public mission of research universities, need to endorse and support what are now well-established paths to open access for this body of knowledge. They also need to be open to innovation and leadership in scholarly publishing models, given how fast these online knowledge economies and technologies are developing and reshaping knowledge production.

There are principally two methods for improving access to research. The first is referred to as *author self-archiving*. That is, authors take a few moments to upload copies of their published work to open-access sites, such as their own website or a library-run archive, under terms set out by their publishers. The second path is *open-access publishing*. This usually applies to journals that have found a means to make their content free to readers immediately upon publication or some period of time after their subscribers receive their copy of the journal.

I would be the first to acknowledge that *free access* is not the whole issue. Getting on a bus and handing out offprints of Talcott Parson's "The School Class as a Social System" would result in little more than a mess of paper on the floor of the bus, doing little for university's public mission. To start making public the latest studies in sociology or biology carries with it responsibilities pertaining to the full meaning of *accessible*. That is why some of us are designing and analyzing new online reading environments that support greater engagement with scholarly work for both scholars and the wider readership among the related professions as well as the public. Accordingly, journal articles could be accompanied by tools that give readers additional context and background tailored to the specific article they are reading.[43] These tools encourage readers to ask whether there are other studies that come to a similar conclusion, whether the concept in question can be further understood by reading about it in other contexts (including encyclopedias and the media), or whether there are government policies or materials on this topic. We may have only begun to design effective tools for this purpose, and the research on this is still under way, but I hope it is clear that the preliminary nature of this work is not a reason not to provide public and global access to research and scholarship. This is about a right to know, to dig as deeply as one is inclined and able into all that is known, rather than a matter of establishing that the public has a proven ability to take advantage in every case of this right to know. It also is good to remember that what makes this body of work valuable is how it is addressed to other researchers able to build on, extend, and challenge.

In the case of author self-archiving, the viability, not to mention the legality, of this path to greater access has now been guaranteed by a majority of journal publishers. These publishers, including some of the biggest, such as Elsevier and Springer, now permit their authors to post the work on their own website or an institutional repository.[44] Some of these publishers permit posting while the paper is in review, and others ask authors to wait until they submit their final peer-reviewed copy, which they can then post (rather than posting the publishers' final PDF, which they may not be permitted to post). Some ask authors to wait six to twenty-four months after publication before posting this postreview version. This means, in effect, that the archives represent a parallel universe of research papers, made up of work that is not quite identical in time and version to what has been published. This suggests, to me at least, that authors archiving their own work is more about establishing the principle—as well as the value—of open access. The risk that needs to be acknowledged with this approach is whether author archiving will simply (1) extend current levels of executive- and coach-class access to knowledge, much as the subscription-pricing model sustains both well-funded and hard-pressed research libraries, or (2) provide a temporary intermediate step toward establishing open access to all research and scholarship.[45] Still, Stevan Harnad is right to insist that this form of self-archiving, an initiative to which he has contributed perhaps more than anyone, currently stands as the most direct and easily realized route to open access for a good proportion of the literature.[46]

It is true that this right-to-archive has not yet been widely embraced by the authors of research articles. It is as if researchers have learned the publish-or-perish lesson all too well, that to have had their work published is the end of the story, and on to the next study. Taking advantage of the Internet to make the work available globally has begun, however, to register among busy and productive researchers, despite the evidence that it helps the work and its new readers. In 2005, Alma Swan found that nearly half the faculty she surveyed reported that they were doing some form of self-archiving with their publications, with that number having doubled from the year before.[47] Beyond the rather unsystematic approach of individual faculty, a number of funding agencies and a few universities in various parts of the world have instituted archiving mandates requiring authors to post copies of their published work in an institutional repository some months after its publication.[48]

The self-archiving mandate, however, has brought to a head the issue of public and private rights in controlling access to this research. After an initial trial period with voluntary archiving, to which the response was decidedly underwhelming,[49] in April 2008 the U.S. National Institutes of Health (NIH) embarked on a public-access policy requiring by law that NIH grant holders deposit a copy of their final, peer-reviewed article in PubMed Central immediately upon its publication for release no later than twelve months after publication (terms similar to many publishers' policies). Still, a number of scholarly publisher associations, including both commercial and scholarly society publishers, are treating this as encroaching on their otherwise exclusive copyright over the published literature. Within six months of the NIH policy, publishers had presented a bill to Congress that would outlaw government efforts to provide public access to publicly funded research. The publishers' position was that even the second-class access provided by the NIH's public-access policy threatened the sustainability of scholarly publishing by diminishing the publishers' ability to protect their return on investment.[50] This, then, is the battle emerging over access rights to the published record of research and scholarship and on which I believe the universities need to take a principled stance while pushing for a balance between funding the journal system in ways that maximize the circulation of knowledge in light of these new web-based publishing systems.

At this point, the universities can reasonably step in and support the value of open access, that is, after the initial swell of interest and support has demonstrated the value and viability of open-access archiving and publishing models, and when the publishers, after initially permitting archiving, are now turning against it in order to retain exclusive ownership over this work. If the universities were to declare their renewed public mission as including greater access to the knowledge they foster, it would offer a considerable incentive for those involved in scholarly publishing to make open-access work. There is much that universities, departments, and research units can do to get behind this idea, even if they are understandably reluctant to put authors' self-archiving mandates into place, given the need to respect faculty's autonomy and rights to their intellectual property (which the same faculty are only too happy, cynics might note, to turn over to commercial publishers).

The first step that a university needs to take is to establish a repository for such archiving, so that faculty have a reliable, well-indexed place to turn to make their work open access. A number of well-supported open-source software systems for archiving are available to help with the uploading, management, and indexing of such materials.[51] With a repository in place, the university can then promote this new public access point by featuring archived research on library, department, or institute websites. It can build collections of its faculty's archived papers that pertain to issues of interest to the public and professional communities, with follow-ups to the media on particularly timely topics. In light of its additional contribution to the global academic community, as well as to the public sphere, it can ask its faculty to state in their annual reports that part of their work that has been archived. In this way, the university can greatly improve its position, given growing public and media expectations that access to information is a basic right and a necessary aspect of life in the twenty-first century.

Likewise, scholarly societies first should make sure that their journals have simple, easy-to-follow, self-archiving policies that are clearly posted and actively supported as a point of pride for the association, as they represent a recognition of authors' rights and opportunities as well as a service to the global community. The societies could feature archived articles on their websites, as the universities do.[52] This greater openness will help the journals have a greater impact and also add to the authors' citation count, as a number of studies have shown.[53] As for the impact of self-archiving on a journal's subscriptions, the longest-standing example is high-energy particle physics, whose arXiv.org Eprint Archive is now a dozen years old and archives almost all the current literature. The publishers of the relevant journals report no decline in subscriptions, at least none over and above the general decline that journals are experiencing as more titles come on the market.[54]

THE OPEN-ACCESS JOURNAL

The mandating of author self-archiving is the most straightforward means of achieving open access to research, but the public mission of the universities would also be served through institutional support for scholar-published and small society open-access journals.[55] This provides a publishing alternative to growing corporate concentration among commercial publishers (namely, Elsevier, Springer, Wiley-Blackwell, and Taylor & Francis), with resulting higher subscription costs affecting research library holdings.[56] An alternative is needed, as scholarly societies turn their journals over to these commercial giants (in return for highly professional publishing services, online and in print, as well as a considerable increase in revenue for the society, beginning with a cash advance in some cases).[57] New approaches to open-access publishing are also strengthening journal publishing in developing countries.[58] Whereas once these journals struggled to publish a print journal with only a handful of subscribers (including donor-supported subscriptions), they are now publishing a journal online that is available worldwide and indexed in Google Scholar, with its articles immediately and freely available to readers. Creating new journals and helping existing ones go online would revitalize the research and review culture in this academic community.

The university's public mission can be advanced, therefore, by not only supporting the archiving of published articles but also participating in journal publishing. For universities and their libraries to support the publishing efforts of scholarly societies and groups of faculty speaks to the current economics of publishing. It also creates a responsive channel for new intellectual developments and thus serves as a source of academic freedom and innovation, as open-access publishing allows journals that form around new ideas to circulate immediately within the global academic community.[59]

We could refer to the economic viability of open-access journals as an unproven model. Three thousand active, open-access journals may be listed in the *Directory of Open Access Journals*, but none is older than the Internet itself, which made this form of publishing possible. Among those titles, a substantial number in the biomedical field and related sciences (which are relatively rich in grants) are able to charge author or publication fees (much as some of the subscription journals in these fields do, with "page charges") of, currently, $2,000 to $3,000.[60] Open-access journals in other fields, however, are not in a position to charge authors a fee, given the level of research grants in other areas.

The key economic strategy of open-access journals is to substantially reduce publishing costs by forgoing a print edition, which is increasingly making sense, since many research libraries are dropping print editions (when they have a choice) because of storage and processing costs but principally because their patrons now prefer using digital titles. As part of this cost reduction, many open-access journals are also tapping into another element of this revitalized public sphere: using open-source software to manage and publish journals, which further reduces their costs while offering a sustainable means of keeping up with technical developments by taking advantage of this new publishing medium.[61] The costs that remain, whether for copy editors or layout, are then covered by institutional or association subsidies, perhaps to hire a graduate assistant to do this work.

For those journals that cannot imagine not having a print edition, there is the example of those journals offering what is known as *delayed open access*, with content released for free reading some period after its initial publication. The *New England Journal of Medicine* is a leading instance, with its research articles made free six months after publication. It is hosted by Highwire Press, a division of Stanford University Libraries, which has more than one thousand journals and from which it is able to give readers free access to more than two million articles, largely because the journals offer delayed open access to their content (a process that can be readily automated online).

A real issue for the nonprofit scholarly association journals is that for a number of societies, subscriptions generate a "surplus" that funds the society's other activities.[62] Enormous surpluses can be generated in the biomedical field by pharmaceutical and medical device advertising, which raises its own ethical issues for scholarly publishing.[63] Societies in other fields have grown dependent on these library subscriptions. While recognizing the importance of societies to establishing the highest standards for scholarly work in their fields, this may not be an insurmountable problem for those research universities interested in increasing access to research and scholarship.

A common thread here, from Highwire Press at Stanford University Libraries to Open Journal Systems at Simon Fraser University Library, is the new role of research libraries. They are becoming actively involved in scholarly publishing, developing software, hosting journals, and operating repositories of work published elsewhere. Library associations like the Association of Research Libraries and the American Library Association have been active lobbyists for open-access initiatives. It is tempting, then, to conclude this chapter by talking about the library's central role in increasing public access to knowledge.

A number of universities, including Harvard and Michigan, have established offices of scholarly publishing in association with their libraries. These offices are in an excellent position to offer interested faculty suggestions for and support of new publishing technologies that could lead to increased access and readership for journals, working papers, and conferences. They could, for example, help faculty members introduce authors' archiving policies for their scholarly associations that strengthen the associations' service to their members and the larger community. These offices could help faculty who edit journals by hosting open-source journal management systems and advising on financial models, such as self-archiving, delayed access, and article-processing fees. The university libraries at Rutgers, Vanderbilt, Emory, Simon Fraser, and Toronto are just a few of those contributing to an alternative library-based publishing economy for journals that offer open access. Not only do the journals benefit, but so do the libraries, as they reduce publishing costs for research and contribute in very public ways to the university's public mission.

Now I would like to introduce a more radical version of library participation in scholarly communication. After all, while libraries have every reason to support high-quality open-access journals, they end up supporting only those journals that charge reasonably priced, not to mention higher-priced, subscriptions. Any money the library saves when a journal becomes open access goes, in effect, into the higher subscription prices. It does not seem like such a large step, then, to imagine libraries, which are already forming consortia to negotiate discounts with big corporate publishers, forming an open-access publishing cooperative with scholarly associations and other academic groups. That is, the libraries would contribute to the cooperative the equivalent of subscription fees to cover the journal's editing costs, in addition to providing hosting and cataloging services, as well as library-supported publishing software and distribution networks, while the societies would provide highly professional open-access journals that would reach the widest possible readership with the library's assistance.[64]

University libraries are already involved in establishing open-access endowments that have the same effect, as in the case of *Stanford Encyclopedia of Philosophy*, an online, open-access, peer-reviewed reference work of the highest caliber. In the course of raising $4 million in an endowment to ensure its sustainability, the encyclopedia has managed to secure commitments of $15,000 from 75 of the 118 institutions offering a doctorate in philosophy (in addition to major allocations from Stanford and the National Endowment for the Humanities). The libraries at these institutions recognize that they are primary benefactors of this work, with the open access it affords being a bonus to the library's public mission, rather than representing some sort of loss of proprietary interest in exclusive access. Although we cannot discount the special institutional situation of Stanford in this case, there is still no reason to think that universities could not do more to ensure that access to research and scholarly work is made as widely available as possible. Outside the academy, new models for creating public intellectual resources are appearing. *Wikipedia* and *The Encyclopedia of Life* provide two delightful instances, both of which draw heavily on research and scholarship—more of which could be made public for interested readers to follow up on—that reflect the university's expanded public mission for the digital era.[65]

The time is right for those who believe that the research university's public mission is to support approaches to scholarly publishing that increase access to this knowledge, despite the challenges, risks, and objections. They are bound to hear concerns that open access will undermine the economic stability of scholarly publishing, placing peer review and journal quality in jeopardy.[66] Of course, if the traditional subscription model were faring well, libraries would not be forced to cut subscriptions in the face of rising prices, while the idea that open access poses a threat is belied by the growing number of open-access ventures such as Oxford University Press's Oxford Open, Springer's Open Choice, and the Public Library of Science's top-ranked *Biology*, as well as the *New England Journal of Medicine* and many of the publications handled by Highwire Press, which make their content open access, albeit some months after their initial publication. It is true that in the decade of experimentation, no single economic model for open access has come to dominate the market in the way that subscriptions did in the past. Yet what is common to the various open-access approaches is a recognition of what it contributes to research and scholarship, as well as to the larger community.

That still leaves reasonable concerns about potential abuses of this knowledge now to be made so readily available, and there have been instances of the public's running ahead of the proper research clinical trials.[67] Again, this risk needs to be compared with whether it is responsible to, in effect, restrict physicians' and patients' access to research, leaving them only a web that offers health information that has not been subjected to the standards for evidence and peer review.

We have technologies and demonstration projects, amid a variety of economic models, that seem to hold promise for enabling scholarly societies, research groups, and university libraries to increase the amount of research and scholarship that is publicly and globally available. Through author-archiving mandates and open-access journals, the public sphere can be stocked with a new wealth of intellectual resources. These are the resources that are critical to education and with which we work so hard to help our students critically engage during their brief time with us.

Having taught students how to think and reason using a dynamic body of knowledge, why would we not want to take advantage of these new technologies? Why would we not want to help these students, as well as others who did not attend university, to see that this open and shared pursuit of knowledge becomes part of a democratic culture? Such initiatives, I state yet again, will first and foremost improve access for scholars around the world—as they will remain the primary audience for this work—and at the same time, and at no additional expense, they will stock the open shelves of the public sphere with a growing body of breakthrough knowledge, demonstrations, challenges, critiques, and reviews, as well as the most ordinary works of science. It will bring to the knowledge economy and the age of information a much needed infusion of learning worthy of any claim to be made on behalf of the research university's public mission.

NOTES

This chapter has benefited from the thoughtful comments of the book's editors, other contributors, and a university press reviewer, as well as the assistance of Anne White. This work was supported by the Pacific Press Endowment at the University of British Columbia.

1. Jennifer Washburn, *University, Inc.: The Corporate Corruption of Higher Education* (New York: Basic Books, 2005), 171. In regard to the public status of research, Washburn's focus is on patent law, but her concerns apply no less to scholarly publishing: "The question of who owns academic research has grown increasingly contentious, as the openness and sharing that once characterized university life has given way to a new proprietary culture more akin to the business world" (xi).

2. At the root of this commercialization and privatization in higher education is a loss of state support, or as Edward P. St. John and Michael Parsons put it, "In the late twentieth century the underlying rationale for the public funding of higher education in the United States broke down." See their introduction to *Public Funding of Higher Education: Changing Contexts and New Rationales*, ed. Edward P. St. John and Michael Parsons (Baltimore: Johns Hopkins University Press, 2004), 1. On the reduction of government support leading to an increasing dependence on tuition and earned income, see Douglas Priest, Edward P. St. John, and Rachel Dykstra Boon, introduction to *Privatization and Public Universities*, ed. Douglas M. Priest and Edward P. St. John (Bloomington: Indiana University Press, 2006). On the broader commercialization that has affected the teaching, athletics, and research funding of public and

private institutions, see Derek Bok, "Benefits and Costs of Commercialization," in *Buying In or Selling Out? The Commercialization of the American Research University*, ed. David Stein (New Brunswick, N.J.: Rutgers University Press, 2004).

3. Roger L. Geiger, *Knowledge and Money: Research Universities and the Paradox of the Marketplace* (Stanford, Calif.: Stanford University Press, 2004), 265.

4. Andrew Delbanco, "Academic Business: Has the University Become Just Another Corporation?" *New York Times Magazine*, September 30, 2007, 25–29.

5. For a formal definition of open access, see Leslie Chan, "Budapest Open Access Initiative" (New York: Budapest Open Access Initiative, 2002), available at http://www.soros.org/openaccess/read.shtml (accessed September 26, 2006).

6. See Paul A. David, Matthijs den Besten, and Ralph Schroeder, "Will *e-Science* Be *Open Science*?" in *World Wide Science: The Promises, Threats and Realities of e-Research*, ed. William H. Dutton and Paul Jeffreys (Cambridge, Mass.: MIT Press, in press).

7. Paul F. Uhlir and Peter Schröder, "Open Data for Global Science," *Data Science Journal* 6, Open Data Issue (2007): 36–53.

8. Jean-Claude Bradley, "Open Notebook Science," Drexel CoAS E-Learning (Blog), available at http://drexel-coas-elearning.blogspot.com/2006/09/open-notebook-science.html (accessed September 26, 2006).

9. Alexander P. Bock, "Scientific Blogging as an Important and Innovative Research Tool to Get Health Data in a Changing Societal Environment" (paper presented at the American Health Association, Washington, D.C., 2007), available at http://apha.confex.com/apha/135am/techprogram/paper_156533.htm (accessed September 26, 2006).

10. For statements on scholarly publishing's current lack of sustainability from the research library's perspective, see L. Leonard et al., "Letter to All UC Faculty from Lawrence Pitts, Chair of the Academic Senate, and the Head Librarians of the 11 UC Campuses," University of California at Berkeley, 2004, available at http://libraries.universityofcalifornia.edu/news/facmemoscholcomm_010704.pdf (accessed September 26, 2006); J. E. Davies and H. Greenwood, "Scholarly Communication Trends—Voices from the Vortex: A Summary of Specialist Opinion," *Learned Publishing* 17, no. 2 (2004): 157–67; A. Byrne, "Digital Libraries: Barriers or Gateways to Scholarly Information?" *The Electronic Library* 21, no. 5 (2003): 414–21. For publishers' concerns about scholarly publishing's sustainability, which they see as dependent on at least current revenue levels, see "An Overview of Scientific, Technical and Medical Publishing and the Value It Adds to Research Outputs" (Oxford: International Association of Scientific, Technical and Medical Publishing, 2008), available at http://www.stm-assoc.org/documents-statements-public-co/2008–04%20Overview%20of%20STM%20Publishing%20%20Value%20to%20Research.pdf (accessed September 26, 2006).

11. On professionals' use of research, see John Willinsky and Mia Quint-Rapoport, "How Complementary and Alternative Medicine Practitioners Use PubMed," *Journal of Medical Internet Research* 9, no. 2 (2007), available at http://www.jmir.org/2007/2/e19 (accessed September 26, 2006); and Sarah Twomey, "Teacher Centered Professionalism: A Teacher Reading Group and New Forms of Access to Knowledge from a Feminist Perspective" (PhD diss., University of British Columbia, 2007); on policymakers, see John Willinsky, "Policymakers' Use of Online Academic Research," *Education Policy Analysis Archives* 11 no. 2 (2003), available at http://epaa.asu.edu/epaa/v11n2/ (accessed September 26, 2006); on contributors to *Wikipedia*, see John Willinsky, "Socrates Back on the Street: *Wikipedia*'s Citing of the *Stanford Encyclopedia of Philosophy*," *International Journal of Communication* 2 (2008): 1269–88, available at http://ijoc.org/ojs/index.php/ijoc/article/viewFile/439/248 (accessed September 26, 2006).

12. John Willinsky, "Open Access: Reading (Research) in the Age of Information." In *51st National Reading Conference Yearbook*, ed. C. M. Fairbanks et al. (Oak Creek, Wis.: National Reading Conference, 2003), 32–46.

13. George C. Herring, ed., *The Pentagon Papers* (Boston: Beacon Press, 1971). It is not that I imagine that information can somehow be free in any economic sense. Rather, the costs associated with printing, binding, and distribution are now borne by Internet access and computing expenses.

14. See n. 8.

15. B. Björk, A. Roos, and M. Lauri, "Global Annual Volume of Peer Reviewed Scholarly Articles and the Share Available Via Different Open Access Options" (Toronto: Proceedings ELPUB2008 Conference on Electronic Publishing, 2008), available at http://www.oacs.shh.fi/publications/elpub-2008.pdf (accessed September 26, 2006); Chawki Hajjem, "L'objet de cette étude est d'évaluer la variation de l'avantage de l'impact de citations des articles en accès libre" (University of Quebec at Montreal, 2005), available at http://www.crsc.uqam.ca/lab/chawki/graphes/EtudeImpact.htm (accessed September 26, 2006).

16. Ted Bergstrom, "Journal Pricing Page," University of California at Santa Barbara, available at http://www.econ.ucsb.edu/~tedb/Journals/jpricing.html (accessed September 26, 2006).

17. M. H. Black, *Cambridge University Press 1584–1984* (Cambridge: Cambridge University Press, 1984), 8, 16. At the very origins of scholarly publishing, with the founding, for example, of Cambridge University Press (the oldest press publishing in English), the university was very much involved in ensuring that fair rates were charged for printing services and working closely with the trade guild, sometimes lending capital.

18. R. Crow, "Description of Mixed Market for Peer Reviewed Scholarly Journals," unpublished paper (Washington, D.C.: SPARC, 2005).

19. For example, the Pew Internet and American Life Project has established that 36 percent of those online consult *Wikipedia* (Lee Rainie, "Wikipedia Users," Pew Internet and American Life Project [2007], available at http://www.pewinternet.org/PPF/r/212/report_display.asp [accessed September 26, 2006]), and 87 percent have sought scientific information (John Horrigan, "The Internet as a Resource for News and Information about Science," Pew Internet and American Life Project [2006], available at http://www.pewinternet.org/PPF/r/191/report_display.asp [accessed September 26, 2006]).

20. For a bibliography and a discussion of studies that measure the impact of open access on citations, see Steve Hitchcock, "The Effect of Open Access and Downloads ('Hits') on Citation Impact: A Bibliography of Studies" (Southampton: University of Southampton, 2007), available at http://opcit.eprints.org/oacitation-biblio.html (accessed September 26, 2006).

21. Henry Malden, *On the Origin of Universities and Academic Degrees* (London: John Taylor, 1835), 2.

22. Harold T. Shapiro, *A Larger Sense of Purpose: Higher Education and Society* (Princeton, N.J.: Princeton University Press, 2005), 4–5.

23. Ibid.

24. Ibid., 5–6.

25. Ibid., 158.

26. Ibid., 159.

27. Bok, "Benefits and Costs of Commercialization," 32.

28. Ibid.

29. Ibid., 46. In an op-ed piece in the *Boston Globe*, while noting that only 10 percent of faculty pay any attention to the research on teaching and learning in higher education, Derek Bok observed that "empirical studies command respect only when they are used to investigate institutions and professions other than those to which professors themselves belong." See his "Are Colleges Failing? Higher Ed Needs New Lesson Plans," *Boston Globe*, December 18, 2005, available at http://www.boston.com/news/globe/editorial_opinion/oped/articles/2005/12/18/are_colleges_failing/ (accessed September 26, 2006).

30. The sterling exception here is David E. Shulenburger, who as provost of the University of Kansas, has applied his economic training to devising ways of increasing access to scholarly publishing. See David E. Shulenburger, *Moving with Dispatch to Resolve the Scholarly Communication Crisis: From Here to NEAR* (Association of Research Libraries Proceedings, 1998), available at http://www.arl.org/arl/proceedings/133/schulenburger.html (accessed September 26, 2006).

31. Adrianna J. Kezar, Tony C. Chambers, and John C. Burkhardt, *Higher Education for the Public Good: Emerging Voices from a National Movement* (San Francisco: Jossey-Bass, 2005), xiii.

32. Ibid., xv.

33. Ibid.

34. Judith A. Ramaley, "Scholarship for the Public Good: Living in Pasteur's Quadrant," in *Higher Education for the Public Good: Emerging Voices from a National Movement*, ed. Adrianna J. Kezar, Tony C. Chambers, and John C. Burkhardt (San Francisco: Jossey-Bass, 2005), 166–81.

35. Ibid., 167.

36. Ibid., 178–79.

37. I would argue against limiting the goals of research in the way, for example, Kelly Ward states that "to fulfill the goals of the scholarship of engagement, scholars must link their teaching, research, and service to community problems, challenges and goals." See Kelly Ward, "Rethinking Faculty Roles and Rewards for the Public Good," in *Higher Education for the Public Good: Emerging Voices from a National Movement*, ed. Adrianna J. Kezar, Tony C. Chambers, and John C. Burkhardt (San Francisco: Jossey-Bass, 2005), 231.

38. Ward, "Rethinking Faculty Roles and Rewards for the Public Good," 180.

39. A similar stance is found in higher education's efforts to support "moral and civic learning" as a means of ensuring that universities exercise "a powerful influence in reinvigorating the democratic spirit in America." The goal is to teach students to become better citizens so that they can "see the moral and civic dimensions of issues, to make and justify moral and civic judgments and to take action when appropriate." See Anne Colby et al., *Educating Citizens: Preparing America's Undergraduates for Lives of Moral and Civic Responsibility* (San Francisco: Jossey-Bass, 2003), 8, 17. Such a well-educated citizen would also seem likely to benefit from continuing access to research and scholarship.

40. Michael Burawoy, "For Public Sociology," in *Public Sociology: Fifteen Eminent Sociologists Debate Politics and the Profession in the Twenty-first Century*, ed. Dan Clawson et al. (Berkeley: University of California Press, 2007), 56.

41. Ibid., 57.

42. Ibid., 58. By the same token, making public a greater part of this knowledge will address William Julius Wilson's concern that "some of the best sociological insights never reach the general public because sociologists seldom take advantage of useful mechanisms to get their ideas out"; and Immanuel Wallerstein's apprehension that there will not be "a more plausible historical social science, a more reasonable accommodation of multiple readings of the good, and therefore ultimately a demo-

cratic political system if there is not greater openness in our public discussion." See William Julius Wilson, "Speaking to Publics," in *Public Sociology: Fifteen Eminent Sociologists Debate Politics and the Profession in the Twenty-first Century*, ed. Dan Clawson et al. (Berkeley: University of California Press, 2007), 118; and Immanuel Wallerstein, "The Sociologist and the Public Sphere," in *Public Sociology: Fifteen Eminent Sociologists Debate Politics and the Profession in the Twenty-first Century*, ed. Dan Clawson et al. (Berkeley: University of California Press, 2007), 174–75.

43. See n. 5.

44. To examine Taylor & Francis's authors' self-archiving policy, which stands as a strong statement on the publisher's sense of contribution and control, see http://www.tandf.co.uk/journals/authorrights.pdf. For a database of more than three hundred publishers' archiving policies, see SHERPA, available at http://www.sherpa.ac.uk/romeo.php (accessed September 26, 2006).

45. The self-archiving model offers the additional irony that while a good number of developing countries have full access to the published articles online, those outside these regions at less-than-well-endowed institutions will have access to the partial record of the author's final unedited (but peer-reviewed) copies.

46. Stevan Harnad, "Is OA (Gold) Really a Desirable Goal for Scientific Journal Publishing?" (American Scientist Open Access Forum, 2007), available at http://users.ecs.soton.ac.uk/harnad/Hypermail/Amsci/5957.html (accessed September 26, 2006). Harnad has also contributed to the development of the open-source software Eprints.org for setting up institutional repositories that include a "request eprint" button for work that is embargoed until a certain subscription-protecting period has passed.

47. Alma Swan, "Open Access and the Progress of Science: The Power to Transform Research Communication May Be at Each Scientist's Fingertips," *American Scientist* (2007), available at http://www.americanscientist.org/template/AssetDetail/assetid/55131 (accessed September 26, 2006).

48. See the ROARMAP (Registry of Open Access Repository Material Archiving Policies) maintained by Eprints.org, available at http://www.eprints.org/openaccess/policysignup/ (accessed September 26, 2006).

49. Four percent of the eligible papers were archived by authors in the first eight months of the voluntary policy initiative. See National Institutes of Health (NIH), *Report on the NIH Public Access Policy* (Washington, D.C.: U.S. Department of Health and Human Services., January 2006), available at http://publicaccess.nih.gov/Final_Report _20060201.pdf (accessed September 26, 2006); and National Institutes of Health (NIH), *Policy on Enhancing Public Access to Archived Publications Resulting from NIH-Funded Research* (Washington, D.C.: U.S. Department of Health and Human

Services, 2005), available at http://grants.nih.gov/grants/guide/notice-files/NOT-OD-05–022.html (accessed September 26, 2006).

50. See the Partnership for Research Integrity in Science and Medicine (PRISM), which was established by the American Association of Publishers to counter open-access mandates, or as PRISM puts it: "Various initiatives and proposals have been put forth by special interest groups and some legislators that would force private sector publishers to surrender to the federal government all peer-reviewed articles that report on research supported by federal research grants." See Partnership for Research Integrity in Science and Medicine (PRISM), *Current Issues* (New York: Association of American Publishers, 2007), available at http://www.prismcoalition.org/ (accessed September 26, 2006).

51. There are somewhat fewer than one thousand institutional repositories registered with the Directory of Open Access Repositories at the University of Nottingham (http://www.opendoar.org/index.html). See Open Society Institute (OSI), "A Guide to Institutional Repository Software" (New York: Soros Foundation, 2004), available at http://www.soros.org/openaccess/pdf/OSI_Guide_to_IR_Software_v3.pdf (accessed September 26, 2006).

52. Scholarly societies are having to rethink their service to members now that they are no longer offering members exclusive access to their journals (which are available to everyone online through the research library).

53. See n. 7.

54. Alma P. Swan, "Self-Archiving: It's an Author Thing" (paper presented at the Southampton Workshop on Institutional Open Access Repositories, University of Southampton, Southampton, 2005), available at http://www.eprints.org/jan2005/ppts/swan.ppt (accessed April 4, 2005).

55. Stevan Harnad argues that efforts to increase access are most effectively directed toward government funding agencies and institutionally mandated self-archiving and that open-access journal publishing "is and remains premature until and unless publishing costs are cut and institutional subscriptions are terminated so they can be redirected to cover the institutional publication costs [associated with the authors' fees that some open-access journals charge]." Harnad, "Is OA (Gold) Really a Desirable Goal?" My involvement in open access has been largely on the side of supporting open-access journal publishing through my work with the Public Knowledge Project on open-source software development as a cost-cutting measure, and my arguments here should be seen in that light.

56. Raym Crow, "Publishing Cooperatives: An Alternative for Non–Profit Publishers," *First Monday*, 11(9) (2006), available at http://www.firstmonday.org/issues/issue11_9/crow/index.html#c1 (accessed September 26, 2006). "Commercial pub-

lishers now play a role in publishing over 60 percent of all peer–reviewed jour-nals, owning 45 percent outright and publishing another 17 percent on behalf of non–profit organizations."

57. Moving a journal from a nonprofit society to a commercial sector can lead to a fivefold increase in price, according to Ted Bergstrom's analysis of the differences in economic journals on a per-page basis. See Ted Bergstrom, "Journal Pricing Page," University of California at Santa Barbara, available at http://www.econ.ucsb.edu/~tedb/Journals/jpricing.html (accessed September 26, 2006). That is, the commercial publishers charge more than five times what the societies charge for peer-reviewed published articles. Even if the articles were five times as good (and Bergstrom provides evidence based on citation counts that this is not the case), it would be difficult to account for the difference, as the authors are unpaid and select the journals to which they submit.

58. For example, we have been working through the Public Knowledge Project, largely in collaboration with the International Network for the Availability of Scientific Publications, to provide and support the use of our open-source journal software (Open Journal Systems) to enable journals in developing countries to achieve a far greater distribution within the region as well as globally.

59. John Willinsky et al., "Doing Medical Journals Differently: Open Medicine, Open Access, and Academic Freedom," *Canadian Journal of Communication* 32, no. 3 (2007), available at http://pkp.sfu.ca/node/776 (accessed September 26, 2006).

60. BioMed Central is a commercial version of the open-access author-fee model, with 180 titles that are published only online. The Public Library of Science is a nonprofit that has managed to use this open-access model to establish very quickly some of the highest-ranked journals in their field. In addition, a number of publishers offer an open-access option for their otherwise subscription journals, with authors able to purchase open access for their article alone. Springer has struck deals with the University of Göttingen and a Dutch library consortium to ensure that their faculties' work is open access in Springer journals. See Peter Suber, "Springer Deal with U of Goettingen," *Open Access News*, October 5, 2007, available at http://www.earlham.edu/~peters/fos/2007/10/springer-deal-with-u-of-gttingen.html (accessed September 26, 2006). This purchased-open-access approach has led Oxford University Press to reduce the subscription price for some of its journals, as the costs are now borne by authors purchasing open access. See Mithu Mukherjee, *Full Year Results from Oxford Open Show Wide Variation in Open Access Uptake Across Disciplines* (Oxford: Oxford University Press, 2006), available at http://www.oxfordjournals.org/news/2006/08/30/full_year_results_from_oxford_op/full_year_results_from_oxford_op.html (accessed September 26, 2006).

61. An example of this open-source software is Open Journal Systems from the Public Knowledge Project, with the principal technical development coming from Simon Fraser University Library (http://pkp.sfu.ca). See John Willinsky, "Open Access: Reading (Research) in the Age of Information," *51st National Reading Conference Yearbook* (Oak Creek, Wis.: National Reading Conference , 2003), 32–46.

62. John Willinsky, "Scholarly Associations and the Economic Viability of Open Access Publishing," *Journal of Digital Information* 4, no. 2 (2003), available at http://jodi.ecs .soton.ac.uk/Articles/vo4/io2/Willinsky/ (accessed September 26, 2006).

63. Willinsky et al., "Doing Medical Journals Differently."

64. SPARC recently explored the fiscal power of publishing cooperatives through Raym Crow's perceptive economic analysis: "Publishing Cooperatives: An Alternative for Non–profit Publishers," *First Monday* 11, no. 9 (2006), available at http://www.first-monday.org/issues/issue11_9/crow/index.html#c1 (accessed September 26, 2006). Where this leaves the university press remains an interesting question, although in the case of open access, some presses, such as the University of Michigan Press, work closely with the library, while at Stanford, the press is overseen by the library. The Public Knowledge Project is creating the Open Monograph Press to address the parallel of open-access monographs and scholarly editions, traditionally the purview of the press, that might also involve pluralistic economic models.

65. *The Encyclopedia of Life* (http://www.eol.org/) provides research sources in various formats, , for example, the yellow fever mosquito. The "Literature References—PDF Links" provides access to those historical articles, dating back to the 1920s, that have been scanned and made freely available, whereas those references that are not freely available are optimistically marked "pdf not yet available." On *Wikipedia's* use of open access research, see Willinsky, "Socrates Back on the Street."

66. PRISM, *Current Issues.*

67. For example, Evangelos Michelakis of the University of Alberta learned that based on his studies that DCA was found to shrink tumors in mice, cancer patients were ordering it online rather than waiting until the proper trials on humans had been conducted. This made him concerned that this premature use of the drug might not only harm patients but also make it harder to carry out the trials if through this uncontrolled use, it were found to do damage. See Evangelos Michelakis, "Untried Cancer Drug Bought on Web," *BBC News*, March 29, 2007, available at http://news .bbc.co.uk/2/hi/health/6506113.stm (accessed September 26, 2006). The University of Alberta has set up a website to offer information about DCA as well as to accept donations to advance this research (DCA Research Information, University of Alberta, http://www.depmed.ualberta.ca/dca/).

From Land Grant to Federal Grant

to Patent Grant Institutions

DIANA R. RHOTEN

AND WALTER W. POWELL

According to the historian Thomas Bender, "No institution in the West, save the Roman Catholic church, has persisted longer. From small medieval beginnings [the university] has become diffused throughout the world, assuming everywhere principal responsibility for advanced teaching and, more often than not, research."[1] Despite the university's persistence as an institution, however, he argues that "the terms of the university's connection to society . . . have of course changed."

The American public research university is no exception to Bender's rule. Public universities emerged in the United States in the nineteenth century as a core social organization designed to deliver higher education teaching and research as well as other public services to individuals of the nation-state. Thanks to the growing demand for expanded educational opportunities and increased research outputs, this mission was further formalized in the twentieth century as the public research university became even more central to the American landscape. The global expansion of higher education is truly remarkable: there are more university students in Kazakhstan today (100,000) than there were in the entire world in 1900.[2] In the twenty-first century, however, the public university is no longer only a provider—nor the only provider—of human capital and basic research to society; it is itself a contributor to and a competitor in the increasingly intertwined global marketplace of knowledge production and innovation.

We argue that while the American public research university has endured and prospered as an institution, its organizational missions of research, teaching, and service have been challenged in the wider society as calls for commercial engagement, broader impacts, and economic development have echoed throughout the country. Clearly, these new values and behaviors have implications for both public and private research universities, but we contend that they carry greater potential conflict and consequence for the latter. As tensions emerge between historical missions and contemporary demands, we find that the public research university's efforts to adapt an old set of activities to new a theory of action are inhibited by the very structural models and cultural myths that make it uniquely "public." At first glance, then, while the public university may appear chameleon-like, seemingly susceptible to and changing its colors in response to environmental shifts, we conclude that beneath the surface, the public research university may be more clam-like, dug in and resilient in the face of changing tides.

In this chapter, we provide a very brief history of the public research university and the development of its mission in the United States, examining the dominant myths and models that have guided public research university activities over time as a way to contextualize the present. We then interrogate the degree to which recent changes in the broader environment of higher education have led to a reorientation of assumptions about and enactments of what public research universities should do, for whom, and how. To do so, we explore key trends involving intellectual property, industry partnerships, and the professoriate. We conclude by discussing implications of the tensions between historical visions and current realities for the public university and the public interest. Although our focus is on American universities, public universities throughout the world have been exposed to similar environmental demands and may thus face somewhat similar organizational dilemmas.[3]

HISTORICAL MYTHS, MODELS, AND MISSIONS OF THE PUBLIC RESEARCH UNIVERSITY

An organization's mission is defined, and its activities directed, by the prevailing worldviews of its key members and constituents. These worldviews are based on preexistent myths (assumptions) and models (actions) of the organization that are shaped and tempered by the wider environment. Changes in the environment can surface anomalies or provoke disorder in these myths and models, as well as disrupt or alter an organization's worldviews, mission, and activities.[4] In this section, we show how the public research university's organizational mission has expanded over time, shaped in large part by exogenous factors.

The Land Grant Institution

The American roots of the public research university can be traced back to the turn of the nineteenth century, with the founding of the University of Georgia (1785), North Carolina (1789), Vermont (1800), South Carolina (1801), and Virginia (1819) all in a relatively few decades. Shortly thereafter, the University of Michigan (1841) set the pace for the large midwestern universities. But the real signal of public commitment to university-based research came with the passage of the Morrill Act in 1862. With this legislation, the federal government donated public lands to a number of states and territories for the purpose of establishing at least one institution of higher learning in the areas of agriculture and mechanical arts, without excluding other scientific and classical studies.[5]

After the Civil War, sixty-seven land grant institutions were founded in this spirit, and the modern American public land grant university was born. With the Second Morrill Act (1890), the federal government extended this commitment to public higher education by providing additional financial endowments for all land grant institutions, except those that made distinctions by race in admissions. The land grants were also given responsibility for research and extension, primarily in the area of agriculture. In this regard, the Hatch Act of 1887 provided for permanent annual appropriations to each state to establish an agricultural experiment station, thus marking the advent of public universities' responsibilities to help generate research that both enhanced agricultural productivity and supported agricultural communities. With the passage of the Smith-Lever Act of 1914, federal funding also became available for the dissemination of such research for public use and service.

These laws did more than grant land to institutions of higher education. Collectively and with remarkably few strings attached, they established the first formal mechanisms for the public funding of institutions of higher education. Thus, although they are not responsible for creating the American public research university, they are largely responsible for distinguishing "public" from "private" universities in the United States and making permanent the role of state and federal support to the former for teaching, research, and service.[6]

The public aspects of teaching and research, long viewed as coequal in the land grant model of the public university, proved to be prescient responses of the government to the needs of the rapidly developing agricultural and industrial sectors of the late nineteenth-century United States. By the early twentieth century, scientific research had become a major avenue of growth and expansion. Scholarly publication was emerging as a source of prestige for universities, and the production of scientific knowledge beyond subjects initially introduced by land grant policies represented a potent new opportunity for university research. By the 1930s and the arrival of the Great Depression, a number of major universities were convinced that sustained engagement with the nation's pressing issues could not be their concern alone but was perhaps something for which both government and industry should pay.

THE FEDERAL GRANT INSTITUTION

Before World War II, the federal government played a significant role in establishing teaching, research, and service activities in certain fields, particularly agriculture and mechanical arts. During the war, both public and private universities contributed vitally to scientific and technical research, most notably in the areas of engineering and the physical sciences related to national security. But land grant endowments and wartime investments were a long way from a coherent, statute-based federal science policy.

After the war, American higher education expanded rapidly. With returning veterans supported by federal funding through the G.I. bill, public universities became wellsprings of education. With the institutionalization of federal policies and agencies, public universities also became major founts of public research. As Gustavo E. Fischman, Sarah E. Igo, and Diana Rhoten discuss in chapter 2, this postwar period is often nostalgically considered the golden age of the university generally. The same can be said of academic science more specifically. Understanding this period's influence on the growth and norms of research helps explain the myths and models of the public research university's mission.

Motivated by the critical wartime advances in science and engineering achieved by the Office of Scientific Research and Development and justified by national defense and health needs, Washington came to favor a postwar science policy that emphasized an active role for the federal government in cultivating and expanding scientific research, both basic and applied. The foundations of this strategy were outlined in Vannevar Bush's famous 1945 report, "Science—The Endless Frontier." Bush applauded the government's support of directly useful, applied research but argued that immediately applicable studies were not enough and that the nation needed to redefine its pursuit of scientific knowledge with an emphasis on continued basic research. To spur and support basic research, Bush specified the importance of a federal role in university-based science:

> There are areas of science in which the public interest is acute but which are likely to be cultivated inadequately if left without more support than will come from private sources. . . . [W]e are entering a period when science needs and deserves increased support from public funds. . . . As long as [colleges, universities, and research centers] are vigorous and healthy and their scientists are free to pursue the truth wherever it may lead, there will be a flow of new scientific knowledge to those who can apply it. . . . [B]asic research is essentially noncommercial in nature. It will not receive the attention it requires if left to industry.[7]

Though not entirely explicit about how academic science would ultimately be converted into technological advances and industrial applications, Bush's report was rooted in the belief that federally funded basic research and scientific training conducted by the universities would be the engine of economic progress and national development. The postwar era essentially defined the research university as a public entity and scientific knowledge as a fundamental public good, destined to enjoy government patronage. This logic fueled the creation of such federal units as the Office of Naval Research (1946), the National Institutes of Health (1944–1946), the Atomic Energy Commission (1946), and the National Science Foundation (1950).

With the emergence of the cold war and the Soviet Union's launching of *Sputnik*, federal support of higher education research continued to grow, as did the budgets of these newly formed agencies. Federal spending for research and development doubled in just four years, rising from $15.3 billion in 1953 to $31.1 billion in 1957 (in 2000 U.S. dollars).[8] These halcyon days of the federal grant institution bolstered the physical and biological sciences, health sciences, and engineering on public university campuses. As with other dimensions of higher education life, however, 1968 also proved to be a year of disruption, marking the first downturn in total federal spending for research and development since 1945.

THE PATENT GRANT INSTITUTION

If the 1950s and 1960s marked the era of public and federal support for higher education and research, the 1970s and 1980s witnessed its erosion. In the early 1970s, the widespread belief was that as a matter of necessity as well as opportunity, spending for public universities would continue to rise. Expectations for and expansions of higher education were multiplying exponentially, resulting in unprecedented increases in student enrollment, academic faculty, scholarly fields, research capacities, and campus resources, all of which translated into amplified costs and expenditures.[9]

Rather than a steady increase, however, the 1970s ushered in the onset of decades of decline and stagnation in per capita funding for research and education, particularly at the state and local levels, from which public universities, compared with private universities, receive a disproportionately greater share of their funding.[10] In the 1970s, on average, about 50 percent of public higher education budgets were state supported. By the twenty-first century, this average had dropped to roughly 30 percent and, in some cases, had fallen to as low as 10 percent. For example, at the University of Illinois, state funding shrank from 37 percent of the institution's budget in 1990 to 20 percent in 2004, and at the University of Virginia, the share of its operating budget coming from the state fell from about 28 percent in 1985 to 8 percent in 2004.[11] In the 2002, the University of North Carolina at Chapel Hill received 25 percent of its general funds budget from the state; the University of Missouri, 21 percent; Ohio State University, 18 percent; and the University of Michigan, 10 percent.[12] This downward turn in per capita funding for higher education was sparked by several factors, including an expanding student enrollment, a declining tax base, and a series of national recessions.

Somewhat ironically perhaps, policymakers at the time openly blamed the worsening economy on two factors, both of which they blamed on Vannevar Bush's linear model of innovation. The first factor was the failure to move ideas from the university lab into the market economy, and the second was the ease of access to U.S. research results by foreign firms.[13] To many scholars, this critique was, and still is, puzzling. How could ideas be both simultaneously accessible to foreign competitors and not sufficiently useful to domestic companies? In actuality, the buildup of basic research in academia was not the main motivating problem. Rather, policymakers were flummoxed primarily by the idea that American science was not matching the technological innovations of Japan and West Germany. Fueled by concerns of global economic competitiveness, U.S.

policymakers and industry captains demanded more economic bang for their American research buck, so federal research spending—particularly for basic research at universities—came under increasing scrutiny in Washington.

Shortly thereafter, as government interests shifted from sponsoring basic research justified by national concerns to promoting applied research targeting global competition, a series of new federal legislative initiatives emerged. The earliest and most commonly cited is the Bayh-Dole Act of 1980, which transferred the rights of ownership of federally funded inventions from the government to the recipient of the federal funds.[14] As a virtual equivalent of the transfer of land grant rights under the Morrill Act, the Bayh-Dole Act turned over intellectual property rights emanating from federally funded research to all universities. With a growing family of policies behind it—including the Stevenson-Wydler Technology Innovation Act of 1980, the Economic Recovery Tax Act of 1981, the Small Business Innovation Research Act of 1982, the National Cooperative Research Act of 1984, and judicial decisions granting expansive rights to intellectual property claims—Bayh-Dole sent a clear and concerted signal for universities to promote technology transfer and pursue property rights.

While prompted by economic concerns and facilitated by legal regimes, the incorporation of such commercial and entrepreneurial activities into the university also was accelerated by technological change and the rise of venture capital financing, particularly in the areas of biomedical and computer science.[15] Under these new conditions—which essentially underpin the global knowledge economy—universities moved away from older models of practice in which the university pushed publicly funded research out to industry toward newer models in which scientists collaborated with industry on publicly and privately supported research. In an array of technologically sophisticated sectors, from biotechnology to semiconductors, design and apparel, and telecommunications, a dense web of affiliations between universities and commercial firms were spawned.[16] To be sure, such relationships are not entirely new. The assumptions and actions surrounding them, however, are different in subtle but potentially significant ways, which can place such activities at odds with the historical myths and missions of the public research university.

University technology transfer has prompted an array of new metrics by which universities are evaluated. The generation of licensing income is one. For public universities, the number of spin-off companies is regarded as a contribution to local economic development. Likewise, some universities underscore patenting as a measure of their contribution to commercial science. These new metrics of accomplishment trigger novel forms of competition among universities and generate new criteria by which universities are assessed.[17] State legislators are much more prone to ask public universities whether they are having an impact on job creation and employment growth in their communities. Indeed, some states tie funding to these goals and allocate resources to commercial engagement. Thus, the embrace of technology transfer has altered the way in which universities are regarded by various key constituencies, and the creation of measures of entrepreneurial accomplishment has led to more intensive efforts inside universities to manage and publicize such activities. Critics, ranging from those who allege the corporate capture of universities to others who contend that bureaucracy and public relations deter the actual transfer and application of knowledge, note that this new regime can conflict with long-standing goals of knowledge production and teaching.[18]

In sum, the missions of the American public research university have shifted over the last 150 years, imbuing the institution with multiple myths and endowing it with different models from one period to the next. As a land grant institution, the public research university was in many ways the "local servant" responsible for homesteading a new field of higher education, democratizing teaching and learning, conducting mission-oriented research, and rendering services directly to local communities and citizens. This nineteenth-century ideal of the public research university was captured in the "Wisconsin Idea," which, as expressed by the then president of the University of Wisconsin, states that the public university should "never be content until the beneficent influence of the university reaches every family in the state."[19]

As a federal grant institution, the public research university took on more of a "national scholar" persona. In this role, the public research university graduated from a set of loosely connected pioneering organizations to a federated system of professional organizations responsible for integrating research with teaching, supplying rigorous basic science for industrial innovation, and leveraging its well-resourced base to advance the country socially and economically. This view of the twentieth-century public research university was best encapsulated in the "Social Contract for Science," which embodied the expectation that in exchange for the government's investments, universities would produce public good research that served the nation's interests and solved its ills.[20] As a patent grant institution, the public research university assumed yet another identity, that of the "international salesman" responsible for taking knowledge products directly from laboratory to the market, reinvesting earnings to enhance prestige and reputation, and carrying the country forward into a globally competitive knowledge economy. Michael Crow, president of Arizona State University, best summarized this vision for the twenty-first-century public university:

"The modern university is the ideal environment for the creation and transfer of knowledge that drives national competitiveness in an increasingly global era."[21]

THE PUBLIC RESEARCH UNIVERSITY: CLAM OR CHAMELEON?

Although our broad sketch of the historical context of the U.S. public research university draws on a wide range of sources, the periods and shifts we have emphasized are generally agreed on by both scholars and commentators. Debate remains, however, over whether recent shifts in mission and the wider environment have translated into alterations and disruptions in the internal activities of public research universities. In this section, we take up these concerns, focusing specifically on activities closely associated with shifts to the "patent grant institution."

On the one hand are those who believe that the work of the university has not changed significantly, although they do not always necessarily agree on its starting point. For example, Clark Kerr, former president of the University of California, suggested that markets and market logic have always been a part of the academic landscape. Describing the tension between the acropolis, with its focus on values and mission, and the agora, the marketplace, Kerr commented:

> The cherished academic view that higher education started out on the acropolis and was desecrated by descent into the agora led by ungodly commercial interests and scheming public officials and venal academic leaders is just not true. If anything, higher education started in the agora, the market, at the bottom of the hill and ascended to the acropolis at the top of the hill. . . . Mostly it has lived in tension, at one and the same time at the bottom of the hill, at the top of the hill, and on the many pathways in between.[22]

Echoing the theme of engagement, Richard Nelson and Nathan Rosenberg argued that science in the United States has always had a more practical character than its European counterpart, and thus contact with industry and involvement with industrial applications has long been a distinguishing feature of the U.S. university.[23]

On the other hand are those who believe that the mission of the public research university has shifted, particularly over the last two decades, creating a sea change in the institution's norms and logics regarding the purpose of knowledge and practice of science. In this view, the once separate streams of public (often academic and/or basic) and proprietary (often industrial and/or applied) science have breached the levies, thereby altering the landscape, particularly of the public research university.[24] Within this camp, there is some disagreement about the incredulity versus the inevitability of these changes. Some believe this intermingling has led universities to be dominated by market interests, thereby undermining its capacity to serve its public purposes and sometimes even its fundamental mission.[25] Others feel "given that reality, . . . the key to making the more modern university more publicly relevant lies in making it, ironically, even more market responsive—or, to use the term we have come to favor, more market-smart."[26]

Next we explore recent trends that characterize and challenge the "patent grant institution": intellectual property, industry partnerships, and the professoriate. We argue that the activities themselves are not entirely new to the public research university but that many of the emergent values and behaviors surrounding them are. We suggest that the current embrace of market mechanisms provokes discussions and conflicts that reveal the core tensions of the twenty-first-century public university. These debates and their resolutions suggest which worldviews are prioritized and which constituents are rewarded.

Intellectual Property

As we pointed out earlier, a number of today's public research universities were established by the Morrill Land Grant Act, with a specific mandate to conduct locally useful research in agriculture and the mechanic arts. Given the immediate economic potential of such mission-oriented research, land grant institutions were among the first universities to address the issue of ownership of government-funded research results.[27] The protection of intellectual property has been a regular activity at most public research universities since the late nineteenth and early twentieth century, whereas private research universities had more ambivalent, if nonexistent, patenting policies for much of the first half of the twentieth century. For example, as early as 1890, the University of Wisconsin sought and secured a patent for Stephen Babcock's test for butterfat. In 1912, Frederick Cottrell, a chemist at the University of California, at Berkeley, obtained a patent for developing an electrical method of recovering valuable materials from smokestack emissions. In 1923, Harry Steenbock, again at the University of Wisconsin, patented an irradiation process to enhance vitamin D in foodstuffs.[28] Moreover, while it is true that technology transfer offices (TTOs) diffused rapidly across universities and that patents began to mushroom in the post-Bayh-

Dole era of the knowledge economy, we should not forget that thirteen of the twenty universities that established such offices before 1980 were public.[29]

Even though patenting efforts are not altogether new, the dominant values and behaviors now attached to patenting and licensing seem to be. This has implications for both public and private universities, but arguably more so for the former. The historical land grant legacy carries with it the view that patenting for commercial intent and individual gain was inappropriate. The motivations for taking patents in earlier times were largely institutional and societal. Take the examples of Frederick Cottrell and Harry Steenbock. They used their first patents to establish the Research Corporation of America (RCA) and the Wisconsin Alumni Research Foundation (WARF), respectively, each with the purpose of managing and supporting their and other public-minded inventors' research. Not only did RCA and WARF protect the rights of products specifically designed to serve the interests of the public, but the organizations also plowed patenting incomes back into their universities to seed new research before World War II when federal monies were limited. In 1925, WARF took over managing Steenbock's patented irradiation technique to prevent its use by producers of oleomargarine (which does not naturally contain vitamin D) and thereby to protect his local state's dairy industry. WARF executed its first licensing agreement on this patent in 1927 with Quaker Oats, to fortify breakfast foods, and subsequently licensed the invention to various pharmaceutical companies while at the same time denying requests from manufacturers wishing to use the process for nonnutritional purposes. The revenues from Steenbock's patent provided the financial base for continued work on vitamin D for several decades.[30]

The contrast with the objectives of current patenting activities is considerable. Today, greater priority is often given to commercial "payoff" and individual incentives over institutional "payback" or public benefit.[31] This is particularly true in the area of biotechnology, for example, where the race for licensing dollars has driven patenting progressively "upstream" to embrace gene and protein sequences, despite the known threats this poses to slowing, restricting, or even eliminating the "downstream" development of new therapies or diagnostic products. Consider the story of the BRCA1 and BRCA2 genes. In 1994, with funding from the National Institutes of Health, a team led by Mark Skolnick at the University of Utah identified the first of these breast-cancer susceptibility genes and filed for a patent on portions of the BRCA1 gene, as well as on the probe to detect mutation in it. The patent was issued three years later to the university and to Myriad Genetics, a company founded by Skolnick in 1991. NIH was left off the patent, and the patent was licensed exclusively to Myriad, which insisted on doing all U.S. testing for the presence of unknown mutation in this and the related BRCA2 gene. Those women who have a mutation in either gene are said to have as high as an 86 percent chance of getting cancer, and the cost for the complete two-gene analysis is now $2,975.[32] In addition to being cost prohibitive for many, exclusive control of the intellectual property (IP) precludes other companies from developing the test and creating competing, possibly superior, tests. Moreover, as a clinical consequence of this proprietary control, some women are undergoing mastectomies on the basis of false positive results.

On the face of it, the lure of potential profit as a rationale for patent-licensing activities is not surprising, given the explosive growth of science-based industries and the regressive state of public financing for public universities. Assessing the pursuit of potential profit as the primary goal for patent-licensing activities requires deeper consideration, however. Despite the uptick in patent-licensing activities at public universities, very few academic patents actually generate considerable revenue.[33] While university-licensing income rose from $123 million in 1991 to slightly more than $1 billion in 2002, only a handful of public universities have had blockbuster successes, most notably University of Florida, Florida State University, and Michigan State University.[34] Most public research universities either make a paltry sum or lose money when the costs of running an office are included. In fact, as Lori Turk-Bicakci and Steven Brint show, public universities are less likely to receive licensing income than are their private counterparts.[35] We believe this is due at least in part to the structural models and cultural myths that define research universities as "public" (in both source and service) and constrain them in ways distinct from that of their private counterparts.

David Mowery, Bhaven Sampat, and Arvids Ziedonis argue that public research universities can and do learn over time how to focus on high-value patents. But by virtue of their mission, public research universities must do more than generate revenue; they must also disseminate knowledge.[36] Sometimes these goals correspond, and other times they clash. Whereas generating revenue often requires restricted access to key research, disseminating knowledge generally entails open access to such research. Thus, embedding new commercial behaviors and values into the core assumptions of the public research university and becoming a successful patent grant institution may introduce conflicts between past and present missions. How these conflicts are ultimately resolved can reveal much about the true state of organizational change. Donald Siegel, Leanne Atwater, and Albert Link discovered through site visits and interviews that universities, especially public ones, are quite sensitive to the charge that they are "giving away" university-based, taxpayer-funded technologies that subsequently yield substantial profits for companies. As a result, many TTOs are adopting a hard line in licensing negotiations.[37] And, indeed, in some cases, state legislatures are demanding that universities strike "better" deals.

Nonetheless, some universities are turning to an emphasis on the social value of innovation. We see steps toward improving access to important technologies that serve underdeveloped nations or underrepresented groups. Some universities are still and again plowing back licensing income into valuable but decidedly noncommercial pursuits. Florida State's revenues, for example, have helped build a first-rate theater department, and the University of Iowa's income supports its noted writers' workshop. This does not mean that concern about the expansion of intellectual property claims on public university campuses is not warranted. To be sure, new values and behaviors with respect to patenting and licensing activities have been broadly introduced at public research universities, but the consequences of these activities are highly varied and, in some cases, reinforce traditional pursuits rather than enter new commercial territory.

INDUSTRIAL PARTNERSHIPS

Public universities have long had partnerships with industry. From their very beginning in the late nineteenth century, land grant universities have been expected to contribute to the economic vitality of their states by training students in the agricultural and mechanical arts to meet the needs of industry and technology.[38] By the turn of the twentieth century, university professors were already routinely working with industry in fields like chemistry and engineering, moving back and forth between the two sectors through either contract or consulting arrangements.[39] These cross-sector relationships accelerated with World War I as academic scientists in these and other fields like physics often temporarily vacated university labs to work with industry on military endeavors. Although they were facilitated by organizations like the National Research Council or philanthropic foundations like Rockefeller or Carnegie, these early university-industry relationships applied to individual-level assignments or connections.

Institutional-level agreements and arrangements with industry initially arrived at public university campuses after World War I and in the form of corporate-sponsored research. In 1920, Michigan was the first to establish a department of engineering with the purpose of coordinating major industrial projects, with Minnesota and Illinois following closely behind.[40] During World War II, federal agencies like the Department of Defense, the Atomic Energy Commission, and even the National Aeronautics and Space Administration (NASA) supported a number of university-industry-government research projects on public university campuses.

After a lull in industry sponsorship and partnership during the 1960s and 1970s, industry investment and involvement both multiplied and diversified over the last few decades.[41] Although universities still receive a very small fraction of their research funding from industry (estimated at around 5 percent), industry investment in public university research increased fourteenfold to $1.16 billion between 1977 and 1997.[42] This compares with private schools, where industry investment increased only tenfold to $555 million.[43] Notably, by the turn of the twenty-first century, eight of the top ten industry-funded universities in the United States were public.[44] More interesting, however, is how industry involvement with the twenty-first-century university has morphed, moving well beyond traditional relationships based on student training, academic consulting, or research services to new complicated marriages set forth in research parks, cooperatives, joint ventures, and strategic alliances. Thus, whereas twentieth-century university-industry partnerships involved corporations with extensive in-house corporate R&D labs that invited basic research inputs from universities, twenty-first-century partnerships are more likely to involve joint R&D between company and university scientists.

The idea of the science park first gained traction shortly after World War II with the founding of the Stanford Research Park in Palo Alto, California (1951), University Research Park in Norman, Oklahoma (1957), and Research Triangle Park in Raleigh-Durham-Chapel Hill, North Carolina (1959). Fifteen research parks were established before 1980, with the express purpose of creating jobs for university-trained youth. In a second wave of foundings, another 110 parks were created before the turn of the century. Unlike their predecessors, these later parks were dedicated to incubating new firms based on and for university-produced research.[45] Many of these newer parks are focused on the life sciences, such as the Virginia BioTechnology Park in Richmond (1992), the Colorado Bioscience Park Aurora (1999), and the University of Maryland BioPark at Baltimore (2003).

In addition to science parks, numerous industry-university cooperative research centers (IUCRC) and research joint ventures (RJV) began popping up across campuses in the 1980s. The primary purpose of both IUCRCs and RJVs is to engage in ongoing collaborative research and foster rapid technology transfer between universities and firms. In contrast to the older linear model of innovation in which university research essentially moved downstream to industry, these partnerships involved simultaneous inputs by academic and industry scientists. The number of IUCRCs on university campuses increased by 154 percent during the 1980s and to more than a thousand by 2000.[46] IUCRCs cover a range of traditional engineering and manufacturing fields to newer areas in biotechnology, information technology, and green technology. University participation in RJVs has also risen steadily since the National Cooperative Research Act of 1984, with the share of all RJVs in the United States involving at least one university doubling from 8 percent (1984–1992) to 17 percent (1992–1999). The bulk of the university RJVs are in electronic and electrical equipment and industrial machinery (including computer manufacturing).

A more recent development in university-industry relationships is the widespread appearance of strategic corporate alliances (SCAs) in the 1990s. Unlike science parks, IUCRCs, or RJVs, these alliances do not create third-party organizations. Instead, in this partnership model, firms pay millions of dollars directly to university labs for research programs that align with their needs and interests. Notable examples include MIT's $30 million alliance with the biotech company Amgen to fund biology researchers; Stanford University's $225-million partnership with Exxon Mobil and others to create the Global Climate and Energy Project; and the University of California at Berkeley's $500-million contract with the energy giant British Petroleum (BP) for its new Energy Biosciences Institute. Generally speaking, the SCA model is used by high-technology firms to access cutting-edge basic science. Companies that are familiar with this form of partnering have multiple alliances with different faculties and universities. The universities, for their part, increasingly have an array of corporate alliance partners, although individual faculty rarely have multiple affiliations with corporate sponsors. Thus, from the faculty side, such connections are more likely to be monogamous, but from industry they are polygamous. While SCAs are typically designed to foster ongoing, open-ended relationships and replace the need for complex legal negotiations, the terms of these alliances vary significantly from case to case. For example, Amgen and MIT simply agreed that patents resulting from work specifically funded by Amgen would be jointly held. In contrast, the Berkeley-BP alliance specifies that nearly a third of the annual financing is designated for confidential research by BP, and it gives BP the rights to negotiate exclusive licenses on the "public" part of this alliance.[47]

Clearly, then, the nature of the public university's relationship to industry has been neither static nor universal; and the dominant values and behaviors surrounding these ties have evolved along with the development of different industries and the changing ideologies of the day. Beyond the education and training objectives of early arrangements, many of the nineteenth- and early twentieth-century projects resembled an outsourcing arrangement in which industry contracted for university research but owned all property, responsibility, and liability for the outcome. In more recent collaborations, which involve joint technological development in third-party centers or a firm's strategic outsourcing of research interests and needs directly to a university, the outcome is often the result of mutual efforts and may yield jointly owned assets between industry and university.[48] The complexity of these new alliances has prompted debate over the publicness of research universities. On the one hand, these alliances bring much needed revenue to the public university, allowing them to carry out their historical missions by delivering better-resourced research programs. On the other hand, with such alliances, universities can run the risk of being captured by and beholden to a private corporate partner's research agenda, threatening the scientific integrity of the university and its ability to serve the public interest independently and without bias. Resolving this debate requires understanding the extent to which industry relationships are altering or disrupting core university actions and assumptions.

At the institutional level, Lawrence Cote and Mary Cote found that despite the increase in industry-university relations, land grant schools had a greater involvement in industry-sponsored contract research or technology extension activities than in science parks or spin-offs.[49] Similarly, in a more recent comparative study, Turk-Bicakci and Brint suggested that public research universities are less likely than private research universities to be highly active collaborators with industry.[50] At the individual level, in a survey of university and industry participants in RJVs, Yong Lee found that faculty gave priority to two things when discussing their motivations: obtaining funds for research assistance, lab equipment, and their own research agenda; and obtaining insights into their own research by being able to conduct field tests.[51] Faculty members viewed opportunities to place students, obtain patents, or start businesses as less important motivations.[52] Even though the empirical basis is limited, the results indicate that as with intellectual property activities, new values and behaviors of entrepreneurialism are influencing industry partnerships at public universities but that business goals and proprietary claims may not yet be fully institutionalized into the core actions and assumptions of the university and its faculty.

THE PROFESSORIATE

The historical missions of nineteenth-century land grants established a strong public purpose for public research universities, seeking to balance responsibilities in its faculty for teaching, research, and extension as services to the community. While still seeking to maintain this three-way balance, the twentieth-century role of public university faculty emphasized national science over local service. This repriortization was evident with the mobilization of national wartime science, and these efforts took faculty off their campuses and away from their communities. After the war, faculty returned to their local institutions, but the "professionalization of scholarly allegiance" and the "institutionalization of higher education" caused professors to turn inward to their research and their scholarly invisible colleges and away from their local or national publics.[53]

As Christine Musselin describes in chapter 14, the onslaught of fiscal retrenchment and the response of new managerialism in the 1970s yielded another redefinition of scientific scholarship and a reconceptualization of academic life. Apart from dedicating significantly more time to research and less to service in their activities, faculty today have also taken up new roles and positions that their predecessors could have never imagined. Some faculty look more and more like entrepreneurs, juggling start-ups and consulting gigs with classrooms and lab work.[54] Others resemble contingent workers, piecing together postdocs, lectureships, and adjunct posts from one institution to the next.

The upshot of this period is a marked diversification in and stratification across career trajectories, research priorities, and fiscal opportunities for American faculty. To be sure, academia has always been competitive and status driven, with rewards and incentives motivating and accruing to the most successful scientists and scholars. As fame and fortune have gained greater currency in the new world of commercial and entrepreneurial returns, however, these new behaviors and values may be altering the twenty-first-century university's compensation, prioritization, and evaluation of faculty work on campuses everywhere, but with particular disadvantages for public universities.

The 1940 Statement of Principles of the American Association of University Professors (AAUP) noted that tenure is a means not only to academic freedom but also to "a sufficient degree of economic security to make the profession attractive to men and women of ability" by providing sufficient financial rewards to maintain commitment and loyalty (AAUP, 1940). Although 2006 faculty salaries outpaced inflation for the first time in a long time, the growing financial disparity between public and private institutions may well be straining the financial commitment and loyalty of public research university faculty. In the late 1970s, across all fields, the average full professor at a public university earned 91 percent of what her private university counterpart earned.[55] Today they earn only 78 percent; or, on average $30,000 less: $106,495 compared with $136,689 (AAUP salary survey,

2006–2007). Indeed, the average salary for *assistant* professors at private universities is more than the average for *associate* professors at publics. According to the results of a recent faculty survey, private university professors are also more satisfied than their public counterparts in the number of courses they teach, the number of students in classes, and the quality of students they advise.[56] Other evidence points to the negative effects of bureaucratic meddling, political constraints, and dwindling public support on faculty morale at public research universities.[57]

In addition to the growing differences in faculty benefits between public and private research universities, there also are yawning gaps in the salary and support offered to faculty whose skills are in demand by the private sector—computer and life sciences, as well as business, law, engineering—and their colleagues in the humanities and social sciences. By 2006, for example, full professors in engineering earned on average about $20,000 more than full professors in social sciences and almost $30,000 more than humanities faculty.[58] These disparities between what are sometimes called the "have" and the "have not" fields are even wider among new assistant professors. Start-up packages for new tenure-track faculty right out of graduate school can average about $300,000 or more in any of the physical or life sciences and engineering fields. By one account, the going annual rate today for sought-after theoreticians in physics is $400,000 to $600,000 at the level of assistant professor, including salary and research support. The price tag for top experimentalists, who have far more extensive laboratory needs, is $1.5 million to $2 million.[59] Whether in hot or traditional fields, private universities are able to offer more customized, lucrative packages than public universities can, which have to consider issues of equity and public scrutiny in ways that private universities do not. When we turn from recruiting to retention, we find private universities again at a considerable advantage.

The intersection of these trends has powerful ramifications for which faculty and fields research universities can and will pursue. Obviously, institutions with larger endowments are in a better position to offer and maintain these types of high salaries and cutting-edge facilities. In 2006, Harvard, Yale, and Stanford had the three largest endowments, which totaled $61 billion dollars, or 125 percent of combined endowments of the fifteen largest public universities. Harvard's endowment alone was $29 billion, more than twice that of the entire University of Texas system and almost five times that of the University of California or the University of Michigan.[60] Absent significant endowment funds, investments in faculty and university facilities must come from either the university budget or the state. The comparative endowment-driven spending power of the privates, combined with the limitations of public budgets and the complications of state financing, which handicap even the finest public research universities, begins to reveal the disadvantages the latter might face when competing for faculty in the new academic marketplace.

As the total costs of hiring and retaining faculty in the sciences are rising across all research universities while the relative salaries, satisfaction, and scientific purchasing powers are falling at public research universities, these institutions are finding it more and more difficult to compete with private universities for "star" faculty in "leading" fields. The expanding incongruence between faculty costs and fiscal conditions at public research universities may have prompted comments such as the following from Harvard University President Drew Gilpin Faust: "One thing we all must worry about—I certainly do—is the federal support for scientific research. And are we all going to be chasing increasingly scarce dollars?" Not that Faust seems worried about Harvard or other top-tier research schools. "They're going to be—we hope, we trust, we assume—the survivors in this race," she says. As for the many lesser universities likely to lose market share, she adds, they would be wise "to really emphasize social science or humanities and have science endeavors that are not as ambitious" as those of Harvard and its peers.[61]

In response, the provosts of eleven public universities in the Midwest (the "Big 10" except for Northwestern University, which is private, plus the University of Illinois at Chicago) argued in an op-ed that "collectively, our institutions educate more than 380,000 students, produce 1 in every 8 American PhDs, and conduct more than $4.5 billion worth of research every year." The provosts also argued that

> what's imperiled goes beyond the public research universities themselves. The relative impoverishment of these schools threatens to upset the public-private balance that is at the core of America's status as the world leader in higher education and academic-based research. That balance underwrites our ability to meet global competition with social, scientific, and economic leadership.[62]

Clearly, the leaders of research universities in our nation's heartland are not willing to be relegated to the backseat by Harvard's president. Nevertheless, the fiscal challenges are very real.

Most of the academic literature views faculty actions and assumptions as inputs to, rather than outcomes of, the tension between historical visions and current realities.[63] We are interested in understanding the extent to which changes in the environmental values and behaviors surrounding the professoriate are altering or disrupting how public university faculty pursue and perform their work. Reflecting the need to legitimate the type of extreme spending decisions described earlier and to demonstrate the broad research contributions of public research universities to global competition mentioned earlier, universities are increasingly deploying performance appraisal systems that rely on easy-to-count and easy-to-report bibliometrics and scientometrics, including publications, research dollars, patents, startups, spin-offs, and licensing revenues, to name but a few.[64] Simon Marginson and Imanol Ordorika discuss the rise of this audit and ranking paradigm within higher education chapter 3. In a recent study using a subset of these metrics, James Adams and J. Roger Clemmons found that the research productivity in private universities was roughly twice that of their public counterparts.[65] The disparities in research output between public and private institutions was further supported by new data from a company, Academic Analytics, that ranks research universities on the basis of per capita faculty productivity. Only one public university—the biomedical powerhouse University of California at San Francisco—is on Academic Analytics' list of top ten large research universities.[66]

While these calculations could suggest a reversal of fortune for public research universities, many of these metrics are rather superficial and account for activities that are more closely aligned with commercialism and entrepreneurialism than with historical missions of teaching, research, and service. Thus failure on these measures might suggest a reluctance by faculty at public universities to accept some of the "new" values and behaviors into their core actions and assumptions. While there has been a general and significant increase in the time that faculty dedicate to research at all universities since the 1970s, twenty-first-century faculty also report spending more time teaching.[67] In public institutions, however, by their very definition of the university, faculty still continue teach and perform service at greater rates than do their private university colleagues. These demands on their time inevitably detract from attention to activities that are captured by simple metrics. Thus, the very structural models and cultural myths that define institutions as "public" and differentiate them from their private counterparts, which many fear are at risk in the present climate, may in fact be the key factor in faculty's maintaining some resiliency in this new political economy of academic science.

BENDER'S RULE AND THE NET IMPLICATIONS FOR THE PUBLIC RESEARCH UNIVERSITY

In a 2004 lecture entitled "Building and Sustaining Excellence in the Public Research University: The American Model," Chancellor Richard Herman of University of Illinois at Urbana-Champaign observed that "universities are constantly refashioning themselves."[68] As we have tried to show in this chapter, over time there have appeared many apparent alterations or disruptions in the way that public research universities do things. Most recently, such changes can be identified in the new concerns about intellectual property, alternative forms of industrial partnerships, and sharp changes in faculty compensation and composition. At first glance, the diffusion of activities in these three areas suggests that public research universities are running fast to adapt to the latest environmental trends and fads driving the evolution of the "patent grant institution." On closer examination, however, the adoption, or perhaps the lack thereof, of values and behaviors like commercialism and entrepreneurialism identified with being a "patent grant institution" suggests that public research universities lag behind private universities.

We do not see efforts to pursue investments in intellectual property or industrial partnerships or to privilege star faculty as new evidence of public research universities' trying to radically reengineer themselves. In fact, we have demonstrated that public research universities have long legacies of activity in each of these areas. Moreover, we do not interpret the halting steps of public research universities toward the "patent grant institution" to be primarily a matter of resources, even though their motivation might be explained this way. Rather, we believe the public research universities' ability to adapt as rapidly and as robustly as their private counterparts are doing to the demands of the twenty-first-century knowledge economy and ecology is inhibited by the very structural models and cultural myths that make this institution "public."

Whether the public research university's difficulty in morphing fully into a "patent grant institution" is qualitatively good or bad depends in part on where one sits. What concerns us are the net implications of being betwixt and between for the public research university and the publics it serves. For example, by establishing technology transfer offices and entertaining large-scale alliances with industry, public research universities signal to their constituents that they can be proprietary and commercial. In so doing, they may jeopardize their position as neutral and objective sites of public good science. Likewise, by offering unparalleled incentive packages to "star" faculty and making ever larger investments in property and facilities to stay on the vanguard of research and discovery, public universities indicate to legislators and Congress that they can survive in competition with private universities. But the very pretense of entrepreneurial viability could threaten their protected status as "public," which has earned these universities considerable material and symbolic support historically.

On the surface, it looks to many people that public research universities have broken the social compact that both assigned them responsibilities for the democratization, prosperity, and progress of America and allowed them to prosper as a protected species on the landscape of American society. Beyond appearances, it seems to us that these institutions have not fully recoded their organizational genetics so to render themselves completely viable as a "patent grant institution" in this new knowledge ecology and economy. Stuck in evolutionary transition, public research universities risk losing their niche and alienating their advocates. Many analysts are of the mind that the public research universities' competitive advantage continues to rest on their ability to teach and train young scientists as much as, if not more than, their capacity to chase patents, start companies, or house star faculty in leading-edge fields. This should not undermine the research potential of the public research university but, rather, capitalize on its teaching and service aptitude. Nonetheless, it has to be troubling to public research universities in the Midwest and South to recognize that their leading graduates, who publish and patent after receipt of their PhDs, move to the West Coast to create or join technology start-up companies.[69]

Thus, while we find fears of public research universities transforming into privatized entities overstated, we are concerned about the net implications of public research universities trying to adopt superficially, but not adapt successfully, to the new, current environment. In the end, this situation may only further disadvantage the public institutions and accentuate a stratification order among public and private universities. In order to assess these implications and weigh our concerns, however, more focused scholarship is needed. A significant challenge in writing this chapter was the lack of current studies that compare and control for public versus private universities when looking at issues of intellectual property, industrial partnerships, or faculty compensation. More comparative research on public-private differences and similarities would offer insight into key policy questions: Would public research universities be better off pursuing a more expansive public role than trying to compete with wealthy privates? What would be the consequences for public education and research science? Most critically, in the current environment, can public research universities do more to protect the public interest by playing the game or by not playing the game?

NOTES

1. Thomas Bender, introduction to *The University and The City: From Medieval Origins to the Present*, ed. Thomas Bender (Oxford: Oxford University Press, 1988), 3–12.

2. Evan Schofer and John Meyer, "The Worldwide Expansion of Higher Education in the Twentieth Century," *American Sociological Review* 70 (2005): 898–920.

3. David Frank and Jay Gabler, *Reconstructing the University: Worldwide Shifts in Academia in the 20th Century* (Stanford, Calif.: Stanford University Press, 2006).

4. Hasan Simsek and Karen Seashore Louis, "Organizational Change as a Paradigm Shift: Analysis of the Change Process in a Large, Public University," *Journal of Higher Education* 65 (1994): 670–95.

5. U.S. Statutes at Large 12 (1862): 503.

6. John Thelin, *A History of American Higher Education* (Baltimore: Johns Hopkins University Press, 2004).

7. Vannevar Bush, *Science—The Endless Frontier* (Washington, D.C.: U.S. Government Printing Office, 1945).

8. National Science Board, *Science and Engineering Indicators* (Arlington, Va.: National Science Board, 2008), fig. O-30.

9. Patricia Gumport, "Sociology of Higher Education: An Evolving Field," in *Sociology of Higher Education: Contributions and Their Contexts*, ed. Patricia Gumport (Baltimore: Johns Hopkins University Press, 2007), 17–52.

10. Whereas public research universities receive almost 10 percent of their funding for research from state and local governments, private research universities receive only 2 percent. See National Science Board, *Science and Engineering Indicators*, fig. 5-10.

11. Richard Herman, "Building and Sustaining Excellence in the Public Research University: The American Model" (lecture presented at the Royal Irish Academy, Dublin, Ireland, March 24, 2004); Survey: Higher Education, *The Economist*, "Higher Ed Inc," *The Economist*, September 8, 2005.

12. John Kronholz, "Schools Trim State Ties," *Wall Street Journal*, April 18, 2003, B1.

13. Michael Dertouzos et al., *Made in America* (Cambridge, Mass.: MIT Press, 1989); Richard Nelson and Gavin Wright, "The Erosion of U.S. Technological Leadership as a Factor in Postwar Economic Convergence," in *Convergence of Productivity: Cross-national Studies and Historical Evidence*, ed. William Baumol, Richard Nelson, and Edward Wolff (Oxford: Oxford University Press, 1994), 129–63.

14. Rebecca Eisenberg, "Proprietary Rights and the Norms of Science in Biotechnology Research," *Yale Law Journal* 97, no. 2 (1987): 177–231; Alicia Dustira, "The Funding of Basic and Clinical Biomedical Research," in *Biomedical Research: Collaboration and Conflict of Interest*, ed. Roger J. Porter and Thomas E. Malone (Baltimore: Johns Hopkins University Press, 1992), 33–56; Arti Rai, "Regulating Scientific Research: Intellectual Property Rights and the Norms of Science," *Northwestern University Law Review* 94 (1999): 77–152.

15. Paul Gompers and Josh Lerner, *The Venture Capital Cycle* (Cambridge, Mass.: MIT Press, 1999).

16. Walter Powell, "Neither Market nor Hierarchy: Network Forms of Organization," *Research in Organizational Behavior* 12 (1990): 295–336; Walter Powell and Jason Owen-Smith, "Universities and the Market for Intellectual Property in the Life Sciences," *Journal of Policy Analysis and Management* 17 (1990): 253–77.

17. Jeannette Colyvas and Walter Powell, "Measures, Metrics, and Myopia: The Challenges and Ramifications of Sustaining Academic Entrepreneurship," *Advances in the Study of Entrepreneurship, Innovation and Economic Growth* 19 (2008): 79–112.

18. See, for example, Jennifer Washburn, *University Inc.: The Corporate Corruption of Higher Education* (New York: Basic Books, 2005).

19. University of Wisconsin at Madison, "The Wisconsin Idea: History of the Wisconsin Idea," Board of Regents of the University of Wisconsin System, available at http://www.wisconsinidea.wisc.edu/history.html (accessed March 13, 2010).

20. David Guston, *Between Politics and Science: Assuring the Integrity and Productivity of Research* (Cambridge: Cambridge University Press, 2000).

21. Michael Crow, "The World Is Catching Up," *Newsweek International*, August 20–27, 2007.

22. Clark Kerr, "A General Perspective on Higher Education and Service to the Labor Market," unpublished paper excerpted in "Distillations," *Policy Perspectives* (Philadelphia: Institution for Research on Higher Education, 1988).

23. Richard Nelson and Nathan Rosenberg, "Technical Innovation and National Systems," in *National Systems of Innovation. A Comparative Analysis*, ed. Richard Nelson (Oxford: Oxford University Press, 1994), 3–21.

24. Parthia Dasgupta and Paul David, "Toward a New Economics of Science," *Research Policy* 23 (1994): 487–521; John Ziman, *Real Science* (Cambridge: Cambridge University Press, 2000).

25. See, for example, Sheila Slaughter and Larry Leslie, *Academic Capitalism: Politics, Policies, and the Entrepreneurial University* (Baltimore: Johns Hopkins University Press, 1997).

26. See, for example, Robert Zesty, William Massey, and Gregory Wegner, *Remaking the American University: Market-Smart and Mission Centered* (New Brunswick, N.J.: Rutgers University Press, 2005), 7.

27. David Mowery and Bhaven Sampat, "University Patents, Patent Policies, and Patent Policy Debates, 1925–1980," *Industrial and Corporate Change* 10 (2001): 781–814.

28. Mitchell Wallerstein, Mary Mogee, and Robin Schoen, eds., *Global Dimensions of Intellectual Property Rights in Science and Technology* (Washington, D.C.: National Academy Press, 1993).

29. AUTM U.S. Licensing Survey, *FY 2005 Survey Summary* (Deerfield, Ill.: Association of University Technology Managers, 2005.

30. Wallerstein, Mogee, and Schoen, *Global Dimensions of Intellectual Property Rights.*

31. Scott Shane, *Academic Entrepreneurship: University Spinoffs and Wealth Creation* (Northampton, Mass.: Elgar, 2004); Phillip Phan and Donald Siegel, "The Effectiveness of University Technology Transfer: Lessons Learned from Qualitative and Quantitative Research in the U.S. and U.K.," Rensselaer Working Papers in Economics 0609 (Troy, N.Y.: Department of Economics, Rensselaer Polytechnic Institute, 2006);Frank Rothaermel, Shanti Agung, and Lin Jiang, "University Entrepreneurship: A Taxonomy of the Literature," *Industrial and Corporate Change* 16 (2007): 691–791.

32. Clifton Leaf , "The Law of Unintended Consequences," *Fortune* 152 (2005): 250–68.

33. Walter Powell, Jason Owen-Smith, and Jeannette Colyvas, "Innovation and Emulation: Lessons from American Universities in Selling Private Rights to Public Knowledge," *Minerva* 45 (2007): 1573–81.

34. Jason Owen-Smith, "The Expanding Role of University Patenting in the Life Sciences: Assessing the Importance of Experience and Connectivity," *Research Policy* 32 (2003): 1695–711.

35. Lori Turk-Bicakci and Steven Brint, "University-Industry Collaboration: Patterns of Growth for Low- and Middle-Level Performers, *Higher Education* 49 (2005): 61–89.

36. David Mowery, Bhaven Sampat, and Arvids Ziedonis, "Learning to Patent? Institutional Experience and the Quality of University Patents," *Management Science* 48 (2002): 73–89.

37. Donald Siegel, Leanne Atwater, and Albert Link, "Assessing the Impact of Organizational Practices on the Relative Productivity of University Technology Transfer Offices: An Exploratory Study," *Research Policy* 32 (2003): 27–48.

38. Neil Tudiver, *Universities for Sale: Resisting Corporate Control over Canadian Higher Education* (Toronto: James Lorimer, 1999).

39. Dorothy Nelkin, Richard Nelson, and Casey Kiernan, "Commentary: University-Industry Alliances," *Science, Technology, & Human Values* 12 (1987): 65–74.

40. Roger Geiger, *To Advance Knowledge: The Growth of American Research Universities, 1900–1940* (Oxford: Oxford University Press, 1986).

41. David Mowery and Nathan Rosenberg, *Paths of Innovation: Technological Change in 20th Century America* (Cambridge: Cambridge University Press, 1998).

42. National Science Board, *Science and Engineering Indicators*, fig. O-30. This 5 percent estimate is conservative; some studies put the figures as high as 12.5 percent. Certainly, in areas like biotechnology and information technology, the figure would be

even higher. See Daniel Kleinman and Steven Vallas, "Science, Capitalism, and the Rise of the 'Knowledge Worker': The Changing Structure of Knowledge Production in the United States," *Theory and Society* 30 (2001): 451–92.

43. Patricia Gumport and Stuart Snydman, "Higher Education: Evolving Forms and Emerging Markets, in *The Nonprofit Sector: A Research Handbook*, ed. Walter Powell and Richard Steinberg (New Haven, Conn.: Yale University Press, 2006), 462–84.

44. Andrew Lawler, "Last of the Big-Time Spenders," *Science* 299 (2003): 330–33.

45. Albert Link and John Scott, "Science Parks and the Academic Missions of Universities: An Exploratory Study" (paper presented at Georgia Institute of Technology Roundtable for Engineering Entrepreneurship Research Conference, Atlanta, March 21–23, 2002).

46. Wesley Cohen, Richard Florida, Lucian Randazzese, and John Walsh, "Industry and the Academy: Uneasy Partners in the Cause of Technological Advance," in *Challenges to Research Universities*, ed. Roger Noll (Washington, D.C.: Brookings Institution Press, 1998), 171–200.

47. Goldie Blumenstyk, "BP Gets Good Terms in U. of California Deal," *Chronicle of Higher Education*, November 23, 2007, A21.

48. Joanna Poyago-Theotoky, John Beath, and Donald Siegel, "Universities and Fundamental Research: Reflections on the Growth of University-Industry Partnerships," *Oxford Review of Economic Policy* 18 (2002): 10–21.

49. Lawrence Cote and Mary Cote, "Economic Development Activity Among Land-Grant Institutions," *Journal of Higher Education* 64 (1993): 55–73.

50. Turk-Bicakci and Brint, "University-Industry Collaboration."

51. Yong Lee, "Technology Transfer and the Research University: A Search for Boundaries of University-Industry Collaboration," *Research Policy* 25 (1996): 843–63.

52. Bronwyn Hall, *University-Industry Research Partnerships in the United States*, EUI working paper ECO no. 2004/14, 2004.

53. R. Eugene Rice, *Making a Place for the New American Scholar* (Washington, D.C.: American Association for Higher Education. 1996), 128.

54. Steven Vallas and Daniel Kleinman, "Contradiction, Convergence and the Knowledge Economy: The Confluence of Academic and Commercial Biotechnology," *Socio-Economic Review* 6, no. 2 (2008): 283–311.

55. Ronald Ehrenberg, "Going Broke by Degree: A Review Essay," *Journal of Labor Research* 26 (2005): 739–52.

56. Scott Jaschik, "The Public (Non-Salary) Advantage," available at Insidehighered. com, http://www.insidehighered.com/news/2007/09/18/coache (accessed September 18, 2007).

57. Anthony Bianco and Sonal Rupani, The Dangerous Wealth of the Ivy League, *Business Week*, November 29, 2007, available at http://www.businessweek.com/print/magazine/content/07_50/b4062038784589.htm (accessed March 13, 2010).

58. Scott Smallwood, "Salaries Rise 3.8 Percent for Professors," *Chronicle of Higher Education*, March 16, 2007, A13.

59. Bianco and Rupani, "The Dangerous Wealth of the Ivy League."

60. Available at http://www.nacubo.org/documents/research/ 2006NES_Listing.pdf (accessed March 13, 2010).

61. Bianco and Rupani, "The Dangerous Wealth of the Ivy League."

62. Rodney Erickson et al., "Educational Excellence, Without Ivy State," *BusinessWeek*, January 3, 2008, op-ed, available at http://www.businessweek.com/magazine/content/08_02/b4066075132603.htm?chan=magazine +channel_opinion (accessed March 13, 2010).

63. Saul Lach and Mark Schankerman, "Royalty Sharing and Technology Licensing in Universities," *Journal of the European Economic Association* 2 (2004): 252–64.

64. Colyvas and Powell, "Measures, Metrics, and Myopia."

65. James Adams and J. Roger Clemmons, *The Growing Allocative Inefficiency of the U.S. Higher Education Sector*, National Bureau of Economic Research Working Paper Series, no. 12683, November 2006.

66. Elizabeth Redden, "Are Public Universities Losing Ground?" available at http://www.insidehighered.com/news/2007/03/14/analytics (accessed March 14, 2007).

67. Jeffrey Milem, Joseph Berger, and Eric Dey, "Faculty Time Allocation: A Study of Change Over Twenty Years," *Journal of Higher Education* 71 (2000): 454–75.

68. Richard Herman, "Building and Sustaining Excellence in the Public Research University: The American Model" (lecture presented at the Royal Irish Academy, Dublin, March 24, 2004).

69. Paula Stephan, "Wrapping It Up in a Package: The Location Decisions on New PhDs Going to Industry," in *Innovation Policy and the Economy*, ed. A. Jaffe, J. Lerner, and S. Stern (Cambridge, Mass.: MIT Press, 2007), 71–98; Caroline Simard, "From Weapons to Cell Phones: Knowledge Networks in the Creation of San Diego's Wireless Valley" (PhD diss., Stanford University, 2004).

German Universities in the
New Knowledge Ecology

ELEVEN

*Current Changes in Research Conditions
and University-Industry Relations*

STEFAN LANGE
AND GEORG KRÜCKEN

Compared with many other countries belonging to the Organization for Economic Cooperation and Development (OECD), Germany is a latecomer to adapting its university system to the changing knowledge economy. The internationalization, massification, and commodification of teaching and research, as well as the blurring of boundaries between the academic world inside the university and the outside world of industry, clients, NGOs, and the state as the central stakeholders, demand a new quality of organizational actorhood from German universities. In many aspects, this actorhood would break with the governance traditions and organizational features for which German universities were well known in the past. According to the ideal dichotomy introduced by Richard Whitley, German universities are currently pushed from "bifurcated hollow organizations" toward some sort of a "state-chartered employment organization" in order to meet the demands of the new knowledge economy.[1]

The traditional governance regime and organizational bifurcation of the German university system was described by Burton Clark as a combination of political regulation by the state and professional self-control by an academic oligarchy.[2] At the beginning of the nineteenth century, the Humboldtian idea of "solitude and freedom" of teaching and research was granted to universities in return for the political subordination of professors by an authoritarian state that also funded the universities' infrastructure, administrative services, and the salaries of the professors and their staff.[3] Despite radical changes in government since World War II, the German university system still is characterized by this historical compromise. In legal terms, this is expressed by the recognition of the dual nature of universities as both public institutions and autonomous corporations.

Until recently, the university had relatively little institutional autonomy in its relationship to the state. Individual professors, however, in all matters concerning research and teaching, were very independent. Indeed, professors were the most important pillars of the German academic oligarchy, a "chair-based organization" of "small monopolies in thousands of parts."[4]

From the chair's point of view, the university and the department were a local corporation of colleagues—the other chairs—all of whom had a basic equality of rights and opportunities. Professors could normally expect that their colleagues, including the deans and members of the rectorate, would not make any decision violating their interests. Such implicit nonaggression pacts transformed a formal structure of majority rule into a structure of informal veto powers.[5] The consequences were obvious: decision making took a lot of time, and the status quo could be changed only when everybody profited, or at least no one suffered a significant loss. Although compromises were reached, they often led to insufficient solutions or merely to symbolic politics.

This inflexible and conservative bias of German university governance has been the object of political discussion for more than thirty years and led to a rising discontent of state actors with the universities because the latter seemed to be more and more unable to adapt to changing environments and societal demands. For quite a long time, however, nothing changed. On the contrary, the number of university members who claimed that German universities were basically "healthy" and only needed more funding from the state increased steadily. Although German reunification in the early 1990s seemed to briefly open a window of opportunity for a holistic change in higher education structures through the necessary reform of East German universities, it did not greatly help reform-oriented actors.[6] As in other societal sectors in East Germany, the enormous pressure on universities to agree to the installation of a working system allowed only the substitution of politically discredited persons; those German professors who acted as temporary or permanent agents of renewal did nothing more than implement the West German status quo. Serious efforts of reform started only in the late 1990s, thus change is still at the very beginning.

PUBLIC RESEARCH UNIVERSITIES AND THEIR ECOLOGICAL ENVIRONMENT IN GERMANY

The Higher Education Sector

With a population of more than 80 million, Germany is the largest country in the European Union and one of the world's largest economies. In 2008/2009, there were 1.97 million students in the German higher education system, which has a binary structure. Of the 364 institutions of higher education, 118 are research universities, and the rest are professional education institutions (Fachhochschulen, etc.). The German higher education sector employed about 184,797 full-time academics in 2008, of which 20.9 percent were professors. About two-thirds of the students are enrolled in universities. In 2005, the universities' total finances made up 1.1 percent of Germany's gross domestic product.[7] Of the 364 institutions of higher education, 235 are public and are funded by the Bundesland (the state) in which they are located.[8]

The Political Coordination of Higher Education and Science Policies

According to the German constitution, the sixteen states are responsible for all education and culture issues, including the universities. The federal government plays only a subordinate role in the higher education system. The states coordinate their policies with respect to universities and higher education in general at the Standing Conference of the Ministers of Cultural Affairs (Kultusministerkonferenz, KMK), and the states coordinate with the federal government at the Joint Science Conference (Gemeinsame Wissenschaftskonferenz von Bund und Ländern, GWK). Finally, the Council for Sciences and Humanities (Wissenschaftsrat, WR) is the advisory body for all matters of higher education and science policy. The council has two boards, one consisting of representatives of science, and the other is made up of representatives from the states and the federal government.

The German system has three intermediary actors between the universities, on the one hand, and the government, on the other. The Deutsche Forschungsgemeinschaft (DFG) is the most important agency promoting research and funding projects. In fact, DFG funds account for more than 40 percent of the German universities' entire external income.[9] The DFG's public funding budget is financed nearly equally by the states (42 percent) and the federal government

(58 percent). The German rectors' association (Hochschulrektorenkonferenz, HRK) is the organized interest group of universities, and the Deutsche Hochschulverband (DHV) is the university professors' professional association.

All these actors have a say in the external university governance, which is carried out by several administrative actors from the federal and state levels, the intermediary organizations, and the scientific elites. This network structure is, and always has been, a dominant governance pattern in the German higher education system. The reason for its dominance is the "semisovereign" character of the German state, which is characterized by a huge amount of joint decision making between the federal government and the sixteen states as well as the close involvement of corporatist actors in formulating policy.[10] The same holds true for the German system of public sector research outside the universities.[11]

The Extra-University-Research Sector

Many research tasks that in other countries are typically located inside the public research university also are public in Germany but are not included in the higher education sector. This research system is divided into four pillars, most of which developed since World War II and provide different "research services" as public goods in return for state subsidies.

The Max Planck Gesellschaft (MPG)

The oldest and internationally best-known pillar is represented by the Max Planck Gesellschaft (MPG),[12] whose institutes carry out basic research that cannot be conducted in universities because of its innovative cutting-edge character or its size and required resources. The MPG is an umbrella organization with a global lump-sum budget of €1.2 billion annually (plus more than 20 percent external funding), consisting of eighty specialized institutes with 13,300 employees (of whom 4,800 are researchers). The institutes are organized according to the "Harnack principle."[13] The MPG is famous for producing the greatest number of Nobel Prize winners in German public-sector research.

The Fraunhofer Gesellschaft (FhG)

The second pillar is represented by the Fraunhofer Gesellschaft (FhG), founded in 1949, whose institutes conduct mostly applied science and contracted research for industry and public purposes. Along with the DFG and MPG, the FhG is the third umbrella organization with a large central administration, consisting of fifty-six institutes with more than 14,000 employees and an actual annual budget of €1.2 billion, of which €394 million is provided by federal government (90 percent) and states (10 percent). The FhG's public mission is focused on contract applied-science research. The state's subsidies to the FhG depend on the amount of third-party funding via research contracts with external partners. For every three euros of external income, the FhG receives one euro in state subsidies. The additional one-third in state funding is to provide a strong economical base and flexibility for the institutes to prepare ideas and solutions for basic research (with a strong bias on future application) that will be valuable to potential contract partners. The FhG, therefore, not only fulfills public and industrial demand but also tries to generate this demand by using the state funding it receives as seed money for innovative research projects.

The Wissenschaftsgemeinschaft Gottfried Wilhelm Leibniz (WGL)

The third pillar in German public-sector research is the Leibniz Gemeinschaft. After World War II, many existing or new research institutes had research tasks of "nationwide interest" and were cofunded by the federal government and the state in which they were located. These independent institutes were merged in the Wissenschaftsgemeinschaft Gottfried Wilhelm Leibniz (WGL) in 1997, which has a secretary and a corporate body of decision making. These institutes form a much looser confederation than those of the MPG or FhG. The WGL today consists of eighty-two research institutes with 13,930 employees (6,347 researchers), has an annual public budget of €852 million (plus more than 20 percent in external funding), and is now described as "conducting problem-solving-oriented research of national interest." This includes basic research as well as applied research, and the well-being of the WGL institutes today depends heavily on third-party funding via contract research (mainly for state and federal ministries) and on DFG-project grants.

The Helmholtz Gemeinschaft Deutscher Forschungszentren (HGF)

Last but not least, the Helmholtz Gemeinschaft Deutscher Forschungszentren (HGF) represents the fourth pillar in the German extra-university research landscape and is by far the biggest research organization in Germany in personnel (27,913 employees, of whom 9,043 are researchers), infrastructure, and state funding (with an annual public budget of €2.1 billion, plus more than 30 percent in external funding). The HGF is a product of Germany's efforts in the 1950s to concentrate nuclear reactor research in big research centers outside the universities. Since then, several new centers focusing on other interdisciplinary tasks of strategic relevance to the German state and industry have been founded, for example, for aerospace or polar research. In 1995 fifteen independent research centers joined under the HGF umbrella. Although a powerful president and collegial bodies of self-governance were installed, the institutes remained legally independent. As in the WGL, the conditions of funding and the evaluation of research became the HGF's main tasks as a corporate research organization.

Other Organizations

Other entities belonging to the German public sector research are the Ressortforschungsinstitute, research institutes that service the needs of and provide information for specific federal ministries; the academies of science; and several smaller organizations. Outside the public sector, industry research provides two-thirds of the funding for R&D in Germany. Nevertheless, the public university is still regarded and idealized as the natural home of basic research in Germany, and recent political reform strategies have tried to reestablish this "natural state."

NEW PUBLIC MANAGEMENT DISCOURSES (NPM) AND STRATEGIES IN THE GERMAN UNIVERSITY SYSTEM: HOW THEY SHIFT RESEARCH CONDITIONS

Political and managerial talk is different from concrete action regarding the introduction of NPM instruments and new governance structures in the German university system. Furthermore, even if action is taken—for example, the reform of state laws, new funding directives, or the establishment of new managerial units in the university organization—their impact on the real behavior of academics in universities may not always be what policymakers and managers expect. Next we discuss the causal nexus between talk, action, and the impact of NPM reforms in German universities with regard to the question, whether researchers in universities adapt to NPM-caused changes in funding, and, if so, with what consequences for their research.[14]

To analyze the adaptation of university management and academics to changes in university governance, we interviewed researchers in six disciplines—

mathematics, biology, geography, physics, history, and political science—in eight Australian and two German universities, as well as top and middle managers.[15] Here we present the results of interviews we conducted at two German universities in the state of North Rhine Westphalia. In each of the two case studies, we interviewed thirty researchers, three deans, and three members from the university management. We tried to find out whether the actual political reforms and changes in the university governance concerning research had affected their research work and how well the researchers had adapted to changing conditions of their knowledge ecology.

Inclusion Pressures: The Call for "Relevance" and "Responsiveness" of University Research

Universities are dual-purpose organizations and, as such, have functions in both the educational and the research system of modern society.[16] Since the 1960s, universities in all Western countries have become subject to increasing pressures for inclusion. Not only industrial production, health care, and the military, but also political decision making, for instance, in environmental protection, and even sports and family life, were supposed to become more rational by the application of knowledge gained from scientific research. These hopes directed an increasing amount of public money into research, much of which went into the basic funding of universities. Therefore, science policymakers felt the need—and public pressure—to make sure that not all this money was entirely spent on research motivated only by scientific curiosity. In this respect, inclusion pressure means that university research should become more responsive to societal demands for extra-scientific "relevance." The self-exclusion of university research into the notorious "ivory tower" was supposed to end.[17]

Universities and their professors had to meet this demand primarily for their self-interest. They had to confirm and, to some extent, also practice "relevance" (under the heading of technology transfer, among others) because they anticipated that otherwise a research drain could continue from the universities to the state-financed extra-university sector. In the end, universities and their professors might lose most of their share of research to the Max-Planck Gesellschaft, the Fraunhofer Gesellschaft, the large research centers of the Helmholtz Gemeinschaft, and other kinds of institutes. This would mean that university professors would lose the work that was most interesting to them and also their reputation among colleagues and society at large. Moreover, the universities then would no longer be different from Fachhochschulen or other polytechnical and professional higher education institutions. In turn, the universities would no longer be able to delegate research focused on "relevance" to the Fachhochschulen. If universities wanted to maintain their position as the ultimate "home of science," where basic research without immediate application value had a safe refuge, they could not ignore "relevance." Problems stemming from the inclusion pressures in research could not be resolved, however, but continued to accumulate after the higher education system stopped expanding in the mid-1970s while the traditionally slow and risk-aversive mode of collective decision making in the universities was maintained.[18] These problems regarding research included the declining international visibility of research conducted in German universities, the lack of attractiveness for foreign researchers, a fragmented system of quality control, complaints from industry, and other extra-scientific users of research results about the unresponsiveness of university research to their needs. All these were problems plaguing higher education and research policymakers, although it took a long time until they began solving these issues systematically and coherently.

The Rise of the New Public Management Regime in the German University System

Whereas university rectors and professors claimed that the problems were caused mainly by the growing scarcity of public funding and demanded significant budget increases, governments began criticizing this attitude as unrealistic with regard to their financial possibilities and, even more important, as a diversion from the real causes of performance deficits. Both the federal government and many state governments became convinced that the central cause of all of these problems was the inability of German universities to reform themselves, which in turn was seen primarily as a result of the professors' unwillingness to change the status quo, which would have meant at least a partial loss of individual and collective privileges. Although the need for a change in university governance had been on the agenda since the Council for Sciences and Humanities passed a "recommendation on structure and administrative organization" in the German higher education system in 1968, the federal political actors' first move toward reform, on still a purely discursive level, can be traced back to the "sixteen theses from Bonn" by Dorothee Wilms, the federal minister for education, in 1983.[19] Here, words like *competition*, *profile building*, the desirability of more *third-party funding*, and *incentive systems* for the best professors first had an impact on the political debate. After all, from government's perspective, universities should become organizations that could adapt to the changing societal demands on teaching and research.

In other European countries and international organizations like the Organization for Economic Cooperation and Development (OECD), New Public Management (NPM) has been debated since the 1980s as a governance regime that should shape public organizations in general toward becoming responsive and even more efficient performers.[20] In Germany, NPM arrived in the mid-1980s through the discussion and propagation of model projects in the Netherlands to reform municipalities. Debates about NPM began to spread to other areas of the public sector until they reached the German universities in the second half of the 1990s. Two streams of literature and reports were influential. The first stream consisted of diagnoses of decline and pathology. In this perspective, "the German university was rotten to the core", "blocked," or simply in deep "misery."[21] The other stream provided the remedy for all the many diseases associated with the German university: As already implemented in other OECD countries, NPM should be more or less adapted to the unique organization distinguishing German universities from other national public organizations, on the one hand, and from private enterprises, on the other hand. Two influential proposals of NPM in this respect were from the president of the University of Kassel, Hans Brinckman, who proclaimed a "new liberty of the university" and Detlev Müller-Böling, who demanded the "unchaining of the university" from direct state control as well as from professorial amateurism with regard to questions of management.[22] Müller-Böling was then the director of the Center for the Improvement of Higher Education (Centrum für Hochschulentwicklung, CHE), a think tank initiated by the German Rectors Conference (HRK) and the Bertelsmann Foundation, a private donation with the mission of acting as an intellectual leader for reforms in German society at large. Other private foundations played a significant role, too, in pushing the reform agenda of NPM in German higher education policies. For example, the Volkswagen Foundation,[23] initiated a commission that brought together some respected and reform-oriented university rectors/presidents, who developed "milestones for a sustainable German science system." Another important private actor promoting NPM is the Association of Donors for the German Sciences and Humanities (Stifterverband für die Deutsche Wissenschaft), which supports the NPM agenda in the German university system through the (co)funding of focused study courses, featuring and initiating memorandi, and awarding scholarships for management qualification matters or grants for conferences and meetings concerning higher education and science management reform. Finally, political bodies like the Enquete Commission of the Federal German Parliament, with its report "Globalisation of the World Economy"[24]—including a chapter on higher education—have attempted to turn public attention toward the need of NPM reforms in the German university system.[25]

The rise of NPM in Germany was a complicated process in which many coincidences played a sometimes decisive role. To understand the NPM reform model and systematically compare it with the German university system's traditional governance regime, we found five mechanisms:[26]

- *Bureaucratic regulation* concerns the traditional notion of top-down authority vested in the state. This dimension refers to regulation by directives, in which the government prescribes, in detail, behaviors under particular circumstances, for instance, in financial or personnel issues.
- *External guidance* refers to activities that direct universities' goal setting and advice. In public university systems, the government is usually an important, but not necessarily the only, stakeholder. It may delegate certain powers to guide to other actors, such as intermediary bodies or representatives of industry in university boards.
- *Academic self-governance* concerns the role of professional communities within the university system. This mechanism is institutionalized in collegial decision making within universities and in the peer review–based self-steering of academic communities, for instance, in funding agencies' decisions.
- *Hierarchical management* refers to the role of university leadership—rectors or presidents on the top level, deans on the intermediate level—in internal goal setting, regulation, and decision making.
- *Competitive pressure* with respect to scarce resources—money, personnel, and prestige—within and between universities mostly takes place not in real but in "quasi markets" whose performance evaluations by peers or quantitative indicators substitute for the demand pull from customers.

In all five mechanisms, the NPM regime differs sharply from the traditional governance regime of the German university system. Traditionally, as shown, strong academic self-governance existed alongside strong bureaucratic regulation by the state. In contrast, NPM strengthens the hierarchical management by rectors and deans, the external guidance of state authorities and external stakeholders (e.g., university boards), and also competitive pressure. At the same time, NPM implies a marked deregulation in budgeting and personnel management and in the approval of study programs. This is what government usually means when it promises greater "autonomy" to universities. Strictly speaking, it promises greater *organizational* autonomy, which should not be confused with the individual autonomy of professors. Indeed, a reduction of academic self-governance is another explicit goal of current NPM policies in the German higher education system.

The core issue of NPM in German higher education policies is the increase of competition among and within universities for resources, students, and national as well as international reputation. Deregulation is one prerequisite for organizational competitiveness; another is the establishment of an organizational leadership that can act on behalf of the university as a corporate actor. Finally, greater external guidance is supposed to give broad long-term orientation to a university's competitive strategy.

The Reform of Research Funding in German Universities: From Basic Supply to Competition

How has NPM actually been implemented in the German university system? The answer is difficult because NPM is still being implemented and also because each of the sixteen states sets somewhat different priorities and uses even the same measure differently.

Individual researchers at universities have always felt competitive pressure, which has become stronger with increasing dependence on funds from the DFG, the Federal Ministry of Research and Education, the European Union (EU), and industry. The share of these funds in the overall university budget has increased steadily and in 2002 was about one-quarter of the budget spent on research.[27] The success rate of project proposals from individual researchers fell from 68 percent in 1995 to 51 percent in 2006. What made this trend even worse is the fact that funded projects were able to cover less and less of their real costs with a DFG grant.[28] This growing dependence on project money has meant greater competition and thus fewer projects on the individual level.

The second big pillar of the German research funding scene is the thematically focused and often mission-based funding programs of the German Federal Ministry for Education and Research (BMBF), the state ministries, and the framework programs of the European Commission. During the past decade, the DFG partly adapted to this model of program funding. In an evaluation of its funding processes by an international expert commission in the late 1990s, the DFG was criticized for its grants for small individual projects and was advised to concentrate more on thematically focused, strong programs: "In principle, resources should be concentrated on a few thematic fields and on fewer more visible projects."[29] In addition to the already existing "large collaborative research areas (SFB), the DFG introduced funding for large decentralized research groups, thematically focused programs, and research centers."[30]

In sum, German funding is developing a bias toward thematically focused, collaborative, or otherwise "big" research. One important corollary of this trend is that the influence of politicians, funding administrators, and academic elite involved in funding is increasing while individual researchers may lose their agenda-setting power in the long run.

Because universities' basic funding has become more and more inadequate for the demands of internationally competitive research in many fields of science, researchers have been forced to search for other sources of money. Otherwise, they would have to reduce or shift their research or maybe stop doing research altogether. Researchers in the natural sciences, who need expensive equipment, materials, and research personnel, often prefer the mission-oriented programs of the federal ministry or the EU framework programs because these funds allow them more flexibility in how to spend the money than DFG grants usually do.[31] That is, the DFG grants do not cover the cost of basic research equipment, which, according to DFG policy, must be provided by the universities. The budget of cost-intensive disciplines is not sufficient to maintain expensive laboratory equipment or even to modernize. So professors need external funding to keep their equipment up to date and to maintain employment contracts with their laboratory staff. Although some sources, such as the EU, have been used more extensively than before and have increased their funding, overall funds have dropped because the demand has grown faster than the supply from all available sources.

The reasons for this rising demand are as follows: First, professors have become "experts in fund-raising" and have devised certain adaptation strategies for different funding sources. Usually the best researchers manage a complex funding-source portfolio in order to guarantee an uninterrupted flow of grants necessary for the smooth continuation of their research. The actual research work often must be done—if the proposals are successful and the money is awarded— by relatively inexperienced young researchers because professors have no time for supervision and advice.[32] Second, some of our interviewees stated that the quality of research has suffered because inadequate financing and time pressures do not allow better work.[33] Third, not only bad research is eliminated by stronger competition for resources, which is an intended effect, but also much good to mediocre research is eliminated as well. Modern science rests on a broad basis of unspectacular routine research, certainly in applied fields but also in basic research. But if this kind of research work cannot be done any longer, the really excellent cutting-edge research also might suffer.

The trend toward a more selective bias in research funding and the preference for big science was reinforced by the "excellence initiative" introduced in 2005 as a joint project by the federal government and the states.[34] The initiative was organized by the DFG and the Council for Sciences and Humanities (WR) as a competition in which universities, instead of individual professors, compete for their share of a budget of €1.9 billion. This money was spent on successful proposals for graduate schools, clusters of excellence (which means the close collaboration of universities with local or regional extra-university research institutes such as the Max Planck, Fraunhofer, Leibniz, and Helmholtz institutes), and outstanding concepts for the university's future development.[35] Success in the last category—which required success in the other two categories as well—led to mass media–driven public recognition as a German "elite university." Since the results of the first cycle of the excellence competition were announced in 2006 and 2007, nine universities hold the "elite" label. One of the driving motives—especially of the federal ministry—for the "excellence initiative" was the observation that more and more public spending on research went into the extra-university research institutes. Universities as the "natural home of science" seemed to have been forgotten in regard to research. This was seen as a shortcoming in the German higher education and research system because only the universities train and graduate young academics and only the universities supply industry and the extra-university research sector with promising and innovative personnel. The federal government feared that a decline in university research could have a bad long-term effect on its teaching and the labor market, too. But one of the best effects of the "excellence initiative" so far is the partial breakdown of the rigid five-pillar structure of the German research system with its narrow mission targets for each of the pillars, which hinders the international visibility of research conducted in Germany. Universities now work, or try to work, more closely with the regional Max Planck, Fraunhofer, Leibniz, or Helmholtz institutes. Even those universities that failed in the excellence initiative's category of building "excellence clusters" have tried to tighten their ties to the extra-university research sector because these ties and collaborations are now regarded as an advantage in the national and international competition for external resources and recognition.

Another tool to boost competition in the German university system is the substitution of some of the basic funding of universities by performance indicator–based funding. Most states now distribute part of the universities' basic funding according to performance criteria, such as the number of graduates or the size of the university's project funds.[36] About three-quarters of a university's budget are fixed personnel costs, however, and the university's possible gains or losses due to performance indicators are usually limited to 1 to 5 percent of the preceding year's budget. This prevents weak performers from getting into financial trouble. Thus, only a very small part of the budget is available for incentives, and their potential effects on motivation are small as well.[37]

Most of the mechanisms of competition do not have a direct monetary influence on demand or supply. Accordingly, because most markets in the system are merely "quasi markets," evaluations of research and teaching have become necessary in order to ascertain the relative position of a university, a faculty, or an individual professor. All states have started making evaluations, and some, for example, Lower Saxony, have created own evaluation agencies.[38] Although the methods and criteria differ considerably, in most cases, the evaluation is some kind of informed peer review.

In accordance with these recent developments, German universities began establishing certain research profiles and—in most cases, interdisciplinary—research centers to fit these profiles. This new form of NPM-driven research organization pushes the universities toward corporate actors, with the aim of changing research from individual to collaborative projects and to the development of "critical masses" inside the universities as well as in cooperation with the neighboring extra-university research institutes. These actions should offer an advantage in the competitive bidding for external research grants and in research areas that have priority on the government's funding agenda. All the universities in our sample invested in building research centers based on certain profiles, shifting financial resources from nonpriority areas to the centers. In many cases, however, universities can provide only a little start-up money for these centers. The model for these research centers is the DFG-funded SFB, and most universities try to imitate the SFB-structure in their priority areas, hoping that the professors involved will collaborate under the umbrella of the center and write a proposal for the establishment of a SFB or some other coordinated program that attracts third-party funding. The institutional funding of the centers by the universities themselves is highly diverse. In most humanities departments, the newly established centers consist of only those resources that the professors agreed to move from the recurrent funding of their chairs to the center. These centers therefore usually have only a little money to invite guests or hold special seminars. Conversely, in many natural science departments the university management is willing to invest large sums to establish collaborative structures that are predicted to bring high returns from third-party funding in the future. Often such centers are financed by matching funds: the central university management is willing to give money if the dean of the respective faculty or department will give money, too. In most cases, though, all money allocated to newly established research centers is just start-up money for a few years and is expected to be replaced by third-party funding later. Because this development has just started, we do not know whether the university managements' hopes of creating competitive and self-supporting research entities will be fulfilled.

Most German universities try to invest heavily in special funds to boost and reward researchers' activities in the competition for external grants and to support grant applications and the preparation of proposals. Special funds for these issues are available at both the central and the faculty/department levels. Again, the money that universities can spend on these issues is scarce. In the two universities we investigated, we found efforts by the central administration to support researchers bidding for large collaborative research grants from the DFG or for grants from the "Framework Programs" of the European Commission.

In most German universities, finding replacements for vacant chairs is no longer solely a task for representative boards and commissions on the faculty or department level. All the university managers we interviewed claimed that strategic recruiting according to predefined core areas of research—often with regard to certain profiles on which the university and government decided in so-called target agreements—was the most important tool for a proactive university management. International collaborations, "big" third party–funded research projects, publications in prestigious international journals, and, last but not least, the fit of the candidates' research priorities to the profiles of the departments or institutes all ranked high on the university managers' list. Most of the faculties/departments in our sample weighted excellent research performance higher for candidates to fill vacant chairs and professorships than excellent teaching performance, despite the claims by all interviewees that they still favored the Humboldtian ideal of the nexus between teaching and research.

Researchers' Adaptation Patterns to Their Changing Environment

University researchers' adaptation to the new ecology of research funding can be observed in four interconnected dimensions, in which the reforms in university governance in general and especially the changing conditions for research funding are mainly seen as problematic: the availability of time for conducting research, the funding situation, adaptation to profile-building activities, and the influence of evaluation schemes.

Time

Time was German university researchers' most frequently mentioned restriction for proper research. Much more than the teaching load, the professors and associates we interviewed saw rising bureaucratization and the resulting increase in administrative work as the greatest restriction of their research activities. Most conspicuous were the increasing accountability accompanying the Bologna Process,[39] the delegation of previously centralized administrative tasks to institutes and chairs in accordance with internal change management, and the bureaucratic drift of externally funded research itself. Competitive bidding for grants and meeting the demands of targeted funding schemes were regarded as time-consuming exercises.

Funding

German university professors are still regularly given basic funding for research. Whether they can conduct research with this funding or whether they are dependent on external funding varied strongly among the disciplines. Nearly all history professors and a majority of the political scientists we interviewed declared that it was hard but not impossible to conduct their research projects by themselves without additional grants. Since this funding does not cover research expenses, most historians reported that they used their own money to get needed books, copies, or microfilms or to visit national and foreign archives and libraries. Political scientists did not report spending much of their own money on research.

The situation of mathematicians was very similar to that of the historians and political scientists. The majority were classic "solitary and free" researchers who conducted low-cost research by solving mathematical problems with "paper and pencil." They did not obtain outside funding because their basic funding was sufficient to supply them with the few things they needed, including a small amount of travel money for attending international conferences.

While basic funding appeared to be sufficient for much historical, political science, and mathematical research, the majority of academics from geology, biology, and physics and those political scientists conducting empirical research, which requires the collection of new quantitative or qualitative data, depended heavily on external funding. Professors in biology and physics declared that they could not perform effectively without much external funding. They claimed that they could conduct successful and internationally visible research in the highly competitive environments of their specialties only if they could work on several related projects at the same time and had access to up-to-date expensive laboratory equipment or radiation sources. Our observable adaptation was primarily a kind of lip service: researchers in all disciplines who depended on external funds were able to adapt to the "proposal lyrics" of the funding agencies without changing their research substantially. An adaptation pattern like dropping unfashionable and, in the end, unfundable research—which we observed in Australia and Great Britain—we have not yet seen in Germany.[40]

Profile building

Profile building through the establishment of research centers in universities is a new form of research organization introduced by NPM. Its purpose is changing research behavior from individual to collaborative projects and to the development of "critical masses," providing advantages in the competitive bidding for external research grants. We observed in our German case studies that especially in the humanities, a majority of academics dealt strategically with these centers but did not commit to them. Most important was that many professors in unfashionable (but for teaching purposes still necessary) specialties inside their disciplines were sidelined by their universities' profile- and center-building strategies and had to cope with a steady reduction of staff. Their adaptation pattern was in many cases a kind of "inner emigration": they left the university's governance regime and did what they wanted with their limited resources because they did not see any advantage in participation.[41]

Evaluation schemes

We found no adaptation to evaluation-based funding formulas. In the two German cases, the amount of money allocated through performance indicators in the universities was still too small to have an observable effect. No professors would change their research behavior for an annual gain or loss of approximately €2.000 to €4.000 for a chair. Even those who obtained additional money through incentive systems and research performance indicators reported that it was a nice benefit but that they would have conducted the same kind of research without these incentives. In the end, the allocation system of German universities did not have enough money to have a significant impact.

The boundary between academic research and the managerial rationality of the new university governance has started to blur but has not yet changed the academic ethos. The discipline still is a strong principle for almost all researchers in our German sample, and the need of many researchers for external funding has not substantially influenced the contents of research. How far recent political moves like the "excellence initiative" might change the university's influence on the selection of research topics or the way that research would be conducted remains to be seen.

SHIFTS OF UNIVERSITY-INDUSTRY RELATIONS: THE CASE OF TECHNOLOGY TRANSFER

When dealing with university-industry relations, we had to take into account different levels of analysis. Using two research projects, we will try to show that the pace of change differed according to what we analyzed.[42] We found the pace of change at the discursive level was not accompanied by an equally dramatic change in practice at both the organizational and individual levels. German universities only slowly transform radically new ideas into practice because the influence of historically entrenched concepts remains stronger. As a result, we had to take into account very different speeds of change. We illustrate this by first reconstructing briefly the political and academic discourse on university-industry relations. We then discuss actual practices analyzing technology transfer offices, bibliometric data on publication patterns, and interview data with different constituencies in German universities.

University-Industry Relations: The Discursive Side

German universities have interacted with industry since at least the late nineteenth century.[43] The strong ties between academia and industry were especially successful in chemistry. But medicine, physics, and engineering also had strong ties to industrial applications, which resulted in a series of remarkable scientific and technological innovations and, ultimately, economic competitiveness. The historian Margrit Szöllisi-Janze speaks of an early knowledge society when describing the situation in Germany between the 1870s and the beginning of World War I.[44] At that time, though, the ideal of the university did not favor strong and direct university-industry linkages. Instead, the Humboldt ideal of a remote, socially isolated community of students and professors, happily bound together in a unity of teaching and research, prevailed. In this institutional setting, theoretical advancements in the natural sciences were widely recognized, while empirical research and industrial applications were regarded as considerably lower in status. Engineering received much less recognition. It had been taught at polytechnical schools, which had, despite their increase in status in the 1870s and 1880s, a far lower status than universities did. In addition, the links between academia and industry were not institutionalized; instead, the transfer was limited to those persons directly involved on both sides. The process, political programs, organizational infrastructures, and university's active involvement were not subject to empirical analysis or theoretical reflection during this early stage of university-industry interactions.

Our findings on the discourse between universities and industry from the 1950s until the present must be examined against this background. We distinguished three ideal models of university-industry linkages: the information and documentation (I&D) model, the cooperation model, and the blurring-of-boundaries (BoB) model.[45]

In the I&D model, the key problem in linking up science and industry is the accelerating pace at which scientific knowledge is produced. The solution to the related problem of knowledge "superabundance" is the creation of information infrastructures that make knowledge available in a methodological and technologically advanced way. Thus, the emphasis is on the creation of new infrastructures designed to improve the flow of knowledge across different institutions. Science-industry relations are supposed to be linear according to the I&D model, so the generation of knowledge is followed by dissemination and then utilization. Personal contacts between scientists and industry do not seem to be necessary. A scientist's primary role is that of a producer of knowledge, whereas industry is mainly seen as using and applying this knowledge. The I&D model arguably was dominant in Germany between the 1950s and the first half of the 1970s. Specialized archival journals (like *Nachrichten für Dokumentation*, first issued in 1950) can be seen as early advocates of the national I&D model. In 1962 the federal accounting office (Bundesrechnungshof) issued the first major national public policy statement clearly expressing a federal commitment to the I&D model: "The solution to the problem of how latent knowledge can be brought to interested parties is essential to the competitiveness of modern industrial communities and so falls under the purview of government responsibility. The retrieval of knowledge . . . is a tool to considerably improve performance in science, the economy, and public administration."[46] About a decade later, dissemination agencies like the Fachinformationszentren, which were created in the 1970s under the auspices of the federal government, and political programs like the I&D program (Programm zur Förderung der Information und Dokumentation) launched by the Federal Ministry for Research and Technology in 1975, were established to make academic knowledge more visible to the industrial world.

In the 1970s, the underlying idea of the I&D model—that with sufficient support by dissemination structures, research outcomes would more or less automatically "fall out" or "spill over" from the academic to the industrial domain—was met with increasing skepticism. Many critics maintained that potential users' access to documented knowledge was not, by itself, enough to stimulate industrial innovations based on this knowledge. Therefore, the cooperation model, which gradually replaced the I&D model, emphasized bringing together researchers and practitioners. Actual or perceived "cultural gaps" between science and the economy were regarded as the main problem. In contrast to the I&D model, the cooperation model regards knowledge and technology transfer as a dialogue among partners from different institutional backgrounds. That is, transfer was no longer seen as a one-way street between universities and industry. This model gained prominence in German science and technology policy during the second half of the 1970s and dominated the discourse during the 1980s. During that period, several political programs aimed at facilitating personnel exchanges between academia and industry were set up. Even more important, since the late 1970s, technology transfer offices were established at almost every German university. Transfer offices were seen as the central mediators between the academic and the industrial world, and they were supposed to establish contacts and clear up misunderstandings in interactions between the university and industry. Because these offices are important to understanding the cooperation model and, more generally, technology transfer in Germany, we will describe them more extensively later.

Whereas the cooperation model assumes and even emphasizes clear institutional boundaries between the university and industry, the blurring of boundaries (BoB) model assumes that these boundaries are becoming increasingly permeable, diffuse, and, in some cases, "blurred." The BoB model sees universities as economic actors, engaging in licensing and patenting activities and fostering spin-offs. By becoming entrepreneurial, the university transcends its institutional identity and traditional boundaries. Whereas the cooperation model focuses on mostly dyadic relations between academic researchers and practitioners, the more complex network model makes it harder or even impossible to differentiate a well-defined academic role from an economic one. In the German discourse, the BoB model emerged in the 1990s, particularly in the federal government and in policy papers by the European Union. It could be found in diverse programs and policies, supporting universities as economic actors and their participation in innovation networks. In 2002, for example, the legal situation changed, and the titles to all patentable innovations being developed at universities shifted from the individual professor to the university organization, to encourage the latter to become actively entrepreneurial with regard to intellectual property and its exploitation. In addition to the emphasis on entrepreneurial activities, the BoB model conceptualizes universities as nodes in broader innovation networks. The European Union, for example, explicitly supported networks by financing "networks of excellence" within the Sixth Framework Program. In Germany, networks of all kinds—regional networks, innovation networks, excellence networks, and competence networks—are promoted by the states and the federal government. "Innovations require networks" is a typical slogan of such programs, or "All parts of the innovation process, starting with basic research up to the diffusion of new products and procedures, should be linked."[47]

The discursive shifts traced back here are remarkable. Beginning in the 1950s, three different models of how to conceptualize university-industry relations emerged, each accompanied by political programs, legal changes, and institution building. According to our analysis, the BoB model of science and knowledge production, which currently dominates, is very different from both the I&D model and the cooperation model. Further analysis, however, will show whether new concepts like "universities as economic actors" being embedded in "innovation networks" are mainly radical new labels, which divert from the role that historically entrenched ideals and practices still play. At present we do not know much about the impact of the more recent initiatives. Nevertheless, with the help of our bibliometric and interview data, we are able to offer some preliminary empirical evidence regarding continuity and change in practices and attitudes at German universities.

Transfer Offices at German Universities: A Watershed in the History of Technology Transfer?

A central aspect of establishing closer links between universities and industry was the creation of technology transfer offices at German universities. From a comparative perspective, the institutionalization of transfer occurred in many countries at the same time, the 1980s. The authors of *The New Production of Knowledge* state: "There was at the turn of the 1980s a watershed in the history of technology transfer in the universities in the United States and Europe."[48] According to them, the transformation of technology transfer from dyadic relations between individual professors and industry toward an organized practice at the university level is an indicator for far-reaching institutional change. The question, however, is, What does a phenomenon like the quantitative growth of transfer offices indicate? Qualitative empirical data on the institutionalization process at German universities show how changes at the discursive level, which led to organizational capacity-building, were separated from actual practices.

In that project, we interviewed forty-one representatives from universities (the heads of the university administration or their deputies), the universities' transfer offices (typically the directors), and representatives from the local chambers of industry and commerce. In addition, we tried to validate our findings through written documents (statistical yearbooks, reports, related studies, and the like).

Based on the findings of our general discourse analysis, we could identify a strong political commitment starting in the mid-1970s from the North Rhine Westphalia's government and its ministry for science and technology to promote technology transfer and related offices. A "transfer gap" was widely perceived, and the "missing link" between the potential supply from the universities and the potential demand from industry was seen in the universities' transfer offices as bridging that gap and bringing together transfer-oriented partners from both sides. Following the implicit assumptions underlying what we labeled the "cooperation model," political programs and initiatives were set up, and universities were given budgetary incentives to create their own technology transfer offices. Beginning with an innovative pilot project in 1976 at the Ruhr University Bochum, other universities followed, eventually leading to the complete institutionalization of transfer offices at all public universities in North Rhine Westphalia. After little more than a decade, in 1988, what had begun as an innovative pilot project had become completely institutionalized.

This institutionalization process was seen as a political success. But since the political initiatives helping create transfer offices were not always met with an equally strong commitment from the universities and industry, what at first sight seemed to be an unequivocal success story needs to be seen in a different light. When asked about the process of institutionalization, interviewees at ten of the fourteen public universities claimed that either the state's government or its department for science and research was the driving force. In only three instances was the motivation located within the universities: twice from the administration and once from transfer-oriented professors. Local and regional industry played hardly any role at all. In only one case was industry's demand visible, but that demand was not considered to be a primary source of motivation. Although the state's government and its department for science and research did not directly insist on the creation of transfer offices at universities, many interviewees felt strong political pressure to comply. This perceived pressure on the universities was met with a widespread lack of interest by the potential transfer partners. Transfer-oriented professors and industrial firms mostly did not perceive the necessity for a new organizational unit. On the contrary, some even feared that an additional bureaucratic layer would stifle well-established informal transfer activities. To put it differently, the institutionalization of transfer offices in large part neither emerged from within the universities, nor was it a response to industry's demand. Transfer offices were mainly a political role model. As a result, the rapid institutionalization process was much more problematic than at first sight. Although the process met with little open resistance, it lacked the required support from all relevant actors outside the political realm.

This lack of support is reflected in their small size and the concrete task structure, which heavily depends on local circumstances. The activities range from assisting start-up companies and offering advice on public funding to extended professional training. Some of the transfer offices even take part in activities, which, like public relations, only remotely resemble tasks of an organizational subunit specializing in technology transfer. Advice on patenting and licensing plays only a limited role. These activities are not as important in Germany as they are at U.S. universities,[49] due to the legal situation. Until 2002, the title to all patentable inventions belonged to the researcher if he or she were a civil servant. Because of the so-called university professor exemption clause (Hochschullehrerprivileg), universities had no incentive to engage in patenting and licensing activities. As a result, transfer offices mainly recruited personnel with an academic background or from within the academic administration. Business-related experiences and specialized legal expertise were hardly to be found. It comes as no surprise that under these circumstances, transfer offices have to deal with an academic clientele with little or no contact with industry, whereas those with strong links to industry do not turn to transfer offices. Compared with traditional informal and dyadic patterns between university professors and industry, German transfer offices' contribution to university-industry relations has always been marginal. Different studies of this have come to the same conclusion by estimating that less than 10 percent of transfer projects between universities and industry have been achieved through transfer offices.[50]

Given these sobering accounts, the institutionalization of transfer offices can hardly be seen as a watershed in the history of technology, indicating far-reaching institutional change. On the contrary, the institutionalization process allowed German universities to adapt to broader societal expectations, mainly from the political realm, without risking too much institutional change. Conceptually, the process may be thought of as a typical example of what John Meyer and Brian Rowan call the loose coupling between the formal structure and the activity structure of an organization.[51] According to their new institutional perspective, organizations need to be understood as embedded in broader social contexts. They are bound to these contexts through material resources and legitimation. Both are granted by conforming to these external expectations. The conformity is reflected in the formal structure of an organization, which serves as a kind of display window for external parties. The formal structure is only loosely coupled with the organization's activity structures, which serves to buffer it from external pressures. Applied to our case, it is obvious that universities' behavior can be understood only by their dependence on the state's government, which actively promotes technology transfer and the institutionalization of transfer offices as role models. Universities conform to these expectations by creating a new and externally visible subunit, the transfer office, which is part of the formal structure. Transfer offices serve as display windows for the universities' political environment. They effectively guarantee external legitimation and resources without heavily altering the organizations' activity structure. Although transfer offices only slightly affected the practices of the universities and their academic staff vis-à-vis industry, with the help of bibliometric data we could nevertheless detect some behavioral changes.

Bibliometric Analysis, 1980 to 2000: The Increasing Role of Copublications Between Academic and Industrial Partners

The cooperation between academic researchers and industry can be measured by bibliometric tools. Our analysis is based on longitudinal data taken from the online version of the bibliometric data bases SCI, SSCI, and A&HCI of Thomson ISI. We measured the overall publication output (articles) of all universities of the federal state North Rhine Westphalia—the federal state where we conducted our research on universities' transfer offices—as well as those publications produced jointly with industrial partners.[52] We found the following results:

Based on our bibliometric data, we can see a striking increase in university-industry cooperation between 1980 and 2000. While we found only 85 copublications in 1980, this number rose sharply over the years, leading to 711 copublications in 2000 (see figure 11.1).

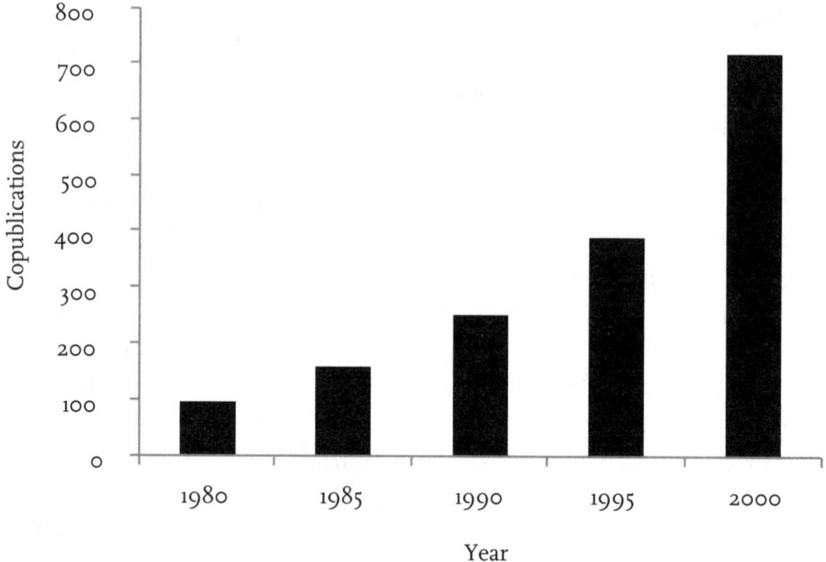

Figure 11.1 Total Sum of Copublications
Source: Authors' elaboration based on Thomson ISI's SCI, SSCI, and A & HCI databases.

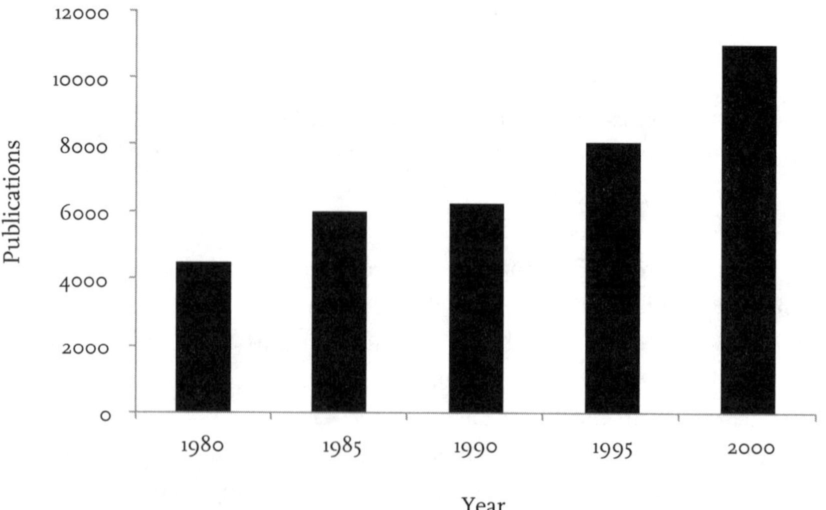

Figure 11.2 Total Sum of Publications
Source: Authors' elaboration based on data from Thomson ISI.

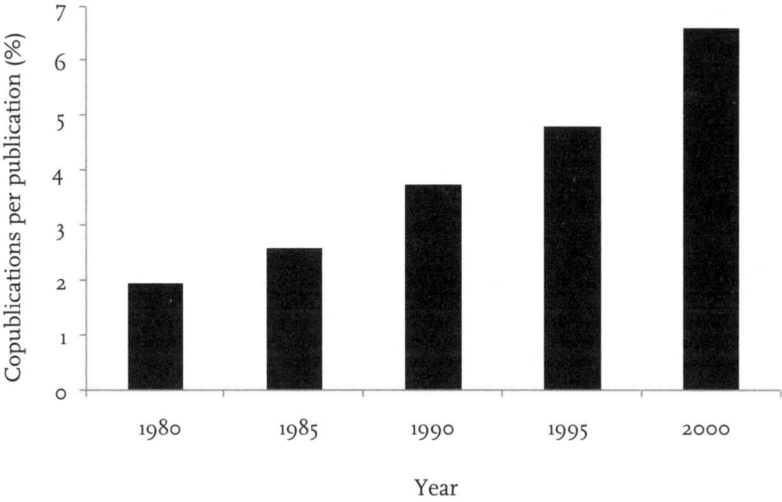

Figure 11.3 Number of Copublications with Industry Compared with Overall
Number of Publications

Source: Authors' elaboration based on data from Thomson ISI.

To interpret these data, we compared them with the total publication output between 1980 and 2000. On the one hand, these figures show that the increase is part of a general trend toward more journal publications, as covered by Thomson ISI (see figure 11.2). On the other hand, the number of copublications with industry, compared with the overall publication output of the fifteen universities in our sample, increased steadily over time (see figure 11.3).

In 1980 only 1.9 percent of all publications were cowritten with an industrial partner, and in 2000 the share tripled to 7.1 percent. Given the strength of our bibliometric indicator, the results certainly indicate a stronger university-industry nexus over time. The relations strengthened noticeably in certain knowledge areas like medicine and engineering, as universities with a medical school and/ or an engineering school seemed to be at the forefront of those university-industry relations that jointly published their research results.

Recent Trends in University-Industry Relations and Their Effects on German Universities: The Perspective of the Academic Stakeholders

To obtain a more comprehensive picture of the apparent changes in university-industry relations, as well as of the effects on both the professors involved and the overall university, we interviewed three main constituencies: six professors with several copublications with researchers from industry, four university rectors or their deputies, and two deans of humanities departments, whose subjects might be indirectly affected by closer links between academia and industry.

First, we were able to assess some of the impacts of the more recent trends on the management of intellectual property rights in German higher education. As we pointed out earlier, the so-called university professor exemption clause, which caused serious problems for universities' patenting and licensing activities, was abolished in 2002. The titles to patents then shifted from individual professors to the university organization. The new law both permitted and encouraged universities to become more entrepreneurial. As we pointed out, the existing transfer offices did not meet the professional requirements for patenting and licensing, so the federal government created new organizational infrastructures, the patent exploitation agencies (Patentverwertungsagenturen, PVAs), in each of the German states. Even though some of the transfer offices at the university level were abolished, most of them remained untouched. Transfer-oriented professors confirmed that these offices were not involved in their interactions with industry.

We still do not know what role the university's transfer offices will play in the new ecology of organizations dealing with university-industry relations. While some of our interview partners can imagine a role for them, others see them as outdated. Apparently, the PVAs have become major players in the field. Transfer-oriented professors see as critical both of them as well as the universities' new entrepreneurial spirit. All our interviewees reported encountering more bureaucratic procedures when collaborating with industry. The preparation of contracts with industry requires significantly more time, since the university often is willing to engage in tough negotiations over property rights with its industrial partner. In particular, some professors criticized university officials' unrealistic expectations of revenues from inventions. Even though the university rectors did not confirm this impression, the criticism was widespread. We still do not know what impact the shift of the intellectual property rights from the individual professor to the university organization will have on the overall patent rate. Policymakers' expectations were high, but at least in the short run, the rate might fall as an unintended consequence of the new, entrepreneurial university's meddling in the traditional patent arrangements between individual professors and industry.[53]

Second, those professors who, according to our bibliometric data, have very strong ties to industry have maintained the traditional image of the professor's role. The "third academic mission,"[54] that is, economic development through technology transfer to industry, did not figure prominently. Instead, our interviewees emphasized research and teaching. Doctoral students acted as the bridge between research and teaching and also between professors and industry. Asked about their reasons for cooperating with industry, our interviewees typically pointed to the necessity for continuing their research. Likewise, the criteria for success are seen as scientific, not economic. In addition, publications also act as signals to industry. "Publish or perish" hold true for structuring the academic field and also is important to maintaining and creating external contacts. Accordingly, the conspicuous changes in the rate of copublications with industry do not necessarily imply equally strong changes in scientists' role models and identity concepts.

From our empirical findings, we found that German research universities still have a long way to go to adapt to the changing knowledge ecology, especially when we compared them with top research universities in the United States. What is striking with regard to the German case is that nearly all reform exercises are formulated and pushed by actors from outside the universities. Private donations and think tanks have had a great impact on higher education and research policy, and state actors tend to conceptualize and implement reform policies in a top-down manner against the resistance of a majority of university teachers and researchers. Policymakers regularly meet members of university organizations, which still have too little managerial capacity to cope with the many reform inputs they are given. Conversely, the new demands are met by a type of public organization that fulfills its two functions of teaching and research under the burden of a steady decrease of basic public subsidies since higher education policies stopped the system's expansion in the mid-1970s. We are not surprised, therefore, that the adaptation to a new knowledge ecology still has not had a great impact on the content of academic work and on the role models and identities of academics in German research universities. In basic research as well as questions of technology transfer, the model of the academic driven by intrinsic motivation, following the norms and regulations of his or her discipline and disciplinary community, remains strong. German academics still see themselves as autonomous and self-determined nodes in the research and technology networks of their choice. It remains to be seen whether actual policies and management strategies trying to push German research universities toward "state-chartered employment organizations"[55] will change that perception (for better or worse) in the near future.

NOTES

1. Richard Whitley, "Constructing Universities as Strategic Actors: Limitations and Variations" (paper presented to the Academia Europea / Werner Gren Foundations Symposium, "The University in the Market," Stockholm, November 1–3, 2007).

2. Burton Clark, *The Higher Education System: Academic Organization in Cross-National Perspective* (Berkeley: University of California Press, 1983).

3. Joseph Ben-David, *The Scientist's Role in Society: A Comparative Study* (Englewood Cliffs, N.J.: Prentice-Hall, 1971).

4. Clark, *The Higher Education System.*

5. Uwe Schimank, *Hochschulforschung im Schatten der Lehre* (Frankfurt: Campus, 1995).

6. Renate Mayntz, *Aufbruch und Reform von oben: Ostdeutsche Universitäten im Transformationsprozess* (Frankfurt: Campus, 1994).

7. All information about the German higher education system presented here is updated from Uwe Schimank and Stefan Lange, "The German University System: A Late-Comer in New Public Management," in *University Governance: Western European Comparative Perspectives,* ed. Catherine Paradeise et al. (Dordrecht: Springer, 2009), 145–70; and Statistisches Bundesamt, *Bildung und Kultur: Personal an Hochschulen 2008,* Fachserie 11, Reihe 4.4 (Wiesbaden: Statistisches Bundesamt, 2009).

8. The sixteen German "Bundesländer" are states in the federation of the German nation state with their own constitutions, legal powers, and public administrations. The Bundesländer also execute federal laws through their public administrations and courts.

9. Stefan Kuhlmann and Thomas Heinze, "Evaluation von Forschungsleistungen in Deutschland: Erzeuger und Bedarf. Teil 1 u. 2," *Wissenschaftsrecht* 36 (2004): 53–69, 126–49.

10. Peter J. Katzenstein, *Policy and Politics in West Germany: The Growth of a Semi-Sovereign State* (Philadelphia: Temple University Press, 1987).

11. All data in this section are from the websites of the research organizations cited in the following section and from (WR) Wissenschaftsrat, *Basisdaten Hochschulen/Forschungseinrichtungen in Deutschland,* Stand, August 5, 2009 (Cologne: WR, 2009). On German public-sector research outside the universities, see Hans-Willy Hohn and Uwe Schimank, *Konflikte und Gleichgewichte im Forschungssystem: Akteurkonstellationen und Entwicklungspfade in der staatlich finanzierten ausseruniversitären Forschung* (Frankfurt: Campus, 1990).

12. First founded as the Kaiser Wilhelm Gesellschaft (KWG) in 1911, it was reestablished in 1948 under a new label as the MPG.

13. The Harnack principle refers to a Max Planck Institute (MPI) being organized around an outstanding researcher, who is established as the director of the MPI and independently decides on its research agenda.

14. This research project, "The Impact of Evaluation Based Funding of Research in Universities on the Contents of Research," was funded by the German Ministry for Education and Research (BMBF) and the Australian Research Council (ARC). The research team in this project consisted of Jochen Gläser, Stefan Lange, Grit Laudel, and Uwe Schimank.

15. For findings, see Jochen Gläser and Grit Laudel, "Evaluation Without Evaluators: The Impact of Funding Formulae on Australian University Research"; and Stefan Lange, "The Basic State of Research in Germany: Conditions of Knowledge Production Pre-Evaluation," both in *The Changing Governance of the Sciences: The Advent of Research Evaluation Systems*, ed. Richard Whitley and Jochen Gläser (Dordrecht: Springer, 2008), 127–52, 153–70.

16. Dietmar Braun and Uwe Schimank, "Organisatorische Koexistenzen des Forschungssystems mit anderen gesellschaftlichen Teilsystemen: Die prekäre Autonomie wissenschaftlicher Forschung," *Journal für Sozialforschung* 32 (1992): 319–36.

17. For this section, see Schimank and Lange, "The German University System," 145–70.

18. Since the mid-1970s, the oil price shock and a weakening economy made less money available for German higher education. In 1977 the KMK decided not to react to increasing enrollment rates by expanding the universities' infrastructure and personnel. Instead, the ministers relied on the false—as it soon turned out—prognosis that enrollment would decline to the status quo ante by the early 1980s. Although the number of entering students has kept growing until today, the universities' infrastructure and personnel still have not expanded significantly.

19. WR (Wissenschaftsrat), *Empfehlungen zur Struktur und Verwaltungsorganisation* (Cologne: WR, 1968); Dorothee Wilms, "Hochschulpolitik für die neunziger Jahre," *DUZ* 23 (1983): 11. Bonn was the (West) German capital then, and still today the Federal Ministry for Education and Research (BMBF) is divided into two big departments: one is located in the new capital, Berlin, and the other remains in Bonn.

20. Christopher Hood, "A Public Management for all Seasons?" *Public Administration* 69 (1991): 3–19; (OECD) Organization for Economic Cooperation and Development, *Governance in Transition: Public Management Reforms in OECD Countries* (Paris: OECD, 1995); Ewan Ferlie, *The New Public Management in Action* (Oxford: Oxford University Press, 1996); Christopher Pollitt and Geert Bouckaert, *Public Management Reform: A Comparative Analysis* (Oxford: Oxford University Press, 2000); and Tom Christensen and Per Lägreid, eds., *New Public Management. The Transformation of Ideas and Practice* (Burlington: Ashgate, 2002).

21. Michael Daxner, *Die blockierte Universität* (Frankfurt: Campus, 1999); Peter Glotz, *Im Kern verrottet? Fünf vor zwölf an Deutschlands Universitäten* (Stuttgart Deutsche Verlags-Anstalt, 1996).

22. Hans Brinckmann, *Die neue Freiheit der Universität. Operative Autonomie für Lehre und Forschung an Hochschulen* (Berlin: Edition Sigma, 1998); Detlev Müller-Böling, *Die entfesselte Hochschule* (Gütersloh: Bertelsmann Stiftung, 2000).

23. Volkswagen Foundation (Volkswagen Stiftung), *Zwölf Empfehlungen für ein zukunftsfähiges deutsches Wissenschaftssystem* (Wolfsburg: Volkswagen Stiftung, 2005).

24. Enquete-Kommission-Globalisierung, *Schlussbericht der Enquete-Kommission-Globalisierung der Weltwirtschaft—Herausforderungen und Antworten* (Berlin: Deutscher Bundestag, 2002).

25. For an analysis of discourse, see Carsten von Wissel, *Hochschule als Organisationsproblem: Neue Modi unversitärer Selbstbeschreibung in Deutschland* (Bielefeld: Transcript, 2007).

26. These five dimensions are derived from Burton Clark's well-known initial "triangle of coordination" ("state," "market," "academic oligarchy"), to which he himself later added a fourth mechanism ("organisation"). See Clark, *The Higher Education System*; and Burton Clark, *Creating Entrepreneurial Universities: Organizational Pathways of Transformation* (Oxford: Pergamon Press, 1998). In addition, the "state" dimension can be further split into two different dimensions ("regulation" and "guidance"), according to Dietmar Braun and François-Xavier Merrien, "Governance of Universities and Modernisation of the State: Analytical Aspects," in *Towards a New Model of Governance for Universities? A Comparative View*, ed. Dietmar Braun and François-Xavier Merrien (London: Jessica Kingsley, 1999), 9–33. For the use of these governance mechanisms in comparative research, see Stefan Lange and Uwe Schimank, "Zwischen Konvergenz und Pfadabhängigkeit—New Public Management in den Hochschulsystemen fünf ausgewählter OECD-Länder," in *Transfer, Diffusion und Konvergenz von Politiken, Sonderheft 38 der Politischen Vierteljahresschrift*, ed. Katharina Holzinger et al. (Wiesbaden: VS, 2007), 522–48.

27. Barbara Kehm and Ute Lanzendorf, "Germany—16 Länder Approaches to Reform," in *Reforming University Governance—Changing Conditions for Research in Four European Countries*, ed. Barbara Kehm and Ute Lanzendorf (Bonn: Lemmens, 2006), 135–86.

28. This situation has changed recently, as the DFG is now allowed also to cover a part of the overhead costs of approved research projects. Until 2007 the universities had to cover all overhead costs for DFG-funded projects from their regular state funding, which could lead to severe financial troubles for strong research universities with many DFG-approved projects. In the "Hochschulpakt 2020" from July 14, 2007,

the federal and state governments declared that they would begin to institute full-cost financing for competitive research projects, starting with 20 percent of the total amount of money granted by the DFG for an approved project.

29. Kehm and Lanzendorf, "Germany—16 Länder Approaches to Reform," 135–86.

30. A DFG-funded "Sonderforschungsbereich" (SFB) is an interdisciplinary coordinated research program proposed and conducted by several professors (and their associates) from several institutes or departments in one university, usually including external collaborations. Such a research program has a framework consisting of several smaller projects that are peer reviewed and evaluated by the funding agency. One of the involved professors acts as the SFB's speaker and coordinator. These programs are evaluated by the DFG every four years and can last up to twelve years. The SFBs' establishment was politically enforced, especially by the federal ministry, to boost cooperation and the building of research profiles in German universities. With regard to their duration and the pooled resources, these coordinated programs provide more support for cutting-edge research than the usual two-plus-one-year funding for individual research projects usually provided by the DFG. The SFB programs have been successful and have been role models for all recent funding instruments, such as TransRegio and other new research programs, which aim to bring together researchers from different universities in coordinated programs to boost nationwide (and international) research collaboration.

31. Grit Laudel, "The Art of Getting Funded: How Scientists Adapt to Their Research Conditions," *Science and Public Policy* 33 (2006): 489–504.

32. This has consequences for the efficacy of research as well: As a postdoc in biology stated in an interview, doctoral students and postdocs in third party–funded projects often have good results in laboratory work but lack the experience and skills to publish their results in journal articles. Because there is no one available to support them in these matters, many results are never communicated to peers and public.

33. What makes things even worse is that the excellent research staff employed in short-term third party–funded projects often leave a project for a better or more secure job while the project is continuing.

34. Uwe Schimank und Stefan Lange, "Hochschulpolitik in der Bund/Länder-Konkurrenz," in *Das Wissensministerium. Ein halbes Jahrhundert Forschungs- und Bildungspolitik in Deutschland*, ed. Peter Weingart and Niels C. Taubert (Weilerswist: Velbrück, 2006), 311–46; Peter Strohschneider, "Über Voraussetzungen und Konzeption der Exzellenzinitiative," *Beiträge zur Hochschulforschung* 31 (2009): 8–25. Since the first excellence initiative was terminated from 2006 until 2011, the federal government and the states recently passed a new agreement to establish a similar initiative from 2012 until 2017, with an increased budget of €2.7 billion. The new initiative is

open for new proposals from the winners of the last initiative as well as for those of new candidates.

35. The "excellence initiative" does not, though, mitigate the significant reduction in financial support for German universities that has taken place over the last three decades and that has made an increasing proportion of German university research dependent on external funding. The proposals for all three categories in the competition are reviewed by commissions made up of international peers. The experts for the review commissions are selected by the DFG as the German organization most experienced in peer-review processes.

36. Michael Jaeger et al., "Formelgebundene Mittelvergabe und Zielvereinbarungen als Instrument der Budgetierung an deutschen Universitäten: Ergebnisse einer bundesweiten Befragung," *HIS Kurzinformation A/13/2005* (Hannover: HIS, 2005); Michael Leszczensky and Dominic Orr, "Staatliche Hochschulfinanzierung durch indikatorgestützte Mittelverteilung. Dokumentation und Analyse der Verfahren in 11 Bundesländern," *HIS-Kurzinformationen A/2/2004* (Hannover: HIS, 2004). However, in most cases there is no nexus between the formula the state uses for distributing money to universities and their internal allocation rules.

37. Lange, "The Basic State of Research in Germany"; Heiner Minssen et al., *Kontextsteuerung von Hochschulen? Folgen der indikatorisierten Mittelzuweisung* (Berlin: Duncker & Humblot, 2003).

38. Christof Schiene and Uwe Schimank, "Research Evaluation as Organizational Development: The Work of the Academic Advisory Council in Lower Saxony (FRG)," in *The Changing Governance of the Sciences: The Advent of Research Evaluation Systems*, ed. Richard Whitley and Jochen Gläser (Dordrecht: Springer, 2008), 171–90.

39. The "Bologna Process" is a politically enforced reform establishing a three-tier study program structure (Bachelor/ Master/ PhD) in all German universities, which requires several curricular reforms and time-consuming involvement in accreditation processes.

40. Gläser and Laudel, "Evaluation Without Evaluators"; Norma Morris, *Scientists Responding to Science Policy. A Multi-Level Analysis of the Situation of Life Scientists in the UK* (Enschede: CHEPS, 2004).

41. They are able to adapt via "inner emigration" because of their employment status as civil servants with tenure. No matter how badly they might perform and how many duties they might neglect, as civil servants they cannot be sanctioned by the university or be dismissed.

42. The first project concerned technology transfer offices at universities in the German state of North Rhine Westphalia. It was conducted by Georg Krücken between

October 1997 and April 1999 with the support of the Department of Sociology at Bielefeld University. See Georg Krücken, "Mission Impossible? Institutional Barriers to the Diffusion of the 'Third Academic Mission' at German Universities," *International Journal of Technology Management* 25 (2003): 18–33; and Georg Krücken, "Learning the 'New, New Thing': On the Role of Path Dependency in University Structures," *Higher Education* 42 (2003): 315–39. The second project, conducted by Georg Krücken, Frank Meier, and André Müller, was larger in scale, as it compared technology transfer discourses and practices at German and American universities. This project was funded from March 2003 until February 2006 by a grant from the DFG. For findings, see Georg Krücken et al., "Information, Cooperation, and the Blurring of Boundaries—Technology Transfer in German and American Discourses," *Higher Education* 53 (2007): 675–96.

43. Wolfgang König, "Technische Hochschule und Industrie—Ein Überblick zur Geschichte des Technologietransfers," in *Handbuch des Wissenschaftstransfers*, ed. Hermann J. Schuster (Berlin: Springer, 1990), 29–41; Georg Meyer-Thurow, "The Industrialization of Invention: A Case Study from the German Chemical Industry," *ISIS* 73 (1982): 363–81.

44. Margrit Szöllösi-Janze, "Wissensgesellschaft in Deutschland: Überlegungen zur Neubestimmung der deutschen Zeitgeschichte über Verwissenschaftlichungsprozesse," *Geschichte und Gesellschaft* 30 (2004): 277–313.

45. Interestingly, one can find similar models in the American discourse. In contrast to Germany, where the three models followed one another in chronological order, the American picture was more strongly marked by overlapping models, to which, beginning with the I&D model, aspects of subsequent models were added in piecemeal fashion.

46. Bundesrechnungshof, *Untersuchung über die wissenschaftliche Dokumentation in der Bundesrepublik Deutschland* (Frankfurt: Bundesrechnungshof, 1962).

47. BMWi (Bundesministerium für Wirtschaft und Technologie) / BMBF (Bundesministerium für Bildung und Forschung), *Innovationspolitik—Mehr Dynamik für zukunftsfähige Arbeitsplätze* (Bonn: BMWi / BMBF, 2002).

48. Michael Gibbons et al., *The New Production of Knowledge: The Dynamics of Science and Research in Contemporary Societies* (London: Sage, 1994).

49. Donald S. Siegel et al., "Assessing the Impact of Organizational Practices on the Relative Productivity of University Technology Transfer Offices: An Exploratory Study," *Research Policy* 32 (2003): 27–48.

50. Krücken, "Mission Impossible"; Michael Reinhard and Heinz Schmalholz, *Technologietransfer in Deutschland: Stand und Reformbedarf* (Berlin: Duncker & Humblot, 1996); Norbert Kluge and Christoph Oehler, "Hochschulen und Forschungstransfer,"

Werkstattberichte 17 (Kassel: Wissenschaftliches Zentrum für Berufs- und Hochschulforschung der Gesamthochschule Kassel, 1986).

51. John Meyer and Brian Rowan, "Institutionalized Organizations: Formal Structure as Myth and Ceremony," *American Journal of Sociology* 83 (1977): 340–63.

52. Before presenting our results, we would like to say a few words about the indicator. On the one hand, it is quite clear that the indicator only brings to light a very limited fraction of the actual collaborations taking place. On the other hand, coauthorship is a very strong indicator for collaboration. It points to a form of cooperation that goes beyond sporadic contacts but is characterized by a certain degree of depth and intensity. Moreover, the indicator measures collaborations that are not taking place somewhere in the periphery of academic work but are reflected in the central process of scientific communication: the process of publication.

53. Here one can see striking similarities to (in theory) and differences (in practice) from the Bayh-Dole Act that the U.S. Congress passed in 1980, which enabled universities to patent and to issue licenses for inventions developed with public funding. Although the Bayh-Dole Act was not directly modeled on that example, German policymakers saw it as a means of increasing universities' patenting and licensing activities. The Bayh-Dole Act certainly has had a strong symbolic impact on the role that universities are supposed to play. But the effects on the actual rate of patents are not as strong as expected in the policy discourse. See David C. Mowery et al., *Ivory Tower and Industrial Innovation. University-Industry Technology Transfer Before and After the Bayh-Dole Act* (Stanford, Calif.: Stanford University Press, 2004).

54. Henry Etzkowitz et al., *Introduction to Capitalizing Knowledge: New Intersections of Industry and Academia*, ed. Herny Etzkowitz et al. (Albany: State University of New York Press, 1998), 1–17.

55. Whitley, "Constructing Universities as Strategic Actors."

The Micropolitics of Knowledge
in England and Europe

The Cambridge University IPRs Controversy

and Its Macropolitical Lessons

VOLDEMAR TOMUSK

TWELVE

Redefining university-based knowledge as intellectual property—particularly since the U.S. Congress's passage of the Bayh-Dole Patent and Trademarks Act in 1980 and the increasing commercialization of higher education over the past ten to fifteen years—has led to criticism from intellectuals both inside and outside U.S. universities and beyond. The vigor of the academics' neoliberal onslaught on the university's public mission, if not always in deeds then at least in words, has tended to mask the universities' success in helping their governments' and policymakers' economic development around the world. Indeed, both the People's Republic of China and European countries have sent PhD students to U.S. research universities; the whole world seems to envy U.S. higher education.[1] Over the past decade, the reason that the European Research Area and the European Higher Education Area were created was to compete against

I would like to thank Dr. Timothy J. Mead, former registrary of the University of Cambridge, and Mrs. Anne Lonsdale, deputy vice-chancellor of the University of Cambridge, for introducing me to the case presented in this chapter and for their informative comments on the matter.

and overcome the United States in the global economic competition. In the view of the European Commission, Europe may be too closely attached to the organizational forms and practices that were successful in the nineteenth century but are not any longer.

As Europe gradually absorbed the shock caused by the fall of the Berlin Wall, the Common Market became permanent with the adoption of the Maastricht treaty in 1991, and the agenda was set for the further expansion of the European Union (EU). Also in the 1990s, Europe began looking for ways to shift from "a cold war academic science and technology policy coalition to a competitiveness one."[2] The new agenda for Europe was defined at the European Council meeting held in Lisbon on March 23 and 24, 2000: "The Union has today set itself a new strategic goal for the next decade: to become the most competitive and dynamic knowledge-based economy in the world capable of sustainable economic growth with more and better jobs and greater social cohesion."[3]

Despite the EU members' declared commitment to the Lisbon strategy, its actual success seems, at best, to have been limited. As a result, in 2005, at a council meeting in Brussels, the Lisbon strategy (for Europe's economic takeover of the world) was called to be resumed "without delay."[4]

Democracy is among the many reasons, followed closely by law and transparency, that the European Commission's good intentions do not always materialize. As Johan Olsen noticed, "The Commission . . . sees itself surrounded by ignorance and lack of commitment."[5] Instead of promptly implementing the plans devised by the experts hired by the commission, Europe's academics became mired in endless debates over meanings, purposes, and values. From the commission's point of view, these debates were a waste of precious resources and a further loss of competitiveness. Even though the commission promotes public consultation, discussion, and debate as a formal part of its policy formulation, statements made by individual commission members often are unusually strongly worded. For example, regarding the implementation of the so-called Bologna Process (i.e., the creation of a European higher education area), former commissioner Vivienne Reding declared, "Bologna cannot be implemented à la carte, it has to be done across the board and wholeheartedly. If not, the process will leave European higher education even less strong and united than before."[6] Nonetheless, the legality of the Bologna Process under European law has been legitimately questioned.[7]

The economic agenda of the Bologna Process (it also has political and cultural agendas)[8] is twofold: (1) restructuring European higher education to allow shifting to Europe some of the fee-paying students from other countries, such as the United States; and (2) hiring the most talented third-country students studying in European universities to work in Europe (as opposed to the United States).[9]

Messages scolding European universities for their lack of responsibility and the weakness of their entrepreneurial spirit also have come through other channels, which the commission has been able to mobilize for its purposes, such as the European University Association.[10] To spread the orthodox views of the Bologna Process throughout the academic community, each of the signatory countries have made available trained Bologna advocates, individuals who under a different regime a few decades earlier might have been referred to as the *kommissary leningradskovo processa*.[11] Despite the rhetoric of a democratic and bottom-up organization of European policy, the experience of higher education suggests a different reality. That is, European policies formulated in Brussels policy circles are not necessarily related to everyday university life. At least in regard to higher education, these policies instead seem to be made up of directives and reports exchanged between high officials in Brussels and academic experts.

Next I offer a glimpse into one of the great European universities—one of the two European universities that, according to Lord Chris Patten, compare well with any of the top 150 American universities[12]—to illustrate the university-level debates responding to the European governments' borrowing U.S. policies and passing them down to their universities. The following case from the University of Cambridge shows the complexity of arguments when there was still an opportunity to make those arguments, which in many places, particularly in most of British universities, is no longer possible. Individual faculty members' positions in defense of their property rights also suggest that any desire to return to a previous era—a golden age or just better than our own time—is unrealistic. As Jason Owen-Smith pointed out, "Commercial engagement may corrode the academy's core, but the features that are at risk are not natural, they are outcomes of distinctive and contingent historical processes."[13]

Even without a grand policy, the universities seem to have changed, in that putting something *back* (e.g., values) does not look like a viable way forward, unless academics are forced back into their ivory tower. The strategy of force would mean commercial separation from the university sector and the full commercialization of biomedicine, computer science, and other fields of applied knowledge. Ironically, however, some of the recent changes have partially restored the attraction of a secluded contemplative life for higher purposes to those who just a few decades earlier saw it as an undeserved luxury and worked hard instead to enhance the social and economic relevance of higher education.

A SUMMARY OF EVENTS IN CAMBRIDGE

In July 2002, the Joint Report of the Council and General Board of the Cambridge University[14] launched a debate that took more than three years to complete and that revealed the university's growing difficulties in trying to balance the traditional values of the scholars with the interests of its various constituent groups: disciplines as well as organizational units and individuals, governmental policies, and the interests of the businesses relying on university-produced knowledge for their technologies. As described by Prof. David Secher, very soon the debate overheated: "I have found the extreme polarization of staff in Cambridge and mistrust of the administration by many academics to be the most disappointing experience in joining the University."[15]

The Joint Report was intended to resolve an obvious discrepancy in Cambridge's intellectual property rights (IPRs) regulations, that is, IPRs rising from research supported by the Medical Research Council and other similar funding agencies assigned to the university. If the research had been funded by the university, the researcher was free to exploit the results for his or her own personal financial benefit, with "no obligation to tell [his or her] colleagues, . . . Head of Department, or anyone else in the University what [he or she] is doing, or even disclose the existence of this intellectual property."[16]

For longer than any other major British university, Cambridge had enjoyed a liberal intellectual property rights policy, according to which the rights to intellectual property—patents and copyrights—were created by faculty members, unless stipulated differently in the funding agreements imposed by a particular funding agency, and were assigned to those persons who created that intellectual property. Since the late 1980s, when the monopoly of the National Research Development Corporation / British Technology Group over the exploitation of the government-funded research outcomes was broken, the research councils have insisted that the universities own the IPRs resulting from their funding.[17] Charities, however, often did not follow this policy, so it left the universities' self-funded research intact. One of the main reasons that Cambridge was able to maintain its liberal policies against external and sometimes internal pressures was the so-called Cambridge phenomenon: the massive development of businesses in the Cambridge area since the 1970s, relying on knowledge produced by the university, which arguably benefited from the same liberal policies. After 1979, under the Conservative government, many British universities were forced to increase and centralize their funding from all types of extramural activities, just to survive. This was the context in which the proverbial entrepreneurial university, the University of Warwick, rose and was made famous by Burton Clark.[18] Aggressive entrepreneurialism left little room for the Cambridge-like *laissez-faire* policies of middle-ranking British universities. Cambridge, however, was not one of those, but twenty years later the change was finally on its way there as well.

In 1977 the then vice-chancellor of the University of Cambridge, Alan Cottrell, had rejected the proposal by the Council of the Vice-Chancellors and Principals (CVCP) that would have changed intellectual property ownership in favor of the university. He claimed that

> academic staff in Cambridge are under contract to devote themselves to the advancement of the subject, to give instruction to students, and to promote the interests of the University as a place of education, learning, and research. Such a contract recognizes the basic principles of academic freedom. Cambridge is unwilling to adopt a more restrictive form of contract as suggested. . . . Freedom of expression is fundamental to universities and the University would be unwilling to put any constraint on an individual who may wish to publish the results of his work on the grounds that the University rather than the researcher wished to explore the possibility of obtaining a patent, as is recommended by the Working Party.[19]

Although the university was able to get away with this for almost twenty-five years, its IPR policy became increasingly unique among British universities, and it is likely that at least some leading members of the of ruling Labour Party would have gladly seen "the goose that lays golden eggs," as many of the speakers described the university with its liberal IPR regime, served on their own dinner table in order to complete the proletarian mission of industrializing British higher education and increasing its contribution to British society and its economy. Following the government's assurance of accountability in the use of public funds, the university was expected to "exercise due diligence in the proper expenditure and exploitation of those public funds. The unfettered exploitation for private gain of these public funds is clearly unacceptable."[20]

As of October 1, 2002, the University of Cambridge assumed the rights over its entire intellectual property, not only the patents, but also the "database rights, semiconductor design rights, performance rights, e-mails, lab notebooks, and everything else following from externally funded research (with a narrow exception of research publications)."[21] This, however, was merely a formal move, as it confirmed the practices of most British funding agencies, and in those cases when it did not, third-party agreements would still be honored.

The new policy was to establish equal treatment of IPRs rising from internally and externally funded research and also from internally funded teaching when the university wanted to use its teaching materials in online teaching activities. What was previously seen as a mere formality had paved the way to a complete redefinition of the role of academics at the University of Cambridge, from the members of an independent community of scholars to hired knowledge workers whose IPRs were to be regulated in a way similar to that of the industrial sector. This outcome was too extreme for many of the members of the university, who thereby initiated a campaign against the proposed regulation. Under the pressure from a large majority of the faculty of the University of Cambridge, the CVCP and the General Board of the University of Cambridge revised its proposal twice.

The third joint report was circulated in May 2005 and discussed on June 7. The version of the ordinance that was put to a vote was a mirror image of the initial proposal. It stipulated: "Copyright is assigned to the creators; in the case where the inventors decide IPR should be protected, the right to apply for a patent is assigned to the University."[22] This meant that although the creators had the right to place an invention in the public domain, if they chose not to do so, the IPRs would go to the university. Another concession was a provision for an inventor, or inventors collectively, who agreed not to involve the university in the exploitation of the intellectual property. This agreement did not leave the university much room to disagree as long as the inventors agreed on whom to assign the IP: "The only grounds for refusing to make such an assignment are a disagreement among the creators or if such an assignment would place the University in breach with a third-party agreement."[23] After being notified by the IP's creators, Cambridge Enterprise had thirty days to decide whether it wanted to exploit the property. If it decided not to pursue it, Cambridge Enterprise and the inventors were to decide together how to proceed.

What also was significant about the third version of the proposed ordinance was that with regard to IPRs, students were to be treated equally with other members of the university, meaning that unless there was an agreement with a third party, a student could decide the fate of an intellectual property that he or she had created.

Despite the university's efforts to reach an agreement, the hard-line opponents from the computer laboratory and the Campaign for Cambridge Freedom movement continued their resistance, using the traditional arguments and adding the following qualification to the report: "We are unable to support this policy as it will undermine academic freedom and will have a chilling effect on the commercial exploitation of research. We hereby give notice that amendments will be introduced to the Regent House in due course." [Three signatures][24]

The ordinance was put to a vote at Regent House on October 5, 2005. The voting ended on December 12, 2005, and the results were announced on January 11, 2006. Of a total of 1,098 votes, 790 were for approval of the ordinance without amendments, 259 for approval with amendments, and 49 against the ordinance. The ordinance therefore was approved without amendments.[25] The people had won. Whether there was anything actually to celebrate, however, was a different matter.

THE CAMBRIDGE PHENOMENON, THE AMERICAN DREAM, AND EUROPEAN POLICIES

The Cambridge phenomenon refers to the development of knowledge-intensive industries, the most significant perhaps being Cambridge Display Technology Ltd. established in 1992, in the Cambridge region. This company credited its size and fame to the university's liberal intellectual property rights (IPRs) policy that had created the freedom and provided the incentives for the academics to commercialize their inventions. According to the first major report on the Cambridge phenomenon by Segal Quince Wicksteed (a Cambridge-based consultancy company) in 1985, the liberal IPR regime had supported the emergence of the Cambridge phenomenon by making it easy for academics to enter commercial activities and to interact with local firms on technical matters.[26]

According to the *Cambridge Phenomenon Report*, "Cambridge was responsible for over 10 percent of the revenue generating technology ventures from UK universities between 1949 and 1984."[27] The updated report from June 2000 noted that Cambridge employed 32,000 people in 1,250 technology firms. By 2002, the IPR debate had exploded, with the number of firms having risen to 1,500, employing some 45,000 people.[28]

Until the twenty-first century, the Cambridge phenomenon had been a major source of pride not only for the university but also for all of British academia and the British government. But then, perceptions changed suddenly and dramatically. The government took the position that more had to be done to translate university research into a competitive British economy worldwide, and Vice-Chancellor Sir Alec Broers, who had long been touting the phenomenon, pulled back drastically, stating in a radio interview on September 19, 2002:

Well, if you take twelve hundred companies and, whatever it is, twenty or thirty thousand jobs, it's not very big is it? We could be much bigger in my mind. When you have only got to have an international company close one plant, they do away with that number of jobs. So the Cambridge phenomenon is a sparkling thing, but it's a sparkling little thing at this stage, and I'd like to see it much bigger. I mean not in the immediate region, as I always argue, but it would be thrilling to me if the big international players were created that could go and employ a hundred thousand people up in Peterborough.[29]

We may wonder whether this view had anything to do with the general change in attitude in Europe around the turn of the century to worrying about its economic competitiveness, first with the United States but also with the growing East Asian economies and India and China on the top of that. Brussels' policy goal to take over the world within a decade had been passed on to the universities:

The Government is rightly concerned to ensure that exploitable outcomes from university research should lead to actual innovation for the benefit of the British economy. Evidently this means that Funding Councils and other official bodies will require quantitative statements concerning technology transfer, including such measures as the number of patents applied for and revenue generated. There are indications that there will be financial incentives to improve performance (through so-called Third Stream Funding).[30]

The irony is that in order to turn the universities toward the markets, additional nonmarket incentives are being introduced, which may well undermine the role of the very same markets, by strengthening the bureaus distributing the financial incentives. This seems to support Rhoades and Slaughter's argument that the core of the neoliberal program is not the reduction of public subsidies but their redirection.[31] While sympathizing with their position regarding the United States, I believe it likely that Europe's excessive reliance on bureaucracy contributes less to its economic competitiveness than does the United States' support of knowledge-intensive production. As practiced in Europe, market socialism is likely to have inherent internal disincentives for initiative and productivity, as well as for leakages of resources.

Another example of the scale of the knowledge transfer in Cambridge was offered by Prof. Secher:

RSD [Research Services Division of the Cambridge University] now manages an annual research income of more than £140m, negotiates 250 contracts for academic researchers, advises on around 150 inventions, and has a technology transfer turnover of more than £3m. Over the past five years the University has made £4.7m from licensing its IPR. Of this, £2m has been paid to inventors, £1.8m to Departments, and £0.8m to the Chest. Over the same period MIT [Massachusetts Institute of Technology] has made more than ten times as much, most recycled through Departments and centrally to fund research, including graduate Studentships and endow Professorships.[32]

Comparability, or the lack thereof, with MIT seems to have been a problem in the United Kingdom and Europe.

Centralizing control over IPRs and technology transfer was seen as one way to catch up with the United States and so was an increasingly popular argument in Europe at the beginning of the twenty-first century. To do this, Cambridge expanded the RSD to where it was thought to cost at least £1 million a year. Many of the staff complained that this made no economic sense, at least not directly. The vice-chancellor's office suggested that pleasing the government in this way would open access to additional research funds, which would be the real benefit and put the universities on a par with European policies for global competition. But this leads to another European problem. Although Europeans love playing the market game with the United States, they do not fully appreciate its rules. Or perhaps in order to accelerate the process, the high offices offer a few additional *market signals*, which eventually create a whole different set of motives, as in the European Union's joint agricultural policies, and undermine the entire exercise.

THE MAIN ARGUMENTS

Of the several arguments presented, most were intended to defeat the university's initiative. The following summarizes the main themes in order to reveal the complexity of the situation and the interests involved.

Freedom of Expression

A group called "Campaign for Cambridge Freedoms" was the greatest organized force opposing the university's plan to assume ownership of all intellectual property produced at the university. The group contended that the university's ownership of IPR would allow it to suppress views with which the university itself or any of its sponsors disagreed, by removing them from public circulation. Prof. Ross Anderson stressed the same position throughout the debate:

I have a direct experience of academic censorship, having been on the program committee of the Information Hiding workshop that accepted the Felten paper, which the Recording Industry Association of America tried to suppress. Other examples might include an economist criticizing a policy dear to the government of the day, or an English lecturer who writes a novel attacked by religious extremists.[33]

The group argued that as proposed by the university, the policy constituted a "draconian intellectual property policy, which would significantly curtail the freedom at Cambridge."[34] This implied that the mission of the university was indeed to promote free expression. But by adopting the new policy, it was either assuming for itself the function of suppressing free expression or was, at the least, putting itself in a position in which it could be forced by any of its sponsors to censor positions publicly expressed by its members.

Although the opponents of the university's policy described in rather colorful terms the dangers it posed to public interests and academic freedom, the vigor by which the group led by the computer laboratory defended academic freedom seemed to have taken some by surprise. During the fourth year of the debate, one of the speakers, Prof. Nick Boyle, finally addressed the issue directly:

Personally speaking, when I hear the phrase "academic freedom" I reach not for the revolver but for the air-freshener—in this context, as in others, it suggests something is concealed beneath the stairs. What is really at issue here is not academic freedom but money. We are being asked to decide how much of a certain pot of money we should use for the public and charitable purposes of the university and how much of it we should pay ourselves for our private benefit.[35]

In 2006, a year after the university's proposal was defeated, Prof. Anderson, the founder and leader of the group, summarized its achievements:

Even though we did not get everything we campaigned for, the outcome was worth the effort. Scholars in the arts and humanities now own the copyrights in popular books they write; scientists and technologists similarly own the software they write; and if you patent an invention, then you can develop it yourself rather than giving it to Cambridge Enterprise.[36]

Computer software clearly has a significant economic value. In addition, in regard to public benefit, as long as intellectual property has not actually entered the public domain, it does not really matter whether the university or an individual suppresses the flow of information or exploits it economically. According to Sir John Sulston, by whose effective campaigning the Human Genome Project was rescued from corporate ownership,[37] "the patenting of DNA sequences has unquestionably lead[led] to a failure of discoveries to be exploited for the common good,"[38] and here it does not matter who owns that patent.

The university may have been wrong to try to make society pay a second time for what it had already paid through its funding to the university: "Charging a high royalty on a patent based on publicly funded research is equivalent to charging the public twice for the same product. They first pay the University to do the research; why should they then pay the University again for access to the product?"[39]

During the campaign, it was argued that the university's attempt to assume ownership of IPRs was wrong, as it did not respect the inventors' freedom to place the inventions in the public domain.[40] Indeed, Prof. Anderson's later statement shows that he did not really consider this as one of the campaign's achievements. Instead, the achievement for him was the individual ownership of intellectual property.

Sharing the Income from IPRs

During the years of the debate, all the parties agreed that the issue of money, if it had any prominence at all, was secondary or tertiary and that the public interest and the public good were the highest priorities.[41] The records, however, show a different picture, which would become obvious when comparing the plan finally adopted with the university's initial plans to share the proceeds from IPRs between the university and the inventor.

According to the final settlement, the inventor was to receive 90 percent of the net royalties of the first £100,000; 60 percent of the second; and 34 percent of the third £100,000 and above.[42] The university's initial plan was quite different. According to this plan, the inventor was to receive 90 percent of the first £20,000; 70 percent of the next £40,000; 50 percent of the next £40,000, and 33.3 percent of the amount over £100,000.[43] It was clear that members of the University of Cambridge had spent more than three years fighting for their own interests first. They did this by using a variety of arguments, the most fundamental of which was built on a human rights approach declaring that the inventor could not be separated from the invention.

As Prof. Dame Marilyn Strathern observed, finding a simple and *natural* solution in such a situation is neither easy nor perhaps even possible:

When the University of Cambridge says that it wishes to assert ownership of the intellectual products of its employees it looks as though a corporation is taking away from the individual what naturally belongs to him or her, and the individual creativity of the scientist seems under assault. But if I were to ask whether a university or an individual were more likely to secure protection in relation to commercial interests, I would answer the university. If I were to ask whether a university or an individual were more likely to see that benefits flowed back to the community at large, I would probably answer the university. Yet if I were to ask whether a university or an individual were the natural owner, I would hesitate. Because the truth is that neither are, and natural ownership is a fiction.[44]

The few statements addressing the issue of faculty compensation imply that at least in relative terms, it had stagnated since the 1980s and that to some members of the university, the university's attempt to obtain IPRs was equal to taking from them money that was rightfully theirs. Even more than that, this money often made working for the university not only financially rewarding but also survivable. For example, Prof. Richard J. Evans reported:

> I depend for a living not just from my salary, which I have seen decline drastically in relative terms over the thirty years during which I've been an academic, but also on additional income from journalism, broadcasting, and commercial publication. This is not just the case with senior academics; I know a number of junior colleagues who are in this position too. Not only would it be wrong for the University to grab this income, it would also drive many of us away and do desperate harm to recruitment of the leading young academics on whom we depend for the maintenance of our position as Britain's leading University.[45]

Prof. Frank M. Stajano's explanation likewise noted that while the additional income from IPRs, consulting, and copyrights was relatively modest, there always was a chance that a person like Stephen Hawking would write a book like *The Brief History of Time* or somebody would invent something generating millions. Such cases, though rare, were still real:

> The liberal policy that existed at the time [in 1992] when I accepted my post here was what allowed the University to attract and retain the brightest and most entrepreneurial researchers. The low wages were somehow compensated by the perspective of a chance to strike it rich. It was a win-win situation that allowed the University to pay a lot less than market price for the best minds.[46]

The university denied any direct economic interest throughout the debate: "The motivation for the policy is not primarily financial. The Council and the General Board wish to see the results of research conducted in Cambridge exploited for public good and for economic growth of the country. They also wish to help the university's academic community achieve these goals."[47]

Despite the university's repeated assurances, a conspiracy theory circulated that there was a rather vicious idea behind the university's plan. Many of the academic staff tended to think that while the new regulation was to give the university's ownership over the last and, most likely, the least valuable 10 percent of the intellectual property created in Cambridge, the fact of having complete ownership would have created an opportunity to sell that property in bulk. Such a universal policy would have given the university an opportunity to "mortgage its intellectual property, in return for a substantial payment by an investment company."[48] Such a bulk sale of IPRs, it was thought, could have financed a university's building project in times when its financial difficulties were apparent. Similar deals had already been made by Imperial College in London as well as Oxford University. The universities' leaders vehemently denied any such possibility.

Nonetheless, many of the faculty did not trust their leadership's capacity to manage that property. According to Boyle's suggestion, there was a finite amount of cash generated from intellectual property to be shared, which meant a zero-sum game. Money that the inventors took home could not be invested in a new laboratory building. A few speakers, however, noted that what the university was heading toward in its inability to handle the IPRs was not even a zero-sum game but a minus-sum game, that the mismanagement resulting from the university's ownership of the IPRs would have reduced the amount of funds to be generated in comparison to what the individuals would have been able to gain. With this, as Prof. Thomas W. Körner noted, the Praesidium of the Poldovian Academy of Literature (i.e., the CVCP and General Board of the University of Cambridge) were following a Poldovian proverb: "Better ten zorbals on my pocket than a hundred in yours."[49]

Teaching and Intellectual Property

The new policy was to establish equal treatment for IPRs rising from internally and externally funded research and, when university was interested in using teaching materials in online teaching activities, also from internally funded teaching. Literally understood, the new IPRs policy in Cambridge could have led as far as lecturers trying to ensure that their "lectures did not cover which

[they] intended to publish [in books]."[50] This created a rather strange situation in a university in which each unit of knowledge was to be separately priced and paid for before it was transferred. That would, of course, make meaningful teaching impossible. But it would also make impossible any discussion within the academic community. Such a policy would mean the end of the university as a "communication community."[51] It also assumes that students are mere customers of the university, which is not necessarily the case. At least the best students, particularly doctoral students and also undergraduate students in some of the better universities, do contribute to the common knowledge pool. Making all knowledge into property would mean that students, too, would calculate the price before opening their mouths in a seminar.

The Public Interest

The extent to which the public interest could be used to justify policies, including those related to higher education, seems to have no limit. Who exactly is the public whose interests many of us are defending is not clear. Is it the two of us or you and your brother or I and my mother-in-law? Despite the claims made by some schools of policy studies, there are always winners and losers emerging from policy implementation, so nonpolitical policy remains mainly a politically inspired myth. It is therefore no surprise that in the Cambridge IPRs debate, the arguments related to the public interest went in all directions and often contradicted one another.

We often assume that the public interest could be best served by posting knowledge in the public domain. This argument was made several times made during the debate, as the following statement suggests: "All Cambridge staff and students should continue to be free to contribute to the free software community, by writing new software or improving existing packages."[52] Unfortunately, as it appears from a distance, the argument was often used to frighten the university away from what the individuals thought belonged to them.

When Prof. Sumeet Mahajan proposed creating a third option as an alternative to either the inventor's or the university's retaining the IP, or placing it in unrestricted public domain, it was ignored. He then proposed creating a *public patent pool*, from which "patents would be licensed royalty-free on conditions that support further sharing."[53] The apparent lack of enthusiasm to pursue this option reveals the gap between the rhetoric and action with regard to the university's public mission when the latter coincides with nobody's interests except those of the anonymous and voiceless *public*.

To remain fair to all sides in the argument, I should make clear that patenting knowledge does serve the public interest, although it is difficult to see how it would require the unsophisticated approach taken by the University of Cambridge's leaders in their initial proposal. "A patent," they explained, "is a right to stop others from making a similar product, and it can be used to demand payment for a license to copy an invention."[54] A patent permits the creation of incentives to invest in turning university knowledge into goods and services that, one would assume, would meet market demand and serve society's needs. Unless the state decided to centralize control over economic resources, as in countries like the former Soviet Union and its satellites, some sort of economic incentives would be needed. After all, despite having control over knowledge as well as economic resources, centrally planned economies proved to be surprisingly inefficient in bringing the two together. I believe that the public's access to material goods may be considered a public good. Production of those goods requires some kind of mechanism that would create incentives to produce the necessary knowledge. Many other kinds of knowledge, however, also need to be produced, although their contribution to the public good might be less material at first glance. The principal problem for universities today is producing these different kinds of knowledge in the same organization.

FURTHER DISCUSSION

Walter W. Powell, Jason Owen-Smith, and Jeanette A. Colyas confirmed this in the case of Stanford University, the biomedical cluster in Boston,[55] as well as the University of Cambridge. That is, the largest majority of university IPRs success stories predate their respective government policies by a decade or more. It appears likely that the reactive legislative initiatives contributed little to the already existing successes and proved to be mostly inefficient in spreading that success. For Stanford, "a mere five licenses accounted for 72 percent of more than $450 million in revenue generated by Stanford's technology transfer activity over a thirty-year period."[56] According to the same source, three of these inventions, covering 63 percent of the total revenue generated between 1970 and 2000, were made back in the 1970s. The simple moral seems to be that government initiatives spreading and borrowing those practices and policies are all but irrelevant to creating and transferring useful knowledge. They also are largely irrelevant to generating additional research funding for the universities. Technology transfer offices hardly ever break even, and licensing the technology covers "only a small fraction—typically less than 5 percent—of the overall costs of university research."[57]

Similar to the biomedical cluster in Boston, the Cambridge phenomenon was not launched when politicians decided to encourage the creation of useful knowledge but when that knowledge became available within the academic community. The effects of large-scale government initiatives appear to have been marginal in creating further success stories, as they were likely to serve other goals, such as changing the distribution patterns of public subsidies, accumulating political capital, strengthening bureaus, and allowing the rise of new generations of officeholders. In that sense, the recent complaints about technology transfer policies and about neoliberalism are grossly exaggerated. But two other concerns deserve closer attention.

The very notion of the university is changing when hordes of business consultants using new terms like *the entrepreneurial university*,[58] *triple helix*,[59] and *mode-2 research*[60] enter university organizations softened by the sweet talk of politicians. Even though only a few of the highest-ranking research universities will ever gain any benefits from those ideas, they must moderate their expectations of the state. The use of such concepts themselves is better understood as a particular kind of political poetry, whose metaphors and rhymes mobilize the troops to conquer new promised lands of consumers. A recent policy paper by the Oxford-based Higher Education Policy Institute made it clear that without the fees paid by non-EU students, who provide 8 percent of higher education funding in the United Kingdom, many British universities would have major financial difficulties.[61]

The second concern is the university's increasing fragility as a community of academics, as demonstrated by the recent debate in Cambridge. While the university's motives for introducing a new IPRs policy remain dubious and the possible national and supranational incentives not properly thought through, the final outcome of the dispute was that academics as a group of individuals defeated the university as a community of scholars and sacrificed the academic community's solidarity for their individual interests. The irony of this situation is that the University of Cambridge still functions as a community of scholars so that it can make such decisions by the vote of all members of the community. But it is a Pyrrhic victory, and a few more victories like that and the community will disappear. At the same time, fixing the university according to any of its historical models is likely to lead to only monstrous and wasteful organizations. While stressing the value of the narrow scientific and technical inventions, the importance of an open exchange of knowledge among all branches of inquiry to even the most technical findings has been underestimated. Once the community is broken, nothing will bring it back, so that it may well be time to make an effort to strengthen it. Merely limiting the patents' role in the academic rewards' system, as opposed to citations,[62] would not necessarily reverse the recent development toward the commercialization of knowledge. The world has changed so that both patents and citations represent a direct cash value, leading in the latter case to higher faculty compensation and, even more important, reputation and competitiveness in the grant market.

Nonetheless, we should also remain aware that the goods and services materialized because of the academics' findings and that despite being sold in the market, they usually add to the public good. One of the lessons of the 2008/2009 financial crisis is that economic growth also is a public good. Accordingly, significant work is needed to better understand the complex contribution of the contemporary university to society and to find ways to allow universities to continue contributing in a way that will not reduce human existence to the concepts found in biology or computer science, or perhaps see life merely as a capacity to consume for the higher purpose of economic growth.

NOTES

1. For example, see Walter W. Powell, Jason Owen-Smith, and Jeanette A. Colyas, "Innovation and Emulation: Lessons from American Universities in Selling Private Rights to Public Knowledge," *Minerva* (2007) 45: 121–42.
2. Garry Rhoades and Sheila Slaughter, "Academic Capitalism and the New Economy: Privatization as Shifting the Target of Public Subsidy in Higher Education," in *The University, State, and Market*, ed. Robert A. Rhoads and Carlos Alberto Torres (Stanford, Calif.: Stanford University Press, 2006), 116.
3. Lisbon European Council, "Presidency Conclusions" (Brussels: Council of the European Union, March 23 and 24, 2000).
4. European Council, "Presidency Conclusions" (Brussels: Council of the European Union, March 22 and 23, 2005).
5. Johan P. Olsen, *The Institutional Dynamics of the (European) University* (Oslo: University of Oslo, ARENA-Center for European Studies, 2005), 22.
6. Vivienne Reding, "Address to the Berlin Meeting of Ministers for Higher Education," Berlin, September 17–19, 2001.
7. Sacha Garben, "The Bologna Process from a European Law Perspective," EUI working paper LAW no. 2008/12 (Florence: Department of Law, European University Institute, 2008).

8. Voldemar Tomusk, "Three Bolognas and a Pizza Pie: Notes on Institutionalization of the European Higher Education System," *International Studies in Sociology of Education* 14 (2004): 75–95.

9. For example, see Pavel Zgaga, *Looking Out: The Bologna Process in a Global Setting: On the "External Dimension" of the Bologna Process* (Oslo: Norwegian Ministry of Education and Research, 2006).

10. For example, see Tomusk, "Three Bolognas and a Pizza Pie."

11. The Commissaries of the Leningrad Process. Similarities between the European Union and the Soviet Union have been noticed by several commentators. Consider, for example, the following statement by Tony Judt:

> The Soviet Union once attracted many western intellectuals as a promising combination of philosophical ambition and administrative power, and "Europe" has some of the same seductive appeal. For its admirers, as for many politicians and businessmen in the advanced regions of western and central Europe, the "Union" is the latest heir to enlightened despotism of the last great reforming era before the coming of national states. For what is "Brussels," after all if not a renewed attempt to achieve that ideal of efficient, universal administration, shorn of particularisms and driven by rational calculation and the rule of law, which the great monarchs—Catherine, Frederick, Maria Theresa and Joseph II—strove to institute in their ramshackle lands? (Tony Judt, *A Grand Illusion? An Essay on Europe* [New York: Hill & Wang, 1996], 115)

12. Chris Patten, *Not Quite the Diplomat: Home Truths About World Affairs* (London: Allen Line, 2005), 288.

13. Jason Owen-Smith, "Commercial Imbroglios: Proprietary Science and the Contemporary University," in *The New Political Sociology of Science: Institutions, Networks, and Power*, ed. Scott Frickel and Kelly Moore (Madison: University of Wisconsin Press, 2006), 65.

14. "Joint Report of the Council and the General Board on the Ownership of Intellectual Property Rights," available at http://www.admin.cam.ac.uk/reporter/2001–02/weekly/5894/15.html (accessed September 28, 2007).

15. "Report of Discussion," Tuesday, October 15, 2002, available at (http://www.admin.cam.ac.uk/reporter/2002–03/weekly/5901/16.html (accessed September 28, 2007).

16. Anthony C. Minson, "Report of Discussion," Tuesday, October 15, 2002.

17. "Report of the RPC Working Group on Ownership of Intellectual Property Rights (IPRs)," available at http://www.admin.cam.ac.uk/reporter/2002–03/weekly/5933/26.html (accessed September 28, 2007).

18. Burton R. Clark, *Creating Entrepreneurial Universities: Organizational Pathways of Transformation* (London: Pergamon Press, 1998).

19. Quoted in Simon Deakin, "Report of Discussion," Tuesday, October 15, 2002.

20. Anthony J. Badger, "Report of Discussion," Tuesday, October 15, 2002.

21. Ross J. Anderson, "Report of Discussion," Tuesday, October 15, 2002.

22. Ian M. Leslie, "Report of Discussion," Tuesday, June 7, 2005, available at http://www.admin.cam.ac.uk/reporter/2004–05/weekly/6004/15.html (accessed September 28, 2007).

23. Ibid.

24. "Third Joint Report of the Council and the General Board on the Ownership of Intellectual Property Rights (IPRs)," available at http://www.admin.cam.ac.uk/reporter/2004–05/weekly/6001/17.html (accessed September 28, 2007).

25. Result of Ballot, grace 1 of October 5, 2005, available at http://www.admin.ac.uk/reporter/2005–06/weekly/6022/27.html (accessed September 28, 2007).

26. Stephen Allott, "Report of Discussion," Tuesday, October 15, 2002.

27. Ibid.

28. Ibid.

29. Quoted in Richard J. Stibbs, "Report of Discussion," Tuesday, October 15, 2002.

30. "Report of the RPC Working Group."

31. Rhoades and Slaughter, "Academic Capitalism and the New Economy," 103–40.

32. David Secher, "Report of Discussion," Tuesday, October 15, 2002.

33. Ross J. Anderson, "Report of Discussion," Tuesday, October 15, 2002.

34. William R. Cornish, "Report of Discussion," Tuesday, May 11, 2004, available at http://www.admin.cam.ac.uk/reporter/2003–04/weekly/5964/20.html (accessed September 28, 2007).

35. Nick Boyle, "Report of Discussion," Tuesday, June 7, 2005, available at http://www.admin.cam.ac.uk/reporter/2004–05/weekly/6004/15.html (accessed September 28, 2007).

36. Available at http://www.cl.cam.ac.uk/~rja14/ccf.html (accessed October 11, 2007).

37. Michael E. McIntyre, "Report of Discussion," Tuesday, October 15, 2002.

38. Sir John Sulston, "Report of Discussion," Tuesday, October 15, 2002.

39. Michael R. Clark, "Report of Discussion," Tuesday, October 15, 2002.

40. David J. C. MacKay, "Report of Discussion," Tuesday, October 15, 2002.

41. "Third Joint Report of the Council and the General Board."

42. Ibid.

43. "Joint Report of the Council and the General Board."

44. Dame Marilyn Strathern, "Report of Discussion," Tuesday, October 15, 2002.

45. Richard J. Evans, "Report of Discussion," Tuesday, October 15, 2002.

46. Frank M. Stajano, "Report of Discussion," Tuesday, June 7, 2005.

47. "Third Joint Report of the Council and the General Board."

48. Sir John Sulston, "Report of Discussion," Tuesday, October 15, 2002.

49. Thomas W. Körner, "Report of Discussion," Tuesday, October 15, 2002.

50. Evans, "Report of Discussion," Tuesday, October 15, 2002.

51. Jürgen Habermas, *The New Conservatism* (Cambridge: Polity Press, 1989).

52. MacKay, "Report of Discussion," Tuesday, October 15, 2002.

53. Sumeet Mahajan, "Report of Discussion," Tuesday, May 11, 2004.

54. Clark, "Report of Discussion," Tuesday, October 15, 2002.

55. Powell, Owen-Smith, and Colyas, "Innovation and Emulation."

56. Ibid., 128.

57. Ibid., 130. See also Jennifer Washburn, *University, Inc.: The Corporate Corruption of Higher Education* (New York: Basic Books, 2005).

58. Burton R. Clark, *Creating Entrepreneurial Universities: Organizational Pathways of Transformation* (London: Pergamon Press, 1998).

59. Henry Etzkowitz, *The Triple Helix: Industry, University, and Government in Innovation* (London: Routledge, 2008).

60. Camille Limoges et al., *The New Production of Knowledge: The Dynamics of Science and Research in Contemporary Societies* (London: Sage, 1994).

61. James Cemmell and Bahram Bekhradnia, *The Bologna Process and the UK's International Student Market* (Oxford: HEPI).

62. Jason Owen-Smith, "Trends and Transitions in the Institutional Environment for Public and Private Science," *Higher Education* 49 (2005): 91–117.

Playing the Quality Game | **THIRTEEN**

Whose Quality and

Whose Higher Education?

JOHN BRENNAN

AND MALA SINGH

Increasingly demanding regulatory systems are a common feature of the changing face of higher education worldwide, despite marked differences of context and history. External quality assurance arrangements are an integral part of such regulatory mechanisms for higher education governance in both the developed and the developing world.[1] These arrangements are reshaping the public orientation of higher education, making the public accountability of higher education more exacting and bringing about far-reaching changes to traditional higher education cultures. They also are reconfiguring key relationships and power balances, for example, between government and the higher education sector, between higher education and its diverse stakeholders, and between institutional managers and academics. Quality assurance, it is argued, is essentially about power.[2] More specifically, it is about the exercise of power of four agents: governments, markets, academic "workers," and academic "managers." In arguing that quality regimes are becoming central arenas for struggles over the exercise of power and values in higher education, this chapter examines important aspects of the quality evaluation mechanisms through which higher education systems are regulated and changed.

Viewed from an international comparative perspective, quality assurance systems across national contexts demonstrate both variety and similarity in their rationales and purposes, in the instruments and methodologies that are used, and in their effects on higher education. What are the factors that shape variety and similarity across evaluative regimes? How are the public missions of higher education institutions in different national systems influenced by contextual pressures and system choices in their evaluative regimes? This chapter compares and contrasts external quality assurance in the higher education systems in the United Kingdom and South Africa in light of these questions. The comparison makes possible an understanding of how the power dynamics of quality assurance are manifested in two different national contexts: in an established system in a developed country and in a new system in a developing country. The higher education and quality assurance systems in South Africa reflect colonial and postcolonial influences from the UK's higher education system[3] but also significant political and educational differences from it. Our analysis seeks to throw light on the purposes and effects of quality assurance in two public accountability regimes in higher education. The systems are located in quite different political projects but employ similar evaluation strategies. The focus of the analysis is the changing relationships between higher education and the state (how changes in the values and agendas of the latter impact on higher education) and shifts in the internal distributions of power within higher education (especially as they affect the status and working lives of academics).

The two national contexts demonstrate variety in the evaluation regimes but also have instructive similarities. One clear difference relates to the scope of quality-related accountability in the two systems, for example, the connection between quality imperatives and "consumer" satisfaction in the United Kingdom, and between quality and equity in South Africa. There also are common reference points in the unfolding of the quality assurance systems in the UK and South African cases, despite differences in their political history, educational priorities, and time sequences. One of these common reference points is the similarity of changes in the power relations between the state and higher education and among different actors within institutions. The second has to do with the politics of quality assurance in attesting to "sameness" or "difference" within the higher education system. Contrasting the case of a well-established system that has gone through several (often controversial) versions of quality assurance and that reflects clear shifts in the power nexus between state, market, and academe with a relatively new system that is in its first cycle and within which emerging power relationships are already tilting away from academe provides a useful study of how the public orientation of higher education is interpreted and shaped by evaluation systems.

THE REGULATORY ROLE OF INTERMEDIARY BODIES

The analyses of Guy Neave and other researchers have demonstrated how the rise of the "evaluative state" and its policy of steering higher education at a distance has necessitated the emergence of intermediary bodies with dedicated mandates (often from government) to hold higher education institutions to public account.[4] Quality assurance structures feature prominently among such intermediary bodies. Quality accountability is measured by hard and soft external evaluation systems, regular reporting requirements, and systems for demonstrating efficiencies and value for money. These systems are intended to satisfy government concerns about the cost-effectiveness of publicly funded higher education as well as stakeholders' demands for greater responsiveness to their specific needs and interests. Ownership and control of these intermediary bodies as well as their direct and indirect relationships with government and academe differ across country systems. What is clear, however, is that many governments, especially those in Organization for Economic Cooperation and Development (OECD) countries, have moved from direct forms of regulation to steering indirectly through intermediary bodies, including quality assurance agencies. This development has positioned the quality-related intermediary structures in a hugely influential way in the changing regulatory regime for higher education. The powers of such agencies, their reporting lines and composition, and their evaluation requirements and consequences reveal a great deal about the shifts in the balance of forces among various centers of power, especially in relation to the often-cited Clark triangle of state, academe, and the market.[5]

The changes to higher education brought about by external evaluation systems have been not only internally far-reaching but also have brought higher education institutions firmly into the public spotlight. Askling and Henkel point out that the "British experience was that quality assurance was the most potent of the change agents among the elements of the New Public Management policy. A major reason for this was the external, transparent and compulsory nature of the quality assurance policies established."[6] The publicity attached to the Research Assessment Exercise (RAE) and the Teaching Quality Assessment (TQA), as well as their funding and reputational consequences, rendered quality assurance "among the most important drivers of the policies and structural arrangements of almost all higher education institutions," leading to new policies, structures, conditions of service, and management interventions designed to maximize performance in the different external evaluation systems. In South African higher education, quality assurance has become prominent in its directive role and impact as one of three statutory policy instruments to steer higher education toward a post-apartheid dispensation that aspires to be more equitable, responsive, and effective than its apartheid predecessor. Without yet having the same measure of public exposure of quality findings or funding overdetermination, as in the case of the UK, the quality assurance system in South Africa has, nevertheless, started to change institutional arrangements and behaviors in response to the requirements of the regulatory body, as well as influencing the relationship between the state and academe and among institutional actors. In both instances, the external quality assurance regimes have brought higher education more explicitly and answerably into the public domain. How has this development helped reframe the public orientation of higher education, and what have been its intended and unintended consequences?

In the case of these two country systems, the powerful role and impact of quality assurance in forging new relations of power and changing the traditional cultures of higher education is very clear. The jurisdictions and power of quality assurance systems derive in the first instance not so much from concerns about the quality of higher education (and its associated accountabilities) but from the social purposes and goals postulated for higher education by governments and other external stakeholders. In a global context shaped by the discourses of efficiency, productivity, and competitiveness and in which economic growth is viewed as synonymous with social development, social policy frameworks, including those for higher education, have explicit emphases on client responsiveness, value for money, and public accountability. Hence they are prominent in quality assurance requirements, as in other areas of regulation of social provision.[7] Evaluation regimes are increasingly focused on the public responsiveness of higher education, although it is not always clear that this advances quality learning, teaching, and research or leads to a power balance that improves the conditions for academic work.

In the United Kingdom, the policy trajectory from Conservative Prime Minister Margaret Thatcher through to New Labour has been characterized by an emphasis on deregulation, privatization, entrepreneurialism, efficiency, consumerism, and accountability. These values found easy reference in higher education in the face of massification and shrinking public subsidies, helping create a form of state-fostered, market-driven understanding of the public orientation of higher education. This increased demand for public responsiveness required higher education to report to a range of external stakeholders and operate in different markets in the search for new sources of financing and reputation building. Quality assurance regimes made it possible to determine the extent to which higher education was fulfilling the demands of public accountability. However, it is worth noting that ambivalence in the relationship between the discourses of efficiency, on the one hand, and quality improvement, on the other hand, gives quality assurance the potential to be more than a mere new public management tool. Initially at least, some academic staff in the UK "bought" into these processes with considerable enthusiasm, seeing in them much needed stimuli for change and improvement. Over time, however, the response has shifted more to a combination of compliance and acute anxiety as the consequences of evaluation outcomes (for both funding and reputation) and the angst associated with them have steadily grown.

In post-apartheid South Africa, higher education policy reflects a complex mix of social justice and efficiency imperatives, which also is encapsulated in the relatively young quality assurance system. This system has flagged equity and transformation issues in its quality criteria, given the need to transcend the legacies of racially based historical advantage. The quality agency's emphasis on capacity development at the start of its work had been welcomed by many academics, albeit accompanied by criticism that the accountability discourse had already grown more pronounced in the system's implementation phase. It remains an open question as to whether in the next cycle of external quality assurance, new contextual pressures and different strategic choices will result in the evolution of the quality regime in a direction similar to that of the United Kingdom. The biggest challenge for the quality assurance system is continuing to exercise its regulatory authority on the basis of a meaningful connection and balance of public accountability, academic authority, quality improvement, and social justice. This requires negotiating the conceptual, methodological, and strategic tensions relating to the attempt to insert broader notions of the public good into external evaluation systems. Such systems are themselves part of accountability arrangements that often privilege efficiency and competitive edge over considerations of social justice,[8] as is evident in the case of the UK.

This chapter argues that the public orientation of higher education as evaluated, reported on, and often "naturalized" by external evaluation systems is vulnerable to being shaped by the common interests of states and markets in cost-efficiencies, competitiveness, and consumerist notions of higher education responsiveness, as strongly indicated in the UK. The nature of evaluation itself and of evaluation systems has been skewed by what such systems are required to measure and what they do not or cannot measure. This leaves a number of social dimensions in higher education underaddressed by formal evaluation systems. Such dimensions could usefully be included if evaluation is intended to advance a broader social and intellectual development agenda in and through higher education. The dominant evaluation approach also marginalizes important constituencies, including academe, in defining appropriate modes and mechanisms for giving expression to the public orientation of higher education.

Quality regimes, however, have the potential to broaden the public orientations of higher education in ways that take account of issues of social transformation, as indicated in the South African case. This may require new thinking about the nature and purposes of evaluation as well as about the policy foundations, actors, and interest groups that shape the operations of intermediary quality assurance bodies. It may also open up new arenas of struggle in engaging government and other stakeholders on the values and content of what constitutes the public accountability of higher education. For example, the growing phenomenon of cross-border provision, in which public institutions become private providers as they go beyond their national public policy jurisdictions, has complicated the issue of the public accountability of higher education. Such developments require broadening the notion of the public orientation of higher education institutions, given that different, possibly conflicting, public policy agendas for higher education (of the importing and exporting countries) have to be aligned in some mutually beneficial way.

We next look at the recent histories of quality assurance in each of the two countries before attempting to reach some conclusions about their role in responding to, shaping, and managing the relationship between higher education and larger public and social interests.

THE CHANGING AIM OF THE QUALITY GAME IN THE UNITED KINGDOM

National quality assurance arrangements were well established in higher education in the UK before their widespread introduction across the rest of Europe during the 1990s. All higher education institutions used an external examiner system in which experienced academics from outside the institution were used to appraise the academic standards achieved by students in the institution and to oversee the awarding of degrees. This was essentially a voluntary system run by the institutions themselves, with the examiners' reports confined to the institutions that they were examining. In addition, beginning in the late 1960s, in the expanding polytechnics and colleges sector of higher education, a national body, the Council for National Academic Awards (CNAA), awarded the degrees and "validated" the degree programs that were developed, taught, and examined in the institutions. It did so through a mechanism of peer review in which academics—from universities, polytechnics, and colleges outside the institution— periodically visited to question the institution's faculty members about their courses and their teaching. Other external quality arrangements included professional accreditation processes—again mainly using an external peer-review process—and, for the polytechnics and colleges sector, a government inspectorate authorized to "visit" institutions and inspect the teaching. All these quality mechanisms focused on the teaching function of higher education. Research was, of course, subject to a peer-review process for both grant applications and publications, and during the mid-1980s this was augmented by a national "research assessment exercise."

This mix of arrangements existed until the early 1990s, after which we saw what has been aptly described as the "UK quality wars"[9] raging throughout the rest of that decade. It is not the purpose of this chapter to tell the story of those "wars"[10] in any detail but to consider what they tell us about the regulatory functions of quality assurance systems in higher education. Although the quality arrangements currently in place bear a passing resemblance to their predecessors, their aims and functioning are very different. Whereas the earlier quality arrangements were meant to demonstrate that quality was "all the same" across higher education in the UK, the objective of the current arrangements is providing evidence that quality is "different" in different parts of the higher education system. This apparent reversal of function reflects both political and educational change during this period.

Quality assurance systems provide a form of external regulation that is shaped to a considerable extent by the prevailing distribution of power while being, to an extent, independent of it. It is relevant to remember the well-known triangle of coordination systems suggested by Burton Clark in the 1980s. According to him, authority in higher education was exercised by a balance of three forces: the academic oligarchy, the state, and the market, which formed the three corners of the triangle. Historically, UK higher education was situated in the "academic oligarchy" corner, whereas other European systems were firmly in the "state" corner. As far as the latter was concerned, it did not need quality assurance because the state had many forms of direct control over its higher education systems. It owned them, it employed the faculty, it set the curricula, and it oversaw the examinations. None of these features could be found in the United Kingdom. Although they were dependent on state funding, UK universities enjoyed very high levels of autonomy right until the 1990s. One of the ways that this began to be challenged was through the creation and expansion of a rival sector to the universities in the form of the polytechnics. These were initially owned and administered by local governments in the UK. It is interesting to recall that they were often referred to as the "public sector" of higher education. The inference was clear: the universities constituted a "private sector." We should note, though, that the quality and standards of the polytechnic sector were intended to be comparable to those of the universities. This was an initial requirement of the CNAA charter and justified the widespread use of university academics in the peer-review processes employed by that council. (The CNAA was an independent body established by royal charter and financed by a small fee paid by or on behalf of students who received its awards.) Standards in the polytechnics were intended to be the same as those in universities. This was what the system of quality assurance was meant to achieve. At least until the end of the 1960s, the United Kingdom had a "binary elite" system: in regard to participation rates, all higher education, whatever the type of institution, constituted an elite.

In a sense, quality assurance had always been used as a prerequisite for institutional membership in the "elite club" of higher education. Most universities had served an apprenticeship under the tutelage of an established institution before they were admitted to the club. The exclusivity of the club partly justified the autonomy and prestige of its members. Quality assurance still performs that role,[11] although the club itself has lost most of its autonomy and prestige. Today, quality assurance also contributes to a much larger role in differentiating institutions within a reputational hierarchy spanning the elite, mass, and universal forms of Martin Trow's 1974 formulation.[12] Whereas quality assurance had traditionally played a unifying role, its present function had become essentially divisive.

The United Kingdom lost its binary system of higher education in 1992 when the polytechnics and some of the larger colleges were redesignated as universities. The change reflected the Conservative government's growing dissatisfaction with the "old" universities, their perceived lack of responsiveness to changing economic and social needs, their lack of accountability for the large sums of public money bestowed on them, and the suspicion that some of them contained "hotbeds" of Marxist opposition to the Thatcherite project. During the 1980s, universities saw many of their traditional autonomies eroded.[13] The University

Grants Committee—the traditional buffer organization between the universities and the state—was abolished in 1981 and replaced by the Universities Funding Council, an unambiguously state organization. This body established regular research assessment exercises (RAEs) in 1986 and oversaw a steady reduction of public funding of universities coupled with greater controls over how the funding was used. (The University Grants Committee had administered a block grant system of funding to universities, and the institutions had almost complete freedom to use the funding as they saw fit.) In regard to accountability for the teaching function, the universities—through the Committee of Vice Chancellors and Principals (CVCP)—took the "defensive" step of creating a quality assurance process through the establishment of an academic audit unit in 1987, whose main purpose was to prevent the state from establishing similar but more powerful mechanisms. The inevitable was delayed until 1992 when a system of external quality assessment of teaching was established by the new higher education funding councils (separate councils for England, Scotland, and Wales).

The point to emphasize is that quality assurance mechanisms were central to the shift in authority and control of higher education away from the universities, first to the state and more recently to the market. Although the 1992 reforms saw the creation of more than forty new universities in the United Kingdom, many perceived the reforms as being about creating new "polytechnics"—more "managed" institutions, responsive to economic requirements and less engaged in research—and the gradual establishment of a smaller elite system of "research universities" within an expanded "mass" system. Quality systems were to play a crucial role in supporting the "vertical differentiation" of the system necessary to its fulfilling both mass and elite functions simultaneously.

At the time of their demise and redesignation as universities in 1992, the polytechnics had achieved some popularity with the government and key interest groups such as employers' organizations. In part, this reflected the perception that they were under effective control and were therefore more responsive to social and economic needs. They were certainly a much cheaper form of higher education than that provided by the universities. If higher education were to expand further, it needed to follow the cost model of the polytechnics rather than that of the universities. At the same time, the differences between polytechnics and universities should not be overstated. In a large part due to the quality assurance mechanisms that had existed since their creation—the external examiner system and the Council for National Academic Awards—the polytechnics were not much different from the universities in the curricula offered to students and the standards of achievement required for a degree. That there was remarkably little controversy about their redesignation as universities is testimony to the status equivalence that they had attained by the end of the 1980s. By this time, the polytechnics and colleges had become the larger of the two sectors of higher education in the UK.

If the historical role of quality assurance had been to play down differences, starting in the 1990s it was all about creating and legitimizing them. The RAE was already demonstrating that not all universities were equivalent in research standing, and the public funding of research based on the RAE results ensured that the differences continued and, indeed, were accentuated. It also ensured that any research aspirations in the former polytechnics that might have been created by their redesignation as universities were kept firmly under control.

The quality assessment regime introduced in 1993 was set to create a similar reputational differentiation for teaching. The system's essential and novel feature was grading the quality of university teaching on a subject basis. Visiting teams of "peers" observed classes and met with faculty members and students to question them about their intentions and experiences. Reports of the assessments were published and contained an explicit statement of "relative" quality, initially on a three-point scale—excellent, satisfactory, and unsatisfactory—then later on a twenty-four-point scale based on six separate dimensions of teaching quality. Rankings and league tables followed, although the assessment agencies never published them. The national newspapers were left to do this part of the job.

It was not just in their published and graded outputs that the quality assessment system of the 1990s differed from its predecessors. Although nominally based on a system of "peer review," its features were very different from the system operated by the Council for National Academic Awards in the polytechnics. Whereas the latter was firmly under academic control through an elaborate system of committees made up of experienced academics from both university and polytechnic sectors, in the new quality assessment arrangements, academics were effectively the "hired help" of the administrators who organized the assessment process. In the new system, the peer assessors had to be "trained" (in order to understand the criteria they should use in the assessment process and also how they should behave during that process). They also were paid for their services, reflecting the contractual nature of their role. (A decent meal or two were the only "rewards" for being part of the old CNAA system.) Perhaps a fundamental difference was that much of the time spent during assessments was devoted to the observation of teaching (a feature that was totally absent from the CNAA process). Collegial conversations over a single day were replaced by three-day "inspections" of teaching practice. Confidential discursive reports were replaced by public gradings of quality.

These radical changes in quality assessment processes reflected a sea change in the relations between the universities and the state and wider society. In many ways, they reflected a new sense of the universities' importance that was to be underlined by their further expansion during the 1990s. Their contribution to the public good required that they respond to public need, first as interpreted by the state but increasingly as interpreted by the market. This implied a shift in the locus of authority from inside the universities to the world outside them.

These arrangements were the focus of continuing "quality wars" during the 1990s. While the main protagonists were the universities and the state, each had their own allies, agendas (hidden and public), and supporters. A messy compromise between a subject-based quality assessment system operated by the funding councils and a continuing academic audit process operated by the institutionally owned Higher Education Quality Council continued until the late 1990s when the two systems were merged, and a single, nominally independent, quality assurance agency was created. In reality, the agency was owned by the institutions but took its orders from the funding councils. Research assessment remained the direct responsibility of the funding councils.

The most recent evolution of the UK's quality assessment regime has been the replacement of the peer review of teaching by an annual student satisfaction survey. All final-year students complete a questionnaire, and the results are published. League tables are constructed. The market has arrived. The underlying belief—central to other areas of public service under Tony Blair's government—is that informed consumer choice is essential to driving up quality and standards. The satisfaction levels of existing consumers should be conveyed to prospective consumers, who will draw the obvious conclusions, and their resulting decisions on university applications will force the universities to improve their quality if they are to survive in an increasingly competitive marketplace. (There is plenty of evidence, however, that students decide on where they want to study for all sorts of reasons and are hardly affected by this student survey information.)

Table 13.1 shows the twenty-year evolution of quality assurance arrangements in the UK and the changing power relationships underlying them. It should be remembered, though, that new arrangements never wholly replace those that preceded them. External examiners continue to ply their trade. The CNAA's culture and processes are much in evidence in the former polytechnics. Open warfare may have gone underground in the UK quality wars. No clear

Table 13.1 Changes in Quality Assurance Arrangements and Their
Power Relationships

Phase 1: Academic authority	External examiners, CNAA
Phase 2: Managerial authority	Institutional audit
Phase 3: State authority	Quality assessment, RAE
Phase 4: Consumer authority	National student survey, teaching quality information

winner can yet be discerned. But the important change is that whereas at the start of the process, quality mechanisms were about ensuring that quality and standards were broadly the same, they now are about demonstrating that they are different.

In this "underground war," different higher education groups (managers, faculty, etc.) may try to subvert the policy intentions of quality assessment in order to achieve their own goals, which generally pertain to change or resistance to it. Current arrangements for the quality assurance of teaching that emphasize the importance of effective institutional procedures and codes of practice tend to favor the interests of centrally placed managers and administrators within the institution, although in some subject areas the existence of professional accreditation partially redresses the balance. Conversely, research assessment, with its main focus on peer-reviewed academic production, tends to favor the interests of faculty members. There are, however, considerable differences among types of institution—and, indeed, among individual institutions—in the precise ways in which quality processes affect local power games.

There also are, of course, important questions to be asked about how much the "game" actually influences the processes and experiences of education. Does it change what is learned and how learning takes place? Phase 1 in table 13.1 emphasizes conformity to subject-based professional authority, arguably conservative and consensual. Phase 2 is likely to be bureaucratic and procedural, affecting the lives of academics rather than students, tending to be about rules, codes, and procedures. Phase 3 brings in the "public good," concern about society's return on its investment and may involve higher education headed toward economic benefit and/or social equity. This could affect the content of higher education, for example, benchmarks and employability. Phase 4 takes this one step further with consumers' and market notions of the public good replacing state authority. It may place positional advantage in a pole position, emphasize vertical rather than horizontal differentiation, and impact on individual academics in relation to issues like "service standards" and pedagogical training.

THE EVOLVING QUALITY ASSURANCE DISPENSATION IN SOUTH AFRICA

A single national quality assurance system for all higher education institutions in South Africa came into being as part of education reform in the political transition to a democratic dispensation in 1994. The new quality evaluation system was one of three steering mechanisms used by the state (together with planning and funding) to reconfigure higher education to be more responsive to the social and economic needs of an emerging democracy. The Higher Education Quality Committee (HEQC) was established in 2001 as part of an independent statutory body (the Council on Higher Education), which also advises the minister of education on higher education. The quality agency started its work in a highly consultative mode, seeking to ensure the widespread involvement of senior administrators and academics in the development and implementation of the new evaluation system. Coming rather late into the world of formal quality assurance, the agency sought positive and negative lessons about quality assurance from both the developing and the developed world (including the United Kingdom). At the same time, it paid close attention to the requirements of local context, concentrating on quality-related capacity development in the face of apartheid quality deficits and signaling its intention to link its evaluation requirements to social transformation within higher education.

Its statutory mandate for both institutional audits and program accreditation gave it a huge reach into institutional and academic life. Still in its first decade of work when external quality assurance in the UK was already in its fourth decade, it had to address inherited differences in quality that were part of the apartheid exclusionary legacy, as well as the binary divide between universities and vocational training institutions (*technikons*). It also had to deal with quality compromises showing up in the post-1994 period as a result of entrepreneurial responsiveness and uncontrolled growth on the part of some institutions, a small but growing private provider sector of uneven quality, and the struggles of recently merged institutions to create new academic identities and systems. Facilitating access to acceptable levels of quality, especially for the disadvantaged majority black population, became an important objective of the new evaluation regime, an objective leading it to link its work to social justice imperatives in the post-apartheid restructuring of higher education. This meant that the establishment and comparability of at least minimum standards of quality across the system were principal political and academic goals in the larger policy project of constructing a single, integrated, higher education system in the country.

Before the HEQC was created, various quality assurance arrangements for different sectors were in place, few of which involved the government directly. This left the higher education institutions largely in control of academic matters in what would be the equivalent of phase 1 of the British system, dominated by "subject-based professional authority." This "freedom" was, nevertheless, framed by the values and agendas of the apartheid state. It included racially and ethnically based higher education institutions, segregated classes, curricula, and worldviews complicit or coexistent with apartheid ideology, security surveillance and harassment of staff and students, international academic isolation, censorship of books and academic materials, and both acquiescence and resistance to apartheid. All this gave texture to the existing regulatory framework and inevitably shaped the meanings, practices, and possibilities of quality within a fragmented and stratified higher education system. Despite the apartheid mythology of "separate but equal," there was little doubt that the fragmented system was academically unequal, unevenly capacitated, and differentially funded and with a variety of quality assurance arrangements in place across the racial divide as well as between the university and technikon sectors.

A few historically advantaged universities were research-intensive institutions, with the other universities and technikons functioning mainly as teaching institutions. No RAE type of system was in place. Funding for research and teaching in public higher education came mainly from government, usually in the form of block grants with little earmarking. Community service, the third core function of higher education, was variously interpreted by different universities and did not operate under any regulatory framework or subsidy-funding arrangement.

The universities had the greatest measure of freedom from formal statutory evaluations, with voluntary, peer-based systems as the model in cases in which external evaluation was used. For a brief period between 1996 and 1998, the universities had a system of voluntary institutional audits, using collegial peer review for quality improvement and the dissemination of good practices. The system was based on the view that "ownership of the quality assurance systems should rest with the universities rather than with the government or an independent body."[14] Its work was, nevertheless, beset with disagreements about its quality findings and soon came to an end. In fields like engineering, statutory professional councils had responsibility for ensuring program quality, setting requirements for practitioner registration but sometimes also scrutinizing curricula and examinations. The technikons had less academic autonomy than the universities and were evaluated formally by a statutory body established in 1986. The evaluation system was linked to state funding and drew on expertise from technikon peers, industry representatives, and representatives from relevant professional councils. As in the United Kingdom, an external examiner system was in place in some parts of the system, but it was often voluntary and ad hoc.

Mobility across institutions and institutional sectors was limited, given the concerns among historically advantaged universities about the quality and standards of qualifications from technikons and historically black institutions. The prevailing (often unstated) perception was that quality was clearly and uniformly high at historically white institutions and doubtful at best at the other institutions. These claims of good and poor quality were never formally validated by any external evaluation system. In 1997, new legislation laid the basis for a nonracial dispensation in higher education, followed in 2004 by the ending of the binary divide and the redesignation of the technikons as universities of technology. In the construction of a new national evaluation system, the issue of building and demonstrating the equivalence and comparability of quality and standards across the different institutions and sectors, amid the legacies of the racial and binary landscape, was a major challenge.

This account demonstrates that as the apartheid era was drawing to a close, higher education institutions, especially the universities, enjoyed a large measure of institutional autonomy in relation to academic matters. They had control over new program and qualification offerings, syllabi, examination and certification systems, student fee levels, arrangements for quality assurance and reaccreditation, and the utilization of research funds. This was accompanied by a loosening of racial controls that brought significant numbers of black students to formerly white higher education institutions. Analysts[15] have pointed to the ironies of a situation in which until the mid-1990s, the apartheid struggle kept higher education in South Africa fairly insulated from the impact of many neoliberal restructuring policies, which had greatly changed the values and power relations between government and higher education in many countries since the Thatcher-era policies in the United Kingdom. Overall, the higher education system bore the legacies of racial advantage and exclusion. It was a spectrum that, at one end, had a cluster of "elite" research institutions; in the middle, a number of predominantly teaching institutions; and, at the other end, institutions offering greater mass access but, in many instances, with faltering academic and financial viability. The disparities in access, quality, and reputation across the different subsectors were academically as well as politically unacceptable, making almost inevitable wide-ranging state policy directives to reconfigure higher education.

Between the end of apartheid and the effective implementation of new regulatory mechanisms by government, the market gained a more visible presence in higher education. A number of public institutions responded to increasing "consumer" demands by expanding their program profiles in search of new student markets, often without the requisite capacity and quality safeguards in place. The decline in state subsidy income in real terms, increasing levels of student debt, the pressure to be more socially responsive, the entrepreneurial search for new student and research product markets, and a still fluid regulatory regime all led higher education institutions to turn to the market in the search for nontraditional students and third-stream income. The number of private providers also grew, up to three hundred, often targeting students who did not have the necessary admission requirements for higher education. Unlike the UK, the turn to the market was not yet directly sponsored by the state but occurred in a regulatory vacuum, which was soon addressed by the education authorities. The legacies of the apartheid past, combined with a veritable explosion of free-ranging higher education responsiveness in the 1990s, set the scene for a new regulatory regime that was more explicitly directive of academe, certainly in comparison to what had been in place before. The regulatory shift changed the power balance from academe to the state and the intermediary bodies established by it while at the same time reining in the free-for-all market responsiveness of the higher education institutions.

The beginning of the new political dispensation saw the development of policy frameworks and regulatory instruments that were intended to align all areas of social provision with the new democracy's values and goals. At the start of the HEQC's work, there was a consensus on the broad values and principles that underpinned the restructuring of higher education amid the general recognition of the necessity of reform. This consensus made the introduction of formal external evaluation less overtly contested by the institutions. These principles included enhanced equitable access, especially for black and women students, redress for the previously disadvantaged, and greater responsiveness to social and economic development priorities through new research themes, new programs and curricula, and new relationships with social partners. Forging a relationship between social justice and efficiency goals had been a challenge to regulatory policy and practice right from the start, especially in building common benchmarks for quality across different higher education sectors. Many of the restructuring goals had to be pursued at a time when the pressures of a globalizing market-friendly world were impinging strongly on the domestic reform agenda, limiting and reshaping the reconstructive ambitions of the state in ways that made the achievement of social justice more ambivalent and the strategies to get there more contested.[16]

South Africa's higher education policy framework and implementation plan after 1994 ended the era of relatively free institutional decision making and almost unqualified academic sovereignty by laying down statutory requirements for system-level and institutional planning, funding, student enrollments, and program scope and quality, many of which previously had been decided internally. The introduction of the new South African quality assurance system coincided with the implementation of an ambitious, state-driven restructuring plan for higher education. To transcend the apartheid landscape in higher education, government reduced the number of public institutions from thirty-six to twenty-two through compulsory mergers and incorporations that cut across historically advantaged and disadvantaged institutions (although some historically advantaged institutions were left intact), abolishing the binary divide and creating comprehensive institutions to offer both general and vocational programs. The government set targets for undergraduate and postgraduate enrollments in different science domains in order to increase the numbers of black and women students and graduates in fields like science, engineering, and technology; put in place a more explicit performance- and output-driven funding formula; and regulated the mix of programs and qualifications in each institution in order to create a more coherent landscape out of the system's duplication, wastage, and uneven quality. The state-driven reconfiguration of public higher education was accompanied by a corresponding regulatory intervention in private provision, reducing the sector from three hundred to one hundred providers, requiring them to be registered by government and accredited by the HEQC, and preventing them from calling themselves universities.

In a succession of far-reaching regulatory demands, especially on public higher education, two kinds of concerns emerged. One was that in higher education, state interventions had come close to interference in many instances (with accompanying dangers for academic freedom and institutional autonomy).[17] The other was that the neoliberal values of cost-efficiencies and output-driven conditionalities were threatening the social justice agenda in higher education reform.[18] How did this reflect on the quality agency, which had entered what had been previously been almost the sole domain of institutional and academic decision making? Complaints about the onerousness of the evaluation system, concerns about the inclusion of social transformation in quality issues, and criticisms about its usefulness to actual quality improvement coexisted with acknowledgment of the strong involvement of academic peers, the agency's programs for capacity development and quality improvement, and the benefits of positive first-cycle attention to quality issues by academics and administrators alike. The current absence of open and deeply divisive "quality wars" may, however, not hold in the next quality cycle, depending on how the quality regime evolves and the changing power relations become clearer.

The state's entry into quality assurance signaled a new era characterized by the reshaping of academic sovereignty by formal stipulations of public accountability. Although the new evaluative arrangements drew strongly on peer review and emphasized academically driven quality improvement, it was clear that public accountability demands were becoming more insistent, invoked at different levels by the state as well as by institutional managers. The role of institutional managers in interpreting and setting quality requirements is, as in the case of the UK, clearly mediating the messages and impact of the external agency. This is already becoming a new "battle line" in some institutions. The reconceptualization of academic authority in response to post-apartheid demands for new forms of public responsiveness from higher education in the social reconstruction was, in many respects, unavoidable. The expansion of social and political freedoms in a new democratic society saw academic freedom enshrined in the country's constitution but circumscribed by discourses and practices linked to the notion of democratic accountability. The role of evaluation systems in reconfiguring academic freedoms and sovereignties while facilitating required forms of democratic accountability is an issue that still awaits greater conceptual clarification as well as fuller empirical investigations in South Africa and beyond. We could argue that in South Africa, the premises and goals of the current evaluation approach might hold the potential to connect social justice imperatives with quality issues. This approach also carries many risks for achieving an appropriate balance among new public accountabilities, necessary academic autonomies, and genuine quality improvement. The risks are likely to be exacerbated if the notion of the public orientation of higher education grows increasingly impoverished through the ascendancy of narrow, market-driven goals of efficiency and performativity and if the evaluation technologies themselves begin to subvert broader social and academic objectives.

As in many countries, the role of higher education institutions in South Africa has assumed heightened social and economic importance, given the knowledge and human resource needs of a massive social reconstruction agenda. The demands of social accountability and the orientation of higher education more explicitly toward public needs have emerged as distinct themes in the changing relationship between the state and higher education in the construction of a more inclusive and diverse society. Quality assurance is one of the areas where, despite the widespread involvement of academics, the authority of the state (through the intermediary agency) has been asserted over academic authority in defining and setting the parameters for new forms of public orientation and social accountability of higher education. The protagonists are the state and the higher education institutions. The battle line is the extent to which the institutions and academics will be full partners in the construction of publicly accountable institutions or whether they will simply be implementers within state-set parameters and increasingly directive state strategies. In the quality assurance regime's mix of academic, managerial, and state authority, academic authority is the most vulnerable, exacerbated by academic compliance and insufficient academic mobilization.

The facilitation of consumer choice is not yet an overarching, state-driven strategy in higher education. The quality agency has indicated that in the current cycle, it is not in favor of ranking institutions, although the local media have been ranking programs like the MBA. Some of the research-intensive institutions have indicated their ambition to get into or improve their positions in global-ranking systems. The HEQC publishes only executive summaries of its findings, urges institutions to themselves make full reports available to their multiple publics, and has started a quality literacy campaign to make students more aware of quality issues. There are as yet no national student satisfaction surveys with published findings. The market may become more powerful in the second cycle of external quality assurance. For now, the social justice imperative to make access to quality education in every part of the higher education system is a dominant value in the evaluation regime. The evaluation systems still must ensure that quality and standards, at least at minimum levels, are broadly equivalent in all the subsectors of higher education in order to transcend the perverse quality differences of the apartheid past. In the evolution of the quality regime and the changing relationships among the protagonists, many struggles lie ahead. Prominent among them is holding on to the social justice imperatives in the "quality wars" that may come, as well as negotiating a substantial presence and role for academic authority in defining and implementing multiple forms of social accountability for higher education.

CONCLUDING REFLECTIONS

The two case studies provide instructive insights into the roles, purposes, and impacts of quality evaluation regimes in different contexts. The differences in the two systems pertain to imperatives of political history, chosen evaluation purposes, and the respective stages of systems development. The creation of "quasi markets" by the state, the power of consumer choice, the pressures of national and global reputational competitiveness, and increasing institutional differentiation are strong features of the UK system. In South Africa, just over a decade and a half after apartheid, the struggle to hold on to a social justice agenda within quality assurance continues, in addition to other, more conventional evaluation objectives. The process, nevertheless, reflects the increasing strain in holding together an acceptable balance between state interventions on behalf of social transformation, the legitimate claims of academic authority and institutional autonomy, and the increasing weight of financial, market, and reputational pressures.

Three issues emerge from our analysis of the two case studies: (1) the role and implications of quality regimes in demonstrating equivalence or difference within higher education; (2) the quality regimes' role and impact on the changing power relationships between the state and higher education and among internal higher education stakeholders; and (3) the role of evaluation systems in shaping the public orientation of higher education. The first relates to the shift in the UK from the role of quality evaluation in demonstrating "sameness" in quality across all of higher education in the country until the early 1990s to its role in demonstrating differences within reputational hierarchies from 1993 onward. In South Africa, quality assurance is still focused on quality equivalences, at least at the level of minimum standards, across the higher education system because of the importance of equity and redress in both its political and educational dimensions. The evaluation processes, however, cannot avoid exposing the stark differences in quality across the system. In addition, the overall policy framework provides for the creation of a more integrated as well as a more differentiated higher education system. It is perhaps only a matter of time before institutions locate themselves in more formalized reputational hierarchies alongside or in place of the current informal ones. It remains to be seen whether in a new configuration of elite and mass elements in the higher education system, the purposes of quality assurance in South Africa will change to the UK trajectory of demonstrating differences over and above broad quality equivalences.

At the institutional and system levels in many countries, quality assurance is increasingly playing a differentiating role. Higher education courses, institutions, and individual academics are "not all the same," and the "differences" among them need to be given increasing visibility. This is partly to do with the maintenance of both elite and mass functions of higher education, but it also has much to do with neoliberalism and its obsession with choice and competition. International league tables and rankings are only the most visible part of this move toward the differentiation of higher education and its legitimization in quality measures. We need to investigate whether reputational, market, and financial pressures create "inevitable" trajectories in quality assurance regimes from early emphases on quality equivalence to later pressures to demonstrate quality differences or whether different political values and choices and stronger academic power could provide alternative possibilities.

The second issue concerns the changes fostered by quality regimes in the power relationships between the state and academe and within higher education institutions. The literature on the politics of quality assurance shows this to be a familiar and almost inevitable dimension of quality assurance regulation in the different higher education systems across the world. Despite arm's length and intermediary regulation, there is little doubt that evaluation systems are tipping the balance away from academe toward external stakeholders. The power of these stakeholders has been reinforced by state policy frameworks setting the parameters for the social purposes of higher education. The changed relationships are not necessarily uniform, predictable, or fixed across different contexts. They often are mediated by the intermediary agencies, their evaluation systems and reporting lines to the state, the power of different stakeholders, the links to funding, and so forth. What is clear, however, is that the discourse of public accountability as articulated in higher education and quality assurance systems has resulted in the restructuring of state/higher education relationships in ways that have opened up higher education to external scrutiny and judgment. The terms of such restructured relationships often have had the effect of disempowering academe.

Changes in relations of power are not confined to the nexus between state and higher education. The strategic preparations for external evaluations and the reputational and resourcing weight of the outcomes of evaluation also have made deep inroads into institutions' traditional teaching and research structures and have altered the relationships among internal role-players. This is evident in both the UK and South Africa and also has been documented in some of the literature on evaluation. Clearly, far-reaching changes within institutional relations are not due solely to the preparations for external quality assurance but are part of a larger set of market-oriented reforms of higher education and the corporatization of higher education institutions. Notions about how quality is to be attained and demonstrated are being shaped increasingly by a layer of academic managers who, one could argue, play a double mediating role, between the state and the institution, and between the institutional management and rank-and-file academics. "Institutional leaders and managers can be considered mediators between policy and practice. In higher education systems, they can be looked upon as potential agents for change. They form the preconditions and define the space of action for academics' work and perhaps too for their norms and values."[19]

Very clearly in the United Kingdom and slowly becoming evident in South Africa, quality processes have led to the empowerment of institutions' academic administrators and middle management. Matters that traditionally had been left to the professional judgment of individual academics and the "basic units" in which they worked are now required to be institutionally managed, with an eye on the requirements and rules of external agencies and on the possible consequences of fulfilling them or breaking them. Managers can also use external quality systems as a tool or legitimizer of internally driven change: someone and something to blame when unpopular decisions are made. They can also be used to legitimize internal differentiation and the unequal treatment of different basic units and individuals. No longer are all formally equal. The "excellent" need their rewards and incentives, and the "weak" need to be brought to face the consequences of their weakness. This is also an issue that could benefit from further research investigations in different institutional and country contexts, as a way of deepening our understandings of the shifting power balances and changing academic environments produced by evaluation systems.

The third issue relates to the ways in which evaluation systems help shape the public orientation of higher education. As is clear from both the case studies, the issue of quality education is no longer solely an internal academic matter but one framed also by the needs and expectations of external stakeholders. Quality assurance regimes are helping set the parameters of the public accountability of higher education and steer the nature and extent of its public responsiveness to broader societal interests and specific stakeholder demands. What constitutes the social or public interest is itself open to stipulation by powerful role-players, including governments and intermediary bodies like quality assurance agencies. It can be defined broadly (social justice for the majority population, as in South Africa) or more specifically (consumer satisfaction, as in the United Kingdom).

The issue of how and why higher education orients itself to different publics in and through external evaluation systems is more usefully viewed as a domain of choice, contestation, and negotiation among different internal and external role-players rather than settling for a predominantly statist or market-based interpretation of the public interest. The former approach could better accommodate a more visible role for academics in helping define the different ways in which higher education and its evaluation systems could respond to and serve the broader public interest.

How far do changes in the balance of power lead to changed behaviors and values among key actors? Does quality assurance not sufficiently measure what academics consider prestigious, but only what the state finds valuable? It is difficult to generalize about this issue, although some trends can be discerned in both countries. In the South African MBA evaluation, the top university business schools were very pleased that the external evaluation exercise confirmed the quality of their MBAs and hence their reputational standing while withdrawing the accreditation of several private providers and other poor-quality public provider programs. Often a great deal depends on the substantial presence and caliber of the peers involved in the evaluations. What may also be disputed by academics is whether what is measurable (especially in a quantitative way) is central to the definition of quality.

There is likely to be a greater divergence between the state and higher education in the type and purposes of the evaluation. According to the OECD Thematic Review of Tertiary Education, there is

> a mismatch between governments' and institutions' approaches to quality assurance, with governments putting more emphasis on summative approaches while institutions have more inclination for formative approaches. On the one hand, governments aim to demonstrate to the society that they make justifiable decisions on tertiary education policy—such as the allocation of funding or termination of academic programmes. On the other hand, the main objective of institutions is quality improvement within the conditions set by government, and they aim to convince the public that the quality of their educational provision is the best possible.[20]

The belief in quality improvement may be the ideal position, but in most places it is found alongside a mixture of institutional compliance and the pursuit of reputational gain.

Both governments and academe have their own—and different—motives for "believing" the results of quality measures. For government, these provide a rational basis for decision making (top universities get a lot more public money because they are "better," not because they are "well connected") and accountability for the use of public funds. For academe, the motives of individual academics and institutions are to maximize the rewards that can flow from the quality game, whatever one thinks of the processes and evidence on which they are based. These rewards are reputational as much as they are financial. While there might be an opposing "collective" rationale that might wish to undermine the quality systems, most institutional leaders would see that as a politically risky move that could hurt higher education as a whole. The view is that it may be better to play to win by the rules rather than subvert them, whatever one thinks about them in practice. On the whole, however, it is probably largely true to say that academics have maintained relatively more control over what counts as "good research," whereas the state has had more influence over teaching—stressing skills and employability and introducing increasing client responsiveness and consumerism.

While power and differentiation may be central to understanding the role of quality processes, they should not be regarded as uncontested forces. Quality processes also must help ensure minimum threshold standards and the public protection that goes with them. When subject communities have some control over the quality exercises, they may use it to spread and enforce a standardized conception of quality and standards in their subject. In addition, the capacity of academics, individually and collectively, for resistance and subversion should not be underestimated. "Quality wars" in different forms but with similar political and educational values at stake may be expected to continue across higher education for some time to come.

NOTES

1. In 2007, the International Network of Quality Assurance Agencies in Higher Education had 189 member organizations from more than eighty countries across the globe.
2. See, for example, Martin Trow, *Managerialism and the Academic Profession: Quality and Control* (Oxford: Quality Support Centre, Oxford University Press, 1994); Guy Neave, "The Evaluative State Reconsidered," *European Journal of Education* 33, no. 3 (1998): 265–84; Marylyn Strathern, *Audit Cultures* (London: Routledge, 2000); Louise Morley, *Quality and Power in Higher Education* (Oxford: SRHE and Oxford University Press, 2003).
3. In quality assurance, for example, some South African institutions use external examiners, while the national agency carries out quality audits.

4. See, for example, Neave, "The Evaluative State Reconsidered."

5. Burton R. Clark, *The Higher Education System: Academic Organization in Cross-National Perspective* (Berkeley: University of California Press, 1983).

6. Berit Askling and Mary Henkel, "Higher Education Institutions," in *Transforming Higher Education: A Comparative Study*, ed. Maurice Kogan, Marianne Bauer, Ivar Bleiklie, and Mary Henkel (London: Jessica Kingsley, 2000), 120–21.

7. See Guy Neave, "The Temple and Its Guardians: An Excursion into the Rhetoric of Evaluating Higher Education," *Journal of Finance and Management in Colleges and Universities* 1 (2004): 211–27.

8. See Mala Singh, "Bundy Blues: Contradictions and Choices in South African Higher Education," in *Kagisano*, vol. 4 (Pretoria: Council on Higher Education, 2006); Lis Lange and Mala Singh, "Equity Issues in Quality Assurance in South African Higher Education," in *Equity and Quality: A Marriage of Two Minds*, ed. M. Martin (Paris: UNESCO / IIEP, 2010), 37–74.

9. David Dill, "The Colonel Bogey March: Roger Brown's History of the UK Quality Wars," *Higher Education Digest*, no. 49 (2004): 2–3.

10. Roger Brown, *Quality Assurance in Higher Education : The UK Experience Since 1972* (London: Routledge Falmer, 2004).

11. Approval by the national Quality Assurance Agency is prerequisite for degree-granting powers and the title of university.

12. Martin Trow, "Problems in the Transition from Elite to Mass Higher Education," in *Policies for Higher Education. General Report to the Conference on Future Structures and Post-Secondary Education* (Paris: OECD, 1974).

13. Kogan et al., *Transforming Higher Education*; Peter Scott, *The Meanings of Mass Higher Education* (Buckingham: Open University Press, 1993).

14. Council on Higher Education, *Evaluation of SERTEC and QPU* (Pretoria: Council on Higher Education, 2000), 23.

15. See, for example, Colin Bundy, "Global Patterns, Local Options? Changes in Higher Education Internationally and Some Implications for South Africa" in *Kagisano*, vol. 4 (Pretoria: Council on Higher Education, 2006), 9. Lange points out that the post-apartheid "grand narratives of rights and social justice also helped to mediate the impact of neo-liberalism in South African higher education in the early days of the transition. See Lis Lange, "'Symbolic Policy and 'Performativity': South African Higher Education Between the Devil and the Deep Blue Sea," in *Kagisano*, vol. 4 (Pretoria: Council on Higher Education, 2006), 44.

16. Peter Maassen and Nico Cloete, "Global Reform Trends in Higher Education," in *Transformation in Higher Education: Global Pressures and Local Realities*, ed. Nico Cloete et al. (Dordrecht: Springer, 2006), 12.

17. See Council on Higher Education, *Academic Freedom, Institutional Autonomy and Public Accountability in South African Higher Education* (Pretoria: Council on Higher Education, HEIAAF no. 5, 2008), 2.

18. See Bundy, "Global Patterns, Local Options?"

19. Kogan et al., *Transforming Higher Education*, 109.

20. OECD Thematic Review of Tertiary Education, 2008, available at www.oecd.org/edu/tertiary/review, p. 37 (accessed December 5, 2008).

The Academic Workplace | **FOURTEEN**

What We Already Know

What We Still Do Not Know,

and What We Would Like to Know

CHRISTINE MUSSELIN

In this chapter, my aim is not to analyze the academic workplace and its transformation but to review the existing literature and suggest new research perspectives. Because of the many publications on the academic profession, I have chosen a representative, but not extensive, review of the field and have organized the literature according to two main perspectives. The first consists of the research on the structure, composition, description, and analysis of the academic profession and/or academic labor markets in different countries. Most of the works I studied concern the academic profession in the Europe and North America. The second perspective deals with academic activities, the conditions under which they are produced, how they are assessed, and what they produce. Last, I focus on issues not addressed by the two first perspectives but seem relevant to understanding the academic profession in public institutions, its evolution, and its forthcoming developments.

DIFFERENT COUNTRIES, DIFFERENT ACADEMIC PROFESSIONS, BUT SOME COMMON TRENDS

Most of the publications on the academic workplace describe the specific situations of the academic profession in different countries, with some of them (the

United States and, to a lesser extent, certain European countries, such as the United Kingdom and Germany) covered more extensively than others. Many recent publications combine country reports into specific regions of the world and outline the main convergences and/or divergences as well as the relevant developments during the last decades. Even if these publications often juxtapose national situations rather than truly compare them, they provide information that helps identify the main trends.

Comparing National Settings to Identify Common Trends

Recent comparative contributions (the special issue of *Higher Education* directed by Philip Altbach and Richard Chait, the book published by Jürgen Ender on European countries, the book coordinated by Altbach on the academic profession in middle-income and developing countries, and the book edited by Altbach and Damtew Teferra on Africa) all lead to rather similar conclusions, despite the strong Euro–North American bias.[1]

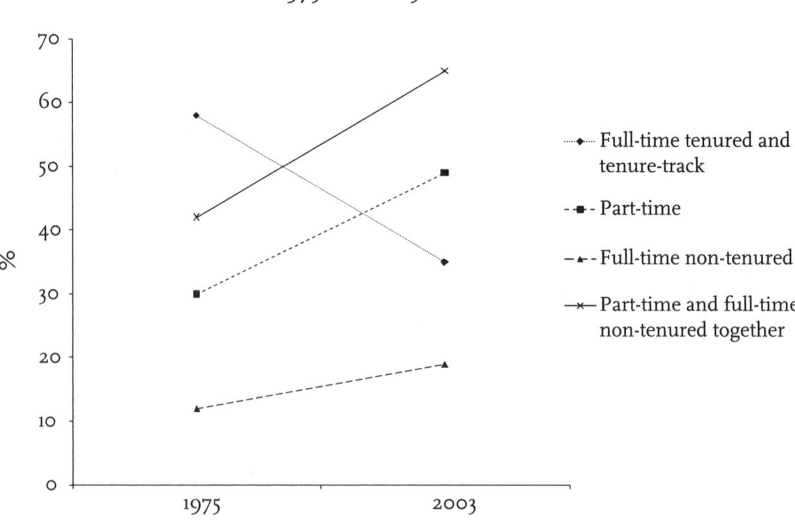

Figure 14.1 Evolution Between 1975 and 2003 in the United States
Source: Author's elaboration based on Ronald G. Ehrenberg, "The Changing Nature of the Faculty and Faculty Employment Practices" (unpublished manuscript, Cornell Higher Education Research Institute, 2005).

Most of these publications show that the academic profession is waning and is facing great changes. The increase in casual positions is easy to document and quantify.[2] The United States is probably the best documented on this issue and shows spectacular transformations. Figure 14.1 shows the dramatic change in the composition of "the American faculty."[3]

This same trend is mentioned in almost all country reports that the proportion of tenure-track positions in the overall academic population is declining.[4] In a comparative report written by David Robinson on higher education teaching personnel in five English-speaking countries, he estimates that in Australia, the number of so-called casual positions more than doubled between 1990 and 2001 but that the number of full-time and part-time positions remained unchanged. Thus, casual positions now account for 20 percent of total academic employment, compared with 9 percent in 1990. In Canada, estimations show a decline in the number of full-time faculty by 7.5 percent between 1990 and 1997, and the number of part-time positions increased by about 10 percent. New Zealand's Association of University Staff estimated that 25 to 30 percent of its academic staff had fixed-term appointments. Both the number of fixed-term contracts and part-time staff rose, with fixed-term contracts representing 39 percent of the academic staff in 1994 and 44.8 percent in 2003, and part-time staff representing about 12 percent in 1995, rising to nearly 18 percent in 2002.[5]

Over the same period, the total number of academic staff generally increased, which had two other impacts. First, what was previously considered a "normal career path" became more an exception, since casual positions do not always become permanent or tenure-track positions; rather, they tend to become a labor market on their own. Second, the varying status among academics is increasing because the employment of casual staff generally is less regulated and less normalized and is governed by local rules. In positions such as research assistants, postdocs, and adjuncts, I found a variety of status, employment contracts, work contents (some specializing in teaching, others in research, and even some in administration), and duties.[6] According to Jürgen Enders, one of the three major trends in higher education systems today is heterogenization, which directly affects academic staff through the increase in casual personnel.[7]

Closely associated with this first trend is the growing share of female academics. Even though their access to the academic profession almost everywhere has improved, the academic workforce nevertheless remains dominated by males (see table 14.1).[8] The number of women holding casual positions is higher than the number of women holding permanent positions.[9] For instance, women held more than 55 percent of casual positions in Australia in 2003[10] and 45 percent

Table 14.1 Percentage of Women Among Academic Staff

Australia[a]	Canada[a]	New Zealand[a]	UK[a]	USA[a]	France[b]	Germany[c]	Japan[d]	India[e]
36	30	36.6	35	40	31.6	17.5	11.6	17

Notes:

[a] For full-time faculty in 2003, see David Robinson, "The Status of Higher Education Teaching Personnel in Australia, Canada, New Zealand, the United Kingdom and the United States" (paper presented at the International Higher Education and Research Conference, Melbourne, December 2005).

[b] Note d'information MEN, 2005, available at ftp://trf.education.gouv.fr/pub/edutel/dpd/ni/ni2005/ ni0535.pdf (accessed March 24, 2010).

[c] My own estimates, from various sources.

[d] For all Japanese R&D staff,, see http://www.stat.go.jp/english/data/kagaku/1531.htm (accessed March 24, 2010).

[e] For universities, see N. Jayaram, "The Fall of the Guru: The Decline of the Academic Profession in India," in Philip G. Altbach (Ed.) *The Decline of the Guru: The Academic Profession in Developing and Middle-Income Countries*, ed. Philip G. Altbach (New York: Palgrave Macmillan, 2003), 199–230.

Source: Author's elaboration based on data from Schuster and Finkelstein, *The American Faculty*.

of part-time instructors in the United States in 1992, as opposed to 33 percent of full-time faculty.[11] Women also had less prestigious careers, advanced more slowly than men did,[12] and earned less than men on average. In addition, disciplines employing higher proportions of women offered lower wages in countries where salaries were negotiated at the institutional level.[13] Among the reasons for these discrepancies may be "voluntary" discrimination[14] or nonconscious, or indirect,[15] discrimination, leading to lower salaries and fewer promotions, everything else held constant.[16] Another reason may be the lower productivity of women compared with men, but this, too, can be interpreted in various ways.[17] Some explanations emphasize women's lower productivity because they spend more time on family and domestic duties; their attitudes toward their career and professional success might be colored by their cultural environment;[18] or they prefer topics or activities (like teaching) that are less highly regarded in the academic sphere.[19] Other critics deny (or downplay) the role of social factors and instead stress institutional obstacles such as hiring barriers, women's lack of mentors, gendered allocation of work, and the poor match between the timing of academic careers and the timing of maternity.[20]

Another important trend is the threat to "permanent" positions, that is, positions held by civil servants or those protected by tenure or leading to tenure. These positions have always been criticized,[21] but now they have led to the implementation of new practices. Sometimes permanent positions are maintained, but the terms of employment are renegotiated[22] to include, for instance, post-tenure reviews.[23] Some countries have limited or redefined permanence, either by suppressing the notion of tenure (in the United Kingdom) or by deciding that newcomers to the professoriate will not be civil servants but private employees (as in Austria or Japan).[24]

Yet another change concerns the development of institutional management that expands along with and supersedes academic (i.e., professional) self-regulation and therefore interferes with it. Some writers have depicted academics as "managed professionals," using terms like "academic workers" or "knowledge workers" to describe the increase in control over academic activities and the standardization and rationalization of teaching and research exercised by higher education institutions.[25] All this is related to the "restructuring" of academic work.[26]

Last but not least, the academic profession has lost some of its prestige. The opening up of the profession following the greater access to higher education has led not only to a decline in the profession (as Altbach stressed in the 1980s)[27] but also to a "more rapid loss of status that in the past" and "related losses of income,"[28] which David Robinson pointed out in the five countries he studied.[29] In some countries (particularly those where the academic profession is regulated by the state), this applies to the whole profession,[30] whereas in those countries where employment arrangements are regulated by institutions, widening discrepancies can be observed among disciplines.[31] Garry Rhoades and Sheila Slaughter, for instance, concluded that salary discrepancies by field and gender are extensive, with some disciplines having both low salaries and little support.[32] Ronald G. Ehrenberg, Marquise McGraw, and Jesenka Mrdjenovic wrote that "the average salary of full professors in economics relative to the average salary of full professors in English language and literature at these institutions grew from 114 percent in 1985/1986 to 128 percent in 2001/2002."[33]

These issues and trends can be found around the world and therefore also affect the developing and middle-income countries. According to Philip Altbach, this generalized evolution is linked to the fact that universities in industrialized countries set the patterns for all countries.[34] Developing countries are therefore in a world of "peripherality" or, to put it more crudely, in a situation of dependence on resources, importation of knowledge, access to technologies, attractiveness, value setting, and the like.[35] As a result, the academic profession in those countries is the same as the academic profession in the industrialized countries writ large: "There are more part-time staff. Full professors have less clear job security and sometimes insecure terms of appointment. They are not as well qualified, and they come from more modest backgrounds. . . . [M]assification has meant that qualifications have not kept up with the need for more teachers."[36]

Moreover, academics are mainly teachers, with research and service a minor or negligible part of their work.

The recent expansion and success of Indian and Chinese higher education nevertheless reveal some current and profound transformations of the world situation. A reframing of the traditional North-South divide may be expected with the constitution of multiple (rather than a single) centers of excellence.[37] But the gap between regions of the world growing economically, scientifically, and technologically, on the one hand, and those regions of the world whose academics are left out, on the other hand, will probably increase.

Limits and "Shadow" Issues

Despite the huge literature on the structure of the academic profession and its evolution, some issues have not yet been adequately addressed. The first issue is measuring this evolution over time within a single country and between countries. Only a few dimensions (such as the percentage of women or the number of casual staff) have been measured. Despite the usual claim that times used to be better, publications from the 1960s reveal very pessimistic views of the development of the academic profession even at that time. Even though the 1960s were often presented as "the triumph of the academic man,"[38] some writers in the 1970s began to develop more critical views, describing the change and turmoil for academics in industrialized countries. For instance, Philip Altbach's conclusions in 1980, in an article entitled "The Crisis of the Professoriate," are very close to those of the current literature, and the driving forces (or explanatory factors) he lists also are similar to those of today.[39] According to Altbach, the academic profession was already facing major changes owing to causes such as the greater number of students; the increasing pressure for more accountability and responsiveness;[40] the decline of the community caused by the diversification of the profession; the institutional reforms of the 1970s and their threat to professors' power; retrenchment policies concerning academic positions; the critics of academic freedom and tenure; and the advancement toward more "hierarchy" in the academic system. There is, however, one main difference from the current situation: in the 1970s, the increase in accountability and responsiveness was interpreted as a consequence of the rising share of public funding in university budgets.

Only a few years later (1986), the plea addressed by Eugene R. Rice for an adjustment of the assumptive world in which academics were said to be still living also points to the major transformations in American higher education through the introduction of a managerial culture in universities.[41]

We therefore should be more cautious about our assessment of change and improve our analytical tools to empirically "measure" what is stable and what is changing and how and where, in order to control the bias introduced by the myth of the "golden age" and the shadows it has cast on the problems of the past.[42]

Another issue insufficiently addressed by the literature on the structure of the academic profession concerns what has been called the "invisible"[43] or "shadow" workforce.[44] Again, the academic profession is currently described as losing permanent positions and gaining casual staff.[45] But with the exception of some North American studies, we lack descriptions and analyses of those working in this "secondary academic labor market," that is, the nonpermanent, non-tenure-track positions. They still constitute a "shadow" population for researchers: Information about their salaries, their employment conditions, their trajectories, their demographic characteristics (age, gender, nationality), their social background, the way they are managed, their activities, and their professional identity all is scarce and is the main subject of only a few works. Those studies that do exist all come from the United States or Canada, but even these offer incomplete information, mostly because of the diversity of status and because their hiring and employment conditions are informal departmental affairs not coordinated at the institutional level. Therefore, these data rely on nationwide faculty surveys and do not contain very recent figures. These two countries also seem to have more information about part-time faculty than other temporary positions. In the United States, for instance, besides Judith M. Gappa and David W. Leslie's book on part-time faculty based on the 1988 National Survey of Postsecondary Faculty,[46] there is a more recent study based on the 1993 National Survey,[47] and a newer book based on the 1998 National Survey.[48] But comparable information about adjuncts is lacking. Among the most recent publications, I found only the study by Daniel C. Feldman and William H. Turnley, which shows the relative deprivation of adjunct faculty in a large public university and documents its effect on job satisfaction, professional commitment, the performance of organizational citizenship behavior, careerist attitudes toward work, and job searches.[49] More broadly, issues such as the ability of part-timers or adjuncts to graduate from secondary (temporary positions) to the primary (tenured or tenure-track positions) academic labor market or the nonacademic job market have not been studied sufficiently. In the 1990s, Gerald Rosenblum and Barbara Rubin Rosenblum concluded (from research based on Canadian universities) that secondary labor market appointees were an important pool for the recruitment of permanent faculty,[50] but more recent work indicates that this probably is no longer true.[51] As a whole, however, such studies are rare and even nonexistent for many countries, thus preventing any kind of comparison.[52] We need to know more about this increasing sector of the academic profession.

Another shadow aspect of the academic profession, even if less crucial to understanding the current changes, concerns faculty members as citizens or private persons. Here we find a great contrast with the literature on students. Students are considered as a subcategory of youth, and there is much published on their attitudes and behaviors toward political parties, associated activities, family, consumption, hobbies, jobs, religions, and so forth. Similar data about academic staff are rare, however, with the exception of the United States.[53] Altbach has some comparative information about professors and politics, but we do not know who the academics are; how they differ from or are similar to other segments of the population; and how they differ from one country to another.[54] For example, how do those working as adjunct staff in teaching institutions, private universities, and industrialized countries differ in age, gender, party affiliation, lifestyle, social background, and so on from those working in permanent positions in research universities, public institutions, and developing countries? After the academic profession opened up, have the lifestyles of academic staff become more similar to that of the average citizen than they were previously, or are they still different? Are the differences among academics greater than among other parts of the population? In other words, who are academics? How do they feel about being an academic nowadays?

ACADEMICS AT WORK: PARTIAL VIEWS TO BE COMPLETED

Another fundamental perspective in the existing literature about the academic workplace concerns academic activities and how they are rewarded.

Analyzing Academic Activities

In many countries, the interaction between teaching and research is said to be crucial to the development of contemporary higher education institutions, but analyses of academic work rarely consider both activities simultaneously. That is, researchers in sociology and the anthropology of science study research activities and usually ignore other academic tasks. And those interested in teaching at higher education institutions concentrate on training and neglect the research component.

The divide between research and teaching

Sociology, anthropology, and philosophy of science have contributed much to the understanding of scientific activities. Two rather different schools of thought and analysis have emerged. First, those belonging to the "Mertonian" school study scientists as members of a professional community built around a common ethos that is a prerequisite for science as an autonomous sphere. Most of the writers in this school first focused on the identification of the conditions for this ethos to be acquired (through socialization) and maintained (through professional control) and then determined whether the scientific practices, institutions, and procedures do or do not conform to this ethos. We could say that rather than describing scientific activities, they described how to make science as independent as possible. In the 1970s, another school developed around the "strong program,"[55] which was critical of the Mertonians. Arguing against the Mertonians' differentialist conception of science,[56] the writers, particularly its French contingent, espousing this second perspective first proposed another conception of scientists, not as members of an autonomous community, but as network builders enrolling actors from different spheres of society.[57] Second, they conducted many ethnographical studies on scientific activities and provided concrete descriptions of what "doing research" meant.[58]

Both perspectives have radically improved our understanding of scientific work (more of the physical sciences than the social sciences) and of the way that institutional arrangements (career patterns, reward principles, etc.) may affect such activities. But both still ignored teaching duties and training activities in general. They also seldom addressed the divide between public and private and looked at privatization from the standpoint of intellectual property rights or patenting rather than its impact on academic activities.

The same conclusion can be made about the publications and works focusing on teaching in higher education institutions. Besides not being as developed as those of scientific activities, these concrete investigations of teaching generally ignore other activities. There is more to be found on curricula, on the evaluation of teaching, and on pedagogical methods than on teaching practices. They also are often rather normative, first looking at improving teaching performance and identifying good methods.

A last kind of work looks at the complementary and/or conflicting divide between research and teaching. As summed up by K-H. Chiang, there are three different positions.[59] Some writers emphasize the complementary relationships between teaching and research;[60] others describe them as competing activities;[61] and still others stress they are independent of one another.

Academics from a more comprehensive perspective

Besides neglecting academics' administrative responsibilities (despite their increasing importance, according to the 1994 Carnegie survey), these studies also ignore the diversification of academic activities.[62] "Teaching" is more than the preparation and presentation of lessons. It also includes using new technologies, finding and organizing internships, producing e-learning, and so forth. Research also refers to a range of tasks such as writing proposals, negotiating contracts, and transferring technology. Finally, seen as a set of different activities, academic work has not been fully explored.[63] I propose three perspectives to better understand the academic profession today.

In a paper identifying what makes universities specific organizations, I argued that the nature and characteristics of academic work are crucial for two reasons.[64] First, both "teaching" and "research" (in the broad meanings just defined) are loosely coupled activities: both can be achieved with low coordination and cooperation with other actors achieving the same tasks. Furthermore they are "unclear technologies" (using the terminology suggested by Michael D. Cohen, James G. March, and Johan P. Olsen), which means that they are difficult to describe and even more difficult to reproduce.[65] Also, the causal relationships between these activities and their results are complex (what do the students really learn from what is taught?). Therefore we need to look more closely at academic activities to better assess how they differ from other productive activities and whether they could become closer. Such a perspective should be able to differentiate among types of institutions.

Second, examining the content of academic activities is not sufficient. Not enough attention has been paid to how academics articulate the tensions and complementarities between the many different tasks to be achieved. Academic work must be studied as a whole rather than split into different independent functions. But we lack studies that consider academic activities in different institutional situations or of different status and at different career stages and also explain the variations and the role and scope of faculty discretion.[66]

Third, there is much to gain from using in academia those concepts used in the sociology of work. Most of the time, academic activities have been approached as the sociology of professions. Not much attention has been paid to issues such as the division of work among peers and the principles organizing the allocation of tasks. We assumed that peers were "doing about the same" and that they were divided by their disciplinary and institutional affiliations. The multiplication and diversification of academic tasks have forced academics to specialize or focus more on some tasks than on others. As a result, faculty members with the same status in the same type of institution may emphasize different tasks. For instance, the study by Jason Owen-Smith and Walter W. Powell of tenured and tenure-track biologists clearly shows that they do not spend as much time and do not have the same activities and the same perceptions about technology transfer activities.[67] But such different organizations of their time can also result from institutional choices. Universities in some countries (e.g., the United Kingdom and the Netherlands) are, for instance, creating academic positions with clearly different missions, some dedicated to teaching and others devoted to research. This development leads to further questions: What explains these variations among peers? What explains the division of work among them? Is it a result of the increasing managerial pressure exercised by higher education institutions? What is the impact of the interaction between academic scientists and new forms of industrial research (in scientific districts, start-ups, etc.)? Last, we must investigate the new division of work introduced by the differentiation and "hierarchization" of the academic profession resulting from the increased number of research assistants, adjuncts, and part-timers. As already mentioned, another characteristic of this population is its specialization, such as postdocs for research, adjuncts, and part-time teaching staff.[68] One way, then, to measure, analyze, and understand the changes affecting the academic profession is to look closely at the nature, content, and determinants of academic work.

Academic Productivity

The study of academics at work is closely linked to the issue of academic productivity and the way it is measured. Scientometrics and bibliometrics have produced data on the scientific productivity of academics, which has led to many studies of the validity of such techniques. But less has been achieved on the impact of the transformation of the academic profession on productivity (in quantitative and qualitative terms). Different issues could be addressed according to this perspective.

In countries where salaries are not set by state bureaucracies but by institutions, many studies have shown that salary incentives are related to productivity. Thus they confirm the relationship between the quantity of scientific production and the differences among salaries,[69] whereas institutional factors (such as the organization of work or the type of governance exercised by the department chairs) also affect the wages of academics in the same department.[70] Evidence regarding the quality of the scientific production is generally more difficult to document, although Ronald G. Erhenberg, Marquise McGraw, and Jesenka Mrdjenovic concluded that the quality of faculty in a university's various fields explained the field differences in average faculty salaries.[71]

Similar issues apply to the impact of managerial control and/or evaluation procedures on productivity. There is some evidence concerning their effects on quantity. In the United Kingdom, for instance, the introduction of the Research Assessment Exercise influenced the number of papers published and academics' attention to research.[72] Again, the effects on quality are much more difficult to measure.

Determining the qualitative and quantitative impact of the transformation of academic work and employment conditions also is difficult. Some scholars, such as Paula Stephan, have observed that the current transformation of academic labor markets is jeopardizing quality. Relying on evidence showing a positive correlation between age and major scientific contributions (e.g., leading to the Nobel Prize), Stephan argues that the delayed access to tenure-track positions, the decreasing possibility of obtaining such positions, and young scholars' dependence on research assistant positions or postdocs make it difficult to obtain independent research support, preclude innovation, and discourage major scientific productions.[73] In other words, the current situation will probably hurt scientific quality.

Similar conclusions were reached about teaching and the impact of adjuncts and part-time instructors on students' completion rates and attainment of graduate degrees. Ronald Ehrenberg and Liang Zhang, for example, offer evidence of the negative impact of the increasing number of non-tenure-track instructors teaching undergraduate classes on students' graduation rates.[74] Accordingly, we need more research on the impact of the "industrialization" of teaching (e.g., through the standardization and rationalization of the contents on which e.learning relies).

Such conclusions provide an opportunity for renewing and enlarging issues crucial to the Mertonian view of the sociology of science concerning the impact of the science system on production.[75] Most of the criticism of the current work situation concerns the priority given to short-term rather than to long-term research objectives, to instrumental rather than abstract topics, to directly applied rather than purely fundamental research, to managerial objectives (such as the reduction of salary costs) rather than science-friendly conditions, and so on. But what evidence validates or invalidates these threats? Some publications on the research relationship between the university and industry suggested that recent developments have had both benefits and risks for universities, but they did not find a clear correlation between the existence of such relationships and faculty behaviors. David Blumenthal and his colleagues[76] agreed with these conclusions and observed that faculty who had research support from industry (as long as they did not receive too much industrial support) published more than those who did not but that their research agenda was influenced by commercial considerations.[77] Nevertheless, such findings remain rather rare and, again, are limited to mostly the American case. These studies also do not address other issues, for example, whether public systems better protect against a decrease in quality. What evidence can we find for domains not related to the university-industry relationship?

A NEW RESEARCH AGENDA FOR THE ACADEMIC PROFESSION?

This third and last section discusses four issues: the lack of attention paid to the divide between public and private; the interaction between academic and other productive activities; the careers and trajectories of academics in relation to career theories; and a combined understanding of labor markets, employment relationships, and organization of work.

The Divide Between Public and Private

The divide between public and private is not often addressed by studies of academics. The reason for this lack of interest may be that most academics are active in public systems, and in countries with a private higher education system, it is often less prestigious than the public system. But the same lack of interest is also found in countries with a strong and well-regarded private sector.[78] In the United States, for instance, the status of institutions is brought up only in papers dealing with salaries and employment relationships; otherwise, it is, at best, one of the explored variables,[79] often with no assessment of potential differences. In addition, we have no systematic account of the differences introduced by the institutional status of both sectors, and only a few extensive comparisons of private and public universities on dimensions such as the profiles of the recruited academics, the recourse and impact of the secondary labor market, the divide between teaching and research, the use and effects of managerial tools, the influence of academic capitalism, the behaviors and attitudes of academics toward technology transfers, recruitment in both sectors, the content of academic activities and the division of work, and academics' trajectories, careers, and conceptions of their activities and identities.[80] More systematic and extensive comparisons across the two sectors are needed to determine whether there is a difference between working in a private or public institution and also to evaluate the level of privatization of public institutions (or the discrepancies between the two) in countries with a dual system.

The main bias introduced by such a perspective provides a static picture when a dynamic one also is necessary to gauge whether the distance or closeness observed today is getting narrower or wider than in the past. For many issues, it is almost impossible to obtain valid views from the past and to avoid reconstructing a mythic golden age. But for others, data may be available and could allow some historical perspective and comparison. This would help define what privatization means and would help measure the accuracy of this process for the management of academic staff. The notion of privatization is usually vague and is applied in a general way without specifying the various degrees and forms it can take.

International comparisons could also help identifying factors explaining, favoring, or reducing the privatization process. For instance, we do not know whether the diffusion of practices, rules of the game, and norms of the private sector are stronger in countries where private universities are at the top of the rankings than in countries where the most prestigious sector is public, or in countries where there is no private sector?

Finally, we should take advantage of the different rates and degrees of privatization of public systems in groups of comparable countries in order to better account for its effects. From this perspective, the European case with its many situations and reforms is a huge laboratory for higher education researchers interested in the divide between public and private and in the privatization process.

The Academic Profession and Other Activities

Most of the time, the academic profession has been studied as an autonomous and specific, albeit not exceptional, population. It has seldom been compared with other professions, but some publications invite us to reconsider this position.

The first group of research deals with the transformation of work in firms. It concludes that work situations in firms (or at least some of them) are beginning to resemble the characteristics of academic tasks. First, the deconstruction of hierarchy tends to transform firms into less vertical structures and therefore more bottom-heavy organizations (a characteristic of scientific organizations). Second, the drift from qualifications (related to specific degrees and credentials) to competences (which are linked to the individual, acquired on the job, and related to knowledge, know-how, and know-how-to-be) increases workers' ability to develop their autonomy at work, to be responsible for their tasks, and also to develop "individualization" (the ability to assess their own contribution). Third, some workers are less often assigned to some specific tasks than to collective projects on which different people having different competences and belonging to different divisions work together during the time needed to achieve a specific mission. As a result, the definition of each job is no longer defined by only the organization but also by the workers themselves. Such considerations led Pierre-Michel Menger to conclude that the arts (but also scientific activities to a lesser extent)

> are more and more considered as the more advanced expression of the new modes of production and of the new employment relationships. . . . The artist comes closer to a potential incarnation of the future worker, through the image of a professional who is inventive, mobile, resistant to hierarchies, intrinsically motivated, embedded in an economy of uncertainty, and more exposed to the risks of competition among individuals and to the new insecurities of professional trajectories.[81]

For Menger, the multiplication of different employment contracts (or the decreasing proportion of permanent positions in firms) brings artists and workers closer. Many of Daniel Lee Kleinman and Steven P. Vallas's conclusions are similar: they observe the "collegialization" of industrial research by which "academic norms are increasingly governing the work practices of selected knowledge workers in high technology firms and industries."[82] In turn, this leads to "a shift away from the hierarchical constraints . . . toward a newer, more flexible, and egalitarian organizational pattern that grants expert employees much higher levels of autonomy than before" and to a regression of linear career models in favor of projects. This is linked to the transformation of the industrial systems themselves and their increased reliance on networks rather than on organizations, to the externalization of tasks that knowledge experts take over, as well as to the increasing complexity and specialization of workers' activities, which limits the efficiency of vertical control.[83] This transformation of knowledge work in firms led Jason Owen-Smith and Walter W. Powell to conclude that biotechnology firms and universities belong to the same scientific community.[84]

Another group of research focuses on the opposite trend, the transformation of academic activities into academic work, of scholars into knowledge workers. This perspective sheds light on the transformation of universities into organizations and on its impacts on the management of academic staff, the content of work, and employment relationships.[85] Considering the consequences of "new managerialism" on academics, some writers observed that faculty members have less autonomy and less control, are submitted to regular evaluation, must be more accountable, and so on.[86] Although universities tend to develop incentive mechanisms and build better-equipped internal labor markets, they transform the nature of their relationships with their faculty, becoming closer to that of the relationship between employer and wage earner while at the same time expecting their academic staff to remain committed to their institution and participate in its performance.[87] Kleinman and Vallas also observed the transformation of research units into profit units, the development of standardized quantitative measures of production, and the emergence of a system of stratification between those engaged in commercially relevant research and "those who undertake scholarly work with no obvious economic benefits."[88] Thus they conclude that the industrialization of academic research expands along with the collegialization of industrial research, and they attribute this simultaneous occurrence to the influence of the two sectors on each other's codes and culture.[89] Their conclusions differ from those of most other scholars, who find only one of the two processes (the influence of research or artistic activities on work or the influence of work on academia). Kleinman and Vallas also argue (rather than provide evidence, unfortunately) for the existence of two opposite forces pushing each sphere closer to the other and for the crossed diffusion of norms and codes between firms and universities.

The third group of publications of interest here deals with either academic or nonacademic work on the same phenomenon, but do not quote each other. Most of the public discourse on the academic profession and higher education today point to the necessity of enhancing mobility (geographical, institutional, or thematic), promoting flexibility within the system, welcoming the development of networks (especially for research activities), and announcing the rise of new technologies in training programs. The managerial literature on firms stresses the same issues and is sometimes depicted as neocapitalism, with some having rather pessimistic views about society today.[90] Richard Sennett, for instance, emphasizes the devastating effects not only on work situations (dilution of authority, loss of control on the tasks achieved by each worker, etc.) but also on family lives and on the construction of the self.[91] In higher education studies, mobility, networking, and flexibility are more rarely criticized, for two reasons: first, organizational affiliation has never been very strong nor very valued (being a "local" is less valued than being a "cosmopolite");[92] and, second, refusing to be international and to be involved in networks and ready to move has negative connotations in academia today. Nevertheless, some scholars fear that it will exacerbate the loss in the sense of community.

Besides determining how these trends will or will not affect the public and the private sectors in different ways, we should also consider the transformation of work in firms and the evolution of academia. Some of the driving forces apply to all or most of the work situations in firms as well as in higher education institutions. Others seem more specific to the academic world and in many aspects contradict the developments outlined earlier. It seems difficult to associate stronger institutional affiliation and stronger leadership with more mobility, flexibility, and networks. Last, the academic profession is experiencing changes because its situation vis-à-vis other professionals or other workers is evolving: what was confined to academia yesterday is now shared by other professionals or workers, including its expertise in knowledge and science. Accordingly, we need more comparative works on academics and nonacademic knowledge workers.

Academic Trajectories

The notion of careers has developed according to two perspectives. The first concentrates on organizational careers and describes how organizational settings frame career possibilities. This perspective led to many developments. According to Rachel Rosenfeld, many of these developments concerned job-shifting events,[93] which she explains as the results of the (organizational) opportunity structures, as defined by the vacancy chains models (with vacancy depending on the availability of empty positions)[94] and by segmentation theory ("labour market divisions [being] seen as locating types of vacancies, vacancy chains, or vacancy-influenced promotion structures").[95] This approach relies mostly on quantitative methodology, which is based on database analysis or historical event analysis.

The second perspective focuses on individuals and how they construct and understand their trajectories, perceive the existing possibilities, and calculate them. This approach gained a large audience with the development of the "new career theory." Observing the declining part of the "bounded" careers (i.e., careers that develop within an organization and are managed by internal labor markets), some writers created the notions of "boundaryless," "protean," or "intelligent" careers to reflect the developments in the labor markets in the 1980s.[96] These writers took into account that careers were becoming more horizontal than upward but also more interorganizational than infraorganizational, thus leading to more fragmented individual identities and a shift in the management of career developments, from the firm to the single worker. In contrast with the first perspective, the second one often relies on qualitative instruments like biographical interviews.

This distinction between bounded (organizational) and boundaryless careers in fact opposes and separates what interactionist sociologists from the Chicago school proposed and considered as interdependent. Thus, for Howard Becker and Everett Hughes, careers are simultaneously objective and subjective, so their interactions should be studied. They are objective because careers are made up of a series of positions and jobs (and rely on organizational/structural settings). They are subjective because they also are related to each person's interpretation of his or her life as a whole and of the different changes he or she has experienced. For Becker and Hughes, careers are defined by the social worlds in which they take place but, in return, define them.[97]

Surprisingly, such perspectives have seldom been used to study academic careers. In fact, most works on the academic profession and labor markets describe how careers are structured by national regulations or institutional practices and thus how they are supposed to develop. But scholars rarely apply this formal description to academics' trajectories. Nevertheless, there are some exceptions: some studies have tried to identify some of the determinants of academic careers by using databases, historical event analysis, or other quantitative methods. Some studies show the relationships between the training trajectory (where the graduate degree was awarded) and access to the most prestigious institutions;[98] the relationships between the entry point and career prospects, establishing that the better the institution one enters first, the easier it will be to move later to a more prestigious place;[99] or the factors influencing mobility.[100] But these studies usually do not shed much light on the discrepancies between private and public institutions and whether and how such discrepancies change. They also provide little information about the evolution of trajectories because they do not compare cohorts over time. Second, they all are based on American cases, which are useful for the U.S. academic professional model but probably not for other models. The lack of comparable studies with other countries thus precludes international comparison.

The interactionist approach and the new career theory have been applied even less often to academics, particularly from an empirical point of view. But some writers have suggested that artistic and scientific activities are today becoming a model for work and have established a parallel between academic careers and boundaryless nonacademic careers. Nonetheless, two partly incompatible versions have been developed in this literature.[101] On the one hand, some texts present academic careers as a typically traditional example for the boundaryless career and as "a model for future careers in other sectors." Arguing that the academic labor market has not changed much since the seminal book by Theodore Caplow and Reece McGee, Yehuda Baruch and Douglas Hall observed that some of the traits traditionally characteristic of academics also are characteristic of boundaryless careers and can be observed in firms today: especially individualism, the importance of networking within and across organizations, participants' ability to choose their own partners or projects, and the possibility of working on many projects at the same time.[102] On this basis, they conclude that careers outside academia are becoming more and more boundaryless and therefore are more and more similar to academic careers. But other writers, mostly in higher education studies, state that academic careers are becoming boundaryless, thus implicitly assuming that they were not so before. Their arguments are based on the increase in non-tenure-track staff, the push for institutional and geographical mobility, and the trend toward multiorganizational affiliations and portfolios.[103] These two views do not completely contradict each other, as it could be argued that the academic profession has always been "protean" but that academic careers are more so than before. Nevertheless, each view comes to rather different conclusions. According to the first one, current academic careers become a model for nonacademic careers. It is rather "challenging" to read that Baruch and Hall present as a model for the future of firms some of the same academic features (particularly autoregulation) that politicians, academic leaders, administrators, and stakeholders often describe as problematic and "to be reformed"! The second view often comes to less optimistic conclusions and offers arguments close to Sennett's fears about the deconstruction of workers' identities if boundaryless careers become the norm. As the academic profession becomes (more) protean, the risks for dilution, loss of attractiveness, and diminishing quality are expected to rise.

Beyond their contradictory arguments, these two views invite us to examine empirically the hypothesis of academic careers as boundaryless or as becoming more boundaryless than before.

First, we should focus on the transformation of organizational careers, using cohort analysis for different cohorts of academics to compare trajectories and the odds of entry, promotions, and institutional and international mobility. An ongoing study of access to full-professor positions for French men and women faculty members shows, everything else held constant, that there is discrimination against women but also that men and women who do become full professors do not follow the same career pattern (women invest more in publications and academic criteria, and men invest more in project and group management) and that when comparing cohorts, the determinants for becoming a full professor varied over time.[104]

Such approaches are, of course, less applicable to non-tenure-track staff. A second group of studies should therefore investigate which academic careers are boundaryless or more boundaryless than others and also what the new boundaries are. Stephen R. Barley and Gideon Kunda maintain that

> it is unlikely that boundaries are any less socially constructed today than they were in the past. To determine whether organizational boundaries are constructed differently today requires data on where people work, with whom they work and, most importantly, how they conceptualize their identities and the social groups of which they are part. In short the issue is not whether boundaries do or do not exist, but *where and how people draw boundaries in the world of work and whether the nature of boundaries they draw has somehow changed.*[105]

Such questions should guide studies of academic trajectories and produce more precise descriptions of the diversity of situations and the different boundaries. They probably are different for those who are on traditional career tracks than for those who are closer to being knowledge workers and for those who have non-tenure-track positions.[106] Such studies would require more qualitative studies, observation of work practices, and socialization processes[107] and would rely on work biographies and "how people interpret both."[108]

Bringing Together Labor Markets, Employment Relationships, and Organization of Work

Even if some parts of the academic labor markets (namely, the market for postdocs in certain disciplines, or the market for "world-class" academics) are generally international, they remain mostly national in at least two ways. First, both the formal regulations and the informal rules that drive these markets remain national, which in turn builds strong barriers to internationalization. Second, most academics see their national, if not their regional, territory as their "natural" hiring and promotion space. Questions need to be addressed concerning the interaction among the characteristics of the academic labor markets, the employment relationships between academics and their university, and the organization of work and the division of labor in higher education institutions. For example, we should understand how the required institutional mobility in the German academic labor markets for professors "is linked" to the hierarchical organization of work between professors and assistants, to the weak capacity of German universities in the management of their staff, and to these universities acting as "buyers" of human capital when they recruit employees but not as employers vis-à-vis their professors.[109] Until the reforms of 2001, these were the pillars on which the German academic profession relied and that characterized the German academic labor market.

This empirical example illustrates the interest in investigating the linkage of specific types of academic labor markets to specific forms of employment relationships and specific models of organizing work. It also reveals the need for theoretical tools and developments to better conceptualize such an interplay.[110] First, we need more analytical (less descriptive) approaches to the academic labor markets, looking at how they work rather than at what they "produce" or at what makes them special.[111] In a recent book, I suggested that four mechanisms can analytically help in understanding (in the Weberian meaning of *verstehen*) the German, American, and French labor markets for permanent or tenured and permanent or tenure-track faculty members: the selection principles used to sort out the candidates;[112] the length and role of the prepermanence period; the balance between the internal and external labor markets in each country;[113] and the type of mechanisms used to set the "price" (salaries, working conditions, etc.) of each academic when he or she is recruited. This analytical approach to academic labor markets, based on mechanisms rather than on descriptive data, offers a starting but incomplete basis for discussion, which could be revised and modified for other national markets and extended to casual faculty.

We also need to investigate further the organization of academic work and to study the allocation of tasks, forms of control over academic activities, and the like. Finally, we need, as suggested by Sandra Harley, Michael Muller-Camen, and Audrey Collin, to pay more attention to the exercise of power in the employment relationships and to better account for the variety of the relationships linking higher education institutions and their staff.[114] In some countries, universities behave more or less as employers toward their faculty, but in others (e.g., Germany until 2001), universities cannot manage their staff and act as buyers of human capital, investing in some professors when they recruit them and hoping for a return on investment. In still others, as in France, universities are mainly host institutions for their academic staff (even if recent acts intend to transform universities as employers). Conceptualizing the interaction of labor markets, employment relationships, and the organization of work has two objectives: first, a better understanding of what a "national" system is, what makes them robust, and how strong they remain and, second, how this would contribute to the empirical and theoretical analysis of academic work and labor markets and thus to the general analysis of work and labor markets.

Although the academic profession has benefited from research, today it needs to reorient its research agenda for at least two reasons. The first relies on scientific issues and pleas for the extension of methods, concepts, and theories. This extension should lead to new perspectives on, and a better understanding of, the academic profession itself. It would also lead to contributions to the theories of work and organization. But the second reason, which is just as important, concerns the relevance of this renewed research agenda. The ongoing transformations of the academic profession require us to adapt our research questions to new issues. The extension of non-tenure-track staff and the redefinition of the academic profession require more studies. We also need a better understanding and analysis of the new careers and trajectories for academics and how they can be related to the overall transformation of work in our societies. Last, we need to investigate the effects of the redefinition of the division between private and public in higher education systems and the current society at large.

NOTES

1. Philip G. Altbach and Richard Chait, "The Changing Academic Workplace: Comparative Perspectives," *Higher Education* (special issue) 41 (2001). Jürgen Enders, ed., *Academic Staff in Europe: Changing Contexts and Conditions* (Westport, Conn.: Greenwood Press, 2001). See also Jürgen Enders, ed., *Employment and Working Conditions of Academic Staff in Europe* (Frankfurt: Materialen und Dokumente, Hochschule und Forschung, 2000); and Jürgen Enders and Egbert de Weert, eds., *The International Attractiveness of the Academic Workplace in Europe* (Frankfurt: Materialen und Dokumente, Hochschule und Forschung, 2004). Philip G. Altbach, *The Decline of the Guru: The Academic Profession in Developing and Middle-Income Countries* (Chestnut Hill, Mass.: Center for International Higher Education, Boston College, 2002). Damtew D. Teferra and Philip G. Altbach, eds., *African Higher Education: An International Reference Handbook* (Bloomington: Indiana University Press, 2003).

2. In the United States, where this trend is particularly strong, this is explained by the cost of tenured staff in general and also the cost of abolishing mandatory retirement. See Paula Stephan, "Job Market Effects on Scientific Productivity" (paper presented at the Sciences Po seminar on Higher Education, February 2005); and Ronald G. Ehrenberg, "Key Issues Facing Trustees of National Research Universities in the Decade Ahead" (working paper, Cornell Higher Education Research Institute, 2005).

3. Jack H. Schuster and Martin J. Finkelstein, *The American Faculty: The Restructuring of Academic Work and Careers* (Baltimore: John Hopkins University Press, 2006).

4. Enders and de Weert, *The International Attractiveness.*

5. Stephen Court, "Academic Tenure and Employment in the UK," *Sociological Perspectives* 41 (1998): 767–74.

6. For instance, Martin Finkelstein signals the development of positions devoted to program development and management. See Martin Finkelstein, "The Morphing of the American Academic Profession," *Liberal Education, Association of American Colleges and Universities,* fall 2003, available at http://www.aacu.org/liberaleducation/le-fa03/le-sfa03feature.cfm (accessed March 24, 2010).

7. Enders, *Academic Staff in Europe,* 4. The two others are decentralization and marketization.

8. This is generally more striking in industrialized countries than in developing ones. The case of Turkey is interesting because the percentage of academic women is exceptionally high owing to the converging effects of different causes. See Mustafa Özbilgin and Geraldine Healy, "The Gendered Nature of Career Development of University Professors: the Case of Turkey," *Journal of Vocational Behavior* 64 (2004): 358–71.

9. Gerald Rosenblum and Barbara Rubin Rosenblum, "Segmented Labor Markets in Institutions of Higher Learning," *Sociology of Education* 63 (1990): 151–64.

10. David Robinson, "The Status of Higher Education Teaching Personnel in Australia, Canada, New Zealand, the United Kingdom and the United States" (paper presented at the International Higher Education and Research Conference, Melbourne, December 2005).

11. Valerie Martin Conley and David W. Leslie, "Part-time Instructional Faculty and Staff: Who They Are, What They Do and What They Think," *Education Statistics Quarterly* 4 (2002), available at http://nces.ed.gov/Pubsearch/pubsinfo.asp?pubid=2002163 (accessed March, 24, 2010).

12. The case of France is illustrative: Permanent positions (*maîtres de conférences*) are available to those around the age of thirty-three, and the number of women recruited, compared with men, is not very different at that stage of their career (in 2004, 41.1% of the newly recruited *maîtres de conférences* were women). But when looking at the

promotion from *maître de conférences* to professor, fewer women enter the competition. Even in disciplines like biology, where the percentage of women holding the position of *maître de conférences* is about comparable to those of men (49.6%), the share of women professors remains very low (16.8%). In 2004, in biology, only 31.5% of the newly recruited professors were women.

13. Marcia L. Bellas, "Comparable Worth in Academia: The Effects on Faculty Salaries of the Sex Composition and Labor-Market Conditions of Academic Disciplines," *American Sociological Review* 59 (1994): 807–21.

14. Barbara Bagilhole, "How to Keep a Good Woman Down: An Investigation of the Role of Institutional Factors in the Process of Discrimination Against Women Academics," *British Journal of Sociology of Education* 14 (1993): 261–74; and Lewis Solmon, "Women in Doctoral Education: Clues and Puzzles Regarding Institutional Discrimination," *Research in Higher Education* 1 (1973): 229–32.

15. In this case, discrimination does not result from the behavior of the deciders but from the gendered criteria used. In other words, although men and women are equally subject to the same norms, these norms favor men. Norms like "continuity in publication flows" or "high productivity in the early thirties," are more difficult for women with children.

16. Mariane A. Ferber and Carole A. Green, "Traditional or Reverse Sex Discrimination? A Case Study of a Large Public University," *Industrial and Labor Relations Review* 35 (1982): 550–64.

17. J. Scott Long., Paul D. Allison, and Robert McGinnis, "Rank Advancement in Academic Careers: Sex Differences and the Effects of Productivity," *American Sociological Review* 58 (1993): 703–22; Eugene A. Hammel et al., "Gender and the Academic Career in North American Anthropology: Differentiating Intramarket and Extramarket Bias," *Current Anthropology* 36 (1995): 366–80.

18. Namrat Gupta and Arun K. Sharma, "Women Academic Scientists in India," *Social Studies of Science* 32 (2002): 901–15.

19. Hammel et al., "Gender and the Academic Career."

20. Henry Etzkowitz, Carol Kemelgor, and Brian Uzzi, *Athena Unbound: The Advancement of Women in Science and Technology* (Cambridge: Cambridge University Press, 2000); Bruce Keith et al., "The Context of Scientific Achievement: Sex, Status, Organizational Environments, and the Timing of Publication on Scholarship Outcomes," *Social Forces* 80 (2002): 1253–82.

21. Armen A. Alchian, *Economic Forces at Work: Selected Works of Armen A. Alchian*, (Indianapolis: Liberty Press, 1977); Philip G. Altbach, "An International Crisis? The American Professoriate in Comparative Perspective," in *Comparative Higher Education: Knowledge, the University and Development*, ed. Philip G Altbach

(Greenwich, Conn.: Ablex, 1998), 75–91; Richard P. Chait and Andrew T. Ford, *Beyond Traditional Tenure: A Guide to Sound Policies and Practices* (San Francisco: Jossey-Bass, 1982).

22. Richard P. Chait, ed., *The Questions of Tenure* (Cambridge, Mass.: Harvard University Press, 2002); Garry Rhoades and Sheila Slaughter, "Academic Capitalism, Manage Professionals, and Supply-Side Higher Education," *Social Text* 51 (1997): 9–38.

23. Chait, *The Questions of Tenure*; Robinson, "The Status of Higher Education Teaching Personnel."

24. Court, "Academic Tenure and Employment in the UK"; Hans Pechar, "The Changing Academic Workplace: From Civil Servants to Private Employees," in *The International Attractiveness of the Academic Workplace in Europe*, ed. Jürgen Enders and Egbert de Weert (Frankfurt: Materialen und Dokumente, Hochschule und Forschung, 2004); Atsunori Yamanoi, *A Study of the Non-Tenure System for Faculty Members in Japan* (Hiroshima: Research Institute for Higher Education, Hiroshima University, 2003).

25. Rhoades and Slaughter, "Academic Capitalism"; Sheila Slaughter S. and Larry L. Leslie, *Academic Capitalism: Politics, Policies, and the Entrepreneurial University* (Baltimore: John Hopkins University Press, 1997); Sheila Slaughter and Garry Rhoades, *Academic Capitalism and the New Economy* (Baltimore: John Hopkins University Press, 2004); John Dearlove, "The Academic Labour Process: From Collegiality and Professionalism to Managerialism and Proletarianisation?" *Higher Education Review* 30 (1997): 56–75; Rosemary Deem, "New Managerialism in Higher Education: The Management of Performances and Cultures in Universities," *International Studies in the Sociology of Education* 8 (1998): 47–70; Albert H. Halsey, *The Decline of Donnish Dominion* (Oxford: Clarendon Press, 1992); Patricia J. Gumport and Brian Pusser, "A Case of Bureaucratic Accretion: Context and Consequences," *Journal of Higher Education* 66 (1995): 493–520; Michael Reed and Rosemary Deem, "New Managerialism—The Manager-Academic and Technologies of Management in Universities—Looking Forward to Virtuality," in *The Virtual University*, ed. Kevin Robins and Frank Webster (Oxford: Oxford University Press, 2002), 126–47.

26. George Lafferty and Jenny Fleming, "The Restructuring of Academic Work in Australia: Power, Management and Gender," *British Journal of Sociology of Education* 21 (2000): 257–67.

27. Philip G. Altbach, "The Crisis of the Professoriate," *Annals of the American Academy of Political and Social Science* 448 (1980): 1–14.

28. Enders, *Academic Staff in Europe*, 2.

29. Robinson concludes that most countries show a decline in the real value of academic salaries compared with those of other professions, even though in the United

States, United Kingdom, and Australia, academic salaries rose in recent years. See Robinson, "The Status of Higher Education Teaching Personnel."

30. But as Enders and de Weert stressed, the stagnation of public salaries "provokes academics to earn an additional income outside academia," a practice already common in eastern Europe, South America, and developing countries. See Enders and de Weert, *Academic Staff in Europe*, 18.

31. Ronald G. Ehrenberg, Marquise McGraw, and Jesenka Mrdjenovic, "Why Do Field Differentials in Average Faculty Salaries Vary Across Universities?" (working paper, Cornell Higher Education Research Institute, 2005); Schuster and Finkelstein, *The American Faculty*.

32. Rhoades and Slaughter, "Academic Capitalism."

33. Ehrenberg, McGraw, and Mrdjenovic, "Why Do Field Differentials in Average Faculty Salaries Vary," 3.

34. Altbach, *The Decline of the Guru*.

35. This is confirmed by the paper by Leong and Leung on Asian academics, in which they observe that while Asian academics in theory can choose to adopt the Western approach (assimilationism), to retain the Asian approach (separationism) or to use both (integrationism), they usually prefer the first strategy and are even encouraged to follow it. See Frederik T. L. Leong and Kwok Leung, "Academic Careers in Asia: A Cross-Cultural Analysis," *Journal of Vocational Behavior* 64 (2004): 346–57.

36. Altbach, *The Decline of the Guru*, 7.

37. Jürgen Enders and Christine Musselin, "Back to the Future? The Academic Professions in the 21st Century," *OECD Higher Education 2030*, vol. 1, *Demography* (Paris: OECD Editions, 2008), 125–50; Robert B. Freeman, "Does Globalization of the Scientific/Engineering Workforce Threaten U.S. Economic Leadership?" (working paper no. 11457) (Cambridge, Mass.: NBER, June 2005).

38. Chris Jenks and D. Riesman, "The Triumph of the Academic Man," in *Campus 1980: The Shape of the Future in American Higher Education*, ed. Alvin C. Eurich (New York: Delacorte Press, 1968), 92–115.

39. Altbach, "The Crisis of the Professoriate."

40. This also is stressed by Wilson in the same journal issue, but in both cases this is linked by the authors to an increase in public funding and involvement: "The trend is one of increased governmental entwinement in both the finance and control of educational institutions." Logan Wilson, "Dialectic aspects of Recent Change in Academe," *Annals of the American Academy of Political and Social Science* 448 (1968): 21.

41. Eugene R. Rice, "The Academic Profession in Transition: Toward a New Social Fiction," *Teaching Sociology* 14 (1986): 12–23.

42. For instance, does "accountability" in the 1980s and today mean the same, does it refer to the same practices, and is it stronger today than previously?

43. Judith M. Gappa, *Part-Time Faculty: Higher Education at a Crossroads* (Washington, D.C.: Association for the Study of Higher Education, 1984); David W. Leslie, Samuel E. Kellams, and G. Manny Gunne, *Part-time Faculty in American Higher Education* (New York: Praeger, 1982).

44. Rosenblum and Rosenblum, "Segmented Labor Markets."

45. Court, "Academic Tenure and Employment in the UK"; Enders and de Weert, *Academic Staff in Europe*; Ronald G. Ehrenberg, "The Changing Nature of the Faculty and Faculty Employment Practices" (working paper, Cornell Higher Education Research Institute, 2005).

46. Judith M. Gappa and David W. Leslie, *The Invisible Faculty: Improving the Status of Part-timers in Higher Education* (San Francisco: Jossey-Bass, 1993).

47. Conley and Leslie, "Part-time Instructional Faculty and Staff."

48. Schuster and Finkelstein's book provides an interesting table on the composition of the subgroup of "part-time" faculty, showing its great diversity in status (17.5% are retired; more than 20% have no other employment; and 9.5% are employed full-time outside higher education). See Schuster and Finkelstein, *The American Faculty*.

49. Daniel C. Feldman and William H. Turnley, "Contingent Employment in Academic Careers: Relative Deprivation Among Adjunct Faculty," *Journal of Vocational Behavior* 64 (2004): 284–307.

50. Gerald Rosenblum and Barbara Rubin Rosenblum, "The Flow of Instructors Through the Segmented Labor Markets of Academe," *Higher Education* 31 (1996): 429–45.

51. McBrier, for example, studied the structure of opportunity for non-tenure-track academics in law and found that the passage from the secondary to the primary labor market was even worse for women. Using event history analysis, McBrier shows that women's rates are slower and that this sex difference reflects a mixture of factors: supply-side factors resulting from geographic constraints, family ties, scholarly productivity, levels of social capital, employment origins in various fields of nonacademic law practice, and the structure of opportunity in non-tenure-track law academia. See Deborah B. McBrier," Gender and Career Dynamics Within a Segmented Professional Labor Market: The Case of Law Academia," *Social Forces* 81 (2003): 1201–66.

52. There is little information about fixed-term assistants in Germany and even less on the "vacataires" in France who are paid by the hour, teach at French universities, and are a very diverse population: Some are permanent faculty members working supplementary hours; some are permanent researchers teaching a few hours; some

are young academics waiting for a permanent position; and some are practitioners teaching a specific topic at the university.

53. Clark's book about academic life provides interesting insights. See Burton R. Clark, *Academic Life, Small Worlds, Different Worlds* (Princeton, N.J.: Carnegie Foundation for the Advancement of Teaching / Princeton University Press, 1987). Recent studies of political and social attitudes include Stanley Rothman, S. Robert Lichter, and Neil Nevitte, "Politics and Professional Advancement Among College Faculty," *The Forum* 3 (2005): 2. In 2006, N. Gross (Harvard University) and S. Simmons (George Mason University) organized a survey, "Politics of American Professoriate," and Harvard's Graduate School of Education launched a huge survey on the satisfaction of tenure-track faculty members; available at http://gseacademic.harvard.edu/~coache/downloads/COACHE_Report_20060925.pdf (accessed March 24, 2010).

54. See, e.g., Philip G. Altbach, "Professors and Politics," in *Comparative Higher Education: Knowledge, the University and Development*, ed. Philip G. Altbach (Greenwich, Conn., Ablex, 1998), 93–103. With the opening up of the academic profession, we can, of course, expect the recruitment of a greater diversity of faculty.

55. David Bloor, *Knowledge and Social Imagery* (London: Routledge & Kegan Paul, 1976).

56. Terry Shinn and Pascal Ragouet, *Controverses sur la science: Pour une sociologie transversaliste de l'activité scientifique* (Paris: Raisons d'agir, 2005).

57. Michel Callon, ed., *La science et ses réseaux: Genèse et circulation des faits scientifiques* (Paris: La découverte, 1989); Bruno Latour, *Science in Action: How to Follow Scientists and Engineers Through Society* (Cambridge, Mass.: Harvard University Press, 1987).

58. Bruno Latour and Steven Woolgar, *Laboratory Life: The Social Construction of Scientific Facts* (Beverly Hills, Calif.: Sage, 1979); Karin D. Knorr-Cetina, *Epistemic Cultures: How the Sciences Make Knowledge* (Cambridge, Mass.: Harvard University Press, 1999).

59. K-H. Chiang, "Relationship Between Research and Teaching in Doctoral Education in French Universities: The Case of Economic and Management, and Chemistry" (report to the Ministry of Education and to the CNRS Direction for European and International Affairs) (Dijon: IREDU, University of Dijon, 2006).

60. An example is Christopher Ball, "Teaching and Research," in *Research and Higher Education: The United Kingdom and the United States*, ed. Thomas Whiston and Roger Geiger (Buckingham: Open University Press, 1992), 130–37; Stephen Rowland, "Relationships Between Teaching and Research," *Teaching in Higher Education* 1 (1996): 7–20.

61. See, e.g., Shirley M. Clark, "The Academic Profession and Career. Perspectives and Problems," *Teaching Sociology* 14 (1986): 24–34; Mary Frank Fox, "Research, Teaching and Publication Productivity: Mutuality Versus Competition in Academia," *Sociology of Education* 65 (1992): 293–305.

62. Philip G. Altbach, ed., *The International Academic Profession: Portraits of Fourteen Countries* (San Francisco: Jossey-Bass, 1996).

63. Denis Bertrand, *Le travail professoral reconstruit: Au-delà de la modulation* (Sainte Foy: Presses de l'Université de Québec, 1993); Denis Bertrand et al., *Le travail professoral remesuré: Unité et diversité* (Sainte Foy : Presses de l'Université de Québec, 1995). Mathias Dewatripont, Ian Jewitt, and Jean Tirole, "Multitask Agency Problems: Focus and Task Clustering," in *The Strategic Analysis of Universities*, ed. Mathias Dewatripont, Françoise Thys-Clément, and Luc Wilkin (Brussels : Editions de l'Université de Bruxelles, 2001), 1–8.

64. Christine Musselin, "Are Universities Specific Organisations?" in *Towards a Multiversity ? Universities Between Global Trends and national Traditions*, ed. Georg Krücken, Anna Kosmützky, and Mark Torka (Bielefeld: Transcript Verlag, 2006), 63–84.

65. Michael D. Cohen, James G. March, and Johan P. Olsen, "A Garbage Can Model of Organizational Choice," *Administrative Science Quarterly* 17 (1972): 1–25.

66. William F. Massy and Robert Zemsky, "Faculty Discretionary Time: Departments and the 'Academic Ratchet,'" *Journal of Higher Education* 65 (1994): 1–22.

67. Jason Owen-Smith and Walter W. Powell, "Careers and Contradictions: Faculty Responses to the Transformation of Knowledge and Its Uses in the Life Sciences," *Research in the Sociology of Work* 10 (2001): 109–40.

68. Martin Finkelstein and Jack H. Schuster, "Assessing the Silent Revolution. How Changing Demographics Are Reshaping the Academic Profession," *AAHE Bulletin* 54 (October 2001): 3–7; Schuster and Finkelstein, *The American Faculty*; Finkelstein, "The Morphing."

69. Howard P. Tuckman and Jack Leahey, "What Is an Article Worth?" *Journal of Political Economy*, 83 (1975): 951–67; Art M. Diamond, "What Is a Citation Worth?" *Journal of Human Resources* 21 (1986): 200–215.

70. Jeffrey Pfeffer and Nancy Langton, "Wage Inequality and the Organization of Work: The Case of Academic Departments," *Administrative Science Quarterly* 33 (1988): 588–606.

71. Ehrenberg, McGraw, and Mrdjenovic, "Why Do Field Differentials in Average Faculty Salaries Vary."

72. Mary Henkel, *Academic Identities and Policy Change in Higher Education* (Philadelphia: Jessica Kingsley, 2000); Sandra Harley, "The Impact of Research Assessment

Exercise on Academic Work and Identity in UK Universities," *Studies in Higher Education* 27 (2002): 187–205.

73. Stephan, "Job Market Effects." For biology in the United States, the probability recently declined from 10.3% to 6.9% (p. 6). Quoting Schulze and Warning, Stephan writes that in Germany, "the ratio of new applications to job openings rose from roughly 3/2 to 5/2 during the 14-year period" studied by the two authors (p. 11). See Günther Schulze and Susanne Warning, "Federalism and the Production of Professors" (paper presented at the conference "Scientific Competition, Theory and Policy," Saarbrücken, Germany, October 2005). "The average age at first major independent research support has increased from 37 in 1980 to 41.9 in 2002 for PhDs" (Stephan, "Job Market Effects," 6).

74. Ronald Ehrenberg and Liang Zhang, "Do Tenured and Tenure-Track Faculty Matter?" (working paper, Cornell Higher Education Research Institute, 2004).

75. Barney G. Glaser, *The Organizational Scientist: Their Professional Careers* (Indianapolis: Bobbs-Merrill, 1964); Joseph Ben David, *Centers of Learning: Britain, France, Germany and the United States* (New Brunswick, N.J.: Transaction, 1977).

76. David Blumenthal et al., "Participation of Life-Science Faculty in Research Relationships with Industry," *New England Journal of Medicine* 335 (1996): 1734–39.

77. According to Whittington and Smith Doerr, women are less involved than men in these kinds of activities. See Kersten Whittington and Laurel Smith-Doerr, "Gender and Commercial Science: Women's Patenting in Life Sciences," *Journal of Technology Transfer* 30 (200): 355–70. Azoulay, Ding, and Stuart come to similar conclusions. See Pierre Azoulay, Waverly Ding, and Toby Stuart, "The Impact of Academic Patenting on the Rate, Quality and Direction of (Public) Research Output" (working paper no. 11917) (Cambridge, Mass.: NBER, 2006).

78. With a few exceptions, e.g., Patricia J. Gumport, "Public Universities as Academic Workplaces," *Daedalus* 126 (1997): 113–36.

79. A few examples based on papers already quoted in this text: Pfeffer and Langton have one hypothesis (p. 8) on the relationships between the wage variation in departments and institutional status (Pfeffer and Langton, "Wage Inequality and the Organization of Work"). Stephan has a table showing that the ratio between "full-time non-tenure-track faculty and total full-time faculty" is higher in private research institutions than in public research universities, etc. (Stephan, "Job Market Effects").

80. There is, however, a large literature on private universities. See Alma Maldonado et al., *Private Higher Education: An International Bibliography* (Chestnut Hill, Mass.: Center for International Higher Education and PROPHE, Boston College, 2004).

81. Pierre-Michel Menger, *Portrait de l'artiste en travailleur: Métamorphoses du capitalisme* (Paris: Seuil, 2002), 8–9, my translation.

82. Daniel Lee Kleinman and Steven P. Vallas, "Sciences, Capitalism, and the Rise of the 'Knowledge Worker': The Changing Structure of Knowledge Production in the United States," *Theory and Society* 30 (2001): 451, 460.

83. Walter W. Powell, "Neither Market nor Hierarchy: Network Forms of Organization," *Research in Organizational Behavior* 12 (1990): 295–336.

84. Walter W. Powell and Jason Owen-Smith, "Universities and the Market for Intellectual Property in the Life Sciences," *Journal of Policy Analysis and Management* 17 (1998): 253–77.

85. Nils Brunsson and Kerstin Sahlin-Anderson, "Constructing Organisations: The Example of Public Reform Sector," *Organisation Studies* 21 (2000): 721–46; Georg Krücken and Frank Meier, "Turning the University into an Organizational Actor," in *Globalization and Organization*, ed. Gili Drori, John Meyer, and Hokyu Hwang (Oxford: Oxford University Press, 2006), 241–57; Patricia J. Gumport, "Academic Restructuring: Organizational Change and Institutional Imperatives," *Higher Education* 39 (2000): 67–91; Musselin, "Are Universities Specific Organisations?"

86. See Halsey, *The Decline of Donnish Dominion*; Dearlove, "The Academic Labour Process"; Slaughter and Leslie, *Academic Capitalism*; Deem, "New Managerialism in Higher Education"; Lafferty and Fleming, "The Restructuring of Academic Work in Australia"; and Reed and Deem, "New Managerialism."

87. Christine Musselin, "European Academic Labor Markets in Transition," *Higher Education* 49 (2005): 135–54.

88. Kleinman and Vallas, "Sciences," 468.

89. The question of the impact of industry (and its new forms) on academic organization is central to the doctoral work of Simcha Jong, "How Industry Ties Shape the Organization of Science; Reorganizations at Berkeley and Stanford After the Birth of the Biotech Industry" (paper presented at the "European Forum on the Role of Universities in Innovation Systems," European University Institute, Florence, June 2005).

90. Luc Boltanski and Eve Chiapello, *The New Spirit of Capitalism* (New York: Verso, 2005).

91. Richard Sennett, *The Corrosion of Character: The Personal Consequences of Work in Late Capitalism* (New York: Norton, 1998).

92. Alvin W. Gouldner, "Cosmopolitans and Locals: Toward an Analysis of Latent Social Roles 1," *Administrative Science Quarterly* 2 (1958): 281–306; Alvin W. Gouldner, "Cosmopolitans and Locals: Toward an Analysis of Latent Social Roles 2," *Administrative Science Quarterly* 2 (1958): 440–80.

93. Rachel A. Rosenfeld, "Job Mobility and Career Processes," *Annual Review of Sociology* 18 (1992): 39–61.

94. Harrison C. White, *Chains of Opportunity, System Model of Mobility in Organizations* (Cambridge, Mass.: Harvard University Press, 1970); D. Randall Smith and Andrew Abbott, "A Labor Market Perspective on the Mobility of College Football Coaches," *Social Forces* 61 (1983): 1147–67.

95. Rosenfeld, "Job Mobility and Career Processes," 45.

96. Michael B. Arthur, "The Boundaryless Career: A New Perspective for Organizational Inquiry," *Journal of Organizational Behavior* 15 (1994): 295–306; Michael B. Arthur and Denise Rousseau, eds., *The Boundaryless Career: A New Employment Principle for a New Organizational Area* (New York: Oxford University Press, 1996); Douglas T. Hall, *Career Development in Organizations* (Thousand Oaks, Calif.: Sage, 1986); Michael B. Arthur, P. H. Claman, and R. J. DeFillipi, "Intelligent Enterprise, Intelligent Careers," *Academy of Management Executive* 9 (1995): 7–22.

97. Howard Becker, *Outsiders: Studies in the Sociology of Deviance* (Glencoe, Ill.: Free Press, 1963); Everett Hughes, *Men and Their Work* (Glencoe, Ill.: Free Press, 1958). As Bastin stressed in his stimulating study of the careers of EU journalists, this makes a significant difference in the new career theory, which focuses only on the way the environment is transforming careers. See Gilles Bastin, "Les professionnels de l'information européenne à Bruxelles: Sociologie d'un monde de l'information (territoires, carrières, dispositifs)" (PhD diss., École normale supérieure de Cachan, 2003).

98. Diana Crane, "Social Class Origin and Academic Success: The Influence of Two Stratification Systems on Academic Careers," *Sociology of Education* 42 (1969): 1–1; Dwight Lang, "Equality, Prestige, and Controlled Mobility in the Academic Hierarchy," *American Journal of Education* 95 (1987): 441–67; Stephan Baldi, "Prestige Determinants of First Academic Job for New Sociology PhDs 1985–1992," *Sociological Quarterly* 36 (1995): 777–89.

99. J. Scott Long., Paul D. Allison, and Robert McGinnis, "Entrance into the Academic Career," *American Sociological Review* 46 (1979): 816–30.

100. Paul D. Allison and J. Scott Long, "Interuniversity Mobility of Academic Scientists," *American Sociological Review* 52 (1987): 643–52; Mathew P. Nagowski, "Associate Professor Turnover at America's Public and Private Institutions of Higher Education" (working paper, Cornell Higher Education Research Institute, 2004).

101. Not to mention more refined analysis stressing contradictory evolutions resulting from a comparable force transforming universities into managed organizations: writers like Harley, Muller-Camen, and Collin conclude that managerialism in the United Kingdom tends to render academic careers less boundaryless, whereas by freeing young academics from the chair-professors, the German managerial reforms tend to make academic careers less bounded as well. See Sandra Harley, Michael

Muller-Camen, and Audrey Collin, "From Academic Communities to Managed Organisations: The Implications for Academic Careers in UK and German Universities," *Journal of Vocational Behavior* 64 (2004): 329–45.

102. Theodore Caplow and Reece McGee, *The Academic Marketplace* (Garden City, N.Y.: Doubleday, 1958); Yehuda Baruch and Douglas T. Hall, "The Academic Career: A Model for Future Careers in Other Sectors?" *Journal of Vocational Behavior* 64 (2004): 241–62.

103. See Mark Kaulisch and Jürgen Enders, "Careers in Overlapping Institutional Contexts: The Case of Academe," *Career Development International* 10 (2005): 130–44; also Susan C. de Janasz and Sherry E. Sullivan, "Multiple Mentoring in Academe: Developing the Professorial Network," *Journal of Vocational Behavior* 64 (2004): 263–83. They argue that the transformation of academic careers into intelligent careers weakens the traditional model of academics guided by one single mentor (usually their dissertation adviser) and instead encourages having several mentors.

104. Myriam Carrère et al., *Les carrières des chercheurs de l'INRA: Analyses et interprétations* (Paris: Monograph, 2006).

105. Stephen R. Barley and Gideon Kunda, "Bringing Work Back In," *Organization Science* 12 (2001): 78 (italics added).

106. This distinction in three groups borrows from a recent paper from Enders and Musselin (2008) but is also quite close to Handy's predictions for the future workplace. According to Handy, the future workplace will consist of three groups: a group of core professionals with organizational affiliation, a group of free-lance professionals with fixed-term contracts, and a group of contingent workers paid by the hour. Enders and Musselin, "Back to the Future"; Charles Handy, *The Age of Unreason* (Cambridge, Mass.: Harvard University Press, 1994).

107. Patricia J. Gumport, "Learning Academic Labor," *Comparative Social Research* 19 (2000): 1–23.

108. Barley and Kunda, "Bringing Work Back In," 78.

109. For a more detailed description of the interplay between these three components in the German, American, and French cases, see Christine Musselin, *The Markets for Academics* (New York: Routledge, 2009), first published as *Le marché du travail universitaire: France, Allemagne, États-Unis* (Paris: Presses de Sciences Po, 2005), chap. 7.

110. In a stimulating paper published in 1994, Sørensen found a similar reflection on the interaction of firms, employment relationships, and wages. See Aage B. Sørensen, "Firms, Wages and Incentives," in *Handbook of Economic Sociology*, ed. Neil J. Smelser and Richard Swedberg (Princeton, N.J.: Princeton University Press and Russell Sage, 1994), 504–28.

111. Aloysus Siow, "The Organization of the Market for Professors" (working paper no. UT-ECIPA-SIOW-95–01, Toronto University, 1995).

112. Musselin, *The Markets for Academics*. One can compare those situations in which several candidates are competing for one position with those in which the competence of one candidate is assessed to evaluate whether he or she fulfills the expected requirements.

113. In other words, does each higher education institution provide career and promotion possibilities (internal labor markets), or must academics return on the job market to obtain a better salary and career?

114. Harley, Muller-Camen, and Collin, "From Academic Communities to Managed Organisations."

Cultural Formations of the
Public University

*Globalization, Diversity, and the State
at the University of Michigan*

MICHAEL D. KENNEDY

FIFTEEN

Most of universities' transformations do not challenge the centrality of excellence to university work, but their public mission may be at risk with the globalization of knowledge cultures, the multiplying frames of diversity and justice informing their mission, and the relative decline in the state's capacity to support university excellence. This risk is magnified when relatively anachronistic conceptions of the public inform the mission and practice of university work.

By considering the relationship among proximate publics, the value of diversity, and the significance of global reference in university work, I clarify in this chapter the cultural formations (those incipient sensibilities that do not necessarily reflect institutional structures)[1] of the public that might inspire new articulations of the cumulative public good in universities. In particular, I propose that service to core and proximate publics (campus and local/state residents) or undifferentiated publics (the world, learning, etc.) in the mission of the public university should be supplemented by elaborations of the value of engaging particular publics. I make this case by drawing on a particular university.

The University of Michigan (U-M) is one of the oldest, largest, and most influential public universities in the United States, and its experience and example have helped shape the very notion of what a U.S. public university is, or even can be, about.[2] We therefore might look at U-M as a strategic research site for understanding the U.S. public research university,[3] to consider in more depth the empirical conditions and normative models shaping questions about the future of public universities. This university also is familiar to me.

The University of Michigan was my employer when I wrote this chapter. I composed this then as an insider, trying to make sense of some of the challenges facing my own institution. That means that I have a familiarity that external analysts might not have. But I also am constrained by the politics of my location; I discuss only those issues that I think can be addressed in existing frameworks of legitimate university practice.

Some readers thus may regard this chapter as more prescriptive than descriptive or analytical, its data more suggestive than systematic, and its conclusions more pragmatic than transformational. These readers are right.

I have learned a great deal from the scholarly literature on public universities as I moved into this research domain from my principal focus on intellectuals and transformation in the communist and postcommunist worlds. I have found interesting data and inspiring rigor in particular scholarly niches. I also recognize an abundance of transformational voices in academic work for those who broadly share their vision. At the same time, their opponents are often able to pull transformers into ideological muck, forcing work and debate that reinforce ideological divisions rather than enable scholarship that moves that ideological opposition. I have found, too, that most notions of "the public" at work in shaping the mission of public universities tend to be flatter and less explicit about the variety of publics than is productive for innovation. In practice, many public universities are working across multiple publics already, but without sufficient academic justification for why they invest in particular publics and especially without an explanation of how those various public engagements cumulate in the development of university work. I believe that by focusing on the transformation of the public/university relationship, we might find new ways to articulate university value and distinction beyond commercial effect and career preparation.

U-M is, of course, distinctive, and because I draw on my own experience in addition to my analysis of this university's various documents, I do not pretend to offer more general prescriptions for other universities in the United States, much less across the world. In fact, the articulation of universities with multiple publics requires grounding in their own locales to be legitimate. But by making explicit some of the challenges, and promises, I hope to stimulate additional and better reflection on what publics we support, and why, in research universities generally.

My experience at U-M is skewed. I have been most involved in articulating the university's international engagement, somewhat involved in exploring diversity's meaning before and after the 2006 referendum prohibiting affirmative action in the state of Michigan's higher education and state employment, and mostly an observer of the university's relationship to the state of Michigan. In this chapter, I move from least to most informed readings and, arguably, from the least to the most complicated of the university's sense of "public." But to what category of university do I refer when I imply something more than this particular University of Michigan?

MEANINGS OF THE UNIVERSITY

Craig Calhoun and Diana Rhoten elaborate more than I will the ways in which this volume elaborates on previously understood usages of "university" and "public," but given my focus on a single university, I will begin by reflecting on what this single case can offer to those interested in the bigger picture.

Because I focus on U-M first and foremost, some of the issues I explore are more appropriate to those universities that share with it a categorical identification or family resemblance. U-M's challenges and opportunities may have more in common with other American universities than with Canadian universities, and more with North American than European, and so on; more with other public universities than private universities; more with other public universities with few branch campuses than those with many; with other research-focused schools than universities that have community engagement leading their mission; more with other universities belonging to the Committee on Institutional Cooperation[4] than schools in the Atlantic Coast Conference (ACC); more with other universities belonging to the American Association of Universities than those who do not belong; more with other universities in the Shanghai Jiao Tong's top 100 than with those beyond that number;[5] and more with other universities that use international references on their homepage and in their practice than do those that struggle to find a place for less commonly taught languages in their teaching. But these questions are not, I believe, limited to any particular category and instead should find suitable translation for other contexts. Indeed, I found similar values in analyzing a single university with whom Michigan shares fewer than half of these qualities.

Rebecca Lowen's analysis of the making of the cold war university focuses on Stanford and raises issues that are peculiar to elite private universities.[6] At least they were peculiar in the last century. Stanford, led by Harvard, Chicago, Columbia, and Yale, received significant private foundation support in the 1920s to develop academic science but, with financial ruin in the 1930s, had to transform one of its ideological self-understandings: its independence from government. Initially, Harvard, Yale, and more than 130 other private institutions refused government support, arguing that to be private, a university had to be independent of all political influence, to remain "remote from the pressures of democratic society."[7] But economic crisis overwhelmed this argument and led to new sensibilities about what it meant to be a great private university, and to new mechanisms, like contract overhead, that allowed previously more acceptable industrial patronage to be linked to federal support without changing the university's sense of private self.

With more and more of the university's budget depending on external sources and not on university endowment, new questions emerged about academic freedom, departmental autonomy, military patronage, and, ultimately, who might define excellence. But these debates have occurred across all universities, both private and public. From depression to world war to cold war, Stanford University came to exemplify the cold war university in the fusion of big science, external support, and national need. This was a private university working to support the national good, struggling at the same time to define itself above and outside political interests (even if its founding conservative bent meant that those with socialist and liberal leanings were at greater risk of being punished for that identification).

Beyond observing that the making of the cold war university at a private university made it look more like a public university, I take two methodological inspirations and two points of departure from Lowen's work. First, her interest in exploring a university as a whole, rather than its departments or schools, suggests the promise and problems of this grander focus. There is great variation in any university, especially large, research-based ones, but when budgets are managed, senior hires and promotions reviewed, and relationships with publics coordinated by central authorities, some universitywide basis for meaningful public engagement must be cultivated.

Second, Lowen's analysis of the ways in which agency and historical context combine to account for the transformation of knowledge production is most suggestive for this chapter. If agency can be found anywhere, it is in the case study, but for Lowen, contexts of depression, war, and academic competition wound up structuring agency far more than academic entrepreneurs could redefine the rules of the game. Hers, of course, is a post-hoc account, designed principally to explain the limits of strategic action.

Thus, while this chapter also looks backward, principally at the last decade of U-M's engagement of publics, it does so in order to expand the range of strategic action rather than to identify its limits. Taking some inspiration from my past work on intellectuals and transformation,[8] as well as those inspiring cultural sociological histories of eventful change,[9] I have found that those who recognize the value of translating schema from one setting to another and can recognize the conditions and contradictions of their various milieus can also extend their own range of possible effect. By recognizing how the engagement of publics in one setting might find amplified resonance in another, universities could extend their efficacy in developing necessary knowledge for the public good.[10] That requires rethinking the public for university work.

MEANINGS OF THE PUBLIC FOR THE UNIVERSITY

As this volume indicates, the sense of public varies considerably across the world. In most places, public refers to the state as such, with universities an expression of state responsibility, power, and employment. Such an institutional emphasis deflects from the sense of public I intend here, one of communicative space and associational life that is neither private nor state owned but that implies both an everyday American sense and a Habermasian rational-critical democratic perspective of identification and open engagement around issues among members of committed collectivities.[11] The theoretical implications of such a notion of public are especially useful for recognizing the peculiarity of the public around and through the university.

With Habermas's elaboration of open and undistorted communicative practice as a normative guide for identifying truthful discourses, we might review university practice to see how well its research, teaching, and administration reflect such principles of reason and communicative rationality rather than, or over and above, power and exchange. Given that the legitimacy of universities depend in part on such idealized claims, Calhoun's invitation to consider qualities of public spheres may be especially appropriate to researching the qualities of publics around and through universities:

> We need to ask how responsive public opinion is to reasoned argument, how well any potential public sphere benefits from the potential for self correction and

collective education implicit in the possibilities for rational-critical discourse. And we need to know how committed participants are to the processes of public discourse and through that to each other. Finally, and not least of all, we need to ask how effectively the public opinion formed can influence social institutions and wielders of economic, political, or indeed cultural power.[12]

These questions are useful for those assessing the corporatization of the university and other power-laden influences on academic practice, but I find another dimension of Habermasian public spheres more useful. Beyond the qualities of any particular public sphere, we should attend to the ways in which different publics inform one another through their constitutive discourses and how those constitutive discourses radiate and have variable impacts.

One of the most productive developments in studies of the public sphere is discovering how different publics around various issues and identifications are constituted and how they combine, contest, and cumulate to create higher aggregations of public discourse that in turn have different effects on those with power, those guiding institutions of consequence. How do various class, regional, and other differentiated publics, for instance, help constitute national publics? Under what circumstances? Or how might particular French, Polish, and German publics shape European public spheres? On which issues? With what strategies?

With these examples, I do not seek to develop a general theory of the conditions under which various publics have consequence. Rather, I use them to illustrate that thinking about the multiplicity of relationships among publics is a useful sensitizing scheme to compare the differing qualities and uneven impacts of the relationship among publics and universities. We might even extend this relational question to the inner life of universities themselves.

While it may be difficult to consider a departmental faculty meeting an expression of the public sphere, given the familiarities of ties and the disciplinary or professional direction of conversation, it could be useful to look at the larger schools in a university as particular kinds of publics with special issues organizing identification and discourse, perhaps law, business, liberal arts, or technology. Furthermore, we might combine those school discourses into a broader university public and then into the associational and public life of the academic sector per se, to be that very aggregation that experts in the public sphere's study look at when they move across class and regional publics into more generalized discussions defining national publics. Studying universities and publics therefore invites us to consider the qualities of each public discourse and then how these different publics shape one another in the larger public of which they are a part. Ultimately, we also can explore how particular university members call on these discourses to claim the authority to speak for the university as a single constitutive actor. And we might also compare universities across space and over time to see which kinds of discourses have public resonance and institutional authority.

Whether in the utterance of a university president, faculty member, or student senate representative, claims are constrained by a broader academic field of discussion, in which the values of scholarship and the kinds of authoritative arguments and credentials have their own quality. But like any organization or occupational field, universities must appeal to logics and values beyond the common sense of their members. In this case, the achievements of investment funds, the costs of laboratory equipment, the priorities of legislators, and the career expectations of students, among other markers, shape the constitution of any university's public sphere. Universities risk their legitimacy, or their distinction, to the extent that principles derived from other systems dominate their practice, whether based on state direction, commercial motivation, or students' career expectations. Somehow, these external principles must be translated into common public sense in the university to support this most immediate public; and the values of the university must be transferred to those whose powers enable the university to function.

Thus, in addition to examining how public discourses within a bounded organization or community combine and cumulate, we should also see how those publics in adjacent spheres intersect. How, in particular, do discourses in one sphere translate into the other, and vice versa?

As the costs of higher education rise and the capacities or willingness of states to support their universities decline, the challenge and importance of this translation grow. In addition to communicating the value of the public university more effectively to legislators, expectations of reaching out to alumni and others philanthropically inclined also increases. While we might regard them as merely investors in the university, I prefer to think of both state and philanthropists and the public within the university as three of the most "proximate" publics whose engagement with one another over the university's value and contribution are among the most consequential discourses for the university's institutional reproduction. Associations of universities and of public media that engage this work, like the *Chronicle of Higher Education* in the United States, reflect and extend those particular engagements.

These are the publics to which we usually refer when speaking about the public university, but there are others that we should keep in mind with the globalization of knowledge cultures and the multiplication of frames of diversity and justice shaping university work. Indeed, beyond the translation of university value to proximate publics, we might also examine the translation of globalization and diversity into the framework of public mission among the discourses to be cultivated among those interested in the transformation of public universities.

With the compression of time and space as a consequence of changes in information and communication technology and with the growing competition to realize on national and even global scale the stature of academic leadership, universities cannot rest easy with their proximate publics. Academic excellence increasingly requires global reference in collaborating with and recruiting faculty and students. To the extent that these global references imply public engagement, they are typically presented as vague and general worlds at large or knowledge in general, which need only to fulfill the demands of scholarly excellence. The sense of public obligation, or public discourse, fades in favor of a kind of participation more like the consumer's than the interlocutor's. Instead of a university with public obligation and engagement, we have a global university with virtual audiences voluntarily consuming scholarly work.

Public reference also changes with the university's varying relationship to groups differentiated by power and privilege. When U.S. universities excluded women, people of color, and non-Christians from their student body and faculty, higher education's variation in public address was manifest. With the appearance of open access, despite differences in participation rates, new conflicts over including disenfranchised publics in higher education emerged on a new scale. But rather than debate how the university might serve those distinctively disenfranchised publics, the discussion often turns on how individual consumers receive, or are denied, rights of entry to scholarly learning.

In both cases, the only public that remains in this globalizing and apparently diverse university is the immediate public constituted by membership. But this is not the meaning of the public university made by engaging those beyond the proximate. Is there a way to extend the forms in which universities classically engage their proximate external publics to global and disenfranchised publics? And are there lessons for how we might reframe the university's public mission so that it serves not only its proximate constituents but also globalizing knowledge cultures and the multiplication of diversity and justice claims simultaneously?

First, I examine the ways in which the proximate public functions in the University of Michigan and then how diversity and globalization offer opportunities to extend and enrich the sense of public that more typically informs the university mission.

THE STRAIGHTFORWARD PUBLIC UNIVERSITY OF MICHIGAN

The U.S. public university is made up of large numbers of students with a full range of infrastructure dedicated to their residential learning. Their campus identification is enhanced through campus-associated arts and entertainment (most evident in sports). Campuses tend to be distributed throughout a state so as to extend access to its regionally, demographically, and economically diverse population; but campuses vary in their dedication to research. Public universities have an especially wide range of research and teaching functions under one roof, from the liberal arts to professional schools, even though these schools usually have unequal financial capacities. Nonetheless, the quality of graduate and professional education is typically the most prominent indicator of research/teaching excellence, enabling excellence to be measured in relatively objective and self-fulfilling prophetical fashion. Dedication to the public is more complicated.

Scholars have identified the ways in which academic excellence and public commitment generate tensions: focusing on state residence rather than overall excellence, and on practical means of study even if they are not the most prestigious or scientifically valuable; and providing services to the public, even when they distract from other definitions of academic accomplishment.[13] The University of Michigan (U-M) is one of the most research-driven public universities. Mindful of its public commitments, it does what it can to represent its academic accomplishment itself as a public good on websites,[14] in brochures, and by its individual leaders. Still, those generic tensions are evident but easily overlooked if we look only at the immediate public that benefits: students.

Founded in 1817 and originally located in the Detroit area on land ceded by the Chippewa, Ottawa, and Potawatomi peoples, U-M moved to Ann Arbor in 1837 and by 1866, with 1,255 students, became the largest university in the United States.[15] By 2006, U-M had more than 52,000 students and more than 5,500 faculty at three campuses, in Ann Arbor, Dearborn, and Flint. The Dearborn and Flint campuses are especially integrated in their communities and differ somewhat from the more research-driven and nationally/globally referenced Ann Arbor campus. When considered together, U-M has one of the largest communities of alumni in the world, 420,000.

The students and alumni of U-M, like those of most public universities, are the clearest and most proximate "public" to which the university might appeal. It also is presumed that such a public should bear close resemblance to and affinity with the political body associated with it: for U-M, this is those in the state of Michigan.

In U-M's mission statement, the university is specifically charged to "serve the people of Michigan and the world through preeminence in creating, communicating, preserving and applying knowledge, art, and academic values, and in developing leaders and citizens who will challenge the present and enrich the future."[16] Accomplished graduates are the most obvious public good, and admissions is the most prominent scarce good over which universities have control. This flow of learners becomes the most obvious public value, and the good stewardship of this valuable resource is the most important demonstration of good leadership.[17]

Various accrediting documents state that Michigan residents should "continue to be the principal beneficiaries of these programs." There is also some informal discussion about what the proper percentage is. After all, U-M's "out of state" tuition is much higher than its in-state tuition. By admitting more students from out of state, U-M could improve its financial profile. But this is never an explicit and public bargaining chip, even though it is an obvious recourse for enhancing U-M's budget should state support ever decline too much.

The public mission also assumes that U-M should help supply the "physicians, dentists, lawyers, teachers and other professionals needed within the state." There is some anxiety that in recent years, too many graduates left the state,[18] but it is also recognized that U-M should train leaders for national and international roles. Indeed, by having such a prominent institution, U-M leaders suggest that the citizens of the state have a greater chance to become prominent in the United States or the world as a consequence of this university's quality.[19]

The demographics of the student body are therefore the easiest way to recognize U-M's special commitment to its public, defined as the residents of the state of Michigan. The trajectory of the student body is the easiest way to identify U-M's special commitment to the world. By associating the private benefit of individual state residents who matriculate at U-M with the public good, the problem of the "public" university is relatively easily addressed. This public association can become problematic, however, because the public value of this education depends on citizens of the state recognizing affinities, whether personally or through networks or in broader cultural associations, with students who enroll and graduate and finding in those affinities a public good.

Another straightforward attempt by the university to articulate its public mission rests in its Public Goods Council. Composed of museums, libraries, performance programs, experiential learning, and other programs serving constituencies within and beyond the academy itself, the council regards its public as "students, faculty and staff at the University . . . public-school students and their teachers, residents of Ann Arbor and the State of Michigan, arts and cultural organizations, public-service units, and countless other community groups."[20] In this, the proximity of the local public is reinforced. But even this impressive articulation is not U-M's best-known public good.

Athletics may be the most prominent public face of many, if not most, of the prominent U.S. public universities. It is also one of the most substantial parts of their economy. U-M expects its athletic department revenues to be $87.4 million in 2008, enabling it to be self-supporting and also to contribute to student fellowships beyond its own mission.[21] The value of success on the gridiron or court can also contribute directly to the popularity of the university in student recruitments or in alumni or fan donations to private endowments. Of course, the relationship between this aspect of university life and the university's educational mission is itself complicated.

The former U-M president James Duderstadt has called the commercialization of intercollegiate athletics a "corrosive example of entertainment culture"; he found that intercollegiate basketball, in particular, had values alien to the university's educational mission.[22] Still, a regional newspaper might signal the importance of collegiate sports to the public with this simple sentence: "Most people know Ann Arbor as a funky college town and the home of Wolverine football."[23] The "Big House," the largest American football stadium in the world, is a virtual shrine at U-M. Attempts to change its architecture[24] or introduce special "luxury box seats"[25] always lead to heated debates about public goods and the public university.

For a volume dedicated to the public university, sports may seem insignificant, but their value should be apparent in helping us recognize the ways in which the university becomes part of the public imaginary, produces goods the public values that extend beyond individual careers, and appeals to those without necessary ties to any particular university. In fact, the authors of the article describing Ann Arbor as the home of Wolverine football themselves recognized the linkage: beyond funk and football, Ann Arbor should also be known as "an economic engine for the state."[26] That is certainly the public good most university spokespersons reach for when justifying the public university. In fact, its cultural articulation shares some important qualities with sports.

THE ECONOMIC VALUE OF THE PUBLIC
RESEARCH UNIVERSITY

Over the last two decades, most public universities suffered relative losses in state appropriations, with the University of California system being the best example.[27] U-M also suffered this loss but for most of this period remained relatively well off through an aggressive privatization of resource streams (raising tuition and private endowment).[28] In recent years, however, the state budgetary environment has worsened dramatically. At the time of this writing, the state of Michigan faced a budget shortfall of some $700 million, whose remedy threatens to cut state allocations to the state's fifteen public universities.[29]

In fact, thirteen of fifteen Michigan public universities already received less funding in 2005/2006 than they did in 2001/2002.[30] Michigan's Governor Jennifer Granholm recently considered an innovation in this formula: breaking the universities into two categories, with "research universities" (U-M, Michigan State University, and Wayne State University) receiving different consideration than the others. They do already, receiving more than half of the state's allocation to higher education, even though they educate less than one-third of the students.[31]

This preference for research universities is a difficult position to sustain in the state legislature, given the coincident geographic dispersal of representatives and of the other twelve public universities. After all, the opponents of the two-category model argue, if public universities are about access, which is one of the public values of public universities, then we should disperse the universities and their benefits across the state.

To counter this popular appeal, others contend that much more has to be done to "talk up business successes" associated with the public research universities.[32] The best example of this is the University Research Corridor, an alliance of the University of Michigan, Michigan State University, and Wayne State University dedicated to generate jobs and investments through scholarly research.[33]

Envisioned as part of the postindustrial economic transformation, Michigan's public university leaders argue that its academic research generates tangible and immediate economic benefits. Michigan State University's president, Lou Anna Simon, for instance, pointed out that for each research dollar brought in, another $26 are generated for the state. This is realized in a variety of ways, above all through the recruitment and retention of the most talented to the state.

This University Research Corridor (URC) emphasizes that universities bring in the most accomplished employees from abroad. And better than some other states, these Michigan universities help these and other professors and their students start companies. The URC celebrates how a student and his adviser set up a medical imaging firm, Xoran Technologies of Ann Arbor, that in 2006 added 171 jobs to the economy. But universities are not involved only in start-ups, they also work to hold onto valued taxpayers.

When Pfizer cut 2,410 jobs, mostly around Ann Arbor, the state teamed up with the University of Michigan and other actors to keep some of these highly skilled workers in the region.[34] U-M President Mary Sue Coleman described the alliance between the state and the university directly:

> Within hours of the Pfizer announcement, leaders from throughout our community and state, including Gov. Jennifer Granholm, gathered in Ann Arbor to say: We will work together to overcome this loss. We have since formed several Strategic Working Action Teams focused on issues such as redeveloping the Pfizer site, creating new jobs for displaced employees, and identifying new funding for area nonprofits at risk because of a drop in charitable giving by Pfizer. U-M is committing $3 million over three years to recruit and hire Pfizer scientists who can enrich our research faculty in biomedical, pharmaceutical and other fields.... Collaboration is critical to our future; it is absolutely essential that government, industry, nonprofits, entrepreneurs and venture capitalists all be players. Collaboration also is essential to a strong, rapid response, which is how communities must act to survive and thrive in the 21st century. This is one reason why U-M, Wayne State University and Michigan State University have come together to form the University Research Corridor. The URC will play a key role in helping transform our state into a technology and innovation leader, using the intellectual capital of our institutions.[35]

Beyond direct economic benefits, the quality of health care, especially cutting-edge health care, is another public benefit that public universities provide the state. Whether in the study of genes that underlie nicotine dependence or in the development of new techniques that allow radiation-treated patients to bear children, universities obviously contribute substantially to the public good. Perhaps the clearest argument for the value of a public university comes in reference to a product that is simultaneously profitable, has broad public value, and is something that the private sector would have never developed:

> Hunein "John" Maassab, a native of Damascus, Syria, came to the University of Michigan for graduate school so that he could study under Dr. Thomas Francis,

developer of the first effective influenza vaccine and leader of the Salk polio vaccine trials.

Shortly after finishing his PhD in 1956, Maassab joined the U-M faculty and began to work on a challenge laid down by Dr. Francis: Make a better influenza vaccine.

The effort became Maassab's lifework, consuming more than forty years of laboratory work, replete with false starts, dead ends, and frustrating disappointments. Had Maassab worked in a pharmaceutical company or another for-profit venture, his project would have been abandoned after only a few years because it was such a long shot.

But at the University of Michigan, with bright students, collaborative colleagues, and excellent resources, Maassab was able to see his vision through to fruition.

His improvement on influenza vaccine is now sold as FlU-Mist, and it is the first live-attenuated influenza vaccine delivered by a nasal spray. FlU-Mist has become an important new weapon against seasonal flu and is expected to reach $500 million in annual sales. It could not have happened anywhere else.

This last example illustrates the more general public good of research in public universities. Its value is most apparent when (1) it extends beyond the manifest function of research and teaching university students; (2) it is provided best, or only, by university work; and (3) it serves an undifferentiated public, or any potential member of it. Intercollegiate sports manage a similar translation. In both circumstances, sports and research can be performed by for-profit organizations, but both enjoy a certain desirable quality when kept distant from commercial taint and the bias it introduces.

The scholarly analysis of the commercialization of public research universities is substantial and beyond my purpose here.[36] For many critics, this close relationship between university mission and economic growth in the (local) private sector is dangerous,[37] as the commodification of college sports may pervert the university's values.

We might caution against essentializing commercial and/or academic values themselves, their differences, and their overall university effects. We should, for example, recognize the variation in commercial/academic ties within the university and the effects that those with particularly close ties have on other parts of the university.[38] Too, recent research suggests that universities wind up having the most successful commercial work when they pursue that interest as open, public, nonprofit organizations dedicated to long-term research rather than short-term benefits.[39]

Another example of promising fusion between commercial and academic aims is Google's partnership with the University of Michigan library to digitize the latter's seven million print volumes.[40] Google promises to provide some local benefits, investing in a major research and development center that will hire about one thousand employees between 2007 and 2012,[41] but the principal academic value comes in making this library globally accessible, as one of the university's greatest public goods. Appropriately, there is some debate about the dangers of a commercial search engine shaping access to these volumes,[42] but the example only reinforces the point that commercial investment does not necessarily limit the academic, or public, values of university work.

Despite the tenor of most of the debate about commercialization, one issue apparently unites all these straightforward public engagements: the *general* conception of the public itself. One of the reasons that economic engines and sports machines offer productive ways to envision the university's public engagement is because prosperity, athletic victories, or even global digital public goods rely on visions of publics that should be unified in their appreciation of what the university is supposed to do. Universities apparently demonstrate that public good by supplementing the general public's sense. But that is not the only way in which universities might engage the public, especially when one of the most important questions is the differentiation of publics themselves.

Rather than presume a general public good in these university engagements, we might ask which publics are served, what value is provided, and why. Consider, for example, another project identified in the University Research Corridor that was distinctive for its identification of the particular public it was designed to serve: a program dedicated to helping seventh-grade girls master science and math.[43] That certainly moves beyond the university's manifest function of serving college students, even though it demonstrates a new public good that can be provided by extending the potential pool of applicants for science and math. This particular commitment, however, also challenges another definition of the public university's public mission in its defiance of a public referendum on U-M's commitment to diversity.

DIVERSITY, EXCELLENCE, AND THE PUBLIC UNIVERSITY

Although public research universities have historically been the higher education leaders in integrating American society across gender, racial, and class lines, their distinction regarding diversity is declining as private universities are competing better for greater resources for the most prestigious representatives of diversity's commitment. Public universities suffer in this competition, however, not only because of relatively fewer resources, but also because of their susceptibility to political influence.[44] Once again, the University of Michigan is a good example of this.

Perhaps more than any other university in the United States, U-M has come to be associated with affirmative action and the politics of diversity because of the 2003 U.S. Supreme Court cases, *Gratz vs. Bollinger* and *Grutter vs. Bollinger*. The latter alleges unlawful preference given to minorities for law school admissions, and the former, for undergraduate admissions to the liberal arts college. These lawsuits, initiated in 1997, used an extraordinary amount of U-M's financial, scholarly, and political resources. One of the most valuable by-products of this was a much finer appreciation of the meaning and value of diversity and the publics that this diversity reflects.

This extensive appreciation of U-M's commitment to diversity was apparent in various amicus briefs from, for example, the Fortune 500,[45] retired military leaders,[46] and a well-known University of Michigan graduate, former President Gerald R. Ford, whose editorial in the *New York Times* argued on behalf of his alma mater's commitment to diversity.[47] But President George W. Bush did not agree and made that clear in various public statements emphasizing that it was the method to realize diversity, not diversity's goal, that was important.[48]

Beyond the debates about the value of a diverse body of business, academic, or military elites, and the means to realize them, the university also developed substantial arguments about the educational value of diverse classrooms themselves. Through both these arguments and the emphasis on contributing to the diversity of the nation's leadership, the case for diversity drifted away from justice per se toward a case for excellence for the workforce, the nation, and the learning process of every student enrolled in the university.[49]

While the results of the Supreme Court case were mixed in their appreciation of U-M's methods, the Court affirmed the university's value and commitment to diversity, along with the importance of linking excellence to diversity. But the opponents to affirmative action were not finished. They took up another method, building on successes in California, to put to a referendum an initiative that would ban affirmative action altogether. Under the title "Michigan Civil Rights Initiative," this movement put before the citizens of the state this question: "Should the state ban preferential treatment to groups or individuals based on their race, gender, color, ethnicity, or national origin for public employment, education, or contracting purposes?"

On November 7, 2006, the voters passed the Michigan civil rights initiative, with 58 percent in favor. Although efforts continue to challenge this outcome, two other developments from this referendum are worth noting in regard to the relationship between public and university.

First, on the day after the vote, U-M President Mary Sue Coleman reiterated the commitment she made during the campaign:

> Diversity matters at Michigan, today more than any day in our history. It matters today, and it will matter tomorrow. It will always matter because it is what makes us the great university we are. I am deeply disappointed that the voters of our state have rejected affirmative action as a way to help build a community that is fair and equal for all. But we will not be deterred in the all-important work of creating a diverse, welcoming campus. We will not be deterred. . . . This applies to our state as much as our university. Michigan's public universities and our public bodies must be more determined than ever to provide opportunities for women and minorities, who make up the majority of our citizenry. . . . I will not stand by while the very heart and soul of this great university is threatened. We are Michigan and we are diversity.[50]

This passion inspired those committed to the defense of the university's practice, but it also led others to wonder just how public this university was. Klaus H. Huser, a resident of nearby Ypsilanti, wrote on November 12, 2006, to the *Ann Arbor News*,

> I find the arrogance of the University of Michigan, as represented by President Mary Sue Coleman, astounding. What audacity to push aside the will of 58 percent of the electorate. Perhaps the liberal eggheads need reminding that it is a public university supported by public funds. Selecting who gets to feed at the trough has been decided by the voters. Everyone is welcome, regardless of race, color, etc. [51]

This concern about university arrogance was by no means a local affair. Picked up in the *Chicago Tribune*, editorial writer Steve Chapman reinforced this resentment of apparent arrogance: "It's no surprise that Coleman doesn't welcome the new ban or the constraints it puts on her enlightened discretion. But if the head of a state university can't respect a legally valid policy approved in a binding referendum by the people she serves, here is the speech she should give: 'I quit.'"[52]

Mary Sue Coleman has not quit and in fact presides over a university deeply committed to rethinking the meaning of diversity in the aftermath of this decision. The meaning of a public university, while not explicitly labeled as such, is implicated in this rethinking, for while the vote must be respected, unless and until overturned by judicial procedures or other political action, it also reflects a failure by the public university to communicate its mission to the public. One reason for that failure rests in the conception of the public underlying the research university.

As the straightforward public university suggests when understood as an economic engine or sports machine, the public thrives when it is undifferentiated. But we recognize, too, that the Big House football stadium and the Pfizer recovery privilege certain parts of the public (the fans and those who might be hired after being laid off), with implied promises of trickle-down value to the rest of the public. In regard to diversity, particular publics are recognized before the general good, and some replace the trickle-down assumptions of other public engagements with zero sums in this one. In order to address this problem of the relationship between particular publics and general goods, university discussions tend to move in two directions when addressing the diversity of diversity.

THE DIVERSITY OF DIVERSITY AND THE PUBLICS THEY ENGAGE

On the one hand, the public university continues to work the diversity dimension by emphasizing the ways in which it is linked to excellence. Among the most innovative aspects of this work has been an exploration of how diversity and complexity are linked.[53] This linkage has, in part, laid the foundation for the "diversity blueprints" strategy that has emerged at U-M to figure out how to move ahead after affirmative action was prohibited.[54]

Diversity as excellence once again, however, presumes a relatively undifferentiated public, much like the public research university as an economic growth engine or a sports machine. At least this argument about diversity is not defined by the challenge of difference around the definition of excellence.

On the other hand, the "diversity blueprints" and other discussions demonstrate that a university committed to diversity is about excellence as well as engagement.[55] The blueprints reflect diversity advocates' commitment to activism by reaching out to communities excluded from the rights and privileges of a democratic but increasingly unequal society. They seek to

> establish fully coordinated educational and community outreach and engagement activities. The University of Michigan has a long tradition of successful educational

outreach and community partnerships. U-M faculty, staff, and students increase our effectiveness as a public body, as well as our institutional visibility, by participating in local communities, state realities, national priorities, and global possibilities while gaining the benefit of the rich diversity of experience and perspective such engagement affords. . . . At this time, greater synergy is needed among these varied efforts in order to make them a stronger signature of our mission as a public university. Specifically, a University center for educational outreach and engagement is needed to coordinate, synthesize, cross-fertilize and strengthen substantive partnerships between the University and its many communities by promoting collaboration among academic and administrative units, fostering the development of new community outreach initiatives, leveraging existing partnerships, and administering outreach and engagement programs of its own. Through these activities, U-M would expand its reach into the communities of the state of Michigan and beyond, bringing resources, opportunities, intelligence, and commitment and broadening and developing the pipeline for students, faculty, and staff. Such coordination would also support well-informed and highly effective university involvement in communities and help ensure that the partnerships developed through these activities are true partnerships: ones that reflect the priorities of the communities being served and that fully recognize the resources, opportunities, expertise, and commitment of people and institutions beyond our campus.

As this passage indicates, there are implied commitments to particular publics, but they are only implied. That, I would propose, is because outreach to these communities is treated as self-evidently necessary and just for those active in the struggle for social justice. For that reason and others, there is no academic agenda that explains sufficiently why university resources should be devoted to particular publics in compelling and general terms. As a consequence, they are left as implicit political goals, unlikely to generate broader support and seen as part of the university's politicization. Indeed, these implicit charges imply another problem, suggested by a later passage in the diversity blueprints.

Reflecting on some people's perception that U-M has generated a certain "political correctness" in its discussions of diversity (to be countered immediately by others claiming intimidation in the reverse direction), the diversity blueprints have called for greater openness, transparency, and free discussion so that diversity's embrace results from voluntary engagement rather than institutional conformity.

The articulation of diversity with the university's public mission illustrates the diversity of diversity, as well as the challenge of identifying the university's proper publics and their constitution. It is clear, for example, that the apparently simple equation of the public with the state of Michigan is inadequate to a discussion of diversity and hardly recognizes the question of under what conditions certain publics deserve recognition and engagement. It also reflects the problem with public governance.

Universities cannot present themselves simply as servants of the public, not only because the university should be, and is constitutionally recognized as, autonomous from the public of the State of Michigan and therefore self-governing. Furthermore, it is not evident what the boundaries of that public are and how the diversity and inequality of the state's publics should be recognized.

To the extent that the university legitimates its public value in the dominant discourses, which in the state of Michigan today is coded as investing in general economic returns more than the welfare of particular publics identified through an intellectually rigorous procedure, the logic of diversity can hardly be apparent in public mission. Excellence has to be the code word, because it is generic and linked to the university's mission. Diversity winds up being elevated only to the extent that it is linked to producing more jobs, greater status, or additional economic opportunities for the people of the state. This is why the amicus brief of Steelcase and other Fortune 500 companies became so compelling during the Supreme Court trials. They argued,

> Now more than ever, the ability of universities, such as the University of Michigan, to consider all of an applicant's attributes is essential to create the educational environment necessary to best train all their students to succeed. The students of today are this country's corporate and community leaders of the next half century. For these students to realize their potential as leaders, it is essential that they be educated in an environment where they are exposed to diverse ideas, perspectives, and interactions. In the experience of the amici corporations, today's global marketplace and the increasing diversity in the American population demand the cross-cultural experience and understanding gained from such an education. Diversity in higher education is therefore a compelling government interest not only because of its positive effects on the educational environment itself, but also because of the crucial role diversity in higher education plays in preparing students to be the community leaders this country needs in business, law, and all other pursuits that affect the public interest. . . . The experiences of the amici corporations demonstrate the need for the cross-cultural education that a diverse educational institution provides, as well as the talented diverse graduates it produces. The changing face of America is reflected in the marketplace, as both the work-

place and the purchasers of products and services become increasingly diverse. For example, the combined spending power of racial minorities in the United States is $600 billion annually (Expert Report of William G. Bowen at 14 [December 9, 1998]). The individuals who run and staff the amici corporations must be able to understand, learn from, collaborate with, and design products and services for clientele and associates from diverse racial, ethnic, and cultural backgrounds. American multinational corporations, including amici, are especially attuned to this concern because they serve not only the increasingly diverse population of the United States, but racially and ethnically diverse populations around the world. . . . In the opinion of amici, individuals who have been educated in a diverse setting are more likely to succeed, because they can make valuable contributions to the workforce in several important ways. First, a diverse group of individuals educated in a cross-cultural environment has the ability to facilitate unique and creative approaches to problem-solving arising from the integration of different perspectives. Second, such individuals are better able to develop products and services that appeal to a variety of consumers and to market offerings in ways that appeal to these consumers. Third, a racially diverse group of managers with cross-cultural experience is better able to work with business partners, employees, and clientele in the United States and around the world. Fourth, individuals that have been educated in a diverse setting are likely to contribute to a positive work environment, by decreasing incidents of discrimination and stereotyping. Finally, an educational environment created by consideration of the potential promise of each applicant in light of his or her experiences and background is likely to produce the most talented possible workforce.

This kind of argument that links excellence and diversity so powerfully in the Supreme Court cases could not be heard in the fall 2006 referendum campaigns that marked affirmative action first and foremost as something that violates the rights of individuals. When the principal public good of the University of Michigan is understood as a private good acquired by in-state residents who enroll as students, and when excellence is understood as an individual quality rather than an institutional accomplishment, the public good of diversity on its own terms becomes hard to defend. For every student benefiting from this public good, many more are denied that benefit; for every argument about how diversity produces excellence, nowhere is it explained which kind of difference is most valuable for the production of that excellence. Diversity and excellence do go together, but excellence demands that we determine which kind of difference is important and why.

When the criteria for admission are universally recognized and legitimate, there is less likely room for contest. But a commitment to diversity, understood less through the politics of student recruitment than the engagement of diverse publics, leaves little room for the solidarity critical to validating the university's excellence and autonomy. For this reason, in the 2006 referendum, diversity's link to excellence could not trump a certain sense of fairness among Michigan's voters, reinforced by an emotional power that the corporate rationales themselves could not offset. There was, however, an alternative evident in the Supreme Court amicus briefs that were not part of the fall 2006 discussion.

The military leadership suggested that kind of affective power of diversity's embrace with this basic claim: "The officer corps must continue to be diverse or the cohesiveness essential to the military mission will be critically undermined."[56] This brief was compelling in part because it not only validated individual success but also linked diversity's value to the solidarity essential to a common national interest. The nation's security, realized through the diversity of an officer corps reflecting the diversity of the enlisted personnel, sutured military excellence, individual accomplishment, and the value of affirmative action as institutional practice in a compelling emotional and logical presentation. But it was also slightly different from the Fortune 500 logic.

The bounds of diversity for the military reflect the nation above all, as well as the diversity of enlisted personnel. Corporate logic reflects the world. These are two very different publics, with two very different kinds of ties between the university-educated and their diverse clienteles. From these differences, we can anticipate the various articulations of diversity emerging in University of Michigan discussions.

On the one hand, in the corporate discussion, engaging diversity was a sign of excellence, anticipating future problems with the current learning. This resonated powerfully with the research by Patricia Gurin and others, emphasizing that diversity is, simply, inextricably woven with scholarly and teaching accomplishment.

On the other hand, the military's national reference was clearly an invocation of the public good, the national mission, and the solidarity that needs no explication, of which the university is or should be a part. Justice is the basis of this solidarity, excellence of the former. But justice is simple only when the bonds of solidarity are obvious, as military cohesiveness demands or as social movement commitments activate. That obviousness is hard to realize in a diverse and contentious university, especially in a global university. Lessons from the struggle to articulate public engagement with the diversity of the world's publics, however, could lead to the reformulation of the state of Michigan's own various publics.

GLOBAL PUBLICS

My predecessor as director of the International Institute, David William Cohen, and I organized a seminar at U-M in the summer of 2002, at which the question of how a global public university might be described was discussed at length.[57] The presumption of U-M's ambition to be a global university reflected one dimension of the problem, followed by a second: how can one escape the constraints of provincial publicness? Should we not recognize the obligation and possibility of moving beyond obvious and obliging public reference?

Globalization and its attending cosmopolitan ethics made the problems involved in these questions seem relatively slight. With increasingly open borders and open minds, universities can facilitate the flow of information and ideas with cyberinfrastuctures that compress time and space, animated by increasingly transnational epistemic communities where national origins hardly play a role in developing bibliographies. Former U-M president James Duderstadt has been a major advocate of this kind of academic transformation and remains among the most forceful of those who seek the development of new organizations of higher education premised on the technological transformations fueling globalization.[58]

In this sense, globalizing knowledge is only an extension of existing dispositions in the commitment to learning, driving the boundaries of the campus into the world itself, without necessarily bringing publics from across the world into the heart of the university. This is evident in the language spoken, in which English typically serves as the lingua franca, or in the mobilizing questions that are asked in metropolitan sites. Globalizing knowledge thus could be seen as a smooth extension of the academic mission to realize excellence.

At the same time, this ambition has hidden the implicit politics of recognition that go into international collaborations. European partnerships come much more easily than those south of the equator, unless that location happens to be Australia. English-language ability facilitates collaborations, too. China and India seemed to be on the rise in globalization of knowledge cultures, for their markets for higher education and for the ways in which state investments and diasporas seemed to create universities whose greater purpose was becoming world class. New strategic alliances across the world formed, tied into these individual institutional strategies in order to move up the excellence ladder, thereby confirming the wisdom of their investors in this assurance of betting wisely on futures. And then came the attacks on September 11, 2001.

With the securitization of everyday life and of knowledge cultures, visas to the United States were no longer so easily obtained. The globalization of knowledge now became tied to a renationalization of knowledge production, asking why universities could not predict better these attacks and how we might ensure protections for the future. New debates took place about training enough people for intelligence and security agencies, replete with the language and cultural skills that could help recognize the threats and the enemies. Knowing other publics of the world became critical in ways that globalizing knowledge frameworks hardly acknowledged.

Kathleen Canning, David William Cohen and I produced a white paper identifying these very logics, and invited five distinguished intellectuals from across the world—Veena Das, Konstanty Gebert, Elizabeth Jelin, Nurcholish Madjid, and Lamin Sanneh—along with U-M graduate students, to comment on the paper and write their own papers inviting us to rethink the global university with public commitments. Cohen and I proposed the problem this way:

> Through the production of basic knowledge in virtually every field and its application to the betterment of lives around the world, the North American research university has professed—especially over the past half century—a privileged location in that world. Not only has the university claimed a unique position in the transfer of learning across generations, but it has also sought to overcome national boundaries and the limitations of its own national or regional formation through the international exchange of learning and through the articulation of universal values.
>
> Yet here lies the essential challenge for the North American research university: how to be both of and in the world, pressing universal values and underlining the indivisible and transcendent nature of knowledge while irrevocably located within the histories, constituencies, and demands of the nation. For some, this challenge may be but a pause in the globalization of institutions of research and learning around the world; for others, the challenge represents an essential contradiction within the very nature of the North American research university's project in the broader world. The challenge, simply put, is the following: should the university transcend its national foundations as it engages the broader world? Can it?

That volume's underlying debate reflects the very problem to be found in diversity's articulation, too, and even in the discussion of the public university's value to its legislated constituency: How can we recognize the university's proper public(s), and which public should be prioritized and when?

UNIVERSITIES CONSTITUTING GLOBAL PUBLICS AND SOLIDARITIES

In the University Research Corridor site, the relatively limited appeal of publics abroad is apparent in the citation of only one project focused on another country: a Michigan State University project led by agriculturalist Dan Clay. He returned to Rwanda in 2001, after having fled in 1994 at the time of the genocide, and helped develop cooperatives in the production, processing, and marketing of specialty coffee for global markets. The largest cooperative, called Maraba, is made up of many widows of the genocide.[59] The report even invites the reader to buy coffee from this operation. While this public work does not significantly enhance proximate economic fortunes, it clearly elevates university work by demonstrating the public good provided for a community that few are likely to disparage as undeserving of university engagement. This, however, is the exception, even when genocide is the problem.

The University of Michigan has been participating in discussions about the 1915 forced migrations and executions of Armenians in the collapsing Ottoman Empire, which many label genocide. Three U-M faculty—Ronald Grigor Suny, Fatma Müge Göçek, and Gerard Libaridian—have been prominent in developing an alternative mode of analysis for this period. Through something called the "Workshop for Turkish/Armenian Scholarship," since 2002 they have held working meetings, produced publications, and maintained a listserv discussion that is the only site where Armenians and Turks can regularly discuss the scholarly questions provoked by this period. This enterprise illustrates some of the challenges and opportunities for research universities and the publics they constitute.

First, this scholarly enterprise cannot be identified simply with any preexisting public, much less national communities. Because of the intensity of nationalized disagreements over whether the events of 1915 count as genocide, this kind of cross-cultural scholarship and transformative dialogue is not easy to carry out. There are relatively few scholars, especially back in 2002, who could cross national divides to engage in substantial scholarly exchange. When such scholars are found, they often are attacked as "anti-Turk" or "anti-Armenian." And because a single word, *genocide*, can inflame such passion even before discussion, it is difficult to begin work across national boundaries without falling into broader political traps overwhelmed by epithets and worse.

While such things are rarely printed, especially in English, while I was U-M's vice provost for international affairs, I was told that the scholars who initiated this work were "suspect" or sometimes even "traitors" to their national cause. Such indictments, of course, do not begin with scholarly evaluations but with interrogations of national correctness, regarding how well they fit certain expectations of national associations. Once, for instance, I was told that Turkish American scholars should be "academic ambassadors" for Turkey. In another time, I was told that Armenian studies should be left to Armenians.

To academics, putting national loyalties above academic expectations is heretical. It is possible to imagine, however, that such nationalist discourses could find more sympathy in light of growing concerns about universities' patriotism in the aftermath of September 11, 2001. To what political community should U-M be patriotic in a discussion of the events of 1915?

While Libaridian, Suny, Göçek, and their colleagues have different national affinities that enable and constrain them in these discussions, they also elevate a commitment to scholarly rigor and ethics to the center of their common efforts. While certainly their work had political effect, they struggled to develop, in the Habermasian terms Calhoun described in chapter 1, reasoned argument and rational-critical discourse. Beyond this, they worked to constitute public solidarities on those bases, implicitly, and sometimes explicitly, challenging the ways in which nationalist presumptions limit the quality of public spheres, whether their origins were Turkish, Armenian, or American. But this cannot be a simple assertion of independence, either.

To claim independence from any national field is, at best, naïve. We might ask instead how claims of national privilege distort academic inquiry and the qualities of rational critical discourse. That kind of question is itself preliminary to, and perhaps even derivative of, the hard work in constituting these various publics through research universities.

To an exceptional extent, global publics, or at least the scholarly collaborations across the world enabling them, are accidental, dependent on the backgrounds and interests of faculty and university leaders. These in turn are structured by larger systems that should be recognized and acknowledged: global markets, political alliances, diaspora commitments, foundation and philanthropic investments, and other forces. But what is neither simply accidental nor overly structural is the development of strategic scholarly interventions that themselves help produce publics and broader solidarities with transformative consequences, albeit with unintended effects, that should be the focus of a much more extended inquiry. I will elaborate on two to illustrate this direction.

The University of Michigan has been substantially engaged in Polish affairs for more than a century, with Polish diaspora faculty and their descendents helping drive interest in that nation at U-M. With the cumulation of scholarly ties, interested faculty, and use of institutional resources to extend engagements, over the last ten years Poland became one of the prominent nations in U-M's global network. It was a particular research question, however, that significantly extended the public value of this relationship.

In the late 1990s, as with many other east European scholarly communities, we tried to imagine the proper way to recognize the tenth anniversary of the end of communist rule in eastern Europe. Brian Porter, Marysia Ostafin, and I thought a focus on the round table negotiations of 1989 would be especially useful, since that would redirect attention to the negotiated moment of that transformation, rather than the familiar imagery of exhaustion that the Berlin Wall's collapse evoked. After pursuing the matter with colleagues in Ann Arbor and with visitors who had been round table participants, we eventually developed a proposal, supported by the university's central administration, to bring more than fifteen participants from all sides of the round table—Solidarity, Communists, and Catholic Church officials, to Ann Arbor to reflect on what enabled this negotiated revolution, and communism's peaceful end.[60]

We succeeded in bringing a distinguished cast to Ann Arbor in part because this question could not be posed in Poland; at least it could not be posed in the same relatively scholarly fashion. In Poland, it would be overwhelmingly politicized. After all, what agency could host such a discussion that did not already have a stake in a particular interpretation of this history? In this sense, the scholarly reputation of the University of Michigan enabled Polish public figures to have an academic conversation that Polish public spheres did not so readily enable.

U-M was not immune from this politicization, either. During our conference and subsequent scholarship, some parts of the Polish and Polish American press vilified me as Adam Michnik's handmaiden. Others thought me to be in the clutch of the pinkos and the reds who negotiated their own golden parachutes in the end to communism.

Some of these criticisms helped. Although my colleagues and I conceived the conference as a way of focusing on how communism's peaceful collapse could have happened, we realized that such a conception privileged a historical narrative that put the hard-line communists' and the Polish far right's narratives to the side. We did not begin with the assumption that this compromise betrayed either socialism or the nation. In this sense, we made a political choice in order to answer a specific historical and social scientific question: how was a peaceful revolution possible at all?

To manage this conference and to accomplish other things, too, my colleagues and I were in 1999 awarded gold crosses of merit by the Polish president. This also was seen by some people to be political. Many of those on the right would view this award by a former communist as only further evidence of political taint. But I could not be called a traitor. I have no Polish blood. And the University of Michigan could not be challenged for such a conference, not only because there are no Polish officials or donors who might punish the university for such an engagement, but also because one of the most prominent Poles in the world endorsed it, hoping that "this disciplined reflection on the spiritual, cultural and political aspects of Poland's peaceful transition to democracy will highlight their ultimate foundation in a moral imperative arising from man's innate dignity and his transcendent vocation to freedom in the pursuit of truth."[61]

This example, however, illustrates the more general point about the constitution of global publics and solidarities through university work. These efforts rely on preexisting capacities and dispositions alongside claims to scholarly excellence; they involve the development of strategic questions that enable scholarly impact on public issues elsewhere; and they require some kind of legitimating discourse that identifies this investment in a distant public worthy of university resources. Asking questions about the peaceful transition to democracy is one such question, especially when the participants in the discussion themselves contributed significantly to the outcome and have so few opportunities to reflect on the conditions and consequences of that very transformation in a scholarly milieu. But not every such issue has a figure like Pope John Paul II to extend that discussion's value, and not every academic subject has such peaceful and democratic dispositions surrounding it, as the events of 1915 illustrate.

Gerard Libaridian, Ron Suny, and Müge Göçek can be called traitors, or suspect, because of their lineages and the questions and collaboration they pose. Those concerns have been magnified dramatically, because one of the participants in these workshops, a friend of Suny, Göçek, and Libaridian, and a man whom I came to appreciate in the meetings I attended, was assassinated in Istanbul on January 19, 2007, for the very principles to which this workshop was dedicated. Hrant Dink was an exceptionally decent man, and more than 100,000 people turned out at his funeral to mourn his loss and to declare that "we are all Hrant Dink."

It was difficult for the University of Michigan to find the right solidarity in this moment. Right after learning of his killing, Müge Göçek wrote on the listserv her first eulogy, a moving tribute to him.[62] The Armenian Studies Program, together with the Center for Middle Eastern and North African Studies, the Center for Russian and East European Studies, and the Department of Near Eastern Studies organized a tribute to Dink on February 6. The discussion centered on the distinction of the man who was killed, the principles for which he stood, and the lessons to be learned.

There were tensions: should he be remembered as an Armenian whom the Turks killed because of his wish to speak the truth about 1915, or was he killed because he wanted, in more general terms, the right to speak truth in his paper, *Agos*? At the same time, while those demonstrating in Turkey could say "we are all Hrant Dink" and "we are all Armenian," it was difficult to determine what made this movement important to the University of Michigan, especially for those who were not in the room, those who were not Armenian or Turkish or who were not invested in the meaning of 1915. This brings us back to the question: which are the university's proper publics?

University officials with a penchant for avoiding complexities might have us turn away from recognizing solidarity with Hrant Dink and the scholarly implications of that recognition. After the commemorative session, a Turkish graduate student, claiming to speak on behalf of "members of the Turkish community," declared that both it and the 2002 workshop meeting in Ann Arbor were a one-sided approach to the meaning of 1915. These massacres, he argued, were the results of war and the Armenian alliance with Russians. They were not genocide. While he and his colleagues decried the assassination of Dink, they also decried the killings of Turkish diplomats by Armenian terrorists in 1994, asking us to remember that Armenians kill as well. These critics, invoking the logic of diversity and fairness, say that their viewpoint is not recognized. They, in effect, moved away from the question of genocide's relevance toward a claim to diversity and fairness and their own imagined public.

If they had attended the 2002 conference, they would have known that Dink challenged the prominence of the "g-word" in such discussions, too. As Dink stated, "Turkish-Armenian relations should be taken out of a 1915 meters-deep well." That topic should be depoliticized and dealt with by historians.[63]

These two examples of global publics and solidarity—around the Polish round table of 1989 and the meaning and causes of 1915—show that the distant public effects of U-M university work are constituted by the questions mobilizing scholarship, even though the meanings of those associations extend far beyond the anticipations of academics. In both these and many other cases, we can see the value of scholarly inquiry on the particular subjects and also that the values associated with scholarly work begin to approximate the quality of transnational discourse and public effect that marks the public sphere that Calhoun uses as a normative and analytical benchmark. This could be another way to assess research universities' public effect.

As we assess university work in engaging publics, we might also examine the ways in which publics are constituted that approximate, and help reinforce, academic values. Here we look for the impact not on jobs created, championships won, or diverse graduates produced for implied and bounded publics, but on the constitution of publics that themselves reproduce and extend university values in their work. Instead of asking how commercialization and commodification are affecting the university, we could ask how the university's values are shaping the qualities of public discourse.

COMPARING PUBLICS, SOLIDARITIES, AND ACADEMIC GOODS

In university discussions, and perhaps even to outside observers and scholarly analysts, discussions of local economies, diversity's expression, and globalizing knowledge belong to different domains of expertise and engagement, to different faculties and offices. But as we rethink the meaning of public universities, I propose that instead of thinking about the pre-given publics to which universities are obligated, we should think about how university work itself helps constitute publics that more and less adopt university values. By comparing these constitutive efforts, we might even find new ways to articulate the public value of research universities.

At the risk of oversimplification and recognizing that these cells are not mutually exclusive, table 15.1 shows how this variety might be rethought.

1. The straightforward core public of U-M and any public university includes members of its own community. Students, faculty, staff, and alumni are obvious members of this academic public. Universities by and large define their own public through principles of hiring and admissions. The main question is who gets to belong, a debate that can easily turn the public question into a matter of which individuals profit from this university public good. This concern declines to the extent that proximate publics identify with, or benefit from, these private gains, in the services that the university and its core public provide or in the more general perception that the members of the academic community deserve their station.

2. Proximate publics are bound to the university in various exchange relationships and therefore rarely require any kind of justification beyond the terms made in the original grant, contract, or law. One can then simply recognize these proximate publics as the university's investments in their economies, workforce skills, and other infrastructural investments. One can also recognize them as their own investments in the universities, as legislative allocations of tax dollars, philanthropic contributions, and so on. Here, the principal debates are whether the exchanges are sufficient to ensure that all partners get what they expect and need in order to do their work well and whether, on the academic side, those expectations enhance, or detract from, the university mission. Because these publics are bound to the university in various extra-academic ties, justifications for public engagement are left implicit.

3. Distant publics of academic choice differ little from the straightforward core public, given that both publics are seen as defined by academic values. The only distinction here, evident in the rationales offered by diversity as excellence and in the celebration of globalizing knowledge, is that academic accomplishment is extended by going beyond familiar and conventional publics to recruit members to the core academic community. Here, however, these distant publics of academic choice are not so obviously embedded in those publics beyond the academy, for their participation in public research universities is defined by their contribution to the academic mission as such more than in their representation of a distant public.

4. Distant solidary publics are the most complex category because their academic values are more easily contested, and the public obligation also can be subject to doubt. Their academic and public justifications therefore vary substantially as well. Compare, for example, the quest to ensure a diverse officer corps for the military or the commitments of universities to engage disadvan-

Table 15.1 University Publics, Proximity, and Rationales

	Academic Values	Public Values
Proximate and obvious	1. Core publics among campus faculty, students, staff, and alumni	2. Local economy, culture, politics, and contractual relationships
Distant requiring justification	3. Diversity as excellence and globalizing knowledge	4. Diversity as national responsibility or as justice; Polish roundtable, Armenian-Turkish workshop

Table 15.2 Distant Public University Work

	Nonconflictual	Conflictual
Membership obligation	1 Diversity/national interest	2. Diversity/social justice
No membership obligation	3. Extending uncontested values like peace and freedom	4. Explaining violence and identifying responsibility

taged communities to whom university actors feel obligated. What do these have in common with a conference on the 1989 Polish round table and the Workshop for Turkish-Armenian Scholarship? In each of these cases, distant publics evoke academic engagement because academic values might be seen to serve those particular public needs and must be justified in those terms.

Viewed simply, one can appreciate why advocates of diversity would frame their defense in terms of excellence, fitting in with a broader recognition that globalizing knowledge cultures are part of the new wave of defining excellence. One can also appreciate why proximate publics fit with university values, given the exchange relationships in which the university is embedded. But for those public issues that involve distant publics, universities must work to constitute their publics on academic grounds in order to justify their investments. This varies with the university's obligation to those distant publics on the strength of its solidarity with them. Again at the risk of oversimplification, table 15.2 compares distant publics.

1. Solidarity was easy to establish with the leaders of the military when they argued that diversifying Michigan's graduates and, by extension, the elite of the military corps and beyond was good for the national interest. Here, diversity was not about individual rights but about the needs of a community. Racism clearly threatens military effectiveness, which in turn is critical to ensuring security for that community to which the University of Michigan must belong. This justification could be effective because solidarity with the national interest can be presumed.

2. Arguments advocating diversity on the grounds of justice, if not supplemented by claims to excellence, are more complicated because the opponents of affirmative action have been able to constitute alternative claims to justice. Nevertheless, given U-M's own commitments to diversity and the university's broader sense of obligation to other U.S. citizens and residents who suffer injus-

tice, substantial initiatives have been undertaken to move the public question away from an exclusive focus on admission to a core public toward reinforcing the value of the university's investments in other publics.

One of the most vivid examples of this is the arts of citizenship project, in which University of Michigan students collected the oral histories of Detroit residents' recollection of the riots in 1967 and turned them into theatrical productions.[64] Projects like these enhance the university's relationship with certain proximate publics, which in turn reinforce legislative support for U-M's distinctive educational and research mission in the state. They therefore do not require substantial justification, at least in comparison to other, more distant publics.

What about those in exchange relationships with the public research university who are neither taxpayers nor citizens and are even in conflictual relations with those with university contracts? The anti-sweatshop movements that have engaged U-M and other universities for at least the last decade illustrate the ways in which the principles of the proximate public can inspire longer-distance solidarities. In response to student movements,[65] U-M created its Labor Standards and Human Rights Committee, composed of faculty and students knowledgeable about these affairs to "provide advice concerning University policies and procedures to address labor issues in the production of U of M goods (items sold with the University of Michigan's name, logos, or other symbols) and to ensure that those corporations manufacturing licensed goods with the University of Michigan name and/or logos, are not engaged in unlawful or unconscionable labor practices."

When inspired by historical ties, claims to social justice can motivate public engagements even when there are no existing exchange relationships. This is most powerfully illustrated by the events following the charges made by Patrick Tierney in the winter of 2001, before the publication of his book *Darkness in El Dorado*. He suggested in private correspondence that two U.S. academics, including one U-M faculty member, "intentionally caused or intensified a deadly measles epidemic among the Yanomami in 1968." The academic community quickly refuted those charges, and Tierney modified his book. U-M went further, however, to dismiss the subsequently published book in its entirety. After the faculty and students protested, the provost's office then acknowledged that while its concern for Tierney's integrity and his research was important, it also was inconsistent with academic practice to settle complex scholarly questions with administrative decisions. With Provost Nancy Cantor's support, U-M anthropologist Fernando Coronil initiated an extended discussion with faculty and students from Michigan and Brazil on the production of knowledge and the university's obligation to those indigenous peoples it engaged in that research.[66]

In each of these cases, the university did not quite choose its public but was, by claims of social justice and its potential implication in an injustice, forced to engage certain publics to which the university, as actor, had an obligation. In both the Polish and Turkish-Armenian cases, the university chose to become implicated by the research commitments of its faculty. There were, however, important differences.

The assets of the Polish case were the political elites and prominent religious authorities endorsing the quest for understanding outcomes more or less universally applauded. In this, the university did not have to choose between mobilized contenders; the academic sense of the case resonated with the power of political and religious authorities on most sides of the debate to pursue this particular initiative. The university had many incentives, therefore, to extend the engagement. In this, it was actually similar to the brief offered by the generals in defense of diversity. If the Poles could teach us, who could argue that we should not better understand the conditions for a peaceful resolution of fundamentally antagonistic claims? That is a universal good to whose pursuit we are bound by universal claims in the condition of our humanity, and not just the obligations of our citizenship.

By contrast, the Turkish-Armenian case was embedded in potentially deadly politics, largely motivated by scholars opposed to political elites. I have witnessed the political pressures mount, threatening university administrators and individual faculty participants to end, or transform, their engagements. With appeals to academic values in their defense and with the promise of genuinely transformative scholarly dialogues in evidence, this workshop has only grown. In this sense, to explain violence and identify those responsible for its proliferation requires even more stringent academic standards and administrative courage to ensure the scholarly enterprise and to avoid having national correctness dominate the academic mission. It is beyond my ability here to show how this case might illuminate the dangers posed by those who would politicize the public university around other, more contemporary conflicts, but the implications should be clear.[67]

My intention in juxtaposing these cases of distant university publics, and more generally with university publics, is to highlight one overridingly powerful point in the public engagement of research universities: There is no overriding sense of public obligation, especially when the public moves beyond the proximate, the obligatory, and the general. But with the increasing complexity of diversity's discussion and the growing significance of global publics in the well-being of even proximate, obligatory, and general publics, we need to think more seriously about the particularities of publics and the reasons that universities should engage them.

We have no explicit method—empirical, normative, or political—that makes rational and/or critical this choice about which publics the universities should engage. Instead, we use familiar patterns of financial influence or political habit, conflicts in which universities are embedded, or simple notions of proximity and scholarly accident in the name of faculty freedom to make those choices. That may be the best we can do, but it also misses an opportunity to reflect on the meaning of the public university in a way that extends appreciation of university work.

Finally, I would like to make a case for envisioning academic work as extending solidarity on academic terms to multiple publics, by asking, How might we encourage distant publics to identify with the academic values offered by a public university? In turn, might that inspire more proximate publics to rethink the value of their own academic engagements?

Public universities are not typically agenda setters of public discourse, nor do they enjoy academic freedom in that political engagement. I have discussed several cases in which academic intervention made a difference: in the frames associated with the Polish round table and the causalities associated with the Armenian genocide of 1915. But the greatest impact by far was how the United States might understand inequality in higher education and affirmative action and how it relates to academic values and the way in which they inform solidarity.

U-M was able to defend its principled approach to diversity in the Supreme Court Case in 2001 and lose the referendum on that same approach in 2006 because solidarity was on its side in the former, but not in the latter. In 2001, former generals could identify racism as responsible for the military's failure and could identify affirmative action as a means of generating the kinds of solidarity necessary for security. In 2006, the opponents of affirmative action could discuss questions of individual fairness, not public goods, thereby effectively banishing solidarity from the discussion of the public research university. When public universities become private goods for the use of student clients, who are one of the university's core publics, universities cannot realize their potential contribution to the public good. When solidarity is lost in the discussion, the excellence of universities comes to be understood as arrogance.

U-M's fiscal challenge, magnified by the state's fiscal crisis, reinforces this problem. U-M cannot defend its relatively greater cost with arguments about the quality of its education alone. If it is just like other public universities, teaching students, it can make only the same claims that other teaching institutions make. To be supported by its state, U-M must do more than teach and provide services. It must somehow demonstrate the collective value of the research it undertakes.

Universities can talk about multiplier effects on local economies; they can partner with the state in developing start-up companies. They can provide for the public good in medical benefits or in bringing science and math competence to girls. These values are important, but they also are indirect, not collective. They require individuals in publics to recognize both their ties to individuals who benefit and their own profit from these expenditures. It relies on a rational calculation of chains of benefit. They are based on a university's contribution to others' needs as others define them. While valuable in themselves, public research universities are less likely to distinguish themselves from other teaching institutions and commercial firms and medical facilities.

In their public engagements, research universities might do more to determine how they contribute to existing publics and how they might help constitute alternative publics and practices through their work, highlighting how their own university values enable distinctive contributions. Here, it may be even more useful to think about university engagements with distant publics than about appeals to diversity as excellence and the intrinsic need to globalize knowledge for academic gain.

By recalling and performing the meaning of the 1967 riots in Detroit, by researching and monitoring the efficacy of labor rights among its licensee's employees in sweatshops across the world, or by addressing various levels of well-being for indigenous peoples engaged as research subjects, the public university transforms its relationship with its more or less proximate publics. Instead of an unseen poor minority, invisible sweatshop laborers, and objects of research, those Detroit citizens, right-bearing workers, and Yanomami research partners join the academic public of the University of Michigan in different ways, newly apparent and implicated in the definition of university values. Especially when those engagements contradict its own commercial interests or needs for prestige, value, or political neutrality, the university's institutional distinction in making the public good becomes apparent if in its engagement of various publics, its academic values lead in the definition of its relationship.

In that drive, we also can see that academic publics extend by obligation as well as by the choices of publics elsewhere to join in the extension of such scholarly identification.

One of the reasons that Polish leaders from the Catholic Church, former communists, and the Solidarity movement came to Michigan in 1999 to talk about their round table negotiations in 1989 was because they valued the research university and wanted to help it apply the lessons about 1989 to other peaceful resolutions of fundamental differences.

One of the reasons that Armenians and Turks dedicated to a historical inquiry into the tragedies of 1915 associated themselves with scholarly priorities rather than political goals of reconciliation was because the commitment to understanding the mechanisms that produced such tragedies must be understood and acknowledged in order for democracy to have a chance to flourish in Turkey and more broadly.

Last, one of the reasons that faculty and students without Armenian, Turkish, or Polish ancestry care about these inquiries is because they can stand in solidarity with the struggle to learn, which in turn can inform other struggles for peace, freedom, and democracy, public goods whose limited value in circumscription becomes more apparent everyday.

I offer these examples of solidarity with distant publics fully aware of the risk that by identifying all these engagements as manifestations of the university's public engagement, I diminish the differences among these relationships. To be sure, U-M owes more to Ann Arbor and to the state of Michigan than it does to Warsaw or Istanbul; there is a contractual relationship between the university and its obligatory political community. To the extent that U-M is implicated in contractual relations that exploit workers or endanger research subjects, it is obligated by those contractual standards to redress grievances and, by academic standards, to take public lessons from them. U-M could not explore the Armenian-Turkish historiography as it has without scholars expert in that catastrophe who also were descendents of those suffering from those struggles. The Polish round table was actually facilitated by a lack of blood ties but dependent on decades of institutional relationship to Poland. Accidents of recruitment channeled these latter global engagements, and the significance of ethnic/national relations to those places varied consequentially. But what ties all these examples together is the positive point: that *forms of university engagement help constitute the character of that university-public relationship.* This becomes more apparent when distant and voluntary and, therefore by necessity, more academic than contractual in tenor. These more exceptional public engagements might help us rethink the more conventional ways in which universities are public.

It may not be the source of funding, faculty employment status, or even statutes of university governance that define the public-ness of the research university. We might instead turn the question on its head and ask how university work itself informs the qualities of public life with the values that motivate scholarship. By this I do not mean to suggest that good academic arguments trump sound operating budgets in the real public university. I only wonder whether part of the good public university's work should be to identify, across the range of its teaching, service, and especially research, in which publics it invests, how its scholarly engagements transform the conditions of life and understanding for others, and how the conditions of public support for its mission affect the public research university's abilities to do its job.

We may face, as Rebecca Lowen described in the 1930s and 1940s, another historical context of economic crisis, war, and academic competition that limits the agency of universities to define their public relationships as they think they ought. By making discursively explicit alternative ways in which public engagement can shape universities' obligation and opportunity to extend their value, we might just create more room for necessary knowledge in shaping the public good.

NOTES

Thanks are due to the workshop participants, especially my discussants Yusef Waghid and N'Dri T. Assié Lumumba; my enduring colleague in the study of higher education, Voldemar Tomusk; other readers, including Jason Owen-Smith, Müge Göçek, Ron Suny, Gerard Libardian, David Lampe; and anonymous reviewers for their comments on earlier versions of this chapter. I am especially grateful to Craig Calhoun and Diana Rhoten for their superb organization of this project and for their special ability to help me move from this insider to in-betweener status in analyzing this place where I was employed for twenty-three years before my move to the Watson Institute at Brown University. My intellectual and life partner, Shiva Balaghi, has moved me to recognize the special privilege, and obligation, of scholarly life in more profound ways than I have previously could have imagined. I am grateful to all these wonderful colleagues for their insights and the solidarity they inspire in pursuit of scholarly consequence. While I continued to revise the chapter's analytical frame through June 2008, I ceased collecting the empirical references for this work in September 2007. Finally, thanks to Daniella Lee-Garcia for her editing prowess in this chapter's final form.

1. Raymond Williams, *Marxism and Literature* (Oxford: Oxford University Press, 1977); Michael D. Kennedy, *Cultural Formations of Postcommunism: Emancipation, Transition, Nation, and War* (Minneapolis: University of Minnesota Press, 2002).

2. Roger L. Geiger, *Knowledge and Money: Research Universities and the Paradox of the Marketplace* (Stanford, Calif.: Stanford University Press, 2004), 65–66, 68–69, 162–65.

3. Robert Merton, *The Sociology of Science: Theoretical and Empirical Investigations* (Chicago: University of Chicago Press, 1979).

4. The member universities of the Committee on Institution Cooperation are Michigan, Illinois, Purdue, Chicago, Northwestern, Pennsylvania State, Ohio State, Indiana, Iowa, Michigan State, Minnesota, and Wisconsin at Madison. See http://www.cic.net/Home/AboutCIC.aspx (accessed September 1, 2007).

5. Available at http://www.arwu.org/rank2008/EN2008.htm (accessed September 1, 2007).

6. Rebecca S. Lowen, *Creating the Cold War University: The Transformation of Stanford* (Berkeley: University of California Press, 1997).

7. Ibid., 33.

8. Ronald G. Suny and Michael D. Kennedy, eds., *Intellectuals and the Articulation of the Nation* (Ann Arbor: University of Michigan Press, 1999).

9. One of the most significant of these is William Sewell, *Logics of History: Social Theory and Social Transformation* (Chicago: University of Chicago Press, 2005).

10. This, of course, is borrowed from the mission statement of the Social Science Research Council, available at http://www.ssrc.org/ssrc_mission/ (accessed September 1, 2007).

11. Craig Calhoun, ed., *Habermas and the Public Sphere* (Cambridge, Mass.: MIT Press, 1992), offers one of the most useful early collections indicating the ways in which the public sphere could be extended to recognize the plurality of publics in the constitution of enlightened democratic goods.

12. Craig Calhoun, "Information Technology and the International Public Sphere," in *Digital Directions*, ed. D. Shuler (Cambridge, Mass.: MIT Press. 2003), 229–51.

13. Geiger, *Knowledge and Money*, 43.

14. News Service, "2006 University Profile," University of Michigan, 2008, available at http://www.umich.edu/news/index.html?profile (accessed June 30, 2007).

15. Howard H. Peckam, *The Making of the University of Michigan: 1817–1992* (Ann Arbor: University of Michigan Press, 1994).

16. Office of the President, "Mission Statement," University of Michigan, 2008, available at http://www.umich.edu/pres/mission.html (accessed June 30, 2007).

17. National Forum on Higher Education for the Public Good, "The National Forum on Higher Education for the Public Good," University of Michigan-School of Education, 2008, available at http://www.thenationalforum.org/ (accessed January 10, 2008); National Forum on Higher Education for the Public Good, "Access and Equity in Higher Education," School of Education, University of Michigan, 2008,

available at http://www.thenationalforum.org/Main/Themes/AccessHE/index.htm (accessed June 10, 2008).

18. Editorial staff, "Michigan Must Find Ways to Make the Best of Higher Ed Investment," *Detroit Free Press*, May 3, 2007.

19. University of Michigan, "Institutional Reporting," available at http://www.provost.umich.edu/reports/slfstudy/ir/criteria/ (accessed June 1, 2007).

20. Public Goods Council, "Promoting Academic Collaboration," University of Michigan, 2006, available at http://www.provost.umich.edu/publicgoods/promot.htm (accessed June 1, 2007).

21. Bruce Madej, "Athletic Revenues Support Financial Aid for Student-Athletes, Capital Improvements," *University Record Online*, 2007, available at http://www.umich.edu/~urecord/0607/Jul23_07/06.shtml (accessed August 1, 2007).

22. James J. Duderstadt, *Intercollegiate Athletics and the American University: A University President's Perspective* (Ann Arbor: University of Michigan Press, 2000).

23. Associated Press, "Ann Arbor Thrives as an Economic Engine," *Traverse City Record-Eagle*, 2006, available at http://www.annarborspark.org/media/files/tcre_annarborthrives_7–13–06.pdf (accessed June 1, 2007).

24. Rebecca Doyle, "Halo Design to Get Second Look, with Public Comments," *University Record*, 1999, available at http://www.umich.edu/~urecord/9900/Sep13_99/2.htm (accessed June 1, 2007); Anna Clark, "Stadium Halo Removed for 2000 Season," *Michigan Daily*, January 7, 2000, available at http://media.www.michigandaily.com/media/storage/paper851/news/2002/04/16/News/Stadium.Halo.Removed.For.2000.Season-1411129.shtml (accessed June 1, 2007).

25. "Save the Big House," available at http://www.savethebighouse.com/index.html (accessed January 1, 2007).

26. Associated Press, "Ann Arbor Thrives as Economic Engine," *Traverse City Record Eagle* July 13, 2006.

27. Geiger, *Knowledge and Money*, 43–44.

28. Ibid., 65–66.

29. Mark Hornbeck and Robert Snell, " Budget Logjam Tarnishes Michigan: Drawn-out Bickering over Finances Hurts State's Image, Ability to Attract Businesses," *Detroit News*, May 18, 2007.

30. Tim Martin, "College-Funding Stats Show Effects of Falling State Aid," Associated Press, May 11, 2007, available at https://clips.vpcomm.umich.edu/index.php (accessed April 2, 2010).

31. Editorial staff, "Editorial: Don't Split 'Big 3's' Budget from Other Schools," *Battle Creek Enquirer*, May 15, 2007, available at https://clips.vpcomm.umich.edu/index.php (accessed April 2, 2010).

32. Doug Stites, " Talk Up Business Successes," *Lansing State Journal*, May 7, 2007, available at https://clips.vpcomm.umich.edu/index.php (accessed April 2, 2010).

33. "Stories from the Corridor," *University Research Corridor*, 2008, available at http://www.urcmich.org/stories/index.html#key (accessed June1, 2008).

34. Regents of the University of Michigan News Service, "Ann Arbor Leaders Create Pfizer Action Teams, Receive $1 Million," 2008, available at http://www.ns.umich.edu/htdocs/releases/story.php?id=3135 (accessed June 1, 2008).

35. Editorial staff, "Editorial: Joint Efforts Can Rebuild Our Region by Mary Sue Coleman," *Crain's Detroit Business*, April 15, 2007.

36. For a general account, however, see Geiger, *Knowledge and Money*.

37. Jennifer Washburn, *University Inc.: The Corporate Corruption of American Higher Education* (New York: Basic Books, 2005); Derek Bok, *Universities in the Marketplace: The Commercialization of Higher Education* (Princeton, N.J.: Princeton University Press, 2004).

38. Geiger, *Knowledge and Money*, 264–65.

39. Jason Owen-Smith and Walter W. Powell, "Knowledge Networks as Channels and Conduits: The Effects of Spillovers in the Boston Biotechnology Community," *Organization Science* 15, no. 1 (2004): 5–21; Jason Owen-Smith, "From Separate Systems to a Hybrid Order: Accumulative Advantage Across Public and Private Science at Research One Universities," *Research Policy* 32, no. 6 (2003):1081–1104; Jason Owen-Smith, "Commercial Imbroglios: Proprietary Science and the Contemporary University," in *The New Political Economy of Science: Institutions, Networks, Power*, ed. K. Moore and S. Frickel (Madison: University of Wisconsin Press, 2005), 63–90.

40. University Library, "MBooks—Michigan Digitization Project," University of Michigan, 2008, available at http://www.lib.umich.edu/mdp/index.html (accessed June 1, 2008).

41. Eliyahu Gurfinkel, "Video: Google's Grady Burnett," *Mlive*, 2007, available at http://blog.mlive.com/ann_arbor_news_extra/2007/03/video_googles_grady_burnett.html#more (accessed June 1, 2008).

42. Wade Rouche, "Coalition of Boston Libraries Chooses the Un-Google Route to Digitization," *X/Conomy—Kendal Square*, 2007, available at http://www.xconomy.com/2007/09/28/coalition-of-boston-libraries-chooses-the-un-google-route-to-digitization/ (accessed June 1, 2008).

43. "Gaining Options, Girls Investigate Real Life," Wayne State University College of Education, 2008, available at http://www.gogirls.wayne.edu/ (accessed June 1, 2008).

44. State of Michigan Constitution, article 8.

45. Regents of the University of Michigan News Service, "University of Michigan Admissions Lawsuits," 2008, available at http://www.vpcomm.umich.edu/admissions/legal/gratz/amici.html (accessed June 1, 2008).

46. Joseph R. Reeder et al., "Consolidated Brief," Supreme Court of the United States, available at http://www.vpcomm.umich.edu/admissions/legal/gru_amicus-ussc/um/MilitaryL-both.pdf (accessed June 1, 2008).

47. Gerald R. Ford, "Inclusive America, Under Attack," *New York Times*, August 8, 1999.

48. George W. Bush, "President Bush Discusses Affirmative Action Case," Office of the Press Secretary, 2003, available at http://www.whitehouse.gov/news/releases/2003/01/20030115-7.html (accessed June 1, 2008).

49. "Expert Report of Patricia Gurin," University of Michigan, 2008, available at http://www.vpcomm.umich.edu/admissions/legal/expert/gurintoc.html (accessed June 1, 2008).

50. Mary Sue Coleman, "Diversity Matters in Michigan," University of Michigan, 2008, available at http://www.umich.edu/pres/speeches/061103div.html (accessed June 1, 2008).

51. Klaus H. Huser, "Letter: How Dare U-M's Coleman Dismiss Voter's Choice?" *Ann Arbor News*, November 12, 2006 available at http://newsclips.vpcomm.umich.edu/article_detail.php?ArticleID=43295 (accessed June 1, 2007).

52. Steve Chapman, "The University of Michigan vs. the People," *Chicago Tribune*, November, 23, 2006, available at http://www.chicagotribune.com/news/columnists/chi-0611230048nov23,1,3074384.column?coll=chi-news-col&ctrack=1&cset=true (accessed June 1, 2007).

53. Laurel Thomas Gnagey, "U-M Explores Diversity from a Complex Systems Approach," *University Record Online*, 2005, available at http://www.umich.edu/~urecord/0506/Nov14_05/05.shtml (accessed June 1, 2007).

54. "Diversity Blueprints Final Report," available at http://www.vpcomm.umich.edu/about/bp-summary.php (accessed June 1, 2007).

55. National Forum on Higher Education for the Public Good, "The National Forum on Higher Education for the Public Good"; National Forum on Higher Education for the Public Good, " Civic Engagement," School of Education, University of Michigan, 2008, available at http://www.thenationalforum.org/Main/Themes/CivicEng/index.htm (accessed June 1, 2007).

56. Available at http://www.vpcomm.U-Mich.edu/admissions/legal/gru_amicus-ussc/U-M/MilitaryL-both.pdf, p. 57 (accessed June 1, 2007).

57. David William Cohen and Michael D. Kennedy, eds., *Responsibility in Crisis: Knowledge Politics and Global Publics* (Ann Arbor: Scholarly Publishing Office of the Uni-

versity of Michigan Library, 2008), available at http://quod.lib.umich.edu/cgi/t/text/text-idx?c=globalpublics;cc=globalpublics;idno=4726364.0001.001;view=toc (accessed June 1, 2007).

58. James J. Duderstadt, "Working Draft of the Quality Subcommittee of the Secretary of Education's Commission on the Future of Higher Education," Millennium Project Papers, 2008, available at http://milproj.ummu.umich.edu/publications/quality _commission/ (accessed June 1, 2008).

59. Newsroom Special Reports, "Strong Coffee," Division of University Relations, Michigan State University, 2008, available at http://special.newsroom.msu.edu/rwanda-coffee/ (accessed June 1, 2008).

60. Organizing Committee, "Communism's Negotiated Collapse: The Polish Round Table Talks of 1989, Ten Years Later," Regents of the University of Michigan, 2001, available at http://www.ii.umich.edu/PolishRoundTable/frame.html. Kennedy (accessed June 1, 2007).

61. Kennedy, *Cultural Formations of Postcommunism*, 289.

62. Fatma Müge Göçek, "Hrant Dink (1954–2007): In Memoriam," *openDemocracy*, 2007, available at http://www.opendemocracy.net/democracy-turkey/dink_memoriam _4272.jsp (accessed June 1, 2007).

63. Ronald Grigor Suny and Fatma Müge Göçek, "Discussing Genocide: Contextualizing the Armenian Experience in the Ottoman Empire," *Journal of the International Institute* 9, no. 3 (2002), available at http://quod.lib.umich.edu/cgi/t/text/text-idx?c= jii;cc=jii;q1=ronald%20suny;op2=and;op3=and;rgn=main;view=text;idno=4750978 .0009.301 (accessed June 1, 2007).

64. Arts of Citizenship Program, "Arts of Citizenship Program Statement," University of Michigan, 2008, available at http://www.artsofcitizenship.umich.edu/about/program.html (accessed June 1, 2008).

65. "Student Power: Sole's Occupation of the U-M President's Office," *Agenda*, April 1999, available at http://www-personal.umich.edu/~lormand/agenda/9904/12.pdf (accessed April 2, 2010).

66. Fernando Coronil, "The Production of Knowledge and Indigenous Peoples," *Journal of the International Institute* 9, no. 1 (2001), available at http://quod.lib.umich.edu/cgi/t/text/text-idx?c=jii;cc=jii;q1=fernando%20coronil;rgn=main;view=text;idno=4 750978.0009.104 (accessed June 1, 2007).

67. Michael D. Kennedy, "Public Relations: How Should the Scholarly and Political Communities Relate to Each Other?" *Newsnet of the American Association for the Advancement of Slavic Studies* 45, no. 2 (2005): 1–6.

Contributors

N'Dri T. Assié-Lumumba is professor in the Africana Studies and Research Center at Cornell University. Her authored and edited books include *Women and Higher Education in Africa: Reconceptualizing Gender-Based Human Capabilities and Upgrading Human Rights to Knowledge* (CEPARRED, 2007), which is being translated for publication in French, Spanish, Arabic, Portuguese, and Chinese.

John Brennan is director of the Centre for Higher Education Research and Information and Professor of Higher Education Research at the Open University in the United Kingdom. He has published several books and many reports and articles on higher education, including the coauthored *Managing Quality in Higher Education* (Springer Netherlands, 2000).

Craig Calhoun is president of the Social Science Research Council and University Professor of the Social Sciences at NYU. He received his doctorate from Oxford University and taught at the University of North Carolina at Chapel Hill, where he served as dean of the Graduate School and founding director of the

University Center for International Studies. At the SSRC he has led an effort to enhance the public role of social science and connect it more closely to its constituencies. His most recent book is *Nations Matter: Culture, History, and the Cosmopolitan Dream* (Routledge 2007); his new book, *Cosmopolitanism and Belonging,* will be published by Routledge in 2011. He is also the editor of *Sociology in America* (Chicago 2007) and *Robert K. Merton: Sociology of Science, Sociology as Science* (Columbia 2010).

Gustavo E. Fischman is associate professor at Arizona State University. He is the author of several books and numerous articles on critical pedagogies, teacher education, and gender issues in education, including *Imagining Teachers: Rethinking Gender Dynamics in Teacher Education* (Rowman & Littlefield, 2000).

Sarah E. Igo is associate professor of American intellectual and cultural history, with affiliate appointments in political science and sociology, at Vanderbilt University. Her first book, *The Averaged American: Surveys, Citizens, and the Making of a Mass Public* (Harvard University Press, 2007), explores the relationship between survey data—opinion polls, sex surveys, and consumer research—and modern understandings of self and nation.

Mark S. Johnson is assistant professor of educational policy studies at the University of Wisconsin at Madison. He has conducted field research and evaluations throughout the former Soviet Union for both public agencies and private foundations on various topics, including civic education; international exchanges and public diplomacy; and strategies for university internationalization in various fields, including the humanities, social sciences, and the sciences and technology.

Michael D. Kennedy is professor of sociology and international studies and Howard R Swearer Director of the Watson Institute for International Studies at Brown University. Among his publications related to higher education are these coedited volumes: *Responsibility in Crisis* (Scholarly Publishing Office, University of Michigan, 2005) and *Intellectuals and the Articulation of the Nation* (University of Michigan Press, 1999).

Andrey Kortunov is president of the New Eurasia Foundation in Moscow. He holds a degree in history from the Moscow State Institute of International Relations and completed his postgraduate studies at the Institute for United

States of America and Canada Studies at the Russian Academy of Science, Moscow.

Georg Krücken is professor of science organization, higher education, and science management at the German University of Administrative Sciences in Speyer. He is the coeditor of *Towards a Multiversity? Universities Between Global Trends and National Traditions* (Verlag, 2006).

Stefan Lange was assistant professor at the German University of Administrative Sciences Speyer until the end of 2009. Since 2010 he has been working as a science officer in the head office of the German Council for Sciences and Humanities in Cologne. His recent publications have been in the areas of higher education governance and research evaluation.

Tukumbi Lumumba-Kasongo is professor of political science at Wells College. He is the author of several books, including *Who and What Govern in the World of the States?* (University Press of America, 2005) and *Japan-Africa Relations* (Palgrave Macmillan, 2010).

Simon Marginson is professor of higher education at the Centre for the Study of Higher Education at the University of Melbourne. He is the coauthor of three books on creativity, imagination, and global creation (Peter Lang, 2009 and 2010) and of *International Student Security* (Cambridge University Press, 2010).

Ka Ho Mok is associate vice president for external relations and concurrently dean of the Faculty of Arts and Sciences at the Hong Kong Institute of Education (HKIEd). Ka Ho is the coeditor of *Changing Governance and Public Policy in East Asia* (Routledge, Taylor & Francis, 2009).

Juan Carlos Moreno-Brid is the research coordinator of the United Nations' Economic Commission for Latin America and the Caribbean (ECLAC-Mexico). His most recent publication is (with Jaime Ros) *Development and Growth in the Mexican Economy: A Historical Perspective* (Oxford University Press, 2009).

Christine Musselin is director of the Centre de Sociologie des Organisations, a research unit of Sciences Po and the CNRS, and lecturer at Sciences Po in Paris. Prof. Musselin's recent publications include *The Long March of French Universities* (Routledge, 2004).

Imanol Ordorika is professor of social sciences and education at the Universidad nacional autonoma de Mexico (UNAM). He is General Director for Institutional Evaluation at UNAM and creator of the online Comparative Study of Mexican Universities, as well as the author of articles, chapters, and several books, including *Power and Politics in University Governance: Organization and Change at the Universidad Autonoma de Mexico* (Routledge, 2003).

Walter W. Powell is professor of education and (by courtesy) sociology, organizational behavior, management science and engineering, and communication at Stanford University and an external faculty member at the Santa Fe Institute. He has published extensively in the areas of organization theory, institutional analysis, and economic sociology.

Diana Rhoten is the cofounder and codirector of a new social enterprise called Startl, as well as the founder and director of the Knowledge Institutions and Digital Media and Learning programs at the Social Science Research Council in New York. Her work focuses on the socio-technical conditions of knowledge production and innovation for the twenty-first century. She has published in a range of academic journals and advises a host of cultural, scientific, and educational institutions on the issues of organizational design, creative collaboration, and adaptive change. For both her theoretical contributions and practical applications in the area of organizational and technological innovation, Diana was named a Sigma Xi Distinguished Lecturer (2005–2007), an award that honors individuals at the leading edge of science.

Pablo Ruiz-Nápoles is professor of economics at the Universidad Nacional Autonoma de Mexico (UNAM) and a current member of the Mexican Academy of Sciences and Sigma Xi. A frequent consultant to ECLAC and the UN, his most recent publication in English is "Protectionism, Free Trade and Preferential Trade: The Mexican Experience 1970–2005" (*Banca Nazionale del Lavoro Quarterly Review*, 2007).

Mala Singh is professor of international higher education policy in the Centre for Higher Education Research and Information at the Open University in the United Kingdom. She has published in the fields of philosophy, higher education, and quality assurance.

Voldemar Tomusk is director for policy and evaluation of the International Higher Education Support Program of the Open Society Foundation, based in

London. He is the author of several books and numerous articles related to the role of higher education in a changing society and is the editor of *Creating the European Area of Higher Education: Voices from the Periphery* (Springer, 2006).

Yusef Waghid is professor of philosophy of education and dean of the faculty of education at Stellenbosch University in South Africa. He is the author of *Community and Democracy in South Africa: Liberal Versus Communitarian Perspectives* (Peter Lang, 2003).

John Willinsky is professor of education at Stanford University and director of the Public Knowledge Project. Much of his work, including his book *The Access Principle: The Case for Open Access to Research and Scholarship* (MIT Press, 2006), is free for downloading on the project's website (http://pkp.sfu.ca).

Index

Porter, Brian, 483

Portuguese language, 87

positional goods, 16

poverty, 159, 166, 241, 270; need for social services and, 274; statistics for Africa, 278; struggle to eradicate, 272, 273; units of analysis and, 279

Powell, Walter W., 391, 433, 437

Princeton University, 72, *107*, 295–96

private universities, 4, 5, 10; in Africa, 238, 275, 281; in Asia, 16–17; assistant professor salaries, 332; in eastern Europe, 16; financial crisis and, 11; in Japan, 105; in Latin America, 30n4, 190n21; minority enrollment, 15; public institutions in relation to, 5–6, 331–34, 336, 337n10; research and development (R&D) in, 162; research productivity, 334; in Russia, 131. *See also* for-profit universities

privatization, 34, 196, 264; African national development agendas and, 273; intellectual property rights (IPRs) and, 431; in Latin America, 44; research agendas and, 436; in Russia, 149; of social services, 269; in United Kingdom, 400

professional schools, 11, 19, 24, 26, 27

professors, 330–34; as "academic entrepreneurs," 217; advising functions and, 26; in African universities, 243; benefits of research to, 27; as civil servants, 5, 24; in German universities, 343, 345, 353; intellectual freedom and, 1, 2; in Latin America, 161; salaries, 332; in Soviet universities, 131. *See also* faculty

Programm zur Förderung der Information und Dokumentation, 360–61

progress, social, 279, 282, 283, 319

property rights. *See* intellectual property rights (IPRs)

Prussia, 5

psychology, 179

publications/publishing: academic-industrial copublications, 365, *366–67*, 367; open-access, 298, 300; "publish or perish," 204, 369. *See also* journals, scholarly; university presses

public good, 2, 70, 242, 391, 466, 494; athletics and, 467; battle for defense of, 220; diversity and, 477; economic benefits and, 469; funding sources and, 4; general conception of the public and, 471; global publics/solidarities and, 481; hegemony and, 93–94; meaning of publicness and, 52–53; national interest and, 255; neoliberal view of, 10, 54–55; "non-rivalrous" goods, 6; open access to knowledge and, 296; quality assurance and, 407, 408; in Soviet higher education system, 132; university as public sphere and, 219

public interest, 53, 316, 390–91, 418

Public Knowledge Project, 313n58, 314n64

Public Library of Science, 305, 313n60

publicness, 3, 52–55, 479–80, 493

public research universities (PRUs), 2–3, 34–36, 315–16; budgets, 11, 13; clam and chameleon metaphors, 323–27; "comprehensive," 130–31; "crisis" of, 48–52, 55; democracy

Sankara, Thomas, 260

Sanneh, Lamin, 480

Santos, Boaventura de Sousa, 50

Sanyal, Bikas, 64n83

São Paulo, Universidad de (Brazil), *182*

São Tomé and Príncipe, 252

Saratov State University (Russia), 140

Sawadogo, Geremie, 270

Sawyerr, Akilagpa, 235, 239

"School Class as a Social System, The" (Parsons), 298

Schwartzman, Simon, 47

science, 1, 3, 439; African universities and, 236, 270, 281; as autonomous sphere, 431; digital technology and, 291; economic development and, 13; girls' competence in, 492; health sciences, 319; hegemony and, 80, 90; industrial applications, 323; intellectual property rights (IPRs) and, 54; Latin American universities and, 160, 163, 178–79; natural sciences, 134, 147, 353, 359; physical sciences, 147, 318, 319; political coordination with German higher education, 344–45; property rights in, 6; publication and, 6–7; public good and, 53; "pure science," 25, 137; religious dissent and, 22; science parks, 328; South African universities and, 413; in Soviet Union, 142, 145; technology-oriented, 11, 19; university rankings and, 22; U.S. federal science policy, 318–19. *See also* Big Science

Science Citation Index (SCI), 204, 206, 207, 212, 365

Sciences Po (France), 16, 23

"Science—The Endless Frontier" (Bush), 319

Scotland, 20, 22, 23, 405. *See also* United Kingdom [UK] (Britain)

Scott, John, 36

Secher, David, 380, 384–85

Segal Quince Wicksteed, 383

segmentation theory, 439

self-determination, 112, 113, 115

semiconductors, 321

Sen, Amartya, 113

Sennett, Richard, 438, 441

September 11, 2001, attacks, 479–80, 482

SFBs (collaborative research areas), 352–53, 355, 373n30

Shanghai Jiao Tong University (SJTU) rankings, 11, 22, 84, 108–10, 162, 459; Center for World-Class Universities, 8; English-speaking nations and, 89; hegemony in higher education and, 106, *107–8*, 108–11; "Hi Ci" researchers, *90*, 91; Latin America universities and, 162, 181, *182*; Times rankings compared with, 106, *107*; U.S. dominance of, 86–87, *107*

Shapiro, Harold T., 295–96

Shulenburger, David E., 309n30

Shulman, Lee, 220

Siegel, Donald, 326

Simon, Lou Anna, 468

Simon Fraser University Library (Canada), 303, 304

Singapore, 86, 88, 210; American research infrastructure and, 96; corporate university governance in, 218; "entrepreneurial university," 202–3; GDP (gross domestic product), *85*; global strategy of,